W9-BXY-870

fifth edition

VICTIMOLOGY

William G. Doerner *&* **Steven P. Lab**
Florida State University   Bowling Green State University

anderson publishing
A member of the LexisNexis Group

Victimology, Fifth Edition

Copyright © 1995, 1998, 2002, 2005, 2008
       Matthew Bender & Company, Inc., a member of the LexisNexis Group
       Newark, NJ
       Phone   877-374-2919
       ISBN-10: 1-59345-506-2
       ISBN-13: 978-1-59345-506-4

Library of Congress Cataloging-in-Publication Data

Doerner, William G., 1949-
    Victimology / by William G. Doerner, Steven P. Lab.
       p. cm.
    Includes bibliographical references and index.
    ISBN-13: 978-1-59345-506-4 (softbound)
    ISBN-10: 1-59345-506-2 (softbound)
    1. Victims of crimes. 2. Criminal statistics. I. Lab, Steven P. II. Title.
HV6250.25.D64 2008
362.88--dc22   2008000280

Cover design by Tin Box Studio, Inc./Cincinnati, Ohio
Photo by Getty Images/James Lauritz

EDITOR Ellen S. Boyne
ACQUISITIONS EDITOR Michael C. Braswell

To Kristina.

WGD

To my future.

SPL

TABLE OF CONTENTS

Chapter 3
The Costs of Being a Victim   **55**

Chapter 4
Remedying the Plight of Victims   **83**

Learning Objectives

After reading Chapter 1, you should be able to:

- Explain how early society handled victim problems.

- Understand the meaning of retribution and restitution.

- Discuss the change from a victim justice system to a criminal justice system.

- Outline the early interest in victim typologies.

- Account for the attention paid to victim precipitation.

- Summarize what Wolfgang found out about homicide victims.

- Report on Amir's victim precipitation study.

- Evaluate the reaction to Amir's victim precipitation study.

- Critique the shortcomings that underlie victim precipitation.

- List the areas that fall under "general victimology."

- Provide an overview of the broad topics victimologists study.

- Talk about the victim movement and tell how it increased public interest in crime victims.

Chapter 1

THE SCOPE OF VICTIMOLOGY

Introduction

Something not very funny happened on the way to a formal system of justice. The victim got left out. As strange as it may sound, the bulk of history has seen crime victims become further removed as an integral part of dealing with criminals. Fortunately, this trend is beginning to reverse itself. Recent years have seen an increased interest in the plight of crime victims and a movement toward reintegrating the victim into the criminal justice system. This chapter will look at the role of the victim throughout history and will trace the elimination of the victim from social processing of criminal acts. We will see how victimology emerged and we will investigate the resurgence of interest in the victim.

The Victim Throughout History

Most people take the existence of the formal criminal justice system for granted. They do not realize that this method of handling deviant activity has not been the norm throughout history. Indeed, the modern version of criminal justice is a relatively new phenomenon. In days gone by, responsibility for dealing with offenders fell to the victim and the victim's kin. There were no "authorities" to turn to for help in "enforcing the law." Victims were expected to fend for themselves, and society acceded to this arrangement.

This state of affairs was not outlined in any set of laws or legal code. With rare exceptions, written laws did not exist. Codes of behavior reflected prevailing social norms. Society recognized murder and other serious affronts as *mala in se* (totally unacceptable behavior). However, it was up to victims or their survivors to decide what action to take against the offender. Victims who wished to respond to offenses could not turn to judges for assistance or to jails for punishment. These institutions did not exist yet. Instead, victims had to take matters into their own hands.

This depiction does not imply there were no provisions for victims to follow. Society recognized a basic system of retribution and restitution for offenders. In simplest terms, *retribution* meant the offender would suffer in proportion to the degree of harm caused by his or her actions. Often times, retribution took the form of *restitution*, or making payment in an amount sufficient to render the victim whole again. If the offender was unable to make restitution, his or her kin were forced to assume the liability.

This response system emphasized the principle known as *lex talionis*—an eye for an eye, a tooth for a tooth. Punishment was commensurate with the harm inflicted upon the victim. Perhaps the most important feature of this system was that victims and their relatives handled the problem and were the beneficiaries of any payments. This arrangement was truly a "victim justice system."

This basic system of dealing with offensive behavior found its way into early codified laws. The Law of Moses, the Code of Hammurabi (2200 B.C.E.), and Roman law all entailed strong elements of individual responsibility for harms committed against others. Restitution and retribution were specific ingredients in many of these early codes. Part of the rationale behind this response was to deter such behavior in the future.

The major goal of *deterrence* is to prevent future transgressions. The thinking is that the lack of any enrichment or gain from criminal activity would make these acts unattractive. Retribution and restitution attempt to reestablish the status quo that existed before the initial action of the offender. Thus, removing financial incentives would make it not profitable to commit crimes.

This basic system of dealing with offensive behavior remained intact throughout the Middle Ages. Eventually, though, it fell into disuse. Two factors signaled the end of this victim justice system. The first change was the move by feudal barons to lay a claim to any compensation offenders paid their victims (Schafer, 1968). These rulers saw this money as a lucrative way to increase their own riches. The barons accomplished this goal by redefining criminal acts as violations against the state, instead of the victim. This strategy recast the state (the barons being the heads of the state) as the aggrieved party. The victim diminished in stature and was relegated to the status of witness for the state. Now the state could step in and reap the benefits of restitution.

A second factor that reduced the victim's position was the enormous upheaval that was transforming society. Up until this time, society was predominantly rural and agrarian. People lived in small groups, eking out an existence from daily labor in the fields. Life was a rustic struggle to meet day-to-day needs.

People, for the most part, were self-sufficient and relied heavily upon their families for assistance. Families often lived in relative isolation from other people. Whenever a crime took place, it brought physical and economic harm not only to the individual victim, but also to the entire family network. This simple *gemeinschaft* society (Toennies, 1957) could rely on the individual to handle his or her own problems.

As the Middle Ages drew to a close, the Industrial Revolution created a demand for larger urbanized communities. People took jobs in the new industries, leaving the rural areas and relocating to the cities. They settled into cramped quarters, surrounded by strangers. Neighbors no longer knew the people living next door. As faces blended into crowds, relationships grew more depersonalized. The interpersonal ties that once bound people together had vanished.

As this *gesellschaft* type of society continued to grow, the old victim justice practices crumbled even further. Crime began to threaten the delicate social fabric that now linked people together. At the same time, concern shifted away from making the victim whole to dealing with the criminal. Gradually, the *victim* justice system withered and the *criminal* justice system became its replacement. In fact, some observers would contend that the victim *injustice* system would be a more apt description.

Today, crime victims remain nothing more than witnesses for the state. Victims no longer take matters into their own hands to extract retribution and restitution from their offenders. The victim must call upon society to act. The development of formal law enforcement, courts, and correctional systems in the past few centuries has reflected an interest in protecting the state. For the most part, the criminal justice system simply forgot about victims and their best interests. Instead, the focus shifted to protecting the rights of the accused.

The Reemergence of the Victim

The criminal justice system spends the bulk of its time and energy trying to control criminals. It was within this preoccupation of understanding criminal activity and identifying the causes of criminal behavior that the victim was "rediscovered" in the 1940s. Interestingly, the victim emerged not as an individual worthy of sympathy or compassion but as a possible partner or contributor to his or her own demise. Students of criminal behavior began to look at the relationship between the victim and the offender in the hopes of better understanding the genesis of the criminal act.

As interest in victims began to sprout and attract more scholarly attention, writers began to grapple with a very basic issue. What exactly was victimology? Some people believed victimology was a specialty area or a subfield within criminology. After all, every criminal event had to include a criminal and a victim by definition. Others countered that because victimology was so broad and encompassing, it deserved to stand as a separate field or discipline in its own right. They foresaw the day when college catalogs would list victimology as a major area of study along with such pursuits as biology, criminology, psychology, mathematics, political science, and other subjects.

Early scholarly work in victimology focused considerable energy upon creating victim typologies. A *typology* is an effort to categorize observations into logical groupings to reach a better understanding of our social world (McKinney, 1950; McKinney, 1969). As we shall see in the following sections, these early theoretical reflections pushed the field in a direction that eventually created an explosive and haunting reaction, nearly crippling this fledgling enterprise.

The Work of Hans von Hentig: *The Criminal and His Victim*

An early pioneer in victimology was a German scholar, Hans von Hentig. As a criminologist, von Hentig spent much time trying to discover what made a criminal predisposed to being a criminal. As he focused on crime victims, von Hentig began to wonder what it was that made the victim a victim. The key ingredient, according to von Hentig, was the *criminal-victim dyad*.

In an early publication, von Hentig (1941) claimed the victim was often a contributing cause to the criminal act. One example would be an incident in which the ultimate victim began as the aggressor. However, for some reason, this person wound up becoming the loser in the confrontation. Von Hentig's message was clear. Simply examining the outcome of a criminal event sometimes presents a distorted image of who the real victim is and who the real offender is. A closer inspection of the dynamics underlying the situation might reveal the victim was a major contributor to his or her own victimization.

Von Hentig expanded upon the notion of the victim as an *agent provocateur* in a later book called *The Criminal and His Victim*. He explained that "increased attention should be paid to the crime-provocative function of the victim. . . . With a thorough knowledge of the interrelations between doer and sufferer new approaches to the detection of crime will be opened" (1948: 450).

Von Hentig was not naive enough to believe that all victim contribution to crime was active. Much victim contribution results from characteristics or social positions beyond the control of the individual. As a result, von Hentig classified victims into 13 categories depending upon their propensity for victimization.

FIGURE 1.1
Hans von Hentig's Victim Typology

Type	Example
1. The Young	children and infants
2. The Female	all women
3. The Old	elderly persons
4. The Mentally Defective and Deranged	the feeble-minded, the insane, drug addicts, alcoholics
5. Immigrants	foreigners unfamiliar with the culture
6. Minorities	racially disadvantaged persons
7. Dull Normals	simple-minded persons
8. The Depressed	persons with various psychological maladies
9. The Acquisitive	the greedy, those looking for quick gains
10. The Wanton	promiscuous persons
11. The Lonesome and the Heartbroken	widows, widowers, and those in mourning
12. The Tormentor	an abusive parent
13. The Blocked, Exempted, or Fighting	victims of blackmail, extortion, confidence games

Source: Adapted from von Hentig, H. (1948). *The Criminal and His Victim: Studies in the Sociobiology of Crime*. New Haven: Yale University Press, pp. 404-438.

Many of von Hentig's victim types reflect the inability to resist a perpetrator due to physical, social, or psychological disadvantages. For example, very young people, females, and elderly persons are more likely to lack the physical power to resist offenders. Immigrants and minorities, because of cultural differences, may feel they are outside the mainstream of society. This lack of familiarity may lead them into situations in which criminals prey upon them. Individuals who are mentally defective or deranged, "dull normal," depressed, lonesome, or blocked may not understand what is occurring around them or may be unable to resist. The acquisitive person and the tormentor are individuals who, due to their own desires, are either directly involved in the criminal act or place themselves in situations in which there is a clear potential for victimization.

The typology that von Hentig created does not imply the victim is always the primary cause of the criminal act. What he does suggest is that victim characteristics may contribute to the victimization episode. According to von Hentig (1948: iii), we must realize "the victim is taken as one of the determinants, and that a nefarious symbiosis is often established between doer and sufferer. . . ."

The Work of Beniamin Mendelsohn: Further Reflections

Some observers credit Beniamin Mendelsohn, a practicing attorney, with being the "father" of victimology. Mendelsohn, like von Hentig, was intrigued by the dynamics that take place between victims and offenders. Before preparing a case, he would ask victims, witnesses and bystanders in the situation to complete a detailed and probing questionnaire. After examining these responses, Mendelsohn discovered that usually there was a strong interpersonal relationship between victims and offenders. Using these data, Mendelsohn (1956) outlined a six-step classification of victims based on legal considerations of the degree of the victim's blame.

The first type was the "completely innocent victim." This victim type exhibited no provocative or facilitating behavior prior to the offender's attack. The second grouping contained "victims with minor guilt" or "victims due to ignorance." These unfortunate people inadvertently did something that placed themselves in a compromising position before the victimization episode.

Mendelsohn reserved the third category for the "victim as guilty as the offender" and the "voluntary victim." Suicide cases and parties injured while engaging in vice crimes and other victimless offenses were listed here.

The next two categories address some of von Hentig's earlier concerns. Mendelsohn's fourth type, "victim more guilty than the offender," represents the situation in which the victim instigates or provokes the criminal act. A person who comes out on the losing end of a punch after making an abusive remark or goading the other party would fit here. Similarly, a victim who entered the situation as the offender and, because of circumstances beyond his or her control, ended up the victim is considered the "most guilty victim." An example of this category would be the burglar whom the home owner shoots during the intrusion.

The last category is the "simulating or imaginary victim." Mendelsohn reserves this niche for those persons who pretend they have been victimized. The person who claims to have been mugged, rather than admitting to gambling his or her paycheck away, would be an example.

Mendelsohn's classification is useful primarily for identifying the relative culpability of the victim in the criminal act. Besides developing this typology, Mendelsohn also coined the term "victimology" and proposed the terms "penal-couple" (a criminal-victim relationship), "victimal" and "victimity" (as opposed to criminal and criminality), and "potential of victimal receptivity" (an individual's propensity for being victimized). Figure 1.2 lists some common terms that victimologists use.

FIGURE 1.2
The Vocabulary of Victimology

Victimhood	the state of being a victim
Victimizable	capable of being victimized
Victimization	the act of victimizing, or fact of being victimized, in various senses
Victimize	to make a victim of; to cause to suffer inconvenience, discomfort, annoyance, etc., either deliberately or by misdirected attentions; to cheat, swindle, or defraud; to put to death as, or in the manner of, a sacrificial victim; to slaughter; to destroy or spoil completely
Victimizer	one who victimizes another or others
Victimless	the absence of a clearly identifiable victim other than the doer, for example, in a criminal situation

Source: Viano, E.C. (1976b). "From the Editor: Victimology: The Study of the Victim." *Victimology* 1:1-7. Reprinted by permission from *Victimology: An International Journal*, Victimology, Inc. All rights reserved.

The Work of Stephen Schafer:
The Victim and His Criminal

Scholarly interest in victims and the role they played in their own demise evoked little interest throughout the 1950s and 1960s. Stephen Schafer, in a playful twist on Hans von Hentig's seminal work, revisited the victim's role in his book *The Victim and His Criminal*. The key concept that undergirded Schafer's thinking was what he termed "functional responsibility." Once again, the victim-offender relationship came under scrutiny.

As Figure 1.3 shows, Schafer (1968) provided a typology that builds upon victim responsibility for the crime. In many respects, Schafer's groupings are a variation of those proposed by von Hentig (1948). The difference between the two schemes is primarily one of emphasis on the culpability of the victim. Where von Hentig's listing identifies varying risk factors, Schafer explicitly sets forth the responsibility of different victims.

FIGURE 1.3
Schafer's Victim Precipitation Typology

1. Unrelated Victims (no victim responsibility)	Instances in which the victim is simply the unfortunate target of the offender.
2. Provocative Victims (victim shares responsibility)	The offender is reacting to some action or behavior of the victim.
3. Precipitative Victims (some degree of victim responsibility)	Victims leave themselves open for victimization by placing themselves in dangerous places or times, dressing inappropriately, acting, or saying the wrong things, etc.
4. Biologically Weak Victims (no victim responsibility)	The aged, young, infirmed, and others who, due to their physical conditions, are appealing targets for offenders.
5. Socially Weak Victims (no victim responsibility)	Immigrants, minorities, and others who are not adequately integrated into society and are seen as easy targets by offenders.
6. Self-Victimizing (total victim responsibility)	Individuals who are involved in such crimes as drug use, prostitution, gambling, and other activities in which the victim and the criminal act in concert with one another.
7. Political Victims (no victim responsibility)	Individuals who are victimized because they oppose those in power or are made victims in order to be kept in a subservient social position.

Source: Adapted from Schafer, S. (1968). *The Victim and His Criminal: A Study in Functional Responsibility*. New York: Random House.

Other Scholarly Efforts

Von Hentig, Mendelsohn, and Schafer were not the only persons to produce significant analyses regarding victims during this time. Most assuredly, some other scholars began recognizing the importance of a victim-based orientation. These early attempts probing the victim-offender relationship signaled the beginning of a renewed academic interest in the victim.

This concern, however, was lopsided. The early victimologists generally failed to look at the damage offenders inflicted upon their victims, ignored victim recuperative or rehabilitative efforts, and bypassed a host of other concerns. In an attempt to understand the causes of crime, they concentrated on how the victim contributed to his or her demise. Eventually, the idea of victim precipitation emerged from this preoccupation with "blaming the victim." As we shall see later in this chapter, the assumption that somehow the victim shared responsibility for or instigated the criminal episode would spark a major ideological confrontation.

Empirical Studies of Victim Precipitation

Victim precipitation deals with the degree to which the victim is responsible for his or her own victimization. That involvement can be either passive (as much of von Hentig's typology suggests) or active (as seen in Mendelsohn's classification). Each typology presented in this chapter implicates victim contribution as a causative factor in the commission of crime. However, none present any empirical evidence to support that point of view. The first systematic attempt to overcome this objection was Wolfgang's (1958) analysis of police homicide records. A few years later, one of Wolfgang's students, Menachem Amir, applied this framework to forcible rape cases. His formulation and interpretation quickly met with a barrage of stinging criticism.

The Work of Marvin E. Wolfgang: *Patterns in Criminal Homicide*

Using homicide data from the city of Philadelphia, Wolfgang reported that 26 percent of the homicides that occurred from 1948 through 1952 resulted from victim precipitation. Wolfgang (1958: 252) defined victim-precipitated homicide as those instances in which the ultimate victim was:

the first in the homicide drama to use physical force directed against his subsequent slayer. The victim-precipitated cases are those in which the victim was the first to show and use a deadly weapon, to strike a blow in an altercation—in short, the first to commence the interplay of resort to physical violence.

Wolfgang identified several factors as typical of victim-precipitated homicides. First, the victim and the offender usually had some prior interpersonal relationship. Typical examples include relationships of spouses, boyfriends-girlfriends, family members, and close friends or acquaintances. In other words, victims were more likely to die at the hands of someone they knew rather than from the actions of a complete stranger.

Second, the homicide act is often the product of a small disagreement that escalates until the situation bursts out of control. That change in degree could be either short-term or may be the result of a longer, drawn-out confrontation. For instance:

> A husband had beaten his wife on several previous occasions. In the present instance, she insisted that he take her to the hospital. He refused, and a violent quarrel followed, during which he slapped her several times, and she concluded by stabbing him (Wolfgang, 1958: 253).

Third, alcohol consumed by the victim is a common ingredient in many victim-precipitated homicides. Several possibilities surface here. It may be that as intoxicated persons lose their inhibitions, they vocalize their feelings more readily. Eventually, these inebriated parties grow more obnoxious and belligerent, and unwittingly provoke their assailants into a deadly confrontation. Another alternative is that alcohol consumption renders these people so impaired that they lose the physical ability to defend themselves in a skirmish. In any event, Wolfgang (1958: 265) points out that "connotations of a victim as a weak and passive individual, seeking to withdraw from an assaultive situation, and of an offender as a brutal, strong, and overly aggressive person seeking out his victim, are not always correct."

The Work of Menachem Amir:
Patterns in Forcible Rape

Several years later, Menachem Amir undertook what perhaps became the most controversial empirical analysis of rape. Amir (1971) gathered information from police records on rape incidents that took place in Philadelphia between 1958 and 1960. Based on details contained in the files, he claimed that 19 percent of all forcible rapes were victim-precipitated.

According to Amir (1971: 266), victim-precipitated rape referred to those situations in which:

> the victim actually, or so it was deemed, agreed to sexual relations but retracted before the actual act or did not react strongly enough when the suggestion was made by the offender. The term applies also to cases in risky situations marred with sexuality, especially when she uses what could be interpreted as indecency in language and gestures, or constitutes what could be taken as an invitation to sexual relations.

Amir proceeded to list a variety of factors that helped precipitate the criminal act. Similar to Wolfgang's homicide findings, alcohol use—particularly by the victim—was a major factor in a precipitated rape. The risk of sexual victimization intensified if both parties had been drinking.

Other important factors include seductive actions by the victim, wearing revealing clothing, using risqué language, having a "bad" reputation, and being in the wrong place at the wrong time. According to Amir, such behaviors could tantalize the offender to the point that he simply "misread" the victim's overtures. At one point, Amir (1971) even suggested that some victims may have an unconscious need to be sexually controlled through rape.

In the concluding remarks of the section on victim precipitation, Amir (1971: 275-276) commented:

> These results point to the fact that the offender should not be viewed as the sole "cause" and reason for the offense, and that the "virtuous" victim is not always the innocent and passive party. Thus, the role played by the victim and its contribution to the perpetration of the offense becomes one of the main interests of the emerging discipline of victimology.

Criticisms and Reactions

The notion of victim precipitation, particularly regarding Amir's claims about rape, came under swift attack. Weis and Borges (1973, 1976), for example, attributed Amir's conclusions to faults implicit in relying upon police accounts, to a host of procedural errors, as well as to ill-conceived theoretical notions. For example, Amir suggested victims may *psychologically* prompt or desire the rape as a means of rebelling against accepted standards of behavior. In contrast, though, the male is simply responding to *social* cues from the female. Despite these different origins of behavior, Amir does not provide any justification for why female behavior stems from psychological factors while male actions derive from social variables. Amir's study attracted blistering rebuttals from academic quarters, along with enraged reactions from women's groups and victim advocates. This reception made many victimologists very uncomfortable with the precipitation argument as it had developed to that point.

Cooler heads soon prevailed. Rather than abandoning the idea of victim precipitation, some scholars began a more sensitive probing. Curtis (1974), for one, suggested that what was needed was a more accurate definition of victim precipitation. For example, one set of researchers might define hitchhiking as a precipitating factor. Other studies may not make such a blanket assumption or may view hitchhiking as substantively different from other precipitating actions.

A more productive approach came from a critical examination of the underpinnings of the victim-precipitation argument. Franklin and Franklin (1976) exposed four major assumptions behind this victimological approach. First, victim precipitation assumes that the behavior of the victim can explain the criminal act. However, some factors often identified as precipitous also appear in instances where no criminal act takes place. For example, many people go to bars at night. Sometimes they drink excessively and then stagger home alone without becoming victimized. Thus, supposedly precipitating acts are not enough, in and of themselves, to cause criminal behavior.

Second, victim precipitation assumes the offender becomes activated only when the victim emits certain signals. This belief ignores the fact that many offenders plan their offenses ahead of time and do not simply react to another person's behavior. For these criminals, crime is a rational, planned enterprise.

Third, Franklin and Franklin (1976) disagree with the assumption that a victim's behavior is necessary and sufficient to trigger the commission of a criminal act. In fact, the opposite is probably closer to the truth. Many offenders commit crimes despite any specific action by the victim. Others will not seize the opportunity to commit a crime, for whatever reason, although a potential victim presents himself or herself.

Finally, victim precipitation arguments assume the intent of the victim can be gauged by the victimization incident. Unfortunately, if intent is equivalent to action, there would be no need for criminal court proceedings beyond the infallible identification of the person who perpetrated the crime. Our criminal justice system, however, explicitly assumes possible variation in intent, regardless of the action.

Although each of these assumptions shows how the victim precipitation argument falters, there is a much larger issue requiring attention. Studies of victim involvement tend to be myopic. That is, they do not address the offender. Instead, they imply all offenders are equal in their drive and desire to engage in deviant activity. This assumption, however, is untenable. Some offenders may actively hunt for the right situation, while others display little or no prior intent. What was needed was an integrated approach that would take both the victim and the offender into account.

Curtis (1974) attempted to do just this when he sketched a simple grid that allows the degree of victim precipitation to vary. As Figure 1.4 shows, Curtis (1974) merged victim provocation with offender intent. This strategy results in recognizing five degrees of precipitation, ranging from pure victim precipitation to total offender responsibility. This presentation shows that even in the position of clear outright provocation by the victim, the offender may still be an equally responsible partner in the final outcome. What is important to remember here is that, at best, one should conceive of victim precipitation as a contributing factor and, certainly, not as the predominant force.

FIGURE 1.4
The Precipitation Grid Outlining the Relative Responsibility
of Both Victim and Offender

Degree of Offender Intent	Degree of Victim Involvement		
	Clear Provocation	Some Involvement	Little or No Involvement
Deliberate Premeditation	Equal	More Offender	Total Offender Responsibility
Some Intent	More Victim	Equal	More Offender
Little or No Intent	Pure Victim Precipitation	More Victim	Equal

Source: Adapted from Curtis, L.A., *Criminal Violence: National Patterns and Behavior*, p. 95, Copyright © 1974 Jossey-Bass Inc., Publishers. First published by Lexington Books. Reprinted with permission. All rights reserved.

A New Approach: General Victimology

The preoccupation with victim precipitation, along with its divisiveness and ensuing fragmentation, threatened to stagnate this fledgling area of interest. The lack of theoretical advances brought genuine worries from some quarters that victimology was bogging down in an academic quagmire (Bruinsma and Fiselier, 1982; Levine, 1978). However, an antidote emerged from the discussions held at an international conference in Bellagio, Italy, during the summer of 1975 (Viano, 1976a). It was the concept of "general victimology."

The remedy proposed by Beniamin Mendelsohn called for victimology to move out of the provincial backwaters of criminology and into its own rightful domain. As mentioned earlier, some scholars wondered whether victimology was a discipline in its own right or if it was merely an attractive subfield of criminology. Mendelsohn attempted to assure victimology of its independence from criminology by devising the term "general victimology."

According to Mendelsohn (1982: 59), victimologists aim to "investigate the causes of victimization in search of effective remedies." Because human beings suffer from many causal factors, focusing on criminal victimization is too narrow a perspective. A more global term, like general victimology, is needed to convey the true meaning of the field.

According to Mendelsohn (1976), *general victimology* subsumes five types of victims. They include victims of:

- a criminal
- one's self
- the social environment
- technology
- the natural environment.

The first category (crime victims) is self-explanatory. It refers to the traditional subject matter that victimologists have grown accustomed to studying. Self-victimization would include suicide, as well as any other suffering induced by victims themselves. The term "victims of the social environment" incorporates individual, class, or group oppression. Some common examples here would include racial discrimination, caste relations, genocide, and war atrocities. Technological victims are people who fall prey to society's reliance upon scientific innovations. Nuclear accidents, improperly tested medicines, industrial pollution, and transportation mishaps provide fodder for this category. Finally, victims of the natural environment would embrace those persons affected by such events as floods, earthquakes, hurricanes, famine, and the like.

In line with Mendelsohn's formulations, Smith and Weis (1976) proposed a broad overview of the areas encompassed by general victimology. As Figure 1.5 illustrates, there are four major areas of concern. They include the creation of definitions of victims, the application of these definitions, victim reactions during the post-victimization period, and societal reactions to victims.

FIGURE 1.5
General Model of the Areas of Research and Application in the Field of Victimology

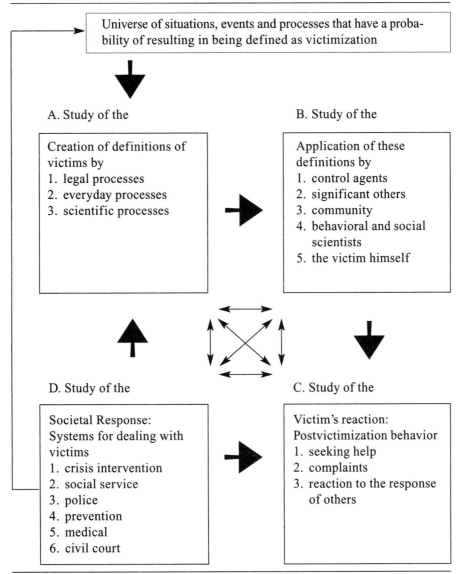

Source: Smith, D.L., and K. Weis (1976). "Toward an Open-System Approach to Studies in the Field of Victimology." In E.C. Viano (ed.), *Victims & Society*. Washington, DC: Visage Press, Inc., p. 45.

When viewed in this context, general victimology becomes a very broad enterprise with extensive implications. As Mendelsohn (1976: 21) explains:

> Just as medicine treats all patients and all diseases, just as criminology concerns itself with all criminals and all forms of

crime, so victimology must concern itself with all victims and all aspects of victimity in which society takes an interest.

Critical Victimology

One recent trend in victimology is the call to shift the focus from the more general approach outlined above to what some people call *critical victimology*. Proponents of this move maintain that victimology fails to question the basic foundations of what crime is, overlooks the question of why certain acts are sanctioned, and, consequently, has developed in the wrong direction. Mawby and Walklate (1994: 21) define critical victimology as:

> an attempt to examine the wider social context in which some versions of victimology have become more dominant than others and also to understand how those versions of victimology are interwoven with questions of policy response and service delivery to victims of crime.

Central to critical victimology, therefore, is the issue of how and why certain actions are defined as criminal and, as a result, how the entire field of victimology becomes focused on one set of actions instead of another. This notion is not entirely different from Mendelsohn's category of "victim of the social environment" outlined previously under the rubric of general victimology. Mawby and Walklate (1994) point out that many crimes committed by the powerful in society are not subjected to the criminal code. Some writers point to the neglect of criminological attention to genocide (Day and Vandiver, 2000; Friedrichs, 2000; Yacoubian, 2000), war crimes (Hoffman, 2000), political campaign law violations (Levine, 1997; Liddick, 2000; Taylor, 2000), clandestine arms sales and weapons of mass destruction (Berryman, 2000; Phythian, 2000; Whitby, 2001), smuggling (Beare, 2002; Bruinsma and Bernasco, 2004; Naylor, 2004; van Duyne, 2003), the human slave trade (Mameli, 2002; Schloenhardt, 1999; Shelley, 2003; Taylor and Jamieson, 1999), deportation (Chan, 2005), investment and consumer fraud (Holtfretter, 2004; Holtfreter, van Slyke, and Blomberg, 2005; Naylor, 2007; Pontell, 2005) as evidence of the overly conservative nature of the field. Consequently, the victims of those crimes do not enter into the typical discussion of victimological concerns.

Under critical victimology, most victim-oriented initiatives tend to perpetuate the existing definitions of crime by failing to question the supportive social factors that give rise to the action and the response (Elias, 1990). The reason for this failure is multifaceted. One contributing factor is the reliance on official definitions and data in most analyses of victim issues. This subjugation inevitably leads to solutions that do not question the underlying social setting. Another factor is the ability of existing agencies to co-opt and incorporate emerging movements (such as children's rights) into existing social control systems. A more radical argument posits that the control of criminal justice and victimology rests in the hands of a powerful few who would view a critical approach as a threat to the status quo.

While critical victimology offers an interesting viewpoint and carries much potential for victimology, debating its merits is beyond the scope of this text. Various points throughout this book, however, will raise issues which are relevant to a critical approach. Examples of this include sociocultural discussions of why violence occurs and investigations of impediments to victim programs. A deeper and more intense examination of critical victimology will be left for other forums.

The Victim Movement

While academicians were debating the victim-precipitation argument, practitioners had pinpointed the victim as someone who deserved assistance from society and the criminal justice system. To some extent, this grass-roots concern for the victim's well-being was a reaction to the charges of victim complicity in the offense. Several different movements occurred simultaneously and contributed to the renewed interest in the plight of the victim. Among them were (1) the women's movement, (2) efforts to establish children's rights, (3) concerns over the growing crime problem, (4) the advocacy of victim compensation, (5) legal reforms, and (6) some other factors.

The Women's Movement

The women's movement, especially in the mid- to late-1960s, included a large component dealing with victims. Victim-blaming arguments often dealt with rape and sexual assault. The female victim found herself and her lifestyle on trial whenever an offender was apprehended. Reformers complained the system dealt with sexual assault victims as if they themselves were the offenders. Advocates pushed for equal treatment. They found the actions of the criminal justice system to be strong ammunition for their arguments. Beyond simply calling for changes in the formal system of justice, the women's movement made many gains. A short list would include the development of rape crisis centers, shelters for battered women, counseling for abused women and their children, and other forms of assistance. As women demanded an equal place in society, they worked to over-come the disadvantages of the criminal justice system.

Children's Rights

A growing concern over the needs and rights of youths blossomed during this period. Many writers point to the mid-1960s as the time when child abuse was "discovered." It was around this time that society decided to define abuse against children as a social problem. However, that does not mean child abuse was a new phenomenon. Child abuse is an age-old practice and, by many accounts, may have been much worse in the past than today. The difference in the 1960s, however, was that many physical and psychological actions used with children began to be questioned and labeled as abuse. States enacted legislation outlining the limits to which a child could be physically "disciplined." Specific children's bureaus within criminal justice agencies were either established or expanded to deal with the growing recognition of child maltreatment. Shelters were created to house children from abusive situations.

Runaways also gained publicity as a serious problem in the late 1960s. The general rebellion of youths in the United States enticed many juveniles to seek freedom from authority. Consequently, runaway shelters appeared in most large cities for the purpose of assisting the youths rather than returning them to their homes. Children were emerging as a new class of victims—both of abuse at home and of society in general.

The Growing Crime Problem

The level of crime in the United States began to register giant strides in the 1960s and throughout the 1970s. According to Uniform Crime Reports (UCR) data, crime in the United States more than doubled from 1960 to 1980. Along with concern over the Vietnam War, crime was the most important issue of the day. Presidential and local elections targeted the problem of law and order as a major concern. In an attempt to identify the causes of the growing problem and possible solutions, President Johnson appointed a commission to examine crime and the criminal justice system. Victim issues were a major focus of the President's Commission (1967) report. Among the victim components of the report were the beginnings of systematic victimization surveys, suggestions for the means of alleviating the pain and loss of victims, ideas for community programs aimed at providing victim services, and calls for involving victims further in the criminal justice system.

Some 15 years after this report was aired, another national task force concluded that victims still had substantial needs that were going unfilled. Many of the identified problems were similar to those noted by the earlier commission.

Victim Compensation

One suggestion made by the President's Commission (1967) was the establishment of methods for compensating crime victims for their losses. Among these techniques were restitution and *victim compensation*. Neither of these ideas, however, originated with the Commission. As was mentioned earlier in this chapter, restitution was the common method for dealing with crime throughout most of history. Victim compensation (state payments made to crime victims) was first introduced in Great Britain by Margery Fry in 1957. Although that early attempt failed, victim compensation fast became a major issue around the world.

New Zealand passed the first compensation legislation in 1963, closely followed by England in 1964. In the United States, California established victim compensation in 1965, New York in 1966, Hawaii in 1967, and Massachusetts in 1968. The federal government enacted legislation in 1984 that outlined compensation in instances in which federal crimes were committed. The statute also provided for monetary assistance to states with compensation programs. By 1989, 45 states had enacted compensation statutes. Other countries, such as Australia and Finland, also have established compensation programs. While each program may differ in its particulars, the basic premise of assisting crime victims remains the same.

Legal Reforms

In addition to the establishment of compensation legislation, a variety of legal reforms aimed at protecting and helping crime victims have appeared since the 1960s. Among the changes that have emerged are statutes that protect the rape victim's background and character in court proceedings. New laws were designed to protect battered spouses and their children. Legislation mandating doctors and teachers to report suspected cases of child abuse represented a bold initiative. Guidelines for informing victims about court proceedings and the legal system, as well as provisions that allow victim impact statements in sentencing and parole decisions, began to surface. In some instances, states passed a "Victims' Bill of Rights." These provisions outline the rights of the victim in a manner similar to those appearing in the U.S. Bill of Rights, which focuses on protections for the accused.

FIGURE 1.6
**Examples of Landmark Federal Victims' Rights Legislation Enacted
in the Twenty-first Century**

2000   *Trafficking Victims Protection Act*
Strengthens criminal enforcement, prosecution, and penalties against human traffickers; provides new protections to victims; and enables victims of severe forms of trafficking to seek benefits and services available to other crime victims.

2001   *Air Transportation Safety and System Stabilization Act*
Creates a new federal victim compensation program specifically for the victims of September 11. The program includes many types of damages normally available only through civil actions, such as payment for pain and suffering, lifetime lost earnings, and loss of enjoyment of life.

2003   *PROTECT Act ("Amber Alert" Law)*
Creates a national AMBER network to facilitate rapid law enforcement and community response to kidnapped or abducted children.

2003   *Prison Rape Elimination Act*
Develops national standards aimed at reducing prison rape.

2003   *Fair and Accurate Credit Transactions Act*
Provides new protections against identity theft and help victims of identity theft recover their financial losses.

2004   *Justice for All Act*
Provides mechanisms at the federal level to enforce the rights of crime victims, giving victims and prosecutors legal standing to assert victims' rights, authorizing the filing of writs of mandamus to assert a victim's right, and requiring the Attorney General to establish a victims' rights compliance program within the Department of Justice.

2006   *Adam Walsh Child Protection and Safety Act*
Increases supervision of sex offenders; also extends the federal Crime Victims' Rights Act to federal habeas corpus proceedings arising out of state convictions, eliminates the statute of limitations for federal prosecution of sexual offenses or child abduction, and extends the civil remedy for child sex crime victims to persons victimized as children, even if their injuries did not surface until the person became an adult.

Source: Compiled from Department of Justice (2006). *National Crime Victims' Rights Week Resource Guide, Crime Victims' Rights in America: A Historical Overview*. Washington, DC: National Center for Victims of Crime. Retrieved on August 17, 2007, from http://www.ojp.usdoj.gov/ovc/ncvrw/2007/pdf/overview.pdf

FIGURE 1.7
President Reagan's Proclamation Establishing the First Victims' Rights Week in the United States

---

April 8, 1981
By the President of the United States of America
A Proclamation

For too long, the victims of crime have been the forgotten persons of our criminal justice system. Rarely do we give victims the help they need or the attention they deserve. Yet the protection of our citizens—to guard them from becoming victims—is the primary purpose of our penal laws. Thus, each new victim personally represents an instance in which our system has failed to prevent crime. Lack of concern for victims compounds that failure.

Statistics reported by the Federal Bureau of Investigation and other law enforcement agencies indicate that crime continues to be a very serious national problem. But statistics cannot express the human tragedy of crime felt by those who are its victims. Only victims truly know the trauma crime can produce. They have lived it and will not soon forget it. At times, whole families are entirely disrupted—physically, financially and emotionally. Lengthy and complex judicial processes add to the victim's burden. Such experiences foster disillusionment and, ultimately, the belief that our system cannot protect us. As a Nation, we can ill afford this loss of faith on the part of innocent citizens who have been victimized by crimes.

We need a renewed emphasis on, and an enhanced sensitivity to, the rights of victims. These rights should be a central concern of those who participate in the criminal justice system, and it is time all of us paid greater heed to the plight of victims.

Now, Therefore, I, Ronald Reagan, President of the United States of America, do hereby proclaim the week beginning April 19, 1981, as Victims Rights Week. I urge all Federal, state and local officials involved in the criminal justice system to devote special attention to the needs of victims of crime, and to redouble their efforts to make our system responsive to those needs. I urge all other elected and appointed officials to join in this effort to make our justice system more helpful to those whom it was designed to protect. And I urge all citizens, from all walks of life, to remember that the personal tragedy of the victim is their own tragedy as well.

In Witness Whereof, I have hereunto set my hand this eighth day of April, in the year of our Lord nineteen hundred and eighty-one, and of the Independence of the United States of America the two hundred and fifth.

Ronald Reagan

Source: U.S. National Archives and Records Administration. *The Ronald Reagan Presidential Library, Proclamation 4831 — Victims Rights Week, 1981*. Retrieved on August 16, 2007, from http://www.reagan.utexas.edu/archives/speeches/1981/40881a.htm

As Figure 1.6 illustrates, Congress has continued its legislative efforts to soften the plight of victims and to bring them back into the criminal justice system. Back in 1981, President Ronald Reagan issued a proclamation, seen in Figure 1.7, establishing victims' rights week. Since then, every sitting President has followed this tradition dutifully.

Other Factors

Other factors have played either a direct or indirect role in emphasizing victim issues. One such source of influence has been the mass media. Rarely a week goes by in which a "crime of the week" does not appear in a special movie or as part of an ongoing series. Shows such as "America's Most Wanted" portray not only the offender but the harm to the victim, often relying on interviews with the victim or victim's family. Such media attention and interest in the victim naturally influences viewers in the audience.

Another factor not to be overlooked is the increasing interest in victims among academics. Four decades ago, there were virtually no books specifically focusing on victims. The publication of Schafer's (1968) *The Victim and His Criminal* signaled an era of increasing interest in victimology. Many texts have appeared since then. They range from general victim topics to specific discussions of compensation, intimate partner violence, child abuse, victim services, and other areas of interest. The first International Symposium on Victimology was held in Jerusalem in 1973. Since then, there have been several more worldwide gatherings and an uncounted number of national, state, and

FIGURE 1.8
Selected Journals Devoted to Victim Issues

Child Abuse & Neglect

Child Maltreatment

Homicide Studies

International Review of Victimology

Journal of Child Sexual Abuse

Journal of Elder Abuse & Neglect

Journal of Family Violence

Journal of Interpersonal Violence

Violence Against Women

Violence & Abuse Abstracts

Violence and Victims

local meetings of academics and professionals working with crime victims. These efforts culminated in the establishment of the American Society of Victimology in 2003. The spurt in college courses devoted to victimology or topical victim issues is encouraging. Some campuses (i.e., California State University–Fresno, Sam Houston State University, University of New Haven) now offer specialized programs in victim services. As Figure 1.8 shows, a variety of specialty journals devoted to victim issues now exist. In short, the victim movement has made strides over a relatively short period and continues to gain momentum.

Summary and Overview of This Book

As you have read, Mendelsohn (1976) saw general victimology as addressing five distinct types of victims. In addition to crime victims, he saw self-victimization, social victims, technological victims, and victims of the natural environment as legitimate focal concerns. All these victims suffer some degree of social or physical pain or loss. Each deserves assistance to offset the devastating effects of the victimization episode.

While Mendelsohn's vision of general victimology is quite impressive, it does cover a huge territory. Because Mendelsohn's approach is such a large undertaking, we will confine ourselves to a more manageable task. For that reason, this text must restrict itself to only the first category—crime victims. By the time you finish this book, we think you will agree with us. Victimology is so broad and complex that it makes sense to look at it in slices.

A glimpse of what lies ahead reveals an ambitious range of topics. This first chapter has laid the foundation for a host of issues and ideas that we will take up in greater detail in later chapters. Many topics will appear in the context of more than one discussion. Chapter 2 examines the extent of victimization and the development of victimization surveys. Victim surveys have become a key measure of crime and contribute a great deal of information to the study of victimization. Chapter 3 looks at the costs associated with being a crime victim and the additional burdens from becoming involved with the criminal justice system. As you will see, many people wrongly assume that victims do not cooperate with the authorities because of apathy. This chapter will demonstrate that the real reason reflects a very sensible cost-benefit analysis. Sometimes it is just too costly and too painful to be a "model citizen." Chapter 4 examines how the criminal justice system responds to victimization, the impact of those responses, and the continuing needs of victims. Chapter 5 continues this interest in making the victim whole again by visiting more recent efforts to bridge the gap between offenders and their victims.

Chapters 6 through 11 turn to discussions of particular forms of criminal victimization. These special topics include sexual assault, intimate partner violence, child maltreatment, elderly abuse, homicide, as well as victimization that takes place on school campuses and in the workplace. Each of these specific victim groupings has developed its own literature about causes and possible remedies. Finally, the book concludes with a look at the changing landscape of legal rights for crime victims.

Another feature that appears at the end of each chapter is the inclusion of selected Internet sites devoted to various victimological topics pertinent to that chapter. People in criminology and criminal justice are becoming much more aware of the wealth of information available through this medium. In order to take advantage of these technological developments, Figure 1.9 contains a listing of sites to get you started in this direction.

FIGURE 1.9
Selected Internet Sites Dealing with General Victim Issues

American Society of Victimology
    http://www.american-society-victimology.us

Amnesty International
    http://www.amnesty.org

International Victimology Web Site
    http://www.victimology.nl

National Center for Victims of Crime
    http://www.ncvc.org

National Crime Victims Research and Treatment Center
    http://colleges.musc.edu/ncvc/index.htm

National Criminal Justice Reference Service
    http://www.ncjrs.org

National Organization for Victim Assistance
    http://www.try-nova.org

United Nations
    http://www.un.org

U.S. Department of Justice, Office for Victims of Crime
    http://www.ojp.usdoj.gov/ovc/welcovc/welcome.html

World Society of Victimology
    http://www.ce.ucf.edu/asp/wsv/default.asp

Key Terms for Chapter 1

agent provocateur

criminal-victim dyad

critical victimology

deterrence

gemeinschaft

general victimology

gesellschaft

lex talionis

mala in se

restitution

retribution

typology

victim compensation

victim precipitation

Learning Objectives

After reading Chapter 2, you should be able to:
- Describe three major data sources for measuring crime.
- Tell what the UCR does.
- Outline three advantages of the UCR.
- Explain three disadvantages of the UCR.
- List the contents of the Index offenses.
- Differentiate personal from property offenses.
- Give a definition of the dark figure of crime.
- Talk about the level of crime and crime trends using the UCR.
- Discuss NIBRS.
- Give advantages NIBRS provides beyond the UCR.
- Specify what a victimization survey is.
- Outline the four generations of victimization surveys.
- Summarize and criticize the findings from the 1967 NORC survey.
- Give an example of telescoping.
- Explain how memory decay affects victim surveys.
- Compare and contrast reverse from forward record checks.
- Identify three assumptions behind the record check strategy.
- Define the term *panel design*.
- Reveal why bounding is important for victim surveys.
- Distinguish a self-respondent from a household-respondent.
- Outline the contributions of second-generation victim surveys.
- Tell why the development of the NCS was so important.
- Address the mover-stayer problem in the NCS.
- Relay a prime difficulty with business victimization surveys.
- Discuss redesign efforts behind fourth-generation victim surveys.
- Provide an example of a screen question in victim surveys.
- Know what the initials NCVS represent.
- Convey the goals and objectives behind the NCVS.
- Explain how the redesign has affected victimization estimates.
- Talk about victimization trends uncovered by the NCVS.
- Link victim characteristics to victimization rates.
- Compare and contrast results from the NCVS with the UCR.
- Discuss the relationship between victims and offenders as found in the NCVS.
- Provide information on the level of reporting victimization to the police.
- Explain what repeat victimization means.
- Discuss the extent of repeat victimization.
- Explain why information on repeat victimization is important.

Chapter 2

GAUGING THE
EXTENT OF CRIMINAL
VICTIMIZATION

Introduction

Gauging the extent of criminal victimization has long been a goal of the criminal justice system and those who study crime. Researchers and policymakers typically rely upon three major data sources for measuring the level of crime (O'Brien, 1985). The first source, official records of police departments, are the traditional depositories for crime information. However, dissatisfaction with police records prompted researchers to look elsewhere. Surveys that ask people about offenses they have committed became a popular alternative. Unfortunately, these surveys are not conducted on an annual or national basis, and they tell very little about the victims of crime. A third tactic is to question individuals about instances in which they were victimized. As we shall see in this chapter, this approach holds much promise.

Despite the common goal of measuring crime, none of these strategies alone yields a definitive answer to the question of how much victimization occurs in society. Each scheme provides a slightly different angle from which to view the crime problem. Each one of these methods has its own distinct advantages and inherent flaws.

This chapter examines some issues involved in measuring victimization, paying particular attention to the development and use of victimization surveys. We also will examine the level of crime and victimization presented by official police reports of crime and the *National Crime Victimization Survey*. As you will see, victim surveys provide a wealth of data that are quite useful for studying victims and related issues.

Official Police Reports

The most widely cited measure of crime is the *Uniform Crime Reports* (UCR) produced by the Federal Bureau of Investigation. The UCR began in 1931 as a mechanism by which police departments in different jurisdictions could exchange relevant information about crime. Police administrators around the country were very supportive of this effort. They felt that such knowledge could help identify the magnitude of the crime problem, map changes over time, and guide actions to combat the criminal element. This reporting system was meant to be a tool for the law enforcement community throughout the United States. As a result, the task of developing and carrying out this innovative program fell to the Federal Bureau of Investigation.

The UCR is characterized by a number of interesting and advantageous features. First, crime data are compiled annually from jurisdictions throughout the country. Such consistency and broad geographical coverage allows crime comparisons from year to year and from place to place. The fact that the UCR has been in operation since 1931 means that it is one of the longest-running systematic data collection efforts in the social sciences.

Second, the UCR has been influential in providing standardized crime definitions. Common definitions make it possible to draw comparisons across different times and jurisdictions. To achieve this goal, the FBI introduced what it calls the *Index, or Part I, offenses*. The FBI divides these serious crimes into two groups. *Personal offenses* include murder, forcible rape, robbery, and aggravated assault. *Property offenses* consist of burglary, larceny-theft, motor vehicle theft, and arson. While state statutes and local codes are not bound to these definitions, the UCR does introduce a common metric among the 50 states.

Third, the UCR gathers a large amount of information and details about the Index crimes. These data are especially useful when attempting to identify patterns and trends about crime and criminals. In addition, the UCR collects data on reported crimes and arrests for an additional 21 categories of offenses, known as the *Part II crimes*. Included in this category are sex offenses (besides rape), offenses against the family, and vandalism. The same level of detail as found in the Part I offenses, however, is not collected for these crimes.

The UCR is not immune from problems or disadvantages. Perhaps the greatest concern is that the UCR overlooks the *dark figure of crime*. In other words, these tabulations reflect only offenses that are known to the police. Any incidents in which victims or witnesses opt not to call the police are excluded from UCR figures. This drawback prompts critics to argue that the UCR grossly underreports the true level of crime in society. The UCR reflects police—and not necessarily criminal—activity.

A second major concern, particularly for our discussion, is the fact that the UCR offers little information on victims and offenders. The UCR gathers detailed data primarily on the more serious personal offenses (murder, forcible rape, robbery, and aggravated assault). Even then, most of the data deals only with persons who are arrested. There is very little information about the victim, the victim's circumstances, the context of the offense, and other potentially valuable information. This fact should not be surprising because law enforcement is oriented more toward dealing with offenders than with crime victims.

Interest in victims and the need to know more about individual criminal events has led to changes in the UCR system over the years. The *Supplemental Homicide Reports* (SHR) provides data on the victim characteristics, location, offender characteristics, relationship between the victim and offender, the use of weapons, and the circumstances surrounding the homicide event. As such, the SHR offers information about the homicide victim and victimization not typically found in the balance of the UCR data.

The most recent set of changes in the UCR has been the introduction of the *National Incident-Based Reporting System* (NIBRS). The NIBRS system grew out of a report completed in the mid-1980s that examined the changing needs for data collection and analysis that could assist law enforcement in combating crime. The NIBRS data has several major advantages over the traditional UCR data. First, NIBRS collects detailed information on 22 categories of offenses (see Figure 2.1) rather than just the eight Index offenses. Second, rather than counting only the most serious Index offense, NIBRS reports on all of the offenses that occur during a criminal incident. Third, NIBRS data includes a wide array of information not found in the traditional UCR data and collects that data on each crime incident. Among the information included in this expanded data collection process is detailed information on the victim, the victim-offender relationship, injuries, and property loss (see Figure 2.1).

The great advantage of the NIBRS data is the ability of law enforcement and researchers to gain a more in-depth picture of the crime problem and to use that information to decide on appropriate courses of action. Unfortunately, participation in the NIBRS system requires increased data entry requirements and data processing abilities on the part of local law enforcement. The agencies must also meet stringent guidelines for participation. Because of these requirements, NIBRS has not been implemented nationally and no nationally representative data are available for study. Local agencies using the NIBRS system, however, are able to undertake more sophisticated analyses of their crime problems.

FIGURE 2.1
Key Victim-related Information Collected by NIBRS for Each Crime Incident

Victim Information:	Offense Categories:
Type of Victim	Arson
Age of Victim	Assault Offenses
Sex of Victim	Bribery
Race of Victim	Burglary/Breaking and
Ethnicity of Victim	Entering
Destruction/Damage/Vandalism	Counterfeiting/Forgery
Resident Status of Victim	Drug/Narcotic Offenses
Homicide/Assault Circumstances	Embezzlement
Justifiable Homicide Circumstances	Extortion/Blackmail
Type of Injury	Fraud Offenses
Relationship of Victim to Offender	Gambling Offenses
	Homicide Offenses
Property Information:	Kidnapping/Abduction
	Larceny/Theft Offenses
Type of Property Loss	Motor Vehicle Theft
Property Description	Pornography/Obscene
Property Value	Material
Recovery Date	Prostitution Offenses
Number of Stolen Motor Vehicles	Robbery
Number of Recovered Motor Vehicles	Sex Offenses, Forcible
Suspected Drug Type	Sex Offenses, Non Forcible
Estimated Drug Quantity	Stolen Property Offenses
	Weapon Law Violations

Source: Compiled from Rantala, R.R. (2000). *Effects of NIBRS on Crime Statistics*. Washington, DC: Bureau of Justice Statistics, and http://www.fbi.gov/hq/cjisd/nibrscat.pdf

Despite the problems with the UCR, the data do have a long history and are helpful in answering a variety of questions. Increased involvement in the NIBRS system will enhance the value of official police crime data. In order to reach a fuller understanding of how the UCR currently contributes to our knowledge of crime, the following section highlights some recent materials published by the FBI.

Statistics from the UCR

According to Table 2.1, the Uniform Crime Reports states that there were more than 11.5 million Index offenses known to the police in 2005. If one considers both personal and property crimes, that number reflects a crime rate of 3,899 offenses for every 100,000 people in the United States. The data also show that there are more than seven times as many property crimes as personal crimes. A closer examination shows that the most common threat of crime comes in the form of larceny, where almost 2,300 individuals out of every 100,000 are victimized. At the opposite extreme, fewer than six persons per 100,000 population are the victim of murder.

TABLE 2.1
National Index Offenses, UCR, 2002

Offense Category	Number	Rate
Violent Crime	1,390,695	469.2
Murder	16,692	5.6
Rape	93,934	31.7
Robbery	417,122	140.7
Aggravated Assault	862,947	291.1
Property Crime	10,166,159	3,429.8
Burglary	2,154,126	726.7
Larceny	6,776,807	2,286.3
Motor Vehicle Theft	1,235,226	416.7
TOTAL	11,556,854	3,899.0

Source: Federal Bureau of Investigation (2006). *Crime in the United States, 2005: Uniform Crime Reports*. Washington, DC: U.S. Government Printing Office. Found at: http://www.fbi.gov/ucr/05civs/data/table_01.html

As mentioned earlier, one great advantage to the UCR is the ability to look at crime over time. Figure 2.2 graphs violent crime rates for the nation from 1979 until 2005. Figure 2.3 presents similar information for property offenses.

FIGURE 2.2
Violent Index Crime Rates, UCR, 1979-2005

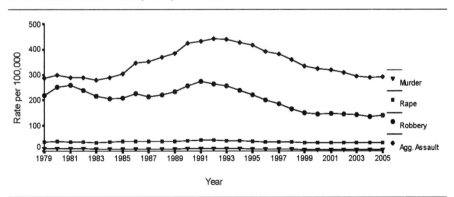

Source: Constructed by authors from UCR data.

FIGURE 2.3
Property Index Crime Rates, UCR, 1979-2005

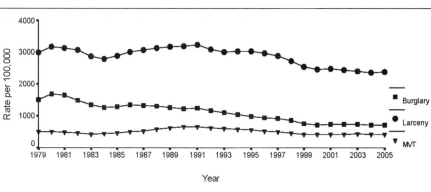

Source: Constructed by authors from UCR data.

In terms of personal crimes, aggravated assault showed a generally upward trajectory until 1991-1993, after which the numbers began to decrease. Robbery, on the other hand, reached similar peaks in both 1981 and 1991. Since 1991 robbery has shown a steady decline. Both homicide and rape have remained relatively flat. Preliminary 2006 data show slight increases in violent crime, particularly murder, robbery, and aggravated assault (FBI, 2007). For property crimes, only burglary has seen a steady drop since 1980. Larceny has experienced two similar peaks in 1980 and 1991, with modest decreases since the early 1990s, while motor vehicle theft has remained relatively unchanged.

The UCR data and similar official records provide interesting, but limited, data for those interested in studying crime victims. Very little information is gathered about victims, and even less is reported in the summary UCR reports. One exception to this fact is the information found in the SHR on victim-offender relationship. Information on the relationship between homicide victims and offenders in 2005 reveals that more than one-fifth of the participants can be considered as acquaintances and 14 percent as strangers, while 5 percent are spouses and 4 percent are boyfriends/girlfriends (FBI, 2006). In 45 percent of the homicides, the relationship between the parties is unknown. Unfortunately, the UCR does not provide such information for other categories of offenses.

While other victim information is collected by the NIBRS program, the lack of national data means that the information is not routinely analyzed and presented in UCR reports. Consequently, the UCR offers little insight for understanding victimization. As a result of the shortcomings of official data, researchers have moved toward other data collection methods for capturing the kind of details important for the study of victimization.

Victimization Surveys

While the UCR has a long history, victimization surveys are just about 40 years old. Victim surveys got their start with the work of the President's Commission in the mid-1960s. The Commission came about because of problems with increasing crime and civil unrest during that era. From its inception, the President's Commission (1967) recognized that an accurate description of the crime problem was lacking. As a result, it authorized a number of independent projects to gather information about crime victims.

From that modest beginning point, victimization surveys have grown into an invaluable data source. A *victimization survey*, instead of relying upon police reports or other official information, entails contacting people and asking them if they have been crime victims. In looking at the development of victimization surveys, one can divide them into various stages or "generations" (Hindelang, 1976). Each successive generation is marked by the way it grappled with several methodological problems raised in earlier phases. Figure 2.4 summarizes the four generations of victimization surveys since their inception in the mid-1960s.

FIGURE 2.4
The Development of Victimization Surveys

First-Generation Surveys
- mid-1960s
- carried out for the 1967 President's Commission
- pilot studies of the feasibility of victimization surveys
- showed much greater victimization than police data

Second-Generation Surveys
- late 1960s and early 1970s
- probe methods to address problems found in First Generation Surveys
- city specific surveys

Third-Generation Surveys
- early 1970s to late 1980s
- National Crime Survey (NCS) initiated in 1972
- Business Victimization Surveys—1972 to 1977
- City Surveys—26 cities from 1972 to 1975

Fourth-Generation Surveys
- 1988 to present
- NCS renamed the National Crime Victimization Survey—initiated 1992

First-Generation Victim Surveys

The initial victim surveys, undertaken at the behest of the President's Commission, represented little more than a set of extensive feasibility studies. These efforts tested whether such an approach could elicit sensitive information from the public. The researchers also wanted to determine how the criminal justice system could use these victim-based findings.

The NORC Survey

Perhaps the best known of all the initial pilot studies was the poll sponsored by the National Opinion Research Center (NORC) and reported by Ennis (1967). This effort was the first national victim survey and targeted 10,000 households throughout the country. Interviewers initially asked participants to report on incidents that happened to them during the preceding 12-month period. Then, the interviewer sought more detailed information on the two most recent and most serious offenses.

What made this survey so well-known was the subsequent claim that the UCR underreported by roughly 50 percent the crime rate indicated by the *NORC Survey*. Table 2.2 contains a comparison of crime rates based upon the NORC data and the UCR figures. The NORC survey uncovered almost four times as many rapes and more than three times as many burglaries as did the UCR. The lone exception to reporting discrepancies was motor vehicle theft. Both data sources produced comparable rates. This similarity was probably due to the fact that most auto insurance companies will not issue a reimbursement check unless the victim files a police report. Combining the offenses into broader categories gave a much clearer picture. The NORC survey unearthed 1.9 times as many violent episodes and 2.2 times more property offenses than official crime statistics had logged. Critics quickly pointed to the NORC findings as definitive proof that official crime records were inaccurate and unreliable because they neglected the "dark figure of crime" (Biderman and Reiss, 1967).

Some Methodological Considerations

While the NORC results were dramatic, there were enough problems to compromise their usefulness. First, the claim that there was twice as much crime than what the police acknowledged was based on a very small number of victim accounts. Under normal conditions, someone conducting a victim survey might anticipate uncovering only

TABLE 2.2
Comparison of NORC Victimization Rates with UCR Rates

Crime Category	NORC	UCR	Ratio of NORC to UCR
Homicide	3.0	5.1	0.6
Rape	42.5	11.6	3.7
Robbery	94.0	61.4	1.5
Aggravated Assault	218.3	106.6	2.0
Burglary	949.1	299.6	3.2
Larceny $50+	606.5	267.4	2.3
Auto Theft	206.2	226.0	0.9
Violent Crimes	357.8	184.7	1.9
Property Crimes	1,761.8	793.0	2.2

Source: The President's Commission on Law Enforcement and Administration of Justice (1967). *Task Force Report: Crime and Its Impact—An Assessment*. Washington, DC: U.S. Government Printing Office.

a handful of rape and robbery incidents. Deriving estimates from a few observations can yield some questionable figures.

Second, the crime instances that victims reported were submitted to a panel of experts to assess whether these events were really crimes. Ultimately, the panel excluded more than one-third of the victim reports. An example of misclassification would be a person who returns home, finds all the furniture gone, and exclaims "Help—I've been robbed!" The real crime here is a burglary, not a robbery. Employing a panel to check victim reports may help validate the results and impart a greater sense of confidence, but it also alerts us to the fact that the survey design had some major flaws in terms of question wording.

A third set of problems dealt with subject recall. Some participants experienced difficulties with telescoping. *Telescoping* takes place when respondents mistakenly bring criminal events that occurred outside the time frame into the survey period. For example, suppose that you are taking part in a victimization survey. The interviewer asks whether you had a car stolen during the past 12 months. In actuality, your automobile was taken 14 months ago. However, because you cannot remember exactly when the incident took place, you advise the interviewer that you were the victim of such a crime.

A related hindrance is faulty memory. *Memory decay* is evidenced when respondents were victimized during the survey time frame, but forgot the event and did not provide the correct answer to the question. Researchers also found that respondent fatigue could influence the results. For example, the level of crime reporting decreased as the length of the survey increased. Because of these considerations, victimization estimates derived from these efforts contained an unknown margin of error. Unless telescoping and memory decay "exactly offset one another, the survey estimate of the amount of crime that occurred is inaccurate" (Schneider et al., 1978: 18-19).

Another major concern emerged from the selection of respondents. The study did not randomly select respondents from households, and individuals under the age of 18 were excluded unless they were married. Additionally, all household offenses were counted as crimes against the head of the household. Each of these facts could add more bias to the results.

Besides the above concerns, a host of other imperfections contaminated the findings. There were definitional problems in the survey questions, an inability to locate where the crime actually took place, a problem in having a count of victims rather than offenses, and other nagging obstacles that plagued first-generation efforts. Despite these weaknesses, an important contribution had emerged. Criminologists and victimologists learned that the public was willing to answer questions about their victimization experiences. These early pilot studies clearly established the need for more refined victimization surveys and the avenues they should travel.

Second-Generation Victim Surveys

Preparations for the second generation of victim surveys began with several exploratory projects conducted during 1970 and 1971. These preliminary studies investigated a variety of methods for addressing the problems noted earlier with the first-generation surveys. Once these concerns received treatment, then it would be time to move on to running the surveys themselves.

Recall Problems

To test the accuracy of respondent recall, researchers in two different locations (Washington, DC, and Baltimore) conducted their own record checks. The strategy here was to compare information derived from police records with victimization survey data. Two types of record checks were involved: reverse record checks and forward record checks.

A *reverse record check* starts by locating crime victim names in police files. The next step is to contact these people and administer a victim survey to them. Therefore, survey responses are checked against the police records to assess the degree to which a respondent confirms offense characteristics that appear in the official files.

The reverse record check comparisons revealed that memory decay grew more problematic as the time period increased. The best recall usually occurred within three months of the incident. After that point, victims became more forgetful about the incident and its details. The results also showed that recall was better for some offenses than others and that there was a noticeable degree of telescoping. In other words, victims erroneously moved up events that occurred outside the time frame and placed them inside the targeted interval. In addition, the wording of some questions and their order of presentation also affected the responses (Hindelang, 1976: 46-53).

Schneider and her associates (1978) approached the very same issues with the exact opposite methodology. They opted to conduct a *forward record check*. After asking respondents in a victim survey whether they had contacted the police about the incident, the researchers combed police records for a written case report. Police reports could not be found for about one-third of the victims who said they had filed such a report. When case records were located, police reports and victim accounts showed a great deal of similarity. However, there was evidence that telescoping could produce some major distortions unless specific steps were taken to counteract this tendency.

Despite the gains that these record check studies provided, there was still a need for caution. Skogan (1981: 13-14) warned of three assumptions imbedded within this strategy. First, there is an assumption that police incident records are the appropriate benchmark against which to assess victim accounts. Just because an officer responds to a call does not mean that an official report will be filed by the officer. Second, record check studies can deal only with situations that have come to the attention of the record keeper. Third, crime victims are a very mobile group whose frequent address changes make recontact difficult. Checking reports at a later time, therefore, becomes problematic.

The problem of telescoping received further consideration in a panel study of households undertaken by the Bureau of the Census in 1971. A *panel design* surveys the same group of households or respondents at regular intervals over a period of time. The repeated interviews or surveys allow for *bounding*. In other words, the first survey serves as the calendar reference point for the second, the second for the third, and so on. The earlier interview gives the respondent a solid referent for separating one time period from the next. It also permits the researcher to check on whether the same victimization instance is reported in more than one time period. This provision can eliminate any obvious repetition in the events that victims report. This panel study found more accurate recall and less telescoping in a six-month time frame than over a 12-month format (Hindelang, 1976)

The San Jose-Dayton Surveys

Incorporating recommendations from earlier exploratory pretests, surveys in San Jose and Dayton sought to compare information gathered from self-respondents with household respondents. A *self-respondent* is a person who reports victimization incidents for himself or herself. On the other hand, a *household respondent* relays information about crimes committed against all members of his or her household. The San Jose and Dayton surveys revealed that self-respondents reported more personal crimes and experienced fewer recall problems than did household respondents (Hindelang, 1976: 57-68).

In addition to interviewing victims from the general population, surveys of businesses and commercial establishments were also being developed at this time. Problems with such things as telescoping, memory decay, question wording, and bounding also existed in these evaluations. Sometimes, particular problems loomed even larger. For example, most reports of a business burglary or robbery would come from an employee who knew about the incident firsthand. Quite often, subsequent efforts to recontact the original informant were hampered by personnel turnover. The contact person, as well as anyone familiar with the episode, sometimes was no longer an employee of the business at the time of the second interview. Thus, the quality of record checks suffered from a lack of continuity among respondents.

The second-generation surveys were useful in identifying several factors that were incorporated into later survey instruments. First, it was found that more specific questions elicited more accurate information and better recall than did very general questions about prior victimization. Second, shorter recall periods (six months or less) significantly limited the problems of telescoping and memory decay. Third, bounding the time period by some concrete event (such as the last interview in a panel design) helped to limit the problem of telescoping. Fourth, interviewing individuals themselves about their victimization experiences was preferable to asking a proxy (a household respondent) about the experiences of others. Finally, through careful wording of questions, it was possible to approximate UCR offense definitions in order to enable comparisons across the two data sources.

Third-Generation Victim Surveys

The third generation witnessed an ambitious schedule of activity. The federal government launched a national victimization survey, a survey of commercial businesses, and a special victimization survey in 26

American cities. The following subsections outline each of these endeavors.

The National Crime Survey

The *National Crime Survey* (NCS) was launched in 1972 with a probability sample of 72,000 households set up in a panel format. The plan was to interview each member within these households. This strategy would produce a study group of approximately 100,000 people after eliminating problems such as refusals to cooperate, incorrect addresses, and others.

Workers contacted each household every six months over a three-year period for a total of seven interviews during this time. To avoid replacing the entire sample at the end of three years, the NCS staggered the beginning and ending points for each wave. Every six months, one-sixth of the households departed the study group and their replacements underwent the initial interview. Roughly 12,000 households were interviewed each month, making the survey process a year-round endeavor.

The NCS incorporated many features uncovered in the earlier exploratory studies. The panel design, for example, established a six-month bounding period for the study. The first interview was not used to estimate crime rates. Instead, it became the starting point or boundary. To guard against telescoping and memory decay, each subsequent interview was checked against previous reports.

One burden that confronted the NCS was the *mover-stayer problem*. Sampling of respondents was built on the residence, not the individual. If the original survey participants vacated the premises and somebody else moved in, the new tenants automatically joined the sample for the balance of the study period. Responses from the new residents were used even though bounding was not possible. The NCS made no effort to track the original respondents. Instead, it was assumed that the impact of relocation upon victimization estimates and the comparability of stable versus changed residences were minimal.

Unlike earlier generations, interviewers talked with each household member rather than just a single household representative. Exceptions to this rule occurred when the contact person was a child, when the parent objected to an interview with a minor, or when repeated attempts to contact an individual family member proved futile. In these cases, one person acted as a proxy for the entire household.

While the above is true regarding individual victimizations, crimes against the household were solicited from only one household representative. This procedure aimed to reduce interviewing time and to eliminate the overlap from talking with more than one person about the same things. Unfortunately, the selected household respondent may not always be aware of all crimes against the household or may not know all the details needed for accurate reporting.

The Business Victimization Survey

Along with the national survey, the NCS also launched a commercial victimization survey. This undertaking gathered information from businesses to assess their level of risk. The commercial survey, though, was discontinued in 1977 for two primary reasons. First, the sample of 15,000 businesses was too small to project reliable estimates. Second, the costs of the survey were not commensurate with the potential payoff.

City Surveys

Twenty-six large cities were selected for special surveys of both residents and businesses. A total of 12,000 households and 2,000 businesses were targeted for interviews in each city. While the single-city findings were interesting, there was a great deal of overlap with the national survey. The costs associated with these multiple projects were astronomical. Eventually, the city surveys were discontinued in 1975 after only three years of operation.

Fourth-Generation Victim Surveys

Today, we are in the fourth generation of victimization surveys. To emphasize this transition, the format and title of the national victim surveys has changed. The name is now the *National Crime Victimization Survey* (NCVS).

The redesign efforts began in 1979, partly as a response to issues raised in a National Academy of Science report (Penick and Owens, 1976). As before, a number of exploratory analyses were undertaken to test potential adjustments. Some of these considerations covered such items as improving accuracy of responses, identifying information by subgroups, adding new questions to tap different dimensions of crime and victim responses, and making the data more useful for researchers (Skogan, 1990; Whitaker, 1989).

Concern over recall accuracy returns to issues of question wording, bounding, memory decay, and telescoping. There was some worry that the *screen questions*—those inquiries that probe possible victimization experiences—could be misleading and in need of revision (Dodge, 1985). Redesign analysts suggested that improved screen questions could result in increased reports of crime by prodding the memory of respondents and providing clearer definitions of criminal victimization. To see how the NCVS does this, Figure 2.5 displays screen questions used in both the individual and household surveys. Each respondent is asked the questions in Figure 2.5 as a means of probing victimization experiences in the past six months. These responses are then used as the basis for in-depth questions about the specific victimization occurrences.

To assess the impact of the changes in screen questions, half the interviews in 1992 were conducted using the old questions while half the subjects were asked the new questions. A comparison of the two formats showed that the revamped queries produced 44 percent more personal victimization reports and 49 percent more property incidents (Kindermann et al., 1997). As expected, reports for robbery, personal theft, and motor vehicle theft did not show substantial gains. However, rapes jumped by 157 percent, assaults rose 57 percent, burglaries increased by 20 percent, and theft moved upward by 27 percent. Inspection of the data led the analysts to believe that the new instrument made inroads into gray-area events. A *gray-area event* pertains to a victimization that does not conform to the usual common stereotype. For example, episodes involving nonstrangers as the aggressors showed marked increases with the new questions. It would appear, then, that the revisions worked as intended.

A shorter reference period was also examined as a means to improve recall. This option, however, was rejected. The increased costs were simply too prohibitive.

The problem of bounding came up in reference to the mover-stayer issue. If you recall, newly relocated respondents at a household marked for inclusion in the NCVS provide unbounded information during their initial interview. One solution called for basing the sample on respondents, as opposed to household addresses. However, such a move would require interviewers to follow sample members to their new residences for subsequent questioning. This option was not feasible because it increased survey costs substantially.

Another exasperating problem has been the inability to examine subgroups within the survey data. Because of legal restrictions protecting respondent identities, it is difficult to analyze victimization data in anything but the national aggregate. The redesign efforts have demonstrated that it is possible to produce limited information based on cities or states without violating subject confidentiality. Such an ability allows for more direct and meaningful comparisons with the UCR and other data sources.

FIGURE 2.5
NCVS Screen Questions*

36a. I'm going to read some examples that will give you an idea of the kinds of crimes this study covers.

    As I go through them, tell me if any of these happened to you in the last 6 months, that is since _____ _____, 20___.

    Was something belonging to YOU stolen, such as—
    a)   Things that you carry, like luggage, a wallet, purse, briefcase, book—
    b)   Clothing, jewelry, or calculator—
    c)   Bicycle or sports equipment—
    d)   Things in your home—like a TV, stereo, or tools—
    e)   Things outside your home such as a garden hose or lawn furniture—
    f)   Things belonging to children in the household—
    g)   Things from a vehicle, such as a package, groceries, camera, or cassette tapes—OR
    h)   Did anyone ATTEMPT to steal anything belonging to you?

36b. Did any incidents of this type happen to you?

36c. How many times?

37a. (Other than any incidents already mentioned,) has anyone—
    a)   Broken in or ATTEMPTED to break into your home by forcing a door or window, pushing past someone, jimmying a lock, cutting a screen, or entering through an open door or window?
    b)   Has anyone illegally gotten in or tried to get into a garage, shed, or storage room? OR
    c)   Illegally gotten in or tried to get into a hotel or motel room or vacation home where you were staying?

37b. Did any incidents of this type happen to you?

37c. How many times?

40a. (Other than any incidents already mentioned,) since _____ _____, 20___, were you attacked or threatened OR did you have something stolen from you–
    a)   At home, including the porch or yard—
    b)   At or near a friend's, relative's, or neighbor's home—
    c)   At work or school—
    d)   In places such as a storage shed or laundry room, a shopping mall, restaurant, bank, or airport—
    e)   While riding in any vehicle—
    f)   On the street or in a parking lot—
    g)   At such places as a party, theater, gym, picnic area, bowling lanes, or while fishing or hunting—OR
    h)   Did anyone ATTEMPT to attack or ATTEMPT to steal anything belonging to you from any of these places?

40b. Did any incidents of this type happen to you?

41c. How many times?

* For each of these questions the respondent is asked to "Briefly describe incident(s)"

Source: Bureau of Justice Statistics (2004). *National Crime Victimization Survey 1992-2002* [Computer file]. Ann Arbor, MI: ICPSR.

A major goal of the redesign was to enhance the analytical worth of the survey. Despite the wealth of information contained in the NCVS, many researchers would like to capture data on other related topics. The redesign team considered the feasibility of adding special supplements that would supply data on selected topics. Examples of these efforts are the Victim Risk Supplement conducted in 1983, the School Crime Supplements carried out in 1989 and 1996, and the Police Public Contact Survey in 1999. Another suggestion was to conduct longitudinal analyses. To date, victimization studies have been restricted to cross-sectional approaches. It has not been possible to match a person's file with responses from an earlier interview. The redesign team strongly recommended that procedures for more longitudinal analyses be adopted. The redesign also suggested the move to *Computer-Assisted Telephone Interviews* (CATI). This technique uses a computer to prompt the interviewer with the proper questions. It automatically skips questions whenever appropriate. Computerization should also eliminate miscoded data by accepting only legitimate responses during the interview.

The NCVS began carrying out the redesigned survey in 1988 and had the full survey overhauled and in place by the end of 1992. Undoubtedly, the NCVS will undergo further modification as victimization surveys continue to evolve and as the need for different sorts of information becomes more apparent. Victimization surveys have become a valuable tool within a very short time. As the next section will show, the information gathered by this approach offers a much different view of criminal victimization than that given by the official records.

Statistics from the NCVS

Recent years have witnessed a growing reliance on victimization survey data for assessing the crime problem. Perhaps the greatest reason for this change is the realization that the UCR suffers from systematic limitations. For some time now, criminologists have recognized that official reports underestimate how much crime there really is. Even the primitive early victim surveys uncovered much more crime than the UCR did. In addition, victim surveys capture data on the victim and the circumstances surrounding the criminal event. As a result, victimization surveys have earned an important niche in the measurement of crime.

According to the NCVS (Bureau of Justice Statistics, 2006), there were more than 23 million crimes committed in 2005. In comparison, the UCR tabulated less than half as many Index offenses in 2005 (Federal Bureau of Investigation, 2006). Even when one takes definitional differences into account, the gap between these two data sources is quite large.

Table 2.3 presents national victimization figures according to incident type. The table reveals that the risks of becoming a property crime victim are far greater than being involved in a violent encounter. This finding mirrors the UCR information discussed earlier.

Victimization surveys also provide additional information not addressed by the UCR. For example, Table 2.4 shows that males are more likely to be violent crime victims than females. Like the UCR, the NCVS reveals that people under the age of 24 are a very vulnerable group. Blacks have higher robbery and aggravated assault rates than do whites. However, they share almost identical chances of becoming simple assault victims. Never-married individuals are also more likely to be victimized. Finally, persons with lower incomes have a higher risk of becoming crime victims in every category than people who are wealthier.

The NCVS has collected victimization data for several years now. This practice permits an inspection of trends. Figure 2.6 graphs personal victimization rates since the NCVS redesign in 1992. A glance at the figure shows that victimization rates for robbery, aggravated assault, and simple assault have slowly declined since 1994. Personal theft and rape/sexual assault, though, exhibit relatively stable offense rates. While the general tendency is for reduced levels of criminal activity in both the NCVS and the UCR since 1993, the reduction in victimization is nowhere near the magnitude of that found in the UCR data. Unfortunately, the short time span since the 1992 redesign makes any trend analyses suspect.

Similar information for household property victimization appears in Figure 2.7 for the 1993-2005 period. Again, the graphs show no major disturbances over time. Household theft displays a consistent and relatively large decline, while burglary and motor vehicle theft show only small reductions. Again, these patterns are somewhat consistent, although less markedly so, with conclusions derived from our earlier examination of UCR crime rates.

TABLE 2.3
National Victimization Levels, NCVS, 2005

Offense Category	Number of Victimizations	Victimization Rate per 1,000
Personal Crimes:		
Rape/Sexual Assault	191,670	.8
Robbery	624,850	2.6
Aggravated Assault	1,052,260	4.3
Simple Assault	3,304,930	13.5
Personal Theft[a]	227,070	.9
Household Crimes:		
Burglary	3,456,220	29.5
Theft	13,605,590	116.2
Motor Vehicle Theft	978,120	8.4

[a] Includes pocket picking and purse snatching.
Source: Bureau of Justice Statistics (2006). *Criminal Victimization in the United States, 2005: Statistical Tables*. Washington, DC: U.S. Government Printing Office.

TABLE 2.4
Personal Victimization Rates by Selected Characteristics, NCVS, 2005

Victim Characteristic	Robbery	Aggravated Assault	Simple Assault
Sex			
Male	3.8	5.6	15.9
Female	1.4	3.1	11.2
Age			
12-15	3.5	8.7	30.6
16-19	7.0	9.7	24.2
20-24	5.5	10.0	30.3
25-34	3.1	4.7	15.2
35-49	1.9	3.2	11.8
50-64	1.4	2.4	7.0
65+	.6	.8	1.1
Race			
White	2.2	3.8	13.4
Black	4.6	7.6	13.0
Other	3.0	2.5	7.9
Marital Status			
Never Married	4.8	7.7	23.5
Married	1.0	2.4	6.6
Widowed	1.4	.5	3.6
Divorced/Separated	3.8	5.2	21.2
Family Income			
$ 0- 7,500	5.6	9.7	20.1
$ 7,500-14,999	4.9	6.8	14.2
$15,000-24,999	3.5	6.4	18.8
$25,000-34,999	2.8	5.2	16.4
$35,000-49,000	2.5	4.3	14.7
$50,000-74,999	1.8	4.3	14.5
$75,000+	2.1	2.6	11.1

Source: Bureau of Justice Statistics (2006). *Criminal Victimization in the United States, 2005: Statistical Tables*. Washington, DC: U.S. Government Printing Office.

FIGURE 2.6
Personal Victimization Rates, NCVS, 1993-2005

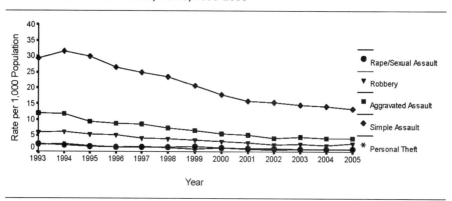

Source: Constructed by authors from NCVS data.

FIGURE 2.7
Household Victimization Rates, NCVS, 1993-2005

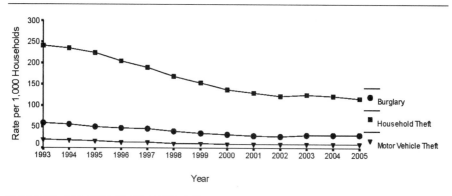

Source: Constructed by authors from NCVS data.

One obvious distinction between the UCR and the NCVS is that victims reveal to interviewers incidents that have not come to the attention of the police. Table 2.5 shows that for most offenses respondents report roughly half or less than half of their victimizations to the police. Aggravated assault (62%) and motor vehicle theft (83%) are those offenses most often reported to the police. Cases of household theft (32%) are the least reported offenses. Figure 2.8 graphically compares crime rates derived from both the UCR and NCVS for 2005. In virtually every category in which even rough comparisons can be made, the NCVS reveals higher offense levels, with the largest differences appearing in burglary and motor vehicle theft.

TABLE 2.5
Percent Victimizations Reported to the Police, NCVS, 2005

Offense	Percent Reported
Personal Offenses:	
Rape/Sexual Assault	38.3%
Robbery	52.4
Aggravated Assault	62.4
Simple Assault	42.3
Personal Theft	35.2
Household Offenses:	
Burglary	56.3
Motor Vehicle Theft	83.2
Household Theft	32.3

Source: Compiled by authors from NCVS data.

FIGURE 2.8
Comparison of 2005 UCR and NCVS Crime Rates

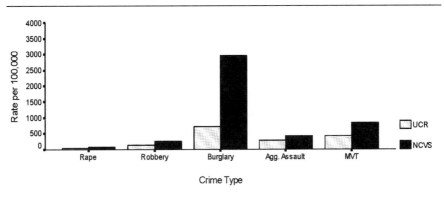

Source: Constructed by authors from UCR and NCVS data.

Victimization data also provide a great deal of information about victim-offender relationships (see Figure 2.9). This information, however, is primarily for crimes in which the victim and offender have personal contact. In 2005, 45 percent of all violent crimes were committed by nonstrangers. Strangers were involved in a high of 66 percent of all robberies to a low of 31 percent of all sexual offenses (Bureau of Justice Statistics, 2006). Acquaintances, either casual or well-known, make up 37 percent of the offenders, according to the NCVS. The NCVS also offers information on the perceived age, race, and gender of the offender.

FIGURE 2.9
Victim-Offender Relationship in Violent Crime, NCVS, 2005

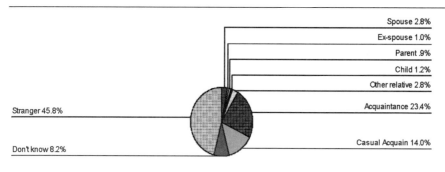

Spouse 2.8%
Ex-spouse 1.0%
Parent .9%
Child 1.2%
Other relative 2.8%
Acquaintance 23.4%
Stranger 45.8%
Don't know 8.2%
Casual Acquain 14.0%

Source: Constructed by authors from NCVS data.

Repeat Victimization

The growth of victimization surveys and the development of new data analysis techniques, particularly through the use of computer mapping, have generated increased interest in repeat victimization or revictimization. *Repeat victimization* can be defined as the repeated occurrence of crime either involving the same victim or the same location. Even casual observation demonstrates that repeat victimization is common with some crimes. For example, it is not unusual for domestic violence victims to drop charges or refuse to cooperate with the prosecution, despite records of ongoing violent episodes. Sherman (1995) points out that police often receive repeated calls for service stemming from domestic violence at the same addresses.

In one of the earliest examinations of repeat victimization, Polvi et al. (1990) noted that the risk of being a repeat burglary victim is 12 times higher than expected, and this risk is more pronounced immediately after an initial burglary. This heightened risk persists for roughly three months and then levels off to normal expected levels.

Major victimization surveys, such as the National Crime Victimization Survey (NCVS), the British Crime Survey (BCS), and the International Crime Victim Survey (ICVS), demonstrate the existence of repeat victimization. The NCVS provides some insight through its questions dealing with *series victimizations*. "A series victimization is defined as six or more similar but separate crimes which the victim is unable to recall individually or describe in detail to an interviewer" (Bureau of Justice Statistics, 2003). The 2005 NCVS reveals that 4.1 percent of all crimes of violence are series victimizations. Similarly, 3.9 percent of all personal crimes and 0.5 percent of all property crimes fall into the series victimization category (Bureau of Justice Statistics, 2006). Analysis of the British Crime Survey (BCS) also shows that multiple victimization episodes are concentrated among relatively few victims. Ellingworth et al. (1995), using BCS data from 1982 through 1992, point out that roughly one-quarter to one-third of all property crime is committed against people victimized five or more times within a one-year period of time. This means that almost two-thirds of victims are repeat victims. Similarly, roughly 50 percent of personal crimes appear as repeat victimizations (Ellingworth et al., 1995). Data from the 2000 ICVS shows that 46 percent of sexual crimes and 41 percent of assaults are repeats (Weisel, 2005). Burglary exhibits the lowest level of repeats, but even there it is 17 percent of offenses.

TABLE 2.6
Estimates of Repeat Victimization from the ICVS

Offense	Repeat Offenses
Sexual Assault	46%
Assault	41
Robbery	27
Vandalism to Vehicles	25
Theft from Vehicles	21
Vehicle Theft	20
Burglary	17

Source: Weisel, D.L. (2005). *Analyzing Repeat Victimization*, Washington, DC: U.S. Department of Justice, Office of Community Oriented Policing Services.

Another way of demonstrating revictimization using victimization data is to compare prevalence and incidence data. *Prevalence data* refers to the number of individuals who experience victimization over a period of time, whereas *incidence data* represents the total number of offenses that are reported during the same period. Any point at which the number of incidents exceeds the number of victims would indicate revictimization. Various analyses of survey data demonstrate the often concentrated nature of victimization. Pease (1998) notes that 2 percent of all respondents account for 41 percent of all property crimes, while 1 percent account for 59 percent of the personal crimes. Farrell and Pease (2003) report that 25 percent of all burglaries in Charlotte, North Carolina, are repeat victimizations and that less than 1 percent of all addresses account for 39 percent of the reported burglaries. Using data on 19 countries from the International Crime Victims Survey, Farrell and Bouloukos (2001) find that more than 40 percent of the sexual assaults and more than 30 percent of all assaults and robberies are repeats.

One problem with identifying repeat victimization involves the impact of short time frames within which repeats can occur. Ellingworth et al. (1995) note that most levels of repeat victimization in the BCS are probably underreported because they rely on repeats only within a one-year time frame, which minimizes the potential for repeats before or after the survey boundaries. The problem of short time frames for repeat victimization is very evident when considering the NCVS. The NCVS reveals significantly lower repeat victimization compared to the ICVS for every category of victimization, including sexual offenses (51% repeats in the ICVS; 23% in the NCVS), assaults and threats (46% ICVS; 26% NCVS), and burglary (40% ICVS; 18% NCVS) (Farrell et al., 2005). The reason for this is the six-month time frame used by the NCVS and the 12-month time frame used by the ICVS. Kleemans (2001) notes that 9 percent of repeat burglaries occur within one month, 30 percent occur within six months, and almost half occur within one year. Thus, the time frame under consideration makes a difference for the finding of repeat victimization.

Beyond documenting the extent of repeat victimization, research also provides information on the time frame of repeats. Pease (1998) notes that a great deal of revictimization tends to occur within a short period of time after the first victimization. Similar results appear in Bowers et al.'s (1998) examination of repeat victimization of nonresidential locations and Johnson et al.'s (1997) burglary study. In both analyses, the risk of repeats remains higher within relatively short periods of time after the initial victimization. Weisel (2005) demonstrates that the time frame for many repeats remains short for a range of offenses (see Table 2.7). For example, 15 percent of domestic violence repeats take place within one day, and 35 percent occur within five weeks (Lloyd et al., 1994). Similarly, 25 percent of repeat burglaries occur within one week, and 51 percent occur within one month (Robinson, 1998). The information on the time frame of repeats can be useful for the introduction of prevention initiatives.

TABLE 2.7
Time Frame for Repeat Victimization

Offense	Proportion of Repeats by Time Period	Where
Domestic violence	15% within 24 hours 25% within five weeks	Merseyside, England
Bank robbery	33% within three months	England
Residential burglary	25% within a week 51% within a month	Tallahassee, Florida
	11% within one week 33% within one month	Merseyside, England
Non-residential burglary	17% within one week 43% within one month	Merseyside, England
Property crime at schools	70% within a month	Merseyside, England

Source: Weisel, D.L. (2005). *Analyzing Repeat Victimization*, Washington, DC: U.S. Department of Justice, Office of Community Oriented Policing Services.

Evidence of repeat victimization, victim recidivism, or chronic victimization is not restricted to survey data or to individuals. Efforts to improve police effectiveness and efficiency have prompted the development of various techniques to identify what are known as crime "hot spots." *Hot spots* are "small places in which the occurrence of crime is so frequent that it is highly predictable" (Sherman, 1995: 36). The use of computer mapping has enhanced the ability of most police departments to identify such places. Sherman et al. (1989) noted that all domestic disturbance calls in Minneapolis came from only 9 percent of the places in town, all assaults occurred at 7 percent of the locations, and all burglaries took place at 11 percent of the places. Similar concentrations of offenses and calls for police service have been found in many other locations (see, for example, Block and Block, 1995; Spelman, 1995). What is not always demonstrated is whether the calls involve the same victims. While domestic violence calls to the same address probably have the same victim and offender (Farrell et al., 1995), repeated assault calls to a bar may involve different patrons every time. In either case, the value of the information is in its ability to inform responses to victimization.

Two basic explanations have been offered for repeat victimization. These are the ideas of risk heterogeneity and state dependence (Farrell et al., 1995). *Risk heterogeneity*, or a *flag* explanation (Gill and Pease, 1998), argues that the victim or location is identified as an appropriate target for victimization due to signs of vulnerability, reputation, or some other factor. The first and subsequent victimizations are all responsive to those factors that make the target attractive. Instances of revictimization may be perpetrated by the either the original offender or by others. Two good examples involve recurring fights at a bar, which attract individuals looking for a fight, and the fact that burglars make choices about what homes to target based on both signs of wealth and perceived effort at completing the crime (Bennett, 1986; Bennett, 1995; Bennett and Wright, 1984; Cromwell et al., 1991). The second possibility, *event dependency*, or *boost* explanations (Gill and Pease, 1998), refers to situations in which the existence of the initial victimization provides input and positive feedback leading to follow-up offenses. The most common form would entail the same offender returning to the same location where he or she committed a successful burglary in the past. This form could also involve different offenders, if the subsequent victimization is the result of shared information between the different offenders. Evidence also exists for the event-dependency explanation (see, for example, Gill and Pease, 1998; Lauritsen and Quinet, 1995; Spelman, 1995).

Revictimization information can be useful for developing responses by both potential victims and community agencies. Pease (1998) offers three conclusive findings based on studies of repeat victimization.

First, "victimization is the best single predictor of victimization." Second, "when victimization recurs it tends to do so quickly." Finally, offenders take advantage of the opportunities that appear in the first offense. These finding do not mean that every victim will be victimized again in the future. Rather, they indicate that victims may be more vulnerable because of circumstances or lifestyle. Past victimization should be used to assess what factors contributed to the crime and what actions can be taken to mitigate future vulnerability. Just as people use knowledge of the victimization of others as a warning sign, so should a victim take heed. Unfortunately, for many victims, "Lightning *does* strike twice!"

The response to victimization can be an important determinant of the possibility for repeat victimization. Pease (1998) argues that targeting prevention activities at past victims has a great potential for reducing the incidence of subsequent offending against those individuals, and may possibly reduce the absolute level of victimization. For example, the Kirkholt Burglary Prevention Program emphasized work with current victims as a means of reducing further burglaries. The project results suggest that this effort successfully reduced repeat victimization.

Despite the increased interest in repeat victimization, there are several issues that require more attention. Perhaps the most pressing issue is to identify the extent of such activity. While the evidence shows that there is a good deal of repeat victimization, not all criminal acts are followed by another one against the same location or individual. Identifying which acts will result in a repeat victimization *prior* to the subsequent act is an elusive task. All of the existing research offers an after-the-fact analysis of the extent of the problem. It is possible, therefore, that interventions targeting past victims may result in a lot of unnecessary effort. On the other hand, such targeting should be more effective than interventions aimed at the general public, many of whom would never become a victim in the first place.

FIGURE 2.10
Selected Internet Sites Dealing with Victimization Statistics

Bureau of Justice Statistics
   http://www.ojp.usdoj.gov/bjs/

FBI Uniform Crime Reports
   http://www.fbi.gov/ucr/ucr.htm#cius

Office for Victims of Crime
   http://www.ojp.usdoj.gov/ovc

Sourcebook of Criminal Justice Statistics
   http://www.albany.edu/sourcebook/

Summary

How much criminal victimization is there in our society? One thing that should be evident after working your way through this chapter is that criminologists and victimologists cannot provide an exact answer. However, by using different data sources, they can give some estimates as to the nature and extent of the victimization problem.

No matter which approach a researcher takes when he or she tackles this question, certain systematic problems have the potential to hamper those measurement efforts. The materials in this chapter shed light on what some of these obstacles are, how they impinge upon the data, and what can be done to minimize these intrusions. As you can see, victim surveys are very much like any other consumer product. People are constantly tinkering, updating, and refining these instruments to take advantage of the most current technology available.

Key Terms for Chapter 2

boost explanations

bounding

British Crime Survey (BCS)

Computer Assisted Telephone Interviews (CATI)

dark figure of crime

event dependency

flag explanations

forward record check

gray-area events

hot spots

household respondent

incidence data

Index offenses

International Crime Victimization Survey (ICVS)

memory decay

mover-stayer problem

National Crime Survey (NCS)

National Crime Victimization Survey (NCVS)

National Incident-Based Reporting System (NIBRS)

NORC Survey

panel design

Part I offenses

Part II offenses

personal offenses

prevalence data

property offenses

repeat victimization

reverse record check

risk heterogeneity

screen questions

self-respondent

series victimizations

Supplemental Homicide Reports (SHR)

telescoping

Uniform Crime Reports (UCR)

victimization survey

Learning Objectives

After reading Chapter 3, you should be able to:

- Talk about why some people do not want to call the police after being victimized.

- Explain how there is "no truth in sentencing."

- Catalog the costs victims sustain as a result of their criminal experience.

- Relay what is meant by "the second insult."

- Chronicle the development of victim-witness management projects.

- Identify some of the recommendations issued by the New Directions project for prosecutors, police, the judiciary, and corrections.

- Outline the planning preparations for instigating a victim-witness assistance program.

- List different types of services usually provided by victim-witness programs.

- Explain how a victim-witness program blunts the "prosecutory assembly line" mentality.

- Talk about the two assumptions that underlie victim-witness service projects.

- Explain how derivative victims have come under the umbrella of victim services.

- Relay why compassion fatigue is an emerging concern.

- Convey how upgrading personnel qualifications and recognizing ethical considerations are professionalizing victim advocates.

- Evaluate whether victim-witness projects work.

- Address the criticism that witness management is simply a tool with which to manipulate victims.

Chapter 3

THE COSTS OF
BEING A VICTIM

Introduction

This chapter takes a look at some of the costs associated with becoming a crime victim. As we all know, victims suffer at the hands of their criminals. Some people may be injured physically. Others may lose property during the attack. All will be gripped to some extent with fear and mental anguish. This aspect of their victimization experience will affect their quality of life and probably will not subside for quite a while.

Victims who turn to the criminal justice system for comfort and solace quickly learn that they run the risk of being exploited. The system, through its impersonal and detached mechanisms for sorting through cases, aggravates the victim's condition. For example, inconsiderate habits may force some victims to wait in hallways for a hearing to start, only to learn later that it has been canceled already. No one bothered to telephone them. Other victims are bewildered by what is transpiring around them. No one has taken the time to explain what is happening in the case or why. Instead, these victims find system officials quickly shepherding them through the courthouse doors without so much as a simple "thank you."

As victim complaints intensified, officials began to worry that continued mishandling would jeopardize the role that victims played when the state presented its case. Prosecutors needed victim testimony to make charges stick. As a result, victim-witness assistance programs materialized. Their goal was to soften the impact of system participation so that victims would make good witnesses at the trial stage.

This chapter will visit some of the problems that victims and witnesses encounter during their treks through the system. We will then focus on what the system is doing to alleviate these problems. Finally, our attention will turn to some criticisms that have surfaced.

FIGURE 3.1
List of Costs Associated with Crime

Costs of Crime	Party Who Directly Bears Cost
Direct Property Losses	
Losses not reimbursed by insurance	Victim
Losses reimbursed by insurance	Society
Administrative cost of insurance reimbursement	Society
Recovery by police	Society
Medical and Mental Health Care	
Costs not reimbursed by insurance	Victim/Family/Society
Costs reimbursed by insurance	Society
Administrative overhead of insurance coverage	Society
Victim Services	
Expenses charged to victim	Victim
Expenses paid by agency	Society
Temporary labor and training of replacements	Society
Lost Workdays	
Lost wages for unpaid workday	Victim
Lost productivity	Society/Employer
Lost School Days	
Foregone wages due to lack of education	Victim
Foregone nonpecuniary benefit of education	Victim
Foregone social benefits due to lack of education	Society
Lost Housework	Victim
Pain and Suffering/Quality of Life	Victim
Loss of Affection/Enjoyment	Family
Death	
Lost quality of life	Victim
Loss of affection/enjoyment	Family
Funeral and burial expenses	Family
Psychological injury/treatment	Family
Legal Costs Associated with Tort Claims	Victim or Family
"Second-Generation Costs"	
Future victims of crime committed by earlier victims	Future Victims
Future social costs associated with above	Society/Victims

Source: Miller, T.R., M.A. Cohen, and B. Wiersema (1996). *Victim Costs and Consequences: A New Look*. Washington, DC: National Institute of Justice, p. 11.

FIGURE 3.2
List of Costs Associated with Society's Response to Crime

Costs of Society's Response to Crime	Party Who Directly Bears Cost
Precautionary Expenditures/Effort	Potential Victim
Fear of Crime	Potential Victim
Criminal Justice System	
Police and investigative costs	Society
Prosecutors	Society
Courts	Society
Legal fees	
Public defenders	Society
Private lawyers	Offenders
Incarceration costs	Society
Nonincarcerative sanctions	Society
Victim time	Victim
Jury and witness time	Jury/Witness
Victim Services	
Victim service organizations	Society
Victim service volunteer time	Volunteers
Victim compensation programs	Society/Offender
Victim time	Victim
Other Noncriminal Programs	
Hotlines and public service announcements	Society
Community treatment programs	Society
Private therapy/counseling	Society/Offender
Incarcerated Offender Costs	
Lost wages	Offender/Family
Lost tax revenue and productivity	Society
Value of lost freedom	Offender
Psychological cost to family/loss of consortium	Family of Offender
"Overdeterrence" Costs	
Innocent individuals accused of offense	Innocent Individuals
Restriction of legitimate activity	Innocent Individuals
Actions taken by offenders to avoid detection	Victim
"Justice" Costs	
Constitutional protections to avoid false accusations	Society
Cost of increasing detection rate to avoid differential punishment	Society

Source: Miller, T.R., M.A. Cohen, and B. Wiersema (1996). *Victim Costs and Consequences: A New Look*. Washington, DC: National Institute of Justice, p. 11.

The Consequences of Victimization

Being victimized results in a number of both direct and indirect costs for the victim, his or her family, the community, and the criminal justice system. Victimization surveys provide insight to the costs associated with the crime. Beyond direct costs from the criminal event, victims and witnesses face additional losses when dealing with the authorities. Figures 3.1 and 3.2 illustrate the range of costs associated with crime for the victim and a host of other people. One consequence of these costs is the need for the criminal justice system to address these issues.

The First Insult: Criminal Victimization

Early victim studies concentrated on documenting the calamity and woes that accompany the victimization experience. The Milwaukee Victim/Witness Project, for example, was undertaken to assess the difficulties stemming from the criminal episode (Knudten et al., 1976; Knudten et al., 1977; Knudten and Knudten, 1981). In addition to sustaining physical injury and property loss or damage, a sizable proportion of victims reported losing time from work and their normal routines. They also endured emotional anguish and interpersonal complications with family members and friends. Despite their perception that these problems were serious, most victims forged ahead alone. Even though many social service agencies were in operation, victims remained largely unaware of service availability. As a result, relatively few victims received help coping with their crime-induced problems (Doerner et al., 1976a).

The 2005 National Crime Victimization Survey offers a host of information on the costs of crime to victims (see Table 3.1). There was a gross loss of more than $17 billion associated with selected personal and property crime victimization in 2005. The bulk of those losses originate in property crimes. At the same time, though, assault victims have losses in excess of $800 million, and robbery victims lose almost $500 million. There also is the untold cost of suffering that stems from physical injury. Estimates are that 33 percent of the robbery victims and 26 percent of the assault victims sustain bodily harm, and not all of these expenses were covered by insurance (Bureau of Justice Statistics, 2006). Compounding these outlays are other ripples, such as time lost from work. Of those who lose time from work, more than 17 percent of all violent crime victims and 7 percent of the property crime victims reported absences extending more than one work week (Bureau of Justice Statistics, 2006:Table 89). Of course, it is very difficult, if not impossible, to gauge the impact on lost productivity from the labor force even after the victim returns to the work site. It should also be borne in mind that these figures do not tap the calamity associated with homicide, child maltreatment, cybercrime, arson, terrorism, fraud, stalking, and the like. In short, what we know about crime losses in the NCVS represents just the tip of the so-called iceberg.

TABLE 3.1
Selected Losses Due to the Criminal Event

Offense	%	% Requiring Medical Injured Care	% w/ Medical Expenses	% Requiring Hospital Care	% w/ Econ. Loss	Gross Loss in Millions	Mean $ loss	Median $ loss
Robbery	33.2	23.4	11.3	9.3	69.1	$494	$791	$120
Assault	25.8	13.4	6.5	5.4	7.3	$836	$192	$50
Rape	--	--	--	--	10.1	$26	$194	$500
Household Burglary	--	--	--	--	89.8	$5,086	$1,471	$250
Motor Vehicle Theft	--	--	--	--	94.3	$5,237	$5,354	$2,500
Household Theft	--	--	--	--	97.6	$5,301	$390	$90

Offense	% loss <$100	% loss $100-$499	% loss >$500	% lost work time	% loss < 1 day	% loss 1-10 days	% loss > 10 days
Robbery	30.3	28.4	18.3	10.2	15.4	72.5	9.0
Assault	36.9	21.5	10.7	7.7	14.8	60.1	11.5
Rape	--	--	--	13.7	20.7	79.3	0.0
Household Burglary	19.0	27.2	35.3	7.7	44.1	48.8	3.4
Motor Vehicle Theft	3.4	7.8	76.2	18.9	29.4	57.7	10.1
Household Theft	39.7	32.2	14.1	4.3	59.8	35.1	1.4

Source: Constructed by authors from Bureau of Justice Statistics (2006).

Miller and his colleagues (1996) combed through a variety of data sources, including the National Crime Victimization Survey, to get a fuller picture of the costs and consequences of criminal victimization. They began by compiling a lengthy list of costs extracted by the victimization experience. As Table 3.2 shows, the annual loss due to just these 10 crime classifications reached $450 billion each year during the 1987–1990 period. These costs include not only medical costs and property loss, but also losses due to time loss, mental health care, and criminal justice system costs.

TABLE 3.2
Annual Losses Due to Crime During 1987–1990, in Millions, Expressed in 1993 Dollars[a]

Type of Crime	Medical	Other Tangible[b]	Quality of Life	Total
Fatal Crime	$ 700	$32,700	$ 60,000	$ 93,000
Child Abuse	$ 3,600	$ 3,700	$ 48,000	$ 56,000
Rape and Sexual Assault	$ 4,000	$ 3,500	$119,000	$127,000
Other Assault or Attempt	$ 5,000	$10,000	$ 77,000	$ 93,000
Robbery or Attempt	$ 600	$ 2,500	$ 8,000	$ 11,000
Drunk Driving	$ 3,400	$10,000	$ 27,000	$ 41,000
Arson	$ 160	$ 2,500	$ 2,400	$ 5,000
Larceny or Attempt	$ 150	$ 9,000	$ 0	$ 9,000
Burglary or Attempt	$ 30	$ 7,000	$ 1,800	$ 9,000
Motor Vehicle Theft or Attempt	$ 9	$ 6,300	$ 500	$ 7,000
Total	$18,000	$87,000	$345,000	$450,000

[a] Totals may appear not to add up due to rounding.

[b] "Other Tangible" includes property damage and loss, mental health care, police and fire services, victim services, and productivity.

Source: Miller, T.R., M.A. Cohen, and B. Wiersema (1996). *Victim Costs and Consequences: A New Look*. Washington, DC: National Institute of Justice, p. 17.

These monetary estimates would escalate considerably if complete information were available on every single crime incident. At the same time, one should realize that these figures refer only to a handful of street crimes. Other statutory violations, tax evasion, white-collar crime, corporate crime, and the like need to be factored in to arrive at a more comprehensive assessment.

To help appreciate the magnitude of victimization costs, consider the following information (Miller, Cohen, and Wiersema, 1996: 1):

- Violent crime causes 3 percent of U.S. medical spending and 14 percent of injury-related medical spending.
- Violent crime results in wage losses equivalent to 1 percent of American earnings.
- Violent crime is a significant factor in mental health care usage. As much as 10 to 20 percent of mental health care expenditures in the United States may be attributable to crime, primarily for victims treated as a result of their victimization.

Beyond such obvious costs as injury, medical expenses, lost days from work, and economic loss, victimization generates a broader public impact. Many citizens, whether or not they have been victimized, report being afraid of crime, and the fear may manifest itself in various ways depending on the person involved and the basis for his or her anxiety. Some individuals fear walking on the streets in their neighborhood while others fear physical attack within their own home. As a result, there may be a shift in physical functioning, such as high blood pressure and rapid heartbeat. Alternatively, the individual may similarly alter his or her behavior in certain places or avoiding various activities. To a great extent, the source of the fear for the individual will determine the response to the fear.

Surveys report that more than 40 percent of the public are fearful of crime (Gallup, 1992; Skogan and Maxfield, 1981; Toseland, 1982). Recent survey results find that roughly 40 percent of the public report that there are areas near their home where they would be afraid to walk alone at night (Gallup, 2006; Pastore and Maguire, 2006). Pastore and Maguire (2006) report that approximately 15 percent of respondents worry frequently or occasionally about being murdered, 45 percent worry about having their home burglarized when they are not home, 24 percent worry about burglary when they are home, 42 percent worry about having their car stolen or broken into, and 28 percent worry about being mugged. More than two-thirds of high school seniors report worrying about crime and violence (Pastore and Maguire, 2006). A 2005 Gallup poll revealed that 47 percent of the participants avoided certain areas, 31 percent own a dog for protection, 23 percent bought a gun for self-defense, 29 percent installed a burglary alarm system, 18 percent carried mace or pepper spray, and 11 percent carried a gun for protection (Maguire and Pastore, 2005: Table 2.40). Obviously, fear of crime has become an added burden affecting both those victimized and the general public.

These figures suggest that many victims, as well as the general public, become the "walking wounded." They endure their problems and tribulations in silence, often without help from external sources. On top of these crime-related losses come more difficulties when a victim's case finds its way into the criminal justice system. As the following section explains, these costs can be substantial.

The Second Insult: System Participation

A victim's problems have only just begun if the case is processed through the criminal justice system. The system extracts further costs as soon as people enter into the halls of justice. In fact, the plight of victims and witnesses has led at least one prosecutor to chastise the system for victimizing its own patrons. Ash (1972: 390) describes typical system encounters in the following terms:

> [T]he witness will several times be ordered to appear at some designated place, usually a courtroom. . . . Several times he will be made to wait tedious, unconscionable long intervals

of time in dingy courthouse corridors or in other grim surroundings. Several times he will suffer the discomfort of
being ignored by busy officials and the bewilderment and
painful anxiety of not knowing what is going on around him
or what is going to happen to him. On most of these occasions
he will never be asked to testify or to give anyone any information, often because of a last-minute adjournment granted
in a huddled conference at the judge's bench. He will miss
many hours from work (or school) and consequently will lose
many hours of wages. In most jurisdictions he will receive at
best only token payment in the form of ridiculously low witness fees for his time and trouble.

A second feature of the Milwaukee Victim/Witness Project (discussed earlier) was to identify problems that the criminal justice system provoked for victims and witnesses (Doerner et al., 1976a;
Knudten et al., 1976; Knudten et al., 1977; Knudten and Knudten,
1981). Interviewers learned that common problems for system participants included time loss, a corresponding reduction in income,
time wasted waiting needlessly inside the courthouse, and transportation problems getting to and from the courthouse. In addition,
court appearances for subpoenaed witnesses translated into lost
wages—a significant concern for many people. Waiting conditions
were another critical problem. At the time of the study, all victims and
witnesses reported to a large waiting room at the courthouse. Bailiffs
would retrieve witnesses when it was time for their testimony. In one
particular case, a sexual assault victim took a seat before the trial began.
A number of other people shuffled in and out waiting for their cases
to start. A few minutes later, much to her chagrin, the victim realized
her suspected assailant was sitting next to her. Intimidation tactics can
be very discomforting (Healey, 1995). In many cases, numerous delays
and postponements can result in cases taking in excess of one year to
resolve (Cassell, 1997). Needless to say, situations such as the one
described here do nothing to alleviate the stress and anxiety associated
with system participation.

Probably the best way to characterize the reactions of victims and
witnesses would be to say that their courthouse experiences leave
them bewildered and frustrated. Although victims have gone there to
discharge a civic duty, they learn the hard way that the system takes
undue advantage of their goodwill. They spend time away from work,
lose money, and are not treated courteously (Norton, 1983:146-147).
As one research team explained:

> [T]here is a serious gap between . . . problems faced by crime
> victims and the help available to them. Unless this gap is
> bridged, victims may come to realize they stand a good

chance of incurring even greater financial losses if they cooperate with the criminal justice system. The anticipated financial loss due to entrance into the system may be sufficient to
deter such citizen involvement. It is ironic that the system
which is designed to protect the constitutional rights of the
offender fails even to recognize the victim's position and
then turns around and wonders why its citizenry is apathetic
(Doerner et al., 1976a: 489).

Rather than claim apathy of the part of victims, it is more realistic to view the lack of participation in the criminal justice system as a
rational choice. That is, victims make a *cost-benefit analysis* and see
exacerbated costs accruing from system participation. Accordingly, the
American criminal justice system is facing a critical loss of citizen trust
and support.

Results from the 2005 National Crime Victimization Survey indicate that more than half the violent victimization episodes and four out
of every 10 property victimizations go unreported to the police (Bureau
of Justice Statistics, 2006: Table 91). When interviewers ask these
victims why they did not call the police, several consistent refrains
emerge. Most often (more than 20% of the time), victims report that
the suspect was not successful and that nothing was lost. Others claim
the police would not do anything or feel that the police would not want
to get involved in the matter. Consequently, victims turn to other officials or individuals besides the police (Bureau of Justice Statistics,
2006). In short, many victims see no benefits to be gained from initi-
ating contact with system representatives.

These sentiments are not confined to the police. Many people harbor genuine doubts that the courts will punish an offender sufficiently
once he or she is apprehended and prosecuted (Maguire and Pastore,
1996: 174; Schneider, Burcart, and Wilson, 1976: 102). They realize
that there is no "truth in sentencing" for convicted felons. Homicide
offenders, for example, usually net a 16-year state prison term from the
courts. However, they typically spend only half this time behind bars.
Judges solemnly pronounce 10-year terms for rapists, but often they
are out in less than seven years. Robbers can expect to fulfill four and
a half years out of an eight-year sentence. Aggravated assault convicts
often serve roughly three years, although their sentences officially
extend for eight years (Maguire and Pastore, 2006: 511). What this boils
down to is that the system is not making good on its promises.

Given this climate, it is not surprising that Gallup reports that only
25 percent of its survey respondents expressed quite a lot or a great deal
of confidence in the criminal justice system (Pastore and Maguire, 2007:
Table 2.11). Citizen reluctance to become involved in the criminal justice system is reaching epidemic heights. A substantial number of vic-

tims and witnesses who have gone through the criminal justice process confide that they would not return if they could avoid doing so in the future (Cannavale and Falcon, 1976; Finn and Lee, 1987: 8; Knudten et al., 1976; Norton, 1983). System personnel complain that citizens are growing increasingly apathetic. However, such a self-serving portrayal is difficult to accept. An alternative description is that victims have grown disenchanted and are rebelling against further abuse. Because of past mistreatment, they are making a very deliberate and rational decision to bypass the criminal justice system.

Victims sustain costs from both the hands of their criminals and then by participating in the criminal justice system. In this sense, they face *double-victimization*. While victims may not be able to avoid the initial criminal victimization, they can choose to avoid the system, thus minimizing their losses. As one victim's mother put it:

> You have already been victimized, and you end up going through the victimization again from the system you are in. So what happens is, with all these choices, you end up trying to maintain integrity and security and sanity in hopes that the truth will come out and you feel good about the result. It is very hard. I don't know if we would go through it again (Cassell, 1997).

Unless these financial needs and system costs and consequences are addressed, victims and witnesses will continue to boycott the criminal justice system.

Prosecutorial-Based Victim-Witness Projects

The criminal justice community has recognized the need to address the looming problem of citizen noncooperation in order to save the system from crumbling. Starting in the mid-1970s, the federal government provided funding for victim-witness assistance programs housed in prosecutor offices. There were more than 265 such programs in place by the end of the decade (Viano, 1979).

Observers refer to these efforts as *victim-witness* or *victim/witness projects*. The underlying ideological thrust is witness management. Prosecutors render services to crime victims not out of compassion, but to cultivate or preserve the worth of the victims as witnesses for the state (Chelimsky, 1981: 83). Thus, the focus is on minimizing witness discontent with system treatment in order to retain testimonial value.

Revised budget priorities and funding shifts saw the federal monies that underwrote victim-witness projects dry up by the beginning of the

1980s. The original federal strategy was to build in funding obsolescence. In other words, the federal government would provide the initial seed money to get new local victim-witness efforts up and running. Then, over the next three or four years, contributions to these projects would dwindle in specific decrements. The goal behind these pre-arranged cutbacks was to wean these fledgling programs away from a complete reliance upon federal funding sources. It was hoped that the early success of these seedling efforts would attract local fiscal support, enabling the projects to become self-sufficient.

To nurture the expansion of victim-witness programs from one jurisdiction to the next, the federal government developed several prescriptive packages. These booklets were blueprints that interested officials could adopt and mold to fit the local terrain. In this way, government could avoid "reinventing the wheel," could bypass obstacles that others had faced already, and would be able to get these programs fully operational with a minimal amount of delay.

Despite a modicum of success, local victim-witness projects languished as federal funds withered. They had not been very adept at becoming institutionalized as permanently funded fixtures within local criminal justice budgets. However, the political landscape underwent significant changes with the release of the report from the President's Task Force on Victims of Crime (1982).

The President's Task Force traveled throughout the country holding public hearings and securing testimony. Time after time, the Task Force received disturbing accounts of how the criminal justice system routinely mishandled victims and witnesses. Citizens relayed the tragic details of their victimization experiences and further explained how their misfortunes had intensified when they turned to the criminal justice system for relief. Victims told how system officials shunned them, how becoming involved in the system had exacerbated or heightened their suffering, and how the halls of justice became just another ordeal to undergo.

Task Force members came to the conclusion that the criminal justice system had become a monstrous operation in dire need of immediate reform. If the plight of victims and witnesses was to be corrected, then the system needed improvement. For this reason, the Task Force issued a number of recommendations aimed directly at victim and witness concerns. Specifically, it urged prosecutors to communicate more closely with victims, seek greater victim input, protect them against any harassment, honor scheduled case appearances, return property promptly, and improve the overall quality of client services.

In 1986, the Department of Justice issued its assessment *Four Years Later: A Report on the President's Task Force on Victims of*

Crime, which monitored compliance with the Task Force's recommendations. The overall tone of the report was quite positive—almost buoyant. Victims and witnesses were making significant strides. Many efforts were underway to address the concerns raised by the Task Force. Assistant Attorney General Lois Herrington (U.S. Department of Justice, 1986: ii-iii) wrote the following message in her transmittal letter to the President of the United States:

> When you created the President's Task Force on Victims of Crime, the Nation began to listen and respond. . . . To date, nearly 75 percent of the proposals have been acted upon, led by a new Office for Victims of Crime in the Justice Department created expressly to implement the Task Force reforms. . . . We hope this document will help assure that the victim of crime will never be overlooked as an integral part of the criminal justice system.

Attention to victim-witness services did not die with these pronouncements. Officials have continued to monitor these efforts and make adjustments wherever necessary. In 1998, the Office for Victims of Crime issued an update, *New Directions from the Field: Victims' Rights and Services for the 21st Century*. This document was the culmination of a three-year project involving more than 1,000 individuals with varied backgrounds and expertise from across the United States. This report noted that, despite the recommendations and efforts proceeding from the 1982 Task Force report, "only a fraction of the nation's estimated 38 million crime victims receive much-needed services, such as emergency financial assistance, crisis and mental health counseling, shelter, and information and advocacy within the criminal and juvenile justice systems" (Office for Victims of Crime, 1998a: vii). Based on this pronouncement, the report called for a renewed emphasis and refocusing on assisting victims of crime.

In order to ensure that the earlier gains won on behalf of victims and witnesses would not be lost and to provide needed impetus for further changes, *New Directions* offered 250 recommendations addressing all parts of the criminal justice system, as well as related fields (such as health care, mental health, education, faith organizations, the business community, and the media). Recommendations specific to prosecutors appear in Figure 3.3. Many of these guidelines reflect the same concerns and needs addressed in the 1982 Task Force Report.

FIGURE 3.3
Selected Recommendations for Prosecutors

1. Prosecutors' offices should notify victims in a timely manner of the date, time, and location of the following: charging of defendant, pretrial hearings, plea negotiations, the trial, all schedule changes, and the sentencing hearing.

2. Prosecutors should establish victim-witness assistance units to ensure that victims of crime receive at least a basic level of service, including information, notification, consultation and participation.

3. Prosecutors should use the full range of measures at their disposal to ensure that victims and witnesses are protected from intimidation and harassment. These measures include ensuring that victims are informed about safety precautions, advising the court of victims' fears and concerns about safety prior to any bail or bond proceedings, automatically requesting no-contact orders and enforcing them if violated, and utilizing witness relocation programs and technology to help protect victims.

4. Prosecutors should advocate for the rights of victims to have their views heard by judges on bail decisions, continuances, plea bargains, dismissals, sentencing, and restitution. Policies and procedures should be put into place in all prosecutors' offices to ensure that victims are informed in a timely manner of these crucial rights in forms of communication they understand.

5. Prosecutors should make every effort, if the victim has provided a current address or telephone number, to consult with the victim on the terms of any negotiated plea, including the acceptance of a plea of guilty or nolo contendere.

6. Prosecutors should establish policies to "fast track" the prosecution of sexual assault, domestic violence, elderly and child abuse, and other particularly sensitive cases to shorten the length of time from arrest to disposition.

7. Prosecutors should adopt vertical prosecution for domestic violence, sexual assault, and child abuse cases.

8. Prosecutors' offices should establish procedures to ensure the prompt return of victims' property, absent the need for it as actual evidence in court.

Source: Office for Victims of Crime (1998). *New Directions from the Field: Victim's Rights and Services for the 21st Century*. Washington, DC: U.S. Department of Justice.

Project Development

An important step in any planning preparation is to determine the feasibility of program implementation. A three-pronged approach is advisable. The first priority is to identify appropriate target groups. The next step is to learn what needs and expectations these clients hold. The final course of action is to assemble a staff to set these plans into motion (Finn and Lee, 1987: 5; Tomz and McGillis, 1997: 11-33).

A major task in any needs assessment is to gain a sense of the size and characteristics of the client population in the area. An important starting block in many instances is to locate or construct demographic projections for the entire population. Analyzing population trends permits profiling by race, age, and gender. As we saw in the last chapter, victimization patterns track demographic variables. Focusing on shifts in various age categories becomes an important exercise. For example, it may be more expedient for an agency housed in a retirement community to concentrate upon crimes against the elderly. Certainly, it would not make good managerial sense to inaugurate an array of services aimed at child maltreatment victims to the exclusion of services for the aged.

Other local resources can provide a wealth of information. For example, crime statistics can indicate some of the more immediate and recurrent problems. Talking with criminal justice professionals, with people who have been victimized, and with existing social service providers can isolate the gaps between what is being accomplished and what clients need. These preliminary efforts can prevent unnecessary duplication.

Following such a series of steps can lead to some very fundamental recommendations. When city officials in Jacksonville, Florida, decided to establish a Crime Victim Intake Center, they turned to a research team for guidance. To assess unmet concerns, Blomberg and his colleagues (1989) analyzed population growth estimates and city crime statistics. They also interviewed staff members from local victim and witness services as well as workers in the criminal justice system. Armed with this information, the evaluators were able to provide officials with an image of what goals and objectives this new agency should strive to achieve.

The decision regarding what services a project should provide must begin with an overview of the models that currently exist. Most victim-witness assistance programs offer a very similar core of services (Finn and Lee, 1987: 17; Tomz and McGillis, 1997: 8; U.S. Department of Justice, 1986: 121-125; Webster, 1988). Figure 3.4 outlines the essential elements that appear in most programs.

While the types of services offered are fairly common, the organizational structure for their delivery can vary. One innovative approach has been to consolidate local victim services into a one-stop center (Blomberg, Waldo, and Chester, 2002). After spending considerable energy developing bonds with criminal justice officials, community leaders, and service providers in Jacksonville, Florida, the Victim Services Center opened it doors to provide an umbrella of resources to victims under a single roof. For example, law enforcement officers can

FIGURE 3.4
Essential Elements to Victim-Witness Assistance Programs

Emergency Services
- _ Shelter/Food
- _ Security Repair
- _ Financial Assistance
- _ On-Scene Comfort
- _ Medical Care

Counseling
- _ 24-Hour Hotline
- _ Crisis Intervention
- _ Follow-Up Counseling
- _ Mediation

Advocacy and Support Services
- _ Personal Advocacy
- _ Employer Intervention
- _ Landlord Intervention
- _ Property Return
- _ Intimidation Intervention
- _ Victim Impact Reports
- _ Legal/Paralegal Counsel
- _ Referral

Claims Assistance
- _ Insurance Claims Aid
- _ Restitution Assistance
- _ Compensation Assistance
- _ Witness Fee Assistance

Court-Related Services
- _ Witness Reception
- _ Court Orientation
- _ Notification
- _ Witness Alert
- _ Transportation
- _ Child Care
- _ Escort to Court

Post-Sentencing Services
- _ Orientation
- _ Notification
- _ Victim-Offender Reconciliation Program
- _ Restitution

System-wide Services
- _ Public Education
- _ Legislative Advocacy
- _ Training

transport victims to this location knowing that these clients will receive any and all of the services they need. This novel approach has been so successful that the National Organization of Victim Assistance deemed it the "Distinguished Program of the Year" in 1998. In addition, the U.S. Department of Justice heralds this approach as a model for other programs to emulate.

Project Performance

Victim-witness projects, like many other social service agencies, keep statistics to track their performance and to justify their continued existence. Reports typically contain such items as the number of persons who used different project features, measures of client satisfaction, individual testimonials praising staff efforts, commendations from system officials, and the like. These process-oriented figures are helpful when describing the level of service delivery and the type of activities in which staff members engage.

When these accounts stretch over time or multiple sites, one can obtain a better idea of the direction in which these ventures are moving. A number of states require prosecutors' offices to make services available to victims and witnesses. While Table 3.3 explains what type of services prosecutors offer, it is also instructive to see the range of services these offices provide. Gaps here could suggest possible areas needing improvement. Another way of looking at the provision of services is to consider the number of victims served. Table 3.4 shows the number of victims served in different capacities in 2003 and 2004 through programs funded by the Victim of Crime Act Assistance Subgrants. It is important to note that many more victims receive assistance from local, state, and private programs that do not receive these funds.

One national assessment surveyed 347 assistance programs to unearth a "state of the art" picture of victim assistance efforts (Webster, 1988). One of the more striking regularities that surfaced from these reports is that victim-witness projects often are swamped with referrals. Both the police and prosecutors are sending more clients to these projects for help, and there has been a sharp rise in victim self-referrals. The number of inquiries has risen so dramatically that some managers have had to expand the number of service providers on staff. In short, these programs seem to have become institutionalized fixtures within the criminal justice system.

Among other things, the survey addressed unmet victim needs and areas that needed improvement. An overwhelming number of respondents felt that victim notification about case status at different

TABLE 3.3
Types of Victim Services Prosecutors' Offices are Required to Provide

Type of Services	All Offices	Full-Time Office Serving Population		Part-Time Offices
		500,000 or more	Under 500,000	
Notification/Alert:				
Notify Victim	82%	87%	85%	73%
Notify Witness	55	67	59	42
Orientation/Education:				
Victim Restitution Assistance	60%	62%	62%	55%
Victim Compensation Procedures	58	73	65	41
Victim Impact Statement Assistance	55	78	60	40
Orientation to Court Procedure	41	57	48	24
Public Education	15	20	17	9
Escort:				
Victim	23%	39%	28%	9%
Witness	17	31	19	9
Counseling/Assistance:				
Property Return	38%	46%	39%	35%
Referral	32	46	37	18
Personal Advocacy	17	26	22	5
Counseling	10	21	12	5
Crisis Intervention	10	19	14	0
Number of Offices	2,282	119	1,480	683

Source: DeFrances, C.J., S.K. Smith, and L.V.D. Does (1996). *Prosecutors in State Courts, 1994.* Washington, DC: U.S. Department of Justice, p. 9.

TABLE 3.4
Number of Victims Served by VOCA Assistance Subgrants

Type of Assistance	FY 2003	FY 2004
Assistance in filing compensation claims	773,420	813,005
Crisis counseling	1,784,588	1,855,996
Criminal justice support and advocacy	2,085,534	2,047,193
Emergency financial assistance	194,502	245,261
Emergency legal advocacy	414,501	418,047
Follow-up contact	2,294,840	2,160,493
Group treatment	470,645	480,406
Personal advocacy	1,385,031	1,375,350
Information and referral (by telephone)	2,599,722	2,908,716
Information and referral (in person)	2,089,112	2,346,796
Shelter/safe house	461,077	432,162
Therapy	340,978	315,512
Other	1,885,191	2,410,625

Source: Office for Victims of Crime (2005). *Report to the Nation, 2005.* Washington, DC: Office of Justice Programs.

junctures of the justice process was a key area of concern (Webster, 1988: 5). Agency directors noted that other prominent concerns included protection from intimidation in domestic violence situations, more victim participation in case decisions, and better training for victims preparing to testify in court proceedings.

Project Evaluation

In the past, some prosecutor offices were so clinical in how they handled witnesses that commentators dubbed these operations "the prosecutory assembly line" (Cannavale and Falcon, 1976). In stark contrast, victim-witness projects now concentrate on making the criminal justice system more user-friendly. For example, prosecutors have redesigned waiting areas to make them more comfortable, and efforts are expended in returning property quickly to owners, filing applications for victim compensation, registering system participants for witness fees, and explaining court procedures to those with questions. Notifying victims and witnesses about cancellations eliminates many unnecessary trips to the courthouse as well as the frustration that accompanies such trips.

Two assumptions have guided these witness service provision attempts (Davis, 1983: 289; Weigend, 1983: 93-94). First, prosecutors want to ameliorate witness conditions because they feel that witness cooperation is essential to winning convictions. Second, the popular view is that victims and witnesses refuse to cooperate with system officials because the anticipated costs are too high. Thus, evaluation efforts gather data aimed at empirically refuting or supporting these two lines of thinking.

Despite the intuitive appeal behind these assumptions, there is some question as to whether these efforts actually carry a commensurate payoff. One jurisdiction established a victim-witness unit that handled only child sexual abuse cases and assessed whether witness cooperation could improve prosecution performance (Dible and Teske, 1993). The victim counselor who was assigned to this unit would follow a case throughout the entire process. This person would meet several times with the victim to establish a rapport with the child and to evaluate the validity of the complaint. Anatomically correct dolls were available so the child could explain what had happened to him or her. Whenever the case went to the grand jury, judges allowed the victim counselor to take the place of the child on the witness stand and explain the details of the case. Finally, the counselor would accompany the child to the trial and offer support in whatever way was necessary. The researchers evaluated the performance of this program using a before-and-after intervention strategy. The results showed that once the program was operational, guilty trial verdicts increased from 38 percent to 72 percent, the severity of the convicted charges increased, and the number of sentences resulting in imprisonment rose. In short, the program was a prosecutorial success.

A recent response to intimate partner violence, the Judicial Oversight Demonstration Project, incorporated a strong victim advocacy/services component (Harrell et al., 2007). The program aimed to protect victims, reduce recidivism, and hold offenders accountable by coordinating community services and justice system action under the oversight of the judiciary. Victim services included a victim advocate working with victims, developing a safety plan for each victim, and providing needed interventions for each victim. The project was evaluated in Dorchester, Massachusetts, and Washtenaw County, Michigan. Results showed that victims reported more contact with victim services and a victim advocate and the receipt of more services (Harrell et al., 2007). Victims also reported satisfaction with the quality of the services and the response of the criminal justice personnel. Unfortunately, reduced repeat victimization is found only in Dorchester, meaning that no clear impact on recidivism is available (Harrell et al., 2007). In this case, the program had mixed results.

What is the key to program success? Why do some programs appear to be more effective than others? One possible explanation is that victims and witnesses seek only humane treatment, and giving them that will increase program effectiveness. Satisfied clients who have had a comfortable experience inside the halls of justice tend to express no reservations about returning again if the need arises (Kelly, 1984; Norton, 1983; O'Grady et al., 1992).

Beyond the Prosecutor's Office

Evidence and research on the effectiveness of prosecutorial efforts may be influenced by other elements and actors in the criminal justice system and societal response to victims. Victim assistance needs to consider a wider range of individuals and agencies beyond the prosecutor's office. Among these are law enforcement, the judiciary, and corrections. While these groups have not been totally ignored in earlier efforts, such as the 1982 Task Force, the bulk of the emphasis and subsequent activity has been at the prosecutorial level. Law enforcement and the judiciary receive a great deal of attention in the *New Directions* report.

Recommendations for police policies and procedures for dealing with victims appear in Figure 3.5. Interestingly, the very first recommendation made by the *New Directions* project for policing is for officers to provide victims with verbal and written notification of their rights at the earliest point in their contact (Office for Victims of Crime, 1998a). In itself, this would be a major change in the operations of most police agencies, and would mirror the concern for offenders' rights currently accorded in the arrest process.

FIGURE 3.5
Policies, Protocols, and Procedures for a Comprehensive Law Enforcement Response to Victims of Crime

Upon first contact with law enforcement, the responding officer should give victims verbal and written notification of their rights according to state or federal law.

Law enforcement agencies should utilize community partnerships to ensure that victims have access to the following emergency services, financial assistance, information and community programs:

- On-site crisis intervention, assistance, and support;
- Immediate referrals to community agencies;
- Transportation and accompaniment to emergency medical services;
- A brochure or other written resources that explain the expected reactions victims have to specific crimes;
- Written information about crime victim compensation and how to apply for it;
- Victims should not be charged for certain medical procedures or for costs arising out of the need to collect and secure evidence.

Protection from intimidation and harm

- Notification about the procedures and resources available for protection;
- An explanation of anti-stalking rights, availability of emergency protection orders;
- Victim notification of the release of the accused and inclusion of no-contact-with-the-victim orders as conditions of the release.

Investigation

- A verbal and written orientation to the investigation process;
- Procedures allowing a victim to choose an individual to accompany them to interviews;
- The name and telephone number of the law enforcement officer investigating the offense;
- A free copy of the incident and arrest report.

FIGURE 3.5—*continued*

If an arrest has been made, victims should be notified of:

- The arrest of the offender;
- Of the next regularly scheduled date, time, and place for initial appearance;
- Any pretrial release of the offender;
- Their rights within the criminal and juvenile justice processes;
- Upon release of a suspected offender, notification of the date, time, and place of the next court appearance.

If there is no arrest within 7 days:

- Information about the right to notification of an arrest, providing the victim maintains a current address.

If the case has been submitted to a prosecuting attorney's office:

- Notification of the name, address, and telephone number of the prosecuting attorney assigned to the case.

Prompt property return.

Source: Office for Victims of Crime (1998). *New Directions from the Field: Victim's Rights and Services for the 21st Century*. Washington, DC: U.S. Department of Justice.

A second major recommendation is that the police should work with and use community agencies and resources to address the needs of crime victims. Emergency services, shelter, financial aid, and information are among the things that victims routinely need. The remaining recommendations revolve around making the investigation, arrest, and case preparation as inclusive of the victim as possible. Victims should be notified of all actions the police take, and the police should explain the process to the victims, both initially and as the case unfolds. In essence, the police should treat the victim as a key stakeholder in the system, rather than as a potential witness to be called if needed.

Recommendations directed at the judiciary often mirror the advice given to prosecutorial offices. They are set forth as a separate set of recommendations to emphasize the importance of judges in recognizing the needs of victims. Many of these recommendations deal with the inclusion of victims at various points in the court process—at pre- and post-release decisions, trial, plea bargaining, and sentencing (see Figure 3.6). As with police, the recommendations open with the need to inform victims of their rights, just as with defendants. Judges also are called on to undergo training and education on victim issues, and to assume a leadership role in addressing the needs of victims.

FIGURE 3.6
Selected Recommendations for the Judiciary

- Judges should advise victims of their rights as routinely as they advise defendants of their rights.

- Judges and all court personnel at all levels of the court system must receive initial and continuing education on the law concerning victims' rights, the impact of crime on victims and their families, and how the judiciary can implement the spirit as well as the letter of these rights.

- Judges should facilitate the rights of crime victims and their families to be present at court proceedings unless the defendant proves that their presence would interfere with the defendant's right to a fair trial.

- Judges should consider victim and community safety in any pre-release or post-release decision.

- Before imposing a sentence, judges should permit the victim, the victim's representative, or, when appropriate, representatives of the community to present a victim impact statement.

- Judges should facilitate the input of crime victims into plea agreements and resulting sentences, and they should request that prosecuting attorneys demonstrate that reasonable efforts were made to confer with the victim.

- Judges have the responsibility to manage their cases and calendars to make victim involvement as feasible as possible.

- Judges should order restitution from offenders to help compensate victims for the harm they have suffered.

- Judges must take a leadership role in conceptualizing and advocating that the justice system encompass not only traditional adjudication and punishment but also holistic problem solving and treatment for victims as well as offenders.

Source: Office for Victims of Crime (1998). *New Directions from the Field: Victim's Rights and Services for the 21st Century*. Washington, DC: U.S. Department of Justice.

The role of the correctional system in aiding crime victims also was addressed in the *New Directions* report. As with the police, prosecutors, and judiciary, the thrust of the recommendations is to recognize the needs and concerns of victims. Again, information provision is a cornerstone of the recommendations, ranging from notifying victims of changes in an offender's status to notification of the release of an offender from an institution (see Figure 3.7). Correctional agencies also are prompted to take an active role in the collection and distribution of restitution, and to use victim impact panels in their work with offenders. Finally, there is a general concern with guaranteeing the safety of victims, as evidenced in calls to protect victims from intimidation and notifying victims and the community of the release of sex offenders.

FIGURE 3.7
Selected Recommendations for Corrections

- Correctional agencies should designate staff to provide information, assistance, and referrals to victims of crime.

- Correctional agencies should notify victims, upon their request, of any change in the status of offenders, including clemency or pardon, that would allow them to have access to the community or the victims themselves.

- Correctional agencies should place a high priority on ensuring the protection of victims from inmate intimidation, threats, or physical or other harm from offenders under their supervision.

- Correctional agencies should collect and distribute restitution payments consistent with the court's order to ensure that victims receive fair compensation from offenders who are incarcerated or released on probation or parole.

- Victims should have input into all decisions affecting the release of adult and juvenile offenders.

- To increase offender awareness of the consequences of their actions on victims' lives, correctional agencies for both adult and juvenile offenders should use victim impact panels and conduct courses about the effects of crime on people's lives.

- Crime victims should be notified of any violation of the conditions of an offender's probation or parole and should be allowed to provide input prior to or during the probation or parole violation hearing.

- When a sex offender is released, uniform community notification practices should be developed and implemented to promote public awareness and provide consistent protection for citizens from state to state.

Source: Office for Victims of Crime (1998). *New Directions from the Field: Victim's Rights and Services for the 21st Century*. Washington, DC: U.S. Department of Justice.

Several clear themes permeate the recommendations targeted at the various parts of the criminal justice system. First, there is a call to recognize the rights of victims and to make certain that victims know about those rights. Second, the recommendations seek actions that will protect victims from further harm, particularly from their immediate offender. Third, victims should be included in virtually all phases of the criminal justice process, if they desire to do so. The system needs to notify victims of their rights to do so and to seek ways to make that participation easier and meaningful. Finally, system employees need to undergo constant education on the needs and rights of victims. Simply outlining the rights is not enough if those persons charged with operating the criminal justice system are not aware of those mandates.

It is the last of these themes that needs the greatest deal of work. Criminal justice personnel are asked to undertake such a wide array of different tasks, often with limited resources. It is not unreasonable to assume that new mandates will receive less than an enthusiastic response when the resources are not forthcoming to successfully implement them. Indeed, the staff of victim-witness projects often struggle to keep pace with staggering caseloads and mounting piles of paperwork. As the victim movement continues to grow and additional tasks are placed on the criminal justice system, agency staff find themselves fielding more requests to apply their expertise to nontraditional clients.

Additionally, many service providers recognize that the victimization experience and its aftermath has ramifications that extend beyond just the person who is victimized. The victim's support system of family members and friends are affected as well. Because these people form an integral support foundation for the victim, extension of services is sensible in these instances. This increased outreach beyond concern for the offender and the immediate victim requires additional expansion of the criminal justice system.

Many criminal justice agencies and victim advocates are called on to offer their expertise to nontraditional victims. *Derivative victims*, while not direct crime victims, usually include persons whose lives have been touched by some tumultuous event (Tomz and McGillis, 1997: 25). The trauma undergone by survivors of an attempted suicide, the processes induced from witnessing a traumatic event, or the emotional upheaval triggered by the unexpected death of a young person are sufficient to propel people into a morass of emotions. It is not unusual for mental health workers and first responders to experience *vicarious trauma* (Pearlman and Saakvitne, 1995; Way, VanDeusen, Martin, Applegate, and Jandle, 2004) or *compassion fatigue* (Boscarino et al., 2004; Figley, 1995; Roberts et al., 2003). Compassion fatigue

> refers to a physical, emotional and spiritual fatigue or exhaustion that takes over a person and causes a decline in his or her ability to experience joy or to feel and care for others. Compassion fatigue is a one-way street, in which individuals are giving out a great deal of energy and compassion to others over a period of time, yet aren't able to get enough back to reassure themselves that the world is a hopeful place. It's this constant outputting of compassion and caring over time that can lead to these feelings (No Author, 2004).

Individuals exposed to a critical incident may find debriefing exercises to be beneficial as they try to sort through and juggle their own emotions. However, such reviews can trigger an adverse reaction if not done properly (Regehr et al., 2003). In short, victim advocates are learning that their skills are needed by a wide range of individuals.

Victim advocates, the people who service victim clients, need the appropriate background and training before they engage in helping behavior. When victim services first emerged as a fledgling area, many service providers were simply well-intended persons with a concern for others. Formal credentials, particularly when victimology was in its infancy, were nonexistent. Today, though, greater attention is being paid to formal pre-service and in-service training for criminal justice personnel and the staff of other agencies who come into contact with victims. Since 1995, roughly 1,800 practitioners have attended the 40-hour course at the National Victim Assistance Academies located on select university campuses (Caliber Associates, 2004). In addition, a number of states have instituted their own programs in an effort to upgrade the training that victim advocates receive. A national assessment of the Academy shows that students acquire the skills they desire and are satisfied with the training they receive. Students further report that the material is applicable to their current work (Caliber Associates, 2004). There is a growing recognition that employee preparation is one mechanism to ensure that quality services are being delivered to victims who need assistance. These efforts echo the recommendations regarding a greater emphasis on personnel development, education, and training found throughout the *New Directions* report.

Dissenting Voices

Not everyone is enamored with the direction that these system-based victim-witness projects have taken. Critics charge that bureaucrats, more interested in organizational survival than in client needs, have replaced zealous advocates. They contend that victim-witness projects have changed so that they no longer remain victim-oriented. In other words, virtually no effort is expended to address what this chapter labels as "the first insult." Instead, these projects concentrate on blunting only "the second insult," problems that stem from becoming involved with the criminal justice system.

Shapland (1983) cautions that many victim-witness programs are erected on what officials think their clients need—not necessarily what victims themselves want or need. Improvement of waiting conditions, provision of witness notification services, distribution of brochures outlining the criminal justice process, and similar strategies can be viewed as peripheral to clients—props designed to appease and manipulate people for ulterior purposes.

Under "ideal" conditions, victim programs would reach out to all victims (Weigend, 1983). However, current operations confine attention to preselected types of criminal victims. This client group is further restricted to just those victims who report the incident to the authorities. As we saw in Chapter 2, the attrition here is considerable.

However, the pool becomes even smaller. Eligibility is reserved for those cases in which the police have identified and apprehended a suspect. Ultimately, the only victims who do get served are those whose cases culminate in the halls of justice.

Skeptics point out that the only value these victims hold to criminal justice officials depends upon how well they can serve those officials. As McShane and Williams (1992: 264) explain, "That which is passed off as victim assistance is, in reality, predicated on the needs of the prosecution rather than on the needs of the victim." Cries of foul from defendant quarters reinforce these concerns. A common complaint from defense attorneys is that granting concessions to victims affords the prosecutor an unfair advantage (Kelly, 1987, 1991). While the evidence to date does not support such an assertion, these statements serve as ongoing evidence to the tensions that victim-witness services elicit.

FIGURE 3.8
Selected Internet Sites Dealing with Victim/Witness Services

American Judicature Society
 http://www.ajs.org

City of Jacksonville Victim Services
 http://www.coj.net/Departments/Community+Services/Victim+
 Services/default.htm

Clark County Victim-Witness Services
 http://www.clarkprosecutor.org/html/victim/victim.htm

Conference of State Court Administrators
 http://cosca.ncsc.dni.us

Federal Judicial Center
 http://www.fjc.gov

Florida Network of Victim Witness Services, Inc.
 http://www.fnvws.org

Green Cross Foundation
 http://www.greencross.org

National District Attorneys Association
 http://www.ndaa.org

Office for Victims of Crime
 http://www.ojp.usdoj.gov/ovc

Psychological Trauma: Treatment, Resources and Biology
 http://www.psychinnovations.com/sitetrau.htm

United States Sentencing Commission
 http://www.ussc.gov

Summary

It is easy to see why victims are reluctant to invoke or to reenter the criminal justice system. Victims initially come into the halls of justice with hopes of minimizing their losses. However, after they complete the circuit and exit the system, they often realize they have maximized their losses instead. As a result, it should come as no surprise that system veterans claim they will avoid the system in the future whenever possible. This decision to boycott the legal system is not the product of an apathetic citizenry. It is a calculated and rational assessment—a silent protest. Avoiding system participation reduces victim exposure to further hardships and liabilities.

System officials have tried to counter this trend by introducing victim-witness management projects into the system. These efforts, though, are reserved for only the small number of victims who eventually testify against their suspects. In addition, they do very little to address economic losses that victims incur from cooperating with the system. As we shall learn in the following chapter, the system has crafted a number of financial incentives designed to lure victims back. It remains to be seen whether these efforts will be sufficient to maintain victim interest in current system operations.

Key Terms for Chapter 3

compassion fatigue	double-victimization	victim advocate
cost-benefit analysis	second insult	victim-witness (victim/witness) projects
derivative victims	vicarious trauma	

Learning Objectives

After reading Chapter 4, you should be able to:

- Define offender restitution.

- Know what a civil restitution lien is.

- Explain the rationale behind restitution.

- Outline four types of offender restitution.

- Evaluate the impact of restitution.

- Explore the ramifications of net-widening.

- Point out some drawbacks of restitution.

- Provide recommendations for improving restitution.

- Grasp why civil litigation is gaining popularity.

- Comment on the benefits of civil litigation.

- Sketch some limitations of civil litigation.

- Outline several recommendations for improving civil remedies.

- Recognize the role of private insurance.

- Explain what victim compensation is.

- Identify highlights in the history of victim compensation.

- Understand the philosophical bases of compensation.

- Know what acts are compensable.

- Define "Good Samaritan" provisions.

- Discuss eligibility restrictions for compensation.

- Define "unjust enrichment" and "contributory misconduct."

- Tell about the awards and funding structures of compensation.

- Debate whether victim compensation works.

- Distinguish macro-level from micro-level effects.

- Describe some program operations.

Chapter 4

REMEDYING THE PLIGHT OF VICTIMS

Introduction

Victims lose not only as a result of the criminal act, but also from participating in the criminal justice process. The criminal justice system alienates the victim, making him or her feel like an outsider to both the offense and the system processes. The victim is little more than a witness for the state. The emphasis is not on making the victim whole. Rather, it is on processing the offender. Judging from citizen disillusionment with the criminal justice system, there is a clear need to take some bold steps to ameliorate the victim's suffering.

The recent proliferation of victim-witness assistance projects represents an attempt to reduce victims' adverse experiences with the criminal justice system. Projects may provide counseling, transportation to and from the courthouse, waiting rooms, prompt notification of court postponements, property recovery assistance, preparation for courtroom testifying, orientation to criminal proceedings, and notification of case disposition. These projects try to soften or reduce the harsh treatment that victims encounter once inside the legal system. Unfortunately, victim-witness assistance programs are not geared toward reducing the economic calamity of the victimization experience. If the victim's decision to avoid formal contact with the criminal justice system stems from a rational cost-benefit assessment, then the system needs to entice victims back into the system with economic incentives.

There are a variety of ways whereby victims may recoup some of their monetary losses stemming from the victimization episode. Some alternatives include restitution, civil litigation, insurance payments, and victim compensation. While each method has the potential to restore the victim to his or her pre-crime state, the victim faces new obstacles when using these methods. Likewise, each option holds a different potential for drawing victims back into the criminal justice system. This chapter will look at restitution, civil litigation, insurance payments, and victim compensation as means of both restoring the victim's losses and bringing the victim back into the criminal justice system.

Offender Restitution

Offender restitution involves the transfer of services or money from the offender to the victim for damages inflicted by the offender. The idea of restitution predates the formal criminal justice system. Prior to the advent of a formal system of social control, victims were responsible for apprehending the offender and exacting payment for any loss or harm. Restitution was clearly outlined in various early laws, such as the Code of Hammurabi and the Justinian Code. The idea of offenders making restitution to their victims largely disappeared once the state assumed responsibility for apprehending and prosecuting offenders. While this new system of justice did not prohibit restitution, the practice gradually fell into disuse and was largely ignored.

The 1960s saw a renewed interest in offender restitution. A variety of factors contributed to this movement. They included the recognition of the victim in the 1967 President's Commission in its reports, the growing concern for identifying alternative methods for dealing with offenders, and the societal movement toward concern for crime victims. The awakening acceptance of restitution at that time was not accompanied by a myriad of new legislation. Rather, it was pointed out that restitution was an already existing sentencing option that the courts very rarely invoked.

The 1982 President's Task Force on Victims of Crime recommended that restitution become the norm in criminal cases. Later that same year, the Victim/Witness Protection Act went so far as to require federal judges to give a written explanation for why they did not require full restitution in a case. By 1990, 48 states had specific legislation dealing with restitution as a separate sentence or as an additional requirement to another sentence (Shapiro, 1990). Today, more than one-third of the states have a constitutional amendment that gives victims a right to restitution (Office for Victims of Crime, 2002d).

Some states have followed the federal lead and now require judges to make offender restitution a mandatory part of sentencing unless there are extraordinary circumstances to suggest otherwise (Office for Victims of Crime, 2002d). At least one state now imposes a civil restitution lien order upon convicted criminal offenders. A *civil restitution lien* means that the sentencing court, at the request of the victim, levies a claim against any real or personal property the convicted offender currently possesses or may come to own (see, for example, Florida Statutes, 1997, §960.29-960.297). What this means is that victims can recover any damages or losses from any assets the offender accrues.

The Rationale for Restitution

The rationale for restitution involves the needs of victims. Victim losses are a key driving force behind the growth of restitution legislation and the use of court-ordered restitution. A survey of Pennsylvania judges revealed that compensating victims was the most important reason for restitution (Ruback and Shaffer, 2005). Other factors, however, are also apparent in the adoption of restitution as a sentencing alternative.

FIGURE 4.1
Competing Rationales for Restitution

- Restoring the victim to the pre-victimization condition
- Rehabilitating the offender
- Providing a less restrictive alternative to incarceration
- Deterring the offender from future criminal activity

Many restitution programs are couched in terms of benefits for the offender. Rehabilitation is hailed as the most potent outcome (Barnett, 1981; Galaway, 1981; Hofrichter, 1980; Hudson and Galaway, 1980). Forcing the offender to pay or perform service to the victim allows the offender to see the pain and suffering that his or her actions caused. Rather than simply punishing the individual, restitution is supposed to provide a therapeutic or rehabilitative response to deviant actions. The rehabilitative argument is particularly appealing whenever restitution is tied to maintaining gainful employment or entering a job training program (Hillenbrand, 1990). In these instances, offenders help their victims while positioning themselves for legitimate opportunities in the future.

Proponents tend to regard restitution as a less restrictive alternative than normal processing, which most often would take the form of incarceration. Labeling arguments, which fault system intervention as the cause of further deviance, support restitution as a means of mitigating future offending. Rather than leading to deviance, restitution assists the offender in refraining from subsequent criminal activity.

Restitution also carries a deterrence effect (Tittle, 1978). Deterrence assumes that people will continue to commit deviant acts only as long as there is a positive payoff. By mandating repayment to the victim, restitution returns the offender—at least financially—to the exact same position held prior to the unlawful act. Coupling restitution with a fine or imprisonment can produce a negative balance between the outcome of the offense (assumed pleasure) and the system's response (pain). Following the basic hedonistic arguments underlying deterrence, the offender would be better off not committing the offense in the first place. Restitution, therefore, can produce a specific deterrent effect on the punished offender and may even provide general deterrence (i.e., influencing others through example).

Types of Restitution

Galaway (1981) outlines four variations on the general theme of restitution. The first, *monetary-victim restitution*, most closely fits the general public's impression of restitution. Under this arrangement, the offender makes direct monetary repayment to the victim for the actual amount of harm or losses incurred. While this is considered direct payment, in practice payments actually are routed through the court or probation office, which then turns the funds over to the victim. This process is particularly useful in cases in which the victim does not wish to have any further contact with the offender.

FIGURE 4.2
Types of Restitution

- Monetary payments to the victim
- Monetary payments to the community
- Service performed for the victim
- Service performed for the community

A second form is referred to as *monetary-community restitution*. This type of restitution entails payment by the offender to the community rather than to the actual victim. This option may be used for several reasons. For example, it may not be possible to identify a tangible victim in cases involving vandalism of public property. A victim may be unwilling to participate in a restitution program. Or the court may be reluctant to use restitution to the victim in the sentencing of an offender. In some instances, this monetary-community restitution may actually be a method whereby the community simply recoups funds it previously made available to the victim. In essence, the community provided "up-front" restitution to the victim that would now be replaced by the offender.

The remaining restitution categories are closely aligned with the first two, except that they substitute service in place of financial payments. Both *service-victim restitution* and *service-community restitution* require the perpetrator to perform a specified number of hours or types of service (or both) in lieu of making cash payments. These forms of restitution are most common in situations in which the offender does not have the ability to make monetary compensation (such as in the case of unemployed individuals and juveniles). Service to the community may act as repayment for restitution that the community made on behalf of the offender, or may be a way to pay for court costs and/or harm to the general populace. In any event, the important feature is that the offender must satisfy the debt established through his or her victimizing behavior.

Evaluating the Impact of Restitution

As with many programs, evaluations of restitution have evolved from simple examinations of attitudes and processes to studies of such outcomes as recidivism, cost savings, and diversion. In general, restitution has enjoyed a warm reception from victims, offenders, the general public, and system personnel (Gandy, 1978; Gandy and Galaway, 1980; Hudson and Galaway, 1980; Keldgord, 1978; Kigin and Novack, 1980; Novack et al., 1980).

However, despite the general acceptance of restitution, relatively few offenders are required by the courts to pay restitution. Table 4.1 presents data showing that in only 18 percent of state felony cases is the felon ordered to pay restitution as a part of the sentence. Even in the case of property offenses, where it is generally easier to document the amount of the loss, fewer than three out of 10 felons are ordered to pay restitution. Restitution orders clearly vary by the type of offense. In Pennsylvania, restitution is ordered more for property offenders, those who have no prior record, whites, and younger offenders (Ruback and Bergstrom, 2006).

TABLE 4.1
Percent of Felons with an Additional Penalty of Restitution

Conviction Offense	Receiving Restitution
All Offenses	18%
Violent Offenses	18
Murder	14
Sexual Assault	16
Robbery	16
Aggravated Assault	15
Property Offenses	27
Burglary	24
Larceny	26
Drug Offenses	37
Weapons Offenses	8
Other Offenses	15

Source: Bureau of Justice Statistics (2007). *State Court Sentencing of Convicted Felons, 2004–Statistical Tables*. Found at: http://www.ojp.usdoj.gov/bjs/pub/scscf04/tables/scs04109tab.htm

The initial wave of restitution evaluations were mostly *process evaluations;* that is, the emphasis was on the number of offenders handled, the amount of time participants took to make restitution, the completion rate for restitution orders, and other similar program achievements. Those eligible to receive restitution include not only the crime victim, but also his or her family, insurance companies, victim support agencies, and government agencies that assist victims (Office for Victims of Crime, 2002d). The losses covered are likewise broad. Beyond costs for property loss or damage, restitution can cover medical expenses, lost wages, funeral expenses, mental health counseling, and other costs associated with the crime and its aftermath (Office for Victims of Crime, 2002d).

Most programs report a high offender compliance rate with restitution orders (Kigin and Novack, 1980; Lawrence, 1990; Schneider and Schneider, 1984). However, success varies according to the type and level of supervision provided to probationers (Ruback and Shaffer, 2005; Schneider and Schneider, 1984). For example, the use of specialized collection units, particularly those located outside of the courthouse, have been found to be less effective at collecting funds compared to those programs located within the courthouse (Ruback, Shaffer, and Logue, 2004; Ruback and Shaffer, 2005). The simultaneous imposition of other sanctions, such as fines and imprisonment, also may hinder or delay offender payments. The Office for Victims of Crime (2002e) suggests that all court-ordered payments be collected under a single system to address this problem. Finally, restitution programs have been found to be quite economical. They can handle a large number of individuals at a relatively low cost (Hudson and Galaway, 1980).

Studies that look at the impact of restitution on victims and offenders are known as *outcome evaluations*. The amount of money collected and funneled to victims is one key result that is assessed. Unfortunately, systematic information on the amount of restitution ordered is not available. What information does exist comes from sporadic reporting from different jurisdictions. In one analysis of felony probation, the Bureau of Justice Statistics reports an average restitution order of $3,368 (Cohen, 1995).

Another major outcome to assess is offender recidivism. Challeen and Heinlen (1978) report 2.7 percent recidivism for restitution clients, compared to 27 percent for similar offenders sentenced to jail. Recidivism declined in three of four programs by 10 fewer offenses per 100 youths (Schneider, 1986). A six-year follow-up of offenders who were diverted into a restitution program also showed significantly lower recidivism (Rowley, 1990). More recently, Ruback and associates (2004), examining the impact of restitution before and after it was made mandatory in Pennsylvania, found that offenders who paid a greater proportion of the ordered restitution had lower recidivism than those who did not make as many payments.

While these results appear encouraging, Schneider and Schneider (1984) caution that the value of restitution depends upon how well the program is administered. When restitution becomes an agency priority, the results are promising. However, outcome measures lag when restitution is handled as an added-on condition and is not a top agency concern. Programs that aggressively target restitution generate more successful performances and lower recidivism rates (Ervin and Schneider, 1990; Ruback, Ruth, and Shaffer, 2005; Ruback and Shaffer, 2005).

Problems and Concerns with Restitution

Despite both the theoretical attractiveness and positive outcomes of restitution, there are a variety of problems and concerns facing the practice. At the very outset is the need to apprehend and adjudicate the offender (Galaway, 1981; Hillenbrand, 1990). The Uniform Crime Reports shows that only approximately 20 percent of crimes are cleared by an arrest, with property crimes (which are most amenable to restitution) having even lower clearance rates. Restitution, therefore, is possible a maximum of one-fifth of the time. Beyond arrest statistics, many offenders are not convicted, thereby mitigating any possibility of restitution.

The Office for Victims of Crime (2002d) notes that a major impediment to restitution is the victim's failure to request such compensation.

While many states require prosecutors or the court to notify victims of their right to request restitution, there is no guarantee that such notification actually takes place. Notification also does not mean that the victims will make the request. One solution to these problems is to make restitution a mandatory part of sentencing in all criminal cases (Office for Victims of Crime, 2002d; Ruback, Ruth, and Shaffer, 2005).

A third stumbling block is the inability of offenders to pay restitution (Office for Victims of Crime, 2002d). Most offenders come from lower-class segments of society. It is naive to assume that these individuals will have the necessary means to make restitution. In some cases, statutes outline provisions in which restitution is ordered but commences at some future date when the offender had the ability to pay (Office for Victims of Crime, 2002d). Another potential solution is assisting offenders in finding employment. The provision of jobs to offenders requires either public funds or substantial cooperation from the private sector, both of which may face problems. First, jobs may not be available. Second, opponents argue that more worthy law-abiding citizens are denied jobs in favor of offenders.

A fourth major issue is demonstrating and calculating the loss and the appropriate level of restitution (Office for Victims of Crime, 2002e). While a dollar figure for stolen or damaged property should be easy to identify, questions arise concerning depreciation for older, used property and the value of sentimental items for which monetary compensation is hard to determine. Some offenses may leave victims with psychological damage, for which setting a dollar figure may be more demanding. Difficulty also arises when attempting to set a level of service for restitution (Harland and Rosen, 1990). How much work or time offsets monetary loss, physical pain, or psychological suffering? In almost every attempt to order restitution, the court is asked to go beyond its legal expertise and become involved in the decisions that would be better made by a doctor, psychiatrist, economist, or accountant.

Another major area of concern deals with the question of the proper philosophy of the criminal court. Thorvaldson (1990) argues that restitution moves the emphasis of the criminal justice system from society to the victim. Under restitution, the victim is seeking personal redress rather than acting on behalf of society. Consequently, restitution diminishes the importance of criminal processing and sentencing (Thorvaldson, 1990). Many individuals also see restitution as inappropriate for cases in which offenders receive a prison or jail term (Office for Victims of Crime, 2002b). Basically, critics claim that restitution shifts the court from a criminal orientation to a civil orientation. Instead of focusing on the offender, the victim becomes the focus of the process.

Several other issues carry potential problems for restitution. The current criminal justice system is not set up to administer such programs

(Shapiro, 1990). Indeed, there is little coordination between agencies on monitoring restitution orders or sharing information on compliance with such orders (Office for Victims of Crime, 1998). Further, there is little evidence that restitution will have a deterrent effect (Barnett, 1981). Clearly, there are still many reasons to question the efficacy of restitution.

While there are several stumbling blocks to restitution, there are many who believe that improving restitution requires taking steps to institutionalize the practice throughout the criminal justice process. Figure 4.3 lists several recommendations made by the New Directions from the Field project (Office for Victims of Crime, 1998). Among these recommendations are making restitution mandatory across the nation and making victims aware of their right to restitution. Of equal importance is the building of methods, techniques, and procedures for monitoring and enforcing restitution orders. Finally, the recommendations also include calls for ways victims can try to enforce restitution payments, notably through petitioning the court and resorting to civil actions.

FIGURE 4.3
Selected Recommendations from the Field for Restitution Programs

- Restitution orders should be mandatory and consistent nationwide.

- A coordinated, interagency response throughout the justice system is essential for the effective collection of restitution.

- Victims should be informed as early as possible in the justice process of their right to receive restitution from the offender.

- At the time of sentencing, courts should have sufficient information about both the victim and the offender to determine the amount of full restitution and a payment schedule.

- The use of technology can greatly enhance the tracking and payment of restitution orders.

- State legislation should make restitution payments a priority over other payments due form the offender, including fines, fees and restitution to entities other than the victim.

- Failure to comply with a restitution order should result in an extended sentence of the offender's community supervision.

- Civil remedies should be applied on a routine and consistent basis to assist crime victims in collecting restitution.

- Victims should have the right to petition to amend the payment schedule for restitution, the amount of restitution ordered, and any failure to order restitution.

Source: Compiled by authors from Office for Victims of Crime data.

Civil Litigation

Another method of redress for crime victims is the civil litigation arena. Civil lawsuits are the modern version of retribution/restitution practices from the past. The victim or the victim's family has the right to take civil action against offenders to recoup losses and to exact punitive damages. People sometimes call a civil lawsuit a tort action. A *tort* refers to a wrongful act that the *defendant* (the criminal) has committed against the *plaintiff* (the victim). This act has produced some type of loss, usually an injury or damage. The purpose of a tort action or civil litigation is for the plaintiff to recover monetary compensation from the defendant for any physical or psychological harm inflicted by the offender (Berliner, 1989). Thus, any civil lawsuit must be concerned with issues surrounding liability of the defendant and collectability or recovery of damages (Office for Victims of Crime, 1997).

There are some important benefits from filing civil suits (Dawson, 1989). Perhaps the most important aspect is the sense of control the victim regains through the court action. As long as the state is prosecuting the case in a criminal court, the prosecutor makes all the key decisions. The prosecutor, not the victim, decides whether to take the case to trial. The prosecutor, not the victim, can negotiate a plea settlement. The prosecutor, not the victim, decides what evidence to bring into court. Once the venue switches from the criminal court to a civil proceeding, the victim is no longer an outsider in the case. Instead, the victim and his or her ensuing problems are the central concern of the court case. The victim has the right to remain in the courtroom throughout the proceedings and has the final say in any settlement decision (National Center for Victims of Crime, 2001).

There are other advantages to pursuing a tort action. In civil suits the level of proof required is "a preponderance of evidence," whereas in criminal cases it is "proof beyond a reasonable doubt" (National Center for Victims of Crime, 2001). Even if the defendant is not found guilty in a criminal trial or if the prosecutor elects not to file charges, civil action may remain a viable alternative. In addition, a unanimous jury decision is not necessary in a civil proceeding. A majority or two-thirds decision is enough to gain a favorable verdict. Berliner (1989) notes that juries tend to be sympathetic to victims in civil cases. Furthermore, the defendant (offender) can no longer refuse to testify by invoking the self-incrimination protection (Brien, 1992; Dawson, 1989; Office for Victims of Crime, 1997). The constitutional privilege against self-incrimination pertains to criminal proceedings, not civil action.

Despite these advantages, there are a number of drawbacks to civil remedies. First, many victims are unaware of the option of pursuing a civil suit or how to find an appropriate attorney. These problems are exacerbated by the fact that many attorneys are unaware of this avenue of redress for crime victims. These problems are slowly being addressed by the establishment of referral agencies or groups around the country and through state legislation that emphasizes victims' rights to civil recourse (Office for Victims of Crime, 1988). Second, as with restitution, the offender must be identified and located. There may be no possibility for civil action if the offender is unknown. Third, civil cases require the victim to hire an attorney and pay some filing fees before the proceedings begin (Barbieri, 1989). In effect, lower-income victims are barred from the civil system. Unless the victim is awarded a sizable sum of money, he or she may actually lose money after paying a guaranteed minimum fee to the attorney. Even with large awards, attorneys typically secure at least one-third of the award as a fee.

Fourth, some victims suffer further damage as a result of the lawsuit. Information about the victim's past behavior, character, and personal situation are all open to detailed scrutiny. This type of examination may cause further psychological and emotional harm to the victim (Barbieri, 1989). Fourth, civil suits are time-consuming and may take a period of years to resolve. During this interval the victim must have continued contact with the offender, which could bring further discomfort.

Finally, because most offenders have little or no income, there is little reason to expect any recovery even if the victim wins his or her suit. One innovation many states have attempted to advance a victim's ability to attach an offender's assets is the passage of so-called *"Son of Sam"* provisions. After New York serial murderer David Berkowitz (nicknamed "Son of Sam") was apprehended, he stood to gain millions of dollars by selling book and media rights to his story while his victims and their families received nothing. The idea that a criminal could gain a small fortune from his heinous acts prompted passage of a new law that allowed the state to confiscate any royalties and place the monies into the compensation fund.

Despite a flurry of similar legislation, these regulations were declared unconstitutional by the U.S. Supreme Court (*Simon & Schuster v. Members of the New York State Crime Victims Board et al.*, 1991). The Court ruled that this statute violated the First Amendment protections against censorship because it "singles out income derived from expressive activity for a burden the State places on no other income, and it is directed only at works with a specified content" (p. 487). As a result, these monies are no longer earmarked for confiscation and payment to crime victims. However, more recent incarnations of "Son of Sam" laws make it easier for victims to bring civil suits to collect any profits made by offenders as a result of their criminal activity. Figure 4.4 displays the revised New York "Son of Sam" legislation.

FIGURE 4.4
The Revised New York "Son of Sam" Provisions

---

1. (b) "Profits from the crime" means (I) any property obtained through or income generated from the commission of a crime of which the defendant was convicted; (ii) any property obtained by or income generated from the sale, conversion or exchange of proceeds of a crime, including any gain realized by such sale, conversion or exchange; and (iii) any property which the defendant obtained or income generated as a result of having committed the crime, including any assets obtained through the use of unique knowledge obtained during the commission of, or in preparation for the commission of the crime, as well as any property obtained by or income generated from the sale, conversion or exchange of such property and any gain realized by such sale, conversion or exchange.

2. (a) Every person, firm, corporation, partnership, association or other legal entity which knowingly contracts for, pays, or agrees to pay, any profit from a crime, as defined in subdivision one of this section, to a person charged with or convicted of that crime shall give written notice to the crime victims board of the payment, or obligation to pay as soon as practicable after discovering that the payment or intended payment is a profit from a crime.

    (b) The board, upon receipt of notice of a contract, an agreement to pay or payment of profits of the crime shall notify all known victims of the crime of the existence of such profits at their last known address.

3. [A]ny crime victim shall have the right to bring a civil action in a court of competent jurisdiction to recover money damages from a person convicted of a crime of which he or she is a victim, or the legal representative of that convicted person, within three years of the discovery of any profits of the crime. . . . Any damages awarded in such action shall be recoverable only up to the value of the profits of the crime.

Source: *McKinney's Consolidated Laws of New York Annotated* (1997), Executive Law §632-a.

FIGURE 4.5
Possible Defendant Resources to Consider When Recovering a Civil Judgment

---

Source of Income:
  Wages
  Benefits (pension payments and annuities)
  Unearned income
  Trust fund income
  Tax refunds
  Government entitlements

Property and Holdings:
  Personal property (cars, jewelry, etc.)
  Real property (home, land, etc.)
  Bank accounts
  All debts owed to the defendant
  Financial holdings (stocks, bonds, etc.)
  Partnership interests
  Future interests in real and personal property through wills, trusts, etc.

Source: Office for Victims of Crime (1997). *Civil Legal Remedies for Crime Victims*, 2nd ed. Washington, DC: U.S. Department of Justice. Found at: http://www.ncjrs.org/txtfiles/clr.txt

Another possible avenue for victims is to file a *third-party civil suit* (Carrington, 1981; Castillo et al., 1979). In these instances, a victim sues a government entity, a business, or corporation, such as a landlord, the managing corporation of a shopping center, or any other responsible body.

The argument developed during litigation of a third-party suit concerns the issue of whether the defendant's negligence failed to establish or to maintain a safe and protected environment. Here the victim must demonstrate two things. First, the criminal episode must be a foreseeable event. One can satisfy this requirement by documenting other offenses that have occurred on the premises or by showing that the area has a reputation for being a high-risk location. Second, the third party must have either failed to take appropriate steps to curtail further criminal events or its efforts must have fallen woefully short.

Suppose, for example, an unknown offender assaults and robs a tenant who is returning to his apartment in a housing complex. Neighbors have complained to the landlord on several occasions that the lighting in the halls is broken, nonresidents have been seen roaming the area, and there have been other similar criminal incidents in the past. Despite this information, the property manager has taken no remedial actions. Under these circumstances, a victim may be able to hold the landlord responsible for ignoring a known hazard.

FIGURE 4.6
Selected Recommendations from the Field for Civil Litigation

- Crime victims should be fully informed of their legal rights to pursue civil remedies.

- State and local networks of civil attorneys who have experience representing crime victims should be expanded.

- Increased efforts should be made to identify consultants with the expertise to testify on issues relevant to victimization in civil and criminal cases.

- Civil attorneys should provide training to victim service providers on civil remedies for crime victims.

- Statutes of limitations for civil actions involving child abuse cases should be extended.

- States should examine statutes of limitations for civil actions relating to other criminal acts to determine whether they should be extended to provide a meaningful opportunity for crime victims to obtain needed relief.

Source: Compiled by authors from Office for Victims of Crime data.

Whether through civil litigation against an individual offender or a third party, victims need to be made more aware of this avenue for recourse. The Office for Victims of Crime (1998) has offered several recommendations to enforce the use of civil litigation (see Figure 4.6). These recommendations range from simply informing victims of this response, to developing consulting networks that can assist in litigation, to changing the laws in order to allow victims more time in which to bring claims in civil court.

Private Insurance

Another method for alleviating the losses due to crime entails private insurance. Most homeowner insurance policies have provisions for recovery of lost and damaged property. Likewise, health insurance policies typically allow payments for injuries sustained as a result of criminal incidents.

The use of insurance to offset the effects of crime does have several shortcomings. Foremost among these is that citizens must purchase the insurance. The fact that many people cannot afford insurance premiums effectively places such protection beyond their reach. Of course, this observation assumes that insurance is available to purchase in the first place. Many inner-city locations are in such crime-infested areas that private insurance companies refuse to do business there. This problem carries enormous ramifications. Lack of insurance leads to further gentrification and more urban decline in these blighted areas. This situation became so grave that the Federal Emergency Management Agency stepped in to fill the gap. The federal government now underwrites crime insurance for commercial enterprises and residents in high-crime areas. There were more than 15,000 such policies in effect at the end of calendar year 1995. These recipients paid approximately $3.3 million in premiums. During the same year, 456 claims were paid out, amounting to a $1.4 million expenditure (Maguire and Pastore, 1996: 390).

Some people also argue that viewing insurance as a means of offsetting crime losses actually penalizes the victim further by assuming that it is the victim's responsibility to take action and avoid crime. A further problem is that most insurance policies have a deductible amount that reduces the cash outlay to victims. Deductibles of $200 or $500 effectively eliminate any insurance payments for many crimes. In general, while insurance is a possible method for recouping losses, it is not an appealing means in many instances.

Victim Compensation

Victim compensation takes place when the state, rather than the perpetrator, reimburses the victim for losses sustained at the hands of the criminal. While it is true that some victim compensation operations derive money from offender restitution, the state is the entity that has direct contact with the victim.

Victim compensation is not a new concept. These remedies once existed in such historical places as ancient Greece and Rome, biblical Israel, Teutonic Germany, and Saxony England (Jacob, 1976: 35-36; Schafer, 1970: 3-7). For a variety of reasons, this practice fell into disuse during the Middle Ages. Modern interest in victim compensation came about as a result of the advocacy efforts of Margery Fry. Fry, an English magistrate, played a prominent role in the passage of victim compensation laws in New Zealand in 1963 and in Great Britain in 1964 (Edelhertz and Geis, 1974: 10-11). In the United States, California launched its victim compensation program in 1966, followed next by New York and Hawaii. As one might imagine, there are a number of parallels between the Great Britain legislation and the American programs (Greer, 1994).

FIGURE 4.7
Landmarks in Crime Victim Compensation

1963	First victim compensation legislation passed in New Zealand
1964	Victim compensation legislation passed in Great Britain
1966	California begins first victim compensation program in the United States
1977	National Association of Crime Victim Compensation Boards created
1984	Federal Victims of Crime Act passed
1986	States receive funding from VOCA for first time
1988	VOCA amended to require states to pay benefits to domestic violence and drunk driving victims

Federal efforts in the United States for victim compensation began in 1964 but did not win approval until passage of the *Victims of Crime Act (VOCA)* in 1984. The VOCA initiated a process whereby the federal government would provide victim compensation for federal offenses and federal funds for state compensation programs. The source of these funds came from fines, bond forfeitures, and special assessments levied on convicted individuals and businesses.

As Figure 4.8 shows, VOCA has been responsible for the flow of significant amounts of money into state compensation programs. The Crime Victims Fund has received more than $6 billion in deposits since it began in 1984 (Derene, 2005). In 2005, the Crime Victims Fund generated almost $834 million for distribution (Office for Victims of Crime, 2005). The fluctuations in deposits since the late 1990s is attributable to several large fines paid by corporations (Derene, 2005). Fund disbursements fall into four categories (Office for Victims of Crime, 2005). First, up to $20 million is set aside for investigating and prosecuting child abuse cases. Second, unspecified funds are set aside to improve services to victims in federal cases. Third, up to $50 million can be allocated for compensating victims of terrorism. Most of the remaining funds are divided between state victim compensation programs and state victim assistance programs (Office for Victims of Crime, 2005). All 50 states, the District of Columbia, and the U.S. Virgin Islands benefit from these funds. In 2002, more than $448 million were paid in state compensation to almost 158,000 claimants, an average of $2,844 per claim (Derene, 2005).

FIGURE 4.8
Crime Victims Fund Deposits

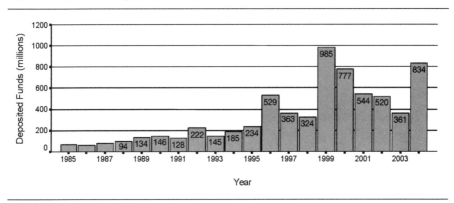

Year

Source: Constructed by authors from Office for Victims of Crime (2005).

In addition to providing money, VOCA helped standardize state crime compensation laws. The initial flurry to pass compensation provisions produced a variety of rules and regulations that differed from one state to the next. To be eligible to receive the federal VOCA funds, states had to follow a series of program guidelines. For instance, some states were granting compensation only to victims who were state residents. VOCA regulations called for the removal of state residency requirements among other things. In order to reach a better understanding of just what victim compensation entails, the following sections describe some of the more salient characteristics of these statutes. Today, victim compensation programs can be found in 35 countries around the world (Office for Victims of Crime, 2007).

FIGURE 4.9
Countries with Crime Victim Compensation Programs

Australia	Italy
Austria	Japan
Belgium	Luxembourg
Bermuda	Netherlands, The
Canada	New Zealand
Cyprus	Norway
Czech Republic	Philippines
Denmark	Poland
Estonia	Portugal
Finland	Republic of Korea
France	Slovakia
Germany	Spain
Great Britain and Northern Ireland	Sweden
Hong Kong (SAR)	Switzerland
Hungary	Taiwan
Iceland	Trinidad and Tobago
Ireland	United States
Israel	

Source: Office of Victims of Crime (2007). Found at: http://www.ovc.gov/publications/infores/intdir2005/alphaindex.html#a

Philosophical Bases

Proponents feel that government has the obligation to provide victim compensation for two distinct reasons. The first view is the *social contract* argument. This perspective maintains that government, through its system of taxation and provision of services, engages in an unwritten contract to care for the safety and well-being of its citizens. Citizens, according to this perspective, have relinquished the power of law enforcement to government in exchange for protection. The experience of being a crime victim, through no fault of one's own, represents an affront to this agreement because the government has failed to keep its promise. As a result, it is incumbent upon government to restore victimized citizens to their former status.

The second philosophical position is the notion of *social welfare.* Government attempts to provide a minimum standard of living for its disabled, deprived, and unfortunate citizens. The position holds that innocent crime victims fall into this category because they suffer deprivations that are not self-induced. As a result, government should extend its welfare practices and come to the rescue of crime victims because they are, in effect, deprived.

The argument one chooses to embrace carries important ramifications for other features of victim compensation. For example, if one adheres to the social welfare view, one might endorse a "financial means test." In this scheme, only poor people should be eligible for compensation benefits. However, if one adopts the social contract notion, then compensation should be available to everybody, regardless of their financial status.

A third reason offered for victim compensation deals with the use of compensation as an enticement to lure victims back to the criminal justice system. Earlier we noted that many victims refrain from contacting the authorities because of the additional costs inherent in doing so. They are responding to a simple cost-benefit analysis. Compensation, however, can alleviate much of the monetary loss associated with the offense. Therefore, it is possible that compensation can tip the balance of the cost-benefit equation and bring victims back into the system. Not only does compensation carry the potential to promote good will between the criminal justice system and citizens/victims, it may also result in more crime clearances and (eventually) lower crime through the apprehension of more offenders.

Compensable Acts

Most programs restrict victim compensation to three categories of victims. The first group includes victims of personal injury crimes and the family members of victims who were killed. All expenses related to physical injuries, including mental health services/counseling and lost wages, are covered (National Association of Crime Victim Compensation Boards, 2007). Payments typically cover medical expenses, losses related to missed work, and mental health treatment of the victim (and family, in the case of the victim's death). Conversely, victims are rarely compensated for losses due to property crimes. Only a handful of states have provisions allowing payment for property loss or damage (Parent et al., 1992).

The second group is "Good Samaritans." Under *"Good Samaritan" provisions,* a person who is hurt or killed during an attempt to prevent a crime from taking place or while attempting to capture a suspected criminal is entitled to compensation. The thinking here is that society owes a special duty to anybody who acts above and beyond the normal duties of citizenship—that altruism should be encouraged, not discouraged.

The final category specifically includes anyone who is injured while coming to the aid of a law enforcement officer. Some states stipulate that people who do not help a police officer when he or she asks for assistance are guilty of a misdemeanor. Thus, it makes sense to compensate citizens when they act on behalf of a police officer.

There also are some people who are specifically not eligible for compensation. For example, most states prohibit compensation for law enforcement officers and fire fighters. The thinking here is that their actions are part of the job and that other programs, such as workers' compensation, are more appropriate vendors (Parent et al., 1992). Other excluded persons include prison or jail inmates and individuals involved in organized crime.

Eligibility Restrictions

One restriction on compensation is to ensure that an offender is not "unjustly enriched." This is primarily a concern in domestic violence cases in which the victim still resides with the offender. Rather than simply exclude domestic violence victims from receiving compensation, the VOCA and its 1988 amendments require states to establish guidelines for determining whether compensation would be "appropriated by [the offender] or used to support him in a *substantial way*" (National Association of Crime Victim Compensation Boards, 2007). States are required to have written guidelines that apply to *all* crimes, not just domestic violence offenses. One way to alleviate such concerns are provisions, such as those in Minnesota, that allow compensation if a domestic violence victim will prosecute the offending party or is in the process of seeking a legal separation or a divorce.

A number of states have a financial means test on the books. In other words, the victim must suffer a serious financial hardship before an award will be forthcoming. As we mentioned earlier, one philosophical basis for establishing a victim compensation program is the social welfare argument. While a financial hardship test stems from this orientation, it is also a mechanism to cap program expenditures. Interestingly, if a state compensation program operates under a financial hardship restriction, it is not eligible for federal victim compensation funds.

Another condition that affects eligibility is victim involvement or *contributory misconduct*. The victim must not share any criminal responsibility for the event. In other words, victim precipitation reduces one's standing for a compensation award. For example, suppose that John challenges Peter to a fight. Peter accepts and during this pugilistic event he breaks John's nose. Depending upon on how the state's provisions read, the compensation board may deny John's claim completely or it may reduce the size of the award in proportion to the amount of victim contribution to the criminal incident.

One additional eligibility criteria concerns the availability of other forms of assistance. Victim compensation is universally viewed as a *source of last resort*. That is, all other avenues for compensation must be exhausted before compensation benefits are forthcoming (National Association of Crime Victim Compensation Boards, 2007). Payments go to victims only after all alternate sources of funds are exhausted. Other sources include workers' compensation, disability benefits, insurance policies, offender restitution, private donations, Medicaid, Social Security, and possibly civil lawsuit awards. Any payments from a compensation program are reduced by an appropriate amount corresponding to funds received from such alternate sources. In order to avoid undue hardship on victims, programs typically make awards and subsequently recover any funds available from other sources.

Awards

States vary in the cap or limit they will pay per claim. Typically, caps range from $10,000 to $25,000, although the state of Washington has a $150,000 maximum while New York has no cap on payments for medical losses. Some states require a minimum loss in order to prevent the program from being inundated by frivolous claims that are costly to investigate. Many states also make emergency awards when victims or survivors face immediate financial hardship (Office for Victims of Crime, 1998).

Crime compensation covers such items as lost wages, medical bills, prosthetics, funeral expenses, and, in some instances, mental health counseling. Most programs do not set aside any monies for pain and suffering or for property damage. Indeed, only five allow for pain and suffering, and eight make awards for property damage (Parent et al., 1992).

A recent addition to the items that victim compensation can pay are costs that arise from forensic medical examinations. A standard police investigatory practice is to transport sexual assault victims to a medical facility for physical examination. As Chapter 6 will explain, this examination consists of two parts, gathering physical evidence from the victim and providing medical treatment to the victim. Some compensation boards reimburse applicants for the medical portion of the examination, but reject payment for the evidentiary aspects. This practice led a U.S. Department of Justice report (1986: 17) to comment that "[f]orcing sexual assault victims to bear this cost is tantamount to charging burglary victims for collecting fingerprints." The Victims of Crime Act of 1984 makes funds available for qualifying victim compensation programs to pay for forensic examinations.

The award itself can take several forms. The payout can be in a lump sum, periodic installments, or in partial amounts. Some states permit victims in dire need to receive a small emergency award, pending the outcome of a full investigation. Some compensation agencies pay vendors (such as doctors and hospitals) directly to prevent victims from skipping out on their bills.

Funding

An important political issue for many people concerns funding sources. While some states extract monies from the general tax structure to underwrite victim compensation, a more popular funding mechanism is the offender. According to the National Association of Crime Victim Compensation Boards (2007), most state compensation programs receive funds primarily from fines and fees levied on offenders, with roughly one-third coming to the states from the Crime Victims Fund. Funding also comes from monies recouped through offender restitution payments to the state. Most programs receive *no* general revenue funds from the state.

Reporting Crime and Applying for Compensation

One prominent feature of victim compensation is its close alliance with the criminal justice system. Virtually every state requires the crime be reported to the police within a relatively short period of time (typically 72 hours). Victims also must cooperate fully with the police investigation, and cooperate completely with the prosecution of the case should the state attorney or district attorney pursue that option. There are also deadlines for when victims must apply for compensation. Failure to abide by any of these requirements results in an automatic claim denial and the repayment of any compensation benefits that the victim may have received already. The Office for Victims of Crime's *New Directions* project (1998) calls for a relaxation of the reporting and claims time frames, and allowing the initial report to be made to non-law enforcement agencies, such as counselors or medical personnel. The current requirements represent a very calculated attempt to bring victims back into the criminal justice system.

Does Victim Compensation Work?

As pointed out in Chapter 2, a substantial number of victims elect not to report their victimizations to the police. Those victims who do contact the police may choose not to prosecute. One reason for this lack of involvement in the criminal justice process appears to be that victims realize they can minimize their losses by avoiding the legal system. If the decision to not cooperate with the system stems from an economic appraisal, then the system needs to lure victims back with financial incentives.

Some observers contend that victim compensation fits this bill. Failure to report the crime to the police, assist in the police investigation, and cooperate completely with the prosecution of the offender can automatically produce a compensation claim denial. Victim compensation, therefore, amounts to an economic incentive that serves to entice the victim back into the legal process. Compensation administrators routinely tout their programs as promoting greater victim cooperation with the legal machinery.

Macro-Level Effects

Victim compensation administrators generally assume that their programs increase victim participation in the criminal justice system. If this is correct, certain macro-level effects should appear. A *macro-level effect* refers to a change in some group or organizational characteristic. Because victim compensation laws mandate crime reporting, cooperation with the authorities, and participation in court cases, certain systematic effects should surface. Victim compensation programs should produce an increased rate of violent crimes known to the police, a higher proportion of known crime that is violent, and an increased proportion of violent crimes cleared by the police.

An examination of four states operating a victim compensation program found no support for any of these expectations (Doerner et al., 1976a). A replication using victim compensation programs from several Canadian provinces did not uncover any evidence for the proposed effects (Doerner, 1978a). Because both studies utilized official data, it is possible that shortcomings within the data influenced the findings. As a result, another analysis examined self-reported victimization data (Doerner, 1978b). Utilizing the National Crime Panel Surveys from 26 cities made it possible to test two hypotheses. First, it was anticipated that compensating jurisdictions would record higher rates of violent crime reporting than would noncompensating areas. Second, it was expected that reporting rates for property crime in compensating and noncompensating jurisdictions would be similar in both types of jurisdictions because these offenses were not compensable. The findings revealed that areas with compensation programs had similar rates of reported violent and property crimes. Thus, these studies suggest that victim compensation did not stimulate an increase in crime reporting.

Although these studies failed to uncover any discernible effects, the possibility still exists that victim compensation programs do influence conviction rates. However, an analysis of Canadian provinces revealed similar conviction rates for violent and for property offenses in both compensating and noncompensating jurisdictions (Silverman and Doerner, 1979). As a result, the researchers concluded that victim compensation did not alter conviction rates.

In sum, these studies do not provide any consistent empirical evidence in support of the contention that victim compensation positively affects other components of the criminal justice system. This conclusion takes on much greater importance in view of the fact that the evidence is derived from studies conducted in two different countries and with data from official, as well as nonofficial, sources. Despite the conclusion of no macro-level or organizational effects, it still remains to be seen whether victim compensation programs generate any micro-level or individual effects.

Micro-Level Effects

Several researchers have pointed out that certain micro-level effects should materialize. A *micro-level effect* refers to any changes in a person, such as being more satisfied with the criminal justice system if a person received compensation. To test this assumption, Doerner and Lab (1980) mailed a questionnaire to victims who had applied for crime compensation in Florida. Following the advice of program officials, they divided the study participants into a group who received compensation and a group who was denied compensation. The expectation was that compensated victims would express more favorable attitudes toward criminal justice personnel and would be more likely to cooperate with these personnel in the future than noncompensated applicants.

The results showed that compensated victims were more satisfied with the crime compensation officials than were noncompensated victims. However, a similar sense of satisfaction did not accrue to the police, to the state attorney, or to the judge. While compensated victims were more likely to say that they would register a claim with the crime compensation program in the event of a future victimization, they were not inclined to cooperate with other system personnel. Thus, it would seem from this study that victim compensation programs do not generate a "spill-over" or a halo effect to the remainder of the criminal justice system.

The foregoing results suggest that victim compensation programs have had little impact on the attitudes and views of the public toward the criminal justice system. This suggests that the future of compensation must not rely on arguments that it benefits the criminal justice system or society. Rather, an appeal to the social welfare and social contract arguments holds much more promise.

Problems and Concerns with Compensation

Besides the potential impact of compensation on the criminal justice system, it is possible to evaluate these operations in terms of the number of victims served and the extent of services provided. Early program evaluations found a number of readily identifiable deficiencies (Brooks, 1975; Doerner, 1977; Meiners, 1978). Just about every program was deluged by the number of claims it had received. Given the small number of staff, some claims required more than a year for processing. Rejection rates exceeded the 50 percent mark and the availability of victim compensation remained a well-kept secret. These observations led one researcher to forecast that unless these problems were corrected, "victim compensation programs will not significantly reduce the plight of the crime victim in our society and will remain a prime example of a misguided social program" (Doerner, 1977: 109). More recently, Newark and associates (2003) reported that 87 percent of claims were approved for payment.

These concerns appear to have diminished as the programs have matured. A phone survey of victims in six states revealed that the average processing time for claims is only 10 weeks (Newark et al., 2003). At the same time, almost one-quarter of the victims believe this processing time is too long. The Office for Victims of Crime (1998) offers several recommendations that could further increase the number of awards, as well as speed up the making of awards. These suggestions include the use of new technologies for filing and processing claims, greater cooperation between agencies in processing claims, and integrating victim compensation closer with other victim assistance functions and programs.

While recent figures on awards appear impressive, they fail to tell us the extent to which all eligible victims are being reached and served by compensation programs. Considering the total number of compensable offenses reported to police, whether the victim was culpable, and the availability of insurance to cover losses, there were roughly 168,000 victims eligible for compensation in 1987 (Parent et al., 1992). Less than half of these crimes, however, resulted in a compensation claim. Many victims are not applying for or receiving compensation. One reason for this gap may be the relative anonymity within which many compensation programs operate (Newark et al., 2003). That is, most victims do not know about the programs (McCormack, 1991). Greater outreach is needed to make victims aware of compensation programs (Office for Victims of Crime, 1998).

FIGURE 4.10
Selected Internet Sites Dealing with the Financial Plight of Victims

---

Federal Office of Child Support Enforcement
   http://www.acf.dhhs.gov/programs/cse

National Association of Crime Victim Compensation Boards
   http://www.nacvcb.org

National Association of VOCA Assistance Administrators
   http://www.navaa.org

Office for Victims of Crime
   http://www.ojp.usdoj.gov/ovc/

Victim Offender Mediation Association
   http://www.igc.org/voma/

Summary

Crime victims face a host of problems, not the least of which are the financial costs accruing from the crime. This chapter has examined several mechanisms that victims can use to recoup some of their losses. There has been a great deal of resurgent interest in restitution over the past few decades. The problems with restitution, however, have prompted moves to other forms of recompense. Both civil litigation and insurance represent methods by which the victim takes an active role.

Unfortunately, each requires a monetary outlay on the part of the victim beyond the loss due to the crime. Many victims simply cannot afford to turn to these alternatives. The final possibility discussed is the use of state victim compensation. Under this scheme, the state makes payments to crime victims. Innocent victims who cooperate with the criminal justice system receive compensation for their crime-related losses. Many victims, however, do not know about these programs and therefore fail to take advantage of these funds. The recent increase in federal participation and funding of victim compensation suggests that this scheme could well become the primary source of monetary aid to crime victims in the foreseeable future.

Key Terms for Chapter 4

civil restitution lien

contributory misconduct

defendant

"Good Samaritan" provisions

macro-level effects

micro-level effects

monetary-community restitution

monetary-victim restitution

net-widening

offender restitution

outcome evaluations

plaintiff

process evaluations

service-community restitution

service-victim restitution

social contract

social welfare

"Son of Sam" provisions

source of last resort

third-party civil suit

tort

unjust enrichment

victim compensation

Victims of Crime Act (VOCA)

Learning Objectives

After reading Chapter 5, you should be able to:

- Define dispute resolution.

- Discuss the rationale for dispute resolution programs.

- Outline and discuss the common elements of dispute resolution.

- Provide evidence on the impact of dispute resolution.

- Provide a definition for restorative justice.

- Compare and contrast the basic premises of retributive justice and restorative justice.

- Discuss the advantages of restorative justice for victims, offenders, and the community.

- Provide a brief discussion of the background (history) of restorative justice.

- Discuss the theory of reintegrative shaming.

- List three major forms of restorative justice.

- Diagram and discuss the six aims of any restorative justice program.

- List the three dimensions that intersect to provide a fully restorative program.

- Define and discuss victim-offender mediation.

- Define family group conferencing.

- Discuss who participates in and the goals of family group conferencing.

- Define circle sentencing and outline the process.

- Compare and contrast victim-offender mediation, family group conferencing, and circle sentencing.

- Show the difference between circle sentencing and healing circles.

- Discuss the impact of restorative justice in terms of participant satisfaction and compliance.

- Outline the impact of restorative justice on recidivism.

- List and discuss at least five problems/issues with restorative justice.

Chapter 5

RESTORATIVE JUSTICE

Introduction

While attempting to compensate victims for their monetary losses is a commendable goal, victims suffer in other ways. Victims of crime may experience a loss of confidence in themselves and their ability to protect themselves and their loved ones, or they may become apprehensive and fear that they will be victimized again in the future. Fear can lead victims to alter their normal routines. Victims may stay home due to fear of future attack; they may lock themselves in their homes to protect themselves; they may shy away from meeting new people due to a belief that they will be victimized; or they may needlessly spend money on security devices or weapons for protection.

Beyond the immediate victim in a crime, one can argue that the criminal act also victimizes society. As noted in Chapter 2, many victims decide to avoid contacting the criminal justice system due to the problem of double victimization. One consequence of this is that the offender may never be caught and may continue to victimize others in the community. The withdrawal of a victim from participation in the community means that the talents and abilities of that individual are lost to the community. Even further, the victimization of one individual may lead others to fear potential victimization (a situation referred to as *vicarious victimization*) and respond the same way as the actual victim. In this way the entire community is victimized.

Responses to victimization, therefore, require more than just attention paid to the financial losses incurred by the immediate victim and his or her family. More is lost as a result of a victimization, both for the victim and his or her family and for the community. A broader response is needed that addresses the needs of the victim and the community. The movement toward restorative justice seeks to address the needs of everyone impacted by the criminal act—the victim, the victim's family, the community, and also the offender.

This chapter examines the idea of restorative justice as a means of addressing the needs of everyone impacted by criminal victimization. Before defining and discussing restorative justice, we will look at the attempt to shift some problems out of the formal criminal justice system and into dispute mediation or dispute resolution programs. Restorative justice techniques have been based on these types of programs, as well as other historical practices used by different cultural groups. These various efforts include victim-offender mediation, family-group conferencing, and circle sentencing. This chapter will examine the emergence of these alternatives for addressing the needs of victims, the community, and the offender.

Dispute Resolution

An immediate precursor to restorative justice, particularly in the United States, is dispute resolution or dispute mediation. One can trace modern dispute resolution back to the early 1970s. During this time, a number of jurisdictions started programs to divert minor disputes out of the formal court system. While many programs were adjuncts to prosecutor's offices and the judiciary, others were sponsored by outside groups or organizations. These initial programs provided an arena in which victims and offenders could meet and work out mutually agreeable solutions. The goal, of course, was to avoid going to court.

Dispute resolution is a mechanism for achieving a number of goals simultaneously. First, the parties involved in the situation work together to resolve the problem rather than having some outside authority impose a solution. Second, any dispute that reaches a settlement is one less case with which the formal justice system must contend. This alternative alleviates some congestion in the court system. Third, this informal approach empowers victims by giving them a direct voice in their own matters. Victims retain complete veto power over the final outcome. Finally, dispute resolution provides the victim with a face-to-face encounter with the offender. This meeting enables the victim to vent anger and seek understanding—something that many victims deeply desire.

The approach of these programs appeals to a diverse audience. Consequently, dispute resolution garners support from many corners and has spread rapidly. Prosecutors and judges welcome the chance to reduce overcrowded dockets, and victim advocates see a tremendous potential to help their clients. More than 80 United States cities had dispute resolution programs in place in 1980 with roughly 4,000 trained mediators (Ray et al., 1986). Six years later, that number swelled to 350 programs with 20,000 mediators (Ray et al., 1986). Its popularity is evident in the proliferation of similar arrangements now operating in Canada, Great Britain, Australia, Denmark, Finland, Germany, and many other countries (Umbreit, 1997).

The types of cases found in dispute resolution take a variety of forms. Interpersonal disputes between family members and friends comprise a large portion of the cases brought to mediation. Domestic disputes, harassment, neighborhood nuisances, and landlord/tenant problems make up the bulk of the disputes. Merchant/customer disputes are more evident in programs that rely heavily on prosecutor's offices for referral. Mediation with juveniles is an attempt to keep the youth offender out of the formal system and eliminate the negative consequences of formal processing (Veevers, 1989).

Common Elements in Dispute Resolution Programs

The basic idea behind dispute resolution is to bring opposing parties together in an attempt to work out a mutually agreeable solution. While dispute resolution programs can vary in terms of the cases they handle or the procedures they use, they typically share five traits in common (Garofalo and Connelly, 1980a):

1. A third-party mediator is involved.
2. Disputants usually know each other.
3. Participation must be voluntary.
4. Processes are informal.
5. Disputants are usually referred to the process by someone in the criminal justice system.

First, these programs involve a third-party mediator who monitors participant interaction. This arbitrator keeps the discussion focused and makes suggestions whenever the need arises. Most mediators are volunteers who are not affiliated with the formal justice system. Because of this independence, some people call these programs "neighborhood dispute resolution."

A second characteristic is that many disputants have known each other over a period of time. Often, they are neighbors, friends, or family members (although store owners and customers can utilize such a program). This familiarity can be helpful when trying to forge a compromise. It can also be a challenge because the dispute may be the result of a long-term issue or problem that may not be amenable to a short-term intervention.

Third, most programs insist that participation be completely voluntary. Both disputants must agree to handle the problem through the program. If either party declines to take part, the dispute moves back to the realm of more formal legal action.

Fourth, the actual resolution of a dispute follows a very informal process. Rules of evidence are not enforced, and attorneys are not allowed to attend these sessions. Instead, the process calls for discussion rather than rigid fact-finding. As one might expect, the mediator has a free hand to conduct each meeting as he or she sees fit.

The fifth and final common aspect is that most disputants enroll in the program after being referred to it by a member of the criminal justice system. Most often, the prosecutor has reviewed the case and decided that the interests of justice can be better served in a nontraditional manner.

Evaluation of Dispute Resolution

Dispute resolution programs are typically portrayed as an effective mechanism for addressing interpersonal disputes. This optimism about the programs would appear to indicate positive results. Unfortunately, evaluations of the programs have provided mixed reviews.

Perhaps the most important possible result of the programs from a victimological standpoint is the ability of the programs to serve the needs of crime victims. Clearly, the ability to arrive at a suitable settlement is a key element for victims. Evaluation efforts typically reveal that more than two-thirds of all participants report a satisfactory resolution, that most of the time the parties live up to the agreement, and most participants are happy with the outcomes (Anderson, 1982; Coates and Gehm, 1989; Cook et al., 1980; Felstiner and Williams, 1982; McGillis and Mullen, 1977; Roehl and Cook, 1982). Similar results have been found for programs geared to juvenile offenders (Bridenback et al., 1980; Reichel and Seyfrit, 1984; Umbreit and Coates, 1993).

Outcome studies that use official data, however, do not paint as consistently optimistic a portrait. These investigations compare recidivism levels for offenders who participate in dispute resolution against those who undergo normal system processing. Various studies report that both adults and juveniles handled through dispute resolution programs have lower recidivism rates (McGillis and Mullin, 1977; Sarri and Bradley, 1980; Smith and Smith, 1979; Vorenberg, 1981). However, other research finds no difference in subsequent court involvement between those who underwent mediation and those who did not (Davis, 1982; Davis et al., 1980; Felstiner and Williams, 1979).

Two factors temper these findings. As we mentioned earlier, participation in dispute resolution is voluntary. What this suggests is that those persons who agree to use this process are hopeful and extremely motivated to find a workable solution. One might expect, then, that voluntary participants would be more likely to abide by the decision and to refrain from similar behavior in the future.

Another stumbling block is that dispute resolution evaluations typically include only successful cases in which both parties agree to a solution. Subsequent program appraisals are based solely on information supplied by "these parties." There is no input from the failures—that is, the people who dropped out because they could not reach a mutually agreeable solution. The inclusion of only successful mediation efforts virtually guarantees a positive outcome.

Additional considerations challenge the use of dispute resolution from a victim's point of view. First, because both parties must agree to participate, many victims never have the opportunity to avail themselves of this service. A hefty number of case referrals never result in a meeting between the parties (Anderson, 1982; Coates and Gehm, 1989; Cook et al., 1980; McGillis and Mullen, 1977). In other words, some victims find themselves shut out of this means of redress. Only those projects that mandate offender participation, such as some Victim-Offender Reconciliation Programs, can guarantee the willing victim a chance to meet with his or her offender.

Another concern is that dispute resolution efforts appear to arrive at lasting solutions only for property matters (Garofalo and Connelly, 1980b). When a property dispute is settled and the victim is made whole again, there is no ongoing problem with which to deal. Personal offenses, on the other hand, are often deeply traumatic events. In many instances, victims and offenders are related to one another or know each other. Dispute resolution settlements are engineered to provide immediate, short-term solutions. They tend not to address long-term root causes of the problem. Thus, dispute resolution may not be an appropriate remedy for all kinds of crime victims. Despite these caveats about the success of dispute resolution, interventions such as these continue to find support.

Restorative Justice

The success of and support for dispute resolution programs has been a major factor in the growth of other programs that seek an alternative to formal criminal justice system intervention. Another factor that has driven the move to alternative interventions is the great growth of victim's rights and awareness. Over the past 30 years there has been an increasing call for programs that pay more attention to the needs of victims. At the same time that victims are receiving more attention, there is a recognition that criminal justice processing of offenders is not effective at deterring crime and reducing victimization (McLaughlin et al., 2003). Consequently, there has been a growing demand for new methods of working with offenders. These apparent competing concerns (i.e., finding an alternative to the system for some offenses, assisting the victim, and intervening with offenders) suggest that any new intervention needs to serve a broader audience. The concept of *restorative (reparative) justice* seeks to use interventions that return the victim and offender to their pre-offense states. For victims, this means repairing the harm done, and for offenders, it means assuring that the action will not be repeated.

Discussions of restorative justice often begin with a comparison between this new idea and that of retributive justice. *Retributive justice* generally focuses on the law breaker and the imposition of sanctions for the purposes of deterrence, vengeance, and/or punishment. The formal criminal justice system operates primarily from a retributive justice approach. *Restorative justice* seeks to repair the harm that was done to both the victim and the community, while simultaneously changing the behavior of the offender. Figure 5.1 contrasts some of the basic assumptions underlying both retributive and restorative justice.

Perhaps the primary difference between retributive and restorative justice is the role of the victim. Under retributive justice, a criminal act is viewed as an offense against society or the state, and the victim is nothing more than a witness for the state. Zehr and Mika (2003: 41) note that "crime is fundamentally a violation of people and interpersonal relationships." Restorative justice sees crime as an act against the victim and community, and the focus shifts from what is best for the state to repairing the harm that has been committed against the victim and community.

This shift in focus to the victim, community, and harm done means that the typical retributive response to crime of punishment and deterrence is no longer appropriate. Instead, restorative approaches seek to repair the harm done to the victim and community (Zehr and Mika, 2003). This requires a focus on the type of harm done and the desire of the victim and community for actions such as restitution and conciliation. The victim and community must be involved in the process in order to identify the harm and the appropriate responses desired by those victimized.

The entire focus of restorative justice, however, is not on the victim and the community. There is also a belief that the offender is also in need of assistance in recognizing the impact of his or her actions and

FIGURE 5.1
Assumptions of Retributive and Restorative Justice

Retributive Justice	Restorative Justice
Crime is an act against the State, a violation of a law, an abstract idea.	Crime is an act against another person or the community.
The criminal justice system controls crime.	Crime control lies primarily in the community.
Offender accountability defined as taking punishment.	Accountability defined as assuming responsibility and taking action to repair harm.
Crime is an individual act with individual responsibility.	Crime has both individual and social dimensions of responsibility.

Punishment is effective.
   a. Threat of punishment deters crime.
   b. Punishment changes behavior.
	Punishment alone is not effective in changing behavior and is disruptive to community harmony and good relationships.

Victims are peripheral to the process.	Victims are central to the process of resolving crime.
The offender is defined by deficits.	The offender is defined by capacity to make reparations.
Focus on establishing blame, on guilt, on past (did he/she do it?).	Focus on problem solving, on liabilities/obligations, on future (what should be done?).
Emphasis on adversarial relationship.	Emphasis on dialog and negotiation.
Imposition of pain to punish and deter/prevent.	Restitution as a means of restoring both parties; goal of reconciliation/restoration.
Community on sideline, represented abstractly by State.	Community as facilitator in restorative process.
Response focused on offenders's past behavior.	Response focused on harmful consequences of offender's behavior; emphasis on the future.
Dependence upon proxy professionals.	Direct involvement by participants.

Source: Adapted from: Bazemore, G.S., and M. Umbreit (1994). *Balanced and Restorative Justice: Program Summary*. Washington, DC: U.S. Department of Justice; and Zehr, H. (1990), *Changing Lenses*. Scottdale, PA: Herald Press.

identifying what needs to change in order to avoid such behavior in the future. Rather than assume that punishment and deterrence are the major approaches to dealing with the offender, restorative interventions seek to understand the causes of the behavior and eliminate those factors.

A quick review of the assumptions in Figure 5.1 demonstrates the centrality of the harm done to the victim and the need for the entire community, including the offender, to participate in repairing the harm. The community, rather than the criminal justice system alone, should shoulder the burden of dealing with crime (Nicholl, 1999). Braithwaite (2003) points out that restorative justice seeks to restore the victims, restore harmony in society, restore social support for all parties, and restore the offenders.

This is accomplished by bringing together a range of interested parties in a nonconfrontational setting, including the victim and the offender, as well as family members or friends, criminal justice system personnel, and members of the general community. The participants, as a group, seek to understand the actions that led to the criminal or antisocial behavior, reveal the feelings and concerns of all parties, negotiate or mediate a solution agreeable to everyone, and assist in implementing that solution (Bazemore and Maloney, 1994). Kurki (2000: 266) notes that "restorative justice is about relationships— how relationships are harmed by crime and how they can be rebuilt to promote recovery and healing for people affected by crime."

The Development of Restorative Justice

While many writers trace the growth of restorative justice in the United States to the dispute resolution/mediation programs from the 1970s, it is possible to go back much further in history and see the elements of restorative justice in everyday practice. Braithwaite (1999: 2) argues that "[r]estorative justice has been the dominant model of criminal justice throughout most of human history for all the world's peoples." As noted earlier in the book, there was no formal "criminal justice system" as we know it today throughout most of history. There were no authorities to turn to for help if an individual was victimized. Victims and their families were expected to take action themselves to address the problems and repair the harm from the offense. The earliest codified laws, such as the Law of Moses, the Code of Hammurabi, and Roman laws, all outlined the responsibility of the individuals to deal with criminal acts committed against them. The development of formal criminal justice systems, particularly the police and criminal courts, shifted the emphasis for taking redress from the victim to the state. It was at this point that the victim became little more than a witness for the state. In essence, restorative justice was replaced by the criminal justice system processes found today.

Many restorative justice practices being used today, however, can be traced directly to historical traditions that have survived in indigenous cultures (Weitkamp, 1999). Of particular note are the practices of the Maori in New Zealand, the Aboriginal tribes in Australia, the Inuits in Alaska, and the First Nations tribes in Canada (Crawford and Newburn, 2003). While there is some debate over the degree to which restorative justice comes directly from the traditions of these groups (see, Daly, 2002), there is little doubt that the ideas underlying restorative justice are not new in the last quarter century.

Theoretical Basis of Restorative Practices

The basic argument underlying restorative justice is that reactions to crime and harmful behavior should seek to repair the harm done to the individual and society while simultaneously reintegrating and addressing the needs of the offender. A number of different theories may be used to underscore the tenets of restorative justice, but the explanation that is most often used is Braithwaite's (1989) reintegrative shaming. *Reintegrative shaming* rests on the assumption that typical processing of offenders through the criminal justice system serves to isolate the offender and stigmatize him or her. This action marginalizes the offender (even more so than he or she may already be in society). In addition, it does nothing to correct the behavior or repair the harm done to the victim. Basically, typical system processing serves only to exact a punishment (retribution) for the criminal act.

The underlying premise of Braithwaite's (1989) theory is that shame can be used in a positive fashion to bring the offender back into society. Under reintegrative shaming, the system needs to express its disapproval of the criminal activity while simultaneously forgiving the offender for the action if the offender is willing to learn from the event and make reparations to the victim and society. The key is on "reintegration," rather than "stigmatization" (Braithwaite, 1989). The ability to employ reintegrative shaming effectively rests on shifting the focus of societal response from solely on the offender to a shared focus on the offending behavior, social disapproval (often by family, friends, and significant others), the needs of the victim and community, and a shared response to make things better (Harris, 2003).

Types of Restorative Justice

Restorative justice takes a variety of different forms, although they all attend to the same basic tenets. Indeed, "restorative justice" is often referred to as "transformative justice," "social justice," "balanced and restorative justice," "peacemaking," or other terms. Braithwaite (2002) notes that many of these terms and programs have been incorporated into the more general idea of restorative justice.

Harris (2003) proposes a model by which to evaluate restorative justice practices (see Figure 5.2). Beyond its use for evaluation, the model contains six aims for any restorative justice program. The four primary aims are:

- Empowerment
- Restoration
- Reintegration
- Emotional and Social Healing

Empowerment reflects the need for all interested parties to be involved in the process. This provides a sense of legitimacy for both the victim and the offender. *Restoration* simply refers to repairing the harm done to all participants. At the same time, retribution is disavowed as

FIGURE 5.2
A Model for Evaluating Restorative Practices

Source: Harris, N. (2003). "Evaluating the Practice of Restorative Justice: The Case of Famiy Group Conferencing." In L. Walgrave (ed.), *Repositioning Restorative Justice*. Portland, OR: Willan.

a legitimate response to the behavior. Restorative justice also seeks to *reintegrate* both the offender and the victim into the community, without the stigma of being an offender or being different from the other community members. Finally, there is a clear need to address the *emotional harm* that accompanies the behavior.

Achieving these primary aims requires that the restorative approach be grounded on two additional factors:

- Procedural Fairness
- Satisfactory Outcome

Procedural fairness refers to the fact that the process must respect all the parties involved. The rights (both legal and human) and wishes of all participants must be recognized as legitimate by the participants. There must also be a *satisfactory outcome* reached. This means that all parties agree with the proposed resolution and are willing to follow through with the plan of action. The failure to achieve procedural fairness and a satisfactory outcome from the process itself will make it

FIGURE 5.3
Restorative Practices Typology

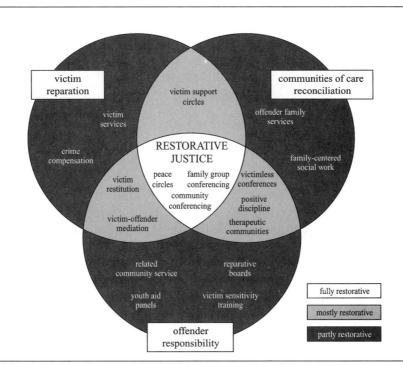

Source: McCold, P., and T. Wachtel (2002). "Restorative Justice Theory Validation." In E.G.M. Weitekamp and H. Kernere (eds.), *Restorative Justice: Theoretical Foundations*. Portland, OR: Willan.

impossible to fully realize the major aims of restorative justice (Harris, 2003).

The degree to which restorative justice programs achieve the results outlined above can vary greatly. Indeed, the diversity in restorative programs can be seen in the extent to which they address the different goals for the varied participants in the restorative process. Figure 5.3 presents a graphic depiction of the types of restorative justice programs and the degree to which they can be considered fully restorative.

The restorative practices typology represents an intersection of three different dimensions—a victim reparation orientation, an offender responsibility focus, and a communities of care domain—all indicated by a separate circle. Each of these dimensions contributes something to address crime and victimization, although each dimension alone offers only limited restoration. Victim reparation, for example, focuses exclusively on the needs of the immediate crime victim through things like victim compensation and victim services, and excludes concerns for the community or the offender. Similarly, the offender responsibility dimension relates to activities that help the offender understand his or her actions and take responsibility.

The intersection of different dimensions brings about greater restoration, with the greatest level of restoration occurring where all three dimensions overlap. It is within this intersection that full restoration can take place. Typical restorative justice practices that appear in this area are Victim-Offender Mediation, Family Group Conferencing, and Circle Sentencing. Each of these are discussed below.

Victim-Offender Mediation

Victim-Offender Mediation (VOM), also referred to as Victim-Offender Reconciliation Programs (VORPs), is a direct outgrowth of the early dispute resolution/dispute mediation programs of the early 1970s and is considered the oldest form of restorative justice (Umbreit, 1999). The first documented VOM program was one run by the Mennonites in Kitchener, Ontario, Canada, in 1973. Victim-Offender Mediation is typically a post-conviction process (although pre-conviction programs exist) in which the victim and the offender are brought together to discuss a wide range of issues. A trained mediator attends these meetings.

The basic premise of VOM is that the criminal incident and its consequences are complex and beyond the ability of the criminal code to address on its own (Nicholl, 1999). Where the formal criminal justice response to crime is to simply impose the sanction outlined in the statutes, VOM seeks to deal with the needs of both the victim and the offender. Perhaps the most important concern addressed in the VOM meetings is to identify for the offender the types and level of harm suffered by the victim as a result of the crime. The victim is given the opportunity to express his or her concerns about the crime and the loss incurred. At the same time, the offender is given the chance to explain why he or she committed the act and the circumstances that may underlie his or her behavior.

The aim of this discussion is for the two parties to gain an understanding of the other person as a starting point for identifying a response to the event. The focus of the meetings is on repairing the harm done to the victim, helping the victim heal (both physically and emotionally), restoring the community to the pre-crime state, and reintegrating the offender into society (Umbreit et al., 2003). Among the potential tangible outcomes for the victim may be the offender making monetary restitution or providing service to repair the harm done. Perhaps of equal importance is changes in behavior and attitude on the part of the offender.

Participation in VOM is voluntary for the victim, but the offender may be required by the court to participate as a part of the court process (Umbreit, 1999). Some programs allow for mediation to occur without the need for a face-to-face meeting between the victim and offender. This typically takes place only when the victim desires to participate in mediation but is reluctant to have any further direct contact with the offender.

Victim-Offender Mediation programs may be a part of the formal criminal justice system, or may be run by other agencies that are not directly connected to the system. In some jurisdictions, mediation may be ordered by the judge in lieu of formal sentencing. A successful mediation may mean that the original conviction is vacated or expunged. On the other hand, the failure of an offender to participate in mediation or the failure of the mediation to reach an agreeable resolution may result in the offender being returned to the court for formal sentencing.

Family Group Conferencing

Family Group Conferencing (FGC) finds its roots in indigenous practices of the Maori in New Zealand. Family Group Conferencing came to prominence in 1989 when New Zealand, responding to the increasing number of Maori youths being handled in the formal justice system, passed the Children, Young Persons and Their Families Act (Crawford and Newburn, 2003). This Act removed all youths ages 14-17 (with only a few exceptions for very serious offenders) from formal court processing and mandated that they be diverted to family group conferencing (Kurki, 2000). Since its inception in 1989, FGC has spread to Australia, the United States, Europe, and other countries.

The greatest difference between FGC and VOM is the inclusion of family members, close friends, and other support groups of the victim and offender in the conferences. There is also the possibility of including criminal justice system personnel, including social workers, police officers, and an offender's attorney (Van Ness and Strong, 2006). The basic ideas of FGC were adapted by the police in Wagga-Wagga, Australia, in 1991 into a process known as *Community Group Conferencing* (CGC) (McCold, 2003). One main difference between FGC and CGC is the possible inclusion of a broader set of support groups and community members to the conference (McCold, 2003). Figure 5.4 graphically depicts the potential involvement of different individuals and support groups in FGC and CGC. The expansion of participants from the victim, offender, and mediator in VOM to support persons and community representatives is very important in a variety of ways.

FIGURE 5.4
Parties Involved in Conferencing

Source: Nicholl, C.G. (1999). *Community Policing, Community Justice, and Restorative Justice: Exploring the Links for the Delivery of a Balanced Approach to Public Safety.* Washington, DC: Office of Community Oriented Policing Services.

The conferences are led by a trained facilitator who serves in various roles. Most often the facilitator will make contact with all participants prior to the conference. At that time he will explain the process and the role of each individual. He will also emphasize the fact that the conference should conclude with a resolution to which all parties are in agreement.

Once the conference begins, the facilitator leads the participants through a discussion of the facts of the case, the impact of the victimization on the parties, the feelings of all participants toward the action and the offender, and the development of a mutually agreed upon resolution (Nicholl, 1999). The families and support persons are very important to this process. They are expected to voice their feelings about the harm that was committed, their concern for the victim of the crime, their disappointment about the offender's behavior, and their suggestions for how to resolve the problem. Of great importance is that the support groups are expected to take some responsibility in monitoring the offender and making certain that any agreements are carried out after the conference (Kurki, 2000).

While most conferences deal with more minor juvenile misbehavior, they can include serious offenses and repeat offenders (Kurki, 2000). Similar to VOM, the emphasis in FGC is on engendering discussion among the parties about what took place, why it occurred, and the most appropriate steps to take to address the harm. Unlike VOM, the conferences do not include a formal mediator who may actively participate in arriving at a resolution. Rather, FGC includes a facilitator who attempts to keep the discussions moving in a positive direction until an agreement can be reached between all parties. Conferences can be held either pretrial or post-trial, and have become a part of police and pretrial diversion programs in many countries (McGarrell et al., 2000; Moore and O'Connell, 1994).

Circle Sentencing

The third type of restorative justice program to be discussed is *circle sentencing*. Circle sentencing, sometimes referred to as healing circles or peacemaking circles (Bazemore and Umbreit, 2001), is based on Canadian First Nation practices and began formal operation in the early 1990s. Circle sentencing invites members from across the community to participate in determining the appropriate sanctions for offenders (Van Ness and Strong, 2006). As a sentencing procedure, this process typically occurs after a case is concluded and the offender is found guilty in court. Participants in sentencing circles typically include all of the parties found in FGCs, as well as general community members who wish to be included.

Sentencing circles may function as either a part of the court or separate from the court. In many jurisdictions, this sentencing alternative is used at the discretion of the trial judge and is not provided for under any statutory authority (Crawford and Newburn, 2003). Most cases handled by sentencing circles involve minor offenses, although some programs will consider more serious crimes (Stuart, 1996). A major difference between circle sentencing and the other forms of restorative justice is that this approach is regularly used with both adults and juveniles (Kurki, 2000).

Because of the fact that this process takes place post-conviction and can include a wide array of participants, circle sentencing normally requires a great deal of preparation before the actual circle convenes (Kurki, 2000). One common requirement is that the offender actively agree to participate, even to the extent of requesting a circle (Nicholl, 1999). The facilitator is responsible for meeting with all participating parties. Those meetings are used to explain the process, outline the facts of the case for those who have more limited knowledge, answer any questions the parties may have, and make plans for the actual meeting. In many cases the offender will work on an initial plan to address the harms he or she committed, which will be presented when the circle meets (Nicholl, 1999). This extensive preparation may mean that the circle takes place months after the crime occurred and the court case concluded.

Every participant in the sentencing circle is given the opportunity to speak, express his or her feelings about the crime, and offer opinions and rationales about the outcome of the discussion. The intended outcome of the circle is consensus on a plan of action that may include a wide array of actions. Plans of action may include further meetings between the victim and offender, apologies by the offender, restitution, community service, treatment/rehabilitation programs (such as counseling or alcohol or other drug treatment), and/or explicit sentencing recommendations to the trial judge (Nicholl, 1999; Van Ness and Strong, 2002). The recommendations of the circles can include recommendations for jail or prison time (Stuart, 1996). The decision of the circles is often binding on the offender (and may be specifically incorporated into the official court record), and a failure to adhere to the decision may result in further criminal justice system processing or being returned to the circle (Van Ness and Strong, 2006). The basic stages of a sentencing circle are depicted in Figure 5.5.

Beyond the reparative plan for the offender, sentencing circles are meant to bring about action by all parties to the crime. The victim is supposed to receive support and be an active participant in healing himself or herself. The community's role is to identify the factors that lead to the offending behavior and seek ways to eliminate those problems. These causal factors may be specific to the individual offender (such as lack of parental supervision or underage alcohol use) or may be larger social-structural issues (such as unemployment or the presence of gangs in the community).

FIGURE 5.5
Stages in a Sentencing Circle

Stage	Activity
Preparation	Identify who will come and remove surprises
Opening	Welcome, ground rules, introductions, creating comfortable atmosphere
Legal Stage	Facts, history, probation report
Clarifying Facts	Anyone can add information, share feelings and concerns
Seeking Common Ground	Identify the issues that underlie the crime, alcohol problems, broken family relationship, exclusion from school, gang memberships
Exploring Options	Examine what must be done to support the victim, what must be done by the offender, what must be done by the community
Developing Concerns	Ensure everyone has been heard and all options understood; probe what options are realistic and will gain shared commitment
Closing	Summarize, even if consensus is not reached; allow people to leave feeling good

Source: Nicholl, C.G. (1999). *Community Policing, Community Justice, and Restorative Justice: Exploring the Links for the Delivery of a Balanced Approach to Public Safety*. Washington, DC: Office of Community Oriented Policing Services.

Not all circles work the same way. In some instances circles can be held without the participation of either the offender or the victim. Because the circles are not meant just to arrive at a sentence for the offender, they may be useful for addressing the individual needs of the three primary parties—offender, victim, and community. In instances in which the circle focuses on only one of the parties, it is typically considered a *healing circle* (Nicholl, 1999).

Summary

While each of the three forms of restorative justice discussed above takes a slightly different approach to repairing the harm done by the criminal act, all are considered fully restorative because they seek to address the needs of the victim, the offender, and the community. The variation between the approaches (outlined in Figure 5.6) brings about restoration by attempting to build understanding between the parties, identifying the factors at work in the behavior, and arriving at a plan of action that is agreed to by all parties. The extent to which these restorative justice programs are successful is addressed below.

FIGURE 5.6.
Restorative Conferencing Models

	Victim-Offender Mediation
Who Participates?	Mediator, victim, offender are standard participants.
Victim Role	Expresses feelings regarding crime and impact. Has major role in decision regarding offender obligation and content of reparative plan. Has right of ultimate refusal; consent is essential.
Gatekeepers	Courts and other entities make referrals.
Relationship to Formal System	Varies on continuum from core process in diversion and disposition to marginal programs with minimal impact on court caseloads.
Preparation	Typically face-to-face preparation with victim and offender to explain process.
Followup	Varies. Mediator may follow up. Probation and/or other program staff may be responsible.
Primary Outcome(s) Sought	Allow victim to relay impact of crime to offender, express feelings and needs; victim satisfied with process; offender has increased awareness of harm, gains empathy with victim; agreement on reparation plan.

Source: Adapted from Bazemore, G., and M. Umbreit (2001). *A Comparison for Four Restorative Conferencing Models*. Washington, DC: U.S. Department of Justice, Office of Juvenile Justice and Delinquency Prevention.

Family Group Conferencing	Circle Sentencing
Coordinator identifies key participants. Close kin of victim and offender invited. Police, social services, and other support persons also invited. Broader community not encouraged to participate.	Judge, prosecutor, defense counsel participate in serious cases. Victim(s), offender(s), service providers, support group present. Open to entire community. Justice committee ensures participation of key residents.
Expresses feelings about crime, gives input into reparative plan.	Participates in circle and decision making; gives input into eligibility of offender, chooses support group, and may participate in healing circle.
Court, community justice coordinators, police, school officials.	Community justice committee.
Primary process of hearing cases in some locations (with juveniles in New Zealand) which requires ceding of disposition power and results in major impact on caseloads. Police-driven process in other locations with possible problems of net-widening and minimal impact on caseloads.	Judge, prosecution, court officials share power with community, i.e., selection, sanctioning, followup. Presently minimal impact on caseloads.
Phone contact with all parties to encourage participation and explain process. Possibly face-to-face contacts with victims, offenders and families.	Extensive work with offender and victim prior to circle. Explain process and rules of circle.
Unclear. May be police, coordinator, or others.	Community justice committee. Judge may hold jail sentence as incentive for offender to comply with plan.
Clarify facts of case. Denounce crime while affirming and supporting offender; restore victim loss: encourage offender reintegration. Focus on "deed not need" (i.e., on offense and harm done, not offender's needs).	Increase community strength and capacity to resolve disputes and prevent crime; develop reparative and rehabilitative plan; address victim concerns and public safety issues; assign victim and offender support group responsibilities and identify resources.

The Impact of Restorative Justice

Restorative justice programs are intended to have a number of different possible outcomes, including repairing the harm done to the victim and rehabilitating the offender. Assessing the impact of the interventions, however, is more difficult to determine. Many evaluations focus on victim and offender satisfaction with the process, and the level of compliance or completion of the agreed upon settlement. Less common are analyses of the impact of the programs on subsequent offending by the offender. In addition, because very little research has been conducted on circle sentencing, most of the comments in this section refer to VOM and FGC.

Satisfaction and Compliance

Assessing the impact of restorative justice within a victimological context suggests that outcomes such as victim satisfaction, feelings of fairness by victims, and the completion of reparations are primary concerns. With very few exceptions, victims (as well as offenders) express satisfaction with the restorative process in which they have participated (Braithwaite, 1999). This is true of VOM, FGC, and circle sentencing. Evaluations of VOM typically reveal that between 75 percent and 100 percent of the participants express satisfaction with the mediation (Kurki, 2000). Similarly high levels of satisfaction arise from FGCs (Bazemore and Umbreit, 2001; Moore and O'Connell, 1994; Umbreit et al., 2003). The level of satisfaction is also reflected in feelings by participants that the process is fair (McCold, 2003; McGarrell et al., 2000; Umbreit, 1999; Umbreit and Coates, 1992; Umbreit et al., 2003). McCold (2003) also notes that most respondents report that they would participate if given a choice to do so. These results contrast greatly with those found in analyses of formal criminal justice system processing, where victims and offenders report lower satisfaction and feelings of fairness.

An important caveat when considering whether a type of program is effective or not is that not all projects are implemented with the same degree of success. Some attempts to establish a restorative justice program may be more successful than others. Given this fact, outcomes may also vary from one evaluation to another. Attempting to address this problem, McCold and Wachtel (2002) rated restorative justice programs according to the degree to which they were fully restorative, mostly restorative, or not restorative. They then looked at reports of satisfaction and fairness by victims and offenders. Their results are very illuminating. In general, participants in fully restorative programs report higher levels of satisfaction and perceived fairness, followed by those in mostly restorative programs. Individuals from programs rated as not restorative report the lowest levels of satisfaction and fairness (McCold and Wachtel, 2002).

A companion to satisfaction is the ability of the meetings to achieve consensus on a solution and whether the parties carry through with the agreement. Again, there is evidence that most meetings culminate in an agreement and most parties comply with the settlement (Braithwaite, 1999; Kurki, 2000; Schiff, 1999; Umbreit and Coates, 1993). Restitution is a common component of many agreements, and evaluations reveal that 90 percent or more of the offenders in FGC comply with the ordered restitution (Wachtel, 1995). McGarrell et al. (2000) note that participants in a conferencing program completed the program at a significantly higher rate than normal diversion clients.

This information on satisfaction and compliance must be tempered somewhat by the fact that participation in the programs is voluntary. This is especially true for victims, although offenders can also opt out of the process in many places. The fact that the program is voluntary may mean that only those individuals who are more amenable to the process to begin with are included in the programs. There may be a built-in bias in favor of positive results. Umbreit et al. (2003), for example, point out that only 40-60 percent of the victims and offenders who are asked to participate in VOM agree to do so. McCold and Wachtel (1998) report that almost six out of 10 FGC cases never materialize due to a refusal to participate. Similarly, an analysis of youth conferencing panels in England and Wales finds that only one-fifth of the victims participate (Crawford and Newburn, 2003). There is no way of knowing if positive results are actually a function of the willingness to participate and effect change, and not just the program itself.

Recidivism

Reducing reoffending is also an important restorative goal. While not always seen as a direct benefit to a victim, the ability to reduce recidivism is advantageous for individual victims and society as a whole. Unfortunately, there is relatively little research on offender recidivism found in the restorative justice literature. Part of the reason for this is the voluntary nature of many programs. One should expect to find lower recidivism from programs where only those who want to participate and want to try and change their behavior are included. Despite this shortcoming, there is some evidence that restorative justice programs are able to reduce the level of subsequent offending. In addition, there is a greater emphasis being placed on assessing the impact of restorative justice programming on recidivism.

Most evaluations of recidivism have appeared in relation to VOM programs. Umbreit and Coates (1993), comparing youths who participated in VOM to those undergoing typical juvenile justice processing in three states, report significantly less recidivism on behalf of the VOM sample. In their analysis of restorative justice conferences for youths in Indianapolis, McGarrell et al. (2000) report a 40 percent reduction in recidivism for the program youths compared to those undergoing normal system processing. Umbreit et al. (2001) provide evidence that youths completing VOM projects in two Oregon counties reduce their offending by at least 68 percent in the year after program participation compared to the year before the intervention. Finally, Nugent et al. (1999) note that both the level of reoffending and the seriousness of subsequent offenses is lower for youths who enter and complete VOM programs.

Examinations of recidivism from conferencing are less common, although those that do exist provide some positive assessments. Daly (2003), examining juvenile conferencing in South Australia, found significantly less recidivism by participants in the conferences. This is particularly true for conferences that are rated as highly restorative. Similarly, Hayes and Daly (2004) uncovered reduced recidivism levels after conferencing. The results are strongest for first-time offenders who are participating in the programs. The results also vary by other characteristics of the offenders, suggesting that conferencing is not equally effective with all individuals and cases (Hayes and Daly, 2004). McCold (2003) claims that recidivism levels after conferencing are no higher than that found in traditional system processing. This suggests that the restorative program has little impact on recidivism, although it may be more desirable than official court processing for other reasons.

Discrepant recidivism results appear in the *Reintegrative Shaming Experiments (RISE)* conducted in Australia. Sherman and Strang (2003) examined the impact of RISE on victims and offenders involved in drunk driving, juvenile property offenses, juvenile shoplifting, and violent youthful offenses. The authors found that conferences reduced recidivism among violent youths by 38 percent. Conversely, there was no impact on either shoplifting or property offenses. Analysis of drunk driving revealed some promising results, but the low number of crimes makes it difficult to adequately evaluate any changes (Sherman and Strang, 2000). Finally, the authors reported that the impact of RISE varies across facilitators, suggesting that the training and preparation of these individuals is key to successful conferencing (Sherman and Strang, 2003).

While positive results on recidivism appear in several analyses, a great deal of additional research is needed on the impact of restorative justice programs. This is especially true for FGC and circle sentencing programs, which have not undergone as extensive evaluations as VOM. It is also important to note that almost all recidivism research has been completed on studies of youthful participants. With the growing interest in using restorative justice approaches with adult offenders, there is an even greater need to assess the potential of the approach. There remains a need to identify and understand the conditions under which different restorative justice programs work and do not work (Braithwaite, 2002).

Problems and Issues with Restorative Justice

Despite the growing popularity with restorative justice approaches, there are a number of problems and concerns that remain unanswered. Figure 5.7 presents a number of concerns with restorative justice. Because a full discussion of critical issues is available elsewhere (see, Ashworth, 2003; Feld, 1999; Kurki, 2000), only a few of the major concerns are presented here.

FIGURE 5.7
Key Concerns with Restorative Justice

Lack of Victim Participation

Emphasis on Shaming and Not Enough on Reintegration/Reconciliation

Inadequate Preparation

Inability to Engender Participation

Problems with Identifying Appropriate Participants

Problems Recruiting Representative Panels

Coercive Participation (particularly coercion of offenders)

Net-Widening

Inadequate Screening of Cases

Inability of Participants (e.g., Families, Communities) to Meaningfully Contribute

Lack of Neutrality by Participants and/or Facilitator

Inability to Address Serious Violent Crimes

Inability to Address Long-Standing Interpersonal Disputes

Too Victim-Oriented

Inability to Protect Constitutional Rights of Offenders

One problem is that restorative justice programs may be too ambitious in their attempt to solve very complex societal problems (Kurki, 2000). Simply gathering common citizens together to talk about a problem and brainstorm possible solutions is only the beginning of a much more complex process to address major social forces that may cause crime. Many problems involve long-standing interpersonal disputes that may not be amenable to simple mediation or conferencing.

A second concern, related to the first, is that restorative justice has been used primarily with less serious and property crimes. There is a great deal of debate over whether this approach can be used success-fully with serious violent offenses (see Bannenberg and Rössner, 2003). This is especially true when offenses such as spouse abuse, sexual assault, aggravated assault, murder, and like crimes are considered. While few programs have directly assessed this question, there is some evidence that restorative justice can be used in these cases. For exam-ple, Umbreit et al. (2003) reported success using VOM with murder-ers and the families of their victims. Corrado et al. (2003) also found positive results (mostly in terms of satisfaction) for a VOM program dealing with serious and violent offenses in British Columbia. The strongest finding in these studies is the need for very lengthy and extensive preparation prior to the intervention.

Third, there exists a concern that, while voluntary, there is an underlying level of coercion in most programs. What makes this truly problematic is that many programs do not allow (or at least frown upon) the presence of defense attorneys, thus raising the issue of an accused's constitutional rights and procedural safeguards (Feld, 1999; Levrant et al., 1999). In some instances, the participation of the offender is actually coerced by the fact that he or she is required to par-ticipate under threat of being processed in court. Compounding this problem is the need for the offender to admit to the act during the process. This is especially problematic if the intervention is taking place pre-adjudication.

A fourth concern with restorative justice is over how the "com-munity" is defined and who is allowed to represent the community (Kurki, 2000). This can be a very important concern because the par-ticipants help mold the outcome and the expectations for the solution. The participants can bring a wide array of differing expectations. This may not be a problem in smaller, more homogeneous communi-ties, such as Maori or Native American communities, but it can cer-tainly be problematic in large, diverse cities.

Fifth, Feld (1999) notes that there is a distinct imbalance of power in most restorative justice programs. This is especially problematic when juvenile offenders must face not only the victim but also the victim's support groups, members of the criminal justice system, and sometimes strangers from the general community. The power differential must be a prime consideration in meetings.

A sixth area of concern deals with the issue of net-widening. *Net-widening* refers to the situation by which the introduction of a new pro-gram or intervention serves to bring more people under the umbrella of social control. This is especially problematic when the new programs are intended to take people currently being served in the formal justice system and divert them to the new program. The expectation is that the new programs will relieve some of the burden from the formal system while simultaneously offering a better response to the problems. It is not clear the extent to which restorative justice has resulted in net-widening, but there is a legitimate concern that this has occurred.

Another concern with restorative justice is the argument that admitting victims into the criminal justice process is threatening to a system that traditionally has been oriented toward offender rights and that identifies society as the victim. Those favoring harsh punishment and those promoting rehabilitation or treatment tend to view the victim as getting in the way of dealing with offenders. The victim may want restitution and community service in lieu of punishment or may be looking for harsh punishment instead of treatment. Clearly, restorative justice proposes a new philosophy for the criminal justice system—particularly the corrections component. The offender-centered correctional system would be replaced by a system that attempts to accommodate diverse needs.

Despite these and other concerns, restorative justice is receiving a great deal of increased attention. Within a relatively short time frame, restorative programming has spread to countries around the world and is being used with a wide array of problems and events. While still used most commonly with youthful offenders and property or minor offenses, advocates are working to include serious and violent acts under the umbrella of restorative justice programming. The increased interest in restorative justice is very evident in the proposal made by the Commission on Crime Prevention and Criminal Justice of the United Nation's Economic and Social Council in 2002 (see Figure 5.8). This proposal recommends that restorative justice practices be used whenever feasible and sets forth guidelines on that use.

FIGURE 5.8.
Economic and Social Council Resolution on Restorative Justice

---

Annex I

Revised draft elements of a declaration of basic principles on the use of restorative justice programmes in criminal matters

Preamble

The Group of Experts on Restorative Justice,

Recalling that there has been a significant increase worldwide in restorative justice initiatives,

Recognizing that those initiatives often draw from traditional and indigenous forms of justice that fundamentally view crime as harm to people,

Emphasizing that restorative justice is an evolving response to crime that respects the dignity and equality of each person, builds understanding and promotes social harmony through the healing of victims, offenders and communities,

FIGURE 5.8—*continued*

Stressing that this approach enables those affected by crime to share their feelings and experiences openly, and aims at addressing their needs,

Aware that this approach provides an opportunity for victims to obtain reparation, feel safer and seek closure, allows offenders to gain insight into the causes and effects of their behaviour and to take responsibility in a meaningful way and enables communities to understand the underlying causes of crime, to promote community well-being and to prevent crime,

Noting that restorative justice gives rise to a range of measures that are flexible in their adaptation to established criminal justice systems and complement those systems, taking into account legal, social and cultural circumstances,

Recognizing that the use of restorative justice does not prejudice the right of States to prosecute alleged offenders,

Recommends that the Basic Principles on the Use of Restorative Justice Programmes in Criminal Matters, annexed to the present resolution, be established to guide the development and operation of restorative justice programmes in Member States.

Annex

Basic Principles on the Use of Restorative Justice Programmes in Criminal Matters

I   *Use of terms*

1. "Restorative justice programme" means any programme that uses restorative processes and seeks to achieve restorative outcomes.
2. "Restorative process" means any process in which the victim and the offender and, where appropriate, any other individuals or community members affected by a crime participate together actively in the resolution of matters arising from the crime, generally with the help of a facilitator. Restorative processes may include mediation, conciliation, conferencing and sentencing circles.
3. "Restorative outcome" means an agreement reached as a result of a restorative process. Restorative outcomes may include responses and programmes such as reparation, restitution and community service, aimed at meeting the individual and collective needs and responsibilities of the parties and achieving the reintegration of the victim and the offender.
4. "Parties" means the victim, the offender and any other individuals or community members affected by a crime who may be involved in a restorative process.
5. "Facilitator" means a person whose role is to facilitate, in a fair and impartial manner, the participation of the parties in a restorative process.

II   *Use of restorative justice programmes*

6. Restorative justice programmes may be used at any stage of the criminal justice system, subject to national law.
7. Restorative processes should be used only where there is sufficient evidence to charge the offender and with the free and voluntary consent of the victim and the offender. The victim and the offender should be able to withdraw such consent at any time during the process. Agreements should be arrived at voluntarily and contain only reasonable and proportionate obligations.
8. The victim and the offender should normally agree on the basic facts of a case as the basis for their participation in a restorative process. Participation of the offender shall not be used as evidence of admission of guilt in subsequent legal proceedings.
9. Disparities leading to power imbalances, as well as cultural differences among the parties, should be taken into consideration in referring a case to and in conducting a restorative process.

FIGURE 5.8—*continued*

10. The safety of the parties should be considered in referring any case to and in conducting a restorative process.

11. Where restorative processes are not suitable or possible, the case should be referred to the criminal justice authorities and a decision should be taken as to how to proceed without delay. In such cases, criminal justice officials should endeavour to encourage the offender to take responsibility vis-A-vis the victim and affected communities and support the reintegration of the victim and the offender into the community.

III *Operation of restorative justice programmes*

12. Member States should consider establishing guidelines and standards, with legislative authority when necessary, that govern the use of restorative justice programmes. Such guidelines and standards should respect the basic principles contained herein and should address, inter alia:

   (a) The conditions for the referral of cases to restorative justice programmes;

   (b) The handling of cases following a restorative process;

   (c) The qualifications, training and assessment of facilitators;

   (d) The administration of restorative justice programmes;

   (e) Standards of competence and rules of conduct governing the operation of restorative justice programmes.

13. Fundamental procedural safeguards guaranteeing fairness to the offender and the victim should be applied to restorative justice programmes and in particular to restorative processes:

   (a) Subject to national law, the victim and the offender should have the right to consult with legal counsel concerning the restorative process and, where necessary, to translation and/or interpretation. Minors should, in addition, have the fight to the assistance of a parent or guardian-,

   (b) Before agreeing to participate in restorative processes, the parties should be fully informed of their rights, the nature of the process and the possible consequences of their decision;

   (c) Neither the victim nor the offender should be coerced or induced by unfair means to participate in restorative processes or to accept restorative outcomes.

14. Discussions in restorative processes that are not conducted in public should be confidential and should not be disclosed subsequently, except with the agreement of the parties or as required by national law.

15. The results of agreements arising out of restorative justice programmes should, where appropriate, be judicially supervised or incorporated into judicial decisions or judgements. Where this occurs, the outcome should have the same status as any other judicial decision or judgement and should preclude prosecution in respect of the same facts.

16. Where no agreement is reached among the parties, the case should be referred back to the established criminal justice process and a decision as to how to proceed should be taken without delay. Failure to reach an agreement alone shall not be used in subsequent criminal justice proceedings.

17. Failure to implement an agreement made in the course of a restorative process should be referred back to the restorative programme or, where required by national law, to the established criminal justice process and a decision as to how to proceed should be taken without delay. Failure to implement an agreement, other than a judicial decision or judgement, should not be used as justification for a more severe sentence in subsequent criminal justice proceedings.

FIGURE 5.8—*continued*

---

18. Facilitators should perform their duties in an impartial manner, with due respect to the dignity of the parties. In this capacity, facilitators should ensure that the parties act with respect towards each other and should enable the parties to find a relevant solution among themselves.

19. Facilitators shall possess a good understanding of local cultures and communities and, where appropriate, receive initial training before taking up facilitation duties.

IV *Continuing development of restorative justice programmes*

20. Member States should consider the formulation of national strategies and policies aimed at the development of restorative justice and at the promotion of a culture favourable to the use of restorative justice among law enforcement, judicial and social authorities, as well as local communities.

21. There should be regular consultation between criminal justice authorities and administrators of restorative justice programmes to develop a common understanding of and enhance the effectiveness of restorative processes and outcomes in order to increase the extent to which restorative programmes are used and to explore ways in which restorative approaches might be incorporated into criminal justice practices.

22. Member States, in cooperation with civil society where appropriate, should promote research on and evaluation of restorative justice programmes to assess the extent to which they result in restorative outcomes, serve as a complement or alternative to the criminal justice process and provide positive outcomes for all parties. Restorative justice processes may need to undergo change in concrete form over time.

    Member States should therefore encourage regular evaluation and modification of such programmes. The results of research and evaluation should guide further policy and programme development.

V *Saving clause*

23. Nothing in these Basic Principles shall affect any rights of an offender or a victim that are established in national law or applicable international law.

Source: Economic and Social Council resolution 2000/14, annex, as amended by the Group of Experts on Restorative Justice. E/CN.15/2002/5/Add.1. Retrieved October 21, 2004, from http://www.unodc.org/pdf/crime/commissions/11comm/5add1e.pdf

Summary

Restorative justice programs offer another method for handling individuals after an offense has occurred. The intent of these programs is multifaceted. There is a desire to restore the victim to the state he or she was in prior to the offense. In addition, the programs attempt to repair the more general harm that has been done to the larger community. Equally important is taking steps to rehabilitate the offender so that he or she does not commit future offenses.

Restorative justice involves various constituencies (Bazemore and Umbreit, 2001; Umbreit, 1997; Van Ness, 1990; Van Ness and Strong, 1997). Under this approach victims are compensated through restitution, are given a voice in the case handling, and become an integral part of the treatment or intervention provided to the offender. The offender is held accountable for his or her transgressions and may be subjected to a wide array of possible interventions.

Communities also may be compensated through offender payments or services. At the same time, the community is expected to assist the victim, work with the offender, and seek to eliminate causes of crime. Finally, the government (particularly in the form of the criminal justice system) is to provide fair and equitable procedures for all parties, while receiving the support and assistance of the public in these efforts (Van Ness, 1990). In essence, restorative justice seeks to bring all parties to the table in a mutual assistance pact. Everyone who comes in with a need is to depart with some degree of satisfaction.

FIGURE 5.9
Selected Internet Sites Dealing with Restorative Justice

Australian Institute of Criminology
 http://www.aic.gov.au/rjustice

British Home Office
 http://www.homeoffice.gov.uk/crime-victims/victims/restorative-justice/

International Institute for Restorative Practices
 http://www.restorativepractices.org/

Nacro
 http://www.nacro.org.uk

New Zealand Ministry of Justice
 http://www.justice.govt.nz/restorative-justice/index.html

Restorative Justice Consortium
 http://www.restorativejustice.org.uk

Simon Fraser Centre for Restorative Justice
 http://www.sfu.ca/cfrj/

Victim Offender Mediation Association
 http://www.voma.org/

It is difficult for anyone to argue against the notion that the offender, victim, criminal justice system, or the community all need and deserve attention. One appeal of restorative justice is the recognition of these varied needs and a concerted effort to address them. Restorative justice certainly speaks to the concerns and interests of victim advocates. It is not surprising that the move toward restorative justice is being led by prominent proponents of victim rights. At the same time, many individuals traditionally concerned with offender rights and treatment can see restorative justice as a means of maintaining concern for offenders amidst the growth of victim rights. The criminal justice system, which is caught in the middle of a tug-of-war between victims and offenders, benefits from a proposal that does not seek to elevate one group's concerns over those of another.

Restorative justice is the most recent entry in a long debate over the proper role of victims in the criminal justice system. However, the increasing interest in restorative justice in recent years has led to the growth of programs around the world. What is still missing, however, is good evaluation of the preventive efficacy of the interventions.

Key Terms for Chapter 5

circle sentencing

community group conferencing (CGC)

dispute resolution

family group conferencing (FGC)

healing circle

net-widening

reintegrative shaming

reparative justice

restorative justice

retributive justice

RISE

vicarious victimization

victim-offender mediation (VOM)

victim-offender reconciliation program (VORP)

Learning Objectives

After reading Chapter 6, you should be able to:

- Give the common-law definition of rape.
- Contrast rape with sexual battery.
- Tie the notion of spousal immunity to the idea of male power and domination.
- Differentiate between acquaintance rape and stranger rape.
- Assemble a picture of forcible rape based on FBI UCR statistics.
- Sketch out the characteristics of sexual assault based upon victimization survey results.
- Compare and contrast UCR and NCVS statistics regarding rape.
- Discuss the shortcomings of the UCR and NCVS databases.
- Explain what the NCVS redesign has meant for sexual assault statistics.
- Critique independent efforts to gauge the extent of sexual assault among women.
- Draw a distinction between the incidence and the prevalence of sexual battery.
- Summarize the National College Women Sexual Victimization Study.
- Provide an overview of the National Violence Against Women Survey.
- Expound upon the problem of sexual violence at the national military academies.
- Talk about why psychopathology is a popular explanation for sexual battery.
- Link a physiological explanation to sexual battery.
- Relate the theme of male domination or power to sexual battery.
- Comment on the categories produced by sexual battery typologies.
- Talk about what a crisis means.
- Understand the stages in the crisis reaction repair cycle.
- Analyze the rape trauma syndrome.
- Amplify some of the concerns surrounding compulsory HIV testing for sexual battery suspects.
- Explain consent and corroboration.
- Outline the purpose that shield provisions serve.
- Talk about sex offender registration laws.
- Distinguish macro-level from micro-level effects.
- Evaluate whether sexual battery reforms are working as intended.
- Provide an overview of the steps involved in the system's response to sexual battery cases.
- Differentiate the medical examination from a forensic examination.
- Raise some issues pertaining to the use of "rape kits."
- List some common pitfalls that the prosecutor's office should avoid in the handling of sexual battery cases.

Chapter 6

SEXUAL BATTERY

Introduction

Sexual battery is a devastating, dehumanizing experience. What makes this crime so crushing is that it is a direct attack on the person's self. Many victims suffer tremendous feelings of humiliation and degradation because of their assailants. Later, many of these same emotions are rekindled when the victim turns to the criminal justice system expecting to find comfort and assistance.

This chapter opens with a brief look at some of the theories that purport to explain why rape occurs. To get a better sense of the prevalence of sexual battery in this country, we will look at official and unofficial data sources. A comparison of information contained in the Uniform Crime Reports with materials from the National Crime Victimization Survey reinforces the discussion held in Chapter 2. Underreporting is a major drawback with this crime category.

The system is not unaware of the widespread reluctance to report sexual battery and to become involved with the authorities. Many states have rewritten their laws in an effort to dismantle the traditional barriers to victim cooperation. For example, rape has become redefined as sexual assault or sexual battery, and attention has been given to concerns with consent, the types of proof necessary to substantiate an allegation of sexual violence, and the character assassination tactics used to discredit victim testimony in court. Whether these reforms are working is an empirical question that we will probe.

Our discussion of sexual battery will delve into the personal tragedy that victims experience, the healing process these people face, and common coping strategies. This material will provide a backdrop for discussing how the police, hospital personnel, and the prosecutor respond to the victim.

Defining Sexual Battery

The definition of rape traditionally has been a matter of utmost concern. The common law view of rape dominated most state statutes well into the 1970s. Common law defines rape as carnal knowledge by a male of a female, who is not his wife, forcibly and against her will (Garner, 1999: 1267). This definition is notable for several reasons. First, the victim status is restricted to females, and only males can be offenders. Second, the only act controlled under this approach is penile penetration. Third, husbands enjoy an automatic exemption from offender status. Fourth, an important element or ingredient is that the victim did not submit voluntarily to the act.

FIGURE 6.1
An Example of a Sexual Battery Statute Containing Provisions
Regarding Aggravating Circumstances

A person who commits sexual battery upon a person 12 years of age or older without that person's consent, under any of the following circumstances, commits a felony of the first degree, punishable as provided in s. 775.082, s. 775.803, or s. 775.084:

(a) When the victim is physically helpless to resist.

(b) When the offender coerces the victim to submit by threatening to use force or violence likely to cause serious personal injury on the victim, and the victim reasonably believes that the offender has the present ability to execute the threat.

(c) When the offender coerces the victim to submit by threatening to retaliate against the victim, or any other person, and the victim reasonably believes that the offender has the ability to execute the threat in the future.

(d) When the offender, without the prior knowledge or consent of the victim, administers or has knowledge of someone else administering to the victim any narcotic, anesthetic, or other intoxicating substance which mentally or physically incapacitates the victim.

(e) When the victim is mentally defective and the offender has reason to believe this or has actual knowledge of this fact.

(f) When the victim is physically incapacitated.

(g) When the offender is a law enforcement officer, correctional officer, or correctional probation officer . . . or any other person in a position of control or authority in a probation, community control, controlled release, detention, custodial, or similar setting, and such officer, official, or person is acting in such a manner as to lead the victim to reasonably believe that the offender is in a position of control or authority as an agent or employee of government.

Source: *Florida Statutes* (2007), §794.011 (4).

Over the years, lawmakers have altered the legal terminology involved with rape in a variety of ways. Many states have replaced the term "rape" with such phrases as "sexual battery," "deviant sexual conduct," and "sexual assault." These changes are more than just semantic. For one thing, they eliminate the gender bias inherent in the common law formulation. Today, it is possible for males to be victims and for females to be offenders. In addition, other forms of sexual abuse now fall under the purview of unwanted criminal intrusions. Some such acts would include oral, anal, and digital penetration, as well as fondling and the introduction of any other foreign objects into the victim's body. Finally, varying degrees of sexual battery replace the former all-inclusive single category of rape. As Figure 6.1 shows, the degree of a criminal act can be distinguished by the extent of injury, use of weapons, presence or absence of penetration, multiple versus lone offenders, and other factors. These aggravating circumstances can raise the applicable penalty allowed under sentencing guidelines.

Spousal Rape

Under common law, a wife cannot accuse her husband of raping her while they are legally married. The underlying assumption is that the marriage vows provide an irretractable contractual arrangement to deliver exclusive sexual services upon demand. The marriage ceremony marks the formal transfer of the woman from her father's possession to the ownership of the husband. The practice of placing a premium on virginity, the institution of the dowry, and the tradition of relinquishing one's maiden name to assume the husband's surname all further reinforce the image of women as a commodity that males can buy and trade. This orientation maintains that a husband is free to do with his "property" as he sees fit (Ryan, 1995).

Despite this legal barrier, society recognizes that some unconscionable husbands do force their spouses to engage in unwanted sexual activity. It is not uncommon for coerced sexual behavior to occur in at least one of every 10 marriages (Finkelhor and Yllo, 1983; Russell, 1982). According to figures from the 2005 NCVS (Catalano, 2006: 9), 28 percent of all rapes and sexual assaults in which females were the targets were committed by intimates (current or former spouses or significant others). A common perception is that a sexual assault by a husband is not as serious as an attack by a complete stranger (Frese, Moya, and Megias, 2004; Monson, Byrd, and Langhinrichsen-Rohling, 1996). However, Yllo (1999: 1060) writes, "When you are raped by a stranger, you live with a frightening memory; but when you are raped by your husband, you live with your rapist."

As mentioned earlier, the common law interpretation, known as *spousal immunity*, is that a husband is incapable of raping his wife. If a jurisdiction follows this line of thinking, husbands enjoy an *absolute exemption* and are not prosecuted for spousal rape under any condition. Many states have relaxed their statutes to reflect the growing awareness that marital rape does exist and can have deep traumatic effects for the victim. These states may allow prosecution if the parties are separated, are in the process of obtaining a divorce, or have taken other steps to void or nullify the marriage. These laws grant what is known as a *partial exemption*. While this modification may appear to be an enlightened and progressive move, it does have its limits. A national survey of rape reform legislation cautions that states that "have removed the traditional immunity for spouses . . . have offset this change by providing relatively low penalties for conviction" (Berger, Searles, and Neuman, 1988: 342). Thus, what may appear at first to be a significant gain is sometimes really a very small concession.

Date or Acquaintance Rape

Another form of sexual assault that has emerged as a major topic of study is the category of *date rape* or *acquaintance rape*. This crime has garnered attention because it does not fit the stereotypical view of rape. To a large degree, many people assume that sexual assault occurs between individuals who do not know one another. They think the offender either stalks his prey or happens upon a victim and violently attacks that person. Date rape, however, does not fit that convenient mold. Rather, the victim and offender know one another and are engaged in friendly, noncombative interaction up until the attack. In many analyses, being "talked into" having sexual relations when the victim did not want to, submitting when inebriated, being made to feel guilty if refusing to have sex, or submitting after being given false promises (such as marriage) fall into the realm of sexual assault, although physical force or threats may not have been involved. The absence of the traditional stranger-to-stranger relationship and physical force sometimes leads some people to believe there must be some degree of consent in date or acquaintance instances, thereby negating a valid claim of rape.

Measuring the Extent of Rape

As we learned in Chapter 2, estimates concerning the nature, extent, and distribution of crime vary considerably depending upon the source of that information. The category of forcible rape or sexual battery is no exception. The typical forums for gathering data on these criminal incidents are the Uniform Crime Reports (UCR) and the National Crime Victimization Survey (NCVS). Information from both these databases, as well as other undertakings, follows in this chapter.

UCR Information

The UCR describes forcible rape as "the carnal knowledge of a female forcibly and against her will" (FBI, 2006). This category excludes statutory rape and other sex offenses. Using this definition, the UCR reveals that there were 93,934 rapes known to the police in 2005. When one transforms the 2005 number into a crime rate, the resulting figure is approximately 62.5 offenses per 100,000 women.

NCVS Information

The emerging women's movement in the 1960s and 1970s assailed official rape statistics as too low and patently inaccurate. This position garnered a great deal of support from the early victimization surveys. The NORC (National Opinion Research Center) victimization survey, undertaken on behalf of the 1967 President's Commission, uncovered almost four times more rapes than what police reports had tallied. Despite a host of methodological problems with first-generation victim surveys, the issue of underreporting fueled skepticism about the reliability and validity of official crime counts.

After a great deal of refinement, the NCVS has emerged as a recognized source of information on crime victims. As you will recall from Chapter 2, the NCVS redesign modified the screen questions so as to more fully measure the extent of certain types of offenses, including sexual assault. Rather than simply probe sexual assault under a general question dealing with being attacked "in some other way," the redesigned survey specifically asks about rape, attempted rape, or any other type of sexual assault (Bachman and Saltzman, 1995). The expectation was that the new survey would uncover substantially more rape and sexual assault incidents than have materialized in the past (Kindermann, Lynch, and Cantor, 1997).

As expected, the level of reported sexual assault did increase under the redesigned format. According to the 1990 NCVS, there were 67,430 attempted rapes and 62,830 completed rapes in the United States. These figures jumped to 148,610 attempted rapes and 167,550 completed rapes in 1994, roughly a 243 percent increase for the combined categories (Bureau of Justice Statistics, 1997: 6). The 1994 figures translate into a combined rape/sexual assault victimization rate of 200 per 100,000 population age 12 and above, compared to a rate of roughly 60 in 1990. However, more recent figures point to a decrease in rape and sexual assault victimization. For the year 2005, the NCVS recorded 51,500 attempted rapes and 64,080 completed rapes (Catalano, 2006: 3), which translate into respective rates of 20 and 30 per 100,000 persons. In addition, the NCVS uncovered another 85,210 sexual assaults.

TABLE 6.1
Selected Characteristics of Rape/Sexual Assault Victimization, NCVS, 2005

Rape/Sexual Assault Rate by Victim Age (rate per 1,000):

12-15	1.2	35-49	0.6
16-19	3.2	50-64	0.6
20-24	1.1	65+	0.0
25-34	0.7		

Rape/Sexual Assault Rate by Victim Race (rate per 1,000):

White	0.6
Black	1.8
Other	0.5

Rape/Sexual Assault Rate by Household Income (rate per 1,000):

Less than $7,500	2.2
$ 7,500 - $14,999	0.6
$15,000 - $24,999	1.4
$25,000 - $34,999	1.7
$35,000 - $49,999	0.9
$50,000 - $74,999	0.5
$75,000 or more	0.6

Rape/Sexual Assault Rate by Victim-Offender Relationship for Female Victims:

Non-stranger	128,440	73%
Intimate	49,980	28%
Other Relative	11,880	7%
Friend/Acquaintance	66,580	38%
Stranger	45,050	26%
Unknown	3,050	2%
TOTAL	176,540	101%

Rape/Sexual Assault Rate by Presence of Weapon:

No Weapon	159,860	85%
Firearm	5,940	3%
Knife	6,360	3%
Don't Know	16,790	9%
TOTAL	188,950	100%

Source: Adapted from Catalano, S.M. (2006). *Criminal Victimization*, 2005. Washington, DC: U.S. Bureau of Justice Statistics.

Table 6.1 presents some selected characteristics of rape incidents outlined in the NCVS. According to this data source, there were more than 191,000 rapes (completed and attempted) and sexual assaults in 2005. Younger females are more likely to become rape victims. Blacks are twice as likely as whites to acknowledge a victimization experience. *Nonstranger rapes* (which include "date rape" and "acquaintance rape," among other things) account for 73 percent of these sexual victimizations. Very few incidents involve a weapon, and there is a marked concentration of episodes among lower-income respondents.

Comparing the UCR with the NCVS Over Time

One way to address any similarities and disparities between police- and survey-derived victimization rates is to look at these data over time. If both sets of crime statistics are subject to similar influences, then they ought to move in unison. Should different forces affect one data set but not the other, then one should observe uncorrelated trends. One intrusion, the implementation of the redesigned NCVS in 1992, created an artificial increase in the number of rapes reported by respondents. As a result, researchers have adjusted the 1973–1991 data to make the entire series more compatible (Kinderman et al., 1997; Rand, Lynch, and Cantor, 1997). Figure 6.2 presents the rape victimization rates for both the UCR and the NCVS from 1973 through 2005.

FIGURE 6.2
NCVS and UCR Rape Rates, 1973-2005

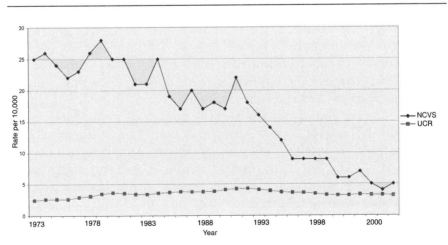

Source: Compilation from annual reports.

The UCR forcible rape rates display a relatively steady climb from 1976 until 1992, at which point the rates started to decline. On the other hand, the victimization rape rates evidence a general downward trend throughout the data, even when considering the sudden jump due to the survey redesign. Both the data from 1976 to 1991 and those from 1992 to 2005 display a downward pattern, with the latter being very pronounced. While the UCR pattern is smooth, the NCVS exhibits steep bounces in both directions. As the two data sources do not track each other until about 1997, the next step is to find what systematic influences affect each data set.

One possibility is that changes in traditional sex-role attitudes have relaxed the taboos once associated with rape. This liberalization, in turn, paves the way for greater reporting of such incidents. The underlying argument is that before this attitudinal shift, women were reluctant to report episodes that departed from "classic rape" stereotypes. For example, victims may have found it easier to report attacks in which the perpetrator brandished a weapon, was a complete stranger, or beat the victim. At the same time, however, victims would hide incidents involving acquaintances or relatives and alcohol use from public view (Fisher et al., 2003a).

To see if this notion was plausible, Orcutt and Faison (1988) analyzed attitudinal trends and victimization reporting habits from 1973 until 1985. They found that broader or more liberated perceptions of acceptable female behavior greatly affected whether the police were notified in nonstranger rape situations. Thus, Orcutt and Faison (1988) maintained that increases in rapes known to the police during this period could very well be a function of changing social mores. Other researchers also lend empirical support to this line of thinking (Bachman, 1993; Bachman, 1995; Baumer, Felson, and Messner, 2003).

Although the notion of an attitudinal shift carries considerable appeal, another alternative is just as lucrative. Criminologists know that organizational changes within the police bureaucracy influence the quantity and composition of official crime. Drawing upon this outlook, Jensen and Karpos (1993) counter that an increased presence of female law enforcement employees changes the quality of police interaction with victims. This gain, in turn, influences agency recording practices. More precisely, dispatchers and officers who are female have a heightened sensitivity toward sexual assault victims. These employees are in a better position to anticipate victim needs. A more sensitive posture, coupled with specialized investigatory units and connections with rape crisis centers, fosters greater citizen reporting and better police documentation of sexual assault cases.

A third reason for the UCR-NCVS discrepancy prior to 1992 is the realization that the victimization survey instrument did not contain any inquiries that deal directly with rape (Bachman and Taylor, 1994; Eigenberg, 1990). The individual screen questions eliciting reports of rape victimization were vague and evasive. This may have been because survey administrators regarded this area as delicate and highly sensitive. The NCVS redesign addresses this deficiency by including an item that uses a screen question asking about rape, attempted rape, and other types of sexual assault. Follow-up questions on any incidents are then conducted. This new procedure resulted in a 157 percent increase in identified incidents compared to the older approach (Kindermann et al.,1997). Consequently, data since the redesign have a better chance of mirroring the patterns in UCR data. However, researchers still must sort through an array of questions regarding validity and reliability before achieving accurate measures of violence against women (Fisher et al., 2003b; Gelles, 2000; Gordon, 2000; Schwartz, 2000).

Other Information on Sexual Assault Levels

In addition to the information and comparisons available from the UCR and the NCVS, independent researchers have attempted to gauge the extent of rape among the total female population for various subgroups of females and for different types of rape. One of the most researched areas deals with date or acquaintance rape. Interest in date rape is not new. In one early survey, one-fourth of the responding college women reported experiencing forcible intercourse over a one-year period of time (Kanin, 1957). More recently, surveys of high school students (Schubot, 2001) and college students have revealed sexual victimization levels that range from 10 to more than 50 percent (Abbey et al., 1996; Bernard and Bernard, 1983; Cate et al., 1982; Kilpatrick et al., 1985; Koss, 1995; Koss, Gidycz, and Wisniewski, 1987; Makepeace, 1983; Schwartz and Pitts, 1995; Shapiro and Schwarz, 1997). Quite often, the aggressor is characterized as an acquaintance. Indeed, Abbey et al. (1996) claim that 95 percent of sexual assaults are committed by an acquaintance. It is also important to note that several studies find significant levels of sexual coercion reported by male respondents (Hogben, Byrne, and Hamburger, 1996; Poppen and Segal, 1988; Struckman-Johnson, 1988; Waldner-Haugrud and Magruder, 1995). The figures for both females and males bespeak of a much greater problem than that suggested by either official data or large national survey data.

In evaluating this information, however, there are several issues that should be kept in mind. First, the magnitude of many figures is inflated by focusing on "lifetime" occurrences or college surveys asking about "since you were 14" or any other similar ages. The data, therefore, appear high when compared to official and NCVS measures that tap only the past year.

Second, while often discussed as "date rape," the actions under consideration typically reflect a much broader category of "sexual coercion." For example, verbal persuasion to engage in sex, promises of marriage, and making someone feel guilty are often lumped together with the use or threat of physical force in defining an experience as sexual assault. While these actions may entail coercion, there is a clear difference in magnitude and potential harm involved in the actions.

Third, most studies of date rape restrict their inquiries to just college students. Furthermore, researchers often rely upon very select groups of students, such as undergraduates enrolled in psychology or criminal justice classes. A college sampling frame, while convenient, is not representative of society nor of the 18-to-22-year-old general population.

Finally, caution must be used in blindly accepting interpretations advanced by "advocates." Gilbert (1993), while reviewing research on the magnitude of date rape, notes that almost three-quarters of the respondents in one study whom the researchers regarded as victims actually reported that they themselves did not think they had been a victim. He also points out that some "rape" questions fail to address whether the behavior was consensual or not—an important criterion to consider. Reliance upon such questionable assumptions results in incidence and prevalence rates that not only dwarf official data but belie even the experiences of crisis assistance groups (Gilbert, 1993). Clearly, rape and sexual assault are greater problems than what official data would lead us to believe (Fisher et al., 2003b). At the same time, though, advocacy data probably errs on the other extreme end of the spectrum by making unreasonable assumptions when measuring the problem. A safe conclusion is that rape is a much larger and more pervasive problem than the UCR and the NCVS figures indicate.

More Recent Efforts

Sensitivity to these and other issues prompted two separate surveys to enlist national samples in an effort to arrive at a more comprehensive understanding of sexual violence. The first project was undertaken to secure sounder information from college women, and the second study focused on American women in general. The release of these details helps round out our current understanding of a number of issues. In fact, the college women survey is touted as "perhaps the most systematic analysis of the extent and nature of the sexual victimization of college women in the past decade" (Fischer, Cullen, and Turner, 2000:

3). Finally, this section visits the problem of sexual violence at U.S. national military academies.

The National College Women Sexual Victimization Study

Acknowledging the limitations highlighted in the previous section, Fischer and her colleagues drew a representative sample of almost 4,500 women enrolled in college during the fall of 1996. This effort, referred to as the National College Women Sexual Victimization (NCWSV) study, borrowed the NCVS two-stage approach of utilizing screen questions and incident-relevant inquiries. However, one enhancement the researchers made was to add a larger number of, and more specific, screen questions. These initial queries avoided using legal terminology and relied more upon behavioral descriptions of the illicit acts. In other words, instead of asking respondents whether they had been raped, interviewers utilized a series of questions that described the exact behavior sought. The purpose behind this approach was to avoid any possible misunderstandings so that respondents could give the most accurate answers possible. It also enabled the investigators to collect data regarding attempted misconduct, threats with and without violence, sexual battery, stalking, and other aspects of sexual coercion.

The extrapolated results indicate that 5 percent of college women contend with rape or an attempted rape annually. If one realizes that many college students take five years to finish an undergraduate degree, then the actual risk rises into the vicinity of 20 to 25 percent. It might be more instructive to place the NCWSV number of incidents in a slightly different context. If a college had an enrollment of 10,000 female students, administrators could anticipate that one sexual battery would take place every day. One must also bear in mind that this estimate does not include other unwanted forms of sexual coercion like harassing comments, obscene phone calls, coercion, voyeurism, and other sexually oriented behaviors. In short, these statistics paint a very unflattering portrait of an environment that many people naively assume is geared more toward intellectual and rational challenges.

The National Violence Against Women Survey

The National Institute of Justice and the Centers for Disease Control and Prevention combined forces to sponsor the National Violence Against Women (NVAW) Survey, which was carried under the guidance of Tjaden and Thoennes (2000). The NVAW Survey, conducted from

November of 1995 through May of 1996, involved 8,000 female and 8,000 male respondents. Its goal was to provide survey data on the prevalence, incidence, and consequences of violence against women.

Like the NCWSV, the NVAW Survey relied upon multiple, behaviorally based queries to generate more detailed victimization information. The results showed that 17.6 percent of the women and 3 percent of the men indicated they had been raped at least once during their lifetimes. In other words, "1 of 6 U.S. women and 1 of 33 U.S. men have been victims of a completed or attempted rape" (Tjaden and Thoennes, 2000: 13).

The researchers were careful to draw a distinction between the *incidence* of rape (the number of victimizations) and the *prevalence* of rape (the number of victims). National estimates based upon the NVAW data generate a total of 876,064 rape incidents with female victims and 111,298 incidents with male victims. By comparison, the 1994 NCVS figures include 432,100 incidents involving female victims and 32,900 cases with male victims. In terms of prevalence, these incidents registered more than 302,000 female victims and almost 93,000 male victims. Obviously, there were a substantial number of victims who reported multiple episodes. In addition, further analyses revealed that intimate partners were responsible for a number of these lifetime rape victimizations (7.7% of the female respondents and 0.3% of the male interviewees). These findings, along with further information regarding physical assault and stalking, confirm that violence against women is a major social problem in the United States.

Sexual Victimization at the National Military Academies

Traditionally, the United States military has been a male bastion. While women have entered the armed services for many years, they typically were relegated to work in stereotypical roles, such as the secretarial pool or hospital nurses. Even when wider access was granted, women were still restricted from entering combat duty, denied posts in other highly hazardous duty areas, and held to different physical fitness standards.

The military academies operate in a dual capacity. In addition to the mission of developing future military leaders, these institutions provide a college education to attendees. In other words, the military academies are institutions of higher education. It was not until the mid-1970s that the military academies began admitting female cadets into their programs. The integration of the two genders met with resistance. For example, the last all-male graduating class of the Air

Force Academy sported tee-shirts and other attire imprinted with the logo "LCWB" or "Last Class Without Broads," one of the more staid euphemisms (Fowler, 2003: 59). Other practices contributed to an atmosphere that was hostile to women. A 2002 survey of the social climate at the Air Force Academy revealed that more than a quarter of the male cadets did not believe women had a place on the campus. Virtually every female cadet expressed concern for their safety when they found themselves alone at night (Fowler, 2003: 59). The practice of not allowing the doors to sleeping quarters to be locked at night fanned these fears.

It was against this backdrop that administrators became aware that sexual assault and sexual harassment were problematic issues. There were 142 allegations of sexual assault at the Air Force Academy during the 1993–2002 interim. Of course, one must balance this number against rampant nonreporting. A survey conducted in 2003 discovered that 80 percent of the female cadets who said they had been sexually assaulted did not report the incident (Fowler, 2003: 1). Almost one in five women said they became sexual assault victims during their stay at the Academy. Another four of five women in a 1995 campus survey were the targets of sexual harassment (Fowler, 2003: 16).

While the Fowler report went on to advance a series of recommendations, Congress considered the problem serious enough to warrant an expanded look at all the national military academies. As a result, a task force was empaneled. Its charge boiled down to a very basic question. Starting with the premise that the military academies recruit only the "cream of the crop," the Task Force posed a simple question: "Why then, with such high-quality youth and high standards of discipline, do acts of sexual harassment and sexual assaults still occur?" (Howeing and Rumburg, 2005: 8).

The Task Force recognized, among other things, the existence of a sexually abusive environment on military campuses. It turned the spotlight squarely on the service academy culture. In an effort to defeat this milieu, the institutions must address social and institutional practices that devalue women. While a variety of reforms are currently being implemented, there is one very important point here. That is, these observations regarding the incidence of sexual violence at the military service academies stem from the very same vulnerable age-groups that both the NCWSV and NVAW isolated.

Theories of Sexual Battery

Any attempt to understand the occurrence of sexual battery must grapple with the causes of such behavior. As with virtually every form of deviant behavior, there is no consensus about the exact etiological or causative factors that underlie sexual assault. A variety of potential explanations have been put forth as capable explanations of this behavior. The following materials highlight selected explanations grounded in the pathology and physiology of the offender as well as the social development of society, with the latter being instrumental in the growth of the women's movement and public interest in sexual assault.

Intraindividual Theories

Most early explanations portrayed rape and sexual violence as stemming from *psychopathology,* or mental imbalances within the offender. The perpetrator was seen as a disturbed or maladjusted individual who failed to exert sufficient control over his actions. Sexual battery was a reaction to repressed desires, past domination by a female figure, or other forces beyond the offender's control (Brownmiller, 1975; Lottes, 1988; Scully, 1990).

These explanations gained quick acceptance because they painted rape as a social aberration. One could attribute such undesirable behavior to the few deranged individuals who committed these acts. What made this perspective so lucrative was that it deflected attention away from society and the victim. In essence, they were blameless for the offense.

Physiological explanations also locate the cause of rape within the individual offender. According to these views, an uncontrollable sex drive, compounded by the lack of available partners, compels the offender to rape (Lottes, 1988). According to Ellis (1989), rape is a consequence of the natural selection process endemic to society. This evolutionary approach maintains that males need frequent copulation as a substitute for the lengthy gestation period experienced by females. According to this theory, females contribute to the species through gestation, while males do so through multiple copulation with more than one partner. Thus, this model contends that rape is the product of a distinctive physiological need on the part of the male.

Sociocultural Explanations

Sociocultural explanations have gained prominence as viable explanations for sexual battery. Sociocultural explanations, frequently labeled as feminist in orientation, focus on the traditional roles of males and females in society.

Brownmiller (1975) brought these arguments to the forefront when she pointed out that the historical place of women in society was one of subservience. Women belonged either to their fathers or to their husbands. Females were property; as such, they were subject to the wishes of the owner. In this context, any attack on a female was actually an affront against her master. Any compensation or retribution due to the possession's devaluation went to the owner, not to the female who was victimized. It is for similar reasons that warring armies use rape as a weapon to terrorize, intimidate, and taunt opposing forces (Brownmiller, 1975).

In updating the sociocultural explanation, rape is simply a means of showing and promoting male domination in a society in which formal ownership of females is no longer permitted. Rape is a means of guaranteeing the inequality between the sexes, with males occupying the upper niches of power. The sociocultural approach emphasizes the argument that rape is *not* a sexual offense. Instead, rape is an offense of *power*—a tool that enables men to exert power and control over women.

The sociocultural explanation borrows heavily from the arena of learning theory. In this approach, behavior is learned through both formal and informal mechanisms, such as imitation, modeling, reinforcement, and explicit training. Proponents who embrace this viewpoint see rape as the result of stereotypical role expectations in society (Brownmiller, 1975; Griffin, 1971; Makepeace, 1981; Sanders, 1980; Schwendinger and Schwendinger, 1983). The "proper" place of males and females is passed down from one generation to the next in everyday behavior and expectations. Rape is a result of males exerting their learned position in society.

As one would expect, the sociocultural explanation gained a great deal of support from the women's movement. It became a clear challenge to the dominant male structure within society. Rape was also identifiable as perhaps the most heinous example of what was wrong with traditional sex roles. The sociocultural problems surrounding rape were highlighted further by the callous methods used by the criminal justice system when handling victims (Brownmiller, 1975; Holmstrom and Burgess, 1978) and by rape myths believed by many individuals (Koss and Leonard, 1984; Lottes, 1988).

The sociocultural approach also receives a great deal of support from discussions of date or acquaintance rape among college populations. Numerous authors point to the influence of peer support in sexual assault (see, for example, DeKeseredy and Kelly, 1995; Koss and Cleveland, 1997; Koss and Gaines, 1993; Martin and Hummer, 1989). Two peer networks often linked to sexual aggression are fraternities and athletics (Armstrong, Hamilton, and Sweeney, 2006; Boeringer,

FIGURE 6.3
Examples of Rape Myths

Rape myths are widely held, inaccurate beliefs about rape. Myths of rape give people a false sense of security by legitimizing sexual assault or denying that it even occurs. They often do this by blaming the victim for their experience or making excuses and minimizing their assault. In effect, these myths perpetuate sexual assault by not addressing the realities of rape.

- Sexual assault does not occur often.

- Women lie about being sexually assaulted to get revenge, for their own benefit, or because they feel guilty afterwards about having sex.

- Sexual assault is committed by strangers.

- The best way for a woman to protect herself from sexual assault is to avoid being alone at night in dark, deserted places such as alleys or parking lots.

- Women who are sexually assaulted "ask for it" by the way they dress or act.

- Rape only happens to young "sexy" women.

- Men who sexually assault women are either mentally ill or sexually starved.

- Rape is a sexual act that is taken too far.

- Men of certain races and backgrounds are more likely to sexually assault women.

- It is only sexual assault if weapons are used.

- Unless she is physically harmed, a woman who has been sexually assaulted will not suffer any long-term effects.

- Women cannot be sexually assaulted by their husbands or boyfriends.

- If a woman consents to have sex at the start of making out with her boyfriend, then she is not assaulted if she changes her mind, but her partner keeps on going.

- If a woman has had many sexual partners then she cannot be sexually assaulted.

- If a man pays for dinner or a movie, the woman owes him sex.

- When men become sexually aroused, they have to have sex and cannot stop.

- When a woman says "no," she really means "maybe" or "yes."

- Women secretly want to be raped.

- A woman cannot be raped if she does not want to be assaulted.

- You can tell if a woman is really sexually assaulted by the way she acts.

- It is only sexual assault if a woman has been physically injured.

Source: Women Against Violence Against Women (2005). *Rape Myths*. Vancouver, British Columbia, Canada: WAVAW. Retrieved August 23, 2007, from http://www.wavaw. ca/ informed_myths.php

1999; Humphrey and Kahn, 2000; Koss and Gaines, 1993; Martin and Hummer, 1989; Stombler, 1994). In both cases, it is argued that offenders are challenged to prove their masculinity, maintain confidentiality, and support one's peers. Intertwined with these peer associations is the use of alcohol. Alcohol contributes to sexual assault in numerous ways. It can reduce inhibitions, thwart the ability of a person to resist advances, increase the possibility of misreading another person's desires or intent, diminish feelings of responsibility, heighten miscommunication, increase offender aggressiveness, and promote "rape myths" (Abbey et al., 1996; Armstrong et al., 2006; Benson, Gohm, and Gross, 2007; Brecklin and Ullman, 2001; Corbin et al., 2001; Davis et al., 2006; Ehrhart and Sadler, 1985; Harrington and Leitenberg, 1994; Lundberg-Love and Geffner, 1989; Martin and Hummer, 1989; Pumphrey-Gordon and Gross, 2007; Ullman et al., 1999). It is important to note that alcohol influences both the offender and the victim. Harrington and Leitenberg (1994) note that the victim was "somewhat drunk" in 55 percent of the sexually aggressive situations they uncovered and that alcohol increased the degree of "acceptable sexual contact" (according to the victim) before the assault. While it is common to assume that most offenders consciously attempt to get the victim drunk, it is probably more likely that alcohol is used willingly by both parties, which, in turn, produces more opportunities for assault. The social setting of college life, coupled with broader social expectations of male and female behavior, enhances the probability of sexually aggressive activity.

Typological Efforts

As discussed in Chapter 1, typologies attempt to organize or classify observations according to what they share or have in common. The goal of a typology is to reach a better understanding of the phenomenon under study by grouping similar items together.

There have been several efforts to construct typologies to reach a fuller understanding of sexual assault. Based upon their clinical experience with offenders, Groth and Birnbaum (1980: 21) warned:

> Rape is complex and multidetermined. It serves a number of psychological aims and purposes. Whatever other needs and factors operate in the commission of such an offense, however, we have found the components of anger, power, and sexuality always present and prominent. Moreover, in our experience, we find that either anger or power is the dominant component and that rape, rather than being primarily an expression of sexual desire, is, in fact, the use of sexuality to

express power and anger. Rape, then, is a pseudosexual act, a pattern of sexual behavior that is concerned much more with status, hostility, control, and dominance than with sexual pleasure or sexual satisfaction.

Drawing upon a scheme developed by Groth and Birnbaum (1980), Schneider (1987) delineates several different kinds of rape. *Anger rape* makes up roughly 20 percent of all sexual battery cases. It involves a conscious attempt to harm and humiliate the victim. *Sexual conquest rape* (more than 50% of all rape offenses) entails the offender's desire to conquer and possess the victim. Offenders feel an overwhelming degree of inadequacy. While not very common (comprising less than 5%), *sadistic rape*, in which sexual gratification is achieved through tormenting the victim, typically involves serious physical harm and sometimes even death. Rapes that are fueled by a desire to prove oneself to peers are considered *gang rapes*. These incidents represent 5 to 10 percent of the cases. The remaining 20 percent of the cases are classified as *impulsive rapes* because they lack any other clear motivating factors.

The ability of these and other typological efforts to alert us to different kinds of sexual assaults has important theoretical ramifications. For example, Ellis has taken the next logical step in understanding rape by promoting a synthesized theoretical model. In essence, Ellis (1989) argues that because no single theory is capable of explaining every case of sexual assault, social scientists must combine a wide variety of variables that hold differing degrees of explanatory power. Some of these key ingredients involve motivational, learning, biological, psychological, and social factors. In short, despite advances in our knowledge, there is still room for continued improvement before we are able to understand what prompts this form of criminal victimization.

A Model of Sexual Assault

Lundberg-Love and Geffner (1989) have developed a model that attempts to explain the occurrence of sexual assault. While primarily targeted at date rape, the model incorporates factors that apply to many forms of sexual aggression. Figure 6.4 outlines four preconditions to date rape, many of which have been discussed already in this chapter. The assumption is that date rape can occur when a motivated offender is faced with few or reduced inhibitions (both internal and external) and a victim who fails to resist or take proper precautions. The authors point out that such a framework can assist in understanding both the offender and the victim in sexual assault situations, as well as inform modes of intervention.

FIGURE 6.4
The Lundberg-Love and Geffner Model

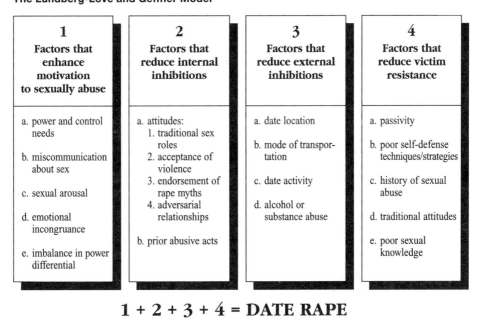

1 Factors that enhance motivation to sexually abuse	2 Factors that reduce internal inhibitions	3 Factors that reduce external inhibitions	4 Factors that reduce victim resistance

a. power and control needs
 	
b. miscommunication about sex
 	
c. sexual arousal
 	
d. emotional incongruance
 	
e. imbalance in power differential
	a. attitudes:
	  1. traditional sex roles
	  2. acceptance of violence
	  3. endorsement of rape myths
	  4. adversarial relationships
	
	b. prior abusive acts
		a. date location
		
		b. mode of transportation
		
		c. date activity
		
		d. alcohol or substance abuse
			a. passivity
			
			b. poor self-defense techniques/strategies
			
			c. history of sexual abuse
			
			d. traditional attitudes
			
			e. poor sexual knowledge

1 + 2 + 3 + 4 = DATE RAPE

Source: P. Lundberg-Love and R. Geffner (1989). "Date Rape: Prevalence, Risk Factors, and a Proposed Model." In M.A. Pirog-Good and J.E. Stets (ed.), *Violence in Dating Relationships: Emerging Social Issues*. New York: Praeger. Reproduced with permission of Greenwood Publishing Group, Inc., Westport, CT.

Summary

As with any other form of behavior, the causes of sexual assault are multifaceted. It is unlikely that any of the various explanations presented above is sufficient in and of itself to explain sexual aggression. The most plausible explanation probably incorporates a variety of factors, such as that suggested by the Lundberg-Love and Geffner model. While most critics would favor a sociocultural orientation, one should not dismiss physiological and psychopathological perspectives out of hand. Indeed, the use of drugs to achieve a "chemical" castration of male sexual offenders has been and continues to be advocated as a means of reducing testosterone-driven sexual assaults. These approaches, however, require a great deal of additional attention before widespread use of such techniques is justified.

The Aftermath of Rape

Although they are enlightening, statistics about the number of offenses, debate over whether one data source is superior to another, and theoretical musing about the causes of sexual battery all present a rather sterile view of the problem. Such a focus loses sight of the victim's personal feelings and experiences. One key area of concern is the emotional repercussion that sexual violence unleashes upon the victim.

As soon as the sexual attack is over, the victim begins the task of facing a bewildering mixture of emotions and concerns. Perhaps the most immediate reaction is one of upheaval and confusion. The victim generally does not know what to do; nor does she know to whom to turn for assistance. Many victims do not call the police right away, particularly if the offender was an acquaintance. If they do talk with anyone, it is often a family member, a close friend, or possibly someone at a rape crisis center.

A great deal of fear and anxiety can accompany this initial disorientation. The victim may second-guess her actions prior to and during the attack. She may fear potential retaliation from the assailant. She may envision disapproval, and even condemnation, from those who learn of the incident. Many victims worry about what will happen if the police and criminal justice system become involved, and how people will respond to them afterwards.

Crisis Reaction

Over the years, psychologists have learned that all these reactions are normal and follow a very typical pattern. A variety of events can contribute to or trigger a state of crisis. They may range from the bereavement or grief associated with death, the loss of a job, an unwanted pregnancy, or any other traumatic event that may surface throughout the course of life (Bassuk, 1980; Lindemann, 1944; Rapoport, 1962). What makes sexual victimization so disturbing is that it is the penultimate violation. As one team of psychological experts explains, "Short of being killed, there is no greater insult to the self" (Bard and Sangrey, 1986: 21).

A *crisis* develops whenever a situation poses a serious danger or threat to the person's self. This hazard is so monumental that the person who is at the center of this crisis has a great deal of difficulty coping with the circumstances. This imbalance, or lack of equilibrium, between what it takes to resolve the problem and the resources to combat the crisis renders the victim unable to climb out of the situation. As Bard and Sangrey (1986: 33) put it:

The sudden, arbitrary, unpredictable violation of self leaves victims feeling so shattered that they cannot continue to function the way they did before the crime. Things fall apart, and victims are unable to pull themselves back together right away.

The severity and duration of a crisis depend upon three conditions. The first consideration is the degree to which the person's self is threatened. Insignificant events require very little, if any, attention or redirection. Devastating intrusions, on the other hand, command many more resources. They need constant attention and can be exhausting. The second factor is the person's ability at that precise moment to deal with a problem of such magnitude. Some people might be worn out from facing a series of calamities prior to this unexpected intrusion. Others might be refreshed and able to muster considerable inner strength to meet the challenge. Finally, the kind of intervention or help that a person receives immediately after the tragedy strikes can determine how long it takes to propel out of this helplessness and into recovery.

The Crisis Reaction Repair Cycle

While the time it takes to recuperate may vary from one person to the next, victims go through a very predictable sequence during their recovery. The *crisis reaction repair cycle* consists of three distinct stages. The first phase is called impact. The second phase is the recoil period. The final stage, reorganization, marks the end of the crisis reaction repair cycle. Although some people contend that this model neglects to explain which victims have these experiences and who will recover more quickly than another (Resick, 1990: 76-77), it does provide a convenient backdrop for understanding the plight of the victim.

Impact

A single word that summarizes the *impact* stage is "shock"; "distress" is another appropriate descriptor. Victims run the entire gamut of emotions during this period. Some people go through denial. Expressions like "I can't believe this happened to me" are common. Other victims blame themselves and ask what they did to deserve this humiliation. Sometimes there are expressions of outrage, anger, and revenge. Confusion, fear, helplessness, guilt, self-pity, and feelings of worthlessness, if left unchecked, can ravage victims during this stage. Many victims seek security and strong emotional support while dealing with and sorting out these feelings. Victims sense that they are vulnerable. They know they have lost control over themselves and their surroundings. As a result, victims sometimes interpret insensitive or judgmental comments as strong condemnations. Remarks such as "I can't believe you went there" or "What do you mean you don't know what happened?" can elicit harsh negative responses and devastate a person in need of some compassionate understanding.

The fear, anxiety, and shame that victims endure during the impact stage are not ill-founded. Sexual assault victims must combat various notions associated with rape and sexual battery. As Chapter 1 explained, the perception of victim precipitation is very much alive— especially in sexual battery situations. One common reaction is to "blame the victim" for the attack by claiming that she was in the wrong place at the wrong time. There might be other hints that the victim acted suggestively, dressed provocatively, or that she originally consented and later changed her mind.

Many victims have to grapple with a number of *rape myths*. These beliefs basically shift responsibility away from the offender and onto the victim. Far from relieving the victim's feelings and problems, they exacerbate them. Among these myths are such ideas as "many women wish to be raped" (Burt and Estep, 1981), "victims who fail to report to the police right away were not really raped" (Costin and Schwarz, 1987; Ehrhart and Sandler, 1985), and the "just world hypothesis" that "only those who deserve to be raped get raped" (Carmody and Washington, 2001; Lerner, 1980).

Recoil

The second phase of the victim's recovery is known as the *recoil* period. At this point, victims begin to adapt to the fact that the violation took place. The mending process helps reduce the sting of the emotions that appeared earlier. While these feelings still resurface from time to time, they are not as intense or devastating as they once were. In some cases, victims may move back and forth between the impact and the recoil stages. Over time, these swings become less frequent and less intense.

Many rape victims experience a condition known as *post-traumatic stress disorder* (PTSD). Clinicians who deal with sexual battery victims sometimes refer to these symptoms more narrowly as the *rape trauma syndrome* (Bassuk, 1980; Burgess and Holmstrom, 1974; Frazier and Borgida, 1992; Giannelli, 1997). In any event, this condition refers to a response to major, sudden tragedies. Figure 6.5 outlines the four key criteria involved in PTSD. First, the stressor or event is such that it brings about a similar result in most people who experience it. Second, the individuals relive the initial experiences through flashbacks, night-

FIGURE 6.5
Diagnostic Criteria for Post-Traumatic Stress Disorder

A. The person has been exposed to a traumatic event in which both of the following were present:

1. the person experienced, witnessed, or was confronted with an event or events that involved actual or threatened death or serious injury, or a threat to the physical integrity of self or others

2. the person's response involved intense fear, helplessness, or horror.

B. The traumatic event is persistently re-experienced in one (or more) of the following ways:

1. recurrent and intrusive distressing recollections of the event, including images, thoughts, or perceptions.

2. recurrent distressing dreams of the event.

3. acting or feeling as if the traumatic event were recurring (includes a sense of reliving the experience, illusions, hallucinations, and dissociative flashback episodes, including those that occur on awakening or when intoxicated).

4. intense psychological distress at exposure to internal or external cues that symbolize or resemble an aspect of the traumatic event.

5. physiological reactivity on exposure to internal or external cues that symbolize or resemble an aspect of the traumatic event.

C. Persistent avoidance of stimuli associated with the trauma and numbing of general responsiveness (not present before the trauma), as indicated by three (or more) of the following:

1. efforts to avoid thoughts, feelings, or conversations associated with the trauma

2. efforts to avoid activities, places, or people that arouse recollections of the trauma

3. inability to recall an important aspect of the trauma

4. markedly diminished interest or participation in significant activities

5. feeling of detachment or estrangement from others

6. restricted range of affect (e.g., unable to have loving feelings)

7. sense of a foreshortened future (e.g., does not expect to have a career, marriage, children, or a normal life span)

D. Persistent symptoms of increased arousal (not present before the trauma), as indicated by two (or more) of the following:

1. difficulty falling or staying asleep

2. irritability or outbursts of anger

3. difficulty concentrating

4. hypervigilance

5. exaggerated startle response

E. Duration of the disturbance (symptoms in Criteria B, C, and D) is more than 1 month.

F. The disturbance causes clinically significant distress or impairment in social, occupational, or other important areas of functioning.

Source: American Psychiatric Association (2000). *Diagnostic and Statistical Manual of Mental Disorders—Fourth Edition, Text Revision* (DSM–IV–TR). Arlington, VA: American Psychiatric Association. Retrieved August 24, 2007, from http://www.psychiatryonline.com.proxy.lib.fsu.edu/content.aspx?aID=3357#3357 Courtesy of the American Psychiatric Association.

mares, and other recollections. Third, those suffering PTSD display a lack of responsiveness and reduced involvement in everyday activities. Finally, the individuals experience a variety of potential problems, such as sleeplessness, headaches, self-blame, fear, and anxiety (Burgess, 1995). Victims often make major lifestyle changes so as to avoid situations similar to that involved in the earlier experience.

Sexual battery significantly affects the victim's self-esteem (Resick, 1987; Shapiro and Schwarz, 1997). Its impact has a lasting effect that diminishes very slowly over time (Murphy et al., 1988; Resick, 1993). Depression is another common problem for sexual assault victims (Atkeson et al., 1982; Marhofer-Dvorak et al., 1988; Murphy et al., 1988; Norris and Feldman-Summers, 1981; Resick et al., 1981; Siegel et al., 1990; Ullman and Siegal, 1993). Sometimes, suicide is a response to the depression brought on by rape experiences (Kilpatrick et al., 1985).

Reorganization

The last stage in the crisis reaction repair cycle is *reorganization*. Victims reach this point once they have sorted through their feelings and are able to place this traumatic event into perspective. As the intensity of their reaction begins to diminish, they are able to move on to other activities. Although from time to time victims will drift back to their unfortunate episode and think about what happened to them, they are no longer as preoccupied with these memories as they once were. These survivors have coped with the situation, reached a point of adjustment, and are now emerging out of the crisis.

Victims never attain a total or complete cure. They carry their emotional scars with them for the remainder of their days. Victims who do complete the repair cycle, however, are able to proceed with the rest of their lives. For those victims who are not able to complete this transition, the future may consist of a continuing struggle to find the answer to the question of "Why me?"

Legal Reforms

As sexual violence and related concerns have grown over the years, societal and criminal justice responses have also changed. One area of reform that we already saw entailed the alteration of statutes governing rape or sexual battery. This section will focus on some of the other more prominent revisions. We have already discussed changes in the definition of rape and the issue of spousal immunity earlier in this chapter.

Compulsory AIDS testing for offenders, removal of the corroboration requirement, and the enactment of shield provisions are additional areas of concern that will be taken up below. After we explore just what these changes are, we will take a look at whether they brought about the desired effect.

Compulsory AIDS Testing

A health concern that worries some sexual assault victims is the threat of sexually transmitted diseases (STDs). Sparking many policy considerations is the growing awareness of the acquired immunodeficiency syndrome (AIDS), caused by the HIV virus, and its devastating effects. One issue is whether the criminal justice system should mandate testing for the HIV virus in sex offenders. According to the National Center for Victims of Crime (1999), just about every state has some type of law governing mandatory HIV testing of sexual offenders. Some states have enacted pretrial compulsory testing for assailants while others restrict this procedure to convicted offenders only. Figure 6.6 contains an example of one such statute.

FIGURE 6.6
An Example of a Compulsory AIDS Testing Statute

---

(1) In any case in which a person has been convicted of or has pled nolo contendere or guilty to, regardless of whether adjudication is withheld, any of the following offenses, or the attempt thereof, which offense, or the attempt thereof, which offense or attempted offense involves the transmission of body fluids from one person to another [sexual battery; incest; lewd, lascivious, or indecent assault or act upon any person less than 16 years of age; assault; aggravated assault; child abuse; aggravated child abuse; abuse of an elderly person or disabled adult; aggravated abuse of an elderly person or disabled adult; sexual performance by persons less than 18 years of age; prostitution; or donation of blood, plasma, organs, skin, or other human tissue] the court shall order the offender to undergo HIV testing, to be performed under the direction of the Department of Health in accordance with s. 381.004, unless the offender has undergone HIV testing voluntarily. . . . The results of an HIV test performed on an offender pursuant to this subsection are not admissible in any criminal proceeding arising out of the alleged offense.

(2) The results of the HIV test must be disclosed under the direction of the Department of Health, to the offender who has been convicted of or pled nolo contendere or guilty to an offense specified in subsection (1), the public health agency of the county in which the conviction occurred and, if different, the county of the residence of the offender, and, upon request pursuant to s. 960.003, to the victim or the victim's legal guardian, or the parent or legal guardian of the victim if the victim is a minor.

(3) An offender who has undergone HIV testing pursuant to subsection (1), and to whom positive test results have been disclosed pursuant to subsection (2), who commits a second or subsequent offense enumerated in paragraphs (1)(a)–(n), commits criminal transmission of HIV, a felony of the third degree, punishable as provided

FIGURE 6.6—*continued*

---

in subsection (7). A person may be convicted and sentenced separately for a violation of this subsection and for the underlying crime enumerates in paragraphs
(1)(a)–(n).

(4) An offender may challenge the positive results of an HIV test performed pursuant
to this section and may introduce results of a backup test performed at her or his own
expense.

(5) Nothing in this section requires that an HIV infection have occurred in order for an
offender to have committed criminal transmission of HIV.

(7) In addition to any other penalty provided by law for an offense enumerated in
paragraphs (1)(a)–(n), the court may require an offender convicted of criminal
transmission of HIV to serve a term of criminal quarantine community control, as
described in s. 948.001.

Source: *Florida Statutes* (2007), §775.0877.

AIDS is spread through interpersonal contact. The usual sources of
contamination include contact with tainted blood, sexual intercourse
with an infected person, and the sharing of needles for injecting drugs.
Medical advances have made it possible to determine whether HIV, a
marker for AIDS, is present within the bloodstream. When a person
tests *seropositive*, he or she is a carrier and has the potential to infect
others.

Despite medical progress, there is still some ambiguity surrounding HIV laboratory testing. For one thing, the presence of HIV antibodies does not mean that a seropositive person has developed AIDS
already. At the same time, a seronegative reading, while reassuring, is
not necessarily conclusive. Once infection occurs, the virus requires an
incubation period. What this means is that it may take several months
for medical screening to detect any antibodies present in the carrier's
bloodstream. Thus, a negative report from one or even two points in
time may not offer a guarantee of being disease-free.

What are the odds that sexual assault victims will become contaminated after the attack? One way to answer that question is to focus
upon two related aspects. The first is to calculate the percentage of HIV
cases within the offender population. The second is to determine the
risk of viral infection from a single act of intercourse.

National health tests administered to military recruits fix the HIV
infection rate at 0.15 percent (Blumberg, 1989: 458). Approximately
90 percent of these seropositive readings come from two groups that
are highly unlikely to attack women: homosexual males and intravenous
drug users (Blumberg and Langston, 1991: 7). It is also estimated
that there is a one in 500 chance of contracting AIDS from a contaminated person during one act of unprotected intercourse (Hearst

and Hulley, 1988). Taking all these variables into account suggests that the odds of a sexual battery victim contracting AIDS from a single incident are minimal. While the Centers for Disease Control and Prevention has identified isolated cases in which a sexual assault victim has contracted HIV, the incidence is so low that statistics are not kept for this means of infection.

An assessment of this situation has led to some protests against mandatory HIV-testing policy as an invasion of constitutional rights. For example, objections have surfaced concerning the suspect's right to privacy, the presumption of innocence, and whether pre-conviction testing violates search-and-seizure standards (McGuire, 1991; Smotas, 1991). At the same time, more than one-half of the states have enacted legislation making the intentional spread of HIV through sexual contact a crime. Florida, in 1996, convicted an HIV-positive man for attempted murder based on his forced sodomy with three boys (Stine, 1996). While there is some indication that media coverage sensationalizes and misrepresents the risk of disease transmission from HIV-related assaults (Flavin, 2000), the case law developing in this area is worth watching over the next few years.

Consent and Corroboration

The common law looked for corroborative or supporting evidence to validate a woman's claim that she had been the victim of a rape. Many juries hesitated to convict solely on the basis of the victim's testimony, especially if the death penalty was involved. They were afraid that the accuser might be harboring a vendetta and, for whatever reason, may try to "railroad" the man into prison (Ellis, 1992).

Typical supporting evidence would involve such things as timely notification to the police, the presence of semen, the use of a weapon by the offender, and (most notably) physical harm (Bourke, 1989; Spears and Spohn, 1996). The assumption was that any victim who was unwilling to submit to a sexual attack should resist to her utmost capacity. It was expected that a woman would submit only if her struggles would bring her to the brink of death. Under this reasoning, the "perfect" case would be the woman who was brutally beaten and exhibited massive physical injuries. Indeed, some people assumed that the absence of physical harm was tantamount to *prima facie* evidence that a rape did not take place.

Legal reforms eliminated the requirement that rape victims must fight ferociously for their lives. The reasoning employed was that no other victims are held to this defensive standard. As Figure 6.7 attests, robbery victims are not expected to resist the robber before giving up their valuables. In the interest of justice, then, it is not fair to impose this extra burden upon sexual assault victims. As a result, when new sexual battery legislation was drafted, the resistance requirement was dropped. Of course, this move is beginning to raise new questions that have yet to be resolved (Stitt and Lentz, 1996).

FIGURE 6.7
The "Rape" of Mr. Smith

The law discriminates against rape victims in a manner which would not be tolerated by victims of any other crime. In the following example, a holdup victim is asked questions similar in form to those usually asked a victim of rape.

"Mr. Smith, you were held up at gunpoint on the corner of 16th and Locust?"

"Yes."

"Did you struggle with the robber?"

"No."

"Why not?"

"He was armed."

"Then you made a conscious decision to comply with his demands rather than to resist?"

"Yes."

"Did you scream? Cry out?"

"No. I was afraid."

"I see. Have you ever been held up before?"

"No."

"Have you ever given money away?"

"Yes, of course—"

"And did you do so willingly?"

"What are you getting at?"

"Well, let's put it like this, Mr. Smith. You've given away money in the past—in fact, you have quite a reputation for philanthropy. How can we be sure that you weren't *contriving* to have your money taken from you by force?"

"Listen, if I wanted—"

"Never mind. What time did this holdup take place, Mr. Smith?"

"About 11 P.M."

"You were out on the streets at 11 P.M.? Doing what?"

"Just walking."

"Just walking? You know it's dangerous being out on the street that late at night. Weren't you aware that you could have been held up?"

"I hadn't thought about it."

"What were you wearing at the time, Mr. Smith?"

"Let's see. A suit. Yes, a suit."

"An *expensive* suit?"

"Well—yes."

"In other words, Mr. Smith, you were walking around the streets late at night in a suit that practically *advertised* the fact that you might be a good target for some easy money, isn't that so? I mean, if we didn't know better, Mr. Smith, we might even think you were *asking* for this to happen, mightn't we?"

FIGURE 6.7—*continued*

"Look, can't we talk about the past history of the guy who *did* this to me?"

"I'm afraid not, Mr. Smith. I don't think you would want to violate his rights, now would you?"

Source: Anonymous, *"The Rape" of Mr. Smith*. Retrieved September 15, 2007, from http://www.geocities.com/Wellesley/3059/smith.html

The modification in the need for corroborative evidence also shows the change in the response to victims. Many jurisdictions no longer require proof of penetration or maximum resistance to the point of physical force. The protocol in effect at Antioch College, displayed in Figure 6.8, makes consent an integral part at each step in order to avoid any possible misinterpretation by either party. These provisions underscore the debate over criminal liability and the absolute last point at which a person can withdraw consent. Essentially, the question is whether the victim can withdraw consent after the sexual act is underway. Common law generally holds that a rape cannot occur if a woman has agreed to participate and sexual intercourse has begun. However, some jurisdictions recognize post-penetration rape in those instances in which force is invoked to complete the act. While legal developments are still taking place in this arena, Illinois has responded to this controversy by enacting a statute that affirms the right to withdraw consent at any time during the sexual encounter. Specifically, that law states "a person who initially consents to sexual penetration or sexual conduct is not deemed to have consented to any sexual penetration or sexual conduct that occurs after he or she withdraws consent during the course of that sexual penetration or sexual conduct" (*Illinois Compiled Statutes,* 2007: 5/12-17).

FIGURE 6.8
The Antioch College Sexual Offense Prevention Policy

Consent is defined as the act of willingly and verbally agreeing to engage in specific sexual conduct. The following are clarifying points:

- Consent is required each and every time there is sexual activity.

- All parties must have a clear and accurate understanding of the sexual activity.

- The person(s) who initiate(s) the sexual activity is responsible for asking for consent.

- The person(s) who are asked are responsible for verbally responding.

- Each new level of sexual activity requires consent.

FIGURE 6.8—*continued*

- Use of agreed upon forms of communication such as gestures or safe words is acceptable, but must be discussed and verbally agreed to by all parties before sexual activity occurs.

- Consent is required regardless of the parties' relationship, prior sexual history, or current activity (e.g., grinding on the dance floor is not consent for further sexual activity).

- At any and all times when consent is withdrawn or not verbally agreed to, the sexual activity must stop immediately.

- Silence is not consent.

- Body movements and non-verbal responses such as moans are not consent.

- A person cannot give consent while sleeping.

- All parties must have unimpaired judgement (examples that may cause impairment include, but are not limited to, alcohol, drugs, mental health conditions, physical health conditions).

- All parties must use safe sex practices.

- All parties must disclose personal risk factors and any known sexually transmitted infections. Individuals are responsible for maintaining awareness of their sexual health.

Source: Antioch College (2005). *Sexual Offense Prevention Policy*. Yellow Springs, OH: Antioch College. Retrieved on August 23, 2007, from http://www.antioch-college.edu/Campus/sopp/index.html

FIGURE 6.9
Polygraph Tests Used to Corroborate Victim Allegations

Ms. Sloan backs up her advocacy with chilling statistics, which she collected from 83 rape-crisis centers in 19 states. Thirty-one of the centers reported that women had to take polygraph tests before police investigations began. Twenty-two reported that if a woman refused to take the test, there were no subsequent investigations into her claims.

Only Illinois and New York have statutes prohibiting law-enforcement officials from requesting or requiring a rape victim to take a polygraph exam. . . . "As long as polygraphing of rape victims can still be requested, then it is not much better than having nothing at all . . . because police can say, 'Well, you're not required to take, and we're not required to investigate or prosecute, either.'"

Polygraphers argue that lie-detector tests help weed out false allegations. According to a Texas examiner, "If a victim is telling the truth, then the polygraph will help prosecutors make the best case possible. If a victim is lying, then an innocent person will not got to jail. And if a victim is exaggerating the circumstances of a story, then it will be detected."

Source: Shecter, J. (1996). "Fighting for Rape Victims." *The Chronicle of Higher Education*, April 19, p. A8.

As Figure 6.9 demonstrates, there is still a reluctance to convict sexual batterers solely on the testimony of the victim for fear of a false claim (Bourke, 1989). As a result, some investigations have included a "lie-detector" test to test the truthfulness of the victim. In light of this disparity, a number of states, including Florida (*Florida Statutes*, 2007: §960.001), have banned the use of polygraph testing to establish the veracity of the victim's complaint.

Shield Provisions

Under common law, the burden of proof in a rape case fell squarely upon the victim. It was up to the victim to show that the accused forced her to engage in behavior to which she objected. A common tactic invoked by many aggressive defense attorneys was to attack the victim's credibility by making an issue of her sexual past. A typical strategy was to imply promiscuity from prior consensual sexual activity with men other than the defendant. Presumably, this information suggested a lack of chastity and, therefore, amply proved the victim's willingness to engage in sexual activity without any reliance on force. In essence, the criminal justice system placed the victim on trial and dealt with her in a callous fashion.

Many victims were reluctant to pursue formal charges under these skewed conditions. No other type of crime victim had to endure this kind of intense scrutiny. For example, lawyers did not probe the history of burglary or robbery victims to show they had a reputation or a proclivity for becoming victimized. As a result, reformers sought to introduce new standards that would protect or shield sexual assault victims from further trauma. To do so required a very delicate balance. As one group of experts explains (Call, Nice, and Talarico, 1991: 784-785):

> The controversy over rape shield laws has presented policy makers with a difficult dilemma: should they permit a defense strategy based on destroying the victim's reputation, a strategy that compounds victim trauma, may discourage reporting rapes, and may enable rapists to avoid punishment. Conversely, a strong shield law may generate complaints that it limits defendants' ability to have an adequate defense, thus violating due process.

The states have varied in their approaches to revising this portion of their sexual battery statutes. Three primary dimensions sprang from these efforts. First, there was the general issue of whether the victim's prior sexual history with others was relevant. Second, there was the more specific concern of whether the victim's prior sexual history with the accused should be admissible. Finally, the court would judge the relevancy of any evidence about the victim's sexual history *in camera*, that is, well out of public earshot. As you can see, the aim of these reforms was to protect the victim's privacy from any unnecessary public invasion.

One can rate a state's shield provisions as either strong (very restrictive and protective of victims) or weak (virtually no change from past practices) depending on how each of these three concerns are handled. While one might guess that more progressive states would respond more favorably to feminist pressures by embracing these changes, such is not the case. There is some indication that having a feminist agenda or strong lobbying efforts has not influenced these evidentiary reforms. Instead, it seems that these modifications reflect the much broader crime control strategy that was presented in Chapter 1 (Berger, Searles, and Neuman, 1988; Berger, Neuman, and Searles, 1991; Call, Nice, and Talarico, 1991).

Sex Offender Registration

The final legislative reform we will discuss is the proliferation of sex offender registration laws. These laws, often referred to as "Megan's Laws" (which will be discussed further in Chapter 7), exist in every state and seek to provide both past victims and the general public with information regarding the presence of a convicted sex offender in the community. The premise underlying these laws is twofold. First, treatment protocols for sex offenders are far from perfect. The common belief is that recidivism rates for these criminals are quite high. Second, warning the public that a sex offender is living in their community alerts residents to take appropriate precautions and to be watchful of these people's activities.

One example of a *sex offender registration* law appears in Figure 6.10. The Florida version shares many of the same features found in other state statutes. The precipitating offense need not be a violent rape. Instead, a host of "sexually oriented offenses" can trigger registration. Such crimes as rape, sexual battery, lewd and lascivious behavior, indecent exposure, other offenses that fulfill sexual needs of the offender (e.g., murder, kidnapping), and various sex crimes against children (e.g., kidnapping, pandering obscenity, compelling prostitution) can trigger these legal provisions. In addition, judges can impose registration requirements on convicted sex offenders because of the likelihood of future violations. Factors that judges can use when making this determination include multiple past convictions, evidence of deviant (not necessarily criminal) sexual behavior, past offenses involving torture or ritualistic acts, or prior nonsexual violent acts.

FIGURE 6.10
The Florida Sexual Predators Act

---

(6) Registration.
   (a) A sexual predator must register with the department through the sheriff's office by providing the following information to the department:
      1. Name, social security number, age, race, sex, date of birth, height, weight, hair and eye color, photograph, address of legal residence and address of any current temporary residence, within the state or out of state, including a rural route address and a post office box, any electronic mail address and any instant message name required to be provided pursuant to subparagraph (g)4., date and place of any employment, date and place of each conviction, fingerprints, and a brief description of the crime or crimes committed by the offender. A post office box shall not be provided in lieu of a physical residential address.
   (f) Within 48 hours after the registration required under paragraph (a) or paragraph (e), a sexual predator who is not incarcerated and who resides in the community, including a sexual predator under the supervision of the Department of Corrections, shall register in person at a driver's license office of the Department of Highway Safety and Motor Vehicles and shall present proof of registration. At the driver's license office the sexual predator shall:
      1. If otherwise qualified, secure a Florida driver's license, renew a Florida driver's license, or secure an identification card. The sexual predator shall identify himself or herself as a sexual predator who is required to comply with this section, provide his or her place of permanent or temporary residence, including a rural route address and a post office box, and submit to the taking of a photograph for use in issuing a driver's license, renewed license, or identification card, and for use by the department in maintaining current records of sexual predators. A post office box shall not be provided in lieu of a physical residential address. . . .
      2. A sexual predator who vacates a permanent residence and fails to establish or maintain another permanent or temporary residence shall, within 48 hours after vacating the permanent residence, report in person to the sheriff's office of the county in which he or she is located. The sexual predator shall specify the date upon which he or she intends to or did vacate such residence. The sexual predator must provide or update all of the registration information required under paragraph (a). The sexual predator must provide an address for the residence or other location that he or she is or will be occupying during the time in which he or she fails to establish or maintain a permanent or temporary residence.
      4. A sexual predator must register any electronic mail address or instant message name with the department prior to using such electronic mail address or instant message name on or after October 1, 2007.

(7) Community and Public Notification.
   (a) Law enforcement agencies must inform members of the community and the public of a sexual predator's presence. Upon notification of the presence of a sexual predator, the sheriff of the county or the chief of police of the municipality where the sexual predator establishes or maintains a permanent or temporary residence shall notify members of the community and the public of the presence of the sexual predator in a manner deemed appropriate by the sheriff or the chief of police. Within 48 hours after receiving notification of the presence of a sexual predator, the sheriff of the county or the chief of police of the municipality where the sexual predator temporarily or permanently resides shall notify each licensed day care center,

FIGURE 6.10—*continued*

---

elementary school, middle school, and high school within a 1-mile radius of the temporary or permanent residence of the sexual predator of the presence of the sexual predator. Information provided to members of the community and the public regarding a sexual predator must include:

1. The name of the sexual predator;
2. A description of the sexual predator, including a photograph;
3. The sexual predator's current address, including the name of the county or municipality if known;
4. The circumstances of the sexual predator's offense or offenses; and
5. Whether the victim of the sexual predator's offense or offenses was, at the time of the offense, a minor or an adult.

Source: *Florida Statutes* (2007).

These laws instruct two main parties to take action. First, the offender must register with the local law enforcement agency where he or she intends to settle. This stipulation includes both the agency that has jurisdiction over the offender's permanent residence and any agency with jurisdiction over a temporary residence. Registration generally must occur within a few days of release from custody, movement into a new jurisdiction, or following a change of address. Second, the law enforcement agency with whom the registration occurs must notify a wide range of constituencies about the presence of the offender. Parties to be notified include neighbors of the offender, local educational institutions, nearby agencies that deal with children, and other local law enforcement agencies. The notification typically includes the name and address of the offender, a physical description, as well as the nature of the conviction offense.

The move to offender registration has not been limited to state action. The federal government passed the Jacob Wetterling Crimes Against Children and Sexually Violent Offender Registration Act in 1995. What this legislation required, among other things, was that states must establish registries of convicted sex offenders or face a reduction in federal criminal justice funding. President Bush signed the Adam Walsh Child Protection and Safety Act into law on July 27, 2006. This initiative created a national sex offender registry, standardized the information each state entered, and integrated all the state files into a single source (White House News Release, 2006). As Table 6.2 illustrates, there has been an enormous growth in the number of persons listed in sex offender registries over a short period of time.

As with any new legislation, several questions and challenges have arisen. One legal concern deals with the potential of these laws to further punish offenders once they have completed their sentences. This worry over double jeopardy, however, has fallen on deaf ears so far, with the U.S. Supreme Court upholding the right of the state to protect cit-

TABLE 6.2
Persons Enrolled in State Sex Offender Registries

Jurisdiction	Offenders in Registry 1998	2001	Jurisdiction	Offenders in Registry 1998	2001
Alabama	440	3,338	Missouri	2,800	7,500
Alaska	3,535	4,107	Montana	1,739	2,088
Arizona	9,200	11,500	Nebraska	640	1,120
Arkansas	958	2,935	Nevada	1,500	2,519
California	78,000	88,853	New Hampshire	1,500	2,168
Colorado	4,326	8,804	New Jersey	5,151	7,495
Connecticut	0	2,030	New Mexico	450	1,171
Delaware	800	1,688	New York	7,200	11,575
District of Columbia	50	303	North Carolina	2,200	5,922
Florida	9,000	20,000	North Dakota	683	766
Georgia	1,200	4,564	Ohio	1,294	5,423
Hawaii	1,000	1,500	Oklahoma	2,303	4,020
Idaho	1,710	1,778	Oregon	7,400	9,410
Illinois	14,300	16,551	Pennsylvania	2,400	4,533
Indiana	9,500	11,656	Rhode Island	273	1,424
Iowa	2,240	3,921	South Carolina	2,500	4,924
Kansas	1,200	1,794	South Dakota	800	1,182
Kentucky	800	2,000	Tennessee	2,800	4,561
Louisiana	3,455	5,708	Texas	18,000	29,494
Maine	275	473	Utah	4,733	5,192
Maryland	400	1,400	Vermont	877	1,509
Massachusetts	7,004	17,000	Virginia	6,615	9,306
Michigan	19,000	26,850	Washington	1,400	15,304
Minnesota	7,300	10,610	West Virginia	600	950
Mississippi	1,063	1,512	Wisconsin	10,000	11,999
			Wyoming	552	682
Total	263,166	386,112			

Source: Maguire, K., and A.L. Pastore (2003). *Sourcebook of Criminal Justice Statistics 2002*. Washington, DC: U.S. Department of Justice, p. 521.

izens in this way (*Kansas v. Hendricks*, 1997). A related concern involves attempts to impose the new laws on those already convicted and serving their sentences. Another issue relates to the impact of such laws on the offender's ability to find a home, locate a job, and be free from intimidation and harassment. There are some instances wherein an offender loses his or her job and must move due to actions taken by community members against him or her (Levenson and Cotter, 2005; Tewksbury, 2005). At what point does the community's right to know impinge on the rights of the offender to be secure in his or her home and to hold a job free from harassment? Each of these various concerns will be addressed in greater detail in Chapter 8.

All these efforts are predicated on the assumption that sex offenders are extremely dangerous to public safety and that they experience unusually high recidivism rates, thereby victimizing even more persons. For example, the legislative intent behind The Florida Sexual Predators Act reads:

> Repeat sexual offenders, sexual offenders who use physical violence, and sexual offenders who prey on children are sexual predators who present an extreme threat to the public safety. Sexual offenders are extremely likely to use physical violence and to repeat their offenses, and most sexual offenders commit many offenses, have many more victims than are ever reported, and are prosecuted for only a fraction of their crimes. This makes the cost of sexual offender victimization to society at large, while incalculable, clearly exorbitant (*Florida Statutes*, 2007: §775.21(3)(a)).

Using this kind of a sentiment as a springboard, Sample and Bray (2003) questioned whether these assumptions are grounded in empirical observations. The researchers relied upon offender criminal history information compiled by the Illinois State Police from 1990 until 1997. Their analysis revealed that sex offenders had one of the lowest rearrest rates for any crime and for the same original crime than did most other criminals. While these data provide little empirical support for the policy efforts that have arisen over the past few years, other commentators are not quite ready to dismiss legislative reactions as groundless or based on hysteria (Pallone, 2003; Wright, 2003). Instead, they suggest that it might be more fruitful to look at other avenues for greater effectiveness.

When dealing with legislative change, the genesis of the reform may not be as important as the impact of the new law. The real question is whether enacted legislative remedies are achieving the desired effects. The following section visits the question of whether legal reforms have worked as intended.

The Impact of Legal Reform

Chapter 4 introduced two concepts that can be of use in addressing the question of whether these legal reforms have had the desired impact. Earlier, we talked about whether victim compensation legislation produced any macro-level or micro-level effects. If you will recall, a *macro-level effect* is a change in such global indicators as crime reporting rates, clearance rates, prosecution rates, conviction rates, and the like. The emphasis is on a broad societal impact. In contrast, a *micro-level effect* entails looking at a much smaller unit to see if there have been changes in such things as worker attitudes, client satisfaction, and so forth.

Both types of effects are helpful to look at when trying to evaluate whether legal reforms have worked. The following material examines whether changes in sexual assault laws have had the anticipated macro-level and micro-level effects.

Macro-Level Effects

The changes that legislators made in the sexual assault regulations were designed to make the criminal justice system more "victim-friendly." Modifying the elements of what constitutes sexual battery, removing some of the overly restrictive evidentiary barriers, and establishing shield provisions should lessen some of the trauma victims experience when seeking justice. These attempts to counteract biases that had come to typify sexual battery cases should encourage greater system participation. As a result, reformers were expecting to find increased crime reporting, higher arrest rates, more effective prosecution, and enhanced conviction rates.

Early studies gave hope that these legal reforms held promise. For example, it appeared that Michigan had experienced some significant gains in arrests and convictions (Caringella-MacDonald, 1984; Marsh et al., 1982). However, subsequent evaluations have been less than enthusiastic about these changes (Bachman and Paternoster, 1993).

One research team studied the effect of definitional and evidentiary reforms in Illinois (Spohn and Horney, 1990). Using court cases from the Cook County Circuit Court allowed the researchers to monitor charges filed by the prosecutor, conviction records, and sentencing outcomes. What Spohn and Horney found was that legislative reforms had very limited, if any, direct impact. They explained that "passage of the rape shield law in 1978 had no significant effects on reports of rape or the processing of rape cases in Chicago. The results of the analysis of the 1984 definitional changes are inconclusive" (Spohn and Horney, 1990: 14).

Conclusions based upon data from a single jurisdiction suffer from an inability to generalize to other locations. One does not know whether the results are idiosyncratic or whether they accurately reflect broad trends. Such a shortcoming points out the need to look at several jurisdictions and various degrees of reform efforts.

After closely examining a number of state statutes, Horney and Spohn (1991) selected six evaluation sites: Atlanta, Detroit, Chicago, Houston, Philadelphia, and Washington, DC. Using records from 1970 until 1984, the researchers gathered information regarding filed reports, indictments, convictions, and sentencing practices. Even after isolating the different types of changes in the various locations, there was no evidence of any systematic or dramatic impact. Another study that looked at the impact of legal reform in Canada upon arrests and subsequent prosecution also found no effect (Schissel, 1996). A reanalysis of the National Violence Against Women Survey (see earlier in this chapter) reveals only subtle changes in reporting practices (Clay-Warner and Burt, 2005). In other words, it appears that rape reforms have not introduced any sweeping changes into system operations.

Micro-Level Effects

The lack of any noticeable macro-level effects perplexed some observers. However, others did not regard these dismal outcomes as being out of the ordinary. They pointed out that the system has a long history of failures in attempting to mend flaws. Whenever outsiders try to correct current practices, system officials have ample opportunities to circumvent the desired goals.

Mindful of the gap between how the law appears on the books and how it is implemented, Horney and Spohn (1991) interviewed judges, prosecutors, and defense attorneys in six cities for clues. What they found was instructive.

While shield provisions outline what types of evidence are considered relevant and provide for *in camera* hearings, private side bars rarely occur. Instead, informal courtroom norms govern the players. Prosecutors, well aware of how the judge eventually would rule, simply concede and do not try to block the admission of certain kinds of evidence. As Horney and Spohn (1991: 155-156) explain:

> If a defendant is acquitted because the judge ignored the law and either admitted potentially relevant evidence without a hearing or allowed the defense attorney to use legally inadmissible evidence, the victim cannot appeal the acquittal or the judge's decisions. If, on the other hand, the judge followed the law and refused to admit seemingly irrelevant sexual history evidence, the defendant can appeal his conviction. All of the consequences, in other words, would lead judges and prosecutors to err in favor of the defendant.

What this finding seems to indicate is that the major players in the courtroom drama have the capability to thwart reform efforts. The results show a huge gap between the law as it appears on the books and the law in action.

Summary

Legislative reform does not guarantee improvement in the plight of the victim or the activity of the criminal justice system. Simply changing the law neither guarantees compliance nor impact. In some cases, the system can accommodate the change by altering procedure rather than outcome. In more recent actions, such as sex offender registration laws, enough time has not gone by yet for an impact to materialize. In still other instances, there has been little, if any, systematic study devoted to the effect of the legislation.

Responding to Sexual Assault Victims

The criminal justice system normally responds to sexual assault cases in the manner outlined in Figure 6.11. After the dispatcher sends a patrol car to the scene, he or she will stay on the telephone with the victim until the responding officer arrives. After arrival, the officer must assess the victim's physical and emotional condition and then initiate appropriate actions. Once this stage is concluded, the officer usually tries to get some details on what has taken place. Victims normally go to a medical facility for treatment. Evidence collection (specially DNA sampling, if possible) takes place at the crime scene as well as at the hospital. At this point, the initial investigation usually concludes with an interview to gather more information about the incident and the assailant.

During the ongoing investigation phase, the police will try to locate witnesses and follow other leads. Building and maintaining case files are important in finding patterns and attempting to link suspects to unsolved crimes. In the event that a suspect is identified and arrested, the final step is to relay all case materials to the prosecutor.

FIGURE 6.11
Ten Stages in a Typical Sexual Battery Investigation

1. Dispatch Officer to Scene
2. Officer Arrival at Scene
3. Initial Assessment at the Scene
4. Transportation to a Medical Facility
5. Initial Police Report
6. Evidence Processing
7. Subsequent Interview
8. Ongoing Investigation
9. Maintenance of Case File
10. Preparation for Prosecution

Source: Carrow, D.M. (1980). *Rape: Guidelines for a Community Response*. Washington, DC: U.S. Department of Justice, pp. 84-87.

This brief overview of case handling emphasizes three groups that become involved in sexual assault matters: (1) the police, (2) medical personnel, and (3) the prosecutor. The following materials examine the role of each in greater detail.

The Police

The view of police indifference and insensitivity toward rape victims is widespread and not without some empirical support. A national survey of police officers uncovered a prevailing attitude of suspicion and lack of concern for rape victims (LeDoux and Hazelwood, 1985). A significant number of police officers, like the general population, subscribe to rape myths. Often, police officers classify rape cases as unfounded based on their perceptions of the offender and the victim (Sanders, 1980). While this decisionmaking is not unlike what takes place in other kinds of cases, it does indicate a consistent style of indifference.

One factor that may reflect the criminal justice system's stance toward rape victims is the level of reporting by victims. As noted earlier, the NCVS reveals that typically almost two-thirds of all rape and sexual assault victims never report their incidents to the police (Catalano, 2006: 10). One possible reason for this nonreporting is the reaction of the police to such allegations. Cumbersome and inappropriate questions can change the emphasis of the case from what the accused did to what the victim did or did not do.

Concern over this callous handling has led many agencies to institute changes in how they process sexual assault cases. Many departments have established specialized investigatory units whose exclusive responsibility is to handle sexual battery calls. Steps have been taken toward training officers to employ crisis counseling techniques, establishing closer ties with rape crisis centers, deploying victim advocates to the crime scene, dispatching female patrol officers to assist sexual assault victims, and developing relationships with doctors and medical services for better treatment of victims. The result of such initiatives is officers who are more sympathetic toward, and hold more positive attitudes about, victims of sexual assault (Campbell, 1995; Campbell and Johnson, 1997; Temkin, 1996).

The Hospital

A standard procedure when dealing with sexual assault victims is to arrange for the provision of medical care. The recommendations contained in Figure 6.12 underscore the fact that the hospital becomes a very crucial link for many victims. The purpose of seeking emergency medical treatment for sexual assault victims is actually twofold. The first goal is to receive medical assistance; the second is to preserve materials for evidentiary purposes.

FIGURE 6.12
Recommendations from the U.S. Attorney General's Office to Medical Care Providers Concerning Victims of Crime

---

- Hospitals should establish and implement training programs for hospital personnel to sensitize them to the needs of victims of violent crimes, especially the elderly and those who have been sexually assaulted.

- Hospitals should provide emergency medical assistance to victims of violent crime without regard to their ability to pay, and collect payments from state victim compensation plans.

- Hospitals should provide emergency room crisis counseling to victims of crime and their families.

- Hospitals should encourage and develop direct liaison with all victim assistance and social service agencies.

- Hospitals should develop, in consultation with prosecuting agencies, a standardized rape kit for proper collection of physical evidence, and develop a procedure to ensure proper storage and maintenance of such evidence until it is released to the appropriate agency.

Source: U.S. Department of Justice (1986). *Four Years Later: A Report on the President's Task Force on Victims of Crime.* Washington, DC: U.S. Government Printing Office, p. 39.

Medical Examination

One of the more pressing needs in a sexual assault case is to attend to the victim's physical well-being. For some victims, this need is rather apparent. There may be bleeding, contusions, bumps, broken bones, or other obvious injuries that require immediate medical treatment. Other victims may be hurt even though they do not display any outward signs of injury.

Many hospitals have established specific procedures aimed at minimizing the emotional trauma that victims experience. A support person—either a victim advocate or a specially trained nurse—will remain with the victim throughout the physical examination. Most hospital procedures allow sexual assault victims to bypass the usual registration procedures in the public intake area. Instead, medical personnel escort the victim to a private room in order to spare the victim further embarrassment and to help the survivor reestablish a sense of control.

A promising development has been the introduction of the Sexual Assault Nurse Examiner (SANE) Program. A *SANE* is a registered nurse who has acquired advanced training and is able to provide specialized service to sexual assault victims. As Figure 6.13 explains, this approach takes a holistic view of victim needs while, at the same time, remaining cognizant of legal and forensic concerns. Essentially, the SANE coordinates service delivery and guides the victim through the entire process. The first SANE program began operating in the mid-1970s. Today, there are more than 100 such programs in place, and that number continues to expand (Ledray, 1999: 1; Littel, 2001: 3), but it is too early to reach a definitive conclusion as to how well these programs are working in achieving their goals (Campbell, Patterson, and Lichty, 2005).

The medical examination addresses the immediate physical injuries, the prevention or treatment of sexually transmitted diseases (STDs), and the possibility of pregnancy. The likelihood of becoming pregnant after a sexual assault ranges from 5 to 30 percent (Shulman, Muran, and Speck, 1992: 205). In addition to external forms of trauma, it is not unusual for sexual assault victims to sustain internal gynecological injuries. These conditions, if left untreated, could lead to long-term complications.

One problem that can have extremely important ramifications is *sexually transmitted disease (STD)*. Because most assailants have not been apprehended or tested at this point, the risk of an STD infection is unknown. Precautionary measures designed to combat gonorrhea, syphilis, chlamydia, or other STDs may be warranted. For example,

FIGURE 6.13
The Sexual Assault Nurse Examiner (SANE) Program

Values Statement

The basis of a SANE program operation is the belief that sexual assault victims have the right to immediate, compassionate, and comprehensive medical-legal evaluation and treatment by a specially trained professional who has the experience to anticipate their needs during this time of crisis. As health care providers, the SANE has an ethical responsibility to provide victims with complete information about choices so victims can make informed decisions about the care they want to receive.

A SANE program is also based on a belief that all sexual assault victims have a right (and responsibility) to report the crime of rape. While every victim may not choose to report to law enforcement, she has a right to know what her options are and what to expect if she does or does not decide to report.

Those who do report also have a right to sensitive and knowledgeable support without bias during this often difficult process through the criminal justice system. Those who do not report still have a right to expert health care. In addition, a SANE program is based on the belief that providing a higher standard of evidence collection and care can speed the victim's recovery to a higher level of functioning, prevent secondary injury or illness, and ultimately increase the prosecution of sex offenders and reduce the incidence of rape.

Mission Statement

The primary mission of a SANE program is to meet the needs of the sexual assault victim by providing immediate, compassionate, culturally sensitive, and comprehensive forensic evaluation and treatment by trained, professional nurse experts . . . .

Program Goals

- To protect the sexual assault victim from further harm.
- To provide crisis intervention.
- To provide timely, thorough, and professional forensic evidence collection, documentation, and preservation of evidence.
- To evaluate and treat prophylactically for sexually transmitted diseases (STDs).
- To evaluate pregnancy risk and offer prevention.
- To assess, document, and seek care for injuries.
- To appropriately refer victims for immediate and followup medical care and followup counseling.
- To enhance the ability of law enforcement agencies to obtain evidence and successfully prosecute sexual assault cases.

Source: Ledray, L.E. (1999). *SANE: Sexual Assault Nurse Examiner: Development and Operation Guide*. Washington, DC: Office for Victims of Crime, pp. 8-9. Accessed on September 16, 2004, from http://www.ojp.usdoj.gov/ovc/publications/infores/sane/saneguide.pdf

Baker and associates (1990) note that almost one-half of the rape victims in their study identified AIDS as a primary worry. However, there is some concern that detection of exposure to the HIV virus is neither timely nor reliable and could impede emotional recovery (Bowleg and Stoll, 1991). Undoubtedly, anxiety over this issue will escalate as the incidence of AIDS and other STDs continues to grow (Ledray, 1999: 73-74).

Forensic Examination

Evidence preservation begins long before the victim reaches the hospital doors. Sometimes sexual assault victims may feel defiled or dirty. They may have a strong desire to take a shower, change clothes, brush their teeth, or wash their hands before going to the hospital. Doing so could destroy potentially valuable evidence. As a result, police investigators normally advise sexual assault victims to delay these activities. They also ask these victims to carry a fresh set of clothing to the hospital so that items worn during the attack can be impounded and preserved as evidence.

A frequent stumbling block to the forensic portion of the emergency room examination has been that it placed physicians in an awkward position (Best, Dansky, and Kilpatrick, 1992). Once the attending physician finished treating the victim, the *forensic examination* was underway (though the victim might not be cognizant of it). Many doctors lacked appropriate training in evidence collection (Carrow, 1980; Hilberman, 1976: 22; Martin and Powell, 1994; Sproles, 1985) or conveyed a less than sympathetic attitude toward the victim (Martin and Powell, 1994; Temkin, 1996). Consequently, they relied upon police investigators for instructions as to what to do in these situations. The outcome, as one might well guess, was often haphazard and far from systematic. These gaps could hinder successful prosecution of the attacker.

Many states responded to a federal initiative and formulated *"rape kits"* to alleviate this evidentiary problem. The Office of the Florida Attorney General (1991), for example, has instituted one such standardized protocol. These kits include a preprinted set of instructions for the physician to follow, report forms to complete, containers for collecting hair samples and fingernail scrapings, swabs and slides for extracting fluid specimens, blood sample containers, and other tools for gathering trace evidence. Although one can order prepackaged commercial "rape kits" from manufacturers, local hospitals can assemble these items for a nominal amount (Carrow, 1980: 109). Once the attending physician completes the forensic examination, the police investigator impounds the kit and submits it to the crime laboratory for evidence analysis.

A related issue that has commanded attention is who should pay for the evidentiary or forensic examination. A follow-up to the 1982 President's Task Force on Victims discovered that it was a common practice for hospitals to bill sexual assault victims for the evidence collection. Today, state victim compensation programs usually underwrite the cost of this evidence gathering. Florida, for example, does not allow providers to bill victims for the medical exam. Instead, the Office of the Attorney General will reimburse vendors up to $500 for these expenses (*Florida Statutes*, 2007: §960.28). If this recourse is not available, then either the investigating agency or the prosecutor's office is usually responsible for payment.

The Prosecutor

In the past, many prosecutors have been reluctant to take sexual battery cases to trial. Prior to the implementation of the legal reforms presented earlier, prosecutors were leery of pursuing cases in which the victim did not sustain any visible physical injuries. The issue of consent was a huge stumbling block, particularly if there was a jury trial. Often, the determining factor in the case was the victim's demeanor and credibility on the stand. In fact, Konradi (1996) reports that the clothes a victim wears to court, the appropriate display of emotion while testifying, rehearsing testimony, and other pretrial preparations help survivors negotiate the criminal justice process and sway the odds in their favor.

Critics have not hesitated to question prosecutorial decisions and case attrition. A common complaint is that prosecutors refused to file charges and failed to prosecute an inordinate number of suspects. In very broad terms, it is typical for only about one-half the victimizations reported to the police to result in an arrest. In turn, only about one-half the arrests culminate in a prosecution, and far fewer end in a conviction.

Some studies indicate that the attrition in prosecution and conviction is due to actions of the victim (Horney and Spohn, 1991; Spears and Spohn, 1996; Spohn and Spears, 1996). For example, victims who take "risks," such as hitchhiking, using alcohol or other drugs, or going to the offender's home, have a greater likelihood of their case being dismissed than other victims. In one sense, these people do not fit the normal profile of a "genuine victim." In terms of the case handling by the system, a detailed comparative analysis has shown that rape cases move through the system just like any other major felony (Galvin and Polk, 1983). Despite this "business as usual" approach, there is still room for improvement in the way prosecutors handle sexual assault cases. Figure 6.14 presents a series of common mistakes for the prosecutor's office to avoid when handling sexual battery cases.

FIGURE 6.14
Pitfalls to Avoid When Managing the Prosecution of Sexual Assault Cases

- Failure to consider organizational arrangements which allow rape prosecutions to be handled by only a few designated prosecutors within the office.

- Failure to allow sufficient flexibility within case assignments so that special sexual assault prosecutors are also given assignments to other major crimes.

- Failure to limit the number of prosecutor personnel coming into contact with the victim.

- Assignment of rape cases to personnel who are insensitive to the victim's needs or biased against victims of sexual assault.

- Assignment of junior personnel to rape prosecutions.

- Designation of female prosecutors as "rape prosecutors" without regard to their skills, experience, or sensitivity to the victim.

- Failure to screen personnel trying rape cases to ensure that individuals who are emotionally or intellectually drained by these cases no longer receive rape prosecutions.

Source: Carrow, D.M. (1980). *Rape: Guidelines for a Community Response*. Washington, DC: U.S. Department of Justice, pp. 95, 97.

The legal reforms mentioned earlier in this chapter are intended to alter the system's response. Shield provisions have become an important part of most recent legislation dealing with sexual battery. No longer is the sexual history of the victim an issue, except as it directly pertains to past consensual sexual behavior with the accused. In essence, the victim is protected or "shielded" from any irrelevant character assassination attempts.

FIGURE 6.15
Selected Internet Sites Dealing with Sexual Assault

American Academy of Experts in Traumatic Stress
   http://www.aaets.org

Feminist Majority Foundation
   http://www.feminist.org

Florida Department of Law Enforcement, Sexual Predator Page
   http://offender.fdle.state.fl.us/offender/registries.jsp

International Association of Forensic Nurses
   http://www.forensicnurse.org

Men Can Stop Rape
   http://www.mencanstoprape.org

Minnesota Center Against Violence and Abuse
   http://www.mincava.umn.edu

National Clearinghouse on Marital and Date Rape
   http://www.members.aol.com/ncmdr/index.html

National Sex Offender Registry
   http://www.nsopr.gov

Sexual Assault Nurse Examiner Sexual Assault Response Team
   http://www.sane-sart.com

Office on Violence Against Women
   http://www.usdoj.gov/ovw

Summary

Sexual violence has been an instrumental rallying point in the growth of the victim movement in the United States. Many of these issues led to the revision of the criminal justice system to make it more protective of victims. Sexual battery victims suffer much emotional trauma and endure a burdensome recovery process. In order to expedite the healing, new legislation and interventions have emerged. These reforms aim to relocate victims from a position where they are blamed to one in which they receive help. Due to the relatively short time since rape and sexual assault have emerged as major policy concerns, there is a need for more research, improved training of system workers, and further development of informed systems of intervention.

Key Terms for Chapter 6

absolute exemption

acquaintance rape

anger rape

crisis

crisis reaction repair
cycle

date rape

forensic examination

gang rape

impact

impulsive rape

in camera

incidence

macro-level effect

micro-level effect

non-stranger rape

partial exemption

physiological
explanations

post-traumatic stress
disorder (PTSD)

prevalence

psychopathology

rape kit

rape myths

rape trauma
syndrome

recoil

reorganization

sadistic rape

SANE

seropositive

sexual conquest rape

sex offender
registration

sexually transmitted
disease (STD)

sociocultural
explanations

spousal immunity

Learning Objectives

After reading Chapter 7, you should be able to:

- Talk about how men have dominated women historically.
- Address historical trends in intimate partner violence.
- Estimate the extent of intimate partner violence.
- Recognize the different types of intimate partner violence.
- Explain how researchers measure intimate partner violence.
- List some shortcomings with how researchers measure intimate partner violence.
- Define intimate partner violence.
- Tie in lethality with intimate partner violence.
- Address the trends in intimate partner violence over the past dozen years.
- Understand what the battered woman syndrome means.
- Link masochism with intimate partner violence.
- Outline the learned helplessness perspective.
- Tell how the cycle of violence builds.
- Explore the role of alcohol in intimate partner violence.
- Connect the power and control wheel with intimate partner violence.
- Summarize how the laws of arrest hampered police intervention in intimate partner violence.
- Assess the nonarrest options available to the police.
- Summarize the Minneapolis Experiment and its findings.
- List three criticisms of the Minneapolis Experiment.
- Relate pro-arrest and mandatory arrest policies to the Minneapolis Experiment.
- Explain how legislatures have relaxed the misdemeanor rule.
- Talk about why there are refuge houses and how they are funded.
- Compare and contrast internal validity with external validity.
- Summarize the replications of the Minneapolis Experiment.
- Explore the prosecutorial response to intimate partner violence.
- Discuss what an injunction is, its provisions, and how it works.
- Address the pros and cons of a "no-drop" prosecution policy.
- Explain the idea of coordinating system responses and their impact.
- Define and discuss the issue of anti-stalking legislation.
- Identify some types of stalkers.
- Incorporate the Lautenberg Amendment into a discussion of intimate partner violence.
- Investigate concerns surrounding court-ordered mandatory counseling for batterers.
- Specify how counseling can aggravate victim concerns.
- Link the battered woman syndrome to executive clemency.
- Comment on the castle doctrine.
- Disclose the role of a fatality review team.

Chapter 7

INTIMATE PARTNER VIOLENCE

Introduction

When one thinks of crime and criminals, the image that most often comes to mind is that of stranger-to-stranger violations. In actuality, however, you are more likely to be killed or beaten by a person you know than by a total stranger. Furthermore, the violent offender is probably not just a passing acquaintance or somebody you nod to at the grocery store. More than likely, that person will be an immediate family member or someone with whom you share a very close personal relationship.

Every day hundreds of husbands brutalize their wives. Much of this violence is hidden from the public eye. It frequently takes place in private, where no one can see the physical infliction or hear the anguished pleas for help. In addition, if people should hear the muffled sounds of a beating, many would not intervene, based on the belief that "a man's home is his castle."

It is only recently that we have come to realize the amount of human suffering that takes place within families. Gradually, this internal domestic strife is becoming more exposed to public view. Society finally is starting to recognize the problem of intimate partner violence (IPV) as a major public health hazard. Twenty-two percent of the nonfatal violent incidents experienced by women from 1993 through 2004 involved altercations with an intimate partner, compared to 3 percent of similar male victimizations (Catalano, 2006).

This chapter deals with violence between husbands and wives, or other conjugal cohabitants. We look at the pervasiveness of this problem and at the types of statutory provisions that govern these behaviors. We also examine how academicians account for IPV. As you will see, the IPV problem has dropped into the laps of law enforcement personnel and they have assumed responsibility as first-responders. The primary reason why the police deal with IPV is because no other public agency operates seven days a week, 24 hours a day, 365 days a year. Because they did not anticipate these tasks, law enforcement agencies often lack the resources and skills required to deal with this form of violence. Despite this shortcoming, police departments and the rest of the criminal justice community continue to look for ways to combat this social problem.

A Brief History of Intimate Partner Violence

The domination of men over women has strong historical roots. Early Roman law treated women as the property of their husbands, a custom reinforced by biblical passages, Christianity, English common law, and the mores of American colonists (Dobash and Dobash, 1977-78; Dobash and Dobash, 1979; Edwards, 1989; Pleck, 1989). As property, women were subject to the control of their fathers or husbands, who held the power of life and death over them.

Women have held no legal standing throughout most of history. Any harm committed against a woman was viewed as an offense against the father or husband, not her. Consequently, it was the male "owner" who sought vengeance or compensation for his loss. At the same time, a female could not be a culpable party. The father or the husband was the one held responsible for any injurious action by his woman. Buzawa and Buzawa (1990) point out that husbands or fathers were expected to punish women. In fact, many Western cultures proscribed official punishment of women in their legal codes.

The legal movement in this country to restrict wife beating fits into roughly three stages. The first period occurred in the mid-1600s when the Puritans in Massachusetts enacted laws against wife beating and family violence (Pleck, 1989). Pleck points out, however, that these laws were rarely enforced. This laxity was due, in large part, to the strong belief in family privacy and the acceptance of physical force by the husband as a valid form of discipline.

A second upswing in concern over IPV appeared in the late 1800s, when states began passing laws restricting family violence. Worries over immigration, rising crime, the use of alcohol, and other factors prompted the passage of laws restricting family conflict and allowing for outside intervention (Pleck, 1989). Some states even mandated public flogging as a punishment for beating women. As with the earlier movement, however, these laws and punishments were seldom enforced (Pleck, 1989).

While these protective actions were evolving, some nineteenth-century state supreme court decisions continued to condone wife beating. However, husbands were advised that physical chastisement should not exceed the boundaries of good taste (Dobash and Dobash, 1977-78: 429-431; Pleck, 1979). It is important to note that it was not until the early part of the twentieth century that women in the United States gained *suffrage*, the right to vote (see Figure 7.1).

FIGURE 7.1
The 19th Amendment to the United States Constitution Granting Women the Right to Vote

---

AMENDMENT XIX

Passed by Congress June 4, 1919. Ratified August 18, 1920.

The right of citizens of the United States to vote shall not be denied or abridged by the United States or by any State on account of sex.

Congress shall have power to enforce this article by appropriate legislation.

Source: The National Archives Experience, *Constitution of the United States*, Retrieved September 14, 2007, from http://www.archives.gov/national_archives_experience/charters/constitution_amendments_11-27.html

The fate of the Equal Rights Amendment (ERA) is another example of the diminished status held by women. The first Equal Rights Amendment (see Figure 7.2) was proposed on December 23, 1923. However, it languished in Congress for years and never got out of committee. Another version of the ERA was approved by the House in 1971 and by the Senate in 1972. However, this effort eventually failed because only 35 out of the necessary 38 states had ratified the ERA when the time for consideration expired. More recently, a resolution reviving the ERA was introduced in the House of Representatives (H.J. Res. 40) and in the Senate (S.J. Res. 10) on March 7, 2007 (Kennedy, 2007; Maloney, 2007) and is currently under consideration. The point remains, though, that women have a lesser status than men and have encountered strong resistance.

FIGURE 7.2
House Joint Resolution 75, Proposing the Equal Rights Amendment,
December 13, 1923

Resolved by the Senate and the House of Representatives of the United States of America in Congress assembled (two-thirds of each House concurring therein), That the following article is proposed as an amendment to the Constitution of the United States which shall be valid, to all intents and purposes, as part of the Constitution when ratified by the legislatures of three-fourths of the several States:

ARTICLE XX.

Men and women shall have equal rights throughout the United States and every place subject to its jurisdiction.

Congress shall have the power to enforce this article by appropriate legislation.

Source: The National Archives, "Martha Griffiths and the Equal Rights Amendment." *Legislative Branch: The Center for Legislative Archives*. Retrieved on September 14, 2007, from http://www.archives.gov/legislative/features/griffiths

The third stage of interest in IPV is the one currently in effect. The 1960s saw the beginning of general social unrest and demands for equality. Concerns over rape, intimate partner abuse, and family violence became rallying cries for the emerging women's movement. Calls for greater police intervention into domestic violence replaced family privacy issues. It was during this time that physicians and social workers became vocal about family violence and brought these problems to the attention of society (Pleck, 1989). Remarkably, not a single research article in the *Journal of Marriage and the Family*, a premiere scholarly outlet in this area, entertained the issue of family violence prior to 1969 (Wardell, Gillespie, and Leffler, 1983). Reflecting on the historical paucity of interest in IPV, Dobash and Dobash (1977-78: 427) pointed out that:

> [W]ife-beating is not, in the strictest sense of the words, a "deviant," "aberrant," or "pathological" act. Rather, it is a form of behavior which has existed for centuries as an acceptable, and, indeed, a desirable part of a patriarchal family system within a patriarchal society, and much of the ideology and many of the institutional arrangements which support the patriarchy through the subordination, domination and control of women are still reflected in our culture and our social institutions.

Perhaps the greatest breakthrough for interest in IPV was the publication in 1984 of the Minneapolis Experiment, which evaluated the effectiveness of arresting abusive husbands. This research, which will be discussed in more detail later in this chapter, generated a great deal of policy change, spawned widespread debate in the academic community and prompted a series of replications.

The renewed interest in IPV has gone relatively unabated. IPV continues to be a leading issue within the larger framework and growth of victimology. The criminal justice system has adapted by altering different policies and procedures for dealing with abusive offenders and their victims. Academic interest has also kept pace. A casual inspection of most library holdings will uncover a large selection of materials dealing with IPV.

The Extent of Intimate Partner Violence

Estimates about how often IPV occurs show some variation from one study to the next. Sometimes the definitions that researchers employ are responsible for these differences. Despite these apparent differences, victimologists would agree that there are several types of IPV. As Figure 7.3 shows, there are least five major forms of IPV. They include physical abuse, sexual abuse, emotional abuse, economic abuse, and psychological abuse.

One well-known survey instrument, the Conflict Tactics Scale (CTS), is used frequently to assess the extent of marital violence. The CTS represents a range of responses to conflict, extending from non-violent to violent actions. Respondents are asked to indicate how often each response was resorted to in the past year. Using the original version of the CTS, Straus and his co-researchers (1980) found that 16 percent of the subjects reported at least one violent episode within the previous year. More than one-fourth of these people acknowledged participating in at least one violent confrontation with their partner during the marriage.

While the CTS enjoyed wide usage when it was introduced, it had some limitations (Dobash et al., 1992). First, only one member of a household was typically surveyed. This shortcoming meant that there were no comparative data against which to gauge the responses. Lack of validation is especially problematic because husbands tend to see less violence than do wives (Browning and Dutton, 1986). Second, these data were limited in terms of assessing the degree of conflict. There was no indication as to the kind of object used in various categories, the number of times an act occurred during each instance, the degree of force used, or differences in the strength of the combatants (Frieze and Browne, 1989). Third, there was no information on the severity of the actual harm, if any, inflicted. Finally, there was rarely any information gathered on the length of the marriage, age of the parties, family socioeconomic conditions, or other demographic characteristics.

FIGURE 7.3
Types of Domestic Violence

Domestic violence can be physical, sexual, emotional, economic, or psychological actions or threats of actions that influence another person. This includes any behaviors that intimidate, manipulate, humiliate, isolate, frighten, terrorize, coerce, threaten, blame, hurt, injure, or wound someone.

- Physical Abuse: Hitting, slapping, shoving, grabbing, pinching, biting, hair-pulling, biting, etc. Physical abuse also includes denying a partner medical care or forcing alcohol and/or drug use.

- Sexual Abuse: Coercing or attempting to coerce any sexual contact or behavior without consent. Sexual abuse includes, but is certainly not limited to marital rape, attacks on sexual parts of the body, forcing sex after physical violence has occurred, or treating one in a sexually demeaning manner.

- Emotional Abuse: Undermining an individual's sense of self-worth and/or self-esteem. This may include, but is not limited to constant criticism, diminishing one's abilities, name-calling, or damaging one's relationship with his or her children.

- Economic Abuse: Making or attempting to make an individual financially dependent by maintaining total control over financial resources, withholding one's access to money, or forbidding one's attendance at school or employment.

- Psychological Abuse: Causing fear by intimidation; threatening physical harm to self, partner, children, or partner's family or friends; destruction of pets and property; and forcing isolation from family, friends, or school and/or work.

Source: Office on Violence Against Women (2007). *About Domestic Violence*. Washington, DC: U.S. Department of Justice. Retrieved on September 20, 2007, from http://www.usdoj.gov/ovw/domviolence.htm

Despite these shortcomings, the CTS carried at least three benefits (Schafer, 1996). First, reliance upon a standardized protocol makes it much easier to compare results from one project to the next and to develop a continuous body of knowledge. Second, using a standardized questionnaire may serve as a tool to minimize subject memory decay. If you remember the discussion in Chapter 2, recall problems are a source of constant worry for survey researchers. Finally, using a standardized set of questions over many different settings makes refinements and improvements possible.

These considerations prompted Strauss and his associates to produce a more refined version of the instrument. The revised scale includes more items pertaining to abuse, documents psychological abuse, delves into different forms of sexual violence, and includes outcome measures such as injury. Efforts at establishing the reliability and validity of this revised protocol are now underway.

Gelles and Straus (1988) claim that approximately 25 percent of all couples will experience abuse during their lifetimes. In terms of numbers, Langen and Innes (1986) estimate that roughly 2.1 million women suffer from abuse each year, while Sherman (1992) reports that police records reflect as many as 8 million cases annually. After reviewing the literature, one researcher extrapolated the number of American women beaten at least once by their husbands during their marriage to be somewhere around 20 million (Pagelow, 1984: 45).

IPV figures, whether official or self-reported, undercount the actual level of abuse and are subject to a great deal of speculation. One reason for inaccuracy may be that many studies fail to register the number of times violence occurs in a relationship, opting instead to simply count whether any abuse has occurred. Looking at the number of times abuse occurred, Straus (1978) reported an average of three beatings a year.

Another problem is that many studies refer only to married couples. Studies of courtship patterns reveal figures of intimate violence ranging from 22 percent to two-thirds of dating partners (Gelles and Cornell, 1985: 65). Apparently, some people view this period as a "training ground" for marital interaction. In addition, researchers tend to overlook the amount of violence that occurs within same-sex couples (Lockhart et al., 1994).

Finally, reconciling disparate research results is often difficult due to differences in study design. Besides using different definitions of abuse, the data sources also vary (such as police records, social service agencies, single-city surveys, or estimates by "experts"). As a result, researchers suspect the actual number of IPV cases is close to 50 percent of all couples (Feld and Straus, 1989). The inescapable conclusion generated from these and other projects is that IPV is an all-too-frequent act.

With the redesign of the National Crime Victimization Survey (NCVS) discussed earlier in Chapter 2 comes more detailed information regarding IPV. The term *intimate partner violence* includes physical episodes involving current and former spouses, boyfriends, and girlfriends (Catalano, 2006). Figure 7.5 displays these figures from 1993 through 2004. While female victimization rates show a decline over the years, the gap between the female and male victimization rates remains pronounced. Females are more likely to experience harm at the hands of their intimates. Females were IPV victims in more than 151,000 cases in 2004. One-half of the female and one-third of the male IPV victims sustained injuries. While most of the injuries were not serious, 5 percent of these victims were shot, cut with a knife, rendered unconscious, exhibited broken bones, suffered sexual battery, or had other extensive wounds.

FIGURE 7.4
Facts About Intimate Partner Violence

- Approximately 1.5 million women and 834,700 men are raped or physically assaulted by an intimate partner each year in the United Stated.
- Nearly two-thirds of women who report being raped, physically assaulted, or stalked since age 18 were victimized by a current or former husband, cohabiting partner, boyfriend, or date.
- In 8 of 10 rape cases, the victim knew the perpetrator.
- According to the National Violence Against Women Survey, 1 in 4 U.S. women has been physically assaulted or raped by an intimate partner.
- Among women who are physically assaulted or raped by an intimate partner, 1 in 3 is injured.
- Each year, more than 500,000 women injured as a result of IPV require medical treatment.
- Intimate partner violence is associated with both short- and long-term problems, including physical injury and illness, psychological symptoms, economic costs, and death.
- Each year, thousands of American children witness IPV within their families. Witnessing violence is a risk factor for long-term physical and mental health problems, including alcohol and substance abuse, being a victim of abuse, and perpetrating IPV.
- The health care cost of intimate partner rape, physical assault, and stalking exceed $5.8 billion each year, nearly $4.1 billion of which is for direct medical and mental health care services.

Source: Adapted from National Center for Injury Prevention and Control (2006). *CDC Injury Fact Book*. Atlanta, GA: Centers for Disease Control and Prevention, p. 55. Retrieved September 22, 2007, from http://www.cdc.gov/ncipc/fact_book/InjuryBook2006.pdf

FIGURE 7.5
Nonfatal Violent Victimization Rate by Intimate Partners per 1,000 Persons of Each Gender, 1993–2004

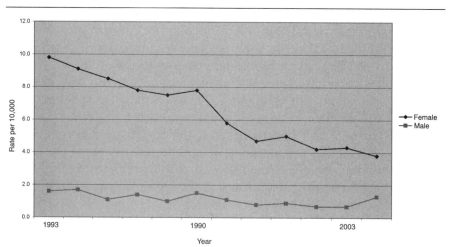

Source: Adapted from Catalano, S. (2006). *Intimate Partner Violence in the United States*. Washington, DC: Bureau of Justice Statistics, p. 2. Retrieved on September 14, 2007, from http://www.ojp.usdoj.gov/bjs/intimate/ipv.htm

Any discussion of IPV must recognize that these incidents have the potential to escalate into lethal confrontations. The Federal Bureau of Investigation (2006) reports that 14,860 homicides occurred throughout the nation in 2005. The Supplementary Homicide Reports, which contain a rich array of data, have information available on 8,136 of these cases. Tabulations based on those files reveal that 75 percent of the victims knew their assailants, while 25 percent were murdered by strangers. Delving further, 34 percent of the detailed homicides were committed by spouses, boyfriends, or girlfriends. Parents, offspring, siblings, and other family members were implicated in 13 percent of these lethal confrontations. Friends, acquaintances, co-workers, and employees accounted for the remaining 52 percent. Thus, based upon the information at hand, homicide victims are more likely to expire from injuries they sustain at the hands of people whom they know rather than complete strangers. This tidbit is exactly what we learned in Chapter 1 from Wolfgang's (1958) classic study of homicide in Philadelphia.

IPV is not restricted to husbands hurting their wives. Sometimes, women batter their mates. When the idea of women striking their mates was first introduced (Steinmetz, 1977-78; Steinmetz, 1978a), some commentators dismissed this notion as a "red herring" or a misleading distortion of the real problem (Fields and Kirchner, 1978). People who adhere to the family violence perspective would welcome greater attention to this and other related topics. However, those who endorse a strict feminist viewpoint would reject this call because it ignores the relationship between gender and power (Stalans and Lurigio, 1995). Perhaps the best summary of this situation came when Henning, Renauer, and Holdford (2006: 6) wrote:

> Those arguing that IPV is a gendered crime with female victims and male offenders will highlight the fact that most of the women in our sample were primary victims. People arguing that women are just as violent as men and that the criminal justice system is biased against males will point to the "female batterers" we identified. Our opinion is that both pieces of information are important and must be acknowledged for the field to advance beyond the highly polarized debate that continues to fuel a growing backlash against domestic violence initiatives.

Part of the reason behind using the more expansive term "intimate partner violence," as opposed to "spouse abuse," is the growing recognition that violence also occurs within same-sex relationships (Kuehnle and Sullivan, 2003; Lockhart et al., 1994; Younglove, Kerr, and Vitello, 2002). Some writers have concluded that violence within same-sex couples takes place at about the same rate as it does in heterosexual pairings (Aulivola, 2004; McClennen, 2005; Stanley et al.,

2006). Instead of painting the issue of spouse abuse along gender lines where women are victims and men are the aggressors, the suggestion these observers make is to recast the issue in terms of intimate partner violence and focus upon violence within primary relationships.

Women sometimes strike back at their assailants. One analysis of women who killed reveals that 86 percent were carrying on an intimate relationship with the victim whom they murdered (Mann, 1988: 38). The fact that some of the men had battered these women has led lawyers to raise the *battered woman syndrome* as a self-defense explanation, a concept we will delve into later in this chapter. The argument is that these women were so traumatized by previous beatings that they simply seized the opportunity to kill their batterers to prevent any further victimization episodes. In any event, situations such as those typified here caused one author to remark, "A man's home may be his castle, but a woman's home too often is her dungeon" (Costa, 1984: 8).

Theories of Intimate Partner Violence

Although there are several theoretical explanations regarding IPV, no clear consensus has emerged as to the root causes of this behavior. For our purposes, the theoretical arguments can be broken down into three general categories: (1) intraindividual theories, (2) sociocultural explanations (patriarchy), and (3) the learned helplessness perspective. The intraindividual approach tries to reach an understanding of the offender's actions. It entertains the question of what makes some people beat their partners and addresses the psychological traits of victims who endure abuse. A second avenue of thought deals with sociocultural explanations, or what some call a feminist perspective. The emphasis here is on the dominant male orientation of society. The final approach, learned helplessness, is also part of the sociocultural tradition. Learned helplessness questions why victims remain in an abusive setting when they can prevent future beatings simply by walking away from the batterer. Despite its intuitive appeal, we shall see that the decision to abandon one's partner is much more complex than just the mere desire to escape a battering relationship.

The status of theorizing on IPV is still haphazard. No single theory has proved the most promising. As a result, the following discussion is meant to be more informative than to advocate the case for any one theoretical perspective.

Intraindividual Theories

Intraindividual theories locate the cause of deviant behavior inside a person. These explanations frequently are referred to as theories of *psychopathology*. They focus on what is wrong within the individual and address a variety of specific issues thought to cause abnormal behavior. Some of these items include substance use, mental illness, stress, depression, low self-esteem, intergenerational transmission of abuse, and other problematic areas.

The earliest theories of IPV often relied on general opinions that the batterer was sick or disturbed. In essence, the offender was an aberration and did not reflect the norm in society. This belief fit well with the idea that IPV was a private matter not to be dealt with outside the home. In those instances where IPV came into the public spotlight, one could dismiss it easily as an isolated incident and of concern only to the immediate family.

While some writers have attributed IPV to the mental illness of the offender, more precise definition can be given to the topic by looking at individual factors that cause or contribute to the behavior. Alcohol and other drug consumption by either or both parties is a common research finding (Brookoff, 1997; Browne, 1987; Collins, 1989; Gelles and Straus, 1979; Hotaling and Sugarman, 1986; Kantor and Straus, 1987; Stuart et al., 2006). However, the fact that substance use is common in IPV cases does not isolate the causal mechanism at work. Two basic possibilities exist. First, the use of alcohol or other drugs may cause the offender to become abusive. The second alternative argues that alcohol and other drugs act as disinhibitors. They break down the barriers that normally would keep the offender from committing the act. Researchers have not yet learned which of these two possibilities is correct.

Stress, depression, low self-esteem, and similar factors are often proposed as causes of IPV (Hotaling and Straus, 1989; Pagelow, 1984). The basic argument is that the offender, when striking out against his or her significant other, is venting frustration or anger at other people or things with which he or she cannot deal directly. For example, one cannot relieve stress at work by attacking the boss. Instead, one might search for a substitute and turn on an available family member who has little recourse. The abuser simply does not possess the tools with which to channel feelings in a more acceptable fashion. Often, socioeconomic conditions of the family are pointed to as a cause of low self-esteem or stress.

Also considered under the heading of psychopathological causes is the idea that some individuals commit abusive acts because they have learned to do so through past experiences. This intergenerational transmission of violence approach is a learning theory. Proponents maintain that an individual who was the victim of abuse or who witnessed abuse as a child often grows up to be an abuser (Hotaling and Sugarman, 1986; Pagelow, 1984; Straus, Gelles, and Steinmetz, 1980). The available evidence favoring the intergenerational transmission approach is weak and is the subject of much debate (Pagelow, 1984).

Besides attributing violence to a pathological condition of the offender, some people would counter that partners who tolerate such behavior are also pathological. In other words, if a person remains in a troubled relationship and still professes to love the batterer after he or she has beaten the partner, the victim must be sick or crazy. The problem with this perspective is the identification of which psychological traits are conducive to remaining in a violent relationship. Some observers point to *masochism*, or a desire to suffer, as the key ingredient. For whatever reason, victims who stay in a battering relationship harbor guilt feelings or other unresolved psychological problems that seem to welcome punishment. As a result, masochistic persons gravitate toward mates who will oblige their needs by hurting them. Another way to rephrase this notion is that these victims induce their partners to beat them to satisfy deep-seated inner urges to be beaten and hurt. This position reminds us of the material presented in Chapter 1, where we discussed the approach that Menachim Amir took when applying the concept of victim precipitation to forcible rape.

As you might imagine, not everyone accepts this orientation unequivocally (Hamberger, 1993; Pagelow, 1992, 1993). One scholar, in assessing this body of literature, notes:

> [T]here is little that would suggest either that women wish to bring the abuse onto themselves or simply that they are trapped in their homes without options. . . . The women were not passively accepting of abuse as most had attempted to get some sort of help but this did not change things. . . . If they are masochistic, they are staying for the abuse. An alternative is that they are staying *in spite* of the abuse or because of the positive aspects of the relationship. A strong possibility is that although women do have options, they do not *feel* that they do (Rounsaville, 1978: 17-18).

Sociocultural Explanations (Patriarchy)

The sociocultural or feminist perspective views the abuse of women as an outcome of their historical treatment and the current patriarchal makeup of society (Brownmiller, 1975; Burgess and Draper, 1989;

Dobash and Dobash, 1979). As has already been discussed, through-out much of history women were the property of the father or husband, subject to control and discipline. Today's society remains predominantly patriarchal, prompting many feminist writers to argue that women's concerns and problems receive little attention. IPV, therefore, is largely ignored by the male-dominated criminal justice system and society. The "man's home is his castle" view has kept the public outside and the vio-lence inside.

Coupled with this view of a patriarchal society is the perception that violence is an integral part of modern society. It is socially accepted as a solution to problems. The increasing level of personal crime, espe-cially among adolescents, is pointed to as evidence of this trend. A world in which violence and aggression are acceptable ways of dealing with disputes leads many feminists to conclude that males rely on violence to exert their position of power and to support the status quo. The patri-archal society benefits from violence against women. This sociocultural argument also surfaces in explanations of sexual battery and rape (see Chapter 6). The theme of dominance in the sociocultural viewpoint has gained support from a wide range of groups due to the ability to apply this perspective to social class (upper-class domination) and racial (white domination) issues (Buzawa and Buzawa, 1990).

The Social Learning Approach: Learned Helplessness

Closely following the historical components of the sociocultural explanations is the idea of learned helplessness. Some professionals con-tend that battered partners remain in destructive relationships for economic reasons. IPV victims may lack the monetary resources that would enable them to depart. They may have no place to go. They may not be able to support themselves financially. They may have young chil-dren that make support even more difficult. They lack marketable job skills. In short, the circumstances are such that some victims are unable to exert control over themselves or their environments. The per-ceived, or actual, inability to support oneself or gain employment may be an outcome of the historic role of women in society.

According to Lenore Walker (1979), many battered women suffer from the syndrome she identifies as *learned helplessness*. The idea of learned helplessness centers upon three components. The first is the information a person has about what is going to happen. The second aspect is the knowledge or perception about what will happen. This component usually comes from past experiences (or lack thereof). The third portion is the person's behavior toward the event that takes place. Some people believe they cannot influence or control what is about to happen to them. As these perceptions mount and grow more overwhelming, the victim comes to believe she is helpless to alter her environment. In other words, she develops a belief that she is not in charge of the world around her and that she cannot change the flow of events. As a result, the victim becomes helpless in her struggle and may appear apathetic to some viewers.

The Cycle of Violence

Contributing to this sense of helplessness is the reality that battered women are not beaten every minute of the day. Instead, there is a *cycle of violence*, which gradually builds the feelings of being powerless and unable to alter their plight. Walker sees this cycle as consisting of three distinct stages: (1) the tension-building phase, (2) the battering episode, and (3) the reconciliation period.

The *tension-building phase* may be accompanied by minor assaults. During this period, the woman believes she can deflect her husband's bullying. She may calm the situation by conceding to his wishes or by staying out of his way. Her goal is not to prevent the battering behavior but to avoid it. She becomes grateful that small displays of abusive behavior are not as serious as what they could be. Sometimes, she may even make excuses for the man's behavior. Her general perception is that these incidents are isolated events that will end once the irritant is removed. Thus, she is able to rationalize these outbursts.

The second part of the cycle, the *battering episode*, is the culmination of the frustrations experienced in the first stage. At this point, the man is out of control and acts in a rage. As Walker (1979: 55) explains:

> He starts out wanting to teach the woman a lesson, not intending to inflict any particular injury on her, and stops when he feels she has learned her lesson. By this time, however, she has generally been very severely beaten.

A common rationalization regarding these volatile outbursts is the man's claim that he did not fully realize what he was doing because he had been drinking. This *disinhibition* account acts to transfer responsibility away from the abuser and to characterize alcohol as the real culprit. In other words, the alcohol weakened the man's normal behavioral restraints, thus triggering atypical and uncontrollable violence. As noted earlier, however, the evidence for alcohol as a cause of IPV is unclear. This fact has prompted some researchers to conclude that although "there is more than a 'kernel of truth' in the drunken bum theory of wife beating, the findings also provide the basis for demythologizing this stereotype" (Kantor and Straus, 1987: 224). One counselor probably had the best handle on this situation when he stated "While I can't say drinking is the cause of domestic abuse, it definitely pours gasoline on the fire" (Healey, Smith, and O'Sullivan, 1998: 6).

The final phase is the *reconciliation period*. Here the batterer transforms himself into a very apologetic, tender, and loving character. Pleas for forgiveness and promises of a better future often cloud the anger and fear the victim has experienced at the hands of her partner. As Walker (1979: 58) puts it:

> The batterer truly believes he will never again hurt the woman he loves; he believes he can control himself from now on. He also believes he has taught her such a lesson that she will never again behave in such a manner, and so he will not be tempted to beat her.

It is not uncommon for the batterer to shower the victim with tokens of affection during this period. A bouquet of flowers may appear unannounced. Declarations of love abound. There may be many little thoughtful things, reminiscent of romantic days gone by, to prove the insistence of a loving relationship. However, the cycle-of-violence perspective implies that this period too shall pass.

As the couple's relationship proceeds through this cycle again and again, the wife's physical and psychological well-being become compromised. As the Power and Control Wheel contained in Figure 7.6 shows, numerous practices trap the victim in this environment. She might assess her marriage as a failure, but not be able to take any remedial steps. There may be strong religious beliefs, family pressures, and other social considerations that prevent action. Postponement of any resolution to the beatings permits the cycle to continue without any end in sight (Eisikovits, 1996). The woman is trapped; she simply learns to live with the violent spasms that characterize the relationship. The learned helplessness perspective centers on the emotional dependency that develops during an intimate relationship. As society expects, the woman becomes more enthralled with her husband. Simultaneously, an economic dependency also surfaces within the household. One writer (Pagelow, 1984: 313) sizes up the situation quite deftly:

> When a woman leaves her abuser, her economic standard of living very likely takes a drastic drop. If she has dependent children, she must take into consideration the lives and welfare of her children, who have roughly one chance out of two of dropping below the poverty level (two out of three for minority children). Is it any wonder that many

battered women remain with their abusers for many years, sometimes until the children have grown up and left home?

FIGURE 7.6
The Power and Control Wheel

The chart below is a way of looking at the behaviors abusers use to get and keep control in their relationships. Battering is a choice. It is used to gain power and control over another person. Physical abuse is only one part of a system of abusive behaviors.

Abuse is never a one-time event.

This chart uses the wheel to show the relationship of physical abuse to other forms of abuse. Each part shows a way to control or gain power.

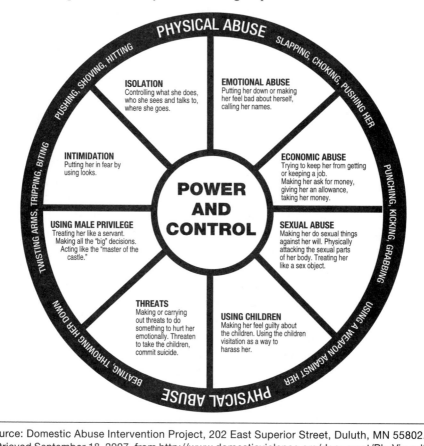

Source: Domestic Abuse Intervention Project, 202 East Superior Street, Duluth, MN 55802. Retrieved September 18, 2007, from http://www.domesticviolence.org/document/PhyVio.pdf Reprinted courtesy of the Domestic Abuse Intervention Project.

Police Intervention

The first point at which society typically becomes involved in domestic disputes is when a police officer is summoned to an abusive episode. Officers who respond to a call involving IPV have a variety of alternatives at their disposal: making an arrest, counseling the parties, referring the couple to professional counseling, threatening to make an arrest, separating the parties, or advising the victim to sign a formal complaint. This portion of the chapter explores some of these options and their limits.

The Arrest Option

While one of the more awesome powers entrusted to police officers is that of arrest, there are several restrictions that limit its utility. The first consideration is the distinction between reasonable suspicion and probable cause. *Reasonable suspicion* permits an officer to intrude into a situation to investigate whether a crime has been committed, is being committed, or is about to occur. *Probable cause*, on the other hand, is more stringent. Probable cause means that the facts and circumstances are sufficiently strong enough to make the officer conclude that the accused is the one who committed the crime under investigation. If probable cause is present, the officer can make a legitimate or lawful arrest. If probable cause is absent, the arrest lacks proper foundation. There is not a lawful custodial situation. Any officer who willfully violates this provision may be the subject of a series of administrative, criminal, and civil penalties.

A second major consideration lies in the distinction between a misdemeanor and a felony offense. The general rule of thumb is that an officer may effect a lawful arrest for a felony offense, either with or without an arrest warrant, as long as probable cause exists. In a misdemeanor case, though, an officer can make a *warrantless arrest* only if the transgression has taken place in his or her presence. This restriction, called the *misdemeanor rule*, can hamper effective police intervention, particularly in situations in which many offenses are misdemeanors, such as IPV.

One recommendation issued by the U.S. Attorney General's Task Force on Family Violence (1984) called for states to revise their provisions concerning arrests in family violence. Most states have responded by relaxing the misdemeanor rule in IPV situations. In other words, an officer can make a legitimate warrantless arrest even though he or she did not observe the crime being committed. The probable cause element, though, has not changed. It still remains the essential ingredient in the decision to take an individual into custody.

Another important determinant in how the police handle a domestic disturbance is whether the suspect is at the scene when the police arrive. If the abuser has left the premises, the officer may not be able to make an immediate arrest. At this point, the officer must assess the extent of injury to the victim. If the injuries are serious and require medical attention, then more than likely the crime is an aggravated battery, which is a felony in most jurisdictions. This classification means the officer can initiate a warrantless arrest. However, if the injuries are minor or nonvisible, then it might be difficult to establish that a crime took place. If probable cause is lacking or if the misdemeanor rule is in effect, then the officer is powerless to make a legitimate warrantless arrest. The only thing that will enable the police to arrest the abuser is if the victim signs an affidavit, and that process usually takes some time.

An *affidavit* is an official complaint in which the victim outlines the details of the offense and swears under oath that the individual named in the accusation is the offender. The completion of this legal document and the issuance of a warrant by a judge give the police proper authority to arrest the suspect on a misdemeanor charge.

Should the suspect be present at the scene when the officers arrive, an evaluation of the arrest option is in order. Bear in mind that if the state legislature has not made IPV an exception to the usual misdemeanor rule, then the officer cannot arrest the abuser for a misdemeanor without observing a violation firsthand. However, if the elements for a felony offense fit, the officer may have probable cause for an immediate arrest.

Nonarrest Options

If an arrest is not possible or if the officer elects not to pursue the arrest option immediately, a variety of other options are at the officer's disposal. The officer may engage in a *mediation* effort. Ideally, this choice involves talking with each party privately to learn each participant's version of what took place. The officer may suggest one or more ways in which to handle disputes of this nature in the future. Alternatively, he or she may try to extract a promise from the disputants that they will not engage in another confrontation after the officer leaves. The officer then exits, in the belief (or hope) that accord has been reestablished.

In other instances, the officer may suggest the couple contact a minister, a counselor, or some other social service agency. The problem with this *referral* option is

that it depends upon the efforts of the citizen for initial contact with the agency to which he is referred. Many of those
involved in domestic disturbances are prevented from seeking assistance by their own fear, ignorance, or lack of initiative (Parnas, 1967: 934-935).

As one psychologist adroitly recognizes, "Regardless of the potential danger, the parties have the Constitutional right to refuse help"
(Bard, 1980: 114). In other words, the police are powerless to compel
individuals to seek family counseling—even if this recourse is in the best
interests of the couple.

Another common tactic is to either threaten or cajole the parties into
peaceful behavior. As one veteran commented, "What can a police officer tell a person who has been married 20–25 years! You just have to
be a good con artist" (Parnas, 1967: 948). Usually this option comes
with the reminder that a return visit by the police will trigger the
arrest of either one or both parties.

Perhaps the most typical response is to separate the combatants.
Officers do not have the legal authority to order an inhabitant out of
his or her own house. However, one prevalent strategy is to request that
the perpetrator leave for a "cooling off" period. Sometimes the request
may go unheeded or the occupant might assert the right to remain on
the premises. In this situation, the officer might try to regain the
upper hand by reminding the uncooperative party of the dire consequences of an arrest. Confronted with a hostile subject and a lack of
legitimate alternatives, the officer might enlist the help of the woman.
The officer might even offer to drive the woman to a relative's house
or to place her and the children, if any, in a domestic violence shelter
for the evening.

The Minneapolis Experiment

Victim advocates and women's groups have long argued that the
police need to take a more proactive role in dealing with domestic violence situations. In particular, they have called for the authorities to
make arrests of offenders rather than resorting to nonarrest alternatives. Underlying these arguments is the assumption that arrest will curb
future IPV acts effectively.

The Minneapolis Police Department, working with the Police
Foundation, agreed to serve as a testing site for an investigation into
the impact of arrest in IPV cases. The purpose of the study was to determine how effective various police responses were in preventing further
episodes of domestic violence (Sherman and Berk, 1984). These

responses included (1) an automatic arrest, (2) having one party leave for a "cooling off" period, and (3) counseling or referral to a social service agency.

Each officer participating in the field experiment received a report pad. This pad instructed him or her about which option to invoke on a particular call. While these actions were predetermined in advance via a randomized fashion, officers could deviate from the guidelines whenever the situation demanded a more appropriate response. Situations allowing for deviation included when the offense was a clear felony, when the officer felt threatened, and when the victim demanded action. To see how well each intervention strategy worked, staff members telephoned civilian complainants biweekly over the following six-month period. The purpose of these telephone contacts was to elicit information about any more domestic violence by the suspect.

Profiles of victims and suspects revealed that 60 percent were unemployed, a considerably higher figure than the area's general 5 percent unemployment rate. Three out of five suspects had a prior arrest record, and almost one-third of the suspected men had a violent arrest history. Eighty percent of the abusers had assaulted the woman at least once during the previous six months. The police had responded to more than one-half of these earlier violent confrontations. One-half of the couples were not married to each other at the time of the study. In short, these men and women appeared to be tormented couples.

Two outcome measures were analyzed. The first indicator tapped whether the police had to return to the residence for another domestic squabble during the six-month follow-up period. The other measure came from the telephone interviews. It indexed any victim reports of repeated violence with the same suspect.

The police blotters showed that officers returned to 26 percent of the households in cases in which the initial strategy was to issue a warning and separate the parties for a brief "cooling off" period. Police recidivism figures reached the 18-percent mark for those settings in which the officer took the counseling approach and registered 13 percent when the officer exercised the arrest option. The telephone accounts showed a high of 37 percent repeaters stemming from the counseling tactic. The low was 19 percent in the cases in which the initial response was an arrest. In short, arrest appeared to be the most efficient way of preventing more IPV between the original combatants.

The researchers combed their data to learn whether an incapacitation effect clouded the results. *Incapacitation* refers to the fact that an offender is unable to recidivate while in confinement. If most of the arrested individuals spent the next six months in jail, the results would not be very impressive. However, further analysis revealed that incapacitation held very little influence on the findings. Almost one-half of the detained suspects were released from confinement within 24 hours of the arrest. Only 14 percent remained in jail one week after their arrest. Thus, it does not appear that an incapacitation effect contaminated or impinged upon the results.

These findings contradict the belief that an arrest merely aggravates an already tense interpersonal situation and that the best course of action is minimal police involvement. First, there was no indication of a revengeful violent escapade once the arrested male returned home. Second, the separation did not produce economic hardships for these women. (Some observers have commented that many wives shy away from the arrest alternative because they rely upon their husbands for a steady income to maintain the household.) Third, the results are even more impressive when one considers the abundant arrest histories—particularly violent confrontations with their wives—that these men had logged.

While proponents embraced these results and used them to lobby for more sustained police action in IPV cases, the researchers themselves were not quite as enthusiastic. Besides reciting the familiar refrain for replicative studies, Sherman and Berk (1984: 270) issued some conservative remarks:

> [A]rrest and initial incarceration alone may produce a deterrent effect, regardless of how the courts treat such cases. . . . Therefore, in jurisdictions that process domestic assault offenders in a manner similar to that employed in Minneapolis, we favor a *presumption* of arrest; an arrest should be made unless there are good, clear reasons why an arrest would be counterproductive. We do not, however, favor *requiring* arrests in all misdemeanor domestic assault cases. Even if our findings were replicated in a number of jurisdictions, there is a good chance that arrest works far better for some kinds of offenders than others and in some kinds of situations better than others.

Reaction to the Minneapolis Experiment

The recognition of IPV as a social problem, as well as the publicity surrounding the Minneapolis Experiment, heralded reaction on several fronts. As one might expect, academicians found flaws in the Minneapolis Experiment. However, mounting public pressure meant the legal system could not sit by idly until scholarly debate resolved these questions. As a result, police enforcement policies changed, and legislatures revamped their criminal codes. What we shall do in this section of the chapter is explore some of these ramifications.

Agency Directives

At one time, many police agencies adhered to a strategy of minimal intervention in IPV disturbances. What this directive amounted to was that officers would not resort to an arrest if they could avoid such action. Such a stance did not tend to bother officers, particularly in light of the mistaken perception that domestic disturbances were the most dangerous calls for police to handle (Garner and Clemmer, 1986; Hirschel, Dean, and Lumb, 1994; Stanford and Mowry, 1990). However, advocacy efforts and lawsuits forced agencies to rescind these informal "no arrest" policies.

The findings from the Minneapolis Experiment forced law enforcement agencies to reconsider their stance. While some administrators maintain a public image of full enforcement, actual field practices fall short of this mark. *Full enforcement* means the police arrest every violator for every illegal act whenever possible. Because such a goal is often impractical, officers engage in selective enforcement. *Selective enforcement* means the police arrest only some violators for some of their actions some of the time. In other words, individual officers are free to exercise their discretion when deciding whom to arrest and whom not to arrest.

Discretion vests officers with considerable latitude in the performance of their duties. It also raises two major concerns (Doerner, 2007: 308). First, the lowest-ranking members of the agency are the ones who determine how official policy translates into action. Second, quite often these decisionmakers are the least accountable members of the agency. That is, their decisions are rarely subject to review. Hence, there are no assurances that actions out in the field correspond to policy guidelines.

One way to circumvent the thorny problem of officer discretion is to remove it. That is exactly what many agencies did when they revamped their IPV guidelines. They outlawed selective enforcement. These new directives, sometimes called *pro-arrest policies* or *mandatory arrest policies*, informed police officers that they must make an arrest whenever feasible in IPV situations. Others, known as *presumptive arrest policies*, assume that an arrest will be made in every case. A decision to not arrest requires a written justification by the officer. Probable cause requirements persist in these new policies. Failure to conform to agency rules and regulations can result in disciplinary action and, if appropriate, termination from employment. In fact, failure to respond appropriately to domestic violence situations also might create a civil liability exposure (Blackwell and Vaughn, 2003). Thus, officers and their agencies have an incentive to adhere to statutory and policy guidelines.

These changes have not come easily. First, many rank-and-file officers resent what they perceive to be an unwarranted encroachment upon their discretion (Steinman, 1988). While there are some indications that mandatory arrest polices work (Simpson et al., 2006), there is other evidence that officers fail to follow mandatory arrest policies (Ho, 2000). For instance, Mignon and Holmes (1995) note that two-thirds of all domestic violence offenders in 24 Massachusetts communities were *not* arrested, despite the existence of a mandatory arrest statute. While arrests increased after the law took effect, compliance remains well below 100 percent. Second, some suspects taken into custody have sued, claiming that mandatory arrest policies unfairly discriminate against males. In other words, if they were not males, officers would not arrest them for IPV. Most of these efforts have faltered.

Some police administrators, in an effort to appease all parties, have shied away from a mandatory arrest policy and have chosen to express a *preference* for an arrest solution. Figure 7.7 contains an example of a written policy directive governing police handling of IPV situations.

FIGURE 7.7
An Example of Police Policy Guidelines Regarding Domestic Violence Arrests

A. Arrest is the preferred response to domestic violence when probable cause exists. That is, when probable cause has been established that an act of domestic violence has occurred, an arrest should be made pursuant to Florida State Statutes Chapter 901. F.S. 901.15(7)(b) and 741.29(5) provide that a law enforcement officer who acts in good faith and exercises good care in making an arrest under this subsection is immune from civil liability that otherwise might result.

B. When determining probable cause, law enforcement officers should consider their observations and any statements by parties involved and any witnesses, including children. Officers shall proactively determine all the crimes for which there is probable cause.

C. Factors which should not be considered in determining whether an arrest will be made include, but are not limited to, the following:
    *   Marital status; sexual orientation; race; religion; profession; age; disability; cultural, social, or political position; or socioeconomic status of either party.
    *   Ownership, tenancy rights of either party, or the fact the incident occurred in a private place.
    *   Victim's request that an arrest not be made.
    *   Belief that the victim will not cooperate with criminal prosecution or that the arrest may not lead to a conviction.
    *   Verbal assurances that the abuse will stop.
    *   The fact that the suspect has left the scene.
    *   Disposition of previous police calls involving the same victim or suspect.

FIGURE 7.7—*continued*

- Denial by either party that the abuse occurred when there is evidence of domestic abuse.

- Lack of a court order restraining or restricting the suspect.

- Concern of reprisals against the victim.

- Adverse financial consequences that might result from the arrest.

- Chemical dependency or intoxication of the parties.

- Assumptions as to the tolerance of violence by cultural, ethnic, religious, racial, or occupational groups.

- Absence of visible injury or complaints of injury.

- Presence of children or the immediate dependency of children on the suspect.

D. The officers making an arrest shall inform the arrestee that domestic violence is a crime and that the State of Florida, not the victim, is responsible for the prosecution.

E. Responding officers shall not initiate discussion of, or accept, a complaint withdrawal or have the victim sign a waiver of prosecution form.

F. Dual Arrests:

1. The Department discourages dual arrests in order to avoid arresting the victim. Where there are allegations that each party assaulted the other, the officer shall determine whether there is sufficient evidence to conclude that one of the parties is the primary aggressor based on the criteria set forth above.

2. If the primary aggressor alleges that s/he is also the victim of domestic violence, then it is imperative that the officer throughly investigate the allegation to determine whether it was an act of self-defense or an act of aggression. If it was a separate act of aggression, then the officer shall make an arrest or request an arrest warrant for the secondary aggressor. If the officer concludes that it was an act of self-defense, no arrest shall be made of the secondary aggressor. If dual arrests are made, the facts supporting each arrest must be clearly documented.

G. Officers shall not threaten, suggest, or otherwise indicate the possible arrest of all parties or the removal of the children from the home, with the intent of discouraging requests for intervention by law enforcement by any party.

Source: Tallahassee Police Department (2007), *Policy Manual.* Tallahassee, FL: City of Tallahassee.

Legislative Reform

Many state legislatures have responded to the problem of IPV with reforms on several fronts. As noted earlier, one popular approach has been to relax the misdemeanor rule. To bypass this restriction, some state legislatures have declared IPV to be an exception to the usual misdemeanor rule. This legislative maneuver removes the "in the presence of an officer" requirement. As a result, a police officer may make a bona fide warrantless arrest for a misdemeanor even though he or she did not witness the violation itself.

Another legislative remedy that gives police officers an immediate response aims to provide safe temporary housing. One fear victims harbor is that the arrested party will return home from jail and embark upon a revengeful rampage. The only alternative available to many women, and one that is often suggested by responding police officers, is to pack their belongings and move their children to a temporary location where they can hide. However, many people do not have the resources to pursue this option. Some are poor; others live too far away from family and friends.

Some social service groups have responded by establishing *refuge houses* or *domestic violence shelters*. The purpose of these places is to provide the battered woman a safe haven where she can live until she decides what to do about the abusive marital situation. The location of these refuge houses remains a well-guarded secret to ensure safety from angry partners who might appear on the premises for retaliation. More recently, some shelters have begun publicizing their presence in an effort to mobilize greater public support (Belluck, 1997). No matter which approach is taken, these havens require considerable finances for housing, furniture, food, clothing, upkeep, and staffing. As Figure 7.8 shows, these escalating costs have prompted some state legislatures to mandate surcharges on marriage licenses and divorce settlements to underwrite IPV centers.

A number of other legislative changes have taken place. Florida police officers who are investigating an incident involving IPV are required by state law to file a written report even if there is no arrest in the matter (*Florida Statutes*, 2007, §741.29). That report must contain an explanation why no arrest was made. In addition, officers must give IPV victims a brochure regarding their rights and remedies, and document that action in the written report.

Other changes are directed at the judiciary. In Florida, persons arrested on a charge of domestic violence are not entitled to bail; they must remain in jail for a mandatory first appearance hearing before a judge who then makes a bail decision (*Florida Statutes*, 2007, §741.2901(3)). In addition, there is a minimum mandatory five-day jail sentence for anyone convicted of domestic violence (*Florida Statutes*, 2007, §741.283). Furthermore, any person convicted of domestic violence in Florida is automatically placed on probation for one year and must attend a batterer's intervention program (*Florida Statutes*, 2007, §741.281).

FIGURE 7.8
How Florida Uses Marriage Fees to Combat the Problem of Spouse Abuse

---

741.01 County court judge or clerk of the circuit court to issue marriage license; fee.—

(1) Every marriage license shall be issued by a county court judge or clerk of the circuit court under his or her hand and seal. The county court judge or clerk of the circuit court shall issue such license, upon application for the license, if there appears to be no impediment to the marriage. The county court judge or clerk of the circuit court shall collect and receive a fee of $2 for receiving the application for the issuance of a marriage license.

(2) The fee charged for each marriage license issued in the state shall be increased by the sum of $25. This fee shall be collected upon receipt of the application for the issuance of a marriage license and remitted by the clerk to the Department of Revenue for deposit in the Domestic Violence Trust Fund. The Executive Office of the Governor shall establish a Domestic Violence Trust Fund for the purpose of collecting and disbursing funds generated from the increase in the marriage license fee. Such funds which are generated shall be directed to the Department of Children and Family Services for the specific purpose of funding domestic violence centers, and the funds shall be appropriated in a "grants-in-aid" category to the Department of Children and Family Services for the purpose of funding domestic violence centers. From the proceeds of the surcharge deposited into the Domestic Violence Trust Fund as required under s. 938.08, the Executive Office of the Governor may spend up to $500,000 each year for the purpose of administering a statewide public-awareness campaign regarding domestic violence.

(3) Further, the fee charged for each marriage license issued in the state shall be increased by an additional sum of $7.50 to be collected upon receipt of the application for the issuance of a marriage license. The clerk shall transfer such funds monthly to the Department of Revenue for deposit in the Displaced Homemaker Trust Fund created in s. 446.50.

(4) An additional fee of $25 shall be paid to the clerk upon receipt of the application for issuance of a marriage license. The moneys collected shall be forwarded by the clerk to the Department of Revenue, monthly, for deposit in the General Revenue Fund.

(5) The fee charged for each marriage license issued in the state shall be reduced by a sum of $32.50 for all couples who present valid certificates of completion of a premarital preparation course from a qualified course provider registered under s. 741.0305(5) for a course taken no more than 1 year prior to the date of application for a marriage license. For each license issued that is subject to the fee reduction of this subsection, the clerk is not required to transfer the sum of $7.50 to the Department of Revenue for deposit in the Displaced Homemaker Trust Fund pursuant to subsection (3) or to transfer the sum of $25 to the Department of Revenue for deposit in the General Revenue Fund.

Source: *Florida Statutes* (2007), §741.

Academic Concerns

Partly due to the tremendous popular and legislative interest in the Minneapolis results, many researchers turned a critical eye toward the project and viewed it as more suggestive than definitive. Flaws in the experiment's design, implementation, and analysis have proved troublesome. In fact, some people considered these limitations serious enough to "make it more appropriate to consider the Minneapolis study a pilot study rather than an experiment with decisive implications for changing national policy" (Binder and Meeker, 1988: 350).

One issue that generated a skeptical reaction involved external validity. *External validity* is another way of asking how generalizable are the results of a study (Campbell and Stanley, 1963: 5). Are the results obtained in Minneapolis applicable to just Minneapolis, or do they apply to other locations? As one critic explains:

> The problem is not that the Minneapolis experiment was a single study; the problem is that it was a *Minneapolis* experiment. Had Sherman and Berk designed a study that collected data from ten cities simultaneously and had the results been consistent across locations, I would not have called for replication. . . . (Lempert, 1989: 155).

A second volley of criticisms focused upon internal validity. *Internal validity* raises the question of whether the treatment caused the outcome or whether outside influences contaminated the experiment (Campbell and Stanley, 1963: 5). For example, the officers who participated in the study volunteered for this duty. Some of these officers became much more extensively involved in producing the data than did others (Binder and Meeker, 1988: 355; Gartin, 1995a). Indeed, three officers supplied the vast majority of all the cases included in the study. Furthermore, officers found it necessary to deviate from the randomly assigned treatment to make an arrest in a number of incidents. While this impact may appear to be negligible (Berk, Smyth, and Sherman, 1988), there is a hint that other complications may be at work (Elliott, 1989: 453-455; Gartin, 1995b; Weiss and Boruch, 1996).

A third area of concern involves a cost-benefit assessment (Binder and Meeker, 1988; Lempert, 1989; Meeker and Binder, 1990). Do the benefits of making a misdemeanor arrest outweigh the costs? What impact do such misdemeanor arrests have on the victim and/or on local jail bed capacities? Is the arrest option an efficient use of scarce police resources? Would other intervention techniques provide more efficient strategies? The following section looks at some of these issues.

The Minneapolis Experiment Replications

The criticisms outlined here, along with a host of other questions, led to the funding of six replication projects. The chosen sites were Milwaukee, Omaha, Charlotte, Colorado Springs, Miami, and Atlanta. While the studies were replications, each site employed a slightly different research design. Rather than use the same battery of possible interventions, the replications tested a variety of police responses, including arrest, mediation, varying lengths of jail confinement, protective orders, and verbal warnings. The most important departure from the Minneapolis study was the increased control over random assignment of responses. In most sites, the dispatcher (or someone else removed from the scene of the disturbance) assigned the response type to officers. In essence, officer discretion was greatly curtailed in the replications.

The results of the replications failed to confirm the Minneapolis findings. In general, there was little evidence that any treatment was significantly better than another at reducing subsequent domestic violence (Sherman, 1992). In Charlotte, for example, arrest did not reduce domestic assaults (Hirschel et al., 1991; Hirschel, Hutchinson, and Dean, 1992), and there is some evidence that recidivism increased after arrests (Sherman, 1992). Similarly, Dunford, Huizinga, and Elliott (1989) reported no difference in recidivism within six months of the initial police contact in Omaha. Further, Sherman (1992) pointed to evidence of escalating abuse in Omaha at the one-year mark.

Sherman (1992), inspecting the reports and data from five of the six replication sites, suggested that arrest has a possible *criminogenic effect*. That is, arresting an offender may cause greater subsequent offending. The only clear deterrent effect of arrest appears in an analysis of apprehensions that resulted from the issuance of an arrest warrant (Dunford, 1990). In this instance, arrest warrants were randomly obtained for Omaha cases in which the offender was not present when police initially responded. Those individuals arrested on a warrant were clearly deterred from further abuse compared to those suspects not arrested. With this exception, arrest had either no effect or was found to increase subsequent abuse.

Sherman (1992) attempted to probe the reasons for the discrepancies between the initial Minneapolis study and the replication projects. First, differences may be due to demographic variation from study to study. Offenders who were employed, married (as opposed to cohabiting), and better educated seem to be deterred by arrest. Individuals with lower stakes in conformity may increase their offensive behavior after an arrest. Second, greater recidivism occurs in longer follow-up time frames, indicating that short-term deterrence may precede even greater long-term abuse. Finally, despite differences and flaws in study designs, there were few consistent differences. Therefore, one cannot attribute variations in results to the research methodology.

While the replication projects greatly tempered the enthusiasm generated by the initial Minneapolis Experiment, Garner, Fagan, and Maxwell (1995) suggested that the conclusions were far from clear. The authors pointed out a variety of questionable assumptions made in the different analyses. A reanalysis of data from all these research sites reported more favorable results. Maxwell, Garner, and Fagan (2001) assert that much more detailed and methodical inspection of the data reveals that arresting batterers appears to reduce future IPV. At the same time, a substantial number of perpetrators who were not arrested did not engage in any subsequent aggressive actions against their partners. A closer look at the pooled data prompted Maxwell and his associates (2002: 66) to conclude that "compared with nonarrest interventions, arrest provides additional safety to female victims of intimate partner assault." However, when offenders did recidivate, they generated approximately seven new assaults within a six-month window. Obviously, the differential impact of arrest on IPV requires further study before researchers can come to a definitive conclusion.

Prosecutorial and Judicial Action

While most attention has been paid to the actions of the police in IPV cases, the victim also can turn directly to the court through the office of the prosecutor. While it is true, then, that not all cases reach the court through an initial police arrest, victims bring few cases (IPV or otherwise) to the prosecutor. The police remain the largest "supplier" of cases for the court.

Evidence exists that there is a high level of attrition in domestic violence cases once they reach the prosecutorial stage. Buzawa and Buzawa (1990) identify a number of reasons for this attrition. First, victims see that there are both immediate and potential costs involved in going through with a case. Among these costs are the possibility of retaliation by the accused, lost time from work, lost income from the accused, lack of companionship, and so forth. Second, many victims change their mind about prosecuting after filing charges. They may no longer see the action as important enough to prosecute or may simply lose interest in the case. Third, victims may feel guilty and assume some of the blame for the abusive act. Fourth, some victims may be using the court for purposes other than to prosecute the offender. They may be trying to teach the accused a lesson, gain revenge, confirm their own status as a victim, or they may have other reasons that do not require completion of prosecution (Eisikovits, 1996; Fischer and Rose, 1995; Gondolf et al., 1994; A. Smith, 2000).

Each of these reasons for case attrition can contribute to yet another factor—pressure by the prosecutor to drop the charges. Based on prior experiences of victims failing to carry through with charges, prosecutors are reluctant to prepare and begin proceedings when they feel it is likely that the victim may withdraw at a later date. Prosecutors, therefore, often influence victims to drop charges by suggesting that the victim was an active participant in the abuse situation. The lack of a clear victim makes a case more difficult to prosecute.

Despite claims that prosecutors often summarily dismiss domestic violence cases, evidence from different jurisdictions reveals that prosecutors make decisions on the basis of case merit more than on the type of case. For example, Schmidt and Steury (1989) note that in cases in which charges were not brought, 45 percent were a result of the fact that victims did not wish to pursue the case, and another 30 percent of the cases rested on questionable legal grounds. Only 14 percent of the cases were deemed not important enough to pursue. Similarly, Sigler, Crowley, and Johnson (1990), in a statewide survey of judges and prosecutors, found the failure to prosecute was due primarily to victims recanting their testimony or a lack of evidence. The most important factor uncovered in the literature is the level of cooperation by the victim. A lack of cooperation often leads to dismissals or a failure to bring charges (Elliott, 1989).

This discussion on whether to prosecute presupposes that such an intervention will make a difference. There have been few studies regarding the impact of prosecution in domestic violence cases. Elliott (1989), in a review of such studies, notes that court actions tend to have little impact on subsequent violence. This conclusion is echoed in one study that shows that no one court sanction was more effective in reducing victim recidivism (Gross et al., 2000). In fact, the evidence is mounting that court-ordered mandatory counseling generally has no impact on subsequent domestic violence. However, it does appear that one subgroup—those men who attend most or all sessions—have much more to lose if they are re-arrested and so they refrain from repeat IPV (Feder and Dugan, 2002; Gordon and Moriarty, 2003). The most notable instance in which prosecution reduces violence is in cases in which past violence was less common and not as serious. These conclusions, however, are drawn from few studies, and much more research is needed before suggesting any significant policy changes.

Besides filing criminal charges against an abusive partner, there is the possibility of taking civil action against the offender. Unfortunately, a woman who has made the decision to leave her partner is usually too destitute to pay the attorney fees and filing costs associated with divorce or other civil petitions. Some states now provide a simplified mechanism to secure an *injunction*, or what some people call a restraining order or a protection order, against the abuser. As of mid-2006, Florida alone had more than 153,000 protective orders in its computerized record-keeping system (Florida Domestic Violence Fatality Review Team, 2007). Under these provisions, the clerk of the court supplies a preprinted, fill-in-the-blanks form to request an injunction or court protection order against the violent party. The clerk also explains how to complete the form. He or she can waive the filing fees if the victim is unable to pay court costs. The clerk also assists in the preparation of these materials. The judge can issue a temporary restraining order on an *ex parte* basis. In other words, the offender does not have to be present in order for the judge to take official action. Any violation of a protective order constitutes a contempt-of-court charge or a separate criminal violation, and any law enforcement officer may then arrest the offender, which is a significant repercussion for men who do not want others to know about their behavior (Eisikovits, 1996; Fischer and Rose, 1995; Sorenson and Shen, 2005; U.S. Department of Justice, 2002; Wallace and Kelty, 1995). In fact, the federal Violence Against Women Act requires judges to enforce injunctions that have been issued outside their states (Eigenberg et al., 2003: 413).

Despite these protections, less than one-half of the women who secure a temporary restraining order go on to obtain a permanent, final order (Zoellner et al., 2000). Perhaps, the process for filing and getting a permanent (as compared to a temporary) court order remains too cumbersome and tedious for these victims (Logan, Shannon, and Walker, 2005). Another possibility is that the experience of obtaining a restraining order might dissuade some women from seeking further formal action. As Wan (2000) illustrates, women may become wary and noncommittal if they encounter court personnel who are intimidating, condescending, or overly bureaucratic. However, there is some evidence that a legislative commitment to combat domestic violence can pay dividends. Dugan (2003) examined various statutory provisions and found that tougher injunction or protective order provisions substantially reduced IPV violence. Figure 7.9 displays an example of a petition form for a court injunction.

FIGURE 7.9
Petition for an Injunction for Protection against Domestic Violence

Before me, the undersigned authority, personally appeared Petitioner
_____(name)_____ who has been sworn and says that the following statements
are true:

(a)   Petitioner resides at: _____(address)_____

(Petitioner may furnish address to the court in a separate confidential filing if, for safety reasons, the petitioner requires the location of the
current residence to be confidential.)

(b)   Respondent resides at: _____(last known address)_____

(c)   Respondent's last known place of employment: ____(name of business
and address)____

(d)   Physical description of respondent:
Race: _____
Sex: _____
Date of birth: _____
Height: _____
Weight: _____
Eye color: _____
Hair color: _____
Distinguishing marks or scars: _____

(e)   Aliases of respondent: _____

(f)   Respondent is the spouse or former spouse of the petitioner or is any
other person related by blood or marriage to the petitioner or is any other
person who is or was residing within a single dwelling unit with the petitioner, as if a family, or is a person with whom the petitioner has had a
child in common, regardless of whether the petitioner and respondent
are or were married or living together, as if a family.

(g)   The following describes any other cause of action currently pending
between the petitioner and respondent: _____

The petitioner should also describe any previous or pending attempts by
the petitioner to obtain an injunction for protection against domestic violence in this or any other circuit, and the results of that attempt _____

Case numbers should be included if available.

(h)   Petitioner is either a victim of domestic violence or has reasonable
cause to believe he or she is in imminent danger of becoming a victim
of domestic violence because respondent has (mark all sections that apply
and describe in the spaces below the incidents of violence or threats of
violence, specifying when and where they occurred, including, but not
limited to, locations such as a home, school, place of employment, or visitation exchange):

FIGURE 7.9—*continued*

_____ committed or threatened to commit domestic violence defined in s. 741.28, Florida Statutes, as any assault, aggravated assault, battery, aggravated battery, sexual assault, sexual battery, stalking, aggravated stalking, kidnapping, false imprisonment, or any criminal offense resulting in physical injury or death of one family or household member by another. With the exception of persons who are parents of a child in common, the family or household members must be currently residing or have in the past resided together in the same single dwelling unit.

_____ previously threatened, harassed, stalked, or physically abused the petitioner.

_____ attempted to harm the petitioner or family members or individuals closely associated with the petitioner.

_____ threatened to conceal, kidnap, or harm the petitioner's child or children.

_____ intentionally injured or killed a family pet.

_____ used, or has threatened to use, against the petitioner any weapons such as guns or knives.

_____ physically restrained the petitioner from leaving the home or calling law enforcement.

_____ a criminal history involving violence or the threat of violence (if known).

_____ another order of protection issued against him or her previously or from another jurisdiction (if known).

_____ destroyed personal property, including, but not limited to, telephones or other communication equipment, clothing, or other items belonging to the petitioner.

_____ engaged in any other behavior or conduct that leads the petitioner to have reasonable cause to believe he or she is in imminent danger of becoming a victim of domestic violence.

(i)   Petitioner alleges the following additional specific facts: (mark appropriate sections)

_____ Petitioner is the custodian of a minor child or children whose names and ages are as follows: _____

_____ Petitioner needs the exclusive use and possession of the dwelling that the parties share.

_____ Petitioner is unable to obtain safe alternative housing because:

_____

_____ Petitioner genuinely fears that respondent imminently will abuse, remove, or hide the minor child or children from petitioner because:

_____

FIGURE 7.9—*continued*

(j)   Petitioner genuinely fears imminent domestic violence by respondent.

(k)   Petitioner seeks an injunction: (mark appropriate sections or sections)

_____ Immediately restraining the respondent from committing any acts of domestic violence.

_____ Restraining the respondent from committing any acts of domestic violence.

_____ Awarding to the petitioner the temporary exclusive use and possession of the dwelling that the parties share or excluding the respondent from the residence of the petitioner.

_____ Awarding temporary custody of, or temporary visitation rights with regard to, the minor child or children of the parties, or prohibiting or limiting visitation to that which is supervised by a third party.

_____ Establishing temporary support for the minor child or children or the petitioner.

_____ Directing the respondent to participate in a batterers' intervention program or other treatment pursuant to s. 39.901, Florida Statutes.

_____ Providing any terms the court deems necessary for the protection of a victim of domestic violence, or any minor children of the victim, including any injunctions or directives to law enforcement agencies.

Source: *Florida Statutes* (2007), §741.30(3)(b).

There are a number of other proposals aimed at improving the prosecutorial and judicial responses to domestic violence. One such idea has been the introduction of victim advocates into the prosecutor's office and the courtroom. The availability of such individuals can help demystify the court process, provide support to the victim, and assist in the successful prosecution of the case. Closely related to this change is the appointment of specific attorneys to handle domestic violence cases and the use of "vertical adjudication" whereby a single prosecutor handles the case from start to finish (Visher, Harrell, and Newmark, 2007: 4). In one jurisdiction, having investigating officers take digital photographs of victim injuries and preserving this evidence resulted in more guilty pleas, a greater number of convictions, and longer sentences (Garcia, 2003). Pretrial domestic violation probation units educate arrested persons about their bond conditions, especially if there is a no-contact-with-victim order, and verify that suspects have acquired an alternative living arrangement (Visher, Harrell, and Newmark, 2007). Finally, many jurisdictions have sought to de-emphasize punishment in domestic violence cases and to promote treatment for both the offender and the victim

Another strategy has entailed efforts to curtail dropping domestic violence cases at the prosecutorial level. Such "no-drop" policies, like the guidelines that appear in Figure 7.10, seek to force victims to carry through with the case and have the state assume the burden of the prosecution (Buzawa and Buzawa, 1990; Davis and Smith, 1995). The thinking behind these no-drop policies is to let the offender know that it is the state, not the victim, pursuing the case and to make abusers accountable for their actions (Berliner, 2003). This practice also extends the time an IPV case is involved in the courts and keeps the batterer under formal scrutiny for a longer period of time (Peterson and Dixon, 2005). Critics, though, question the advisability of coercing victims into prosecution without a fuller understanding of the ramifications (Flemming, 2003; Ford, 2003; Humphries, 2002). Despite the appearance of being harsh, two-thirds of the shelter residents in one study favored mandatory prosecution policies (A. Smith, 2000).

FIGURE 7.10
An Example of a Prosecutor's Domestic Violence Guidelines, Which Contain a "No-Drop" Clause

4. Assistant State Attorney

    A. Charging Considerations

        1. Facts of the case should be considered in light of the following:
            (a) Use of a weapon;
            (b) Seriousness of the injuries and/or threats;
            (c) Defendant's history of violence toward the victim and others;
            (d) Defendant's entire criminal history;
            (e) The potential lethality of the situation.

        2. If a factual basis exists to charge the defendant and there exists a slight corroboration, then the defendant should be charged. Corroboration can be derived from:
            (a) Medical records of the victim;
            (b) Witnesses who overheard sounds that would indicate that a crime occurred;
            (c) Witnesses who observed the offense or injuries, including children;
            (d) 911 tapes;
            (e) Physical evidence at the scene;
            (f) Photographs of the scene;
            (g) Photographs of the victim's injuries;
            (h) Diagram of the scene.

FIGURE 7.10—*continued*

---

3. Prosecutors should be mindful of double jeopardy issues when reviewing cases where an injunction has been issued.

4. If the prosecutor makes a decision not to proceed with prosecution, the file must be documented with a full explanation as to why he or she felt the case could not be prosecuted. Prior to dismissing the case, the Assistant must discuss his or her decision with the Division Chief and the Deputy State Attorney.

5. When a filing decision has been made, the victim is to be notified at each stage of the legal process. The right to appear and to address the Court should be honored. Prosecutors will adhere to all the requirements enumerated in Chapter 960, Florida Statutes.

6. When the case goes to trial, the Assistant State Attorney should meet with the victim and witnesses to thoroughly review their testimony prior to trial.

7. The case should proceed with limited continuances to increase the likelihood of conviction and decrease the opportunity for the defendant to pressure the victim or commit any subsequent violent acts.

8. If a problem surfaces after the case is filed that renders the case unprosecutable, the trial Assistant State Attorney must obtain approval from his or her Division Chief and Deputy State Attorney to *nolle prosequi* the case.

5. Uncooperative Victims

    A. Aggressive prosecution policies have arguably tended to re-victimize the victim by forcing victims to testify against their wills. In some cases where victims fail to appear after being subpoenaed for trial, they have been held in contempt and conceivably have faced a term in jail. The question whether to arrest or incarcerate a victim for failure to appear in court to testify against her abuser is not an easy one to answer. If the victim does not show for trial, the State could choose not to proceed. This action would undoubtedly send the message to abusers that they need only keep the victim away from court with threats or promises and the criminal case will be dismissed. The net result would be to place control of the case in the hands of the abuser. A possible answer is to adopt an official policy that warrants would be requested for victims who fail to appear for trial after being subpoenaed to attend. If such a policy was adopted, it would certainly draw criticisms from victim advocates in our circuit. On the day of the trial, the Assistant State Attorney could decide if he or she could proceed without the victim. If the case cannot be proven without the victim, a continuance could be requested. Then, the Assistant State Attorney could request "An Order to Show Cause" be issued for the victim.

Source: Office of the State Attorney (2007). *Policy Manual*. Tallahassee, FL: Second Judicial Circuit.

Coordinating System Approaches

Instead of thinking that any single agency can have a major impact on IPV, it is more reasonable to assume that coordinated efforts of several agencies will be more effective. Coupling arrest with aggressive prosecution, for example, may reduce subsequent offending more than arrest alone. Indeed, one criticism of the Minneapolis Experiment and its replications was the lack of information on what happened to the offender after the arrest. Unfortunately, relatively few analyses look at broader-based system approaches.

Tolman and Weisz (1995) reported on one coordinated arrest and prosecution program in Illinois. DuPage County instituted a program that included a pro-arrest policy, as well as prosecution based on complaints signed by the police when victims refused to do so. While officers can sign complaints in many jurisdictions, it is not very common, because the refusal of victims to sign generally signifies a future lack of cooperation with the prosecution. In the DuPage program, the prosecution actively worked to gain victim participation in the case. Analyzing 690 domestic abuse cases, Tolman and Weisz (1995) found the highest recidivism levels in cases of arrests with no convictions. Conversely, arrests ending in conviction displayed the lowest recidivism rates. The authors argue that this system approach is more effective than individual agency initiatives.

Another cooperative arrangement holding potential for stemming IPV entails coupling victim or social service agencies with the criminal justice system (Ahmad and Mullings, 1999; Spence-Diehl and Potocky-Tripodi, 2001). The use or inclusion of victim or social service agencies is becoming increasingly common in recent years. Many police departments will call on specially trained individuals to assist in responding to IPV or sexual assault cases. Similarly, prosecuting attorneys often rely on victim advocates and social service agencies to help guide victims through legal proceedings and encourage victims to carry through with a prosecution. In fact, some evidence suggests that this attention enhances victim cooperation immensely (Dawson and Dinovitzer, 2001).

A recent effort in Milwaukee provides a good illustration that the "go-alone" approach often invites failure. Prosecutors in that city unilaterally decided to accept more IPV cases for court action by relaxing the emphasis on victim cooperation. However, there was no corresponding effort to enlist the help of other members of the criminal justice system. Police officers did not receive any training or instruction on how to improve evidence-gathering at crime scenes, victim advocates were not prepared for the increased number of clients, court resources were not increased to handle an expanding docket, and the prosecution staff did not grow. As Davis, Smith, and Taylor (2003: 279) termed it, this situation "was a recipe for disaster." The flood of case filings resulted in substantial delays from start to finish, a rise in pretrial repeat offenses, lower conviction rates, and enormous victim dissatisfaction. These misguided experiences led the authors to warn that "good intentions do not always result in good public policy" (Davis et al., 2003: 280).

Relatively little empirical research has been conducted looking at the use of victim advocates and social service agencies. In one report, Davis and Taylor (1997) analyzed the impact of a program that combined the police with social workers in New York City. This program, the Domestic Violence Intervention Education Project (DVIEP), involved crisis response teams in two main functions. One was to follow up on IPV calls handled by routine patrol. The second function involved educating the public about family violence and invoking system response. The authors were able to make random assignments of IPV cases to either the DVIEP program or normal police intervention. Similarly, the education program was randomly assigned to different households. Unfortunately, the evaluation showed no impact on subsequent self-reports of IPV or on the seriousness of subsequent abuse. On the other hand, the project significantly increased the willingness of respondents to call for police assistance (Davis and Taylor, 1997). It would appear that the project had its greatest impact on altering the amenability of victims to recognize their victimization as a problem and one that required some form of intervention. What is missing from the evaluation is any assessment of the quality of the intervention, especially across cases, and the extent to which the program prompted other positive responses on the part of the victims.

More attention needs to be paid to systemic responses to IPV. These efforts are not uncommon. Unfortunately, few have undergone rigorous evaluation, leaving the programs with little more than faith in their abilities. It would be advantageous to know what type of cooperative intervention works best and in what settings each is most appropriate. As Miller (2006: 1125) explains:

> [A] single solution, such as a single domestic violence intervention program or a mandatory arrest, prosecution, and counseling program for known abusers, is untenable. We know that not all IPV abusers should be arrested. And we know that some abusers, if not incapacitated, will continue a pattern of intimate terrorism that will result in severe, chronic, or permanent injury or death. Imagine a highly curable illness (e.g., bronchitis) that affects 19% of the women in the general population and a different type of illness (e.g., a mutated flu virus) that can threaten the lives of 2% of the women. Are those numbers big enough to warrant therapeutic or preventive strategies? Are they different enough to warrant different responses? (citations omitted).

More Recent Responses

Besides making legislative changes that allow greater police action, such as relaxing the misdemeanor rule, most jurisdictions have responded to IPV by enacting laws aimed at threatening behavior and situations. Perhaps the most notable of these efforts is the growth of anti-stalking laws, outlawing gun possession by domestic violators, court-ordered mandatory counseling for convicted batterers, granting clemency to battered women convicted of killing their partners, installation of a national hotline, and empaneling fatality review teams.

Stalking Laws

While the word "stalking" may bring an immediate picture to mind, there is no single accepted definition of what the term means. According to Wright and colleagues (1997: 487), *stalking* "is the act of following, viewing, communicating with, or moving threateningly or menacingly toward another person." The inclusion of "viewing" and "communicating with" in the definition may surprise some readers. These kinds of actions, however, can create a great deal of anxiety and fear, especially if they are part of a repeated pattern or coupled with other activities. The combination of action with both fear and repetition can be seen in Florida's stalking statute displayed in Figure 7.11.

FIGURE 7.11
The Florida Stalking Statute

---

(1) As used in this section, the term:

    (a) "Harass" means to engage in a course of conduct directed at a specific person that causes substantial emotional distress in such person and serves no legitimate purpose.

    (b) "Course of conduct" means a pattern of conduct composed of a series of acts over a period of time, however short, evidencing a continuity of purpose. Constitutionally protected activity is not included within the meaning of "course of conduct." Such constitutionally protected activity includes picketing or other organized protests.

    (c) "Credible threat" means a threat made with the intent to cause the person who is the target of the threat to reasonably fear for his or her safety. The threat must be against the life of, or a threat to cause bodily injury to, a person.

    (d) "Cyberstalk" means to engage in a course of conduct to communicate, or to cause to be communicated, words, images, or language by or through the use of electronic mail or electronic communication, directed at a specific person, causing substantial emotional distress to that person and serving no legitimate purpose.

FIGURE 7.11—*continued*

(2) Any person who willfully, maliciously, and repeatedly follows, harasses, or cyberstalks another person commits the offense of stalking, a misdemeanor of the first degree, punishable as provided in § 775.082 or § 775.083.

(3) Any person who willfully, maliciously, and repeatedly follows, harasses, or cyberstalks another person, and makes a credible threat with the intent to place that person in reasonable fear of death or bodily injury of the person, or the person's child, sibling, spouse, parent, or dependent, commits the offense of aggravated stalking, a felony of the third degree, punishable as provided in § 775.082, § 775.083, or § 775.084.

(4) Any person who, after an injunction for protection against repeat violence, sexual violence, or dating violence pursuant to § 784.046, or an injunction for protection against domestic violence pursuant to § 741.30, or after any other court-imposed prohibition of conduct toward the subject person or that person's property, knowingly, willfully, maliciously, and repeatedly follows, harasses, or cyberstalks another person commits the offense of aggravated stalking, a felony of the third degree, punishable as provided in § 775.082, § 775.083, or § 775.084.

(5) Any person who willfully, maliciously, and repeatedly follows, harasses, or cyberstalks a minor under 16 years of age commits the offense of aggravated stalking, a felony of the third degree, punishable as provided in § 775.082, § 775.083, or § 775.084.

(6) Any law enforcement officer may arrest, without a warrant, any person he or she has probable cause to believe has violated the provisions of this section.

(7) Any person who, after having been sentenced for a violation of § 794.011 or § 800.04, and prohibited from contacting the victim of the offense under § 921.244, willfully, maliciously, and repeatedly follows, harasses, or cyberstalks the victim commits the offense of aggravated stalking, a felony of the third degree, punishable as provided in § 775.082, § 775.083, or § 775.084.

(8) The punishment imposed under this section shall run consecutive to any former sentence imposed for a conviction for any offense under § 794.011 or § 800.04.

Source: *Florida Statutes* (2007), §784.048.

The three key features of most anti-stalking codes are the existence of threatening behavior, criminal intent by the offender, and repetition in the activity. These three factors are important because there is no other law violation involved in most instances. For example, in the absence of an anti-stalking code, simply following someone around is not illegal, even though it might be construed as harassment (Sheridan, Davies, and Boon, 2001). In fact, some professions, such as private investigation or journalism, typically require one person to follow another. Determining threat or criminal intent is not easy. The usual standard, however, involves recognizing what a "reasonable person" would fear or find acceptable. The requirement for repeated action or a pattern of activity also helps to outline what constitutes stalking. It is important, therefore, for legislation to allow for the distinction between different types of "following" behavior. One example of this evolving notion would be the phenomenon of *cyberstalking*, which refers to harassment conducted via the Internet, e-mail, or other means of electronic communication (Ashcroft, 2001; Office for Victims of Crime, 2002).

As far as IPV goes, stalking often takes place once the victim has decided to end the "cycle of violence." As mentioned earlier, the cycle of violence progresses through three distinct stages: the tension-building phase, the battering episode, and the reconciliation period. However, once the woman is determined to abandon the abusive relationship, the male partner may be at a loss as to how best regain control over her. When the mollifying behaviors that worked so well before fizzle, the male may resort to stalking activity or threats in an effort to thwart her escape (Coleman, 1997; Eisikovits, 1996; Melton, 2007; Roberts, 2005).

The development of anti-stalking laws is relatively recent. Indeed, the first state anti-stalking code was passed by California in 1990, largely in response to the highly publicized murder of actress Rebecca Schaeffer. Since that time, every state and the District of Columbia has enacted some form of anti-stalking legislation.

At the federal level, several pieces of legislation deal with stalking. The 1994 Violence Against Women Act holds offenders civilly liable for violent actions that are based on gender. The Federal Anti-Stalker Act of 1996 addresses stalking that crosses state lines or uses the U.S. mail.

As with any new legislation, many state codes have been challenged on a number of fronts (Bureau of Justice Assistance, 1996). The most strenuous objections have focused on the perceived ambiguity and extensive breadth of the statutes (Bjerregaard, 1996; Sohn, 1994; Thomas, 1997). For example, critics have charged that terminology such as "repeatedly" and "intent to cause emotional distress" is too vague, thus rendering the statutes unconstitutional. Other challenges attack provisions that outlaw such things as "contacting another person . . . without the consent of the other person" or "following" another person. The contention is that this wording is so broad that it criminalizes constitutionally protected behaviors. In almost every case, the courts have rejected these arguments and upheld the constitutionality of stalking laws (Bureau of Justice Assistance, 1996).

Penalties for stalking depend upon past violations, as well as the extent of any injury or threat. Misdemeanor violations typically allow for a jail term of up to one year (Bureau of Justice Assistance, 1996).

Felony violations, however, can carry substantial penalties, particularly if there are aggravating circumstances, such as the use of a weapon, the violation of a restraining order, or a prior conviction. These penalties may include 20 years imprisonment (e.g., Arkansas and Alabama) or fines of $10,000 or more (e.g., Illinois, Kansas, and Oregon). It is also possible that stalking may constitute a violent crime for purposes of "three strikes" laws in some states, resulting in life sentences without parole (Bureau of Justice Assistance, 1996).

Despite the sudden growth of stalking legislation, there is relatively little research on the topic. Most discussions point to media accounts of well-known, spectacular stalking incidents, typically involving celebrities or politicians, or actions resulting in murder (Hickey, 2006; Wallace and Kelty, 1995). Much more common is stalking of women by ex-husbands or ex-boyfriends. Steinman (1993) claims that 5 percent of all women will be stalked at some point in their lives. Similarly, Beck (1992) reports that 90 percent of all women killed by a former intimate had been stalked by the offender prior to the act.

While there is little documentation about the size of the problem, several authors have developed typologies of stalkers and stalking incidents. Geberth (1992), for example, divides stalkers into two basic groups: psychopathic personality stalkers and psychotic personality stalkers. The *psychopathic personality stalker* group is made up of individuals who tend to dominate women and stalk ex-wives or former girlfriends. These individuals are reacting to their loss of control and often intend to commit violence against the victim. On the other hand, the *psychotic personality stalker* haunts television stars or other well-known personalities out of a misplaced sense of love and desire. These individuals delude themselves into thinking that the victim will reciprocate the affections once the offender makes contact.

Holmes (1993) offers a broader-based stalking typology. *Celebrity stalkers* target famous figures with whom there has been no personal contact in the past. Violence may emerge as a response to perceived rejection by the victim. The *lust stalker* targets a series of victims who fit a specific image. This offender seeks sexual gratification from the victim and turns violent when that expectation is not fulfilled. Stalking that involves victims and offenders who know one another falls into two categories: the love-scorned stalker and the domestic stalker. The *love-scorned stalker* knows his or her quarry, but they do not share a past intimate relationship. The offender, however, believes that the victim eventually will come to admire him and return the attention. Failure to do so often results in nonfatal violence. The *domestic stalker* usually crops up after an intimate relationship concludes. The offender haunts the victim as revenge for ending the relationship. A fifth type is the *political stalker*. This offender targets public figures because of their political ideology and often wants to harm the victim. Holmes's

(1993) final category is the *hit stalker*, who trails his or her prey in the role as a paid, professional killer.

Other authors have embarked on similar typological endeavors (Wright et al., 1997; Zona, Sharma, and Lane, 1993). In each case, the researchers are attempting to shed some light on a relatively new area of study. Unfortunately, the categories too often are based on small selected samples of cases and have not been validated in other analyses. The extent to which the results are useful, then, remains a matter for further study.

The extent to which stalking laws will impact the level of domestic abuse is unknown at this time. Most statutes are too new to have undergone extensive impact analysis, although a considerable body of case law is beginning to form (Ashcroft, 2001). It is unclear, for example, to what extent these laws are being used by victims and enforced by the police and the courts. The fact that the statutes have withstood constitutional challenges suggests they should receive attention as a legitimate tool in the fight against IPV.

The Lautenberg Amendment

Congress passed a bill, introduced by Senator Frank R. Lautenberg, that banned gun ownership by any person ever convicted of a misdemeanor domestic violence charge (see Figure 7.12). This amendment to the Gun Control Act of 1968 took effect on September 30, 1996. A number of states followed this federal strategy by either changing their own IPV statutes to prohibit abusers from possessing firearms or by including similar language in the provisions of a restraining order (Nathan, 2000).

The goal behind this initiative is to combat violence against women. IPV homicides made up 11 percent of all homicides committed in this country between 1976 and 2005 (Fox and Zawitz, 2007). Almost two-thirds of these homicide victims were women. More than two-thirds of the spouses and ex-spouses murdered from 1976 through 2005 were killed with firearms (Fox and Zawitz, 2007).

Opposition to this initiative formed very quickly, and a flurry of outcries soon crystallized. Opponents argued that extending a weapons ban to persons *ever* convicted of domestic violence was nothing more than an *ex post facto* law and patently unconstitutional. In other words, additional penalties were being applied to cases that were already concluded and to situations in which individuals had already completed their sentences. Proponents maintained that the critics were wrong: the new laws made possession of a weapon by convicted IPV offenders after the passage date a completely new charge. Because the language outlawed a new behavior, it did not violate the prohibition against *ex post facto* laws.

FIGURE 7.12
An Excerpt from the Lautenberg Amendment

(g) It shall be unlawful for any person—

   (8) who is subject to a court order that—

      (A) was issued after a hearing of which such person received actual notice, and at which such person had an opportunity to participate;

      (B) restrains such person from harassing, stalking, or threatening an intimate partner of such person or child of such intimate partner or person, or engaging in other conduct that would place an intimate partner in reasonable fear of bodily injury to the partner or child; and

      (C) (i) includes a finding that such person represents a credible threat to the physical safety of such intimate partner or child; or

         (ii) by its terms explicitly prohibits the use, attempted use, or threatened use of physical force against such intimate partner or child that would reasonably be expected to cause bodily injury; or

   (9) who has been convicted in any court of a misdemeanor crime of domestic violence, to ship or transport in interstate or foreign commerce, or possess in or affecting commerce, any firearm or ammunition; or to receive any firearm or ammunition which has been shipped or transported in interstate or foreign commerce.

Source: 18 U.S.C. 922.

Observers also noted that the weapons ban meant that law enforcement officers and members of the military with IPV histories fell under these provisions. These persons could not perform essential job functions if they were not allowed to carry a firearm. Efforts to gain a public-interest exemption for these groups have failed (Nathan, 2000).

Finally, others contended that these provisions violated the equal protection clause because harsher penalties were being exacted from misdemeanants than from felons (Nelson, 1999). In other words, convicted felons could petition to have their civil rights restored. If successful, they could lawfully possess a firearm. No corresponding reinstatement procedure exists for misdemeanants. To date, the Lautenberg Amendment has survived these and other challenges.

Court-Ordered Mandatory Counseling

One lingering problem with relying upon mandatory arrest policies as the most appropriate or sole solution to the problem of IPV is that arrest by itself is generally an ineffective response. What an arrest platform amounts to, especially in the absence of any follow-up intervention, is a "Scared Straight" tactic. In other words, fear becomes the overriding motivational factor. While it is true that the deterrence doctrine is an important underpinning for how the criminal justice system operates, it is not always the most efficient practice. As a result, therapeutic interventions that seek to prevent a relapse have become an essential strategy. In fact, Florida, like other states, now requires judges to sentence convicted abusers to participation in a batterer's intervention program (*Florida Statutes*, 2007: §741.281). Although this strategy is appealing, one must bear in mind that there is often a considerable delay between arrest and program enrollment (Healey and Smith, 1998). What this section explores, then, is whether self-initiated or court-mandated participation works better, whether the counseling should deal with only one or both parties in the relationship, and whether therapeutic intervention is a meaningful route to travel.

One scheme for envisioning how treatment produces change within a person is to cast any transformation, whether the topic be abusive action or addictive behavior like cigarette smoking, into a five-step model (Cancer Prevention Research Center, 2007). The initial phase, the *precontemplation stage*, is a point at which the person, although he or she may recognize the need to stop engaging in destructive behavior, has no set timetable nor goals in place. The *contemplation stage* gets the person ready for what is to come. Here, the subject recognizes the need for modification and starts thinking about the best way to embark upon this process. The *preparation stage* occurs when the individual devises a plan and is ready to implement it. The *action stage* comes when the person achieves the goals and makes headway in terms of eradicating the objectionable behavior. Finally, the *maintenance stage* calls for eternal vigilance. At this point, the person must continue the newly learned behavior and not succumb or give in to pressures to revert back to the old destructive behavior.

Abusive partners who wish to alter their violent behavior need a supportive therapeutic environment in which to complete this transition. Up until now, abuser participation in therapeutic activities has been largely voluntary or one-sided. Batterers who seek counseling may start with all the best intentions in the world. Given the myriad of defenses that one may conjure up to defend previous actions, the therapist faces a herculean task with these clients. Usually, a self-referred patient, no matter how energetic and dedicated, is fragile but amenable to treatment (Dutton and Starzomski, 1994). Should the counselor critically confront the client and abruptly challenge his or her fundamental thinking, the chances are that the self-referred person will not return for a second session (Murphy and Baxter, 1997). In such a case, any hopes for change are dashed.

A second important consideration for the therapist is whether to deal with one or both parties in the abusive relationship. Therapists who engage in couple therapy have several focal points in mind. They are aiming to eliminate any psychological or physical violence, to convince the clients to accept responsibility for escalating to violent behavior when arguing, to have clients learn self-control, to establish better communication between the couple, to promote more enjoyable activity for the couple, and to instill the idea that each partner should treat the other with respect (O'Leary, 1996: 451-452).

While this protocol may appear reasonable, critics express serious reservations about it. There is a fundamental disagreement with how the problem is conceptualized. As McMahon and Pence (1996: 453) explain, "such terms as *spousal abuse, physically aggressive couples, or abusive relationships* . . . hide the fact that the phenomenon under discussion is primarily men's violence toward their wives or female partners" [emphasis in original]. When the therapist approaches violent behavior as a symptom of a much larger underlying problem, all the counselor does is deflect attention away from treating the violent behavior. What the therapist should be addressing is the abuser's reliance on violence, not probing for tensions within the relationship, and certainly the counselor should not imply that the wife bears responsibility for helping the male partner change his behavior.

There is some evidence that battered women and mental health workers have divergent perceptions of IPV and that this lack of a common definition undermines the utility of seeking help. The therapist's failure to assess the situation appropriately produces two types of victim disenchantment. They are disenchantment through avoidance and disenchantment through action.

According to Eisikovits and Buchbinder (1996), *disenchantment through avoidance* arises when the counselor sidesteps the issue of violence. Rather than initiate a discussion of the battering, many therapists stand back and wait for the victim to broach the topic. This avoidance or lack of guidance leaves many victims wondering about the therapist's interest. Therapists, on the other hand, try hard to maintain some professional distance when dealing with clients. Instead of seeing this stance as a professionalization strategy, however, victims view it as aloofness or coldness. In other words, what battered women expect from their counselors is quite different from the services they receive.

A second avenue, *disenchantment through action*, further cements the woman's frustration with the therapeutic relationship. Many therapists open a couple session by asking the male to give his version of what is taking place within the relationship. Quite often, the male will make some effort to debunk the woman's rendition. Immediately the woman is thrust into the position of having her truthfulness being evaluated. Furthermore, by transforming the battering into an indicator of tensions within the relationship, the therapist paints the woman as a co-source of the disharmony. As Eisikovits and Buchbinder (1996: 436) explain:

> For battered women, violence is their life, but for the social worker, it is a symptom. Due to self-disclosure, many battered women tend to develop the illusion of interpersonal closeness, whereas social workers respond with "correct," professional role relationships. Social workers attempt to place violence in context, corroborate the women's story, and bring the men into the process to make them part of the solution rather than the problem. Such behaviors are interpreted by the women as evidence of distance and betrayal.

As you can see, there are many complex issues endemic to the role of therapeutic intervention. While the common assumption is that counseling can cure whatever ails the people in an IPV relationship, there are a number of questions that require a critical examination first. At the same time, this discussion has not even delved into the question of which kinds of treatment are more suitable than others, which protocols produce the best success rates, and at what cost (Gondolf, 2000; Healey, Smith, and O'Sullivan, 1998; Jones, 2000; Taylor, Davis, and Maxwell, 2001). While this area will experience further research and greater development, one thing is certain: While court-mandated therapeutic intervention may appear to be a reasonable and satisfactory solution, it is not a simple universal antidote to the problem of IPV. A "one size fits all" approach simply will not work.

Executive Clemency

One post-conviction remedy, executive clemency, provides a course of redress to women imprisoned for killing their husbands or boyfriends. *Executive clemency* means the state governor, either alone or in consultation with a board or panel, commutes or reduces the original court-imposed sentence to a lesser punishment. This humanitarian effort usually comes about after doubts surface regarding the sufficiency of the evidence presented at trial, additional evidence becomes unveiled after the trial is concluded, overlooked aspects of the case gain prominence, the sentence is overly harsh when balanced against mitigating factors, or a host of other reasons (Acker and Lanier, 2000). In capital punishment cases, executive clemency sets aside the death penalty and usually substitutes life imprisonment in its place (Freilich and Rivera, 1999; Pridemore, 2000).

When such a request is filed by an IPV survivor, the claim usually involves the "Battered Woman's Syndrome" (BWS) as an extenuating circumstance or a form of self-defense. Under normal conditions, a person involved in a physical confrontation has the legal obligation to retreat whenever possible. One can become the aggressor and initiate an attack in self-defense only if that person is cornered and has no immediately available avenue of escape. The BWS contends the lethal or violent response by the woman who is in an ongoing abusive relationship represents the culmination of the cycle of violence and learned helplessness. While an opportunity to get out of harm's way might have been present at the time of the incident or the immediate conditions may not have amounted to a genuine threat to the woman's overall health or well-being, her past experiences have convinced her no other feasible alternative exists. In short, she is cornered in her own home (Orr, 2000). Thus, lashing out at the abuser is the only convincing way to end this torment.

The formulation of the BWS as a legal defense had to contend with the portrayal of this phenomenon as either an excuse or a justification. Mental health workers paint BWS as a post-traumatic stress disorder, a mental state. Feminists, on the other hand, object to this depiction. They argue BWS is a normal response to an extremely abusive relationship (Gagné, 1996). This distinction frames the contours of an important legal battle.

The stakes involved here are very high. The excuse route would call for the woman to admit she committed the act but maintain that she lacked responsibility for the deed. Insanity issues would arise here. The justification path requires a similar admission. However, here the perpetrator would point to recognizable mitigating circumstances. The insanity excuse, if believed, could lead to a civil commitment in a mental health facility for treatment. On the other hand, the justification excuse, if compelling, could result potentially in exoneration (Sigler and Shook, 1997: 368).

Generally speaking, five criteria are necessary for clemency consideration under the BWS:

1. the applicant must be a woman;
2. she must be incarcerated for murder of an intimate partner;

3. she must document a history of abusive behavior from her intimate partner;
4. she must have completed a portion of the imposed sentence; and,
5. she must have an acceptable outlook on her experience.

FIGURE 7.13
The Castle Doctrine

Kathleen Weiand was charged with first-degree murder for the 1994 shooting death of her husband Todd Weiand. Weiand shot her husband during a violent argument in the apartment where the two were living together with their seven-week-old daughter. At trial Weiand claimed self-defense and presented battered spouse syndrome evidence . . . in support of her claim. Weiand testified that her husband had beaten and choked her throughout the course of their three-year relationship and had threatened further violence if she left him.

Under Florida statutory and common law, a person may use deadly force in self-defense if he or she reasonably believes that deadly force is necessary to prevent imminent death or great bodily harm. . . . Even under those circumstances, however, a person may not resort to deadly force without first using every reasonable means within his or her power to avoid the danger, including retreat. . . . There is an exception to this common law duty to retreat "to the wall," which applies when an individual claims self-defense in his or her own residence. . . . An individual is not required to retreat from the residence before resorting to deadly force in self-defense, so long as the deadly force is necessary to prevent death or great bodily harm.

The privilege of nonretreat from the home, part of the "castle doctrine," has early common law origins. . . . It is not now and never has been the law that a man assailed in his own dwelling is bound to retreat. If assailed there, he may stand his ground and resist the attack. He is under no duty to take to the fields and the highways, a fugitive from his own home. . . . *Flight is for sanctuary and shelter, and shelter, if not sanctuary, is in the home. . . . The rule is the same whether the attack proceeds from some other occupant or from an intruder.*

Imposition of the duty to retreat on a battered woman who finds herself the target of a unilateral, unprovoked attack in her own home is inherently unfair. During repeated instances of past abuse, she has "retreated," only to be caught, dragged back inside, and severely beaten again.

What [the duty to retreat] exception means for a battered woman is that as long as it is a stranger who attacks her in her home, she has a right to fight back and labors under no duty to retreat. If the attacker is her husband or live-in partner, however, she must retreat. The threat of death or serious bodily injury may be just as real (and, statistically, is more real) when her husband or partner attacks her in home, but still she must retreat.

In conclusion, we hold that there is no duty to retreat from the residence before resorting to deadly force against a co-occupant or invitee if necessary to prevent death or great bodily harm. . . .

Source: Excerpted from *Weiand v. State*, 732 So. 2d 1044 (Fla. 1999).

This post-conviction remedy is an important strategy when attempting to undo previous miscarriages of justice. Once the courts began recognizing BWS as a viable self-defense argument, convicted women started to avail themselves of this new concept. Introducing evidence that documented the existence of an abusive relationship and bringing this new information to an executive clemency board for review offers new hope to women who previously were unable to convince the trial court that this experience was a legitimate justification for the events that had unfolded.

National Telephone Hotline

We often tend to think of crime as an urban phenomenon and forget that problems, such as domestic violence, know no boundaries. These interpersonal difficulties also occur in rural areas and among culturally diffuse groups where remoteness may compound these difficulties (Logan, Walker, and Leukefeld, 2001; Websdale, 1998). Unfortunately, many agriculturally based areas lack a sufficient population density and tax base to support a variety of community service and outreach programs. This recognition has prompted officials to establish a national hotline in an effort to reach out to underserviced constituencies.

The national hotline (1-800-799-SAFE) is available seven days a week, 24 hours a day. Specialists can handle inquiries, make local referrals, and offer advice to callers. Interpreters, who can communicate in more than 140 different languages, ensure that no ethnic group goes unserved. This mammoth effort is an attempt to make sure the problem of domestic violence does not go unanswered in any segment of society.

Fatality Review Systems

Many states have established *fatality review teams* to dissect cases involving domestic violence homicides and suicides (Websdale, Sheeran, and Johnson, 1999). While the exact team composition varies from one state to the next, it is common for participants to hail from the law enforcement sector, prosecutor's offices, medical examiner or coroner staff, victim advocates, probation services, the judiciary, and the academic community. The purpose of these reviews is to study domestic violence deaths and near-fatal incidents in an effort to learn about the underlying dynamics and to improve formal responses. These panels review the history of the participants, examine the events that eventually culminated in such violence, and try to identify possible intervention strategies that could prove useful in preventing future tragedies. While the exact authority of these panels varies, most bodies can gain access to confidential records, such as hospital charts and investigative case files. Usually, the information gleaned from these varying sources is exempt from discovery and legal proceedings. In other words, what is learned from these reviews becomes protected information.

These team reviews try to identify "red flags" or early warning signs so that local agencies can take appropriate action whenever they encounter a situation with similar characteristics (Hassler et al., 1999). For instance, procuring an injunction, fleeing to another state, and prior violence are all tell-tale signs that should alert authorities to the potential for escalation or an elevated risk of violence at the hands of the estranged batterer. As we mentioned previously in the discussion of stalking, the decision to leave an abusive and possessive partner is a critical juncture that often triggers a violent response. Educating health care professionals, judges, prosecutors, victim advocates, and law enforcement personnel about the dangers associated with these and similar circumstances could aid in reaching more accurate lethality assessments and providing appropriate services. For example, some jurisdictions have found that using a dangerousness assessment scale immediately after arrest helps judges decide what steps are appropriate to take in order to ensure the safety of the victim (Goodman, Dutton, and Bennett, 2000; Weisz, Tolman, and Saunders, 2000). Another possibility, electing not to purge expired injunctions from computer files, could provide an extensive data bank that would help social service providers better understand the couple's past and design a more appropriate response to the current crisis. In short, our current understanding of the dynamics that underlie IPV is insufficient when one considers the enormous consequences that all too often accompany this suffering.

FIGURE 7.14
Selected Internet Sites Dealing with Intimate Partner Violence

---

American Bar Association Commission on Domestic Violence
    http://abanet.org/domviol

Domestic Violence Project of Santa Clara County
    http://www.growing.com/nonviolent

Domestic Violence Institute
    http://www.dviworld.org/index.html

Domestic Violence Resources
    http://www.silcom.com/~paladin/madv

FIGURE 7.14—*continued*

Family Research Laboratory at the University of New Hampshire
   http://www.unh.edu/frl/index.html

Florida Domestic Fatality Review Team
   http://www.fdle.state.fl.us/publications/Domestic_Violence_Fatality_Report
   _2006.pdf

Michigan's Battered Women's Clemency Project
   http://www.umich.edu/~clemency

MINCAVA – The Minnesota Center Against Violence & Abuse
   http://www.mincava.umn.edu

National Coalition Against Domestic Violence
   http://www.ncadv.org

National Domestic Violence Hotline
   http://www.ndvh.org

Partnerships Against Violence Network
   http://www.pavnet.org

Office on Violence Against Women (U.S. Department of Justice)
   http://www.usdoj.gov/ovw

Summary

Intimate partner violence is gaining broad recognition as a pressing social problem. People who profess to love one another hurt each other regularly. Abusive behavior appears to be almost an integral part of these relationships. It may be very difficult for an outsider to comprehend why anyone would tolerate being victimized repeatedly in this way. However, as the learned helplessness perspective explains, many people are trapped into staying in an abusive relationship. Fleeing from the abuser is not always a viable option.

Some people look to the criminal justice system—particularly the police—to provide effective relief to IPV victims. While police folklore holds that nonintervention is a more suitable stance, the Minneapolis Experiment suggested otherwise. That study reported less intimate partner violence after the police took the abuser into custody. While there are some doubts over the wisdom of basing public policy upon the outcome of a single study, many law enforcement agencies reacted almost immediately. They instituted policies that instructed officers to make an arrest for IPV whenever possible. More recent studies, however, suggest these policies may have been implemented too hastily. The more prudent path for the criminal justice system to pursue in IPV matters is to retain an open mind and be willing to try different approaches as research and practice dictate. As Davis and Smith (1995:551) explain:

> We have come a long way in changing how the criminal justice system responds to domestic violence cases. Significant reforms have included mandatory arrest policies, no-drop prosecution practices, civil restraining orders, and batterer treatment programs. Unfortunately, research findings on these reforms have not been encouraging, and it is unclear whether these reforms are making victims safer from harm or changing batterers' violent behavior.

Key Terms for Chapter 7

action stage

affidavit

battered woman syndrome

battering episode

celebrity stalker

contemplation stage

criminogenic effect

cyberstalking

cycle of violence

disenchantment through action

disenchantment through avoidance

disinhibition

domestic stalker

domestic violence

domestic violence shelter

ex parte

ex post facto law

executive clemency

external validity

fatality review teams

full enforcement

hit stalker

incapacitation

injunction

internal validity

intimate partner violence

learned helplessness

love-scorned stalker

lust stalker

maintenance stage

mandatory arrest policy

masochism

mediation

Minneapolis Experiment

misdemeanor rule

political stalker

precontemplation stage

preparation stage

presumptive arrest policy

pro-arrest policy

probable cause

psychopathic personality stalker

psychopathology

psychotic personality stalker

reasonable suspicion

reconciliation period

referral

refuge house

selective enforcement

sociocultural explanations

stalking

suffrage

tension-building phase

warrantless arrest

Learning Objectives

After reading Chapter 8, you should be able to:

- Explain the difference between abuse and neglect.

- Understand what is included under the term maltreatment.

- Talk about how child maltreatment was discovered.

- Explain why it took so long to recognize child maltreatment.

- Outline the provisions that appear in child maltreatment laws.

- Relate reporting provisions to the "good faith" standard.

- List the items that should be included in a maltreatment report.

- Discuss the intention behind a central register.

- Identify some problems that still remain in maltreatment laws.

- Gain a feeling for the prevalence of child homicide and child maltreatment.

- Link what we know about maltreatment to its data sources.

- Interpret the relationship between maltreatment, social class, and surveillance bias.

- Compare and contrast theories of why maltreatment takes place.

- Offer some criticisms of the theories that explain child maltreatment.

- Evaluate the "cycle of violence" thesis.

- Present some coping strategies aimed at fighting maltreatment.

- Understand the issues surrounding the registration of sex offenders.

- Sketch some efforts involving legal reform and maltreatment.

Chapter 8

CHILD MALTREATMENT

Introduction

One of the sadder experiences children endure are victimizations perpetrated by family members. Some parents routinely beat their offspring. Others deny them food and affection. Still others sexually molest children. Until recently, these victims had no special legal safeguards. Many states placed the welfare of children under "cruelty to animals" provisions. Fortunately, the diligent efforts of child advocacy groups have changed that picture.

Research in the area of child maltreatment has revolved around three questions. First, how widespread or prevalent are child abuse and neglect? Second, what are the correlates of child maltreatment? Third, what causes people to engage in this type of behavior? In addition to these concerns, this chapter probes what is meant by child abuse and neglect, what child abuse laws cover, and some strategies that people have suggested to combat this problem.

The Discovery of Child Maltreatment

Child maltreatment is not of recent vintage. For most of history, children were looked at as family property. The ancient Romans believed that the father was endowed with the power of *patriae potestas* (Thomas, 1972). In other words, fathers had the right to sell, kill, or allow their progeny to continue to live. The ancient Greeks, especially the Spartans, practiced infanticide and abandonment of physically deformed newborns (deMause, 1974). The story of Oedipus

Rex is testimony to the fact that these practices were accepted among both the lower and higher classes in society. Biblical stories also depict instances of child abuse, such as Abraham's aborted sacrifice of his son Isaac and King Herod's slaughter of the innocents. Other accounts of inhumane treatment have persisted down through the ages. Children were treated no differently from other property owned by the father (Whitehead and Lab, 2006).

Why were children treated in such ways? Both emotional and economic factors help explain this high degree of indifference toward children. First, the life expectancy was very short. The majority of infants died during the first year of life. Therefore, emotional attachments to newborns were avoided as a defense mechanism against the highly probable death of the infant. Second, families simply could not bear the burden of feeding and caring for another member. Children, because they could not work in the field and contribute to the household, represented a drain on the already limited family resources. This status was especially true for female offspring who would need a dowry in order to find a suitable husband.

Children who survived the first few years of life quickly found themselves thrust into the position of being "little adults" (Aries, 1962). There was no status of "childhood" as we know it today. As "little adults," children took part in all adult activities. They were expected to go to work and help support themselves. They received no formal education. Rather, schooling often entailed being sold into apprenticeship in order to bring money into the family and to provide a skill for the child.

This situation persisted into the Industrial Revolution. At that time, the severe economic competition for labor was fulfilled by exposing children to long and arduous work hours under unsafe conditions. The identification of "childhood" as a distinct station in life began to emerge slowly. Infant mortality showed signs of diminishing. Clergy, educators, and other child advocates stepped forward. As the statuses of "child" and "adolescence" emerged, there was a concurrent rise in concern over the treatment of children (Davis, Chandler, and LaRossa, 2004). Society started to realize that youths needed to be handled differently from adults. Local school boards have become enmeshed in long debates over the merits and utility of corporal punishment (Dorne, 1989:21-50; Hyman, 1982; Zirkel, 1990). As the map contained in Figure 8.1 shows, there is a concerted effort to ban the application of corporal punishment in schools. Organizations, such as the American Academy of Pediatricians and the American Psychological Association, have taken a formal stance against corporal punishment. At the same time, Florida courts view corporal punishment as a parental privilege and place disciplinary measures outside the scope of child maltreatment statutes (*Kama v. State*, 1987; *Raford v. State*, 2002; *Wilson v. State*, 1999). In other words, it is not possible for a parent to commit a simple battery against his or her child when administering physical punishment. Of course, if disciplinary measures exceed the level of good taste, then felony charges might be appropriate.

FIGURE 8.1
States Banning Corporal Punishment in Schools

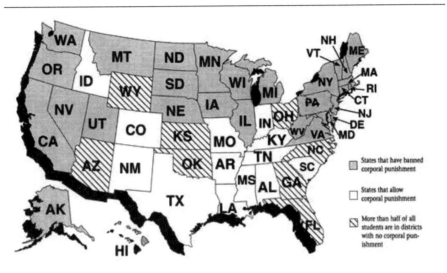

Source: National Coalition to Abolish Corporal Punishment in Schools (2007). "States Banning Corporal Punishment." Columbus, OH: The Center for Effective Discipline. Retrieved on August 30, 2007, from http://www.stophitting.com/disatschool/statesBanning.php Reprinted courtesy of the National Coalition to Abolish Corporal Punishment in Schools.

While the acceptance of maltreatment waned, it did not disappear. The privacy of the home and the assumed sanctity of parental authority allowed much to take place out of sight. What happened within the protected confines of the home was considered to fall beyond the purview of society.

Until recently, child abuse was not easy to detect. John Caffey, a pediatric radiologist, published a study in 1946 outlining bone damage of mysterious origin that he found in some of his young patients. While not accusing parents of being the direct source of these injuries, Caffey (1946) noted that some parental explanations of various accidents were preposterous. Caffey's discovery prompted other physicians to conduct similar investigations. These researchers also stopped short of blaming parents for the intentional infliction of the observed injuries. Eventually, Caffey (1957) came to suspect that parents were responsible for this "unspecified trauma." However, this accusation still did not clarify whether the injuries were intentional or accidental.

The first public denunciation of parents as intentional abusers of their offspring appeared in the early 1960s. In a groundbreaking publication, Kempe and his associates abandoned the term "unspecified trauma" and introduced a new phrase, *the battered-child syndrome*. The Kempe radiological research team (1962: 107) applied this new terminology to "young children who have received serious physical abuse, generally from a parent or foster parent."

This discovery launched a movement aimed at eradicating this newly found concern. Before detailing those efforts, though, two questions arise. First, why did it take so long to discover child abuse, especially because it is such a serious problem? Second, why did radiologists, and not some other medical group, such as pediatricians, discover this phenomenon?

Understanding the Discovery of Child Maltreatment

Four obstacles impeded the recognition of these injured children as victims of abuse (Pfohl, 1977). First, although emergency-room physicians dealt with the physical aftermath of brutal beatings, they did not understand what they saw. Second, physicians were unable to bring themselves to realize that parents would beat their children or inflict such severe wounds deliberately. A third hurdle was the confidential doctor-patient relationship. Physicians generally regarded the parent, not the child, as their client. Disclosing confidential information to the authorities would violate ethical standards. Such action could subject the physician to civil liability and professional censure. Finally, testifying in court would place physicians in the awkward position of having to defend their medical expertise and diagnosis to laypersons.

Concerning the question of why radiologists were the discoverers, Pfohl (1977) explains that radiologists differed from physicians in four important ways. First, radiologists examine X-rays, not people. They can be more objective because they have no direct contact with the patient. Second, the goal of radiology is to discover new diagnostic categories, whereas direct-care providers simply identify a condition and place it into a logical, already existing category. Third, the doctor-patient relationship was not a stumbling block because the patient is the person who is being X-rayed. The fourth and most important point deals with the issue of professional control.

Pediatric radiology was a peripheral medical specialty during the 1950s. It lacked professional prestige. Instead of dealing directly with patients, radiologists conducted research alone in isolated laboratories.

This separation from patients also meant that radiologists did not make glamorous life-or-death decisions. As a result, child abuse offered a unique opportunity for this marginal branch to become more integrated into the mainstream medical profession. After all, it involved the clinical task of diagnosis. Making the correct assessment could spell the difference between life and death for a young patient.

The term "battered-child syndrome" was born. Adding the word "syndrome" after the term "battered child" created a new medical diagnostic category. These facts, coupled with the advances of other professions whose goal was to "cure" abusers through therapy, elevated the discovery of child abuse to prominence. Child abuse became an integral component of medical parlance.

A Survey of Child Maltreatment Laws

Immediately after the "discovery" of child abuse, state legislatures raced to enact new laws. A wave of legislative adjustments followed in the late 1960s and early 1970s. The task was to respond to aspects that were overlooked in the hasty lawmaking process. Except for some minor tinkering, maltreatment statutes have remained largely intact since that time. The passage of a federal law dealing with child abuse and neglect brought greater standardization to state statutes.

Although abuse and neglect fall under the broad and more encompassing term of *maltreatment*, they are two distinct phenomena. *Abuse* is the commission of an act upon the child, while *neglect* refers to the omission of a caretaker function.

To gain a more thorough understanding of child maltreatment laws, our analysis focuses upon a limited range of topics. First, we review the statutory definitions of abuse and neglect. Next, we direct our attention to provisions governing who should report such incidents, what the report should contain, and the central register. Finally, the discussion concludes by pointing out some problem areas that remain.

Statutory Definitions

Most state laws define abuse and neglect in very general terms. The purpose behind this approach is to encourage the reporting of as many suspected cases as possible. By casting out a broad net, the hope is to uncover instances of maltreatment that might otherwise go undetected. Critics, though, charge that such an expansive definition invites excessive governmental intervention.

Abuse generally refers to any nonaccidental infliction of injury that seriously impairs a child's physical or mental health. Most statutory definitions outlaw sexual abuse, sexual exploitation, pornography, and juvenile prostitution. Some jurisdictions make it a point to exclude reasonable disciplinary measures such as controlled spanking of a child by a parent, guardian, or custodian. Although corporal punishment is a common corrective method in this country, there is the fear that it could lead to maltreatment. Most states fail to define emotional abuse explicitly, although virtually every state includes the term in its provisions.

Neglect is the withholding of life's essentials. These necessary ingredients include food, clothing, shelter, and medical treatment. Some states recognize that parents may hold religious beliefs that prohibit them from seeking medical care. They place such persons outside the scope of the neglect definition. However, if the child's condition involves a life-threatening situation or serious disability, the courts will not hesitate to intervene and order the administration of appropriate medical treatment. Some statutes also mention such offenses as failure to make child support payments, alcoholic or substance-dependent parents who cannot supervise their offspring properly, permitting a child to be habitually truant from school, and family abandonment.

The federal Child Abuse Prevention and Treatment Act (42 U.S.C. 5101, *et. seq.*) captures the essence of these statutory details. It defines child maltreatment in terms of three components. First, the act or failure to take appropriate action must produce an unacceptable risk of serious physical or emotional harm, death, sexual abuse, or exploitation. Second, the target of this maltreatment is a child, usually a person under the age of 18 years. Finally, the perpetrator is a parent or caretaker who bears responsibility for the child's welfare and well-being.

As one might imagine, there are a variety of behaviors that fall under the rubric of child maltreatment. Figure 8.2 attempts to capture the breadth of these activities by displaying the major types of child maltreatment along with definitions and examples for each category. Figure 8.3 lists two less common, but just as harmful, behaviors.

The Reporter

A significant element of child abuse laws are the mandatory reporting provisions. Any person who witnesses or learns of a child maltreatment incident has the obligation to report the occurrence to the authorities. Anyone who knowingly fails to make such a report risks a criminal penalty.

FIGURE 8.2
Main Types of Child Maltreatment

Neglect is failure to provide for a child's basic needs. Neglect may be:

- Physical (e.g., failure to provide necessary food or shelter, or lack of appropriate supervision)

- Medical (e.g., failure to provide necessary medical or mental health treatment)

- Educational (e.g., failure to educate a child or attend to special education needs)

- Emotional (e.g., inattention to a child's emotional needs, failure to provide psychological care, or permitting the child to use alcohol or other drugs)

Physical Abuse is physical injury (ranging from minor bruises to severe fractures or death) as a result of punching, beating, kicking, biting, shaking, throwing, stabbing, choking, hitting (with a hand, stick, strap, or other object), burning, or otherwise harming a child. Such injury is considered abuse regardless of whether the caretaker intended to hurt the child.

Sexual Abuse includes activities by a parent or caretaker such as fondling a child's genitals, penetration, incest, rape, sodomy, indecent exposure, and exploitation through prostitution or the production of pornographic materials.

Emotional Abuse is a pattern of behavior that impairs a child's emotional development or sense of self-worth. This may include constant criticism, threats, or rejection, as well as withholding love, support, or guidance. Emotional abuse is often difficult to prove and, therefore, Child Protective Services may not be able to intervene without evidence of harm to the child. Emotional abuse is almost always present when other forms are identified.

Source: Child Welfare Gateway Information (2006). *What Is Child Abuse and Neglect?* Washington, DC: U.S. Department of Health and Human Services. Retrieved on August 31, 2007, from http://www.childwelfare.gov/pubs/factsheets/whatiscan.cfm

FIGURE 8.3
Other Forms of Child Maltreatment

Munchausen Syndrome by Proxy

This syndrome almost always involves a mother abusing her child by seeking unneeded medical attention for him or her. It is rare and poorly understood. The cause is unknown. The mother may fake symptoms of illness in her child by adding blood to the child's urine or stool, withholding food, falsifying fevers, surreptitiously giving emetics or cathartics to simulate vomiting or diarrhea, or using other maneuvers (such as infecting IV lines to make the child appear or become ill). These children are often hospitalized with groups of symptoms that don't quite fit classical disease findings. Frequently, the children are made to suffer through unnecessary tests, surgeries, or other uncomfortable proce-

FIGURE 8.3—*continued*

dures. The affected parent is usually very helpful in the hospital setting and is often appreciated by the nursing staff for the care she gives her child. She is commonly seen as devoted and unusually self-sacrificing, which can make medical professionals unlikely to suspect the diagnosis. Her frequent visits unfortunately also make the child accessible to her so that she can induce further symptoms. Changes in physical exam or vital signs are almost never witnessed by hospital staff and almost always occur in presence of the mother. Munchausen syndrome occurs because of psychological problems in the adult, and is generally an attention-seeking behavior. However, the syndrome can be life-threatening for the child involved because this unusual behavior can escalate to the point of severe physical harm or even death.

Shaken Baby Syndrome

Shaken baby syndrome is a type of inflicted traumatic brain injury that happens when a baby is violently shaken. A baby has weak neck muscles and a large, heavy head. Shaking makes the fragile brain bounce back and forth inside the skull and causes bruising, swelling, and bleeding, which can lead to permanent, severe brain damage or death. The characteristic injuries of shaken baby syndrome are subdural hemorrhages (bleeding in the brain), retinal hemorrhages (bleeding in the retina), damage to the spinal cord and neck, and fractures of the ribs and bones. These injuries may not be immediately noticeable. Symptoms of shaken baby syndrome include extreme irritability, lethargy, poor feeding, breathing problems, convulsions, vomiting, and pale or bluish skin. Shaken baby injuries usually occur in children younger than 2 years old, but may be seen in children up to the age of 5.

In comparison with accidental traumatic brain injury in infants, shaken baby injuries have a much worse prognosis. Damage to the retina of the eye can cause blindness. The majority of infants who survive severe shaking will have some form of neurological or mental disability, such as cerebral palsy or mental retardation, which may not be fully apparent before 6 years of age. Children with shaken baby syndrome may require lifelong medical care.

Source: Van Voorhes, B.W. (2007). *Munchausen Syndrome by Proxy*. Bethesda, MD: U.S. National Library of Medicine. Retrieved on August 31, 2007, from http://www.nlm.nih.gov/medlineplus/ency/article/001555.htm; National Institute of Neurological Disorders and Stroke (2007). *Shaken Baby Syndrome*. Washington, DC: National Institutes of Health. Retrieved on August 31, 2007, from http://www.ninds.nih.gov/disorders/shakenbaby/shakenbaby.htm

As we already mentioned, medical personnel championed the early battle against child maltreatment. However, physicians initially were very reluctant to report suspected cases of abuse or neglect. In fact, when states were drafting their original child abuse laws, the American Medical Association opposed any provision that required doctors to report suspicious cases (No Author, 1964). One reason for this stance was a fear of legal and professional repercussions.

Most states normally regard doctor-patient interaction as a *privileged relationship*. A privileged relationship means there is an inviolable, nonintrudable bond between two parties. The physician cannot reveal any information gathered in that confidential capacity without first obtaining the patient's consent. Should a doctor break that trust, he or she could face a civil lawsuit and professional censure. Some other privileged discussions are conversations attorneys hold with their clients and the confessions that ministers hear from their penitents.

Because the traditional doctor-patient privileged relationship could hinder physician reporting of suspected abuse and neglect, many states created an exemption. Today, the doctor-patient privileged relationship does not exist in child maltreatment cases. In addition, states have extended this protection by granting *legislative immunity* to any person who makes a child maltreatment report in "*good faith*." That is, if a person contacts the authorities out of genuine concern for the child's well-being, he or she cannot be sued if the allegation turns out to be false. However, the obstacles of identifying, understanding, and diagnosing are still challenging steps for attending physicians today (Flaherty, Jones, and Sege, 2004; Flaherty et al., 2006; Leventhal, 1999; Levi, Brown, and Erb, 2006).

The Report

State statutes require that reporters contact authorities about alleged maltreatment as quickly as possible. Some states stipulate that the initial disclosure can be an oral statement, followed a short time later by a written report. The purpose of an oral report is to avoid any cumbersome bureaucratic delays when a child is at risk. The written report must include the victim's name, parents' identity, address, and nature of the injuries. It should also contain color photographs and X-rays, if possible. It also must indicate whether there are other siblings in jeopardy. Figure 8.4 details some of the observations that are useful in trying to establish whether an abusive or neglectful situation exists.

One area of intense legislative debate in some jurisdictions was the issue of to whom to submit the report. Most statutes designate a public social service agency as the primary recipient of child abuse and neglect reports. However, such an arrangement is not satisfactory for at least three reasons. First, most social service agencies conduct their business on a nine-to-five, Monday-through-Friday schedule. Lack of availability and the inability to research family records at night, on weekends, or holidays becomes a key concern. Second, although search-and-seizure guidelines empower the police to make warrantless

FIGURE 8.4
Some Indicators of Child Maltreatment

Physical Abuse

- Unexplained bruises in various stages of healing.
- Unexplained burns, especially cigarette burns or immersion burns.
- Unexplained fractures, lacerations or abrasions.
- Swollen areas.
- Evidence of delayed or inappropriate treatment for injuries.

Physical Neglect

- Abandonment.
- Unattended medical needs.
- Consistent lack of supervision.
- Consistent hunger, inappropriate dress, poor hygiene.
- Lice, distended stomach, emaciated.
- Inadequate nutrition.

Sexual Abuse

- Torn, stained or bloody underclothing.
- Pain, swelling or itching in genital area.
- Difficulty walking or sitting.
- Bruises or bleeding in genital area.
- Venereal disease.
- Frequent urinary or yeast infections.

Emotional Abuse

- Speech disorders.
- Delayed physical development.
- Substance abuse.
- Ulcers, asthma, severe allergies.

Source: The National Children's Advocacy Center (2007). *Physical and Behaviorally Indicators of Abuse*. Huntsville, AL: The National Children's Advocacy Center. Retrieved on August 31, 2007, from http://www.nationalcac.org/families/for_workers/abuse_indicators.html

entries into houses or other structures if an emergency exists, such lawful powers do not extend automatically to non-sworn personnel acting as governmental agents. Third, it is not uncommon for the perpetrator to be present when the social service worker arrives. Because of the potential explosiveness involved and possible violence directed against the social worker, many states also include the police as an appropriate agency to handle child maltreatment reports (Cross, Finkelhor, and Ormrod, 2005). The offender's presence may fuel antagonisms. For example, if the child is in danger, the investigator may place the minor in *protective custody*. In this situation, the worker terminates parental custody for the time being, removes the child from the home, and places him or her in foster care for safekeeping pending judicial review at a later date. In addition to arousing parental anger, this step can stir up resentments within the child. As one victim told the U.S. Attorney General's Task Force (1984: 15):

> Why should I have been taken out of my home? I was the victim. I had [done] nothing. I did nothing wrong. My father should have been taken out, not me.

The Central Register

A critical component of child maltreatment laws is the establishment of a central register. A *central register* is a depository that stores records of all allegations of child abuse and neglect. Register users can index cases by the child's name, parent's name, and perpetrator's name. While many states have had such a tool for some time now, a federal hot-line now exists.

The purpose of this record-keeping system is to help in the diagnosis by tracking relevant case histories. In the past, some enterprising abusers skirted detection by taking the child to a different hospital or a new doctor every time the child needed medical attention. This strategy usually succeeded because the attending physician lacked access to any previous medical records. With the central register, chronic abusers have a more difficult time eluding detection.

Some Trouble Spots

Although child abuse and neglect laws have undergone much revision, some gaps remain. One troublesome area revolves around definitional aspects. Most states have an expansive construction of what constitutes abuse and neglect. However, not everyone views maltreatment in the same way. Social workers and police officers, for example, may regard instances of maltreatment as being more serious than do doctors and lawyers (Giovannoni and Becerra, 1979; Saunders, 1988). Even teachers (Webster et al., 2005) and pediatricians (Levi, Brown, and Erb, 2006) disagree among themselves as to how to categorize cases. Differences also exist between such groups as police, mental health therapists, and child protection services workers (Cross et al., 2005; Deisz, Doueck, and George, 1996; Everson et al., 1996). These divergent definitions can strain already scarce resources by compelling a small staff to investigate a large number of allegations. For example, three out of every five reports alleging child maltreatment during 2005 turned out to be unfounded or unsubstantiated (National Child Abuse and Neglect Data System, 2006: 16). Such a high rate of unfounded allegations is a source of concern that scarce resources are being diverted away from children who really do need attention (Melton, 2005).

A second problem is that not all states place the same degree of emphasis on child maltreatment. Designated violations range from misdemeanors in some states to felonies in other states. Even though the United States does have a national data collection system in place for child abuse and neglect, it may be that variations in state reports stem from differing definitions (Whitaker, Lutzker, and Shelley, 2005).

A third difficulty involves the lack of reporting. Despite statutory protection, many professionals are still reluctant to report suspected instances of maltreatment. Some develop *countertransference*—a sense of guilt, shame, or anxiety that leads to nonreporting (Pollak and Levy, 1988). Others either waiver in their initial assessment that the situation is serious or they fear that an interruption in an ongoing treatment program would halt any progress already made (Kalichman et al., 1990; Willis and Wells, 1988; Zellman, 1990a; Zellman, 1990b).

Finally, the issue of training has not received sufficient attention. Teachers, for example, spend much time in direct contact with children. One might think that teacher preparation courses and state licensing requirements would devote detailed attention to the topic of child abuse and neglect. Perhaps one solution would be for legislation to require specific instruction to all workers whose occupational duties involve routine contact with children (Crenshaw, Crenshaw, and Lichtenberg, 1995; Lamond, 1989; U.S. Attorney General's Task Force, 1984: 74-80).

The Incidence of Child Maltreatment

Measuring child maltreatment is very difficult. These acts usually take place out of the public eye. As a result, it is a very difficult offense to detect. The neighbors rarely see it, and the police have a hard time discovering it. When it is detected, the victim may be too young to explain what happened. As a result, nobody really knows how pervasive child abuse is.`

Although the incidence of child maltreatment remains elusive, the National Child Abuse and Neglect Data System (National Child Abuse and Neglect Data System, 2006: xiv) estimates that 899,000 children were victims of abuse and neglect in 2005. Sadly, 1,460 or 1.96 of every 100,000 American children died from maltreatment in 2005. In other words, four children die from maltreatment every day in this country, with 45 percent being under the age of one. According to the *Uniform Crime Reports*, 182 murder victims in 2005 were infants. Another 328 homicide victims came from the one- to four-year-old age bracket, while an additional 75 criminal homicide victims were between the ages of five and eight (FBI, 2006).

Most observers would agree that these numbers underestimate the true extent of child fatalities due to maltreatment. One review team examined medical examiner records for 1985–1994 in North Carolina. They contended that child abuse statistics actually underestimate the true number of child homicide cases by 60 percent (Herman-Giddens et al., 1999). A similar investigation in Colorado showed that half the maltreatment deaths during 1990–1998 were misclassified (Crume et al., 2002). To combat this problem, some jurisdictions employ *child death review teams* (Durfee, Durfee, and West, 2002). These groups combine the expertise of child protective services workers, law enforcement officers, coroners and medical examiners, health care workers, prosecutors, and others to investigate child deaths to determine whether maltreatment was involved. Some signs that may suggest abuse or neglect would include severe head trauma, the shaken baby syndrome (see Figure 8.4), injuries to the abdomen or thorax areas, scalding, drowning, suffocation, poisoning, and chronic neglect.

NCANDS compiles yearly figures on child maltreatment in the United States based on information provided by state child protective service agencies. According to the best available estimates, authorities received reports involving 3.3 million children alleged to be maltreatment victims in 2005. However, investigators were able to substantiate the allegations in only 29 percent of the cases (National Child Abuse and Neglect Data System, 2006: xiv). A *substantiated allegation* means that sufficient evidence existed to confirm the reporting person's suspicions.

It is important to realize that child maltreatment figures may not reflect actual changes in the level of maltreatment. It is possible that a heightened awareness of child abuse has led to greater reporting of maltreatment by the public, more intensive investigative efforts, and better methods for tabulating the data by interested agencies. Given the historical treatment and place of children in society, it is very likely that the growing numbers are the result of better counting rather than a rampant escalation of abusive incidents. Figure 8.5 contains a visual depiction of the different types of substantiated maltreatment involved in cases handled during 2005. As you can see, neglect tops the list.

FIGURE 8.5
Maltreatment: Types of Victims, 2005

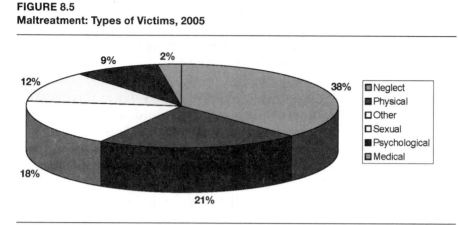

Source: National Child Abuse and Neglect Data System (2006). *Child Maltreatment 2005*. Washington, DC: U.S. Department of Health and Human Services, pp. 41-42.

FIGURE 8.6
Selected Child Maltreatment Statistics, 2005

- An estimated 899,000 children were determined to be victims of child abuse or neglect in 2005

- Children ages birth to 3 years had the highest rates of victimization at 16.5per 1,000 children.

- Girls were slightly more likely to be victims than boys.

- More than 60 percent of child victims experienced neglect.

- While the rate of White victims of child abuse or neglect was 10.8 per 1,000 children of the same race, the rate for American Indian or Alaska Natives was 16.5 per 1,000 children and for African-Americans 19.5 per 1,000 children.

- In 2005, an estimated total of 3.3 million referrals concerning the welfare of approximately 6 million children were made to Child Protective Services agencies throughout the United States.

- More than one-half (55.8 percent) of all reports that alleged child abuse or neglect were made by such professionals as educators, law enforcement and legal personnel, social services personnel, medical personnel, mental health personnel, child daycare providers, and foster care providers.

- 42 percent of child fatalities were attributed to neglect.

Source: National Child Abuse and Neglect Data System (2006). *Child Maltreatment 2005*. Washington, DC: U.S. Department of Health and Human Services.

Figure 8.6 lists some child maltreatment statistics. As alarming as these statistics may be, the reader should bear one thing in mind: no one yet has compiled an accurate count of the number of crippling injuries or the physical and mental retardation cases that stem from this kind of violence. All that we can do at this point is to make ballpark estimates of what suffering our children endure.

Another way to grasp the impact of child maltreatment is to look at the monetary costs associated with this type of victimization. Earlier in Chapter 3, we explained that victims sustain a host of direct and indirect costs as a result of being victimized. If you recall, direct costs pertain to the immediate consequences, and indirect costs include long-term or secondary effects. One national estimate fixes the direct costs of maltreatment victimization in excess of $24 billion annually. This figure includes expenditures for physical health problems and mental health problems, as well as expenses incurred by the child welfare, law enforcement, and judicial sectors. Indirect costs are estimated to be at least $70 billion annually. This category includes special education, long-term health costs, subsequent juvenile delinquency, future adult criminality, and lost productivity from the labor force. All told, this conservative annual estimate totals $94 billion in losses attributable to child abuse and neglect (Fromm, 2001). Another model projects the overall cost of a single child maltreatment case to be around $6 million over the victim's lifetime (Conrad, 2006).

A Word of Caution Regarding Official Maltreatment Statistics

Many people think of child abuse victims as being infants or small children. Quite often, however, the data source itself can influence what one finds. Clinical studies, which are based on counseling records, usually reveal that the very young are victims. Yet, surveys show that child maltreatment spans all ages. Survey data generally record a high proportion of nonwhite victims, whereas clinical studies do not. This relationship probably reflects differential accessibility. Many African Americans, because of their impoverished status, are unable to afford private therapy.

A common finding in family violence research is the relationship between child maltreatment and social class. Reliance upon official records usually shows that maltreatment cases are concentrated at the lower end of the social class spectrum. It is possible that lower-class people resort to violence more often to resolve misunderstandings (Gelles, 1973; Wolfgang and Ferracuti, 1967). At the same time, official abuse and neglect statistics contain an inherent slant. Because members of the lower class come under the watchful eyes of service providers more often, higher rates of detected maltreatment and other problematic conditions should come as no surprise. In other words, it is entirely possible that child maltreatment is just as prevalent in the middle and upper classes as it is in the lower class. "Surveillance bias" may be responsible for this so-called empirical regularity. As Chaffin and Bard (2006: 301) explain, *surveillance bias* "refers to any increased, systematic outcome-related scrutiny that may exist for some individuals or groups but not others." The critical difference is that members of the middle and upper classes have the advantage of more resources. As a result, they can escape monitoring while those of the lower class are not as fortunate. Given this orientation, Gelles (1975; 1980) recommends that attention be focused more upon the "gatekeepers"—the system personnel who have the power to confer the label of child abuse.

At least one researcher has taken this suggestion to heart. Handelman (1979) investigated a variety of alleged maltreatment cases that were referred to a social service agency for official investigation. Taking an organizational approach, Handelman showed how agency emphasis upon certain carefully selected details influenced the degree of intervention required in each case. In other words, the imposition of the label "child abuse" depended upon the presence or absence of certain cues. They included the social worker's interpretation of what constitutes abuse and neglect, the client's amenability to accepting the label of child abuse, and the caseload the worker was currently handling.

Handelman's study shows that the definitional ambiguity surrounding child abuse and neglect, coupled with bureaucratic mandates, may influence the official designation of problem families as abusive families. On the other hand, the system may overlook and discard actual cases of child abuse because the workload is sufficiently high to keep all agency workers fruitfully occupied.

Theories of Child Maltreatment

Explanations for child maltreatment fall into three popular approaches: (1) intraindividual theories, (2) sociocultural explanations, and (3) the social learning approach. Because each way of looking at child maltreatment has its own implications, this section of the chapter will examine each approach briefly and highlight some problems encountered with each model.

FIGURE 8.7
Who Is Committing These Acts?

There is no single profile of a perpetrator of fatal child abuse, although certain characteristics reappear in many studies. Frequently the perpetrator is:

- a young adult in his or her mid-20s

- without a high school diploma

- living at or below the poverty level

- depressed

- may have difficulty coping with stressful situations

- has experienced violence first-hand

Source: U.S. Advisory Board on Child Abuse and Neglect (1995). *A Nation's Shame: Fatal Child Abuse and Neglect in the United States*. Washington, DC: U.S. Department of Health and Human Services, p. 13. Retrieved on September 1, 2007, from http://www.icanncfr.org/documents/Nations-Shame.pdf

Intraindividual Theories

The intraindividual approach views child maltreatment as the product of some internal defect or flaw inside the abuser. Supposedly, this personality deficiency leads "to a lack of inhibition in expressing frustration and other impulsive behavior" (Spinetta and Rigler, 1972: 299). If researchers can identify the disturbances present in child abusers, then the next step is to develop appropriate treatment plans. As one commentator (Melton, 2005: 11) explains, "the assumption [is] . . . that the problem of child maltreatment was reducible to 'syndromes'—in effect, that abusive and neglectful parents were either very sick or very evil and that they thus could be appropriately characterized as 'those people' who were fundamentally different from ourselves." Thus, the psychiatric model is attractive because it tries to locate and treat personality disorders that lead to child abuse.

Steele and Pollock (1974) conducted one of the first attempts to apply the psychiatric model to child abusers. They described their initial patient as a "gold mine of psychopathology." Those insights guided their analyses of 60 families over the next six years. The results revealed that child abusers did not monopolize any one particular diagnostic category. Instead, maltreaters exhibited disorders that spanned the entire spectrum of *psychopathology* or mental disorders. One phenomenon the researchers did focus upon, though, was role reversal.

Role reversal occurs when parents switch roles with children, expecting the child to shower them with nurturance and love, rather than vice versa. When the child fails to provide such emotional support (as evidenced, for example, by crying for a prolonged period, soiling diapers, or being unresponsive), the frustrated parent feels unwanted, rejected, and not loved by the child. Such feelings trigger an aggressive parental response that culminates in maltreatment. Steele and Pollock (1974) trace this infantilism back to the abuser's relationship with his or her own parents. According to them, parents maltreat children because of the inadequate relationship they had with their own parents.

Later research in this vein led Wright (1976) to coin the phrase *"sick but slick" parents*. Child maltreaters do not exhibit serious deficiencies on a battery of traditional psychological inventories. However, closer inspection shows that these subjects were not answering truthfully. Instead, the evaders gave what they thought were socially desirable responses. Thus, child abusers go to great lengths to project an image of themselves as normal parents—probably in order to deflect detection.

Despite these insights, critics point to four concerns that weaken the intraindividual approach. First, the data source is slanted. Most psychiatric inquiries rely upon clinical information as opposed to a random sample from some larger population. As a result, there is no way of knowing whether abusers who seek help form a typical cross-section of all maltreaters. Second, these studies usually lack an appropriate control group. The absence of a benchmark makes it difficult to determine whether attributes isolated as peculiar to abusers are unique or are shared with members of the larger population. Third, there is very little agreement among psychiatric researchers about which exact characteristics distinguish abusers from nonabusers. Finally, much of the research conducted in this vein is *ex post facto*. That is, it occurs after the abuse has taken place and registers very little predictive power.

Sociocultural Explanations

The sociocultural approach looks for events that are external to the individual. This orientation emphasizes the amount of stress found within the family. Such irritants as unemployment, family size, child spacing, and social isolation become focal points.

One typical characteristic of studied abusive families is their location in the lower social strata. Although one possibility is that social service agencies maintain more surveillance over these families, the etiological connection still fascinates researchers. Apparently, other variables act together to aggravate this situation. For example, Gil (1971) reports that one-half the fathers were unemployed when they abused their children. Families that are cut off from neighbors and friends are prime candidates for internal hostilities (Garbarino and Gilliam, 1980). Family size and the amount of spacing between children often create havoc for parents. Unwanted pregnancies, large families, substance abuse, and unsupportive spouses may strain family resources and exacerbate an already tense living arrangement (Gelles, 1980; Smithey, 1997).

The social stress model emphasizes parents' lack of coping strategies (Belsky, 1978). In other words, when parents become stressed, their reactions include a sense of frustration and helplessness. This relative lack of power carries a feeling of not being in control, which makes it very easy for parents to lash out and vent their rage on their unprotected offspring.

The sociological approach to explaining child maltreatment has not escaped criticism. One problem is that the model fails to explain why some stressed families do not turn to child abuse as an outlet. The model also overlooks other available coping strategies. Furthermore, it fails to explain why or how abuse is chosen from all the other alternative strategies.

The Social Learning Approach

Social learning theory focuses upon the absorption of experiences and reinforcement. It means that rewarded activities, or those that go unpunished, creep into the observer's repertoire of what is acceptable behavior. Subscribers find this approach very useful when studying family violence.

Social learning theory has spawned an interest in examining whether maltreatment leads to subsequent impairment. A review of 29 empirical studies analyzing children who witnessed parental violence does find some connection with certain types of developmental problems (Kolbos, Blakely, and Engleman, 1996). There are other indications that being the victim of child maltreatment leads to subsequent delinquent behavior (Doerner, 1987; Doerner and Tsai, 1990; Fagan, 2005; Heck and Walsh, 2000; Kelley, Thornberry, and Smith, 1997; Lansford et al., 2007; Smith and Thornberry, 1995; Thompson et al., 2001; Widom, 1989; Widom and Maxfield, 2001; Zingraff et al., 1993). While researchers have not looked at this linkage thoroughly, it does appear that this relationship might vary according to the kind of maltreatment, the severity of the experience, and the frequency and duration of the victimization episodes. As this body of research becomes more sophisticated over the next several years, investigators should be able to achieve greater closure on this issue.

The principles behind social learning theory also lend credence to the notion of a *cycle of violence*. There is a fear that children who watch their parents engage in violent outbursts toward each other will come to accept these behaviors as permissible. Similarly, children who are maltreated run the risk of thinking that these behaviors are acceptable because their parents performed them. When these children grow up and form their own intimate relationships, these very same acts of violence are likely to surface.

Adherents to the "cycle of violence" thesis more commonly apply it to two forms of family violence (Schwartz, 1989). First, there is the popular notion that abused children will grow up to become child abusers. Second, there is the belief that children who witness spousal violence will become spouse abusers in their relationships. The U.S. Attorney General's Task Force on Family Violence (1984: 2-3) summed up this view when it wrote:

> Children in violent homes "learn" violence in much the same way they learn any other behavior. They observe that violence is a normal way for people to treat one another and a normal way to solve problems. The family violence that occurs today is a time bomb that will explode years later as abused children become abusers of their own children or other children, and as children who watch one parent hitting the other repeat the example in their relationships or the community.

Some family violence researchers feel that this assessment is accurate. While there is limited empirical evidence to support this position (Newcomb and Locke, 2001; Simons et al., 1995), these findings are very tentative. However, this state of affairs did not keep one spokesperson from proclaiming that "[t]he idea that child-abusing parents were themselves victims of abuse, and that wife-beating husbands come from violent families, is now widely accepted" (Straus, 1983).

Not all victimologists share this opinion. There is a great deal of debate over whether past victimization causes future offending. Some scholars maintain that there is still no sound empirical proof for the notion of intergenerational transmission of violence. As far as child maltreatment goes, Gelles and Cornell (1990: 13-17) refer to the "cycle of violence" as a myth that hinders a full understanding of family violence. They reject this idea because it implies that maltreated children are imprinted or programmed to become abusers later in life. Another author explains that her "search of the literature reveals that many writers repeat the claim but few produce any sound empirical evidence to support it" (Pagelow, 1984: 225). In other words, even if the linkage does exist, the definitive research needed to support this claim has yet to appear (Widom, 1989). Pagelow (1984: 254) further chips away at this very point when she concludes:

> [T]here is no scientifically sound empirical evidence that there is a *causal* relationship between being an abused child and becoming an adult child abuser. There is evidence of a weak association, but when up to 90 percent of child abusers cannot be shown to have been abused in their own childhoods, the association can be considered hardly greater than chance.

The existence of contradictory evidence surrounding this unresolved debate suggests that a great deal of additional research is needed prior to making any final decisions about an intergenerational argument. The fact that past victimization may make the individual either an offender or a further victim indicates that different types of intervention may be useful once the initial victimization episode takes place. There is a clear need to identify the causal forces at work here prior to making any fundamental policy decisions for addressing future behavior.

Some Coping Strategies

What can be done to ensure that all children have a safe home and a loving atmosphere in which to grow and develop? One option that the state does exercise is to rescind parental custody and place children in foster homes or in other alternative housing. Such a procedure comes into play in only the most extreme circumstances and is a last-ditch effort. But what else can be done? Some people have suggested public health screening for detection. Others think parenting classes are the key to prevention. Another group advocates the development of profiles of offenders and victims to enhance detection. Further suggestions include more active law enforcement, self-help groups, and legal changes that would increase deterrence. These latter solutions would avoid governmental intrusion into one's domicile. The following materials explore some of these options.

Health Screening

One social policy option that attracts interest is a health screening program. Proponents suggest that public health workers should conduct routine home visits where there are young children and newborns (Leventhal, 2001; National Committee to Prevent Child Abuse, 1996;

Olds, Hill, and Rumsey, 1998). In fact, the U.S. Advisory Board on Child Abuse and Neglect (which no longer exists) is on record as recommending universal implementation of home visits. These home visits would serve a dual purpose. The first goal would be prevention. Workers could help new parents adjust to their offspring by showing them how to care for infants and allaying parental apprehensions. The second objective would be to uncover hidden cases of maltreatment. Such a strategy would avoid the haphazard detection techniques now in use.

FIGURE 8.8
The Hawaii Healthy Start Program

Paraprofessional home visitors call on families weekly (or more frequently, if needed) for the first 6 to 12 months. The first 1¹/₂ hour visit is spent describing the program and the role of the home visitor.

During the first 3 months of weekly visits, the primary focus is on helping the parents with basic family support, such as learning how to mix formula and wash the baby and understanding the baby's early stages of development and sleep patterns, as well as on answering the most common question, "Why does my baby cry so much?"

A great deal of the home visitor's time is spent listening to parents and providing emotional support, helping them obtain food, formula, and baby supplies; assisting them with housing and job application; getting them to appointments; and providing informal counseling on a wide range of issues, including domestic violence and drug abuse. . . .[E]arly in their relationship, the home visitor and the family develop an Individual Family Support Plan, which lists the services that Healthy Start provides, plus assistance available from other social services. The family checks the services they want to receive during the next 6 months. The plan spells out "What we want," "Ways to get it," "Who can help," "Target date," and "What happened."

Source: Earle, R.B. (1995). *Helping To Prevent Child Abuse—and Future Criminal Consequences: Hawaii Healthy Start*. Washington, DC: U.S. Department of Justice.

Although this proposal is appealing to some (Eckenrode et al., 2000; MacLeod and Nelson, 2000), it has some drawbacks. One criticism is that it invites unwarranted governmental intrusion. Two types of errors would surface (Light, 1973: 569-571; Warner and Hansen, 1994). A *false positive error* would occur when a worker misclassifies a nonabused child as a maltreatment case. A *false negative error* entails not diagnosing a child as abused when that child really is a maltreatment victim. Critics fear that these two errors could be high enough to render this approach questionable at best. Proponents counter that a greater emphasis on personnel training and a multistage checking system would avoid the embarrassment of making false accusations and impugning caregivers. However, false allegations can have far-reaching implications for both the accused and the accuser (Hershkowitz, 2001).

The Hawaii Healthy Start Program (HSP) (see Figure 8.8) enjoyed a warm reception from all quarters upon its unveiling. It was heralded as a very promising program, served as a prototype, and was widely imitated in a number of sites around the country. However, some recent appraisals have questioned whether the HSP program is effective in combating child abuse. For instance, Duggan and her associates (2004) found that HSP families did not exhibit significantly lower levels of child maltreatment than families not exposed to similar interventions. In other words, the program had a minimal impact. A second study by the same researchers (Duggan, Fuddy, et al., 2004) noted that the home visitors were not particularly adept at monitoring clients. The overwhelming failure to identify risky behaviors accurately meant that the necessary referrals were not being made, thus curtailing the program's utility in addressing child maltreatment. In other words, gaps between what the program looked like on paper and what it became when put into action compromised the integrity of the model.

These findings have sparked a number of reactions in the literature and have spawned a variety of positions and suggestions (Chaffin, 2004; Chaffin, 2005; Daro, 2005; Hahn et al., 2005; Hassell, 2005; LeCroy and Whitaker, 2005; Olds, Eckenrode, and Kitzman, 2005; Oshana et al., 2005). One spin-off program, Healthy Families America, appears to have sidestepped some of the thorny issues that ensnared the HSP program (Oshana et al., 2005). For instance, the Healthy Families America program is not a "one size fits all" approach. Instead, it continues to adapt to client needs and absorb recommended changes that flow from empirical evaluations. The challenge is to remain focused and continue working toward the goal of making improvements in the lives of children.

Education

The education effort aims to demystify child rearing by providing parents with instruction in child development. Some observers contend that the high school curriculum should contain a family course. Others advocate continuing adult education projects at hospitals, schools, churches, and social service agencies (National Committee to Prevent Child Abuse, 1996; U.S. Attorney General's Task Force, 1984: 68-71).

Although this approach appears attractive, it is not the simple cure one might wish it to be. This option could not be implemented within a very short period of time (Light, 1973: 573). Issues regarding course content, development, and funding have to be resolved. Moreover, once in place, this alternative would require several years before yielding any returns.

Parents Anonymous

Parents Anonymous is a nonprofit national organization with local chapters. Local groups consist of parents who feel they are maltreating or are in danger of maltreating their children. The national organization operates a 24-hour hot-line that parents can call when they need to vent their frustration or anger. Hopefully, talking to a sympathetic person who has encountered similar feelings will curb any violence directed at a child. In some ways, Parents Anonymous resembles

FIGURE 8.9
Parents Anonymous®

Who Attends the Parents Anonymous® Group?

Parents Anonymous® Groups welcome any parent or individual in a parenting role seeking support and positive parenting strategies regardless of the age or special challenges of their children. Parents may be married, divorced, single, grandparents, stepparents, foster parents, teen parents, or even aunts and uncles. Parents at risk or involved with Child Protective Services, domestic violence, homeless shelters, correctional and/or substance abuse programs also attend. In Parents Anonymous®, our important message is "Asking for Help is a Sign of Strength.®"

What Happens in a Parents Anonymous® Group?

- Parents are welcomed to the Parents Anonymous® Group and receive information about how the group operates.

- Parents are invited to share responsibility for planning and operating the Parents Anonymous® Group.

- Parents talk and problem-solve with other parents about parenting issues and challenges.

- Parents determine their own goals and timelines.

- Parents receive a variety of Parents Anonymous® program materials such as the *I Am a Parents Anonymous® Parent* along with newsletters such as *The Parent Networker*, which features stories written by parents for parents.

- Parents give and receive support from other parents during and after meetings.

- Parents expand their network of support with others to help reduce stress and isolation.

- Parents learn about community resources and how to link to them.

- Parents have the opportunity to take on meaningful leadership roles in their family, the Parents Anonymous® Group and their community.

Source: Parents Anonymous® Inc., *Parents Anonymous® Group*. Retrieved on September 7, 2007, from http://www.parentsanonymous.org/pahtml/progNet_p_AdultGroup.html

the Alcoholics Anonymous network. The federal Office of Juvenile Justice and Delinquency Prevention entered into a partnership with Parents Anonymous in the hope that the emphasis on strengthening family ties would help combat both child maltreatment and juvenile delinquency (Rafael and Pion-Berlin, 1999). This partnership builds upon other federal efforts to encourage better parenting skills (Bavolek, 2000).

In order to meet the ideals outlined in Figure 8.9, the members of each local chapter gather for weekly meetings to discuss their successes and failures, both as parents and as crisis interventionists for fellow members. Because membership is anonymous, it is not known just how effective this type of program is in the fight against child maltreatment. As a result, no definitive evaluations have appeared on this self-help project, although such work is currently underway.

Counseling

Another avenue for dealing with child abuse cases emphasizes a treatment or rehabilitation approach. This response seeks to help both the victim and the offender, often involving the entire family. Most treatment interventions revolve around individual and group counseling. Various studies report that treatment programs are successful at engendering more assertiveness in victims and opening up communication about the event and related problems (Maddock, Larson, and Lally, 1991; Owen and Steele, 1991; Woodworth, 1991). At the same time, however, some distrust and suspicion of the offender remains after treatment, and therapy can have a negative impact on the family unit (Levitt, Owen, and Truchsess, 1991; Maddock, Larson, and Lally, 1991; Woodworth, 1991). Wright (1991) evaluated the impact of removing the offender from the home (a common step in familial sexual abuse) and concluded that this action often leads to divorce, distant relations between the missing parent and children, financial hardship, and failed attempts at reconciliation.

Perhaps the most notable result of intervention studies is the almost universal finding that more services are needed than are typically available. Indeed, it may be the absence of available and appropriate services that is the cause of negative treatment outcomes. Among the needs most often cited are increased financial assistance, extended treatment and counseling, more clarity and structure in the expectations of all participants, and the provision of tangential services for related problems such as alcohol and other drug dependence (Levitt et al., 1991; Woodworth, 1991; Wright, 1991).

Sex Offender Laws

Megan Kanka was a seven-year-old girl who resided in a small New Jersey town. Her neighbor, Jesse K. Timmendequas, lived across the street. Timmendequas had a dark secret that nobody in the neighborhood knew about. He had been convicted twice of sex offenses against children and had just been released from prison. He was also living with two other sex offenders whom he had met while in prison. On July 29, 1994, Timmendequas promised Megan that she could play with his puppy if she went inside his house. She did. It was there that he sexually assaulted Megan and strangled her to death with a belt before disposing of her body.

Public outrage over this death spurred state legislatures to pass new laws commonly referred to as *Megan's Laws*. While the exact details vary from state to state, the core requirement calls for public notification whenever a sex offender is released from prison into the community.

These laws typically classify sex offenders into three risk categories with commensurate notification responsibilities (Brooks, 1996). The lowest tier is reserved for convicted offenders who have made numerous adjustments and are least likely to recidivate. The typical requirement is that the state must notify victim and local law enforcement agencies that the offender has been released from custody and is back in the community. The second level is the *sexual offender*. This person is deemed to be a "moderate risk," and an additional notification is made to local schools and youth organizations (e.g., Boy Scouts, Girl Scouts, sports and recreation centers). The highest risk category, *sexually violent predator*, is reserved for the most dangerous offenders with the most proclivity for recidivism. In these instances, the entire community is alerted about the offender's release. Community meetings, press releases, as well as flyers and posters complete with photographs, criminal history, the offender's new address, place of employment, and vehicle tag all serve to advertise this person's presence in the area. The hope, of course, is that enhanced community awareness will spur greater parental supervision over their children and reduce any opportunity for the criminal to re-offend.

Balancing the rights of the offender against the community's concern for protection has ignited considerable debate. Critics have raised a number of objections to these new regulations (Cohen, 1995; Presley, 1999). For one thing, they contend that these practices violate the offender's constitutional right to privacy and the embargo against cruel and unusual punishment. Completing a term of imprisonment, argue some people, satisfies an individual's debt to society. Another worry concerns vigilantism. Beatings, demonstrations, and even arson have greeted some offenders after their much-publicized releases from confinement (Brooks, 1996; Steinbock, 1995). Finally, some commentators maintain that these laws, despite a noble intention, fail to protect children adequately. Steinbock (1995:5) notes that most child molestation is perpetrated by family members and friends, not by strangers. Furthermore, common plea bargaining practices allow many child molesters to sidestep the label of "sex offender" and avoid registration requirements (Pallone, 1995; Pallone, 2003).

These and other issues have brought the dawning recognition that current ways of dealing with sex offenders are ineffective and represent an emotional knee-jerk reaction (Freeman-Longo, 1996; Lieb, 1996; Myers, 1996; Prentky, 1996). Many sex offenders have lengthy criminal histories, are not amenable to treatment, and will recidivate after release. As a result, some states have instituted civil commitment procedures for mentally ill sex offenders in an effort to prevent future victimization. In other words, once a dangerous sex offender completes his or her prison sentence, the state will initiate legal proceedings to confine this person indefinitely in a mental institution.

This strategy came under fire for a number of reasons. First, critics argued that this approach was nothing more than an *ex post facto* law. It imposed additional punishment long after the criminal court had adjudicated the matter. Second, there is the question of *double jeopardy*. Essentially, the offender is being punished twice for the same act. Third, the prospect of a lifetime commitment after completing the terms of incarceration amounts to cruel and unusual punishment. Finally, additional confinement violates plea bargain terms.

The U.S. Supreme Court ruled on this matter in *Kansas v. Hendricks* (1997). Hendricks was a convicted sex offender who had already served a 10-year prison term. As he neared release, the state sought to commit Hendricks to a mental institution as an uncured sexually violent predator. During that trial, Hendricks freely admitted that he quit the therapy program the prison offered, that he had a long history of sexually assaulting children, that he felt that he suffered from *pedophilia* (a sexual attraction toward children), and that he had no control over his urges to molest children. The jury found that Hendricks suffered from a mental abnormality and posed a danger to others; they agreed that he met the criteria for being classified as a sexually violent predator. The judge, then, issued a civil commitment order. Hendricks appealed it on the grounds that Kansas had violated his due process rights and double jeopardy and *ex post facto* protections.

The Supreme Court ruled against Hendricks in a 5–4 decision. It held that the Kansas statute had built in a sufficient number of procedural checks to provide for due process and protect against overzealous application. Furthermore, the Court found that Kansas had distanced the civil commitment procedures from any criminal proceeding and, therefore, the statute was not punitive in nature. The Justices ruled that Kansas was correct to incapacitate Hendricks as a way of protecting society even though no effective treatment was available for his mental abnormality.

Two days after the Supreme Court rendered this opinion, the New York legislature passed a sexual predator act into law. A number of states availed themselves of this protection in quick succession. Figure 8.10 contains excerpts from the Florida version. Today, all 50 states have enacted similar legislation with federal prompting.

FIGURE 8.10
Excerpts from the Florida "Involuntary Civil Commitment of Sexually Violent Predator Act"

394.12 Definitions

   (10)   "Sexually violent predator" means any person who:

      (a)   Has been convicted of a sexually violent offense; and

      (b)   Suffers from a mental abnormality or personality disorder that makes the person likely to engage in acts of sexual violence if not confined in a secure facility for long-term control, care, and treatment.

394.917 Determination

   (2)   If the court or jury determines that the person is a sexually violent predator, upon the expiration of the incarcerative portion of all criminal sentences and disposition of any detainers other than detainers for deportation by the United States Bureau of Citizenship and Immigration Services, the person shall be committed to the custody of the Department of Children and Family Services for control, care, and treatment until such time as the person's mental abnormality or personality disorder has so changed that it is safe for the person to be at large. At all times, persons who are detained or committed under this part shall be kept in a secure facility segregated from patients of the department who are not detained or committed under this part.

Source: *Florida Statutes* (2007), §394.

The U.S. Supreme Court addressed an allied issue in *Smith et al. v. Doe et al.* (2003). Two convicted sex offenders in Alaska protested the fact that their pictures and other personal information were posted on an Internet web site. The respondents argued that because they were convicted and sentenced prior to the passage of this statute, *ex post facto* protections exempted them from the retroactive application of the new law's provisions.

After hearing arguments, the Supreme Court held that the *ex post facto* clause did not apply in this instance for several reasons. First and foremost, the creation of this sex offender registry was done for civil, not criminal, purposes. Because the goal of the statute is to protect the public, as opposed to imposing punitive measures on offenders, this law is civil and not criminal in nature. *Ex post facto* provisions extend only to criminal penalties. Second, many punishments during colonial times were intended to shame or humiliate offenders. The intention of the current register is not to disgrace convicted sex offenders but to provide meaningful information for the greater public good. Third, placing identifying details on the Internet does not expose offenders to a heightened level of ridicule. Widespread publicity is necessary for this notification to be effective and work as intended. Fourth, the register does not restrict the movement of the persons listed on that site. Convicted sex offenders are free to live and work any where they choose, so long as they comply with the registration requirements. Finally, even though the intent is to generate a deterrent effect, one of the hallmarks of criminal legislation, the statute is merely a regulation and not a new punishment. As a result of these considerations, the U.S. Supreme Court upheld the posting of sex offender information as serving a legitimate social function.

In the wake of these and other court rulings, researchers have begun studying the collateral experiences of sex offender registrants (Levenson and Cotter, 2005; Mustaine, Tewksbury, and Stengel, 2006; Tewksbury, 2005; Tewksbury and Lees, 2007). Being stigmatized as a sex offender does carry serious social repercussions. There are reports of registrants being fired from their jobs or enduring other employment restrictions once their status became known. Others have been denied housing, treated rudely, and subjected to other forms of harassment. Additional complaints center around the lack of a process for differentiating between a 10-year or lifetime registration, the inability to get removed from the list if one's risk to society diminishes, and the "one size fits all" mentality that lumps together all types of behavior under the single rubric of "sex offense."

Law Enforcement

Law enforcement action against child maltreatment consists of two general types. There are efforts to enhance police detection abilities, and there are projects aimed at preventing maltreatment. These two activities often overlap.

One suggestion is for law enforcement agencies to construct profiles to identify abusive caretakers and their victims. The construction of offender profiles is a recent, although somewhat controversial, development in crime control. Such tactics help spot drug couriers in airports and assist in other kinds of investigations (Williams and Arrigo, 1999). The Federal Bureau of Investigation, for example, has begun compiling and analyzing data on serial murderers. When applied to child maltreatment, the hope is that this statistical information would target high-risk families for surveillance and therapy.

FIGURE 8.11
Possible Signs of Child Maltreatment

The Child:

- Shows sudden changes in behavior or school performance.

- Has not received help for physical or medical problems brought to the parents' attention.

- Has learning problems (or difficulty concentrating) that cannot be attributed to specific physical or psychological causes.

- Is always watchful, as though preparing for something bad to happen.

- Lacks adult supervision.

- Is overly compliant, passive, or withdrawn.

- Comes to school or other activities early, stays late, and does not want to go home.

The Parent:

- Shows little concern for the child.

- Denies the existence of—or blames the child for—the child's problems in school or at home.

- Asks teachers or other caretakers to use harsh physical discipline if the child misbehaves.

- Sees the child as entirely bad, worthless, or burdensome.

- Demands a level of physical or academic performance the child cannot achieve.

- Looks primarily to the child for care, attention, and satisfaction of emotional needs.

The Parent and Child:

- Rarely touch or look at each other.

- Consider their relationship entirely negative.

- State that they do not like each other.

Source: National Clearinghouse on Child Abuse and Neglect Information (2006). *Recognizing Child Abuse and Neglect: Signs and Symptoms*. Washington, DC: Child Welfare Information Gateway. Retrieved on September 4, 2007, from http:/www.childwelfare.gov/pubs/factsheets/signs.cfm

Unfortunately, a host of compromising factors plagues current efforts. For example, information comes only from known abusers. Without a good data source, this approach has serious limitations. Figures 8.11 and 8.12 display materials developed by the National Clearinghouse on Child Abuse and Neglect Information in an effort to increase public awareness.

FIGURE 8.12
Signs of Specific Types of Child Maltreatment

Signs of Physical Abuse

Consider the possibility of physical abuse when the child:

- Has unexplained burns, bites, bruises, broken bones, or black eyes.
- Has fading bruises or other marks noticeable after an absence from school.
- Seems frightened of the parents and protests or cries when it is time to go home.
- Shrinks at the approach of adults.
- Reports injury by a parent or another adult caregiver

Consider the possibility of physical abuse when the parent or other adult caregiver:

- Offers conflicting, unconvincing, or no explanation for the child's injury.
- Describes the child as "evil," or in some other very negative way.
- Uses harsh physical discipline with the child.
- Has a history of abuse as a child.

Signs of Neglect

Consider the possibility of neglect when the child:

- Is frequently absent from school.
- Begs or steals food or money.
- Lacks needed medical or dental care, immunizations, or glasses.
- Is consistently dirty and has severe body odor.
- Lacks sufficient clothing for the weather.
- Abuses alcohol or other drugs.
- States that there is no one at home to provide care.

Consider the possibility of neglect when the parent or other adult caregiver:

- Appears to be indifferent to the child.
- Seems apathetic or depressed.
- Behaves irrationally or in a bizarre manner.
- Is abusing alcohol or other drugs.

Source: National Clearinghouse on Child Abuse and Neglect Information (2006). *Recognizing Child Abuse and Neglect: Signs and Symptoms*. Washington, DC: Child Welfare Information Gateway. Retrieved on September 4, 2007, from http://www.childwelfare.gov/pubs/factsheets/signs.cfm

Another prevention tactic calls for the licensing of all caregivers who have contact with children. Florida, for example, stipulates that all private and public employees who deal with children must undergo a pre-employment background check. They must submit a set of fingerprints and not be a convicted felon. Applicants must also complete a 40-hour course to become a licensed child care worker. Failure to comply with these standards automatically results in licensing disqualification (*Florida Statutes*, 2007: §402.305).

Other novel approaches are surfacing all over the country. One such imaginative venture has been to enlist the help of robots (Norton, 1987). Besides giving the usual safety presentations to school children, some police agencies use robot celebrities to help talk with abuse victims. The robot can be equipped with a video recorder, television monitor, camera, and microphone to preserve interview sessions for prosecution.

Other departments rely upon "drawing interviews" in which the child constructs pictures to explain graphically what happened to him or her (Farley, 1987). Puppet shows tend to fascinate children and are useful in explaining "good," "bad," and "secret" touches. Local businesses sometimes sponsor fingerprint programs to help combat the missing children problem. Police agencies have started the School Resource Officer Program in which officers are assigned to school counseling programs. Some departments promote "Officer Friendly" outings in which officers meet school-age children and explain how the police like to help children (Klappers, 1985).

The use of anatomically correct dolls as an investigative technique in sexual abuse cases is another frequently employed approach (Berliner, 1988; Boat and Everson, 1988; Maan, 1991; Walker, 1988). Quite often, the victim is too immature or naive to express himself or herself adequately. The child may also feel confused because he or she is pitted against a parent or other adult for whom the victim may maintain a sense of loyalty, love, and concern. The child is faced with denying one set of feelings while emphasizing another. To help quell this trauma, the youngster can indicate what happened by using dolls. Despite its popularity, there is some concern that a standard clinical protocol has not emerged governing the use of anatomically correct dolls (Everson and Boat, 1994; Levy et al., 1995; Skinner and Berry, 1993; Williams, Weiner, and MacMillan, 2005; Wolfner, Faust, and Dawes, 1993). As a matter of fact, the American Psychological Association (1991) passed a resolution warning against the unquestioned reliance of this forensic tool.

Legal Reform

Participation in criminal justice system proceedings can be a traumatic experience for children. In fact, the American Bar Association

(1996) requires attorneys to consider the child's well-being carefully before deciding whether the victim should testify in court. However, victim testimony is a crucial component in an adversarial system of justice. Without a victim's account, most cases are simply not prosecutable. As a result, some jurisdictions employ victim counselors to help combat the emotional upheaval that victims incur and to sustain victim credibility by increasing cognitive recall (Geiselman, Bornstein, and Saywitz, 1992). The content of these disclosures may fall under the protection of victim-counselor privilege laws in some states (Office for Victims of Crime, 2002). Figure 8.13 contains several recommendations issued by the U.S. Attorney General when dealing with child abuse cases.

FIGURE 8.13
U.S. Attorney General Guidelines for Prosecutions Involving Child Victims and Child Witnesses

Closing the Courtroom

When a child testifies, the court may order the exclusion from the courtroom of all persons, including members of the press, who do not have a direct interest in the case. Such an order may be made if the court determines, on the record, that requiring the child to testify in open court would cause substantial psychological harm to the child or would result in the child's inability to communicate effectively.

Speedy Trial

In a proceeding in which a child is called to give testimony, the court may *sua sponte* or on a motion by the attorney for the Government or a guardian *ad litem* designate the case as being of special public importance. Attorneys for the Government should consider moving the court to make such a designation in any case involving a child witness for the Government. In cases so designated, the court shall expedite the proceeding and ensure that it takes precedence over any other. The court shall ensure a speedy trial to minimize the length of time the child must endure the stress of involvement with the criminal justice process. When deciding whether to grant a continuance, the court shall take into consideration the age of the child and the potential adverse impact the delay may have on the child's well-being.

Adult Attendant

A child testifying at or attending a judicial proceeding has the right to be accompanied by an adult attendant to provide emotional support for the child (18 U.S.C. §3509(1)). The statute permits the court, at its discretion, to allow the adult attendant to remain in close physical proximity to or in contact with the child while the child testifies. The court may allow the adult attendant to hold the child's hand or allow the child to sit on the adult attendant's lap throughout the course of the proceeding. The adult attendant shall not provide the child with an answer to any question directed to the child during the course of the child's testimony or otherwise prompt the child. Federal prosecutors should inform children and their guardians of this right and facilitate its implementation.

FIGURE 8.13—*continued*

Testimonial Aids

The court may permit a child to use anatomical dolls, puppets, drawings, mannequins, or any other demonstrative device the court deems appropriate for the purpose of assisting a child in testifying.

Alternatives to Live, In-Court Testimony by Child Victims

Federal statute permits prosecutors to use live testimony by closed-circuit television and videotape depositions as alternatives to live, in-court testimony from child witnesses in cases involving offenses against children, when the court finds that the child is unable to testify in open court for any of the following reasons:

1. The child is unable to testify because of fear.

2. There is a substantial likelihood, established by expert testimony, that the child would suffer emotional trauma from testifying.

Notwithstanding the foregoing statutory authority, prosecutors should be aware that constitutional constraints arguably require three criteria to be satisfied before any alternative to live, in-court testimony can be used:

1. In-court testimony would traumatize the child witness.

2. The trauma would result from the presence of the defendant.

3. The trauma would render the child witness unable to communicate.

If the court orders the taking of the child's testimony by closed-circuit television, the attorney for the Government and the attorney for the defendant (not including a defendant appearing *pro se*) shall be present in a room outside the courtroom with the child and the child shall be subjected to direct and cross-examination. The only other persons who may be permitted in the room with the child during the child's testimony are the child's attorney or guardian *ad litem*; persons necessary to operate the closed-circuit television equipment; a judicial officer, appointed by the court; and other persons whose presence is determined by the court to be necessary to the welfare and well-being of the child, including an adult attendant.

The child's testimony shall be transmitted by closed-circuit television into the courtroom for viewing and hearing by the defendant, jury, judge, and public. The defendant shall be provided with the means of private, contemporaneous communication with the defendant's attorney during the testimony. The closed-circuit television transmission shall relay the defendant's image and the voice of the judge into the room in which the child is testifying.

Source: Excerpted from U.S. Attorney General (2005). *Attorney General Guidelines for Victim and Witness Assistance*, pp. 51-55. Washington, DC: U.S. Department of Justice, Office for Victims of Crime. Retrieved on September 7, 2007, from http://www.usdoj.gov/olp/final.pdf

Any reform effort must weigh victim trauma against the defendant's constitutional rights. The defendant has the right to confront and to cross-examine witnesses under the Fourteenth Amendment of the United States Constitution. There is the right to a public trial under the Sixth Amendment, and the public has the right to access the proceedings under the First Amendment. The difficulty, then, becomes one of balancing victim trauma induced by system participation against the defendant's interests. As we stressed earlier in Chapter 1, this is the criminal's, not the victim's, justice system.

Some states in this country relax the hearsay rule when the following circumstances are present: a child victim is under the age of 11, he or she is involved in a child abuse case, and the trustworthiness of a statement made out of court and not under oath can be established (*Florida Statutes*, 2007:§90. 803(23); Levine and Battistoni, 1991). The *hearsay rule* disallows statements made by a third party because the court cannot evaluate that person's credibility and, thus, the defense is unable to impeach that testimony. Judges waive the hearsay rule only under very narrow circumstances.

Another mechanism to reduce victim trauma is the use of *in camera* proceedings. One such effort has been to allow child victims to testify outside the courtroom in less formal, less threatening surroundings. This practice allows the judge to interview a child in private and to videotape the testimony for the trial. An example of a state statute allowing for this practice is reproduced in Figure 8.14.

FIGURE 8.14
An Example of a Statute Allowing Videotaping of Testimony in Child Sexual Abuse Cases

---

(1) On motion and hearing in camera and a finding that there is a substantial likelihood that a victim or witness who is under the age of 16 or who is a person with mental retardation as defined in s. 393.063 would suffer at least moderate emotional or mental harm due to the presence of the defendant if the child or person with mental retardation is required to testify in open court, or that such victim or witness is otherwise unavailable as defined in s. 90.804(1), the trial court may order the videotaping of the testimony of the victim or witness in a case, whether civil or criminal in nature, in which videotaped testimony is to be utilized at trial in lieu of trial testimony in open court.

(4) The defendant and the defendant's counsel shall be present at the videotaping, unless the defendant has waived this right. The court may require the defendant to view the testimony from outside the presence of the child or person with mental retardation by means of a two-way mirror or another similar method that will ensure that the defendant can observe and hear the testimony of the victim or witness in person, but that the victim or witness cannot hear or see the defendant. The defendant and the attorney for the defendant may communicate by any appropriate private method.

Source: *Florida Statutes* (2007), §92.53.

FIGURE 8.15
Selected Internet Sites Dealing with Child Maltreatment

American Bar Association Center on Children and the Law
http://www.abanet.org/child

American Professional Society on the Abuse of Children
http://www.apsac.org

Child Welfare Information Gateway
http://www.childwelfare.gov

Child Welfare League of America, Inc.
http://www.cwla.org

Childhelp
http://www.childhelpusa.org/index.htm

Court Appointed Special Advocates
http://www.nationalcasa.org

Healthy Families America
http://www.healthyfamiliesamerica.org

Klaas Kids Foundation
http://www.klaaskids.org

National MCH Center for Child Death Review
http://www.childdeathreview.org

National Center of Shaken Baby Syndrome
http://www.dontshake.org

National Center on Child Fatality Review
http://www.ican-ncfr.org

National Children's Advocacy Center
http://www.nationalcac.org

National Children's Alliance
http://www.nca-online.org

National Council on Child Abuse & Family Violence
http://www.nccafv.org

Polly Klaas Foundation
http://www.pollyklaas.org

Prevent Child Abuse America
http://www.preventchildabuse.org

Although the use of *in camera* proceedings is innovative, it has encountered some legal objections. First, some defendants have argued that such proceedings violate their constitutional right to confront and cross-examine witnesses. These complaints have been quashed by allowing the defense counsel to attend the out-of-court questioning. In addition, the courts have ruled that the defendant does not have to be physically present in the same room with the witness. A suitable alternative arrangement is to have the defendant view witness testimony from another location via closed circuit television (Bjerregaard, 1989; Melton, 1980).

A second objection deals with the right of the public to have access to the trial. Sufficient precedent exists that the public has limited access to observe judicial proceedings without jeopardizing the legal process. A similar third objection deals with the defendant's right to a public trial. Precedence is mixed on this point. After reviewing a variety of cases, Melton (1980: 282) concluded that "embarrassment and emotional trauma to witnesses simply do not permit a trial judge to close his courtroom to the entire public." While *in camera* proceedings may avoid inducement of unnecessary trauma, not all courts have reached a definitive conclusion about the conditions under which it is permissible.

Perhaps Vandervort (2006: 1415) captured this dilemma in the following remarks:

> Videotaping has often been opposed by prosecutors and urged by defense advocates. This has largely been a quixotic debate that has taken place in a vacuum with advocates for either side advancing their perceived interests and without consideration of how other investigative methods and tools might complement the use of videotaping. Moreover, the broader community's interests have been largely absent from this debate. Our findings suggest that, at least when used as part of a carefully thought-out investigative protocol, videotaping has a deleterious impact upon defendants' interests and a very positive impact of prosecutor's efforts to successfully prosecute child sexual abuse cases.

Summary

It has taken our society much time to recognize that child mal-treatment exists. Once discovered, states implemented laws forbidding the victimization of children. Maltreatment, however, tends to take place behind closed doors. It often involves victims who are unable to defend themselves, making detection difficult. While reporting laws aim to remedy this dilemma, they have had a boomerang effect. About two-thirds of all child maltreatment complaints are graded as unfounded or unsubstantiated.

Other coping strategies have surfaced. Together, they suggest that the eradication of child abuse and neglect is everybody's responsibil-ity. One way to place this mandate in perspective is to realize that some-where in this country another child probably died from maltreatment during the time it took to read this chapter.

Key Terms for Chapter 8

abuse

battered-child syndrome

central register

child death review teams

countertransference

cycle of violence

double jeopardy

ex post facto law

ex post facto research

false negative error

false positive error

good faith

hearsay rule

in camera

legislative immunity

maltreatment

Megan's Laws

neglect

patriae potestas

pedophilia

privileged relationship

protective custody

psychopathology

role reversal

sexual offender

sexually violent predator

"sick but slick" parents

substantiated allegation

surveillance bias

Learning Objectives

After reading Chapter 9, you should be able to:

- Explain who the elderly are.

- Talk about age patterns in victimization statistics.

- Discuss the objective odds of elder victimization.

- Separate "fear of crime" into two components.

- Understand what is meant by the fear-crime paradox.

- Demonstrate the "graying" of the American population.

- Link changes in life expectancies with population shifts.

- Tie "vicarious victimization" to fear of crime.

- Comment on the political role of the elderly.

- Distinguish risk from vulnerability.

- List four risk factors for the elderly.

- Outline three vulnerability factors for the elderly.

- Compare and contrast elder abuse with elder neglect.

- Estimate how much elder maltreatment takes place.

- Relay various shortcomings with official estimates of elder maltreatment.

- Provide some characteristics of maltreated adults.

- Discuss the extent and possible causes of institutional elder abuse.

- Sketch out some explanations for elder maltreatment that focus upon individual pathological conditions.

- Explain how situational aspects contribute to maltreatment situations.

- Summarize how role reversal impacts elder maltreatment.

- Discuss the relevancy of social exchange theory for elder abuse and neglect.

- Define ageism and explore how it affects maltreatment.

- Evaluate whether mandatory abuse reporting laws are effective.

- Recognize the limitations of current social service provisions.

Chapter 9

ELDER ABUSE

Introduction

Perhaps the most recent concern to emerge in victimology is the topic of elder victimization. The elderly are an expanding segment of the population. There were only 3.1 million persons age 65 or older in 1990, representing roughly 4 percent of the American citizenry (Administration on Aging, 2007). In 2005, that number had grown to more than 26 million Americans age 65 or older (12.4% of the population). The number is expected to rise even further to more than 71 million and make up 20 percent of the population by 2030 (Administration on Aging, 2007), and reach 87 million elderly in 2050.

FIGURE 9.1
Percent Older Population: 1990-2050

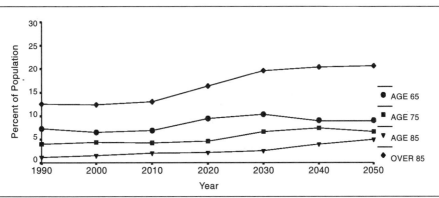

This demographic change is due, in large part, to medical advances that have increased the life expectancy of both men and women. *Life expectancy* refers to the number of years that the average person should live. The life expectancy for a man born in 1900 was 46.3 years; it was 48.3 years for a woman. These numbers soared to 81.8 and 84.8 years, respectively, in 2003 (Administration on Aging, 2007). This steady increase in life expectancies suggests that the absolute number of potential crime victims who are elderly will continue to grow.

Because interest in elder victimization has just begun to sprout, there remain a number of unanswered questions and issues. The entire field of elder victimization is still in the process of defining its parameters. The subject matter can be divided into two major subheadings: criminal victimization and elder maltreatment. For our purposes, criminal victimization refers to the commission of acts against the elderly that would be criminal violations regardless of the victim's age. Certainly, abuse and neglect fall into this category. However, they differ from other crimes in that they specifically target the elderly. The status of being elderly provides the opportunity for this type of victimization.

Defining the Elderly

At one time, it was relatively easy to define elderliness. Most people worked until they reached age 65, and then they retired, subsisting on a pension and social security benefits. Federal legislation eventually lowered the threshold for Medicaid and Medicare to 62 years of age. Suddenly, more and more pension plans opened their retirement windows to younger participants. Companies found themselves in jeopardy of "graying." In order to provide promotional opportunities for younger workers and to restructure their work force, some businesses began offering special incentives for early retirement packages. They attempted to lure younger persons, who were in the mid- to late fifties, into retirement. As you can see, gauging elderliness in terms of retirement eligibility soon lost any intrinsic meaning.

Gerontologists, people who study the aging process, tend to be critical of efforts to link old age to chronological years of life. Much to their dismay, many researchers quickly adopted calendar age as a convenient reference point (Schaie, 1988). This simple definition overlooked the complexity of the aging process. As Maddox and Wiley (1976: 9) explain: "aging connotes three distinct phenomena: the biological capacity for survival, the psychological capacity for adaptation, and the sociological capacity for the fulfillment of social roles."

Victimologists began to realize that lumping all people over the age of 65 into a single category did not produce a homogeneous group (Fattah and Sacco, 1989). There were significant variations that were being masked by this designation. As a result, efforts were made to expand the senior citizen category. Some researchers separated "early old age" (age 64-74) from "advanced old age" (age 75 and older). Other schemes recognized that there were important differences between the "old," the "very old," and those over 85—the "old old" (Fattah and Sacco, 1989). The reader should be sensitive to this concern and be aware that classifying the elderly into a single group can do more disservice than good.

Criminal Victimization of the Elderly

While crime pervades much of modern society, it does not reach all social groups equally. Perhaps the best source of information on who is victimized is the National Crime Victimization Survey (NCVS). Based on NCVS data, the most victimized people are blacks, males, people from the lower economic strata, and the young. The elderly, in contrast, experience relatively low levels of victimization.

An inspection of NCVS data bears out this point. Victimization levels are highest among the youngest age categories and consistently decline with each successive age group. While persons age 65 and over make up about 12 percent of the population, they experience only 2 percent of the violent crime victimizations reported to the interviewers. Similarly, those ages 50-64 comprise roughly 25 percent of the population but report only 11 percent of the total victimizations. Conversely, respondents ages 12-19 make up roughly 17 percent of the population but experience 28 percent of the victimizations. Another way of looking at this data is to inspect the victimization rates for the different age groups. As shown in Figure 9.2, victimization rates for all personal crime categories decrease across age groups from ages 20-24 through age 65 and over. These data show a clear negative linear relationship between victimization and age. Thus, one could conclude that the overall objective odds of falling prey to the criminal element are very small for senior citizens.

FIGURE 9.2
Comparative Rates of Victimization, NCVS, 2005

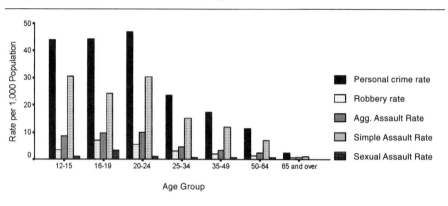

Fear of Crime

While the actual victimization experience directly impacts a finite number of people, a much larger portion expresses a genuine fear of becoming crime victims. *Fear of crime* consists of two parts: (1) the actual odds of being victimized, and (2) the subjective or perceived risk of victimization.

Fear of crime has soared over the past 30 years (Erskine, 1974; Hindelang, 1975; Skogan and Maxfield, 1981; Toseland, 1982). Interestingly, the level of fear consistently outdistances both official and victimization measures of actual crime. For example, Skogan and Maxfield (1981) note that while almost half of all Americans fear crime, official records show only about 6 percent of the population become actual crime victims.

As with actual victimization, surveys find that fear is not constant across demographic groups. In general, fear is highest among urban dwellers, females, blacks, the poor, and the elderly (Baumer, 1985; Clemente and Kleiman, 1977; Erskine, 1974; Gomme, 1986; Greenberg et al., 1985; Hindelang et al., 1978; Lab, 1990; Riger et al., 1978; Skogan and Maxfield, 1981; Smith and Lab, 1991). This elevated fear among the elderly contrasts with the fact they are the least likely to become crime victims. This paradoxical discrepancy between the objective level of victimization and the subjective perception about the odds of becoming a victim has attracted prolonged debate in the research community.

Explaining the Fear-Crime Paradox

One would expect that because crime against the elderly is relatively low, there should be a corresponding reduced fear of crime for that group. When the level of fear is incongruent with the supposed cause of fear (crime in this case), it becomes necessary to find alternative explanations for that fear. Attempts to explain the fear-crime differential typically fall into three related discussions. Those deal with the way fear is measured, and the issues of differences in risk and vulnerability (either real or perceived) among the elderly.

Measuring Fear

No universally accepted definition of fear has emerged in the literature. Consequently, measures of fear vary by the definition used by different researchers. Ferraro (1995) provides one of the most recognized definitions. He defines *fear* as "an emotional response of dread or anxiety to crime or symbols that a person associates with crime" (p. 8). The key to this definition is the required *emotional response* from the victim. As a result, fear can be elicited by different events or situations, depending on what evokes emotions in varied individuals. The elderly, therefore, may respond as being fearful in situations that do not evoke the same response in younger respondents.

Ferraro (1995) points out that fear measures often tap more than emotions. For example, many studies ask respondents to rate their assessment of safety in a specific neighborhood or area, or to provide an opinion on whether crime is increasing or decreasing over a period of time. In both of these cases, the research is tapping more of a value judgement or a person's general knowledge than any real emotional reaction to crime. The emotional component is more directly tested in surveys that ask about how much respondents *worry* about being victimized (Ferraro, 1995; Ferraro and LaGrange, 1988). Unfortunately, many studies claiming great fear of crime rely on questions that do not assess the emotional state of the victim. One example of those questions is the key query from the NCVS, which asks "How safe do you feel or would you feel being out alone in your neighborhood at night?" While bordering on an emotional response, the question is so broad and hypothetical that it would not fit Ferraro's definition.

Does this mean that the fear data are meaningless? Is there nothing to be gained from surveys purporting to measure fear? Does this mean that the elderly really are not fearful? In each case, the answer is no. While no definitive statement can be made about fear, what the varying measures do offer is some insight into the related issues of risk and vulnerability, at least as they are perceived by the elderly. *Risk* typically refers to the chances of becoming a victim of crime, while *vulnerability* deals more with the susceptibility to crime and the harm that accompanies victimization. In some instances, the same factors enhance both risk and vulnerability. For the elderly, there are particular risk and vulnerability factors that may help explain their inordinate fear of crime. It is to these discussions that we now turn.

Risk

Possible risk factors for the elderly include their economic resources, where they live, whether they live alone, and their diminished physical abilities. The economic status of an elderly person can have a great impact on other facets of life. More than 3.5 million elderly individuals had household incomes below the poverty level in 2005, with another 2.3 million living below 125 percent of the poverty level (Administration on Aging, 2007). This equates to 17.7 percent of the elderly U.S. population. Indeed, the median income in 2005 for elderly persons was under $22,000 for males and under $12,500 for females (Administration on Aging, 2007).

Dour economic conditions often dictate that many elderly live in older, deteriorating neighborhoods; in areas that are more ethnically diverse due to turnover of older homes to younger tenants; and in neighborhoods with more transient populations. These types of neighborhoods are often very crime-prone. They frequently attract deviants as residents and draw outsiders who commit crime. The prevalence of crime in these areas, whether directed against the elderly or not, exacerbates feelings of fear and loss of safety among the aged (McCoy et al., 1996).

Additionally, many senior citizens lack financial reserves and live in homes needing repairs. To the extent that confidence games play a role in the level of crime, older people living in run-down housing may respond more favorably to offers of seemingly "bargain" repairs. Economic factors also may force the elderly to walk or to use public transportation, which may increase both real and perceived risks of victimization.

The fact that many elderly live alone also increases risk by making them more suitable crime targets. Roughly 30 percent of all older Americans reside by themselves, with 36 percent of the women over the age of 65 living alone (Administration on Aging, 2007). Dealing with a single individual lessens both resistance and chances of identification of intruders. Hindelang and associates (1978) show a relationship between living alone and victimization. Similarly, Bachman (1992) reports that divorced or separated elderly persons are victimized more often than are married elderly.

The generally diminished physical abilities of the elderly also contribute to actual and perceived risk. If the offender is a young male, an elderly victim is at a clear physical disadvantage. One-third of the violent crime victims age 65 and older report that their assailant was under 30 years old, and half of their offenders were strangers (Bureau of Justice Statistics, 2007). Both the age differential and the anonymity of offenders serve to enhance the fears of the elderly.

Going beyond simply identifying potential risk factors, Stafford and Galle (1984) have considered exposure to risk in assessing fear of crime. They argue that the elderly are overly victimized given their exposure to risk. Stafford and Galle (1984) claim that by adjusting the level of fear in terms of the degree to which different demographic groups are exposed to victimization opportunities, the discrepancy between fear and victimization greatly diminishes. In the study, the elderly still express higher levels of fear than expected, but not to the great extent found in other studies. Ward et al. (1986) present similar evidence that fear is related to the differential risk introduced by varying environmental situations. Warr (1984), however, cautions that fear cannot be totally explained by differences in risk. Age continues to play a role in the level of fear even after accommodations are made for differential risk.

Vulnerability

Because risk alone does not completely explain the level of fear among the elderly, vulnerability helps round out the picture. Vulnerability refers to the ease of being victimized and the impact the crime has upon the victim. The assumption is that people who would suffer the greatest pain or loss from a victimization will be the most fearful. For the elderly, vulnerability is a key concern. Among the many factors that increase elder vulnerability are physical attributes, financial concerns, and social connections.

Declining physical strength and increasing health problems contribute much to a sense of vulnerability. Only 38 percent of the elderly rate their health as excellent or very good, and almost all elderly individuals have at least one chronic health condition (Administration on Aging, 2007). The most common chronic ailments are hypertension (52% of the elderly), arthritis (50%), heart disease (32%), and cancer (21%) (Administration on Aging, 2007). Older people also visit physicians more often, are disproportionately represented among the hospitalized, and account for more than one-third of the health care expenditures in this country (U.S. Senate, 1991).

These medical facts suggest that the elderly are not as capable as younger persons of warding off physical attacks, are likely to be more prone to injury, and are in need of more medical assistance than other segments of the population. Data from victim surveys support this point. For example, the likelihood of injury and medical attention because of a crime increases with victim age (Bachman, 1992; Cook et al., 1978; Hochstedler, 1981; Killias, 1990; Liang and Sengstock, 1983; U.S. Department of Justice, 1992). It is not unusual for crime-related injuries to aggravate preexisting health problems (Burt and Katz, 1985).

Economic liability often accompanies criminal victimization. The elderly have reduced incomes. Much of that money is derived from fixed sources, such as social security, pension funds, and investments (Administration on Aging, 2007). Any loss, no matter how small, can be burdensome to the elderly. Indeed, victimization data reveal that after adjusting for income and insurance, the elderly sustain greater economic losses than any other age group (Cook et al., 1978; Cook et al., 1981). Many elderly cannot afford more medical expenses, insurance premiums, and property replacement costs.

Besides such tangible factors as physical harm and economic losses, social isolation can compound the impact of victimization. As we have discussed elsewhere in this text, social support is an important part of coping with the aftermath of crime. This is no less true for the elderly. Older victims who suffer physical injury may need assistance with normal daily activities during their recuperation. They also may need help repairing damaged property, shopping for replacement goods, or straightening up the mess left by intruders. Sometimes victims blame themselves for the crime. Social support is important for placing the event in its proper perspective and alleviating any guilt feelings. The presence of a support network also can help the victim realize that the world is not all bad, and that the victimization should not be the central focus of what to expect in the future.

Many elderly do not have access to a suitable support system. A number of factors contribute to the social isolation of the elderly. First, the transience of today's society means that the families of the elderly are scattered around the country, often due to employment requirements. Second, old age often brings the death of one's spouse and friends, which results in living alone. Third, due to economics, many elderly live in transient and ethnically diverse neighborhoods. Any one, or a combination, of these factors can make a person feel lonely and isolated. A victimization experience can further fuel these feelings. Social isolation, therefore, intensifies the physical and economic impacts by reducing one's sense of well-being.

Elder Abuse and Neglect

Like victimology in general, it is only recently that abuse and neglect of the elderly has surfaced as a topic worthy of study. Some observers credit Steinmetz (1978b) with introducing the idea of *elder abuse* into contemporary focus. This is not to say that maltreatment of the elderly did not exist prior to this time. There have always been tensions between the young and the old that have resulted in various forms of mistreatment.

An examination of pre-modern Western society shows that disagreements over property rights resulted in physical conflict, including death, between parents and their offspring. Pre-industrial American parents often used economic power to control their adult children, leading to strained family relationships (Steinmetz, 1988). Due to this economic bondage, children often despised and isolated their parents, waiting until such a time that they could rid themselves of the parent. The idea that the young have always venerated their elders down through the ages is a myth.

Family patterns changed during the Industrial Revolution (Stearns, 1986). There were fewer households mixing different generations under the same roof. Retirement support systems made their debut, reducing the financial dependency of the older generation on younger family members. Better economic situations also made medical care more accessible. A new industry of caregivers, such as geriatric nurses and social workers, made it possible for people outside the immediate family to provide suitable alternative living arrangements. All these factors spelled a period of relative calm between parents and their grown children. More than likely, it is this ebb that accounted for the lack of attention paid to abuse and neglect of the aged.

The Reemergence of Interest in Elder Abuse

Demographic Change

Renewed interest in elder abuse and neglect stems from several factors. Perhaps one major reason for the keen interest in elder affairs stems from the graying of the American population. As already demonstrated, there has been a dramatic surge in the number of elderly people in this country since 1900, and projections show that this trend should continue well into the twenty-first century. The increased number of elderly raises a variety of issues and concerns for society, including health care, social security viability, and crime victimization. The absolute increase in the number of elderly should equate with an increased number of crimes against the elderly.

Vicarious Victimization

The sustained interest in crime against the elderly is also a result of the influence of the mass media. Victimologists refer to this phenomenon as *vicarious victimization*. People who have had no actual victimization experiences themselves become acutely aware of others who were preyed upon by criminals. The receiver absorbs this information and speculates that "it could have happened to me." This indirect attribution heightens one's fearfulness, even though the actual odds of victimization may be remote.

Patterns of television viewing and newspaper consumption, both of which portray a great deal of sensationalistic reports, contribute to fear of crime. Victimization of the elderly has emerged as an issue that commands media attention. Different media routinely present stories or issue warnings about con artists operating scams on area residents, particularly the elderly. While some writers claim that fraud and cons are prevalent against the elderly (Geis, 1977; Levin, 1993; McGhee, 1983; Pepper, 1983), there is little evidence to support these claims. Despite the relative rarity of crimes against the elderly, the prominence they receive in the media propels them into the consciousness of the general public.

Political Action

Another factor in the growth in visibility of elder issues is political astuteness. Given their numbers, the elderly form a considerable voting constituency. Age-based advocacy groups have the resources and savvy to lobby elected officials. Perhaps the most notable of these groups is the American Association of Retired Persons (AARP). The AARP is active in promoting legislation on a variety of topics important to individuals age 50 and over. Among the issues addressed by the AARP in recent years are health care benefits and costs, employment opportunities for seniors, improved conditions in group residential living centers, and crime against the elderly.

Social Consciousness

A final reason for increased attention to elder abuse and neglect may be the general trend to take up the causes of oppressed and/or under-privileged segments of society. In this sense, interest in elder abuse is a logical extension of the concern over women's and children's issues.

Defining the Problem

While many commentators point to elder abuse and neglect as a problem, there is little agreement on exactly what constitutes abuse and neglect. A number of problems appear in attempts to provide a definition of abuse/neglect. First, many definitions fail to distinguish abuse from neglect. As we explained in the chapter on child maltreatment, many researchers view abuse as a more active form—and neglect as a more passive form—of mistreatment. Second, some definitions require the perpetrator to act with "intent." They ignore the possibility of abuse or neglect that is unintentional yet still problematic for the victim. Instead, harm may be the result of the failure of a caregiver to provide for needs of the victim. Third, some definitions assume that the victim must depend upon the perpetrator for physical or mental care. One might construe this feature as a legal requirement to provide care before an act is considered abuse. It also ignores the possibility that a perpetrator may be dependent on the victim and commits abusive acts as a means of exerting power. Finally, some definitions include the idea of self-neglect. Many writers, however, view self-neglect as a distinctly different problem from abuse and neglect inflicted by a third party.

Recently, the National Research Council (2003) undertook an analysis of the state of the evidence on elder abuse and offered the following definition of elder mistreatment:

> "Elder mistreatment" ... refer[s] to (a) intentional actions that cause harm or create a serious risk of harm (whether or not harm is intended) to a vulnerable elder by a caregiver or other person who stands in a trust relationship to the elder or (b) failure by a caregiver to satisfy the elder's basic needs or to protect the elder from harm (p. 40).

This definition excludes self-neglect and victimization by strangers. While both of these situations are of interest, they are significantly different from the remaining actions that are encompassed by the definition. The definition includes a wide array of behaviors committed by family members and other caregivers (such as staff at nursing homes), both intentionally and unintentionally, against an elderly individual.

The definition offered above, like many definitions of abuse/neglect, includes a wide range of diverse types of abuse/neglect, with varying degrees of agreement among users. For example, the term "physical abuse" can mean different things to different people. Few would disagree that physical attacks against the elderly represent abuse, particularly when perpetrated by someone who is responsible for the victim's well-being. However, some consider the deliberate withholding of care as physical abuse, while others might call the same act "neglect" (Wolf and Pillemer, 1989). Even when researchers do separate abuse from neglect, they may disagree on the contents of each (Galbraith, 1989). This definitional ambiguity hampers discussion of the issues and the comparison of findings from one study to the next.

Figure 9.3 contains a breakdown of various forms of elder abuse and neglect outlined by the National Center on Elder Abuse. These categories are fairly representative of those found in past research and various state laws. In their categorization, the distinction between abuse and neglect relies mainly on whether the offender is a caretaker of the victim. The failure of a caretaker to fulfill that role generally results in a determination that neglect, either active or passive, is present. Abuse, on the other hand, does not rest on an obligation to provide care. That is, anyone can commit an abusive act. One can divide abuse further into various categories of physical, psychological/emotional, and material exploitation.

FIGURE 9.3
Forms of Elder Abuse and Neglect

Physical Abuse	Inflicting, or threatening to inflict, physical pain or injury on a vulnerable elder, or depriving them of a basic need.
Emotional Abuse	Inflicting mental pain, anguish, or distress on an elder person through verbal or nonverbal acts.
Sexual Abuse	Non-consensual sexual contact of any kind.
Exploitation	Illegal taking, misuse, or concealment of funds, property, or assets of a vulnerable elder.
Neglect	Refusal or failure by those responsible to provide food, shelter, health care or protection for a vulnerable elder.
Abandonment	The desertion of a vulnerable elder by anyone who has assumed the responsibility for care or custody of that person.

Source: National Center on Elder Abuse (n.d.). Frequently Asked Questions. Retrieved September, 10, 2004, from http://www.elderabusecenter.org

Today, most researchers rely on categorizations of abuse and neglect rather than viewing them as a single concept. However, these categorizations do not resolve all definitional problems. Using the categories in Figure 9.3 as an example, one can find several apparent problems. First, the components of a caretaking "obligation" are not always clear. Who decides an individual's obligation? What actions are required, as opposed to being simply "nice to do"? Second, some actions may cause more than one type of maltreatment. For example, physically striking an individual can engender fear and intimidation (i.e., psychological abuse) as well as physical abuse. Similarly, material exploitation deprives the victim of his or her property and may also result in an inability to provide needed care (i.e., neglect). Finally, because much research is based on official records of various government and social service agencies, the categories may not correspond to the legal classifications used to define the problem at that location. It is apparent that definitional problems are an unresolved issue in the study of elder abuse. As a result, we will remind the reader of these issues whenever they affect issues discussed in the chapter.

The Incidence of Elder Mistreatment

Identifying just how much mistreatment of the elderly takes place is not an easy undertaking. The National Research Council (2003) points out several weaknesses that permeate attempts to enumerate the extent of elder abuse/neglect. Among the problems found throughout both published and unpublished reports are unclear and inconsistent definitions, unclear and inadequate measures, incomplete professional counts, lack of population-based data, and a lack of prospective data (National Research Council, 2003: 2).

The first two problems are relatively easy to understand and simply point out that the study of elder abuse has yet to embrace a single definition of abuse and neglect and, as a consequence, tends to use a wide array of different measures when trying to count the extent of abuse/neglect. The problem of "incomplete professional counts" refers to the fact that many attempts to count abuse/neglect rely on the reports of a select group of individuals or agencies. Thus, the results of those counts basically provide anecdotal evidence rather than reliable counts of the problem. The "lack of population-based data" is a similar problem in that, even when an attempt to undertake a broad-based study is undertaken, the results are not necessarily representative of the entire population. Finally, the prospective data issue deals with the fact that most counts are based on review of already collected records and primarily reflect the actions of the agencies. What is needed is to identify a population of elderly individuals and trace their experiences (prospectively) over time in order to uncover the abuse/neglect they experience.

Beyond the problems noted by the National Research Council, measures of abuse/neglect may be hampered by the willingness and ability of elders to report their victimization. Acierno (2003) notes that older adults may be reluctant to report instances of abuse or neglect for a number of reasons. First, the perpetrators of elder abuse often are family members. The victim may want to protect the offender or regard the situation as a private matter not meant for outside viewing. The victim, therefore, may be unwilling to notify anyone. Second, the victim may think that he or she somehow contributed to the situation and, therefore, is at fault. Third, the victim may fear retribution by the offender if the victim reports the abuse. Additionally, the victims may feel embarrassed for allowing the victimization to occur, or may feel stigmatized as a result of reporting the incident. Reporting of abuse may also be impeded by a victim's physical inability to report the event. Eyesight problems, hearing loss, speech impediments, or memory loss can all make reporting problematic (Acierno, 2003). Other reasons why elderly victims may be reluctant to contact authorities are the fact that victims may depend on the offender for daily care and support, or the victim simply does not recognize the abuse as such or, as often happens in financial theft, may not be aware of what has happened. Given these possible influences on reporting behavior, it is safe to conclude that reported estimates mark the lower boundaries of elder abuse and neglect.

The National Research Council (2003) claimed that between one and two million members of the senior population have been the victim of some form of abuse. Projections from other studies reveal that this figure is not far-fetched (Pillemer and Finkelhor, 1988; Tatara, 1990), although the actual figure may extend as high as 2.5 million victims (Hudson, 1988). The National Center on Elder Abuse (NCEA) has conducted several studies on the extent of abuse/neglect.

In 2004 the NCEA surveyed Adult Protective Services (APS) agencies in all 50 states. *Adult Protective Services* are "those services provided to older people and people with disabilities who are in danger of being mistreated or neglected, are unable to protect themselves, and have no one to assist them" (NAAPSA, 2001: 1). These agencies are the clearinghouse for information/data on elder abuse in all states. The NCEA estimates that there were 381,430 cases of abuse in 2004 for a rate of 8.3 cases for every 1,000 persons age 60 and over (see Table 9.1). While these numbers are lower than other figures, it is important to note that these instances reflect only those cases reported to specific government agencies or officials. In relation to the earlier figures, official data appear to include a small minority of all cases.

TABLE 9.1
Reports of Abuse of Persons Age 60+ to Adult Protective Services, 2003

Estimated Total Number	381,430	
Estimated Rate per 1,000	8.3	
Cases Received	253,426	(32 states)
Investigated Cases	192,243	(29 states)
Substantiated Cases	88,455	(24 states)

Source: Constructed by authors from National Center on Elder Abuse (2006) *Abuse of Adults Aged 60+, 2004 Survey of Adult Protective Services.* Washington, DC: National Center on Elder Abuse.

TABLE 9.2
Percent of Different Types of Elder Maltreatment Substantiated by APS Agencies

Type of Abuse	Percent[a]
Self-Neglect	37.2
Caregiver Neglect	20.4
Emotional/Psychological/Verbal	14.8
Financial/Material Exploitation	14.7
Physical	10.7
Sexual	1.0
Other	1.2

[a] Percent does not total to 100 due to the substantiation of more than one type of maltreatment within individual cases.
Source: Constructed by authors from Teaster et al. (2006). *The 2004 Survey of State Adult Protective Services: Abuse of Adults 60 Years of Age and Older.* Found at: http://www.elder-abusecenter.org/pdf/2-14-06%20final%2006+report.pdf

The NCEA study also provides some insight to the various types of abuse and neglect. Relying on data for only substantiated cases reported to APS agencies, Table 9.2 shows that the most common type of mistreatment is self-neglect (37.2% of cases). Caregiver neglect accounts for another 20 percent of the cases, while emotional/psychological/verbal abuse and financial/material exploitation appear in roughly 15 percent of all cases. Interestingly, physical abuse appears in only one out of 10 cases of elder maltreatment. This data suggests that perhaps the most easily recognized form of abuse (i.e., physical abuse) is less common than types of maltreatment that may be easier to hide from view. These findings support the earlier claims of Shell (1982), Sprey and Matthews (1989), and Tatara (1993).

Besides looking at simple raw numbers, many reports offer estimates of the prevalence of abuse in the elderly population. Most estimates place the number of victims between 5 and 10 percent of the aged population (Giordano and Giordano, 1984; Hudson and Carlson, 1999; Hudson et al., 1999; Mouton, 1999). Other studies using small sample sizes from specific locations (Block and Sinnott, 1979; Gioglio and Blakemore, 1983) and from other countries (Schlesinger and Schlesinger, 1988) report victimization rates hovering around 2 to 4 percent of the elderly population.

While there may seem to be some consistency across studies in the reported levels of elder abuse, there are many factors that one should keep in mind when considering the extent of maltreatment. Many social service providers and researchers claim that these estimates grossly underreport the actual level of maltreatment. The greatest difficulty with these estimates is that most are based on official statistics and, as you may recall from Chapter 2, official statistics require notification by the victim or someone else.

Some Characteristics of Victims and Offenders

In addition to looking at the amount of elder mistreatment cases, researchers have tried to learn more about these situations. Some of the more meaningful variables they have examined include age and sex of the victim, the relationship between the victim and offender, and age and sex of the offender.

Data from the NCEA study provide information on victim and offender characteristics for all forms of abuse combined. More detailed information on different categories of abuse/neglect are found in the 1998 National Incidence Study. Tables 9.3 and 9.4 provide results from both efforts. In terms of victims (Table 9.3), females are most often the victims of all forms of abuse and neglect, except abandonment, for which almost two-thirds of the victims are male. Similarly, whites are the more typical victims in all but abandonment situations. Figures for abandonment show that blacks are disproportionately victimized. These findings are similar to those reported by other researchers (e.g.,

TABLE 9.3
Characteristics of Elder Abuse Victims (percents).

			Type of Maltreatment[b]			
	All Forms[a]	Emotional	Emotional/ Psychological	Physical	Financial/ Material	Abandonment
Sex						
Male	34.3%	40.0%	23.7%	28.6%	37.0%	62.2%
Female	65.7	60.0	76.3	71.4	63.0	37.8
Race						
White	77.1	79.0	82.8	86.0	83.0	41.3
Black	21.2	17.2	14.1	9.0	15.4	57.3
Other	1.2	3.8	3.1	5.1	1.6	1.4
Age						
60-69	20.8	8.2	20.3	15.3	12.5	18.4
70-79	36.5	40.0	38.4	41.1	39.5	61.8
80+	43.8	51.8	41.3	43.7	48.0	19.8
Income						
< $5,000	--	2.4	6.2	7.6	1.9	0.0
$5,000-$9,999	--	66.8	37.8	49.5	46.0	96.1
$10,000-$14,999	--	21.4	31.0	18.5	29.8	3.9
> $14,999	--	9.5	25.0	24.5	22.4	0.0

[a] Source: Teaster, P.B., T.A. Dugar, M.S. Mendiondo, E.L. Abner, and K.A. Cecil (2006). The *2004 Survey of State Adult Protective Services: Abuse of Adults 60 Years of Age and Older.* Found at: http://www.elderabusecenter.org/pdf/2-14-06%20final%2006+report.pdf
[b] Source: Administration on Aging (1998). *National Elder Abuse Incidence Study: Final Report.* Found at: http://www.aoa.gov/abuse/report

TABLE 9.4
Characteristics of Elder Abuse Offenders (percents)

		Type of Maltreatment			
	Emotional	Emotional/ Psychological	Physical	Financial/ Material	Abandonment
Sex					
Male	47.6%	60.1%	62.6%	59.0%	83.4%
Female	52.4	39.9	37.4	41.0	16.6
Age					
< 40	20.1	34.3	20.3	45.1	1.4
41-59	34.2	42.4	41.9	39.5	67.5
60-69	9.2	10.4	8.1	3.4	0.0
70-79	18.9	4.8	12.4	1.6	1.5
80+	17.9	8.2	17.4	10.4	29.6
Race					
White	76.6	77.3	83.0	77.1	34.4
Black	20.4	17.8	11.3	18.7	59.0
Other	3.1	4.9	5.6	4.2	6.6
Relation					
Child	43.2	53.9	48.6	60.4	79.5
Sibling	8.7	1.8	4.7	1.3	0.0
Spouse	30.3	12.6	23.4	4.9	6.4
Grandchild	8.8	8.9	5.6	9.2	6.6
Other Relative	4.2	11.7	6.2	9.7	0.0
Other	4.8	11.2	11.6	14.5	7.4

Source: Administration on Aging (1998). *National Elder Abuse Incidence Study: Final Report.* Found at: http://www.aoa.gov/abuse/report

Cazenave and Straus, 1979; Pillemer and Finkelhor, 1988; Tatara, 1993; Wolf and Pillemer, 1989). Levels of abuse also are higher for older individuals. Not surprisingly, income figures show that victims are primarily found in the lower-income groups, particularly the $5,000-$9,999 income range. This may be due to the inability of poorer elderly to acquire competent help and assistance.

The usual perpetrators of most forms of elder abuse and neglect are males, middle-aged, white, and relatives of the victim. Females dominate as offenders in the category of neglect and for the global measures of abuse (largely due to the fact that neglect is the most common form of abuse). The age distribution in offending is not surprising given the fact that people between the ages of 41 and 59 are more likely to have elderly parents for whom to care. This is further borne out in the relationship data, in which children typically make up 50 percent or more of the offenders in almost every category of abuse/neglect. The offender is not a distant relative or someone who lives outside the home. Again, this national data is in concert with a variety of past studies (e.g., Pillemer and Finkelhor, 1988; Quinn and Tomita, 1986; Wolf and Pillemer, 1989).

Institutional Abuse

The living situation of the victim plays an important role in determining possible correlates of elder abuse and neglect. While many think that strangers commit most of the elder abuse and that they do so in impersonal institutional surroundings, such is not the case. Indeed, most senior citizens do not even live in institutions. Only 5 percent of the elderly reside in nursing homes or other institutional settings, although the number increases greatly with age (Administration on Aging, 2006). An inspection of the raw numbers reveals that there are approximately 1.6 million persons living in licensed nursing homes (Administration on Aging, 2006). Consequently, while only a small percentage of elders are at risk of being mistreated in these facilities, there are many elderly at risk on any given day.

Extent of Institutional Abuse

Unfortunately, there has been very little study of abuse/neglect in residential facilities. What data does exist, however, suggest that abuse and neglect are not uncommon. Pillemer and Moore (1989), surveying staff in nursing homes, report that more than one-third of the respondents witnessed at least one episode of physical abuse, while eight out of 10 saw incidents of verbal or psychological abuse in a 12-month period. Interestingly, 10 percent admitted committing physical abuse themselves, and 40 percent admitted verbal/psychological abuse. McDonald (2002) notes that 58 percent of nursing home staff witnessed other staff yelling at residents; 11 percent witnessed staff threatening residents; 21 percent saw residents being pushed or shoved; and 12 percent observed staff slapping residents. The most common form of physical abuse is the use of excessive restraints (MacDonald, 2002).

One problem with surveys of staff is that they often focus on reports of witnessing abuse/neglect. What may occur in these studies is that a large number of respondents may witness the same events, thus resulting in a larger percentage of respondents reporting the abuse. This is demonstrated to some degree by the fact that self-reports of inflicting abuse in the same studies is smaller than the figures for witnessing abuse/neglect. Surveys of residents and their families are an alternative means of gauging abuse/neglect in the institutions. Data from a survey of Georgia nursing home residents and their families reveal that 44 percent of the respondents reported physical abuse, while 48 percent reported rough treatment on the part of the staff (Atlanta Long-term Care Ombudsman Program, 2000).

Theft is another form of abuse believed to be very common in institutional settings. While most of the evidence is anecdotal or based on the impressions of workers in nursing homes (see, for example, Harris, 1999; Harris and Benson, 1996), one survey of nursing home employees found that 4 percent admitted to theft, and 10 percent observed other employees stealing from residents (Harris and Benson, 1998). In one survey of patients, 50 percent claimed to have had property stolen from their room (Kruzich et al., 1992). Other forms of institutional abuse involve fraudulent medical billings, unnecessary physical or chemical restraint, and social isolation.

While these limited survey data suggest that abuse/neglect are common in institutional settings, few nursing homes or residential care facilities are cited for such behavior. Doty and Sullivan (1983) noted that only 7 percent of the nursing homes in the United States were cited for abuse in 1980. A report of the U.S. House of Representatives in 2001 found that only 10 percent of nursing homes were cited for actual harm to residents over a two-year time period (Hawes, 2003). These figures are significantly smaller than those found in surveys of staff or residents. One reason for this may be that the events are not being reported to the authorities or oversight agencies in the different jurisdictions.

Another possible reason for the low numbers of cases in official abuse reports may be the fact that many events are simply not reported in a timely enough fashion, thus resulting in a determination that the event was unfounded. This is the position taken by the General Accounting Office (2002). Despite the fact that the Centers for Medicare and Medicaid Services (the oversight agency for nursing homes) mandates various reporting guidelines for abuse and neglect allegations, the GAO notes that most state agencies are not promptly notified in accordance with regulations. Indeed, almost two-thirds of the reports are made two or more days after the required deadline (GAO, 2002). This delay is problematic because it makes it difficult, if not impossible, for the investigating agencies to undertake a meaningful investigation. After a delay it is often difficult to talk to witnesses, the witnesses or victims cannot recall the event clearly, or the evidence is no longer available for the police or other investigators. Based on these findings, the GAO (2002) made several recommendations to improve the identification and investigation of abuse in residential settings (see Figure 9.4).

FIGURE 9.4
GAO Recommendations for Protecting Nursing Home Residents

- Ensure that state survey agencies immediately notify local law enforcement agencies or Medicaid Fraud Control Units when nursing homes report allegations of resident physical or sexual abuse or when the survey agency has confirmed complaints of alleged abuse.

- Accelerate the agency's [Centers for Medicare and Medicaid Services] education campaign on reporting nursing home abuse by (1) distributing its new poster with clearly displayed complaint telephone numbers and (2) requiring state survey agencies to ensure that these numbers are prominently listed in local telephone directories.

- Systematically assess state policies and practices for complying with the federal requirement to prohibit employment of individuals convicted of abusing nursing home residents and, if necessary, develop more specific guidance to ensure compliance.

- Clarify the definition of abuse and otherwise ensure that states apply that definition consistently and appropriately.

- Shorten the state survey agencies' time frames for determining whether to include findings of abuse in nurse aide registry files.

Source: Government Accountability Office (2002). *Nursing Homes: More Can Be Done to Protect Residents from Abuse*. Washington, DC: U.S. General Accounting Office, p. 27. Retrieved March 14, 2005, from http://www.gao.gov/new.items/d02312.pdf

Causes of Institutional Abuse

What factors contribute to abuse in settings that, at least nominally, exist to care for the well-being of the elderly? Pillemer (1988) offers a model containing four interrelated sets of factors. The first of these are *exogenous factors,* which reflect the influence of the larger community on institutional operations. For example, a relatively small number of nursing homes and available beds means that clients have few choices and that poor quality facilities will still be in demand. Similarly, low unemployment in the community may result in fewer qualified workers available for employment in these settings (Bennett et al., 1997).

The *nursing home environment* is a second source from which abuse may arise. Institutions that have a custodial orientation and fail to emphasize resident needs will tend to have greater levels of abuse. Similarly, poor supervision, low staff-to-patient ratios, lower pay, and high staff turnover can all contribute to less concern for the elderly patient (Pillemer, 1988). A third area of potential concern involves *staff characteristics.* Pillemer (1988) notes that younger staff members and those with less education tend to show less concern for the elderly. These individuals take a more custodial view toward their duties. Workers who experience higher levels of stress and burnout also contribute to the incidence of abuse (Harris, 1999).

The final category of factors reflects *patient characteristics* (Pillemer, 1988). Elderly patients who are in poor health and have poor (or deteriorating) social abilities pose additional challenges and place greater demands on institutional staff. In Ohio, an estimated 600,000 nursing home residents suffer from some form of dementia, making the patient more resistant to care (Ohio State Medical Association, 1994). Consequently, some staff may respond in inappropriate ways. A patient who tends to wander the halls, for example, may be subjected to bed restraints as a means of controlling the behavior (Schramberg and Gaus, 1999). Exacerbating the incidence of abuse may be the social isolation of an elder (Pillemer, 1988). The absence of visitors means that abuse and neglect can take place with little chance of discovery.

Bennett et al. (1997) offer various signs or indicators of potential abuse in institutions. Different indicators correspond to different forms of maltreatment. Signs of physical abuse include unexplained injuries or bruises, poor hygiene, unexplained accidents, or the need for excessive or repeated medication. Heightened anxiety, agitation, withdrawal or fear, isolation from other patients or visitors, and unkempt residents may indicated psychological abuse. Finally, exploitation may be indicated by missing property, the inability of the residents to purchase essentials, and/or the misappropriation of a resident's allowance (Bennett et al., 1997).

Responding to Institutional Abuse

Most jurisdictions have passed legislation specifically to address the incidence of institutional abuse and neglect. Ohio, for example, passed the Patient Abuse/Neglect Law in 1986. Under this statute, "any person who owns, operates, administers or who is an agent or employee of a care facility in the state shall not abuse or neglect a resident of that facility" (Ohio State Medical Association, 1994). The onus for investigating and enforcing criminal violations of this law falls on the state attorney general, not local law enforcement. Claims for civil liability can be handled at either the state or local level. At the federal level, the 1987 Nursing Home Reform Act outlines various forms of prohibited activity, including abuse, neglect, and the unwarranted use of restraints. More recently, as noted earlier, the GAO (2002) made suggestions for improving the reporting and investigation of abuse in residential facilities as a first step to addressing this problem.

Theories of Elder Abuse and Neglect

What causes elder maltreatment? Why does it occur? There are no simple answers to these questions. Researchers have looked at a variety of explanations. Generally speaking, these different approaches fit into five basic groups or categories, based on: (1) intraindividual sources, (2) situational aspects, (3) symbolic interactionism, (4) social exchange, and (5) social attitudes. While some observers might propose alternative groupings, this arrangement is a convenient way to explore the more popular perspectives.

Intraindividual Theories

Intraindividual theories reflect the belief that abusers suffer from some underlying pathological condition. In essence, there is something wrong with the perpetrator that forces him or her to act abusively. Some distinctive factors that fall into this category are alcohol and other drug dependence, mental illness or retardation, intergenerational causes of behavior, and an inability to deal with changing life expectations.

There is considerable support for thinking that abuse stems from intraindividual sources. Perpetrators of physical abuse often have mental and emotional problems, and are more likely to have histories involving psychiatric hospitalization (Wolf and Pillemer, 1989). A heavy reliance upon alcohol or other drugs is a common characteristic among offenders (Anetzberger et al., 1994; Champlin, 1986; O'Malley et al., 1983; Quinn and Tomita, 1986). Fattah and Sacco (1989) point out that substance abuse can impact maltreatment in two ways. In addition to reducing inhibitions against violence or theft, it may limit the caretaker's ability to care properly for the victim. One can make similar claims for the adverse impact of mental illness.

The idea of intergenerational transmission of violence has a fair share of adherents. The notion that parents instill an acceptance of violence in their offspring has appeared in the literature on child abuse and spouse abuse. Applying that same argument to elder abuse and neglect is a logical extension. Indeed, elder abuse researchers rely on child abuse and spouse abuse research to support their arguments (see Quinn and Tomita, 1986). The main difference appears in the outlet for the aggression. Rather than an abused child growing up and abusing his or her child, the abused child grows up and retaliates against the parent who committed the initial abuse (Pillemer, 1986). However, this literature suffers from serious design flaws and weak empirical support. More research needs to be undertaken before reaching a verdict as to whether intergenerational transmission is a reasonable explanation.

Situational Aspects

Situational explanations of elder abuse and neglect reflect an array of factors that deal with the social, environmental, and economic situation of the victim and perpetrator. Some common factors include dependence, stress, and social isolation. The potential influence of each is discussed in turn.

Dependency on other people for daily needs and special assistance often emerges as a major cause of maltreatment. Elder persons may become victims because they rely so heavily upon the caregiver for subsistence. In reality, however, abusers tend to be economically dependent upon their victims (Anetzberger, 1989; O'Malley et al., 1983; Wolf and Pillemer, 1989). It appears that maltreatment is most likely to occur when the caregiver harbors a great deal of resentment toward the older person in his or her guardianship.

Some observers see stress as a leading cause of abuse and neglect (Phillips, 1986). According to this perspective, the perpetrator strikes out at the individual or situation that he or she perceives as causing tension. Some of the more significant stressors include the intensity or burden of caring of another person (O'Malley et al., 1983; Quinn, 1990; Quinn and Tomita, 1986; Schlesinger, 1988; Steinmetz, 1983; Steinmetz, 1988), the economic strain that accompanies extended care (Champlin, 1986; O'Malley et al., 1983; Shell, 1982; Wolf and Pillemer, 1989), insufficient caregiver training (Steinmetz, 1988), and a lack of privacy between cohabiting adults (Anetzberger, 1989; Steinmetz, 1988). Steinmetz (1988) points out that elders sometimes feel they must resort to invading privacy, crying, yelling, or using guilt and other maneuvers to get what they want from their caregivers. A continued reliance upon these tactics can lead to tension, which the abuser may try to resolve by retaliating against the older person.

Another situational factor that contributes to elder maltreatment is the social isolation experienced by the participating parties. Lack of family support can exacerbate both dependency and stress (Anetzberger, 1989; Steinmetz, 1983; Steinmetz, 1988). For example, an offspring who cares for a parent may resent the fact that other siblings are not providing similar assistance. Indeed, studies have found that abusive situations often involve frustrated caregivers with limited support systems at their disposal (Kosberg, 1988; Pillemer, 1986; Quinn and Tomita, 1986; Wolf and Pillemer, 1989). Taken together, dependence, stress, social isolation, and other situational factors can precipitate abuse and neglect as well as contribute to other causes of maltreatment.

Symbolic Interactionism

The symbolic interactionism approach to explaining elder abuse acknowledges that individual roles change over time. Participants alter their expectations and reactions according to the new way in which they see and interpret the changing "reality." In essence, reality is the result of how people interpret what is going on around them and react to their surroundings.

Elder abuse signifies a dramatic *role reversal* for both the parent and the child. At an earlier point in time, the elderly person provided the basic income, made the major decisions, and acted as the head of the household. At that time the child was completely dependent on the parent. As years pass, parents relinquish their dominance. Parents whose well-being withers may come to rely heavily on the child—making extensive new demands and requiring more assistance than ever before. In essence, the parent and the child swap positions and take on new roles. Many individuals are either unprepared or unwilling to accept these new responsibilities; this frequently leads to abuse and neglect (Galbraith, 1989; Phillips, 1986).

As the aging person faces changing needs and begins to rely upon others for basic assistance, he or she redefines the situation in a variety of ways. In one sense, the parent may see himself or herself as a burden to the caregiver (Quinn and Tomita, 1986) and, in turn, may tacitly accept any maltreatment. Alternatively, the elderly individual may feel that the caregiver is too demanding, makes unreasonable requests, fails to do things when and how the parent wishes, or simply ignores the parent (Phillips, 1986; Shell, 1982). The older person may fight, yell, throw tantrums, invade the care giver's privacy, or react in other inappropriate ways (Quinn and Tomita, 1986). The caregiver can similarly define the actions and demands of the elderly as inappropriate. These behaviors by both the older person and the caregiver can easily lead to abuse and neglect, or result in the interpretation of actions as abusive (Phillips, 1986).

Social Exchange

Closely related to both the situational and symbolic interactionist approaches is *social exchange theory*. Parties interact appropriately as long as both sides receive something in the exchange and each side feels that the other is treating him or her fairly (Galbraith, 1989). Typically, there is an assumption of equitable power or resources applied to the situation by both sides of the exchange.

As the elderly grow increasingly dependent on others, they have increasingly less to offer in an exchange relationship (Phillips, 1986). If this inequity continues over a period of time, a strong imbalance may develop between the parties (George, 1986). The parties may allow this imbalance to accumulate because of a past mutual history (Cicirelli, 1986).

The aging person in an imbalanced exchange relationship may respond with feelings of guilt or distress (George, 1986) and recognize that he or she no longer has the power to control the relationship (Phillips, 1986). The caregiver may realize that the relationship is unfair. He or she may resent the fact that a valuable service is being provided with little or no return. That individual may opt to inflict punitive costs on the elderly person through abuse or neglect as a way to rectify the imbalance (Phillips, 1986). The mistreated member of the dyad may quietly accept the abuse or neglect in recognition of his or her dependent position in the exchange.

Social Attitudes

The final theoretical perspective for explaining maltreatment involves social attitudes toward aging and the elderly. Quinn and Tomita (1986) point out that, while attitudes themselves do not cause abuse or neglect, public opinion does make it easier for maltreatment to take place and thrive. *Ageism*, the stereotyping of older individuals and treating them differently because of their age, basically places the elderly in a devalued position (Hudson, 1988). Various factors contribute to a general malaise about the elderly and their plight. The historical record of interaction between the generations provides some insight, just as the past plays a role in the plight of women and children. As noted earlier, older members of society have often kept rigid control over the family, yielding power only through death or major confrontations (Stearns, 1986; Steinmetz, 1988). The animosity that developed between parents and offspring in the past may be reappearing today when the elderly turn to the independent child for care and support.

A second factor may be that old age, particularly very old age, is an unknown in modern society (Quinn and Tomita, 1986). Families in the past century have moved away from extended households, even to the extent of being scattered across the country. This means that most citizens are isolated from aging family members and cannot readily assist them. Coupled with longer life spans and medical advances that allow humans to live longer, people are faced with unknowns about being old. The elderly lack physical and economic power, and because they tend to be out of the work force, they face a perception that they are useless. Social attitudes such as ageism make abuse and neglect more tolerable to society.

Responding to Elder Abuse and Neglect

Societal response to elder abuse and neglect is still very much in the developmental stages. Only within the past decade or so has formal legislation dealt specifically with the rights and needs of older Americans. The Family Violence Prevention and Treatment Act of 1984 was perhaps the earliest legislation to prohibit elder abuse. In the same year, amendments to the Older Americans Act mandated that states assess the need for abuse services, identify existing programs, and address the problem of elder abuse (Rinkle, 1989). The reauthorization of the Older Americans Act in 1993 included new initiatives dealing with the protection of the elderly, including an ombudsman program, abuse and neglect prevention programs, and legal assistance. Of course, the impact of these initiatives will have to be assessed in the future. Amid the growing number of legislative initiatives, perhaps the most noteworthy and successful has been the promotion of mandatory elder abuse reporting laws.

Mandatory Reporting

At first glance, it appears reasonable to assume that mandatory reporting is a good first step in dealing with elder abuse. Interestingly, however, there has been a great deal of resistance to mandatory reporting and numerous criticisms of these efforts. Most states now have some form of mandatory reporting law for abuse that, either implicitly or explicitly, covers elder abuse (Kapp, 1995; Macolini, 1995; Thobaben, 1989). As noted earlier, the Centers for Medicare and Medicaid Services mandates several procedures that facilities receiving federal funds and reimbursement for services must follow, and these regulations require reporting of abuse and neglect to state-level agencies.

Figure 9.5 offers excerpts from both the Ohio and Florida statutes governing the mandatory reporting of elder abuse. A couple of important observations can be drawn from the statutes. First, reporting requirements are restricted primarily to public employees or employees of agencies that would most likely have contact with potential victims. Persons not included in these categories have no legal obligation to make a report of suspected abuse. Second, the specificity of who must report suspected abuse varies somewhat from state to state. In Florida, bank employees and inspectors of public lodging establishments must report. In Ohio, the clergy and attorneys are required to report. Similar differences can be found in statutes from other states.

The greatest criticism of such efforts has been that they do little more than encourage reporting. Often, these reporting laws fail to define elder abuse, to identify to whom abuse is to be reported, to impose penalties for failure to report abuse, and to outline what to do with the reports once they are made (Blakely and Dolon, 1991; Quinn and Tomita, 1986; Thobaben, 1989). A number of other problems also have been identified with mandatory reporting laws. First, the laws typically deal only with the reporting of abuse and fail to provide resources to follow up on the reports or to do something about the problem (Anetzberger, 1989). Second, critics claim that these laws intrude into the privacy of the individual. The best example of this contention involves laws requiring physicians to report suspected cases of abuse, which critics contend violates client-physician confidentiality (Crystal, 1986; Macolini, 1995; Rodriguez et al., 2006). Third, mandatory reporting is seen as reinforcing ageism by focusing on the victim rather than the offender (Anetzberger, 1989; Quinn, 1990; Quinn and Tomita, 1986). These laws identify the victim of abuse and often prompt reactions that may include removing the victim from the home or blaming the victim for the abuse, rather than focusing on the perpetrator (Crystal, 1986). A fourth criticism is that these efforts place the elderly into a category with children, the mentally ill, and others who are incapable of making decisions for themselves. These laws, therefore, fail to treat the elderly as adults and, consequently, degrade the elderly victim.

FIGURE 9.5
Mandatory Reporting Provisions in Ohio and Florida

Ohio Revised Code: Section 5101.61

Any attorney, physician, osteopath, podiatrist, chiropractor, dentist, psychologist, any employee of a hospital . . ., any nurse . . ., any employee of an ambulatory health facility, any employee of a home health agency, any employee of an adult care facility . . ., any employee of a nursing home, residential care facility, or home fo the aging . . ., any senior service provider, any peace officer, coroner, clergyman, any employee of a community mental health facility, and any person engaged in social work or counseling having reasonable cause to believe that an adult is being abused, neglected, or exploited, or is in a condition which is the result of abuse, neglect, or exploitation shall immediately report such belief to the county department of human services.

Florida Statutes: Title XXX, Chapter 415.1034

(1) Mandatory reporting, . . .

    (a) Any person, including but not limited to, any:

        1. Physician, osteopathic physician, medical examiner, chiropractic physician, nurse, paramedic, emergency medical technician, or hospital personnel engaged in the admission, examination, care, or treatment of vulnerable adults;

        2. Health professional or mental health professional . . .;

        3. Practitioner who relies solely on spiritual means of healing;

        4. Nursing home staff; assisted living facility staff; adult day care center staff; adult family-care home staff; social worker; or other professional adult care, residential, or institutional staff;

        5. State, county, or municipal criminal justice employee or law enforcement officer;

        6. Any employee of the Department of Business and Professional regulation conducting inspections of public lodging establishments . . .;

        7. Florida advocacy council member or long-term care ombudsman council member; or

        8. Bank, savings and loan, or credit union officer, trustee or employee, who knows, or has reasonable cause to suspect, that a vulnerable adult has been or is being abused, neglected, or exploited shall immediately report such knowledge or suspicion to the central abuse hotline.

The move toward greater protection for the elderly is evident in the introduction of an Elder Justice Act bill in both the 108th and 109th Sessions of the U.S. Congress. The proposed Act outlines a variety of efforts. Central to the bill is the detection, prevention, and prosecution of elder abuse. Also included is the establishment of an Office of Elder Justice in the U.S. Department of Justice, the collection and dissemination of data on elder abuse/neglect, the creation of an infrastructure at the federal and state levels for addressing elder abuse, the improvement of long-term care, and the screening of employees of nursing facilities. Even if the bill is not enacted, its intent and the breadth of the provisions point to the increasing concern over elder abuse and neglect.

Social Service Provision

One expected outcome of mandatory reporting laws and other legislation is that social service professionals will be alerted to the problem and will take appropriate actions. Surveys of various social service professionals reveal that nurses, social workers, and the clergy are among those who most often deal with and who are most knowledgeable about elder abuse (Anderson, 1989; Dolon and Hendricks, 1989). Interestingly, while one might assume that the police would be a primary source of immediate contact and aid, law enforcement is minimally involved—even when mandated to receive reports of abuse (Dolon and Hendricks, 1989; Fiegener et al., 1989). The relative lack of police involvement may be due to the fact that often the most common form of abuse identified by social service workers is self-neglect (Fiegener et al., 1989). The questionable legal status of self-neglect serves to remove the police from the equation.

Beyond identifying which social service workers are most involved in dealing with elder abuse, research has surveyed these professionals about their views of service needs. The need for additional training in elder abuse issues is perhaps the most common response (Blakely and Dolon, 1991; Dolon and Blakely, 1989; Fiegener et al., 1989). A second commonly expressed opinion is that there is room for more and improved resources to deal with abuse. Blakely and Dolon (1991), based on a national survey, identify a number of other needs, including greater cooperation between agencies, more public awareness, increased numbers of staff to deal with elder abuse, and stronger elder abuse legislation. What these responses tell us is that social service efforts to deal with elder abuse are still in their infancy and that much more remains to be done.

In an attempt to address the issues of elder abuse and neglect, many jurisdictions have established agencies, or offices within agencies, with the specific mandate of responding to those needs (such as Adult Protective Services). Often these efforts are backed by state legislation and are attached to agencies such as health and human services departments. Today, every state has some form of protective service devoted to the elderly. While their primary task revolves around investigations of abuse and neglect, these offices may also be responsible for such disparate activities as licensing nursing homes, funding research, and training social service workers. The fact that every jurisdiction has some form of Adult Protective Services is not indicative of a growing consensus on the problems of elder abuse and neglect. There remains a great deal of diversity in definitions, legislation, legal requirements, and interventions across the different jurisdictions.

FIGURE 9.6
Recommended Research Agenda of the National Research Council

- Basic research on the phenomenology of elder mistreatment is a critical early step in the further development of the field.

- Development of widely accepted operational definitions and validated and standardized measurement methods for the elements of elder mistreatment is urgently needed to move the field forward.

- Population-based surveys of elder mistreatment occurrence are feasible and should be given high priority by funding agencies.

- Funding agencies should give priority to the design and fielding of national prevalence and incidence studies of elder mistreatment.

- [N]ew methods of sampling and identifying elder mistreatment victims in the community should be developed in order to improve the validity and comprehensiveness of elder mistreatment occurrence estimates.

- The occurrence of elder mistreatment in the institutional setting, including hospitals, long-term care and assisted living situations, is all but uncharacterized and needs new study sampling and detection methods.

- Studies are greatly needed that examine risk indicators and risk and protective factors for different types of elder mistreatment.

- Substantial research is needed to improve and develop new methods of screening for possible elder mistreatment in a range of clinical settings.

- Research on the effects of elder mistreatment interventions is urgently needed.

- An adequate long-term funding commitment to research on elder mistreatment must be made by relevant federal, state, and private agencies.

Source: Compiled from National Research Council (2003). *Elder Mistreatment: Abuse, Neglect, and Exploitation in an Aging America*. Washington, DC: National Academies Press.

Increased Research

Perhaps the largest key to responding to elder abuse and neglect is increasing our knowledge about the problem and appropriate responses. The work of the National Research Council (2003) points out the weaknesses and limitations that permeate the current knowledge about the problems. Based on their extensive review of the extant literature, the NRC offers a comprehensive research agenda that, if undertaken and completed, would greatly enhance our knowledge and understanding of elder abuse and neglect (see Figure 9.6). The results of this research endeavor would be improved responses and interventions to help the elderly victims of abuse.

FIGURE 9.7
Selected Internet Sites Dealing with Elder Abuse

American Association of Retired Persons
    http://www.aarp.org

Federal Interagency Forum on Aging-Related Statistics
    http://www.agingstats.gov

National Center on Elder Abuse
    http://www.elderabusecenter.org

National Citizen's Coalition for Nursing Home Reform
    http://www.nccnhr.org

U.S. Administration on Aging
    http://www.aoa.gov

U.S. Census Bureau
    http://www.census.gov

Summary

As the number of elderly persons steadily increases, society faces new problems and issues. For victimology, the elderly emerge as the subject of interest in two broad areas. First, they are victims of the same crimes as everyone else. Second, they occupy a special niche as victims of abuse and neglect.

More is known about general crimes committed against the elderly because of the great similarity to crime against the rest of society. Theft, burglary, assault, and other such offenses are traditional realms of interest for the criminal justice system. The greatest difference regarding crime against the elderly falls not in the crime itself, but rather in the impact of that crime upon the victim.

Elder maltreatment, however, poses a relatively new problem for the criminal justice system. While abuse may not be a new occurrence, it is a phenomenon that is just now gaining attention. Victimologists are beginning to identify the intricacies of the problem, probe its causes, and offer some solutions. However, a great deal of additional work remains to be done at both the theoretical and practical levels. A short decade of work has not been sufficient to do much more than identify elder abuse and neglect as a major problem and offer the sketchiest of responses.

Key Terms for Chapter 9

Adult Protective Services

ageism

elder abuse

elder neglect

exchange theory

exogenous factors

fear of crime

gerontologists

institutional abuse

life expectancy

mandatory reporting

nursing home environment

patient characteristics

risk

role reversal

sentinel agency

Silver Haired Legislature

situational factors

social exchange theory

staff characteristics

symbolic interactionism

vicarious victimization

vulnerability

Learning Objectives

After reading Chapter 10, you should be able to:

- Define criminal homicide.
- Assemble a picture of homicide victimization based upon UCR statistics.
- Explain why African Americans are overrepresented in homicide statistics.
- Offer a profile of youthful violence in America.
- Elaborate on the PERF statement "we have a gathering storm of crime."
- Give some insights based on lifetime murder victimization rates.
- Evaluate the need for a national Firearm Fatality Reporting System.
- Explore the development of the National Violent Death Reporting System.
- Distinguish a primary homicide from a nonprimary homicide.
- Link victim precipitation with the term "situated transaction."
- Describe how routine activities or lifestyle can influence homicide victimization.
- Outline the stages of Luckenbill's situated transaction in a homicide confrontation.
- Show how the mass media can influence violence.
- Convey what is meant by the differential distribution of homicide victimization rates.
- Discuss the "regional culture of violence" thesis.
- Sketch out two sets of challenges to the "regional culture of violence" thesis.
- Introduce the term "trauma" and explain its relevance.
- Establish a connection between trauma and medical resources.
- Offer an explanation as to how medical resources could affect the production of homicide statistics.
- Explore some remaining issues in the medical resources argument.
- Relay the details of the death notification process.
- Discuss the grief process and its different stages.
- Explain some of the adjustments faced by survivors of homicide victims.
- List the five homicide survivor patterns and tell how they differ in response to the homicide event.

Chapter 10

HOMICIDE

Introduction

One aspect of daily life that sets the United States apart from other industrialized countries is the death toll that continues to mount from criminal violence. Murder is a common fixture in our urban landscape. Homicide, for example, is a leading cause of death among youthful African-American males in this country.

This chapter will take a close look at the dynamics that underlie criminal violence. Most killers murder someone they know rather than kill a complete stranger. Victim precipitation and alcohol consumption appear to be almost essential ingredients in any deadly confrontation. While there are different interpretations as to how alcohol actually works in these settings, it is certain that expanding medical resources have done much to keep these mortality figures in check. In fact, one argument developed in this chapter is that medical resources play an important role in the production of homicide statistics.

No treatment of homicide would be complete without looking at the silent or hidden sufferers of homicide: the survivors of the deceased. In this context, we will visit the death notification process and the bereavement process endured by the victim's relatives.

The Extent of Homicide Victimization

According to the FBI's Uniform Crime Reports (UCR) published in 2006, there were almost 16,692 known homicides in the United States during 2005. Unlike most of the Index crimes, the FBI attempts to collect detailed data on reported homicides and makes this information available through the Supplementary Homicide Reports. These reports seek data on both the victim and the offender, as well as the circumstances surrounding the event. Despite this fact, detailed information is not available for every one of these deaths. As a result, the UCR data offers a sketch based upon information derived from 89 percent of the known victim deaths.

The Federal Bureau of Investigation (2006) defines *criminal homicide* as the "willful (nonnegligent) killing of one human being by another. . . . [It] does not include the following situations in this offense classification: deaths caused by negligence, suicide, or accident; justifiable homicides; and attempts to murder or assaults to murder. . . ." The FBI also omits from its tabulations traffic fatalities and deaths resulting from gross negligence.

TABLE 10.1
Age Distribution of U.S. Murder Victims, 2002

Age in Years	Number	Simple Percent	Cumulative Percent
Under 1	182	1.2%	1.2%
1-4	328	2.2	3.4
5-8	75	0.5	3.9
9-12	78	0.5	4.4
13-16	456	3.1	7.5
17-19	1,349	9.1	16.6
20-24	2,834	19.1	35.7
25-29	2,262	15.2	50.9
30-34	1,649	11.1	62.0
35-39	1,257	8.5	70.5
40-44	1,194	8.0	78.5
45-49	938	6.3	84.8
50-54	708	4.8	89.6
55-59	384	2.6	92.2
60-64	272	1.8	94.0
65-69	183	1.2	95.2
70-74	159	1.1	96.3
75+	291	2.0	98.3
Unknown	261	1.8	
Total	14,860	100.1%	100.1%

Source: Federal Bureau of Investigation (2006). *Crime in the United States 2005: Expanded Homicide Data Table 2: Murder Victims by Age, Sex, and Race, 2005.* Washington, DC: U.S. Government Printing Office. Retrieved August 17, 2007, from http://www.fbi.gov/ucr/05cius/offenses/expanded_information/data/shrtable_02.html

Homicide victims are more likely to be males than females. In 2005, 79 percent of the deceased were males. In terms of race, 49 percent of the homicide victims were black and 49 percent white (Federal Bureau of Investigation, 2006). This racial composition means that blacks experience an *overrepresentation* in homicide victimizations. Considering that blacks make up approximately 12 percent of the American population, all things being equal, one would expect that they would account for 12 percent of all murder victims. Because the participation figure of 49 percent clearly exceeds the 12 percent population mark, victimologists regard blacks as being excessively represented in homicide statistics.

Table 10.1 displays the age distribution of murder victims for 2005. Those figures show that 510 deaths can be attributed to *infanticide* (child homicide). Victims under the age of five made up 3.4 percent of the homicide victimization pool. If we expand the upper limit of childhood to 12 years of age, children account for 4.4 percent of all the homicide victimizations in this country. The most likely perpetrator in the majority of these cases is a parent or parent substitute. *Eldercide*, murders involving elderly victims, are less frequent in comparison.

A closer look at Table 10.1 shows that homicide victimization is concentrated among the younger segments of society. More than half of all homicide victims (54.5%) were between 17 and 34 years of age. In fact, since 1969, the leading cause of death among young black males is homicide (Bilchik, 1999: 3). As Figure 10.1 suggests, this frightening observation has led some commentators to conclude that violence, particularly with the use of firearms, has reached epidemic proportions among disadvantaged, urban, black males (Kellerman, 1994; Snyder and Sickmund, 2006; Sorenson, Richardson, and Peterson, 1993). Another commentator (Kellerman, 1994: 541) notes, "the number of 15- to 19-year-old African-American males who died from gunshot wounds in 1990 was 4.7 times larger than the number who died from acquired immunodeficiency syndrome, sickle cell disease, and all other natural causes of death *combined*" [emphasis in original]. At the same time, these figures fail to convey the toll sustained from the combined years of potential life lost whenever a person loses his or life prematurely.

Christoffel (2007), a public health researcher, wryly points out that firearms violence has surpassed epidemic levels and has reached the point of being endemic. In other words, after a disease or public health threat skyrockets (an epidemic), intervention programs involving medical treatment and immunizations cause the phenomenon to level off. There might be periodic flare-ups, however, if surveillance and monitoring efforts lose their vigilance.

FIGURE 10.1
A Profile of Youth Violence in America

- In 2004, 5,292 young people ages 10 to 24 were murdered—an average of 15 each day.

- Homicide was the second leading cause of death for young people ages 10 to 24 years old.

- Among homicide victims ages 10 to 24 years-old, 81% were killed with a firearm.

- Among 10- to 24-year-olds, homicide is the leading cause of death for African Americans, the second leading cause of death for Hispanics, and the third leading cause of death for American Indians, Alaska Natives, and Asian/Pacific Islanders.

- Homicide rates among non-Hispanic, African-American males 10–24 years of age (53.1 per 100,000) exceed those of Hispanic males (20.1 per 100,000) and non-Hispanic White males in the same age group (3.3 per 100,000).

- In 2005, more than 721,000 young people ages 10-to-24 were treated in emergency departments for injuries sustained from violence.

- In a 2005 nationally-representative sample of youth in grades 9 through 12, 35.9% reported being in a physical fight in the 12 months preceding the survey; the prevalence was higher among males (43.4%) than females (28.1%).

- In a 2005 nationally-representative sample of youth in grades 9 through 12, 18.5% reported carrying a weapon (gun, knife or club) on one or more days in the 30 days preceding the survey.

- In a 2005 nationally-representative sample of youth in grades 9 through 12, 5.4% carried a gun on one or more days in the 30 days preceding the survey.

Source: National Center for Injury Prevention and Control (2004). *Youth Violence: Facts at a Glance.* Atlanta, GA: Centers for Disease Control and Prevention. Retrieved August 17, 2007, from http://www.cdc.gov/ncipc/dvp/YV_DataSheet.pdf

The Police Executive Research Forum (PERF) invited police chiefs and mayors from around the country to attend a Violent Crime Summit in October of 2006. After monitoring recent UCR violent crime levels, PERF officials became alarmed that the surge in homicides, robberies, and aggravated assaults might portend another crime spike or epidemic. Those observations, and the information presented in Figure 10.2, prompted Los Angeles Police Chief William Bratton, the head of PERF, to declare "We have a gathering storm of crime" (Rosen, 2006: 2). Fearful of the prospects, the PERF staff performed another pulse check using the latest data available. Once again, the pronouncement was solemn. Crime trends had not abated and, if left unchecked, the prediction was that they would continue upward to unprecedented levels of violence (Police Executive Research Forum, 2007).

FIGURE 10.2
Violent Crime Milestones between 2004 and 2006 in Selected Cities

Alexandria, VA	Homicides doubled from 2004 to 2005
Arlington, TX	5-year high for aggravated assaults
Boston, MA	10-year high for homicides
Cincinnati, OH	20-year high for homicides
Fairfax County, VA	16-year high for homicides
Kansas City, MO	6-year high for homicides
Nashville, TN	7-year high for homicides
Orlando, FL	All-time high for homicides
Prince George's Co., MD	All-time high for homicides
Richmond, CA	10-year high for homicides
Springfield, MA	Nearing a 10-year high for homicides
Toronto (Canada)	10-year high for homicides
Trenton, NJ	All-time high for homicides
Virginia Beach, VA	10-year high for robbery

Source: Rosen, M.S. (2006). *Chief Concerns: A Gathering Storm—Violent Crime in America.* Washington, DC: Police Executive Research Forum, p. 5. Courtesy of Police Executive Research Forum.

Weapon involvement, especially firearms, is a potent predictor of lethal and nonlethal injuries (Saltzman et al., 1992). In fact, despite the recent downturn in homicide rates at the turn of the century, firearms remain the second leading cause of injury-related deaths in the United States (Gotsch et al., 2001; National Center for Health Statistics, 2006). The data in Table 10.2 show that firearms are used in two-thirds of all homicides. Approximately 78 percent of firearms-related homicides involve handguns. Knives and other sharp objects account for an additional 13 percent of the homicides. In only 7 percent of the cases are hands, feet, fists, or other "personal weapons" used (Federal Bureau of Investigation, 2006). Compared to weapon use in aggravated assaults (where, as in homicides, the intent of the offense is bodily harm to the victim), homicides are three times as likely to involve a firearm.

Relying upon annual homicide measures is not a completely accurate way of studying victimization. For example, overall homicide rates in the United States have declined over the past several years. These annual decreases, as pronounced as they are, can generate the impression that this problem is becoming less serious. As a result, researchers have turned to a new way of looking at homicide data. They refer to *lifetime murder victimization rates*—the chances of dying from a homicide—to study this social problem more closely.

TABLE 10.2
Murder Victims by Weapon, 2001–2005

Weapon	2001	2002	2003	2004	2005
Firearms	63%	67%	67%	66%	68%
Knives or cutting instruments	13	12	13	13	13
Blunt objects (clubs, hammers, etc.)	5	5	4	5	4
Personal weapons (hands, fists, feet, etc.)	7	7	7	7	6
Poison	–	–	–	–	–
Explosives	–	–	–	–	–
Fire	1	1	1	1	1
Narcotics	–	–	–	1	–
Drowning	–	–	–	–	–
Strangulation	1	1	1	1	1
Asphyxiation	1	1	1	1	1
Other	9	6	6	6	7
Total %	100%	100%	100%	101%	101%

Source: Federal Bureau of Investigation (2006). *Crime in the United States 2005: Expanded Homicide Data Table 7: Murder Victims by Weapon, 2001–2005.* Washington, DC: U.S. Government Printing Office. Retrieved August 17, 2007, from http://www.fbi.gov/ucr/05cius/offenses/expanded_information/data/shrtable_07.html

Table 10.3 presents lifetime murder victimization rates for the year 1997, the most recently available data. The table borrows a basic demographic procedure known as a life table. The first entry in the table indicates that one out of every 207 Americans under the age of four would become a murder victim. These figures allow several comparisons. First, black persons and males have considerably higher victimization odds of succumbing to lethal violence than do whites and females. Second, death by homicide is a grim reality for black males. Black males face a one out of 35 chance of becoming a homicide victim from birth until the end of their teenage years. In comparison, white males are seven times less likely to die from criminal violence. Third, the likelihood of becoming a homicide victim declines from age 30 onward. As the reader can see, this technique captures tendencies that crude homicide rates overlook.

A growing number of medical experts are becoming increasingly concerned with the implications stemming from firearms and other interpersonal disputes. One research team assembled a variety of data to construct an estimate of the medical costs associated with interpersonal violence during calendar year 2000. Corso and his colleagues (2007) compiled information on the expenses associated with medical care, lost wages due to a lack of labor force productivity, and other considerations. Their best indications are that fatalities due to homicide extracted a staggering $22.1 billion from the American economy.

TABLE 10.3
1997 Lifetime Murder Victimization Rates by Race and Sex for the United States

Age	Total	White Male	White Female	Black Male	Black Female
0-4	207	241	684	35	171
5-9	214	248	731	35	184
10-14	215	249	741	35	186
15-19	217	251	753	35	189
20-24	250	284	825	41	206
25-29	328	356	953	57	243
30-34	419	442	1088	76	290
35-39	534	544	1309	101	368
40-44	678	663	1588	133	481
45-49	860	820	1876	174	638
50-54	1109	1032	2280	231	826
55-59	1388	1304	2714	269	998
60-64	1752	1660	3259	354	1204
65-69	2203	2076	3597	464	1552
70-74	2686	2607	3896	544	2012
75-79	3376	3338	4585	690	2099
80+	4009	3774	5228	856	2375

Source: Federal Bureau of Investigation (2000). *Crime in the United States 1999: Uniform Crime Reports*. Washington, DC: U.S. Government Printing Office, Table 5.2. Retrieved on August 17, 2007, from http://www.fbi.gov/ucr/Cius_99/99crime/99cius5.pdf

One fundamental concern is that the United States does not have a comprehensive national clearinghouse that stockpiles data regarding gun-related deaths. As a result, some physicians implored the federal government to establish a *Firearm Fatality Reporting System*, modeled after the fatal crash data bank operated by the National Highway Traffic Safety Administration. Researchers there have used this information to effect seatbelt laws, child restraint regulations, and other safety considerations aimed at reducing vehicle-related deaths. After a pilot program demonstrated the feasibility of expanding such an approach, the Centers for Disease Control and Prevention (CDC) launched the *National Violent Death Reporting System* (NVDRS) in 2003, involving more than a dozen states. The goal is to collect information for all suicides, homicides, and unintentional firearms deaths. The NVDRS utilizes records from a variety of sources (death certificates, medical examiner reports, police files, crime labs, fatality review teams, etc.) to compile a more comprehensive picture of victims, offenders, and circumstances (Centers for Disease Control and Prevention, 2007).

Findings are starting to trickle in from this innovative data collection system. For example, more than half of the suspects who killed an intimate partner subsequently committed suicide (National Violent Injury Statistics System, 2005a). Ending a romantic relationship stood out as a precursor of suicide among youths in the 18- to 24-year-old bracket

(National Violent Injury Statistics System, 2005b). In Miami, almost half the children killed by their fathers died during a violent attack on their mothers (National Violent Injury Statistics System, 2004). It is anticipated that the NVDRS and its expansion to all 50 states in the near future will add some more interesting findings and will fuel policy developments in the prevention of violence.

The FBI (2006) also reports that homicide is, for the most part, an intraracial event. In other words, victims and offenders tend to share the same racial backgrounds. Black offenders killed 93 percent of the black homicide victims, and white perpetrators murdered 85 percent of the white homicide victims. Similarly, males were more likely to die at the hands of male killers (but so were female victims).

One important distinction that has emerged in the literature is the notion of nonprimary versus primary homicide (Parker, 1989; Parker and Smith, 1979; Smith and Parker, 1980). A *nonprimary homicide* is a situation in which the victim did not know the offender very well, if at all. A *primary homicide* means that both the victim and the offender shared a primary, or face-to-face, relationship. Primary homicides span a variety of relationships. Some examples of primary relationships would include spouses, parents and their children, siblings, and people who are very close to one another. One researcher has dubbed cases involving men who murder their wives or lovers as *intimate femicide* (Stout, 1991). Recognition of the "battered wife syndrome," discussed in Chapter 6, has unearthed situations in which women retaliate by killing their husbands or lovers (Mann, 1988; Mann, 1990). The

FIGURE 10.3
Homicides by Victim-Offender Relationship, 1976–2005

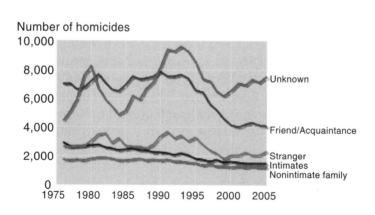

Source: Fox, J.A., and M.W. Zawitz (2007). *Homicide Trends in the U.S.* Washington, DC: U.S. Bureau of Justice Statistics. Retrieved August 17, 2007, from http://www.ojp.usdoj.gov/bjs/homicide/relationship.htm

act of *parricide*, children who kill their parents, has not escaped scholarly attention (Berliner, 1993; Fine, 1993; Heide, 1989, 1993; Mones, 1993). One can subdivide parricide into cases involving *patricide* (where the father is the victim) or *matricide* (where the mother is the victim).

Figure 10.3 plots the homicides that took place the between the years 1975 and 2005 according to the relationship between the victim and the offender. This reinforces an important point that we saw in Chapter 1 when we dealt with Wolfgang's seminal analysis of homicides that occurred in Philadelphia: that is, most victims know their assailants. A person is more likely to be killed by someone with whom he or she is acquainted rather than by a complete stranger.

Theories of Homicide Victimization

Most criminological theories attempt to understand why some people resort to criminal behavior while others do not. Victimologists, on the other hand, take a slightly different approach by focusing upon the not-so-victorious portion of the criminal-victim dyad. As we saw in Chapter 1, this concentration upon the victim led to an early reliance on the notion of victim precipitation. What did the victim do to deserve this type of treatment? While this idea does have some very real limits, victim involvement has yielded some fruitful insights when it comes to homicide victimization. As a result, the following materials focus upon theories that are based upon social interactionism and a cultural perspective.

Social Interactionism

As we mentioned before in Chapter 1, early victimologists gave serious consideration to the idea of *victim precipitation*. They sought to learn what the victim did that triggered such a violent reaction. While Hans von Hentig and others debated how the dynamics of the criminal-victim dyad led to the victim's ultimate demise, it was Wolfgang's (1958) analysis of Philadelphia homicides that provided the necessary empirical support.

Wolfgang (1958) undertook an extensive review of police homicide records for all murders committed during the five-year period of 1948–1952 in Philadelphia. The one thing that struck Wolfgang was the realization that there was a significant amount of victim participation in some of these homicide events. Wolfgang (1958: 254) categorized 150 cases (26% of all the homicides) as victim-precipitated. In other words, the victims in these incidents initiated the violent encounter. They were the first party to display a weapon, throw a punch, or take other physically aggressive actions. When the other party retaliated, the violence escalated to a lethal response.

As we explained in Chapter 1, Amir, one of Wolfgang's students, applied the same thinking to forcible rape situations. The reaction to Amir's treatment of victim precipitation in sexual battery cases drew an intense and bitter reaction. Consequently, this concept remained dormant for many years. It took two decades before other homicide researchers revived this idea.

Homicide as a Situated Transaction

Luckenbill (1977) rekindled interest in victim actions when he addressed homicide as a "situated transaction." What he meant by a *situated transaction* was that the homicide culminated from a chain or series of discrete actions and reactions by the participants. The combination of the two actors, and possibly an audience, contributed to the development of a violent interaction. Luckenbill became intrigued by how the parties reacted to each other and whether the dynamics progressed in any regular patterns.

Tracing the hostilities, as well as the moves and countermoves displayed by the participants, led Luckenbill to conclude that these deadly struggles evolved in a series of predictable stages. What usually initiated these encounters was some type of an insult. The eventual victim may have said something rude, made an unwelcomed remark, or issued an obnoxious gesture toward the other party. The second stage consists of the recipient's assessment of these actions as offensive. The next stage, the response, appears to be absolutely critical to the final resolution of this conflict. The recipient's response could be to ignore the apparent insult, to dismiss the issuer as inconsequential, or to deal with the matter immediately. For instance, direct confrontation could involve a dare for the victim to restate the insult, an issuance of a retaliatory remark or gesture by the aggrieved party, or a physical challenge. The goal at this point is to do something to save face, degrade the initiator, or demonstrate superiority.

If the attempt to salvage one's social appearance fails, then the situation escalates to the fourth stage. At this point, both parties have elected neither to turn away nor to defuse the mounting disagreement. There could be more verbal challenges, accompanied by minor scuffling or further insults. Should neither party break off or end the grievance, a battle is imminent. A common strategy at this point is to assume an intimidating stance as a demonstration of pugilistic superiority or to display a weapon as proof of a tactical advantage. A failure to heed such a warning results in the ultimate demise of one of the parties. Thus, Luckenbill (1977) sees murder as the final outcome in a series of moves and counterstrategies negotiated continuously by the combatants.

Following the lead of Luckenbill (1977), Felson and Steadman (1983) reconstructed the criminal episode that resulted in imprisonment on charges of homicide and aggravated assault. A refinement of Luckenbill's stages lent clarification to the analysis. Victim precipitation was a very prominent characteristic of homicide situations. Combatants who were armed, intoxicated, and aggressive were more likely to be killed than those who were sober. As Luckenbill (1977) explained, these violent episodes usually began with a verbal confrontation. They then moved to the next stage with more threats and evasive actions. If a serious outcome is to be avoided, this is the time to deescalate matters. However, for those incidents that do continue, the physical attack ensues next.

Victim precipitation is a major contributing factor in serious violence. The key feature of these violent encounters is that they are provoked by an attack on one's "honor" and systematically evolve into a deadly "character contest." In essence, the nature of the instigating act is trivial compared to the final outcome. To verify whether this conceptualization was correct, Savitz and associates (1991) reviewed 381 homicides that took place in Philadelphia during 1978. Each homicide was dissected, paying close attention to how the quarrel began and who initiated the challenge or "character contest." Almost two-thirds of the killings fit Luckenbill's description of a "situated transaction"; half of these cases involved victim-initiated circumstances.

Other applications of Luckenbill's "situated transaction" approach have found it to be helpful in reaching a better understanding of intimate partner homicide (Swatt and He, 2006) and how the "code of the street" leads to recurrent violence (Rich and Grey, 2005).

The Routine Activities/Lifestyle Model

An alternative approach for explaining homicide events is through the inspection of routine activities. Routine activities refers to the fact that individuals may place themselves at risk of victimization by their everyday behavior. Cohen and Felson (1979) demonstrate this possibility by examining social changes that have led to increasing property crime. They point out that the move to two-earner households has left homes unprotected during the day and allows for the purchase of more valuable and portable items. At the same time, increased mobility has led to a greater number of targets for offenders. Taken together, this convergence of suitable targets, lack of guardianship, and the increased motivation of offenders has allowed for greater levels of theft. Hindelang, Gottfredson, and Garofalo (1978) refer to this as a function of the lifestyle of the parties involved. That is, an individual's choice of behavior (i.e., lifestyle) influences the chances of becoming a victim. This approach is referred to as the *routine activities/lifestyle model*.

A similar explanation can be used for personal offenses such as homicide. For a homicide to occur, it is necessary that the offender and victim be in the same place and that some event or occurrence precipitate the act. One example of this would be the following scenario:

> Two acquaintances frequent a bar where fights are a common occurrence. On one visit both individuals are cheering for opposing sports teams and make a wager on the outcome. Toward the end of a close contest, a questionable call by an official determines the outcome of the game. Coupled with a good amount of alcohol consumption, the two parties come to blows; one person pulls a knife and stabs the other.

From a routine activities perspective, this offense is partly attributable to the routine of the parties involved.

One example of the applicability of a routine activities/lifestyle model is the apparent tie to the seasonality of homicide. It has long been argued that homicide varies by season of the year (Dexter, 1904; Ferri, 1882; Lombroso, 1968; Quetelet, 1835) and that this variation is attributable to changes in heat and humidity (Baron and Bell, 1975; Durkheim, 1951; Lombroso, 1968). Rather than credit changes in homicide to fluctuating temperature, recent research has relied more on routine activities as an explanation. For example, the warm summer months draw people out of doors and prompt increased use of alcohol. This change in routine activities escalates the chances for personal victimization. Conversely, one can argue that inclement weather reduces outdoor activity, which may lead to greater intrafamilial conflict. Indeed, research has demonstrated that personal crime, including homicide, varies with heat and humidity (Baron and Bell, 1976; Cotton, 1983; Lab and Hirschel, 1988; LeBeau and Langworthy, 1986). Thus, it is feasible to assume that changing routines explain alterations in the level of homicide.

The value of the routine activities/lifestyle explanations is in understanding the social situations in which homicide occurs. These perspectives argue that our choices of where to go, what to do, and how to proceed (even when made innocently) influence the chances of becoming a victim. Recognition of this process may provide insight into homicide events.

Mass Media Influences

One way that culture influences both individual outlooks and behavior is through the images produced in the mass media. The pervasiveness of violence on television and in other popular outlets has led many spokespersons to condemn what they see as an unhealthy trend in our society. A number of professional and self-appointed watchdog groups routinely monitor the level of violence displayed in television broadcasts, movies, and books. Every year these organizations issue counts regarding the number of violent acts shown on television. Their verdict is that the level of violence available for public consumption has climbed beyond any acceptable limit. What these groups fear is that the widespread depiction of violence will desensitize viewers (especially younger and more impressionable children), render turbulent outbursts of behavior more acceptable, and prompt violent actions. In many respects, this argument is a simple extension of social learning theories. Among the various learning theories that would apply here are the ideas behind: (1) modeling (Bandura and Walters, 1963), (2) differential association (Sutherland, 1939), and (3) differential identification (Glaser, 1956).

Modeling is perhaps the simplest form of learning theory. It suggests that people learn by copying or imitating the behavior of others. While it is assumed that most people will duplicate the actions of significant others, it is possible that some nondiscriminating viewers will mimic the activity of characters in the media.

Sutherland's (1939) *differential association* theory argues that most learning comes from interpersonal contacts that vary in frequency, duration, priority, and intensity. Individuals will act in accordance with the dominant input from the people with whom they have direct contact. Sutherland, however, paid very little attention to the media—primarily because television did not yet exist in those days.

Glaser (1956), however, recognized the growing potential of the mass media to influence or mold behavior. *Differential identification* proposes that personal contact is not necessary for the transmission of behavioral guidelines. Both real and fictional presentations in the media, particularly television, can serve to define behaviors as either acceptable or unacceptable. In essence, differential identification is an explicit recognition that viewers can "model" or "imitate" what they see on the screen. This transference becomes problematic when the media grows preoccupied with depicting violence.

There is no dispute that the mass media is enamored with crime and violence. Violent crime is a major theme in both news and fictional media presentations, with 20 percent or more of television broadcast time often devoted to crime-related topics (see, for example, Dominick,

1978; Graber, 1977; Hofstetter, 1976). Even a casual observer cannot escape the centrality of crime to television. Recent years have seen a steady diet, as evidenced by shows such as "America's Most Wanted," "Unsolved Mysteries," "Law and Order," "CSI: Crime Scene Investigation," and the influx of telecasts such as Court TV.

Perhaps the most disturbing aspect of this proliferation of crime-related programming is that the presentations rarely resemble reality. Only the most sensational and horrific offenses make their way into the media. Violent crime, particularly murder, is overrepresented in comparison to its actual occurrence in the real world, and details are often distorted (Colomb and Damphousse, 2004; Dominick, 1978; Gerbner et al., 1980; Graber, 1980; Hofstetter, 1976; Paulsen, 2003; Skogan and Maxfield, 1981; Surette, 1998). In addition, it is rare for a story to focus on the consequences of the crime (e.g., being caught, prosecuted, and punished). Crime is glorified to some extent through its simple dominance in the stories. Such exposure may desensitize the public toward violence.

Various researchers have examined the potential of media presentations to influence behavior. At the simplest level, Gerbner et al. (1978; 1980) and Barrile (1980) have demonstrated that the general public gives answers about crime that are more consistent with what is presented in the media than with what actually occurs. A more important concern, though, is whether media presentations can promote similar behavior among viewers. Belson (1978) reports that individuals with higher levels of exposure to realistic depictions of violence tend to commit more serious acts of violence. Similarly, studies of prize fights and fictionalized suicides find significant increases in homicide and suicide after these media presentations have aired (Phillips, 1982; Phillips, 1983).

The link between video game exposure and violent behavior has not escaped scholarly attention either. While some studies report a significant association, others claim that such an effect does not exist. Despite this lack of closure, some observers immediately pointed to being involved in excessively violent video gaming as a culprit in the 1999 Columbine High School shootings in which 13 people were killed and another 24 were injured and in the 2007 massacre on the Virginia Tech campus that left 32 people dead and 25 wounded (Ferguson, 2007a). According to Ferguson (2007b), the literature on video game exposure is so replete with flaws that it is not possible to reach a definitive conclusion at this time. For one thing, researchers have not linked the measures commonly used to tap aggressive behavior with criminal violence. Another concern is that the typical subject pool of college or high school students overlooks the target group—persons who are predisposed toward violence. Finally, publication bias seems to have exerted an unwarranted impact on what papers make it to print.

In other words, journal editors are more prone to publish articles with significant findings and are more likely to turn down manuscripts that fail to unearth any significant relationships. This editorial slant, of course, predetermines what "knowledge" is readily available for consumption. All these concerns, in conjunction with a fresh look at the literature, led Ferguson (2007a: 481) to the worrisome conclusion that "researchers in the area of video game studies have become more concerned with 'proving' the presence of effects, rather than testing theory in a methodologically precise manner."

There are some claims that exposure to aggressive/violent pornography is coupled with violent criminal behavior (Donnerstein, 1980; Donnerstein and Hallam, 1978; Meyer, 1972; Shope, 2004; U.S. Attorney General's Commission on Pornography, 1986; Zillman, Bryant, and Carveth, 1981). For example, just before his execution, serial killer Ted Bundy blamed pornography for his violent escapades. Moreover, Andison's (1977) review of television violence research concluded there was a positive correlation between media presentations and violence. This relationship has grown stronger in more recent years, possibly due to accumulated exposure to media violence over time (Andison, 1977).

Apart from these macro-level attempts to unravel a media-behavior link, there are numerous individual accounts of instances in which an individual imitates an act of violence seen on television or is prompted to violence by media presentations. While evidence on the media-violence link is not conclusive, there is at least qualified support for a causal connection. Huesmann and Malamuth (1986) suggest that, at the very least, excessive exposure to media violence can force some viewers to become more aggressive. It is uncertain, however, just how this causal mechanism actually works. While it is logical to assume that mass media depictions of violence prod some individuals to be violent, it is equally plausible that people who commit aggressive acts simply enjoy watching violence in the media. Despite the fact that researchers have not firmly established the direction of this relationship, there is little doubt that the mass media plays a major role in the high levels of violence in society.

The "Regional Culture of Violence" Thesis

For years, the southern portion of the United States has held the dubious distinction of leading the country in terms of homicide victimization rates. In fact, the South is still noted for its elevated homicide rate (Federal Bureau of Investigation, 2006). As one might imagine, this *differential distribution of homicide rates* has attracted considerable scholarly interest. What the phrase "differential distribution of homicide rates" refers to is the fact that murder rates are not uniformly dispersed throughout time and space. In other words, if all things were equal, then all regional homicide victimization rates should be equivalent to each other. The observed imbalance leads one to the question of how to account for these differences in murder rates. As Figure 10.4 illustrates, homicides involving firearms are concentrated in the South.

FIGURE 10.4
Firearm Homicides, by State, 1989–1998

■ States at or above the 90th national percentile
▨ States at or above the 75th but less than the 90th national percentile
☐ States less than the national percentile

Source: National Center for Injury Prevention and Control (2007). *Injury Mortality Maps of the United States, 1989-1998*. Atlanta, GA: Centers for Disease Control and Prevention. Retrieved August 19, 2007, from http://webappa.cdc.gov/cdc_mxt3

A variety of theoretical accounts have cropped up in the literature. Some criminologists have tried to explain regional victimization differences by looking at such things as the size of the minority population (Dollard, 1949), the frustration-aggression hypothesis (Henry and Short, 1954), and childhood socialization practices (Gold, 1958). However, a penetrating critique of these and other theories uncovered a number of inadequacies and led to their dismissal. That assessment forced Hackney (1969) to speculate that one promising approach would be to look at the role of culture in the production of homicide victimization rates. That pronouncement opened the door for Gastil (1971) to build upon the Wolfgang and Ferracuti (1967) "subculture of violence" framework by posing such a theoretical perspective.

Gastil (1971) began his inquiry by mapping state homicide victimization rates over a number of years. What he found was a stable and intriguing pattern. Murder rates were quite pronounced in the South. Moreover, these rates declined with distance away from this area. States bordering the South had elevated homicide rates, but these figures were not quite as high as what was found in the Southern states. Areas located just beyond these border states exhibited even lower homicide victimization rates. Finally, the states located furthest away from the South consistently showed the lowest homicide victimization rates. These observations led Gastil (1971: 414) to suspect that "persistent differences in homicide rates seem best explained by differences in regional culture."

According to Gastil (1971), there exists a distinctive Southern culture predating the Civil War that tolerates violence. Gastil points to a number of cultural vestiges as supporting evidence of this area's propensity toward violence, including slavery, gun ownership, dueling, a strong military tradition, frontier living, and an exaggerated sense of honor among males. This violent heritage renders Southerners distinctive from other Americans. The net impact of these cultural remnants is a desensitization toward the use of violence as an acceptable behavioral response.

People who are born and bred in the South become carriers of this "Southernness" culture. Not only do Southerners inculcate their offspring into this normative value system, they also transport these violent tendencies wherever they go. What this contagion model stipulates is that areas settled by Southerners become infected and, in turn, are characterized by corresponding elevations in homicide victimization rates.

Gastil (1971) traced migration patterns out of the South to see how state murder rates mirrored settlement origins. To help track population shifts, Gastil constructed an *Index of Southernness*. States colonized by Southern-born persons receive top scores on this measure. Areas with sparse settlements of Southerners rank at the bottom of the scale. Thus, Gastil's "Index of Southernness" is an attempt to track cultural diffusion through migratory patterns.

An empirical analysis of 1960 homicide victimization rates and census materials revealed a dramatic empirical relationship between the "Index of Southernness" and murder. As a result, Gastil (1971: 425) concluded that Southernness was responsible for the differential distribution of homicide victimization rates throughout the United States.

This pronouncement, referred to as the *"regional culture of violence"* *thesis*, eventually spawned a large body of empirical studies.

Challenges to the "Regional Culture of Violence" Thesis

Gastil's broad assertion linking Southern culture with higher homicide victimization rates sparked several lines of research. The first approach questioned the cultural aspect of this explanation. The second strategy focused on the tenability of the regional component. The following materials examine each of these developments.

Cultural Challenges

The "regional culture of violence" thesis drew an immediate challenge from Loftin and Hill (1974). They noted that instead of measuring culture directly, Gastil (1971) opted to substitute geographical location as a surrogate. These researchers reanalyzed state homicide rates, adding their own *Structural Poverty Index*, which reflected variables such as high infant mortality, low education, and low income. They also added a measure of income inequality to the analysis. Loftin and Hill (1974) found that the statistical power of Gastil's Index of Southernness diminished to virtually nothing. Instead, the Structural Poverty Index and the income inequality measure were the strongest predictors of homicide levels. Essentially, then, these researchers raised serious doubts as to whether Southernness was the key to understanding the differential distribution of homicide victimization rates.

Another tack that researchers took moved away from the macro level and concentrated on the micro level. The thinking here was that Gastil's notion of a "culture of violence" hinges on the existence of a divergent normative value system. In other words, members of a subculture adhere to a distinctive attitudinal system that allows violence as a legitimate behavioral response. This belief system differs from the dominant culture and is directly responsible for higher rates of interpersonal violence among Southerners.

Despite repeated attempts, researchers have not been able to identify a separate Southern tradition conducive to violence (Doerner, 1978a; Doerner 1979; Erlanger, 1974; Erlanger, 1975). In fact, there appears to be no attitudinal differences toward violence between Southerners and nonSoutherners, or between nonSoutherners and migrants who have left the region. Under these conditions, there does not appear to be any support for the existence of a divergent regional attitudinal structure. Thus, Gastil's contagion idea (that Southerners are carriers of a violent tradition who infect receiving areas) lacks foundation.

Regional Challenges

A second line of inquiry has remained at the macro level. The focus has been on examining the ecological distribution of homicide victimization rates. A close look at Gastil's Index of Southernness reveals that all the Southern states receive the same score. What this observation means, then, is that Southernness must be distributed uniformly throughout the entire Southern region. Consequently, if Southernness is responsible for variations in murder rates, the South should display homogeneous or similar homicide victimization rates across the states.

A look at homicide rates from 1940 through 1970 in 10-year intervals uncovers significant intraregional variation (Doerner, 1980). In other words, grave dissimilarities abound. A longitudinal analysis using the same data source that Gastil studied, the same point in time that Gastil examined, and the same spatial unit of analysis did not substantiate the assumption of regional homogeneity. When coupled with an earlier study of regional homicide rates (Doerner, 1975), the following conclusion emerges:

> [I]f a *"regional* culture of violence" ever existed in the South, it existed prior to 1940. Thus, while the term *"regional* culture of violence" is a misnomer when applied to the contemporary South, it does not preclude the possibility that "Southernness" did exist at one time and that remnants exist in scattered pockets throughout the South" (Doerner, 1978b: 93).

Medical Resources as an Emerging Theoretical Dimension

While the empirical evidence mustered in response to Gastil's (1971) formulation was strong enough to cast heavy doubts regarding the adequacy of a cultural explanation, the original concern still remained. Some commentators chided researchers for failing to address the primary question in a meaningful way (Gastil, 1978; Loftin and Hill, 1978). That is, how can victimologists account for the differential distribution of homicide rates? If cultural values are not the answer, then what is? All the scholarly quibbling had yet to generate a meaningful alternative explanation (Hawley and Messner, 1989).

Conceptual Obstacles

Up to this point, past research efforts were hampered because they had glossed over some very important points. For example, the typical conceptualization of homicide was that it constituted a finite and distinctive legal category. This approached overlooked its underlying relationship to other proscribed behaviors. Illegal violent acts range from mere threats or verbal taunts (assault) to minor injuries (simple battery) to very serious bodily harm (aggravated battery) to death (homicide). When viewed in this context, one can locate violent behavior on a continuum. To illustrate this point, the FBI (2006) definition of an aggravated assault is "an unlawful attack . . . for the purpose of inflicting severe or aggravated bodily injury," usually with "use of a weapon or by means likely to produce death or great bodily harm." In one sense, homicide is nothing more than a successful aggravated battery, while an aggravated battery could very well be a failed murder attempt.

A second pertinent point is the obsession with lethality as the only theoretically meaningful outcome of violent social interaction. Riveting attention entirely upon the outcome of an event ignores the fact that violence is a process and that death is only one possible consequence. Just because two combatants engage in a physical confrontation, with or without weapons, does not mean that this clash will culminate automatically in a death. Wounded fighters often sustain non-fatal injuries (Weaver et al., 2004). Furthermore, when they do incur critical, life-threatening damage, death is not necessarily imminent. Timely and appropriate medical intervention can play a key role in keeping an aggravated battery from slipping into a homicide statistic. Firearms were present in seven out of 10 homicide events in 2006, but in far fewer aggravated assaults cases (Federal Bureau of Investigation, 2006). This regularity may be due to the fact that firearm incidents require more medical attention than other injuries. Thus, it would seem that the potential impact of medical resources upon the production of lethality rates stemming from criminal violence deserves further examination.

The Impact of Medical Resources

One specialty area in the medical literature is trauma management. *Trauma*, in the medical sense, refers to any physical injury, without concern for the origin of the damage. Some examples of trauma include traffic accident injuries, industrial mishaps, suicide, poisoning, drowning, heart attacks, burns, stabbings, gunshots, and so forth. One prominent goal of trauma management is to reduce trauma-induced mortality.

In a review of the trauma management literature, Doerner (1983) looked at emergency transportation, field treatment, hospital emergency treatment, and post-operative recovery. One generalization that emerged was that rapid ambulance response time, coupled with the deployment of specially trained paramedics, increased the odds of patient survival. Medical experts refer to a period called the "*golden hour*," the time period in which seriously injured people need medical attention if they are to survive. A second finding is that quick delivery of a salvageable patient to a hospital emergency room does not ensure survival. Most hospitals are not equipped sufficiently to handle serious trauma cases. They lack the appropriate technological facilities and do not have uniquely trained persons on staff. Instead, an ambulance with a critical injury case would be better advised to reroute to a specially designated trauma center. There the patient would receive more intensive care from specialized medical teams acquainted with the most current technology. However, all these measures still do not guarantee an automatic "save" from death. There is the ever-present danger of inaccurate patient assessment, post-operative infection, and other long-term complications.

It is important to realize that medical resources, just like homicide rates, are differentially distributed throughout time and space. In fact, many areas, as seen in Figure 10.5, aim to correct geographical imbalances by offering financial incentives to doctors who agree to practice in certain locations (Rivo, Henderson, and Jackson, 1995). There is recognition, of course, that the concentration and distribution of physicians is influenced by such considerations as degree of urbanization, community size, quality of life, and the availability of hospital facilities (Anderson, 1977; Begun, 1977; Eyles and Woods, 1983; Frenzen, 1991; Marden, 1966; Reskin and Campbell, 1976; Rushing, 1975; Rushing and Wade, 1973). One known outcome of greater medical specialization is a reduction in infant mortality rates and alterations in morbidity or sickness patterns (Anderson, 1977; Begun, 1977; Friedman, 1973). Given this evidence, it would not be unreasonable to expect that areas characterized by relatively fewer medical resources would exhibit higher lethality rates stemming from criminal violence, not because of the impact of Southernness, but due to the limited availability of adequate emergency medical care.

FIGURE 10.5
One Way to Entice Physicians to Practice Medicine in an Area

[Medical-school students] Plum and Albritton were both offered assistance from their local hospitals to graduate from medical school at FSU, complete their three-year residency at Tallahassee Memorial Hospital and return to Perry and Marianna, respectively, to spend at least four years taking care of home.

The deal seemed to make the most sense, Plum said. The community supports the student, and the student gives back to the community.

"There is a shortage of doctors everywhere," Albritton said.

Doctor's Memorial Hospital invested $60,000 in Plum's education, so Plum will provide a solution to a problem in his community once he returns.

Taylor and Jackson counties are both federally designated as medically underserved, primarily because of a lack of physicians.

"It's hard to get doctors to come here," said Diana McRory, human resource director.

Source: Jefferson, J. (2007). "Towns Invest in Medical Students." *Tallahassee Democrat* (May 26):3A. Courtesy of *Tallahassee Democrat*.

Empirical Evidence

Given this orientation, Doerner (1983) pitted the Index of Southernness against several indicators of medical care in an examination of state homicide rates. While the results were not entirely conclusive, they did offer some encouraging support for this line of reasoning. Spurred on by these results, a second study was undertaken using Florida counties (Doerner and Speir, 1986). Once again, modest support for the medical resources argument emerged. Buoyed by these findings, a third study employing more detailed measures of medical resources was initiated (Doerner, 1988). Yet again, there was some indication that medical resources, particularly emergency transportation, partially affected criminally induced mortality.

Concern that the accumulating evidence might be peculiar to the state of Florida prompted Long-Onnen and Cheatwood (1992) to look at the medical resources argument in five other states: Delaware, Maryland, Pennsylvania, Virginia, and West Virginia. Their data showed limited support for the notion that medical resources contribute to the production of homicide rates. In a similar vein, an examination of female homicide offender records in Alabama links racial inequities in emergency medical care with victim demise (Hanke and Gundlach,

1995). In addition, Giacopassi and Sparger (1992) combed through Memphis police homicide files for the years 1935, 1960, and 1985. Looking at the circumstances surrounding these nonsalvageable cases, Giacopassi and Sparger (1992: 256-257) concluded:

> Although the present data are subject to varying interpretations and do not prove that medical care has saved the lives of many who earlier would have become homicide statistics, the evidence seems heavily weighted in favor of this argument. Logic says that increasingly efficient ambulance services, better roads and highways, better trained paramedics, improved communications systems, more hospitals and trauma centers, more skillful physicians, and advances in medicine and medical care all have served to suppress America's homicide rate.

Finally, Harris and his colleagues (2002) undertook an extensive analysis of homicide and aggravated assault rates spanning the 1960–1999 period. Their results add further credence to the notion that medical resources have had a dramatic influence on the production of homicide and aggravated assault statistics. Harris and his research team (2002: 130) concluded:

> Compared to 1960, the year our analysis begins, we estimate that without these developments in medical technology there would have been between 45,000 and 70,000 homicides annually the past 5 years instead of an actual 15,000 to 20,000.

Some Remaining Issues

This initial wave of research activity suggests that the medical resources argument is plausible and deserves further consideration. In fact, a "wish list" assembled by the editorial board of the journal *Homicide Studies* includes a call for further study of this linkage (Smith, 2000: 5-6). Much more work remains to be done before any worthwhile theoretical advances can materialize. Some possible directions include a closer look at the role of alcohol, the application of the "autopsy method," and the use of an *injury-severity index*.

Both the victimological and emergency medical literatures acknowledge that alcohol is a common ingredient in trauma incidents (Brookman and Maguire, 2005; Jurkovich et al., 1993; Lowenstein, Weissberg, and Terry, 1990; Riedel, Zahn, and Mock, 1985; Rivara et al., 1997; Soderstrom and Smith, 1993; Sutocky, Shultz, and Kizer, 1993;

Wilbanks, 1984; Wolfgang, 1958; Woolf et al., 1991). Criminologists typically characterize alcohol as a social lubricant. They maintain that alcohol consumption relaxes people, lowers their social inhibitions, weakens restrictions governing the use of force, and triggers the release of any pent-up hostilities (Hepburn, 1973; Kantor and Straus, 1987; Wolfgang, 1958). A somewhat related corollary is that alcohol ingestion dulls the reflex system and compromises one's physical readiness. It distorts perceptions and increases reaction time, leaving a person incapable of mounting a sufficient self-defense in the event of a violent attack.

One frequently overlooked aspect of alcohol consumption is that it can also hinder timely medical intervention. Drinking can impede the cardiocirculatory system and depress the central nervous system. Sometimes when time is of the essence, these physical reactions make it difficult to reach an accurate or conclusive diagnosis. For example, a common physical reaction after drinking alcohol is for the pupils to dilate. An attending physician concerned with the possibility of a closed-head injury has to decide whether alcohol is masking the patient's true physical status or if the physical conditions are valid symptoms of brain-related damage (Horton, 1986; Jurkovich et al., 1993; Stone et al., 1986; Woolf et al., 1991). In the absence of any further information, the doctor may delay treatment pending more conclusive blood tests or risk error by choosing one course of intervention over another. Indeed, the general consensus in the emergency medical literature is that 20 to 30 percent of all in-hospital, trauma-associated deaths are avoidable (Chan, Ainscow, and Sikorski, 1980; Davis et al., 1991; Dove, Stahl, and Delbuircio, 1980; Haywood and Hofer, 2001; Kreis et al., 1986). While not cognizant of this effect, some criminological studies do show higher alcohol or other drug levels in deceased victims compared to survivors of aggravated battery situations (Felson and Steadman, 1983; Pittman and Handy, 1964).

A common hospital administrative practice is to conduct periodic postmortem reviews to determine whether patients are receiving adequate medical care. This tool is what medical researchers call the *autopsy method* (Pollock et al., 1993; Stohert, Gbaanador, and Herndon, 1990; West, Cales, and Gazzaniga, 1983), and it is used to reduce preventable in-hospital deaths (Hayward and Hofer, 2001). If a systematic problem surfaces, there might be a suggestion that the institution adopt a different treatment protocol as the standard operating procedure in these instances (Enderson et al., 1990; Ivatury et al., 1991). This constant case monitoring enables trauma centers to take advantage of breaking medical developments and new equipment.

Emergency room admissions generally do not receive medical attention on a "first come, first served" basis. Usually, medical personnel triage patients or conduct a screening during the admissions phase. That is, incoming patients receive a grade regarding the extent and seriousness of their injuries. This strategy creates a queue in which the more seriously wounded are assigned a higher treatment priority over less injured persons (Thayer, 1997).

There have been very few victimological efforts that measure the degree of physical injury incurred by violent crime victims. One researcher suggests that application of the "Abbreviated Injury Scale" and an "Injury Severity Score" could provide immense benefits to this line of inquiry. Allen (1986) explains that these trauma scales were developed to help vehicular crash investigators determine automotive safety standards. His suggestion is that one could use these indices to grade the type of and amount of injuries sustained by crime victims and then to monitor survival patterns. While some researchers have expressed qualms about applying these scales retroactively to archived medical records (Giacopassi and Sparger, 1992: 252-253), these criticisms are not insurmountable (Safarik and Jarvis, 2005). With proper training and adequate documentation, these tools could be incorporated into ongoing patient registration procedures. As you can see, it is quite possible that a sustained interdisciplinary effort, such as what is described here, would enhance our understanding of the production of homicide victimization statistics.

Survivors of Homicide Victimization

Death is a topic that many people prefer to avoid discussing. In fact, mortality is a taboo subject. Thinking about it can generate a sense of anxiety, so many people shun the subject. Whenever a person dies, someone must inform the next-of-kin or other survivors of the deceased. The notifier who delivers this message must be prepared to deal with a wide range of responses. The recipients of this communication start the coping process immediately upon hearing of the news. The manner in which the initial notification is made can impact the grieving process. This portion of the chapter will discuss death notification procedures and then move to a treatment of the bereavement process.

Death Notification

Death notification is not a pleasant responsibility. Often, this task falls to law enforcement officers, victim advocates, or representatives from the medical examiner's or coroner's office. Many agencies have adopted formal policies similar to what appears in Figure 10.6 to help their personnel with the delivery of death-related news. Even if an explicit policy does not exist, death notification procedures usually follow a four-step process (Byers, 1991; Hendricks, 1984): (1) information gathering, (2) control and direction, (3) assessment, and (4) referral.

FIGURE 10.6
A Law Enforcement Agency Policy Regarding Death Notification Procedures

A.   Notification Within the City

    1.   When the next-of-kin of a deceased, seriously injured or seriously ill person lives in the City, the officer should make all notifications in person whenever practical. However, if this is not practical, the officer should contact the Communications Center and request another officer be dispatched to the residence for notification.

    2.   The officer delivering the notification should have as much information as possible to enable him or her to carry out the notification in a professional and considerate manner. When possible, contact between officers or with the Communications Center should be via telephone.

    3.   The officer should make every reasonable effort to notify the next-of-kin during his or her tour of duty.

        a.   The officer shall not leave notification up to the hospital or other authorities.

        b.   The officer shall note in the offense report the name of the person notified, relationship and time accomplished.

    4.   The officer, when possible, should stand by after the notification has been made and render additional assistance to the next-of-kin and, when necessary,:

        a.   contact clergy;

        b.   contact medical assistance;

        c.   contact other family members.

Source: Tallahassee Police Department (2007). *Policy Manual: Death Notification*. Tallahassee, FL: City of Tallahassee.

The first step in any death notification is the information-gathering phase. The person who is to deliver the news should anticipate the types of questions that the recipients may ask and determine the appropriate response to those inquiries. The most important element here is to obtain and verify the identification of the deceased. The name of the person, gender, age, address, and any other personal identifiers are of paramount importance. Similar information about the survivor(s) is also essential. Also valuable is information on the circumstances surrounding the death, including time and place. Prior to making the actual notification, the deliverer should confirm that he or she is at the correct location and has reached the appropriate party.

Step two in the death notification process is control and direction. It is the responsibility of the notifier to define the situation for the survivor by informing him or her of the unfortunate news. The deliverer should be factual, honest, and deliberate in the choice of words. Experts advise that it is best to avoid such euphemisms as "He's gone to a better place" or "She is looking down upon us now" (Byers, 1991; Hendricks, 1984). As the impact begins to take effect upon the survivor, the third phase—the assessment stage—begins to unfold.

The primary task of the notifier during the assessment stage is to gauge how the bereaved reacts to the disturbing message. Should the recipient show signs of self-blame, or self-destructive behavior such as suicide, the deliverer will need to rechannel, guide, or prod the person out of this frame of mind. If the situation worsens, other resources (such as a clergy member, a physician, a victim advocate, another survivor, or a neighbor) might be in a better position to assist. The objective of this phase is to ensure the well-being of the survivor(s).

The last stage is called referral. Survivors will become flooded with a number of concerns. They will need immediate information about how to make funeral arrangements, how to get the body released from the medical examiner's office, what police procedures must transpire, and the like. Once the situation is under control, the notifier has completed his or her assignment and may leave the scene.

It is important to realize that leaving the scene does not mean that the situation has ended for the notifier. Emergency responders sometimes become deeply immersed in these events and have their own feelings to sort through once the formal assignment is completed (Hendricks, 1984; McCarroll et al., 1993; Walker, 1990). Many agencies will hold a debriefing session for members after a huge disaster or a major catastrophe has subsided. The intent is to relieve any stress reactions that workers may have developed during the crisis. These sessions allow workers to ventilate their feelings, receive information that they may have lacked during the incident, and begin adjusting back to the daily routine.

The Bereavement Process

As we learned earlier in Chapter 6, people who experience a calamity inevitably find themselves in the midst of a crisis. The death of a significant other, particularly through a homicide, qualifies as a sudden, emotionally shattering event that can quickly propel survivors deep into a crisis state. Based upon what experts know about the crisis reaction repair cycle, recovery usually proceeds in a very predictable fashion.

The complete lack of any warning associated with most homicides denies survivors a chance to prepare beforehand for such excruciating news. Survivors do not have the luxury of *anticipatory grief*—the preparations that people can make to cushion the impact of death when a loss is imminent or expected to take place. For example, the diagnosis of a terminal illness in an elderly relative permits family members to brace themselves for the inevitable. This advance warning alerts people to what is coming, gives them time to search for appropriate coping mechanisms, and enables survivors to adapt expeditiously to the loss. Homicide survivors lack this preparation. They are thrust into a crisis state unexpectedly without any prior warning or any chance to adjust their readiness.

Most homicide victims are men under the age of 40. This demographic profile means that the survivors of homicide victims will face a host of challenges. Generally speaking, it is easier to cope with timely, as opposed to "off-time," deaths (Detmer and Lamberti, 1991; Parry and Thornwall, 1992). At this point in the life cycle, most men have established a family unit. Their children will grow up without their father. The widow must assume all family responsibilities, including financial burdens. While social security and insurance may help defray some expenses, the role structure of the nuclear family unit often changes. Older children may take on more caretaking functions for younger siblings. Some women may find that they must reenter the job market on a more sustained basis. In short, the survivors must make many adaptations to compensate for the loss of a loved one.

Relatively little research has been devoted to the response of homicide survivors to the loss of a loved one. Kübler-Ross (1969) outlined four stages to the *grief process*: (1) shock and denial, (2) anger, (3) isolation, and (4) acceptance/recovery. The first stage is shock and denial. Immediately after being informed of the death, the survivor reacts by denying that the information is true and tends to shut out all input concerning the event. This reaction is a short-term, self-protection mechanism that serves to cushion the blow. The second stage is anger. Here the survivor vents his or her rage, frustration, and anger toward anyone or anything available. This anger may be toward the bearer of the news, the doctors who could not save the victim, the offender, society, or even himself or herself. Third, the survivor tends to isolate himself or herself from others. Isolation reflects different emotions ranging from the uncertainty of how to deal with others to the feeling that there is no one to whom the survivor can turn. Finally, the survivor begins to resume some form of normal activities in the acceptance/recovery stage. While the death remains with the individual, the event is incorporated into the daily routine of the individual as he or she realizes that life must continue.

As mentioned in Chapter 6, there is no predetermined timetable for grief resolution. It may take years before survivors can put the incident behind them. The bereavement process may be continuous and fluid, with members sometimes regressing to early stages. Recovery may be prolonged because of case processing by the criminal justice system. What little research that does exist on homicide survivors, though, suggests that these intense feelings diminish over time and the healing eventually tracks a typical recovery pattern (Horne, 2003; Kitson et al., 1991; Range and Niss, 1990).

There is also evidence that different survivors adapt and cope with the homicide in various ways. Key (1992) identified five *homicide survivor patterns* based on his clinical experience with such individuals. These patterns are highly related to the lifestyle and social setting of the victim and the survivor. The five survival patterns correspond to (1) the alcohol- or other drug-related murder, (2) the domestic violence homicide, (3) the gang-related murder, (4) the isolated sudden murder, and (5) the serial murder. The survivor in each of these situations reacts differently.

For example, in the alcohol- or other drug-related murder survivor pattern, the survivor typically knew of the victim's use and/or trafficking behavior. The survivor had some warning ahead of time that the victim was involved in potentially dangerous behavior and, consequently, was able to prepare somewhat for the loss of the victim. The survivor may even actually feel a sense of relief once the event occurs.

In the domestic violence homicide survival pattern, the survivor may feel some personal guilt for failing to intervene when early signs of abuse and problems emerged. The survivor may believe that if he or she had become involved, the victim may still be alive.

The gang-related homicide is typically expected by the survivor, who feels he or she had no control over the event. In many cases, the survivor may believe that the victim was also a homicide offender and it was only a matter of time until the offender became a victim.

The final two categories, isolated sudden murder survival pattern and the serial murder survival pattern, both reflect situations in which the death was totally unexpected. These are the scenarios that correspond to the classic image of an unsuspected homicide victimization. Here, the survivor experiences the typical grief pattern outlined earlier. There are feelings of denial, anger, self-blame, guilt, isolation, and eventual reemergence to everyday reality. Key (1992) notes that these survival patterns are not exhaustive; not all possible patterns are included. Rather, he offers these patterns as illustrations of how various people respond to a homicide event in different ways based on the circumstances and background of both the victim and the survivor.

Critical to the bereavement process is the provision of support to the survivor. This support most likely begins with the police officer or physician who notifies the survivor and then lasts for a long period of time. An ideal support network can help with a myriad of different things facing the survivor. It certainly would include some offer of counseling, whether in an individual or group setting. While one might assume that these services are common in our society, such assistance is often unknown to the survivor. One method that has emerged in many communities in recent years has been homicide support groups. These groups serve many immediate and long-term needs. In addition, they may involve themselves in community outreach programs, such as those teaching youths about the impact of homicide (Johnson and Young, 1992). Inevitably, the homicide survivor goes on with his or her life. The degree to which survivors receive assistance in that process, however, differs greatly from place to place.

FIGURE 10.7
Selected Internet Sites Dealing with Homicide

Bureau of Justice Statistics
  http://www.ojp.usdoj.gov/bjs

Centers for Disease Control and Prevention
  http://www.cdc.gov

David Baldwin's Trauma Information Page
  http://www.trauma-pages.com

Death Notification and Survivor Care Program
  http://www.ucsf.edu/deathnotification

Doctors Against Handgun Injury
  http://www.doctorsagainsthandguninjury.org

Firearm Injury Center, Medical College of Wisconsin
  http://www.mcw.edu/display/router.asp?docid=186

Harvard Injury Control Research Center
  http://www.hsph.harvard.edu/hicrc

Homicide Research Working Group
  http://www.icpsr.umich.edu/hrwg

Parents of Murdered Children
  http://www.pomc.org

Summary

Homicide, the deliberate killing of one human being by another, claims the lives of thousands of people every year. For some segments of society, murder has reached epidemic levels. For instance, homicide is a leading cause of death for young, African-American males in United States cities. Further compounding the alarming spread of violence is the fact that it does not appear that this bloodshed will disappear any time soon. As a result, our theories and interventions are in need of greater refinement. So far, victimization data have experienced some serious limitations, and policy developments have been negligible. It is the homicide survivors, though (particularly young children), who carry the worst emotional scars. They are forced to make efforts to reclaim their shattered lives and make sense out of the aftermath of the homicide.

Key Terms for Chapter 10

anticipatory grief

autopsy method

criminal homicide

death notification

differential association

differential distribution of homicide rates

differential identification

eldercide

Firearm Fatality Reporting System

"golden hour"

grief process

homicide survivor patterns

Index of Southernness

infanticide

injury-severity index

intimate femicide

lifetime murder victimization rate

matricide

modeling

nonprimary homicide

overrepresentation

parricide

patricide

primary homicide

"regional culture of violence" thesis

routine activities/lifestyle model

situated transaction

Structural Poverty Index

trauma

victim precipitation

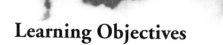

Learning Objectives

After reading Chapter 11, you should be able to:

- Use the routine activities perspective to explain victimization at work and school.

- Explain the many meanings and types of workplace violence.

- Discuss the extent of victimization in the workplace, and what workers are most at risk of violent victimization.

- Describe various sources of data on workplace violence.

- Provide different possible explanations for workplace violence.

- Outline various ways to prevent violence and victimization in the workplace.

- Specify key elements of a workplace violence prevention program.

- Identify and explain different bases for employees to claim employer negligence.

- Talk about the types and extent of victimization at school.

- Compare and contrast individual and school-level data on school crime.

- Visit different responses to victimization at school utilized by students.

- Highlight different ways schools respond to crime problems.

- List potential responses schools can employ to address crisis situations.

- Define sexual harassment and its various forms.

- Discuss the extent of sexual harassment.

- Talk about how victims and employers can respond to harassment situations.

Chapter 11

VICTIMIZATION AT WORK AND SCHOOL

Introduction

Many of the foregoing discussions of victimization revolve around actions tied to the home of the victim and/or the offender. Indeed, as we have seen, one of the perplexing problems with much family violence is how to shed light on actions that take place behind closed doors, hidden from the rest of society. Not all victimization, however, takes place inside the home. One reason we focus on victimization at home is the fact that the home is where many victims and offenders have the most contact. Two other prime locations for victimization are the workplace and school.

The workplace and school are two prime locations for violence and victimization for a variety of reasons. Perhaps the easiest explanation revolves around the idea of routine activities. As we saw in earlier chapters, the *routine activities perspective* posits that crime is more likely where and when three things coincide: (1) a suitable target, (2) a motivated offender, and (3) an absence of guardians. Both the workplace and schools typically bring these three key ideas together. The fact that most adults hold a job and most youths, by law, must attend school satisfies the first condition. This same fact also addresses the second condition of having a motivated offender. Going to work or school brings a variety of individuals together. It is from these groups of individuals that the potential offenders and victims emerge. The third factor, a lack of guardians, may be an unfortunate part of many schools and places of employment. The schools and employers may not focus on or be prepared to offer protection to those parties who frequent their locations. The need to take protective measures may not have arisen in the past. Thus, the employer or school has failed the victim more through ignorance than because of an uncaring attitude.

Paying greater attention to the role of security and prevention at work and at school is a relatively recent phenomenon. The media, researchers, and various agencies have given increased attention to workplace and school victimization, particularly in terms of violent episodes in recent years. The best illustration of this focus can be found in the attention paid to the problem in the media. Shootings at work and at school are headline news, and coverage often persists on television for weeks or months after the event. Violent events, therefore, are seen as part and parcel of going to work or school.

This chapter investigates victimization, particularly violence, at work and at school. The chapter is divided into separate discussions of work and school. For each type of victimization, the chapter attempts to define the problem, provide an overview of the extent of victimization at work and school, offer potential explanations for the behavior, and visit potential responses. Points of similarity between work and school, such as in the case of teacher victimization, are noted throughout the discussion. A separate but related topic, sexual harassment, is considered at the end of the chapter.

Victimization at Work

While many different crimes occur at work against both the agency or the employees, most discussions of workplace victimization revolve around the problem of violence. Interest in workplace violence has increased in recent years, largely due to media presentations of killings at work. Indeed, violence directed by an employee or ex-employee against others at the workplace has popularly come to be known as *"going postal,"* a reference to a few highly publicized incidents of violence by postal workers at the workplace. Workplace violence, however, is not confined to a single action or location.

Defining Workplace Victimization

No single, agreed-upon definition of *workplace violence* appears in the literature. A wide range of actions can be subsumed under the idea of workplace violence, including homicide, assault, robbery, rape, intimidation, harassment, threats, and even verbal and psychological aggression. The National Institute of Occupational Safety and Health (NIOSH) defines workplace violence as "violent acts, including physical assaults and threats of assault, directed toward persons at work or on duty." Unfortunately, this definition fails to address issues of intimidation, harassment, or verbal aggression. The fact that those omitted forms of violence are harder to measure is perhaps the most notable reason for adopting a more limited working definition.

Some definitions limit workplace violence to situations in which the offender is a current or former employee at the workplace. Other delineations consider any violent act committed against an employee on the job, whether the offender is a client, another employee, or a complete stranger. The offender also may be a relative or close acquaintance of the victim who is bringing a problem or confrontation from home or elsewhere into the workplace.

Another consideration in defining workplace violence is identifying what constitutes the workplace. Most people think in terms of a specific location, such as a store, factory, office, or school. At the same time, the workplace can be considered in a broader sense. Many jobs require employees to work outdoors and move around a wide geographic area. Water meter readers, police officers, firefighters, real estate salespersons, taxi drivers, and many others do not have just one "place" of business. Rather, their place of business varies across both time and space. Thus, most investigations of locational violence tend to consider the workplace as being wherever the employee is on duty, and not just an identifiable geographic location.

Based on these considerations in defining workplace violence, a typology of violence has developed over time (see Figure 11.1). Initially developed by the California Occupational Safety and Health Administration, the typology has been modified by others. The current typology offers four categories of workplace violence. Type 1 reflects violence by offenders who intend to commit a crime. Included here are offenses such as robbery, theft, and other actions that are related more to the opportunity to commit a crime than to the individuals involved. Type 2 workplace violence involves actions in which there is a customer/client relationship and violence emerges during the business transaction. Type 3 involves worker-on-worker confrontations. The fourth and final type involves a personal relationship between the victim and offender from outside the workplace. Wives, husbands, boyfriends, girlfriends, children, siblings, friends, and other acquaintances all fall into this group. While explanations for victimization in the workplace are not mutually exclusive across the types (for example, stress at home may impact on altercations between coworkers), these categories provide an organizing theme for looking at causation.

FIGURE 11.1
Typology of Workplace Violence

Type	Description
I: Criminal intent	The perpetrator has no legitimate relationship to the business or its employee, and is usually committing a crime in conjunction with the violence. These crimes can include robbery, shoplifting, trespassing, and terrorism. The vast majority of workplace homicides (85%) fall into this category.
II: Customer/client	The perpetrator has a legitimate relationship with the business and becomes violent while being served by the business. This category includes customers, clients, patients, students, inmates, and any other group for which the business provides services. It is believed that a large portion of customer/client incidents occur in the health care industry, in settings such as nursing homes or psychiatric facilities; the victims are often patient caregivers. Police officers, prison staff, flight attendants, and teachers are some other examples of workers who may be exposed to this kind of WPV [workplace violence], which accounts for approximately 3% of all workplace homicides.
III: Worker-on-worker	The perpetrator is an employee or past employee of the business who attacks or threatens another employee(s) or past employee(s) in the workplace. Worker-on-worker fatalities account for approximately 7% of all workplace homicides.
IV: Personal relationship	The perpetrator usually does not have a relationship with the business but has a personal relationship with the intended victim. This category includes victims of domestic violence assaulted or threatened while at work, and accounts for about 5% of all workplace homicides.

Source: NIOSH (2006). *Workplace Violence Prevention Strategies and Research Needs*, NIOSH Publication No. 2006-144. Found at: http://www.cdc.gov/niosh/docs/2006-144

The Extent of Workplace Victimization

Systematic analyses of workplace violence are rare relative to more general studies of violence and victimization in society. While we hear about crime and violence regularly on television and in other media, very little of that information deals with the workplace. Indeed, workplace violence mainly appears in the media only when a mass shooting or homicide takes place at work. This statement, however, does not mean that data on workplace violence do not exist.

Liberty Mutual produces an annual report on workplace safety. In 2006, assaults and violent acts were the tenth leading cause of injuries at work, accounting for 1.1 percent of all workplace injuries (Liberty Mutual, 2007). The Bureau of Labor Statistics (BLS) reports that homicide is one of the four most frequent causes of work-related fatalities, with 516 homicides occurring at workplaces in 2006. While high, this is the fewest number ever reported by the Bureau of Labor Statistics.

Another way to look at workplace violence is to consider the prevalence of the problem across work sites. According to a BLS survey, 5.3 percent of more than 7.3 million establishments experienced at least one violent incident in 2005 (Bureau of Labor Statistics, 2006). Table 11.1 provides data on the percent of establishments experiencing different types of workplace violence.

TABLE 11.1
Percent of Establishments Experiencing Workplace Violence in Past 12 Months

	Any Incidents	Criminal	Customer/ Client	Coworker	Domestic Violence
Total	5.3%	2.2%	2.2%	2.3%	0.9%
Private Industry	4.8	2.1	1.9	2.1	0.8
State Government	32.2	8.7	15.4	17.7	5.5
Local Government	14.7	3.7	10.3	4.3	2.1

Source: Bureau of Labor Statistics (2006). *Survey of Workplace Violence Prevention*. Found at: http://www.bls.gov/iif/oshwc/osnr0026.pdf

One of the broadest-based attempts to look at workplace violence may be the National Crime Victimization Survey (NCVS). The NCVS asks respondents to identify where their victimization took place. Table 11.2 presents data for the average number and rate of victimizations that occurred while at work or on duty from 1993-1999. The results show that there were more than 1.7 million crimes of violence committed at the workplace or while at work. This number represents 18 percent of all victimizations reported over the seven-year time period (Duhart, 2001). It is noteworthy that most of those violent victimizations are simple assaults, which account for three-quarters of all acts of violence at work. At the other extreme, 900 homicides occur per year, but make up only .1 percent of all violent acts.

TABLE 11.2
Victimization in the Workplace

Type of Crime	Number	Rate per 1,000 Workers	Percent of Workplace Violence
Homicide	900	0.01	.1
Rape/Sexual Assault	35,500	0.3	2.1
Robbery	70,100	0.5	4.0
Aggravated Assault	325,000	2.3	18.6
Simple Assault	1,311,700	9.4	75.2
Total Violent Crimes	1,744,300	12.4	100.0

Source: Duhart, D.T. (2001). *Violence in the Workplace, 1993-99*. Washington, DC: Bureau of Justice Assistance.

TABLE 11.3
Occupations of Victims of Violent Victimization in the Workplace, 1993-1999

Occupation	Number	Rate per 1,000 Workers
Medical		
Physicians	71,300	16.2
Nurses	429,100	21.9
Technicians	97,600	12.7
Mental Health		
Professional	290,900	68.2
Custodial	60,400	69.0
Teaching		
Elementary	262,700	16.8
Junior High	321,300	54.2
High School	314,500	38.1
College/University	41,600	1.6
Special Education	102,000	16.7
Law Enforcement		
Police	1,380,400	260.8
Private Security	369,300	86.6
Corrections Officers	277,100	155.7
Retail Sales		
Convenience/Liquor Store	336,800	58.9
Gas Station	86,900	68.3
Bartender	170,600	81.6
Transportation		
Taxi cab driver	84,400	128.3
Bus Driver	105,800	38.2
Total[a]	4,720,100	38.3

[a] Total includes occupations not otherwise listed in the table.

Source: Duhart, D.T. (2001). *Violence in the Workplace, 1993-99*. Washington, DC: Bureau of Justice Statistics.

While the data in Table 11.2 suggest that victimization at work is not an insignificant problem, they do not indicate who is most at risk of becoming a victim. That is, are all workers equally likely to be a victim at work, or should some workers be more concerned than others? Using data from the NCVS, Duhart (2001) computed the number and rate of victimizations for individuals working in different occupations from 1993-1999. Table 11.3 presents the results of his computations for nonfatal workplace violence.

The information in Table 11.3 shows that some workers are at a much greater risk of being victimized than are other workers. Perhaps not unexpectedly, individuals working in law enforcement are victimized at a higher rate than almost all other occupations. Police officers are the most victimized, both in terms of raw numbers (almost 1.8 million victimizations) and victimization rate (261 per 1,000). Corrections officers, while not second in terms of numbers, are the second most victimized given the number of people in that position (i.e., the rate of violent victimizations). Those working in private security also face a high level of violence. There is also a relatively high rate of victimization for those employed in the mental health field. These results for law enforcement and mental health should not be surprising given the type of job and the kinds of people with whom these employees must deal. Besides law enforcement, the highest rates of victimization appear for taxi drivers (rate of 128.3), followed by those working in retail sales. There also is a relatively high rate for junior high school teachers (rate of 54.2).

Why do certain occupations display higher levels of victimization? Perhaps the best explanation entails the factors outlined under the routine activities perspective. Many jobs put workers into situations in which there is a great deal of contact with the public, and often that contact occurs in isolation from coworkers or some form of supervision. Stores, gas stations, and bars, for example, often have a single employee at work at a time. The worker, therefore, is isolated. That is, there is an absence of guardians. In other settings, such as retail sales and service occupations like taxi driving, there is an assumption that a suitable target (i.e., cash) is available, thus making those individuals good targets for offending. Yet another factor is dealing with special populations.

The varied measures of workplace violence offer a number of important insights. First, the commonly held beliefs about workplace violence are generally wrong. Most of the violence is related to other criminal acts and is not the result of a disgruntled worker or ex-employee. Second, the most dangerous occupations are often those in which the employees have tacitly accepted a degree of risk by the very nature of the job, such as law enforcement or mental health

FIGURE 11.2
Percent of Establishments with Potentially Hazardous Work Environment

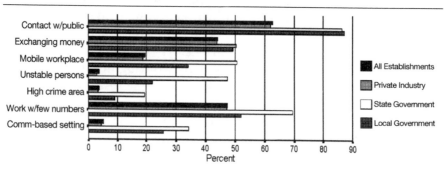

Source: Bureau of Labor Statistics (2006), Survey of Workplace Violence Prevention, 2006. Found at: http://www.bis.gov/iif/oshwc/osnr026.pdf

workers. Third, the level of risk is closely related to occupations in which the victim works alone and/or the job requires employment at night and early mornings when the employee is isolated from others. Fourth, a significant portion of all victimizations, both violent and theft, occur at work or when the victim is on duty. These findings offer insight that is useful for understanding workplace victimization and responses to this problem.

Explanations and Causes of Workplace Victimization

Explanations for workplace violence run the gamut of explanations seen in many of the other chapters in this book. In most respects, the causes for workplace violence are the same as for non-workplace violence, spouse abuse, child abuse, and other forms of victimization. What differs is the location of the transgression. We have already explored one potential explanation in the introduction to this chapter—routine activities. The fact that a person's job may place him or her in a situation where potential offenders are nearby, where the potential victim or the circumstances make for an attractive target, and where there are no other individuals to help provide protection is one good explanation why certain employees and certain occupations experience more victimization.

Most discussion and interest in workplace victimization involves violence perpetrated by current or former coworkers on other employees. This format is the more typical portrayal seen in the news media. One major cause of violence by workers is stress (Braverman, 1999).

Stress may come from a variety of different sources. Among the most obvious are personal conflicts between employees or family problems brought to work by an employee. Another important source of worry is the workplace itself. The downsizing or restructuring of an organization can place a great deal of stress and uncertainty on the workforce (Braverman, 1999). Competition for a position or the feeling that another, less worthy employee attained a position can precipitate conflict between employees. The dismissal of an individual from a job, whether legitimate or not, can make the person feel cheated (Schneid, 1999). Many of these situations can make a worker feel that the workplace is an unfair and unjust place (Greenberg and Alge, 1998). Individuals may feel a great deal of stress when they do not get what they feel is deserved. Greenberg and Alge (1998) note that when people perceive that decisions or procedures are unfair, aggression becomes one avenue of response. Stress also may be enhanced by physical characteristics of the workplace that cause discomfort for the employees (Chappell and DiMartino, 1998), such as extreme temperatures or overcrowding.

Support for the identification of stress as a leading contributor to workplace violence comes from the finding that most instances of violent behavior are not by new employees or employees who have caused trouble in the past (Schneid, 1999). Instead, a good deal of workplace violence is committed by individuals who have been model employees and can be considered dedicated workers. It is easy to see in these cases how changes in the workplace, such as reclassification of jobs, competition for promotion, or the dismissal of an employee, can bring about stress and possible violence. In essence, these types of changes contradict the individual's self-image vis-à-vis the job and his or her place on the job. Thus, the individual may feel betrayed and unfairly treated by the job and others at the place of employment.

Besides work factors that can bring about stress, other factors also play a role in coworker violence. A number of individual factors, such as a history of violence, poor socialization, substance use and abuse, depression, and mental illness, are important predictors (Braverman, 1999; Chappell and DiMartino, 1998). Schneid (1999) points out that ownership of firearms is also strongly related to violent acts on the job. These factors are commonly found in studies of violence in other settings, and the assumed causal mechanism is the same.

Intervention and Prevention

As in any situation in which victimization is a potential concern, the best recourse is to take steps to prevent the problem in the first place. Indeed, the Occupational Safety and Health Act of 1970 addresses the issue of workplace safety in what is known as its *general duty clause*," which states:

> Each employer shall furnish to each of his employees employment and a place of employment which are free from recognized hazards that are causing or are likely to cause death or serious physical harm to his employees (29 *U.S.C.* 645(a)(1)).

This clause is most often used in connection with physical considerations of a workplace that pose a potential hazard to employees, such as hazardous waste, exposed wiring, slippery floors, the lack of railing around open pits, and similar factors. While potential violence is not typically considered under this clause, violent acts clearly fall under this section of the Act. Employers, therefore, have a duty to provide a workplace free from violence, whether that violence is between employees or involves individuals from outside the workforce. The form of the response will vary from workplace to workplace.

FIGURE 11.3
OSHA Recommendations for Protecting Employees Against Violence

---

Employer Actions:

Provide safety education for employees
Secure the workplace—locks, video surveillance, lighting, alarms,
    ID badges, guards
Provide drop safes to limit cash on hand
Provide cell phones and hand-held alarms for field staff
Keep informed of location of field employees
Properly maintain employer-provided vehicles
Develop policies and procedures for home visits and field work

Employee Actions:

Learn to recognize, avoid, or diffuse potentially violent situations
Alert supervisors to any concerns about safety or security
Avoid traveling alone to unfamiliar locations or situations
Carry minimal cash

Source: Occupational Safety and Health Administration (2002). *Workplace Violence.* OSHA Fact Sheet. Retrieved October 6, 2004, at http://www.osha.gov/SLTC/workplaceviolence/solutions.html

The Occupational Safety and Health Administration (OSHA) (2002) provides a list of recommendations for protecting employees against workplace violence (see Figure 11.3). These measures can be grouped into two general categories: those the employer should take and those the employee should enact. Some of the suggestions fall into the realm of physical design changes that can enhance security, such as improved lighting or alarms, protective enclosures, and inaccessible safes. Other recommendations relate to maintaining contact with workers in the field, working in pairs or groups, and making certain that vehicles and equipment are in good working condition. Employees should also learn how to recognize, avoid, and diffuse problematic situations. Beyond these recommendations, OSHA (2002) provides guidelines for what employees should do following a violent incident on the job, including reporting the act, receiving medical attention, and discussing the event with others.

Protective measures, such as those appearing in Figure 11.3, are limited mainly to actions that fit Type 1 violence in which there is clear criminal intent. What they do not address are actions between coworkers or problems brought to the workplace by family members or acquaintances. Braverman (1999) outlines five key elements that all employers should develop for preventing victimization in the workplace. The successful implementation of these factors can address all forms of workplace violence.

First, the employer needs to establish *clear policies and procedures* to guide all elements of the work environment (Braverman, 1999). The absence of policies and procedures leaves both employees and outsiders uncertain about how things are to be done, when they are to occur, and so on. Second, all members of the workplace need *training* on all aspects of the policies and procedures. Third, the employer and the employees need *access to medical and mental health expertise* in order to assess and address potential problem situations and individuals. This expertise can alert the workplace to problems before they get out of hand, as well as give individuals an alternative source of response apart from violent activity. Fourth, the employer needs to establish *clear, commonsense policies and procedures for terminations and layoffs*. This step is especially important for heading off feelings of injustice and a lack of fairness in the decision-making processes at work. Finally, the employer *needs to be able to identify signals for violence* in order to take appropriate actions before the violence actually occurs (Braverman, 1999). This knowledge can be fed back into the mental health and training activities of the overall violence prevention plan.

Chappell and DiMartino (1998) offer several additional measures to consider for violence prevention. The first of these deals with the selection and screening of employees. They suggest that employers need to utilize pre-employment tests, alcohol and other drug screening, and similar measures to identify potentially problematic employees. The employer can then use that information in the hiring process or to work with the employee to deal with any problems. A second suggestion involves training employees in interpersonal and communication skills and in recognizing cues to aggressive behavior. Such training can be used to recognize and defuse situations prior to major confrontations. An additional prevention initiative is simple information sharing between all parties concerned about workplace safety.

Responses to Workplace Victimization

While the prevention ideas outlined above hold the potential of mitigating the level and amount of victimization in the workplace, they do little to address the failures of the workplace to protect victims. What recourse do victims have after being victimized at work? Who can be held accountable for the victimization? As in any other situation in which an individual is a crime victim, the victim can turn to a variety of sources for assistance. Victim compensation, restitution, and civil action against the offender are all possible sources of help. Another possible source of assistance to employees may be workers' compensation. *Workers' compensation* is basically an insurance plan in which employers participate (typically mandated by law) that makes payments to employees who are hurt on the job. The employer pays premiums into the compensation system on behalf of all employees. Workers can draw on the funds if an injury is job-related.

Another source of victim assistance may come from *third-party lawsuits*. As discussed earlier in this book, a third-party lawsuit is one in which a victim can sue someone other than the offender due to the failure of the third party to take action that would have mitigated a foreseeable problem. In the case of workplace violence, the employer has a duty to take action to provide a safe work environment to its employees. The occurrence of victimization at work may signal the failure of the employer to respond to a known problem or a problem about which the employer should have known.

Schneid (1999) lists various bases on which a victim can claim employer negligence in a third-party lawsuit. The first involves *negligent hiring,* in which an employer knew or should have known that the individual posed a risk to others. A second related issue is the *negligent retention* of an employee who already works for the employer and is a known risk to others. Both of these issues raise concerns over the proper screening of potential and current employees. Third is *negligent supervision.* In this situation, the employer may be unable to dismiss a potential problem worker, but should recognize that the person poses an unacceptable risk and needs to be closely monitored on the job. The failure to carry out the needed supervision may allow the violence to occur. A fourth basis for a suit may involve *negligent training.* While the failure to train employees adequately to use equipment or do the job properly is probably the most common form of negligence under this heading, it is also possible that the training should include how to deal with problem clients or coworkers. The failure to provide that training may allow violence to take place. Perhaps the clearest form of negligence would involve *negligent security*. Under negligent security, the employer has a duty to safeguard employees, the workplace, and the public from known problems. These problems may have appeared in the past and the employer simply ignored the problem rather than taking proactive steps to avoid its reoccurrence (Schneid, 1999).

Under each of these forms of negligence, the victim can make a claim against the employer for loss and damages due to the victimization. As discussed earlier in Chapter 4, this recourse does not require the actual offender to be caught, convicted, or to have resources to pursue. The onus falls on the employer. The task for the victim, however, is to hire an attorney and prove that the employer knew, or should have known, of the potential problem. The burden is on the victim to prove the negligence. This action can take time and resources that many victims do not have.

Responding to victimization at work is a relatively new issue for most agencies. While violence and crime at work are not new problems, they have become recognized and studied in recent years. Many organizations have not given the problem of workplace violence much attention in the past. A great deal of additional research and work should be directed at victimization on the job.

Victimization at School

Victimization and violence at school have become major concerns in recent years. This emphasis is due largely to several isolated events that have received major media attention. Perhaps the most notable example is the mass murder at Columbine High School in Colorado, where two students planned and carried out lethal attacks on fellow students. Similarly, heinous crimes on college campuses, such as the rape and murder of Jeanne Clery in her college dorm room at Lehigh University in Pennsylvania, have raised concerns over safety on college campuses. The reality of victimization at schools, however, is far from what is portrayed in the media. Instead, lethal violence is relatively rare, and most victimizations involve property offenses or minor confrontations. In this part of the chapter, we attempt to outline the problem of victimization in schools and discuss the responses institutions should take to address these problems. We will first address victimization in junior and senior high schools before turning our attention to institutions of higher education.

Victimization in Junior and Senior High Schools

In contrast to the our earlier discussion of the workplace, where the emphasis was generally on violent acts, the literature on schools takes a broader approach to victimization. School violence, including acts such as murder, assault, and rape, represent the most serious form of victimization at school. It is typically these acts that find their way onto the evening news and frame the problem for the general public. School victimization, however, includes another entire realm of actions that typically receives less attention. Included here are theft offenses, vandalism, bullying, and verbal altercations. As will be seen, this latter group is much more prevalent in the schools, although it rarely finds its way into the media or many discussions. It is important, therefore, to consider both violent and nonviolent forms of victimization when discussing the academic setting.

Besides listing the types of actions to consider, it is equally important to recognize the targets and the locations of the victimization when discussing schools. One major assumption held by many people is that victimization in schools takes place between students. This assumption, however, neglects the fact that teachers and staff members are also potential victims. Indeed, the discussion earlier in this chapter shows that victimization against teachers is not an insignificant problem. A second consideration is where the victimization takes place. School victimization covers more than just the school building or the playground. Students in transit to and from school, whether walking, riding a school bus, or using public transportation, are generally considered under the auspices of the school. Any action against them in those venues is considered a form of victimization at school. This realization also means that one can extend "victimization at school" to include the time immediately before and immediately after the school bell rings.

Beyond the actual victimization of students, teachers, or staff, it is important to consider the level of fear felt by the members of the school environment. Fear can affect a larger number of individuals besides actual crime victims. Its influence can be particularly debilitating if the fear keeps youths from going to school or concentrating on studies. The purpose of the school can become secondary to the safety concerns of the students. It is important, therefore, to examine the level of fear and the consequences of fear in schools.

The Extent of School Victimization

Recent years have seen an increased interest in assessing the extent of victimization at school. Several large-scale analyses of victimization and crime, as well as numerous smaller projects, provide insight into this problem and how this phenomenon may be changing over time. Luckily, the data do not come exclusively from one source or point of view. Instead, information is available from students, teachers, and administrators. It looks at both individual experiences with victimization and crime experienced as a school (i.e., reports on the level of crime for an entire school).

One major source of data from students is the National Crime Victimization Survey (NCVS). Data from the 2004 NCVS appear in Table 11.4. The data indicate that 55 out of every 1,000 youths ages 12-18 report being victimized at school. The highest rates of victimization across all demographic categories appear in theft offenses, followed by violent crimes. Breakdowns by gender, race/ethnicity, and age reveal some interesting results. First, the rate of victimization is very similar for males and females in all categories except violent crimes. Second, blacks and whites have similar victimization rates, and both rates are higher than those for Hispanics and other ethnic groups. Finally, victimization is generally higher among younger individuals.

TABLE 11.4
Rate of Student-reported Victimization at School by Selected Characteristics, 2004[a]

Student Characteristics	Total	Theft	Violent[b]	Serious Violent[c]
Total	55	33	22	4
Gender				
Male	57	31	27	4
Female	52	35	17	4
Race/Ethnicity				
White	60	35	25	5
Black	60	34	26	4
Hispanic	39	27	12	–
Other	38	29	10	–
Age				
12-14	64	34	30	5
15-18	46	31	15	3

[a] Data for students aged 12 to 18.
[b] Violent crimes include rape, sexual assault, robbery, aggravated assault, and simple assault.
[c] Serious violent crimes include the violent crimes except for simple assault.

Source: Dinkes, R., E.F. Cataldi, G. Kena, and K. Baum (2006). *Indicators of School Crime and Safety, 2006.* Washington, DC: U.S. Department of Justice and U.S. Department of Education.

Based on figures such as those seen here, some people have suggested that the problem of school crime is rather small. Indeed, relatively few students are ever the victim of any serious violent victimization, and the percent of property victimizations is also small. What can be lost in these figures, however, is the number of youths who are victimized. According to the NCVS, roughly 1.2 million students ages 12-18 were victims of nonfatal crimes at school in 2004 (Dinkes et al., 2006). This figure translates into about 706,000 thefts and 556,000 violent crimes. Additionally, the level of reported victimization at school has declined since 1993. What these numbers show is that, despite the relatively low *rate*, the actual number of victims at school is significant.

An important related topic not addressed in Table 11.4 is the extent of homicides at school. Certainly, media portrayals of sensational killings at schools—such as at Columbine High School in Colorado in 1999 and Westside Middle School in Jonesboro, Arkansas, in 1998—lead to the impression that lethal violence is a relatively common event that is occurring with ever greater frequency. The reality of the situation, however, is that homicide at school is a rare event. For the period from July 1, 2004, to June 30, 2005, there were only 21 homicides at schools (Dinkes et al., 2006). These results are not atypical and show that homicide is a very rare event at school, despite the picture drawn in the media.

Students are not the only potential victims at school. Teachers, administrators, and other staff also can be targets. Data from surveys of teachers show that a significant number have been the victims of force or threats of force at school. According to the NCVS, more than 380,000 teachers were physically attacked or threatened with injury by a student during the 2004-2005 school year (Dinkes et al., 2006). This represents approximately 10 percent of all teachers. The level of teacher victimization, therefore, is not insignificant and should not be ignored in discussions of school crime.

Responses to School Victimization

Beyond the immediate problem of victimization at school, we need to be concerned about how individuals respond to both the real and perceived levels of crime and victimization. Typical responses to real or perceived victimization at school generally fall into three categories: fear, avoidance, and self-protection. Each of these has implications for the students and the educational system.

Fear of crime is a common problem expressed by students. According to the 2005 NCVS, 6 percent of students feared attack or harm at school, and 5 percent feared attack or harm on the way to or from school (Dinkes et al., 2006). As we showed in earlier chapters, fear can be a debilitating factor for some people. In relation to students and schools, it can cause youths to focus on noneducational endeavors, thus degrading the learning environment and potentially harming the long-term potential of students to succeed in school or at work. This fear also can lead to other immediate responses.

One of those responses is avoidance behavior. Staying home from school due to fear of victimization is a common response for some youths. The 2005 *NCVS: School Crime Supplement* reports that 5.5 percent of students avoid school, school activities, and/or specific places at school due to fear of attack or harm (Dinkes et al., 2006). A variety of other studies have reported similar proportions of youths who skip school due to fear (Lab and Clark, 1996; Lab and Whitehead, 1994; Metropolitan Life, 1993; Ringwalt et al., 1992). While the youths may be attending school, the quality of the education they receive is diminished. Some students may go hungry, suffer discomfort because they are afraid to use restrooms, arrive late for classes due to using only certain stairways or hallways, or refrain from taking part in enriching extra-curricular activities. In essence, the school experience is far from an ideal nurturing atmosphere. The ultimate form of this avoidance is quitting school. Students who drop out are not included in surveys of students. Thus, the number of youths who report avoiding school due to fear in most studies is an undercount of who is taking this action.

Another form of response involves self-defense actions, particularly carrying weapons for protection. According to data from the Youth Risk Behavior Survey conducted by the Centers for Disease Control and Prevention, 6.5 percent of high school students reported carrying a weapon to school at least once in the past 30 days (Dinkes et al., 2006). Lab and Clark (1996) found that 24 percent of the respondents carried a weapon to school for protection at least once over a six-month time period. Even higher levels of weapon possession at school emerge in studies of inner-city schools (see, for example, Sheley et al., 1995). Among the weapons carried for protection are guns, knives, brass knuckles, razor blades, spiked jewelry, and mace (Lab and Clark, 1996).

Unfortunately, while bringing a weapon to school may make a youth *feel* safer, such devices have the potential of causing more problems than they solve. One negative outcome is that being caught with a weapon can lead to expulsion, criminal prosecution, and other sanctions against the student who is trying to protect himself or herself. A second possibility is that if the student is attacked and does try to use the weapon, the level of violence and victimization may escalate. That is, a fist fight can become a shooting, or a theft can result in an aggravated assault. The victim may be more seriously harmed, or the victim may become the offender. Yet another consequence is that schools can become armed camps where the administration is forced to take progressively intrusive measures to keep the weapons out of school.

Regardless of which response is taken to actual or potential victimization, the atmosphere and the activity in the schools shift away from education. Learning becomes a secondary concern to safety and protection. Students and teachers never quite devote their entire attention to the lesson plan. Everyone in the school is victimized.

Explanations and Causes of School Victimization

Discussions of explanations and causes for victimization at school typically refer to the standard arguments for deviance in society. One set of explanations emphasizes the *strain* that some people feel when faced with others who have more or who are more successful at something. Those strained individuals may strike out at others who are more successful or against society for withholding success from them. *Subcultural explanations* have been useful in explaining the behavior of individuals who fit into an identified group or segment of society, such as youth gangs. In essence, individuals in certain groups may follow a set of values and beliefs that could lead to conflict with the behavioral mandates of society. Thus, if a youth acts in accord with gang dictates, he or she may be in violation of other rules, such as those of the school or community. Yet another set of explanations revolves around the idea that the youths *learn* to use violence as a means of getting what they want and settling disputes. The learning may come from parents, siblings, or others in the community. As you can see, each of these approaches can provide a potential explanation for crime in schools.

One explanation that is particularly germane to in-school crime is the *routine activities perspective*. Schools provide all the necessary factors for crime, according to routine activities theory. By bringing a large number of youths together, the school is making suitable targets (students and their belongings) available to potential offenders (other students) within a location where there is often nobody watching (a lack of guardians). Both the offender and the victim are required by law to attend school. Offenders can pick the time and place within the school for committing an offense. Moreover, despite all the best intentions in the world, teachers and staff cannot be watching every student at all times.

The routine activities explanation receives even more support when one considers the temporal nature of crime. An inspection of when youthful offending occurs shows that most juvenile crime is committed in the afternoon between roughly 3:00 and 4:00 P.M. (Office of Juvenile Justice and Delinquency Prevention, 1999). Specifically, almost 20 percent of juvenile violent crime and 14 percent of youthful sexual assaults take place between 3:00 and 7:00 P.M. on school days. This interval is precisely the time when youths are out of school and generally not under any direct supervision by a parent, teacher, or other adult guardian. In addition, a great deal of this victimization takes place near a school or along major routes used by youths going to or from school. Thus, the connection between schools and victimization is easy to delineate.

Besides trying to identify a specific theoretical argument underlying crime and victimization at school, it is useful to consider the possible factors or variables that may be indicative of potential violence. Many of these factors and variables fit different theoretical points of view. Perhaps their greatest value is their use as warning signs of potential problems for school officials and others. Figure 11.4 presents one list of warning signs identified by more than 500 experts on school violence and victimization, coming from diverse backgrounds and experiences. Among these signs are past violent behavior, verbal aggression, lack of parental supervision, a preoccupation with violence, gang participation, depression or withdrawal, past trauma, and substance abuse. While these traits cannot definitively identify students who will be violent at school, students displaying these signs should be given added attention or referred to appropriate sources of intervention.

FIGURE 11.4
Warning Signs of Potential Violence

- Has engaged in violent behavior in the past.
- Has tantrums and uncontrollable angry outbursts abnormal for someone that age.
- Continues exhibiting antisocial behaviors that began at an early age.
- Forms and/or maintains friendships with others who have repeatedly engaged in problem behaviors.
- Often engages in name calling, cursing, or abusive language.
- Has brought a weapon or has threatened to bring a weapon to school.
- Consistently makes violent threats when angry.
- Has a substance abuse problem.
- Is frequently truant or has been suspended from school on multiple occasions.
- Seems preoccupied with weapons or violence, especially that associated more with killing humans than with target practice or hunting.
- Has few or no close friends despite having lived in the area for some time.
- Has a sudden decrease in academic performance and/or interest in school activities.
- Is abusive to animals.

FIGURE 11.4—*continued*

- Has too little parental supervision given the student's age and level of maturity.
- Has been a victim of abuse or been neglected by parents/guardians.
- Has repeatedly witnessed domestic abuse or other forms of violence.
- Has experienced trauma or loss in their home or community.
- Pays no attention to the feelings or rights of others.
- Intimidates others.
- Has been a victim of intimidation by others.
- Dwells on perceived slights, rejection, or mistreatment by others; blames others for his/her problems and appears vengeful.
- Seems preoccupied with TV shows, movies, video games, reading materials, or music that express violence.
- Reflects excessive anger in writing projects.
- Is involved in a gang or antisocial group.
- Seems depressed/withdrawn or has exhibited severe mood or behavioral swings, which appear greater in magnitude, duration, or frequency than those typically experienced by students that age.
- Expresses sadistic, violent, prejudicial, or intolerant attitudes.
- Has threatened or actually attempted suicide or acts of unfashionable self-mutilation.

Source: International Association of Chiefs of Police (2000). *Guide for Preventing and Responding to School Violence*. Washington, DC: International Association of Chiefs of Police.

Addressing School Victimization

Schools have taken a wide array of actions to deal with actual and potential crime and victimization. Often, the most visible and immediate response is to introduce measures that impose greater physical control over students, teachers, administrators, visitors, and the school grounds. Typical responses include the call for installing metal detectors at entrances, locking all but one door to outsiders, requiring everyone to wear identification badges, installing closed-circuit television monitors, and hiring guards for the hallways and the building. Unfortunately, these prevention efforts typically assume that the offenders and the threats come from outside the school and that most of the problems are addressed once students are screened into the building. What these efforts overlook is that most of the crimes take place between offenders and victims who are students, each of whom has a right (and expectation) to be in the school.

Beyond the simple introduction of physical security devices and methods is the heavy reliance on harsh discipline and control measures. Suspension and expulsion from school are common responses to violence and repeated transgressions by students. Unfortunately, these actions do little to address the factors that may cause the problem and often represent only a quick fix for larger underlying problems in the school. In addition, these responses sometimes force the offending party to drop out of school and cause further problems down the road (Adams, 2000). Closely related to suspension and expulsion are zero-tolerance policies that often lead to a greater reliance on suspension and expulsion. Such stances do not allow the schools to address the differing needs of transgressors (Adams, 2000).

Recognizing the limitations of such physical prevention methods, schools also have attempted to implement a variety of programs and policies to deal with crime and aggression in the schools. One general approach is to institute some form of conflict management or resolution program. These programs appear under a variety of different names, including dispute resolution, peer mediation, conflict resolution, and others. While the approach of the programs may vary, their purpose is to teach students to recognize conflict and learn appropriate ways of channeling aggression and resolving problems before they can escalate further. Several programs of this type have shown success, such as the Resolving Conflict Creatively Program (DeJong, 1993), the Responding in Peaceful and Positive Ways program (Farrell and Meyer, 1997), and the work of Olweus (1994; 1995) to address bullying problems in schools. One advantage of these interventions is that they attempt to address the needs of both the victims and the offenders. The victims are active participants in responding to any actions against them and can seek redress for losses or injuries, while the offender can learn appropriate methods for dealing with antisocial behavior and impulses.

Where these varied responses may address issues of school security, prevent future problems in school, and satisfy the need to assist offenders, they often leave the victim on the outside of the response (the notable exceptions are some forms of conflict resolution). There are differing ways that a school can respond to the needs of the victim, as well as students who are indirectly victimized by criminal actions taking place at school. Many of those responses mirror the responses offered in other chapters. Other responses, however, may be geared to the unique nature of the school, where a large number of individuals must be considered in the wake of different actions.

College Campus Victimization

Crime on college campuses has been vaulted to the forefront of social concern as the result of highly publicized shootings on campus. Perhaps the most notable of these events was the deaths of 32 students at the Virginia Polytechnic Institute and State University (VPI) on April 16, 2007. A more recent event was the shootings of two students at Delaware State University on September 21, 2007.

For years, many colleges and universities were reluctant to reveal crime data. Administrators were concerned about the kind of image such information might project about their institutions. Worries abounded that negative publicity might hurt student recruitment and adversely affect enrollments. Consequently, systematic collection of crime data from colleges was rarely possible, and the information was largely unavailable.

The situation changed with congressional approval of the Jeanne Clery Disclosure of Campus Security Policy and Campus Crime Statistics Act (20 U.S.C. 1092). Jeanne Clery, a 19-year-old college freshman at Lehigh University in Pennsylvania, was raped and murdered in her dormitory room by another student whom she did not know. The suspect, who was apprehended, entered the dormitory through a series of doors that had been left ajar. Later, it was revealed that the university had received numerous complaints about propped-open doors in that same dormitory in previous months. In addition, there were other security lapses and a lack of available information about campus safety.

FIGURE 11.5
Summary of the Clery Act Provisions

- Schools must publish an annual report disclosing campus security policies and three years worth of selected crime statistics.

- Schools must make timely warnings to the campus community about crimes that pose an ongoing threat to students and employees.

- Each institution with a police or security department must have a public crime log.

- The U.S. Department of Education centrally collects and disseminates the crime statistics.

- Campus sexual assault victims are assured of certain basic rights.

- Schools that fail to comply can be fined by the U.S. Department of Education.

Source: Clery Act Summary. Retrieved October 3, 2004, from http://www.securityoncampus.org/schools/cleryact/index.html

Dissatisfaction with how the university handled the investigation and other aspects of the matter prompted the victim's parents to lobby for a campus crime disclosure law. Those efforts were successful at the state level and paved the way for a national campaign. In 1990, a new federal directive took effect mandating that colleges and universities make certain crime statistics public. There have been several modifications and amendments to the original provisions over the years. Figure 11.5 summarizes the currently existing provisions.

The Extent of College Student Victimization

The Clery Act requirements have resulted in more than 6,000 colleges and universities forwarding victimization statistics and other information to the U.S. Department of Education for tabulation. Table 11.5 contains the total number of known crimes that took place on college campuses throughout the entire country during 2004. Those tallies are further divided according to the type of college or university. The counts reveal that burglary is the most common crime on campuses, followed by aggravated assaults, forcible sexual assaults, and robberies. Murder and nonforcible sexual assaults are relatively infrequent events. Interestingly, there does appear to be some variation according to the type of institution. Four-year colleges and universities are responsible for the largest number of violent victimization episodes, followed by two-year schools and other kinds of programs.

While these data are interesting, they are silent on several fronts. For example, the information in Table 11.5 pertains to victimizations that have taken place on college campuses. While the Department of Education now requires schools to document crimes that take place on property adjacent to their campuses, local authorities typically are responsible for recording those reports. The availability and accuracy of these statistics are subject to a host of influences. In addition, these numbers do not provide a full picture of the collegiate experience. Rising enrollments mean that many institutions lack sufficient housing for their students. This shortage forces college enrollees to look for off-campus housing and commute to campus. Victimization episodes that arise from the collegiate lifestyle, but that take place away from the campus gates, tend not to make their way into institutionally generated statistics. Another influence, the dark figure of crime stemming from student-victims not contacting the authorities (Fisher et al., 2003a; Fisher et al., 2003b; Hart, 2003), can also affect the accuracy of these reports.

The counts displayed in Table 11.5 are not part of the FBI Uniform Crime Reporting program; they are generated from campus police and security agencies. As a result, crime statistics on college cam-

TABLE 11.5
Number of Known On-Campus Violent Crimes, 2004, U.S. Department of Education

Type of Institution	Murder/ Nonnegligent Manslaughter	Forcible Sex Offenses	Nonforcible Sex Offenses	Robbery	Aggravated Assault	Burglary
Public, 4-year or above	8	1,452	16	635	1,299	12,981
Private nonprofit, 4-year or above	4	1,026	4	741	853	11,383
Private for-profit, 4-year or above	0	5	0	47	34	491
Public, 2-year or above	3	140	4	233	542	4,144
Private nonprofit, 2-year	0	5	0	84	67	616
Private for-profit, 2-year	0	10	0	95	68	385
Public, less-than-2-year	0	2	0	48	52	81
Private nonprofit, less-than-2-year	0	4	0	94	26	102
Private for-profit, less-than-2-year	0	5	0	83	68	268
Total	15	2,649	24	2,060	3,009	30,451

Source: U.S. Department of Education, *Summary Campus Crime and Security Statistics — 2002-2004*. Retrieved September 16, 2007, from http://www.ed.gov/admins/lead/safety/crime/summary.html

puses suffer from similar limitations that can taint official statistics, in addition to their own idiosyncrasies. As a result, the National Crime Victimization Survey (NCVS) added items in 1995 to distinguish college students from nonstudents. Unfortunately, the NCVS does not differentiate between full-time and part-time students, private as opposed to public college students, or undergraduate from graduate students. In addition, college student victimization experiences are not separated into those incidents that took place on-campus, adjacent to campus, or away from campus.

Table 11.6 presents average annual victimization rates, according to student status, for the 1995–2002 interval. Generally speaking, college students experienced lower violent victimization rates than did nonstudents. Male college students and male nonstudents showed similar victimization rates, while female college students had much lower victimization rates in comparison with their nonstudent counterparts. In terms of race, both white and black college enrollees reported lower victimization rates than nonstudents of the same race. Conversely, Hispanic college students report similar or higher victimization rates than do nonstudents.

TABLE 11.6
Average Annual Violent Victimization Rates of College Students and Non-students, by Gender and Race, 1995–2002

Victim Characteristic	Rates per 1,000 persons age 18-24				
	Rape/ Sexual Assault	Robbery	Aggravated Assault	Simple Assault	Violent Crimes
College Students	3.8	5.0	13.5	38.4	60.7
Gender					
Male	1.4	7.4	21.4	49.9	80.2
Female	6.0	2.7	6.2	27.7	42.7
Race					
White	4.0	4.4	13.2	43.3	64.9
Black	3.2	8.7	15.6	24.9	52.4
Other	2.1	7.0	9.8	18.4	37.2
Hispanic	4.6	2.8	15.4	33.4	56.
Non-Students	4.1	9.5	17.7	44.1	75.3
Gender					
Male	0.4	12.4	22.4	44.0	79.2
Female	7.9	6.4	12.9	44.1	71.3
Race					
White	4.5	7.5	17.6	51.6	81.2
Black	4.9	16.7	22.5	39.1	83.2
Other	3.6	7.5	12.1	20.0	43.1
Hispanic	1.9	10.8	15.7	27.5	55.9

Source: K. Baum (2005). *Violent Victimization of College Students*, 1995-2002. Washington, DC: U.S. Government Printing Office.

Explanations and Causes of College Campus Victimization

Early researchers noticed that campus victimization rates varied from one location to the next. Intrigued by this variation, McPheters (1978) examined UCR data for 38 colleges. Basically, McPheters (1978) learned that an urban location alone did not impact campus crime rates. Other risk variables, such as high unemployment in the surrounding area and being in a large city, were more important influences.

While the McPheters study was interesting, other researchers worried that its small sample size compromised the results. One strategy that subsequent investigators concentrated upon was to include a much larger number of post-secondary institutions in the pool. While these studies tended to confirm the original finding that location had no effect on the overall campus crime rate, the composition of known crime did change. Schools in big cities exhibited greater amounts of violent crime (Fox and Hellman, 1985), although these rates were not as extreme as what was observed in the larger community (Bromley, 1995; Bromley, 1999), crimes involving alcohol and other drug violations were on the rise (Sloan, 1994), and property crime, especially theft, was the predominant violation (Bromley, 1995; Bromley, 1999; Fisher et al., 1998; Henson and Stone, 1999; Sloan, 1992; Sloan, 1994; Volkwein, Szelest, and Lizotte, 1995).

One problem that plagued these initial studies was their reliance upon UCR data, which is restricted to crimes occurring on school property. Another shortcoming was that these inquiries focused solely on student victimization and neglected to include faculty, staff, support workers, and visitors. A third criticism was that most of these studies lacked a sound theoretical base.

Recent efforts have attempted to correct for these deficiencies by incorporating self-report victimization data and by adopting the routine activities/lifestyle model discussed earlier. The routine activities/lifestyle model maintains that the level of crime is a function of the availability of suitable targets, exposure to crime, lack of guardianship, and motivated offenders. Target availability reflects greater pursuit of recreational activities, the drinking associated with leisure time, and other risky behaviors associated with the pursuit of fun. Certainly, the youthfulness of college cohorts, the large numbers of people concentrated into the confines of the campus environment, and dense on-campus living arrangements contribute to exposure to crime. Lack of guardianship is sometimes a hallmark of college living. Students typically leave belongings unattended, leave doors unlocked for their own convenience, and remain generally unaware of crime-prevention techniques. Finally, motivated offenders abound in atmospheres characterized by a lack of primary relationships.

Adopting this framework has enabled researchers to gain further insights into campus crime. For example, Fisher et al. (1998) found that dormitory living (proximity to crime) and student affluence (target attractiveness) was associated with property victimization. Tewksbury and Mustaine (2003) link lifestyle with college student reliance upon self-protection measures. In a similar vein, Fisher and Sloan (2003) tracked fear of victimization among college women and developed recommendations that stem from the lifestyle approach.

Addressing Campus Crime

In the past, most responses to crime on college campuses simply reflected law enforcement and security efforts found in the general community. Prevention activities primarily involved educating and working with students to take precautions and call for assistance when faced with criminal behavior. This general state of affairs has changed greatly since the 2007 Virginia Tech shootings. Most institutions and states have taken steps to develop emergency response plans and proactive efforts to head off serious violent actions on campus.

One example of recent efforts at campus safety is the actions of the Task Force on Ohio College Safety and Security. This task force was charged with ensuring that all college campuses in Ohio are safe and prepared to address security breaches. Several outcomes of this task force include the creation of a clearinghouse on campus safety information, clarification of legal issues facing colleges when identifying and investigating potential offending students, developing safety training courses for security personnel, and workshops on safety issues. The task force also promulgated a Campus Safety Checklist (see Figure 11.6) with which campuses can assess their preparation to address safety problems and concerns.

FIGURE 11.6
Ohio Campus Security Checklist

Does your campus have a safety and security plan? Has it been reviewed and updated since April 2007? Please check all of the following that apply to your campus:

1. Protocols are in place to address the behavior of students, faculty, staff, and guests who are disruptive or pose a significant potential risk of harm and a clear response protocol exists if a student or other person on campus is engaged in or actively threatening violence.

2. Faculty, staff, and students know how to identify and what to do if someone poses a risk of harm to self or others.

3. Campus authorities have a clear understanding of relevant laws.

4. Responses to actual or potential threats are coordinated with on and off campus safety forces.

5. Protocols are established for both internal and external communications with all who need to know, including students, faculty, staff, administrators, safety officials, hospitals, and media.

6. Procedures are in place to mobilize support required during a crisis, including vital staff, mental health personnel, communications staff, and facility operational staff.

7. A plan is in place for business continuity and resumption/ recovery.

8. Resources are available to address emotional, physical, and other human needs following an incident.

9. Plans are developed to return essential staff and personnel to campus.

Source: Task Force on Ohio College Campus Safety and Security (2007). Found at: http://www.regents.ohio.gov/cstf/CSTF-Final_Report.pdf

Sexual Harassment

Another problem facing both employees and students is that of sexual harassment. *Sexual harassment* differs from most other forms of victimization, including sexual assaults, in two primary ways. First, sexual harassment often does not involve an actual physical assault. Rather, harassment can manifest itself in subtle ways, such as sexually suggestive comments, unwanted touching, risqué jokes and pornography, or blatant demands for sexual contact. In most cases, these actions take place within work or educational settings where the both the offender and the victim are required to be in close contact. This consideration means that the offender and victim are acquaintances. The second distinguishing feature of sexual harassment is that the criminal justice system rarely deals with these infractions. Instead, sexual harassment falls into the realm of civil or administrative law and remedies.

While no universally accepted definition of sexual harassment exists, most definitions outline unacceptable actions that fall into two broad categories. The first is *quid pro quo* harassment, wherein the offender requires sexual contact in exchange for employment, better working conditions, high grades, or other favorable treatment. In essence, the offender sets up an exchange arrangement in which sex is the cost to be paid by the victim. Most people would recognize this first category as a violation of the rights of others. The actual threat does not have to be carried out for the action to constitute sexual harassment. The threat is enough in and of itself.

The second category deals with the creation of a *hostile environment*. Under this form, the harassment may be as subtle as displaying calendars of naked people at work, telling crude sexual jokes, touching a person, or commenting about how "sexy" a person looks in certain clothing. In each case the victim, intentionally or unintentionally, is made to feel uncomfortable. While some individuals may not perceive these actions as harassment, others will be impacted negatively by the activity. This second form, therefore, is more difficult to identify and requires individuals to express their feelings about such actions to the offending party. The true problem begins when the offender continues a practice after being informed about the transgression. The hostile environment situation does not require the loss of a job, benefits, or other factors in order to prove harassment (Rubin, 1995).

Both of these forms of sexual harassment appear in Section 1604.11 of the Federal Regulations governing the *Equal Employment Opportunity Commission* (EEOC) (see Figure 11.7). While the definition is specific to employment situations, many institutions have tailored it to fit the unique nature of their own environments. Universities, for example, typically add language that applies the same conditions to actions that interfere with the ability of a student to learn. It is not uncommon to see definitional policies developed to meet the specific needs of different agencies and settings.

FIGURE 11.7
The EEOC Definition of Sexual Harassment

Section 1604.11 Sexual Harassment.

Unwelcome sexual advances, requests for sexual favors, and other verbal or physical conduct of a sexual nature constitute sexual harassment when

(1) submission to such conduct is made either explicitly or implicitly a term or condition of an individual's employment,

(2) submission to or rejection of such conduct by an individual is used as the basis for employment decisions affecting such individual, or

(3) such conduct has the purpose or effect of unreasonably interfering with an individual's work performance or creating an intimidating, hostile, or offensive working environment.

The Extent of Sexual Harassment

Gauging the extent of sexual harassment depends on the definition used and the target of the investigation. There is no ongoing national data collection program for sexual harassment. Rather, what knowledge we have is based primarily on various surveys. Further complicating the measurement of the problem is the fact that most surveys target specific groups, such as students or faculty at a single university, or heavily female-dominated employee groups like nursing. Thus, the results typically are not generalizable to the overall population. Other measurement problems include the failure of respondents to report harassment due to embarrassment or fear of retaliation and the failure of some people to define a sexual situation as harassment even though it may fit the legal definition.

Despite these measurement problems, numerous studies provide insight into the frequency with which sexual harassment occurs. In one early study, 17 percent of the female students reported sexual advances, and 14 percent claimed to receive unwanted sexual invitations. McKinney (1990), studying 156 faculty at one institution, reports that almost 14 percent of the female respondents and 9 percent of the male respondents felt they had been sexually harassed by a coworker. In a national survey of college faculty, 6.8 percent of the respondents reported harassment, with women reporting almost five times more incidents than men (Dey et al., 1996). Using results from female employees, Gutek (1985) advises that 53 percent had been negatively impacted (i.e., being fired, denied promotions or raises) due to refusing sexual advances at work. Studies of the general public, while more rare, have uncovered even greater levels of harassment. For example, Wyatt and Riederle (1995) find 44 percent of women from the Los Angeles area claim to have been sexually harassed at work, and 45 percent report harassment in social settings. Finally, Swisher (1995) notes that the number of sexual harassment claims made to the Equal Employment Opportunity Commission (EEOC) more than doubled from 1991 to 1993 (3,300 complaints compared to 7,300 complaints). EEOC data on the number of sexual harassment charges brought to their agency or Fair Employment Practices agencies around the country show even greater numbers of harassment (see Table 11.7). In 1998, there were more than 15,500 cases filed, and a 2006 tally showed 12,025 cases (Equal Employment Opportunity Commission, 2007). The vast majority of these cases involve a female complainant, although there has been a slight increase in the percent of cases where the complainant is male.

TABLE 11.7
Sexual Harassment Charges, 1998-2006

	FY 1998	FY 2000	FY 2002	FY 2004	FY 2006
Receipts	15,618	15,836	14,396	13,136	12,075
% of Charges Filed by Males	12.9%	13.6%	14.9%	15.1%	15.4%
Resolutions	17,115	16,726	15,796	13,786	11,936
Resolutions By Type:					
Settlements	7.1%	10.0%	10.7%	11.9%	12.2%
Withdrawals w/Benefits	7.7%	8.3%	7.8%	8.3%	9.8%
Administrative Closures	36.8%	27.7%	25.1%	23.6%	23.8%
No Reasonable Cause	42.3%	44.1%	47.1%	48.7%	47.5%
Reasonable Cause	6.1%	9.9%	9.3%	7.5%	6.7%
Merit Resolutions	20.9%	28.2%	27.8%	27.7%	28.7%
Monetary Benefits (Millions)*	$34.3	$54.6	$50.3	$37.1	$48.8

*Does not include monetary benefits obtained through litigation.

The data reflect charges filed with EEOC and cooperating state and local Fair Employment Practices agencies. The total of individual percentages may not always sum to 100% due to rounding.

Source: U.S. Equal Employment Opportunity Commission (n.d.). *Sexual Harassment Charges, EEOC & FEPAs Combined: FY1997-FY2006.* Retrieved on September 20, 2007, at: http://www.eeoc.gov/stats/harass.html

Responses to Sexual Harassment

As noted earlier, responses to sexual harassment generally fall outside the realm of the criminal justice system. Instead, victims can take a variety of steps to address harassment, ranging from taking personal action to invoking the legal system (see Figure 11.8). Most organizations have sexual harassment policies that outline the problem, the expectations for workers, and the procedures for resolving these issues. Where these actions fail, victims can invoke various equal employment statutes and protections or take direct action in civil court. No matter what avenue is chosen, however, the victim is put under additional unwarranted stress and inconvenience.

FIGURE 11.8
Steps for Stopping Sexual Harassment on the Job

You should respond immediately and directly to the offender to indicate that the behavior or remark is not acceptable.

1. Confront the harasser. Tell the harasser clearly that you are offended by the behavior. Tell the harasser you don't like what was said or done and you want it to stop.

2. Talk with other coworkers about it. You might find they feel the same way you do.

3. Keep a journal or diary of the harassing behaviors. Write down time, date, and place of the incidents and the circumstances surrounding it. List any witnesses who can verify your story.

4. Check with the personnel office. Find out what the company's policy is towards harassment. Ask to know your rights.

5. If harassment continues, submit a complaint, including a request for action to a grievance officer, your supervisor, and your harasser's supervisor.

6. Take legal action by filing a complaint with . . . the federal EEOC or seek the advice of a private attorney.

Source: Ohio Civil Rights Commission (1996). *Sexual Harassment in the Workplace*. Columbus, OH: Ohio Civil Rights Commission.

The resolution of sexual harassment cases can take a variety of forms. Table 11.7 provides some insight into the outcomes of cases brought to the EEOC. Interestingly, the number of resolved cases often exceeds the number of new cases due to the fact that some cases are carried over from one year to the next and other agencies transfer cases to the EEOC. Most of the complaints are resolved through administrative closures or "no reasonable cause" (two-thirds or more combined). These categories typically represent findings that harassment did not occur or that the complainant did not follow through with the case. "Merit resolutions" represent the next major form of case resolution; they include situations in which a settlement has been made or a case has been withdrawn because the complainant has received some form of desired benefit. This outcome is a growing form of resolution, with almost 29 percent of the cases during 2006 being settled in this manner. Interestingly, while most cases do not end with a finding that harassment actually occurred, the cases in which claims of harassment are upheld result in significant monetary benefits. In 2006, $49 million was awarded to complainants.

Beyond the responses outlined in Table 11.7, companies can be compelled to take steps in response to harassment by their employees. This action is due to the fact that employers and educational institutions have a legal responsibility to provide a harassment-free environment in which to work and learn. These actions can be divided into two groups: measures to stop the harassment and make certain it does not recur, and measures to correct the effects of the harassment.

The EEOC offers a variety of examples of these actions. To stop harassment, the employer can give warnings or reprimands to offenders, transfer or reassign an individual, force offenders into counseling, demote or monetarily sanction the person, closely monitor the individual in the future, or even discharge the offender (Equal Employment Opportunity Commission, 1999). At the same time that steps are taken to deal with the harasser and the situation, things can be done to help the victim directly. For example, if leave or some other form of time off was taken by the victim due to the incident, the employer can restore that lost time. A victim who left employment due to harassment also could be offered full reinstatement to the job. The employer also may review the personnel file of the victim and expunge any negative comments or evaluations related to the behavior of the harasser (Equal Employment Opportunity Commission, 1999). Various responses should be considered when dealing with harassment cases.

Sexual harassment is a problem that has received increased attention in recent years, particularly with the increase of females in the workplace. As such, many employers and schools are having to deal with this emerging issue and develop new policies and procedures. It is not unusual for businesses and educational institutions to initiate mandatory training on sexual harassment for all staff members. The hope is that such an initiative will limit the number of sexual harassment incidents. At the very least, it helps to mitigate the liability of the employer or school if an incident does occur. Clearly, sexual harassment is a problem that must be addressed.

FIGURE 11.9
Selected Internet Sites Dealing with Victimization and Harassment at Work and School

Bureau of Justice Statistics
http://www.ojp.usdoj.gov/bjs

The Chronicle of Higher Education
http://www.chronicle.com

National Center for Educational Statistics
http://nces.ed.gov

National Institute for Occupational Safety and Health
http://www.cdc.gov/niosh

National Women's Law Center
http://www.nwlc.org

Ohio Board of Regents
http://regents.ohio.gov/security_task_force.php

Security on Campus, Inc.
http://www.securityoncampus.org/index.html

U.S. Department of Education, Office of Postsecondary Education
http://www.ope.ed.gov/security

U.S. Department of Labor
http://www.dol.gov

U.S. Equal Employment Opportunity Commission
http://www.eeoc.gov

U.S. Occupational Safety and Health Administration
http://www.osha.gov

Summary

Being victimized at work or at school can be particularly traumatic because most workers and students assume they are safe at these locations. Except for those individuals employed in the criminal justice system or in another security position, people have a right to expect that their employer or school has taken steps to secure them and their property. Workers and students are pursuing lawful activities, and any form of victimization represents a violation of their expectations. Schools and employers can be held liable for failing to take reasonable precautions that would attempt to guarantee the safety of those in their care or employment. It is important that employers and schools take preventive measures before a victimization takes place, outline remedial actions to take in the event of a victimization, and prepare plans to aid and assist anyone who is victimized (directly or indirectly) while on the job or at school. All of these actions must be dynamic and able to adjust to situations as they arise. As such, no set of responses can consider all possible events. Instead, the responses should outline processes, rather than specific outcomes.

Key Terms for Chapter 11

Equal Employment Opportunity Commission

general duty clause

going postal

hostile environment harassment

National Crime Victimization Survey: School Crime Supplement

National Institute of Occupational Safety and Health

negligent hiring

negligent retention

negligent security

negligent supervision

negligent training

Occupational Safety and Health Administration

quid pro quo harassment

routine activities perspective

sexual harassment

strain

stress

subcultural explanations

third-party lawsuits

worker compensation

workplace violence

Learning Objectives

After reading Chapter 12, you should be able to:

- Explain the constitutional changes proposed by the President's Task Force.

- Understand the pros and cons behind this proposal.

- Outline the strategy behind the proposed Twenty-Sixth Amendment to the United States Constitution.

- Provide details as to what the proposed Twenty-Sixth Amendment encompassed.

- Convey why some people did not support the proposed amendments to the Constitution.

- Understand why the strategy switched to targeting state constitutional reform.

- Discuss the revived interest in a federal victim rights constitutional amendment.

- Trace legislative reforms at the federal level.

- Tell what some of the guidelines are regarding the treatment of federal victims and witnesses

- Relay the provisions of the federal victims' "Bill of Rights."

- Talk about the two court rulings that focused on the federal crime victims "Bill of Rights."

- Explore some of the guarantees that the states have extended to crime victims.

- List some of the concerns and remedies that critics have voiced over victim rights.

- Describe what a victim impact statement contains.

- Communicate the effect victim impact statements have had.

- Understand some of the constitutional issues surrounding the death penalty cases.

- Appreciate how these constitutional issues affect the Supreme Court's reasoning with respect to victim impact statements.

- Outline case developments regarding federal Supreme Court rulings about victim impact statements.

Chapter 12

VICTIM RIGHTS

Introduction

The historic trend in formal systems of justice has been to look at crimes as transgressions against society and victims as witnesses for society. Recent years, though, have seen a gradual movement toward more victim participation in the justice process. Victims are gaining rights that restore them to greater prominence in the criminal justice system. Some of these rights are as simple as recognizing the victim's human dignity. Others outline procedures that allow victims to address the court and parole boards. Even more subtle changes include moving cases out of the formal justice system and into informal settings where victims seek to settle problems with the offenders.

Reasons for these new victim rights are easily identified. First, special interest groups have championed victim causes. They have pushed to balance the rights of the offender with the needs of the victim. Second, the justice system has experienced a great deal of dissatisfaction with how it handles victims. As we demonstrated in Chapter 3, victims derive little, if any, value from contact with the system. Except for fulfilling some vague notion of a "civic duty," victims have very little to gain—and much to lose—from system participation. Many victims never even have the satisfaction of knowing the outcome of their cases. The move toward procedures that give victims a louder voice is a way to make the system more responsive and to lure victims back into the halls of justice. Third, the justice system is overwhelmed by the volume of cases. Plea bargaining strategies, failure to file charges, time delays, inadequate sentences, and early prisoner releases due to overcrowding indicate that the system is not working well. Alternatives need to be developed.

This final chapter looks at the attempt to reverse the historic trend of alienating victims from the resolution of criminal matters. Specifically, the chapter looks at two general trends that seek to make the victim an active participant at various stages of the justice system. We turn first to the passage of constitutional amendments. Then, we will look at statutory provisions for victim rights. While this legal landscape is changing, there is still room for much improvement.

Victim Rights Amendment

Victim rights reform has taken several different paths in the United States. One strategy has involved efforts to gain passage of a federal constitutional amendment, commonly referred to as a *Victim Rights Amendment* (VRA), to guarantee victims certain rights when they participate in the criminal justice system. A parallel movement involved bids to change state constitutions by incorporating VRAs there as well. What we will do in this section is look at how this movement has fared.

Federal Constitutional Reform

At the conclusion of its work, The President's Task Force on Victims of Crime (1982) issued a strong, stirring call for action. The Task Force (1982: 114) explained that "government must be restrained from trampling the rights of the individual citizen. The victims of crime have been transformed into a group oppressively burdened by a system designed to protect them." As a result, the Task Force proposed that the Sixth Amendment to the U.S. Constitution be modified to incorporate a new clause guaranteeing explicit rights to crime victims. As Figure 12.1 shows, advocates envisioned that the addition of a single sentence would balance the constitutional standing of crime victims.

Supporters feel that a strong parallel exists between the historical conditions that spawned the original Bill of Rights and the current predicament of crime victims. Constitutional safeguards originally emerged from the colonists' determination to combat what they considered to be an unjust and oppressive system. The drafters of this document wove the notion of fair treatment for persons accused of crimes into a series of protections. This new formulation promised Americans such things as the right to a speedy trial, the right to confront one's accusers, the right to counsel, and freedom from cruel and unusual punishment. As one writer (Eikenberry, 1987: 33) put it, "The founding fathers wanted to ensure that the evils experienced by many innocent citizens at the hands of the English did not find their way into the newly found government."

FIGURE 12.1
Proposed Change to the Sixth Amendment of the United States Constitution*

In all criminal prosecutions the accused shall enjoy the right to a speedy and public trial, by an impartial jury of the State and district wherein the crime shall have been committed, which district shall have been previously ascertained by law, and to be informed of the nature and cause of the accusation; to be confronted with the witnesses against him; to have compulsory process for obtaining witnesses in his favor and to have the Assistance of Counsel for his defense. **Likewise, the victim, in every criminal prosecution shall have the right to be present and to be heard at all critical stages of judicial proceedings.**

* Proposed changes are highlighted for the reader.

Source: President's Task Force on Victims of Crime (1982). *Final Report*. Washington, DC: U.S. Government Printing Office, p. 114.

Crime victims today find themselves in a posture reminiscent of the situation that this country's early settlers faced. The elevation of rights for the accused, coupled with the declining status of the victim, have left victims in a predicament. Even though victims have endured suffering through no fault of their own, the state is generally more concerned with protecting the rights of their transgressors.

The proposed change to the federal Constitution aims to restore the victim's legal standing and guarantee a certain degree of justice. The inclusion of a VRA in the federal Constitution, just like the extension of suffrage and the abolition of slavery, would provide a corrective mechanism for undoing past harms (Eikenberry, 1987: 48). However, modifying the Constitution involves a slow, deliberate, and tedious process. This was part of the problem with the Equal Rights Amendment, which attempted to resolve gender inequities. As these initial efforts floundered, advocates embraced a new tactic.

A change of direction was heralded during a conference sponsored by the National Organization of Victim Assistance (NOVA) during January of 1986. After reviewing the recommendations proposed by The President's Task Force on Victims of Crime, participants offered an alternate strategy. Rather than trying to add language to embellish the Sixth Amendment, the suggestion was to create an entirely new Twenty-Sixth Amendment. This new amendment read:

> Victims of crime are entitled to certain basic rights including, but not limited to, the right to be informed, to be present, and to be heard at all critical stages of the federal and state criminal justice process to the extent that these rights do not interfere with existing Constitutional rights (Young, 1987: 66-67).

Sponsors were in favor of a new amendment for at least three reasons (Young, 1987: 67). First, forming a separate entry that dealt only with victims made the entire issue less confusing and objectionable. Victim gains would not hinge upon offender rights. Second, the new language was broader and much more inclusive. For example, it earmarked participation throughout the entire criminal justice process as its goal rather than restricting such participation to judicial proceedings. Third, it did not tamper with any rights of the accused. As a result, critics could not argue that victim rights were detrimental to existing protections afforded the accused.

These attempts to tamper with the federal Constitution drew resistance. Some observers countered that the entire effort to establish a national VRA was misdirected. Dolliver (1987) argued that the purpose behind the federal Bill of Rights is to protect against governmental infringement upon personal liberties. Because victim issues do not involve questions of freedom, they simply do not fit here. While one might commiserate with the unfortunate plight of crime victims, the "lack of uniformity in state statutes should hardly be an automatic recipe for a constitutional amendment" (Dolliver, 1987: 91).

Others found the proposed language to be too vague and overly encompassing. Lamborn (1987), for example, raised a number of perplexing questions as to the meaning of each phrase in the proposed federal amendment. His analysis ended with the following pronouncement (1987: 220):

> The failure of the proponents of the various proposals for a constitutional amendment on behalf of the victim to address the many complex issues raised by their proposals does not diminish the need for an enhanced role for the victim in the criminal justice process. That failure does, however, suggest that the campaign for a constitutional amendment is premature.

State Constitutional Reform

Given the lukewarm reception, support for any kind of national constitutional reform quickly dwindled. In fact, an assessment of the inroads gained after the 1982 President's Task Force (U.S. Department of Justice, 1986) ignored the entire issue of a federal VRA. Clearly, a new direction was needed.

The method of reform was revisited and revised. Representatives from several victim advocacy groups had established an informal network for sharing ideas and information. Early in 1987, members of these groups decided to create a coalition called the National Victims' Constitutional Amendment Network (NVCAN). This group dedicated itself to promoting VRAs at the state, rather than the federal, level.

Targeting states became the preferred option for many reasons (Lamborn, 1987: 201; Spencer, 1987). First, state VRAs would generate greater interest and more local support. Second, even though many states already had victim rights statutes on the books, there was no way to enforce these provisions. A state VRA would reinforce these arrangements. Finally, because state constitutions already protected criminals, it was reasonable to extend the same courtesy to crime victims.

FIGURE 12.2
States with Victim Rights Amendments

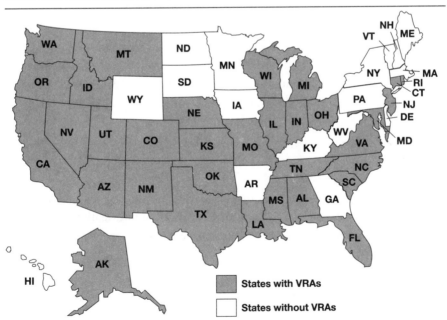

Source: National Victims' Constitutional Amendment Passage, State Victims Rights Amendments. Retrieved September 8, 2007, from http://www.nvcan.org/canmap.html

At the present time, there are no provisions in the federal constitution that deal with victim rights. However, 33 states, starting with

California in 1982, have approved such constitutional measures. The map contained in Figure 12.2 shows the states in which voters have endorsed VRAs in their state constitutions.

State constitutional provisions typically address a set of common rights. Unfortunately, most people remain unaware of these rights, especially when it would be critically important to exercise these safeguards. As a result, NVCAN reviewed state statutes, perused agency policies, and then interviewed key players and victims. This distillation helped NVCAN isolate critical or core rights that are common threads. Building upon this base, NVCAN then constructed a victim version of the popular *Miranda* rights cards that police officers routinely use to inform suspects of their rights. The thinking is that police officers could distribute this information during the initial investigation in order to make victims fully aware of their rights. That model card appears in Figure 12.3 in a generic format. Obviously, it would be up to a local jurisdiction to tailor the exact language to its own state VRA.

FIGURE 12.3
Victims' Rights "*Miranda* Card" Model

We are sorry that you have become a victim of a crime. As a crime victim, you are entitled to specific rights. You have the right to:

- Be treated with dignity and respect.
- Be notified of all critical proceedings and developments in your case.
- Be notified of the status of the alleged or convicted offender.
- Be present at all hearings at which the defendant is entitled to attend.
- Be heard at critical proceedings.
- Restitution to be paid by the offender in cases that result in a conviction.
- Reasonable protection from the alleged or convicted offender before, during, and after the trial.
- Apply for victim compensation in cases involving violent crime (for more information, call [list number for compensation information]).
- Information about and referrals to services and assistance.
- Right to pursue legal remedies if your rights are violated.

Source: National Victims' Constitutional Amendment Network (2004). *Crime Victims' Rights "Miranda Card."* Denver, CO: National Victims' Constitutional Amendment Passage. Retrieved September 8, 2007, from http://www.nvcan.org

In order to gain a better understanding of what a state VRA looks like, Figure 12.4 reprints the Florida version, which was passed by 90 percent of the voters in November of 1988. Notice how the first section mirrors the Sixth Amendment of the federal Constitution and how the second section tracks the language of the proposed Twenty-Sixth Amendment. The construction of the victim addition was done in such a way as to facilitate ratification of the federal VRA once it passed Congress and went before the states.

FIGURE 12.4
Florida Victim Rights Amendment

Section 16. Rights of accused and of victims.

(a) In all criminal prosecutions the accused shall, upon demand, be informed of the nature and cause of the accusation, and shall be furnished a copy of the charges, and shall have the right to have compulsory process for witnesses, to confront at trial adverse witnesses, to be heard in person, by counsel or both, and to have a speedy and public trial by impartial jury in the county where the crime was committed. If the county is not known, the indictment or information may charge venue in two or more counties conjunctively and proof that the crime was committed in that area shall be sufficient; but before pleading the accused may elect in which of those counties the trial will take place. Venue for prosecution of crimes committed beyond the boundaries of the state shall be fixed by law.

(b) Victims of crime or their lawful representatives, including the next of kin of homicide victims, are entitled to the right to be informed, to be present, and to be heard when relevant, at all crucial stages of criminal proceedings, to the extent that these rights do not interfere with the constitutional rights of the accused.

Source: *Constitution of the State of Florida*, Article 1, Section 16, *Florida Statutes* (2007).

The opposition to state constitutional amendments reflects concern over making changes to a document that serves as the basic foundation of our laws. Lamborn (1987) points out that many amendments are proposed without thorough investigation and discussion. Critics fear that victim rights bills tend to be more gut-level reactions than well-thought-out proposals. Consequently, there appears to be a conservative ideology underlying amendments that favor a "lock 'em up" philosophy.

Opponents of constitutional provisions also warn against eroding the rights of the accused in the haste to assist crime victims. Viano (1987) suggests that passage of constitutional amendments favoring crime victims will result in increased litigation over the treatment of victims, similar to what accompanied civil rights legislation. In essence, such constitutional amendments foster conflict between groups in society.

Rekindling Federal Constitutional Reform

The momentum achieved through state-level efforts was bolstered by a series of rulings issued by the trial court judge in the Oklahoma City bombing case. There, the defendant, Timothy McVeigh, was accused of detonating an explosion that toppled the federal building, killing 168 persons and injuring hundreds more. During pretrial motions, Judge Richard Matsch announced that he would set aside 45 courtroom seats for media representatives, 37 for public observers, and 16 chairs for the defense. There were no plans to accommodate any victims or survivors (Howlett, 1997). After the government provided a dozen places for victims, Judge Matsch issued an order on June 26, 1996, barring factual witnesses from the trial proceedings. What this ruling meant was that any victim who did not testify but exerted his or her right to attend the deliberations was not eligible to make a victim impact statement before the court during the sentencing phase.

This controversial decision ignited a number of reactions. The Department of Justice intervened, asking the judge to reconsider his decision. Victims and survivors filed their own motion, arguing that the judge's ruling abrogated or set aside the protections guaranteed under the federal Victims' Bill of Rights. One victim explained: "as it stands, I have to make the excruciating choice between testifying only in the sentencing phase and attending even one minute's worth of the trial" (Cassell, 1997).

The judge upheld his original position in a subsequent hearing, and an appeal to the federal District Court on October 4, 1996, produced no change. Bringing the case before the U.S. Court of Appeals for the 10th Circuit provided no immediate relief either. Judge Matsch steadfastly warned all parties that a potential avenue of appeal would be opened for the defendant if any victim attended the trial proceedings and gave victim impact testimony later during the sentencing phase. His position was that Rule 615 of the Federal Rules of Evidence at that time superseded the provisions of the Victims' Bill of Rights. The fear was that exposure to other victims' testimony during the trial might slant or taint the independent recollection of victims at the later sentencing phase (Cassell, 1997; Myers, 1997a). Essentially, then, the legal protections contained in the federal Victims' Bill of Rights held a deep, hollow clang for the Oklahoma City bombing victims and their survivors.

In response to this controversy, Congress passed the Victim Rights Clarification Act (VRCA) the very next year. The VRCA, which appears in Figure 12.5, removed the obstacle that hemmed in Judge Matsch. Today, victims are permitted to observe both portions of the criminal trial. The thinking behind this legislation is that while seques-tering witnesses is intended to protect the defendant's basic right to a fair trial, impact statements deal with sentencing and bear no rela-tionship to adjudication. As a result, the VRCA clarifies the victim's right to attend the full criminal trial and preserves the victim's right to address the court during sentencing proceedings.

FIGURE 12.5
The Victim Rights Clarification Act of 1997

Rights of victims to attend and observe trial.

1. Non-Capital Cases. – Notwithstanding any statute, rule, or other provision of law, a United States district court shall not order any victim of an offense excluded from the trial of a defendant accused of that offense because such victim may, during the sentencing hearing, make a statement or present any information in relation to the sentence.

2. Capital Cases. – Notwithstanding any statute, rule, or other provision of law, a United States district court shall not order any victim of an offense excluded from the trial of a defendant accused of that offense because such victim may, during the sentencing hearing, testify as to the effect of the offense on the victim and the victim's family. . . .

Source: *The Victim Rights Clarification Act of 1997*, 18 U.S.C. §3510.

These actions propelled a number of victim groups and other interested parties to merge into a unified force. Buoyed by successful campaigns to introduce state VRAs, lobbying efforts resurrected the earlier strategy of seeking support to amend the United States Con-stitution. This work culminated in Senate Joint Resolution 6, a proposal for a new amendment to the federal Constitution.

A mounting wave of criticism quickly surfaced, and opponents echoed many of the concerns mentioned earlier. An editorial in *The New York Times* wondered whether support for constitutional reform amounted to anything more than mere political posturing by elected officials (Lewis, 1996). However, Kansas Attorney General Carla J. Sto-vall (1997) countered that the framers of the Constitution never intended for this document to be so sacrosanct as to not undergo modification. In fact, Congress has altered the Constitution 27 times already, extending protections to persons accused of crimes in 15 of these changes. In Stovall's (1997) view, "I do not believe it just that within our system no rights are guaranteed by the very same document to the victims of the very acts for which the accused have been arrested and guaranteed rights." Ultimately, the proposed amendment failed to gain passage.

Proponents took issue with such a pessimistic forecast and mounted another charge to bolster a consideration of victim rights at the federal level. Advocates went back to the drawing boards and emerged with a new bill for Congress to consider in the following session. Senator Jon Kyl (Arizona) and Senator Dianne Feinstein (California) attempted to rekindle interest in the victim rights issue by introducing a new constitutional amendment on April 1, 1998. This proposal wove its way through the Senate Judiciary Committee and was reintroduced in January of 1999 during the 106th Congress. A companion bill also made its way into the House of Representatives and gathered much support. However, the bill encountered obstacles in April of 2000, forcing the disappointed Senators Kyl and Feinstein to withdraw from further consideration what had become known as Senate Joint Resolution 3.

FIGURE 12.6
Proposed Victim Rights Amendment to the United States Constitution

---

SECTION 1. The rights of victims of violent crime, being capable of protection without denying the constitutional rights of those accused of victimizing them, are hereby established and shall not be denied by any State or the United States and may be restricted only as provided in this article.

SECTION 2. A victim of violent crime shall have the right to reasonable and timely notice of any public proceeding involving the crime and of any release or escape of the accused; the rights not to be excluded from such public proceeding and reasonably to be heard at public release, plea, sentencing, reprieve, and pardon proceedings; and the right to adjudicative decisions that duly consider the victim's safety, interest in avoiding unreasonable delay, and just and timely claims to restitution from the offender. These rights shall not be restricted except when and to the degree dictated by a substantial interest in public safety or the administration of criminal justice, or by compelling necessity.

SECTION 3. Nothing in this article shall be construed to provide grounds for a new trial or to authorize any claim for damages. Only the victim or the victim's lawful representative may assert the rights established by this article, and no person accused of the crime may obtain any form of relief hereunder.

SECTION 4. Congress shall have power to enforce by appropriate legislation the provisions of this article. Nothing in this article shall affect the President's authority to grant reprieves or pardons.

SECTION 5. This article shall be inoperative unless it has been ratified as an amendment to the Constitution by the legislatures of three-fourths of the several States within 7 years from the date of its submission to the States by the Congress. This article shall take effect on the 180th day after the date of its ratification.

Source: *Congressional Record*. Senate Joint Resolution 1, 108th Congress, 1st Session, September 4, 2003.

Undaunted by this experience, determined advocates continued to rally for a federal constitutional amendment. Senators Kyl and Feinstein introduced another resolution on January 1, 2003. That bill was referred to the Senate Judiciary Subcommittee, which held hearings and moved favorably on the proposal. The proposed amendment, which appears in Figure 12.6, is no longer active.

Proponents and supporters came to the painful realization that they lacked a sufficient number of votes to gain Congressional passage. Rather than simply accept defeat and walk away, the decision was made to re-channel interests into the legislative, rather than the constitutional, reform effort. As Senator Feinstein (2004: S4262) explained

> It is clear to me that passage of a Constitutional amendment is impossible at this time. If we tried, and failed, it could be years before we could try again. Victims of crime have waited years for progress, and a compromise approach, resulting in the bill now under consideration, will result in meaningful progress.

While quite a few members of Congress endorse the notion of victim rights, their position is that these rights should be statutorily, not constitutionally, guaranteed. In order to harness these energies, lawmakers mobilized to create a crime victims' bill of rights. As we will see in the next section, these efforts were successful in gaining passage of a bill that incorporated a range of victim rights into already existing federal law.

Victim Rights Legislation

Another avenue to secure victim rights called for the passage of new laws and regulations that spelled out exact protections. Just like VRA reform, legislation was enacted mandating certain rights and privileges for crime victims and witnesses at the federal level. As Figure 12.7 demonstrates, victim issues have garnered much publicity. This activity also prompted a parallel response at the state level. Both the federal and state arenas are visited in this section.

FIGURE 12.7
President Bush's Proclamation Establishing Victims' Rights Week

---

National Crime Victims' Rights Week, 2007
A Proclamation by the President of the United States

National Crime Victims' Rights Week is an opportunity to underscore our commitment to protecting the rights of crime victims and to recognize those who bring hope and healing to these individuals and their families. During this week, we especially remember and mourn the victims of the senseless acts of violence at Virginia Tech. A grieving Nation honors the innocent lives lost in this tragedy, and we pray for the families of the victims.

My Administration is committed to helping safeguard our communities and to ensuring that the rights of those who have been victimized by crime are protected. My Family Justice Center Initiative, announced in 2003, is now providing assistance and services for victims of domestic violence at centers nationwide. Additionally, last year I signed into law the Adam Walsh Child Protection and Safety Act of 2006, which helps protect our youth by increasing the penalties for crimes against children and creating a National Child Abuse Registry. My Administration also supports a Crime Victims' Rights Amendment to the Constitution to further protect the basic rights of crime victims.

During National Crime Victims' Rights Week and throughout the year, we remember and are grateful to our Nation's victim service providers, volunteers, law enforcement, and community organizations that support victims of crime through their commitment and compassion. To find out more information about victims' rights and volunteer opportunities, individuals may visit www.crimevictims.gov. Together, we can help ensure that crime victims have the rights and protections they deserve.

NOW, THEREFORE I, GEORGE W. BUSH, President of the United States of America, by virtue of the authority vested in me by the Constitution and laws of the United States, do hereby proclaim April 22 through April 28, 2007, as National Crime Victims' Rights Week. I encourage all Americans to help raise awareness and promote the cause of victims' rights in their communities.

IN WITNESS WHEREOF, I have hereunto set my hand this twentieth day of April, in the year of our Lord two thousand seven, and of the Independence of the United States of America the two hundred and thirty-first.

GEORGE W. BUSH

Source: Office of the Press Secretary (April 20, 2007). *National Crime Victims' Rights Week, 2007: A Proclamation by the President of the United States*. Washington, DC: The White House. Retrieved on September 9, 2007, from http://www.whitehouse.gov/news/releases/ 2007/04/20070420-12.html

Federal Legislative Reform

One alternative to making constitutional changes is to promote legislation that addresses victim concerns. This approach is clearly more palatable to many people. As Figure 12.8 shows, the federal government has undertaken a variety of initiatives dealing with crime victims over the past three decades. Many of these bills have prompted the states to take parallel steps. A common federal strategy is to make funds available to states only if they incorporate specific features into their statutes and programs. As a result of this strategy, one will find much congruity between federal and state efforts.

FIGURE 12.8
Significant Landmark Federal Victim Rights Initiatives

1974	Law Enforcement Assistance Administration funding establishes the first local victim/witness programs.
1981	President Reagan's signs a proclamation establishing the first Victims' Rights Week.
1982	Omnibus Victim/Witness Protection Act promulgates victim rights for the federal court system.
1982	The President's Task Force on Victims of Crime releases a series of recommendations.
1983	The Office for Victims of Crime opens within the U.S. Department of Justice.
1983	The U.S. Attorney General unveils guidelines for the treatment of federal victims and witnesses.
1984	The U.S. Attorney General Task Force on Domestic Violence releases its report.
1984	Victims of Crime Act establishes the Crime Victims Fund to support compensation programs.
1990	The Crime Control Act creates the federal Crime Victims' Bill of Rights.
1990	Congress passes the Student Right to Know and Campus Security Act, also known as "The Clery Act."
1992	The Hate Crime Statistics Act takes effect.
1994	The Child Sexual Abuse Registry is implemented.
1994	The Violence Against Women Act releases monies to combat female victimization.
1996	The Community Notification Act ("Megan's Law") requires sex offender registration and community notification.
1997	The Victim Rights Clarification Act stemming from the Oklahoma City bombing case.
1998	The Crime Victims with Disabilities Act is passed.

FIGURE 12.8—*continued*

2001   A special federal victim compensation program is created for victims of the September 11th attacks on the World Trade Center and the Pentagon.

2003   Amber Alert (America's Missing: Broadcast Emergency Response) launches a national child abduction response.

2003   The Office on Violence Against Women is established within the Department of Justice.

2003   January is set aside as National Stalking Awareness Month.

2004   Justice for All Act provides rights for crime victims.

2005   A national online sex offender registry is commissioned.

2005   Programs aimed at combating human trafficking and rescuing such victims are launched.

2006   Adam Walsh Child Protection and Safety Act increases sex offender supervision.

Source: Adapted from National Center for Victims of Crime (2007). "Landmarks in Victims' Rights and Services," *2007 National Crime Victims' Rights Week Resource Guide.* Washington, DC: U.S. Department of Justice.

These legislative developments often encourage further action. For example, the U.S. Attorney General originally promulgated a set of guidelines for dealing with and assisting federal victims and witnesses in 1983. These regulations were updated recently to ensure that federal officials were complying with all pertinent federal directives (Office of the U.S. Attorney General, 2005). Figure 12.9 lists the services that federal officials are mandated to deliver when dealing with crime victims. These rules attempt to make federal criminal procedures more accommodating and inviting to victims and witnesses.

Probably the most noteworthy feature in the federal legislative arsenal was the creation of the Crime Victims' Bill of Rights in 2004, which appears in Figure 12.10. It is important to note that although it is called a "bill of rights," it is *not* a national constitutional provision. These provisions illustrate how the federal government has expanded its policies and procedures for informing crime victims of their rights and for protecting their interests (Office of the U.S. Attorney General, 2005).

Passage of the federal Crime Victims' Bill of Rights has been the subject of two recent court cases. In *Kenna v. U.S. District Court* (2006), a father and son investment team had bilked scores of victims to the tune of almost $100 million. Both defendants pleaded guilty to the charges. More than 60 victims submitted victim impact statements. At the father's sentencing hearing, several victims, including the plaintiff Kenna, addressed the court and explained how their retirement savings were drained, businesses bankrupted, and lives ruined by the father's nefarious scheme. The court sentenced the father to 20 years in prison.

FIGURE 12.9
Federal Regulations Regarding Services to Victims

c. Description of services.

1. A responsible official shall

   a. inform a victim of the place where the victim may receive emergency medical and social services;

   b. inform a victim of any restitution or other relief to which the victim may be entitled under this or any other law and [the] manner in which such relief may be obtained;

   c. inform a victim of public and private programs that are available to provide counseling, treatment, and other support to the victim; and

   d. assist a victim in contacting the persons who are responsible for providing the services and relief described in subparagraphs (a), (b), and (c).

2. A responsible official shall arrange for a victim to receive reasonable protection from a suspected offender and persons acting in concert with or at the behest of the suspected offender.

3. During the investigation and prosecution of a crime, a responsible official shall provide a victim the earliest possible notice of

   a. the status of the investigation of the crime, to the extent it is appropriate to inform the victim and to the extent that it will not interfere with the investigation;

   b. the arrest of a suspected offender;

   c. the filing of charges against a suspected offender;

   d. the scheduling of each court proceeding that the witness is either required to attend or, under section 10606(b)(4) of this title, is entitled to attend;

   e. the release or detention status of an offender or suspected offender;

   f. the acceptance of a plea of guilty or nolo contendere or the rendering of a verdict after trial; and

   g. the sentence imposed on an offender, including the date on which the offender will be eligible for parole.

4. During court proceedings, a responsible official shall ensure that a victim is provided a waiting area removed from and out of the sight and hearing of the defendant and defense witnesses.

FIGURE 12.9—*continued*

---

5. After trial, a responsible official shall provide a victim the earliest possible notice of

   a. the scheduling of a parole hearing for the offender;

   b. the escape, work release, furlough, or any other form of release from custody of the offender; and

   c. the death of the offender, if the offender dies while in custody.

6. At all times, a responsible official shall ensure that any property of a victim that is being held for evidentiary purposes be maintained in good condition and returned to the victim as soon as it is no longer needed for evidentiary purposes.

7. The Attorney General or the head of another department or agency that conducts an investigation of a sexual assault shall pay, either directly or by reimbursement of payment by the victim, the cost of a physical examination of the victim which an investigating officer determines was necessary or useful for evidentiary purposes. The Attorney General shall provide for the payment of the cost of up to 2 anonymous and confidential tests of the victim for sexually transmitted diseases, including HIV, gonorrhea, herpes, chlamydia, and syphilis, during the 12 months following sexual assaults that pose a risk of transmission, and the cost of a counseling session by a medically trained professional on the accuracy of such tests and the risk of transmission of sexually transmitted diseases to the victim as the result of the assault. A victim may waive anonymity and confidentiality of any tests paid for under this section.

8. A responsible official shall provide the victim with general information regarding the corrections process, including information about work release, furlough, probation, and eligibility for each.

9. No cause of action or defense.

   This section does not create a cause of action or defense in favor of any person arising out of the failure of a responsible person to provide information as required by subsection (b) or (c) of this section.

Source: *Victims' Rights and Restitution Act of 1990*, 42 U.S.C. §10607.

The son's sentencing hearing took place three months later. However, in this hearing, the judge declined to give any of the victims the opportunity to deliver a fresh set of remarks before the court. The judge stated that he had already listened to the victims at the last sentencing hearing and did not anticipate learning anything new. The judge then went ahead and sentenced the son to a little more than 11 years imprisonment.

FIGURE 12.10
Federal Crime Victims' Bill of Rights

A crime victim has the following rights:

1. The right to be reasonably protected from the accused offender.

2. The right to reasonable, accurate, and timely notice of any public court proceeding, or any parole proceeding, involving the crime or of any release or escape of the accused.

3. The right not to be excluded from any such public court proceeding, unless the court, after receiving clear and convincing evidence, determines that testimony by the victim would be materially altered if the victim heard other testimony at that proceeding.

4. The right to be reasonably heard at any public proceeding in the district court involving release, plea, sentencing, or any parole proceeding.

5. The reasonable right to confer with the attorney for the Government in the case.

6. The right to full and timely restitution as provided in law.

7. The right to proceedings free from unreasonable delay.

8. The right to be treated with fairness and with respect for the victim's dignity and privacy.

Source: *Rights of Crime Victims*, 18 U.S.C. §3771(a).

Kenna filed a writ of *mandamus* in reaction to the judge's behavior. A writ of *mandamus* asks a higher court to order a lower court to act upon or refrain from, as the case may be, upholding the petitioner's rights. Kenna contended that the judge's refusal to allow victim input at the second sentencing hearing violated the fourth provision in the federal Crime Victim's Rights Act listed in Figure 12.8 dealing with the "right to be reasonably heard." That safeguard, according to Kenna, guaranteed him allocution or the right to speak before the court. The presiding judge, on the other hand, relied upon the word "reasonably." His position was that the language vested him with the authority to exercise discretion and limit victim testimony because the victims' views were already known. As a remedy, Kenna sought to have the sentence overturned and demanded that the judge be forced to listen to the victims and then resentence the defendant. The court of appeals agreed with Kenna. It advised the district court to conduct a new sentencing hearing and to allow Kenna and other victims in the cases to make oral presentations.

The federal Crime Victims Bill of Rights was tested again in a second related development (*United States v. Wood*, 2006). There, the defendant Wood had been found guilty of fraud and was scheduled for a sentencing hearing. However, the victims had plans to be out of the country on that day. Hence, they requested a later date for sentencing that would enable them to attend and speak before the court. The defendant objected to the delay, and the case made its way before the district court. After hearing this case, the district court relied upon the *Kenna* decision and found that the minor delay was a reasonable accommodation.

State Legislative Reform

While these federal actions were taking place, many states were devising their own ways to protect and assist crime victims. One prime example of these inroads is that all the states now have active victim compensation programs. Virtually every state in the union has passed its own legislation dealing with victim rights. In many respects, these provisions mirror federal efforts. As Figure 12.11 outlines, Florida victims and witnesses are entitled to a number of rights. The introduction of victim rights legislation has not gone without criticism. For one thing, these additional measures and responsibilities translate into increased loads for beleaguered criminal justice workers. These actions may bring about some delays and greater costs in the court process.

Some people fear that greater participation may exacerbate harm to the victim. A number of states do not allow victims to be completely barred from attending the criminal trial. However, some restrictions usually apply (Office for Victims of Crime, 2002a). More worrisome, though, is that the victim must relive the traumatic events surrounding the crime during both the fact-finding and sentencing phases of a court case. Pointed questions by the defense can be a further detriment. This experience might be a cleansing event for some victims, but for others it may only intensify and prolong the hurt.

Another question involves the situation in which a victim is not notified or accorded his or her statutorily guaranteed rights. What avenues can victims pursue should the system not honor these rights? Many statutes spell out the steps expected of system personnel. Arizona, for example, requires that the prosecutor notify the court that he or she has made an honest effort to confer with the victim prior to arranging a plea agreement (Office for Victims of Crime, 2002b). However, there is little recourse if the prosecution does not comply with these procedures. In fact, some states include an explicit disclaimer that victims cannot take any legal action against system personnel who fail to follow the statute (Office for Victims of Crime, 2002b). Other jurisdictions rely on a more general immunity clause that prohibits the public from suing governmental agents for actions undertaken in good faith or without malice. One possible solution lies in the area of ethics standards. Victims may be able to file complaints with a state ethics board that can levy disciplinary action for failure to comply with the law. However, it is likely that this recourse would bring very little satisfaction to the victim.

FIGURE 12.11
Florida Guidelines for Fair Treatment of Victims and Witnesses

Florida victims and witnesses are entitled to the following considerations:

- Information concerning services available to victims of adult and juvenile crime.
- Information for purposes of notifying victim or appropriate next of kin of victim or other designated contact of victim.
- Information concerning protection available to victim or witness.
- Notification of scheduling changes.
- Advance notification to victim or relative of victim concerning judicial proceedings; right to be present.
- Information concerning release from incarceration from a county jail, municipal jail, juvenile detention facility, or residential commitment facility.
- Consultation with victim or guardian or family of victim.
- Return of property to victim.
- Notification to employer and explanation to creditors of victim or witness.
- Notification of right to request restitution.
- Notification of right to submit impact statement.
- Local witness coordination services.
- Victim assistance education and training.
- General victim assistance.
- Victim's rights information card or brochure.
- Information concerning escape from a state correctional institution, county jail, juvenile detention facility, or residential commitment facility.
- Presence of victim advocate during discovery deposition; testimony of victim of a sexual offense.
- Implementing crime prevention in order to protect the safety of persons and property, as prescribed in the State Comprehensive Plan.
- Attendance of victim at same school as defendant.
- Use of a polygraph examination or other truth-telling device with victim.
- Presence of victim advocates during forensic medical examination.

Source: *Florida Statutes* (2007), § 960.01.

A recent development has been the establishment of special investigative units that look into complaints that system officials have usurped victim rights. An *ombudsman* is a neutral party who provides a checks-and-balances function and cuts through bureaucratic red tape in an effort to rectify problems or resolve disputes expeditiously. The Department of Justice, for example, has founded the Office of the Victims' Rights Ombudsman to handle any federal violations that may arise. Several states (i.e., Alaska, Minnesota, and South Carolina) have also formed similar units. Once again, though, the federal ombudsman has the final voice, and this person's ruling is binding and not subject to appeal or review.

A more perplexing issue involves a debate over the goals of the criminal justice system. Increased attention to victim harm shifts sentencing from a preoccupation with rehabilitation to an emphasis on retribution and restitution. What this change does is refocus attention upon the needs of the victim. Critics protest that this alteration creates an imbalance and invites a diminution of offender rights. Others note that the call for harsher sanctions stretches an already overextended correctional system beyond its capacity (Acker, 1992; Erez, 1989; Ranish and Shichor, 1985). As one writer adroitly put it:

> [I]n some respects, a new battle has replaced the old. Now, it is not victims fighting for a place in the system; the current consensus is that they belong. But a new battle now rages between the state and its own limited resources. Vying for these resources are overcrowded jails, rising crime rates, and competing welfare and infrastructure programs. Clearly, the rights of crime victims will not be secure until these issues are resolved (Calcutt, 1988: 834).

Victim Impact Statements

Perhaps one of the more significant steps in the crusade for victim rights has been the idea of a victim impact statement. A *victim impact statement* (VIS) allows the victim the opportunity to let the court know how the incident has influenced his or her life. Victims can describe the emotional and financial costs associated with the victimization and can outline what they consider to be an appropriate punishment.

A VIS takes one of two forms. The first is a written account that usually accompanies the presentence investigation report. The second format, called *allocution*, is an oral presentation. Here the victim himself or herself addresses the court during the sentencing phase.

Two major streams of interest have trailed the VIS. The first area concerns research dealing with the effect of a VIS upon case processing. The second focus is upon the legal challenges that have risen regarding the use of a VIS in death penalty cases. Both topics are addressed in the following sections.

The Effect of Victim Impact Statements

The most surprising finding in virtually all victim impact statement studies is that large numbers of victims do not avail themselves of this opportunity. For example, while one-half of the felony victims over a four-year span in Ohio provided a VIS, only 6 percent exercised the right of allocution at sentencing (Erez and Tontodonato, 1990; Erez and Tontodonato, 1992). Other studies concur that fewer than 10 percent of all victims make statements at sentencing hearings or parole board deliberations (McLeod, 1987; Ranish and Shichor, 1985; Villmoore and Neto, 1987).

One reason for this stunning lack of participation is that many victims are not aware of the right to be present. In addition, in some instances, they cannot be located when the case reaches that stage of the criminal justice process (McLeod, 1987; Villmoore and Neto, 1987). But even when victims do know about this opportunity, they refrain from using it. Many victims are dissatisfied with the system, do not think their input is critical, fear retaliation, or are concerned for their own emotional well-being (Erez and Tontodonato, 1992; Villmoore and Neto, 1987).

For victims who do use the system, contrary to what skeptics had forecasted, not all of them use the VIS vindictively to seek the harshest punishment possible (Acker, 1992). Critics were concerned that VISs would supersede legal factors and that judicial punishment would comply with these subjective "victim pleas." One study found that the victim's presence in court, a VIS, and a request for incarceration all influenced the use of imprisonment as a sanction (Erez and Tontodonato, 1990). However, the VIS carried far less weight than legal variables and prior offense history in sentence determination. Other studies report that VISs have no impact on sentences, restitution orders, the speed of court procedures, or victim satisfaction (Davis and Smith, 1994; Davis and Smith, 1995; Davis, Henley, and Smith, 1990; Erez, 1990; Erez and Roeger, 1995; Erez and Tontodonato, 1992). In fact, one victimologist caustically commented that "requiring a victim impact statement and recommendation as part of the presentence report is a mere genuflection to ritualistic legalism" (Walsh, 1986: 1139).

There is an emerging body of literature that appears to contradict some of these earlier findings. Parsonage and his colleagues (1994) found that parole boards are less likely to recommend inmates for release prior to sentence expiration when victims oppose such action. Luginbuhl and Burkhead (1995), in an experimental design that utilized college students as subjects, uncovered a tendency for these simulated jurors to vote for the death penalty when they had access to victim impact statements like the one the prosecution proffered in the *Booth* case (see the following section). Finally, Morgan and Smith (2005) reported that victim participation had a decided effect on parole board release decisions in Alabama.

Despite a number of empirical studies that find sentencing practices remain largely unaffected by victim input, VISs have generated tremendous legal concern. As the following section explains, even the federal Supreme Court became embroiled in the use of VISs during capital cases.

Federal Supreme Court Rulings

The practice of allowing a VIS has resulted in three significant U.S. Supreme Court cases. Initially, the Court barred the use of a VIS in death penalty cases. However, the Court later reversed itself to permit such information to be heard during the sentencing phase. A brief look at these three cases will illustrate how case law has evolved in this area. However, first, it might be helpful to revisit some of the major issues that framed the death penalty at that time so we have an appropriate foundation for viewing the victim impact cases.

The U.S. Supreme Court struck down the death penalty as cruel and unusual punishment in *Furman v. Georgia* (1972). Race had emerged as an important determinant of when the death penalty was imposed in rape cases. Black defendants were more likely to receive the death penalty when the victim was white than in intraracial incidents or instances in which the suspect was white and the victim was a minority member. In other words, social considerations, rather than legal variables, predicted sentencing outcomes.

The Florida state legislature reacted to *Furman* by enacting a revised statute aimed at removing any arbitrary or capricious intrusions (Ehrhardt et al., 1973). Essentially, the new law established what are called "mitigating" and "aggravating" circumstances. Four years later, the Court upheld the imposition of capital punishment as constitutional in *Gregg v. Georgia* (1976).

Aggravating circumstances render the crime more heinous or despicable (*Florida Statutes*, 2007: § 921.141(5)). Some examples would include torturing the victim prior to death, a gang-style execution, a murder committed for pecuniary gain, or killing somebody during the course of a felony, and the like. *Mitigating circumstances* are factors that make the crime somewhat more understandable (*Florida Statues*, 2007: §921.141(6)). That would include such items as mental impairment or a low IQ, a history of being abused as a child, being under extreme mental duress at the time of the incident, young age, and other similar conditions.

Judges and juries are obligated to consider both mitigating and aggravating circumstances when deliberating over an appropriate sentence. If the mitigating circumstances outweigh the aggravating circumstances, then the appropriate punishment would be life imprisonment. If, however, the aggravating circumstances are more prominent than the mitigating circumstances, then the death penalty would be the appropriate choice.

In addition to understanding the role of mitigating and aggravating circumstances in capital punishment cases, we should also be aware that the trial court must remain vigilant in protecting suspect rights. Inflammatory statements are not allowed, and items that would unduly prejudice jurors are not admissible. Given this background, we are now in a better position to appreciate the issues that were raised in the VIS decisions.

Booth v. Maryland (1987)

The Supreme Court first addressed the issue of the VIS in *Booth v. Maryland* (1987). Booth was convicted of two counts of first-degree murder in a case involving an elderly couple. During the sentencing portion of the trial, the judge allowed the admission of a written VIS that was read to the jury.

According to Booth's lawyer, the VIS contained a number of inflammatory statements. For example, the VIS described the victims as "loving parents and grandparents," as well as "extremely good people who wouldn't hurt a fly." Family members also stated that their parents were "butchered like animals" and that nobody "should be able to do something like that and get away with it." Furthermore, the victim's daughter said that she "could never forgive anyone for killing them that way." Given the tone of these statements, Booth's lawyer argued that such characterizations were unduly prejudicial to his client.

The Supreme Court delivered a 5-4 judgment and ruled that a capital sentencing jury should not be exposed to a VIS during its deliberations. Drawing upon previous death penalty decisions, the Court noted that a VIS was not a statutorily defined aggravating circumstance. Introducing testimony about the sterling character of the victim runs the risk that the jury could make an arbitrary decision. In other words, instead of focusing completely upon the defendant, the jury might be tempted to impose the death penalty solely because the victim was an outstanding member of the community.

Justice Scalia issued a dissenting opinion. There he wrote:

> To require, as we have, that all mitigating factors which render capital punishment a harsh penalty in the particular case be placed before the sentencing authority, while simultaneously requiring, as we do today, that evidence of much of the human suffering the defendant has inflicted be suppressed, is in effect to prescribe a debate on the appropriateness of the capital penalty with one side muted. If that penalty is constitutional, as we have repeatedly said it is, it seems to me not remotely unconstitutional to permit both the pros and the cons in the particular case to be heard (pp. 520-521).

South Carolina v. Gathers (1989)

In *South Carolina v. Gathers* the U.S. Supreme Court extended this embargo to cover prosecutor comments made to a jury during the sentencing portion of a death penalty case. During closing arguments, the prosecutor emphasized repeatedly that the deceased was an extremely religious person and a self-styled minister. The South Carolina Supreme Court, relying upon the *Booth* decision, overturned the sentence of death. It reasoned that the prosecutor's remarks implied that the death sentence was appropriate because the victim was such a religious person.

An appeal to the U.S. Supreme Court brought a similar rebuff. The federal justices, in another 5–4 split decision, ruled that the prosecutor's description of the victim violated the standards erected in *Booth*. However, the dissenting opinions made it quite clear that there was considerable disenchantment with *Booth* itself. Justice O'Connor, for example, wrote "I remain persuaded that *Booth* was wrong when decided and stand ready to overrule it if the Court would do so. . . ."

Justice Scalia also echoed a similar sentiment in his dissenting remarks. There he wrote:

> Two Terms ago, when we decided *Booth v. Maryland*, I was among four Members of the Court who believed that the decision imposed a restriction upon state and federal criminal procedures that has no basis in the Constitution. I continue to believe that *Booth* was wrongly decided, and my conviction that it does perceptible harm has been strengthened by subsequent writings pointing out the indefensible consequences of a rule that the specific harm visited upon society

by a murderer may not be taken into account when the jury decides whether to impose the sentence of death. . . . I therefore think now the present case squarely calls into question the validity of *Booth*, and I would overrule that case (pp. 823-824) [citations omitted].

The tension among the Justices was quite evident. Even to the uninitiated, it was quite clear that the clouds were gathering prior to the storm. That test would come in the form of another case the Court would visit just two years later: *Payne v. Tennessee.*

Payne v. Tennessee (1991)

The VIS controversy continued until the Court reversed itself in the 1991 *Payne v. Tennessee* decision. Payne had been sentenced to death for murdering a mother and her child. A three-year-old survived the attack, and the jury received a VIS that documented the duress the child was facing. The jury imposed the death penalty upon Payne. Payne's lawyer appealed the sentence, arguing that any reliance upon a VIS in a capital case clearly violated both *Booth* and *Gathers.*

The federal Supreme Court granted *certiorari*, heard the case, and overturned its earlier rulings. As the majority opinion explained:

> We thus hold that if the State chooses to permit the admission of victim impact evidence and prosecutorial argument on that subject, the Eighth Amendment erects no *per se* bar. A State may legitimately conclude that evidence about the victim and about the impact of the murder on the victim's family is relevant to the jury's decision as to whether or not the death penalty should be imposed. There is no reason to treat such evidence differently than other relevant evidence is treated.

As a result of *Payne*, the courts are no longer required to suppress a VIS in a capital penalty case. If state law permits the prosecution to explain what repercussions the survivors have shouldered because of the incident, that information is appropriate for the jury to hear. Nothing in the Eighth Amendment forbids such testimony from consideration.

The controversy surrounding the issue of a VIS in a death penalty case provoked one commentator to recommend a slightly different tack. Finn-DeLuca (1994: 427-428) suggests that a much more beneficial route would be for state legislatures to construct guidelines governing the types of victim impact evidence considered admissible and what kind of information would be inappropriate for juries to hear during the penalty phase. Such a strategy would avoid sentencing practices that rely heavily upon emotional or inflammatory appeal (Newman, 1995).

Florida has followed this recommendation. With respect to victim impact statements in capital punishment cases, *Florida Statutes* (2007: § 941.121(7)) reads:

> Once the prosecution has provided evidence of the existence of one or more aggravating circumstances as described in sub-section (5), the prosecution may introduce, and subsequently argue, victim impact evidence to the jury. Such evidence shall be designed to demonstrate the victim's uniqueness as an individual human being and the resultant loss to the community's members by the victim's death. Characterizations and opinions about the crime, the defendant, and the appropriate sentence shall not be permitted as a part of victim impact evidence.

Some Closing Thoughts

Chapter 1 framed this book in the context of Mendelsohn's rendition of the field as "general victimology." At that point, readers were advised that this book was going to concentrate on a single component of that typology: criminal victimology. After considering so many different topics and broad issues, we think our readers would agree that this restriction certainly did not hinder the amount of materials we have visited and digested.

Several themes have formed the organizational backbone of this text. Perhaps the most important guiding point is the notion of "double victimization" introduced in Chapter 3. The whole idea that the system intensifies—rather than rectifies—victim suffering is a pivotal concern. Each subsequent chapter continued this dialogue by addressing various reform efforts intended to help transform the *criminal* justice system into a more meaningful *victim* justice system. While many of these efforts have blossomed and are making the "halls of justice" more user-friendly, we have tried to retain a critical (but not overly skeptical) eye. Simply put, some legal reforms have not worked. As a consequence, many troublesome areas are still in need of solutions.

Another recurring concept that we have been careful to include wherever possible is the idea of victim precipitation. As the opening chapter explained, the original thrust within victimology was to unveil how victims contribute to their own demise. Despite an intense ideological backlash, remnants of victim-blaming continue to haunt victimological developments. We saw this when we turned to sexual assault, spouse abuse, child maltreatment, elder abuse, and homicide victimization. Rather than shy away from these accounts, we have included them for the reader's own evaluation. In many instances, this intense scrutiny of victim actions has acted as a springboard. It has stimulated a number of theoretical viewpoints. Sexual assault is now interpreted in terms of power and domination instead of sexual gratification. The question of "why doesn't she leave him?" paves the way for understanding how learned helplessness and the cycle of violence immobilize spouse abuse victims. A reinterpretation of how alcohol influences social interaction patterns and impedes the delivery of medical services sheds a different light on homicide victimization. As you can see, the criticisms and flaws associated with the victim precipitation argument have launched many new perspectives.

Another common unifying thread that weaves its way throughout the text has been the inclusion of a distinct practitioner orientation. For example, the sexual assault chapter places the victim's experience within the context of a crisis reaction. It also explores the activities that take place at different junctures throughout the criminal investigation process and introduces the sexual assault nurse examiner program. Similarly, the spouse abuse chapter addresses how research has prompted policy changes in the ways that the police and the courts now provide services to battered women. Coping strategies for lessening the incidence of child maltreatment and elder abuse also make an appearance. Information on the steps involved in a death notification, as well as the bereavement stages that loved ones will encounter, helps to provide a more intense view of what service providers and their clients face during the aftermath of a horrible victimization episode. Victimization in the schools and at the work place, traditionally thought to be safe places, also receives considerable attention. Recent events have made us realize that these locations have their own distinct patterns of victimization. There is also a chapter devoted to dispute mediation and restorative justice, mechanisms that attempt to draw victims closer into the pursuit of a just solution. Finally, progress already made is evident in the efforts to secure victim rights, the debate over the propriety of victim impact statements, and the efforts to search for informal remedies that address individual victim concerns.

Those readers contemplating a possible career in the field of criminal justice should keep in mind that while the victim movement has been responsible for many changes, the ultimate success of these efforts hinges upon the people who work within the justice community. Remaining sensitive and compassionate to each victim's tragedies is the most essential ingredient to any meaningful social service delivery.

FIGURE 12.12
Selected Internet Sites Dealing with Victim Legal Issues

FirstGov: The U.S. Government's Official Web Portal
    http://www.firstgov.gov/Topics/Reference_Shelf.shtml#Laws

Loudoun County, Virginia, Victim Witness Program
    http://www.co.loudoun.va.us/VWP/rights.html

MADD (Mothers Against Drunk Driving) Victim Services & Information
    http://www.madd.org/victims

National Center for Victims of Crime
    http://www.ncvc.org/ncvc/main.aspx

National Victims' Constitutional Amendment Network
    http://www.nvcan.org

U.S. Code, Legal Information Institute
    http://www4.law.cornell.edu/uscode

U.S. Federal Courts Homepage
    http://www.uscourts.gov

U.S. House of Representatives
    http://www.house.gov

U.S. Senate
    http://www.senate.gov

U.S. Supreme Court Decisions
    http://supct.law.cornell.edu/supct/index.html

Summary

The victim movement is maturing. Over the past two decades, there have been a number of serious initiatives to provide victims with rights. These efforts have continued to gather momentum. Laws now cover a wide range of areas, such as restitution, victim compensation, victim impact statements, notification of system procedures, protection of victims and witnesses, and consultation with victims. This coverage suggests that victim rights will continue to gain even more prominence.

Two issues must be kept in mind as this trend continues. First, there is still much to be learned about the plight of victims. Good intentions, no matter how noble, do not automatically guarantee that recipients are better off now than they were in the past. Only through constant monitoring and evaluation is it possible to gauge the effects of change.

Second, in our zeal to help victims, it is important to seek an equitable balance. In the past, many commentators have argued that the system has erred by becoming overly concerned with offender rights. The same argument can be used against victim rights if appropriate precautionary steps are not taken. A middle ground that balances everyone's interests must be sought. Consider Marquart's (2005: 330) remarks:

> The American criminal justice system has come a long way in recognizing and clarifying the rights of both offenders and victims. The exclusion of victims from the process is now a thing of the past. How and where victims are heard and their exercise of power is still an unfolding process in our society.

Only when victims attain equitable footing with offenders will we be able to talk about a true justice system, rather than a *"criminal's* justice system."* That is the challenge facing victimology.

Key Terms for Chapter 12

aggravating circumstances

allocution

mitigating circumstances

ombudsman

victim impact statement (VIS)

Victim Rights Amendment (VRA)

writ of *mandamus*

REFERENCES

Abbey, A., L.T. Ross, D. McDuffie, and P. McAuslan (1996). "Alcohol, Misperception, and Sexual Assault: How and Why Are They Linked?" In D.M. Buss and N.M. Malamuth (eds.), *Sex, Power, Conflict: Evolutionary and Feminist Perspectives*. New York: Oxford University Press.

Acierno, R. (2003). "Elder Mistreatment: Epidemiological Assessment Methodology." In National Research Council,. *Elder Mistreatment: Abuse, Neglect, and Exploitation in an Aging America*. Washington, DC: National Academies Press.

Acker, J.R. (1992). "Social Sciences and the Criminal Law: Victims of Crime—Plight vs. Rights." *Criminal Law Bulletin* 28:64-77.

Adams, A.T. (2000). "The Status of School Discipline and Violence." *The Annals* 567:140-156.

Adams, D.B. (2002). *Summary of State Sex Offender Registries, 2001*. Washington, DC: Bureau of Justice Statistics.

Administration on Aging (1998). *National Elder Abuse Incidence Study: Final Report*. http://www.aoa.gov/abuse/report.

Administration on Aging (1997). *A Profile of Older Americans: 1997*. http:/aoa.dhhs.gov/aoa/stats

Ahmad, J., and J.L. Mullings (1999). "Family Violence Units." *Texas Law Enforcement Management and Administrative Statistics Program Bulletin, Volume 6, Number 5*. Huntsville, TX: Police Research Center, Sam Houston State University.

Aker, J.R., and C.S. Lanier (2000). "May God—or the Governor—Have Mercy: Executive Clemency and Executions in Modern Death-Penalty Systems." *Criminal Law Bulletin* 36:200-237.

Akers, R.L. (1973). *Deviant Behavior*. Belmont, CA: Wadsworth.

Allen, R.B. (1986). "Measuring the Severity of Physical Injury among Assault and Homicide Victims." *Journal of Quantitative Criminology* 2:139-156.

American Academy of Pediatrics, Committee on School Health (2000). "Corporal Punishment in Schools." *Pediatrics* 106:343. Reaffirmed in May, 2006. Retrieved on August 31, 2007 from http://aappolicy.aappublications.org/cgi/reprint/pediatrics;106/2/343.pdf Reprinted courtesy of the American Academy of Pediatrics.

American Bar Association (1996). *Standards of Practice for Lawyers Who Represent Children in Abuse and Neglect Cases*. Chicago: American Bar Association.

American Psychiatric Association (2000). *Diagnostic and Statistical Manual of Mental Disorders—Fourth Edition, Text Revision (DSM–IV–TR)*. Arlington, VA: American Psychiatric Association. Retrieved August 24, 2007 from http://www.psychiatryonline.com.proxy.lib.fsu.edu/content.aspx?aID=3357#3357

American Psychiatric Association (1994). *Diagnostic and Statistical Manual of Mental Disorders—Fourth Edition (DSM-IV)*. Accessed Online Psychological Services, *Posttraumatic Stress Disorder*. Retrieved September 13, 2004 from http://www.psychologynet.org/dsm.html

American Psychological Association (1991). *APA Resolutions Related to Children, Youth, and Families: The Use of Anatomically Detailed Dolls in Forensic Evaluations*. Washington, DC: American Psychological Association. Retrieved on September 4, 2007 from http://www.apa.org/pi/cyf/res_dolls.html

Amir, M. (1971). *Patterns in Forcible Rape*. Chicago: University of Chicago Press.

Anderson, J.G. (1977). "A Social Indicator Model of a Health Services System." *Social Forces* 56:661-687.

Anderson, K. (1982). "Community Justice Centers: Alternatives to Prosecution." Paper presented at the National Symposium on Victimology.

Andison, F.S. (1977). "TV Violence and Viewer Aggression: A Culmination of Study Results, 1956-76." *Public Opinion Quarterly* 41:314-331.

Anetzberger, G.J. (1989). "Implications of Research on Elder Abuse Perpetrators: Rethinking Current Social Policy and Programming." In R. Filinson and S.R. Ingman (eds.), *Elder Abuse: Practice and Policy*. New York: Human Sciences Press.

Anetzberger, G.J., J.E. Kobrin, and C. Austin (1994). "Alcoholism and Elder Abuse." *Journal of Interpersonal Violence* 9:184-193.

Antioch College (2005). *Sexual Offense Prevention Policy*. Yellow Springs, OH: Antioch College. Retrieved on August 23, 2007 from http://www.antioch-college.edu/Campus/sopp/index.html

Aries, P. (1962). *Centuries of Childhood*. New York: Knopf.

Armstrong, E.A., L. Hamilton, and B. Sweeney (2006). "Sexual Assault on Campus: A Multilevel, Integrative Approach to Party Rape." *Social Problems* 53:483-499.

Artingstall, K.A. (1995). "Munchausen Syndrome by Proxy." *FBI Law Enforcement Bulletin* 64(8):5-14.

Ash, M. (1972). "On Witnesses: A Radical Critique of Criminal Court Procedures." *Notre Dame Lawyer* 48:386-425.

Ashcroft, J. (2001). *Stalking and Domestic Violence: Report to Congress*. Washington, DC: U.S. Department of Justice.

Ashworth, A. (2003). "Is Restorative Justice the Way Forward for Criminal Justice?" In E. McLaughlin, R. Fergusson, G. Hughes and L. Westmarland (eds.), *Restorative Justice: Critical Issues*. Thousand Oaks, CA: Sage

Atkeson, B.M., K.S. Calhoun, P.A. Resick, and E.M. Ellis (1982). "Victims of Rape: Repeated Assessment of Depressive Symptoms." *Journal of Consulting and Clinical Psychology* 50:96-102.

Atlanta Long-term Care Ombudsman Program (2000). *The Silenced Voice Speaks Out: A Study of Abuse and Neglect of Nursing Home Residents.* Atlanta, GA: Atlanta Legal Aid Society.

Aulivola, M. (2004). "Outing Domestic Violence: Affording Appropriate Protections to Gay and Lesbian Victims." *Family Court Review* 42:162-172.

Bachman, R. (1995). "Is the Glass Half Empty or Half Full?: A Response to Pollard (1995)." *Criminal Justice and Behavior* 22:81-85.

Bachman, R. (1993). "Predicting the Reporting of Rape Victimizations: Have Rape Reforms Made a Difference?" *Criminal Justice and Behavior* 20:254-270.

Bachman, R. (1992). "Elderly Victims." *Bureau of Justice Statistics Special Report.* Washington, DC: U.S. Government Printing Office.

Bachman, R., and R. Paternoster (1993). "A Contemporary Look at the Effects of Rape Law Reform: How Far Have We Really Come?" *Journal of Criminal Law and Criminology* 84:554-574.

Bachman, R., and L.E. Saltzman (1995). *Bureau of Justice Statistics: Special Report: Violence Against Women: Estimates from the Redesigned Survey.* Washington, DC: Bureau of Justice Statistics.

Bachman, R., and B.M. Taylor (1994). "The Measurement of Family Violence and Rape by the Redesigned National Crime Victimization Survey." *Justice Quarterly* 11:499-512.

Baker, T.C., A.W. Burgess, E. Brickman, and R.C. Davis (1990). "Rape Victims' Concerns about Possible Exposure to HIV Infection." *Journal of Interpersonal Violence* 5:49-60.

Bandura, A., and R.H. Walters (1963). *Social Learning and Personality Development.* New York: Holt, Rinehart and Winston.

Bannenberg, B., and D. Rössner (2003). "New Developments in Restorative Justice to Handle Family Violence." In E.G.M. Weitekamp and H. Kerner (eds.), *Restorative Justice in Context: International Practice and Directions.* Portland, OR: Willan.

Bard, M. (1980). "Functions of the Police and the Justice System in Family Violence." In M.R. Green (ed.), *Violence and the Family.* Boulder, CO: Westview Press, Inc.

Bard, M., and D. Sangrey (1986). *The Crime Victim's Book,* 2nd ed. New York: Brunner/Mazel Publishers.

Baron, R.A., and P.A. Bell (1975). "Aggression and Heat: Mediating Effects of Prior Provocation and Exposure to Any Aggressive Model." *Journal of Personality and Social Psychology* 31:825-832.

Barrile, L.G. (1980). *Television and Attitudes about Crime.* Ph.D. Dissertation: Boston College.

Bassuk, E.L. (1980). "A Crisis Theory Perspective on Rape." In S.L. McCombie (ed.), *The Rape Crisis Intervention Handbook: A Guide for Victim Care.* New York: Plenum Press.

Baumer, T.L. (1985). "Testing a General Model of Fear of Crime: Data from a National Survey." *Journal of Research in Crime & Delinquency* 22:239-255.

Baumer, E.P., R.B. Felson, and S.F. Messner (2003). "Changes in Police Notification for Rape, 1973–2000." *Criminology* 41:841-872.

Bavolek, S.J. (2000). *The Nurturing Parenting Programs*. Washington, DC: U.S. Department of Justice, Office of Juvenile Justice and Delinquency Prevention.

Bazemore, G., and D. Maloney (1994). "Rehabilitating Community Service: Toward Restorative Service in a Balanced Justice System." *Federal Probation* 58:24-35.

Bazemore, G., and M. Umbreit (2001). *A Comparison of Four Restorative Conferencing Models*. Washington, DC: U.S. Department of Justice, Office of Juvenile Justice and Delinquency Prevention.

Bazemore, G., and M. Umbreit (1994) *Balanced and Restorative Justice: Program Summary*. Washington, DC: Office of Juvenile Justice and Delinquency Prevention.

Beare, M. (2002). "Organized Corporate Criminality—Tobacco Smuggling between Canada and the U.S." *Crime, Law and Social Change* 37:225-243.

Beck, J. (1992). "Murderous Obsession." *Newsweek* July 13:60.

Begun, J.W. (1977). "A Causal Model of the Health Care System: A Replication." *Journal of Health and Social Behavior* 18:2-9.

Belluck, P. (1997). "Women's Shelters Disclosing Their Locations, Despite Risk." *The New York Times* August 10:A1, A17.

Belsky, J. (1978). "Three Theoretical Models of Child Abuse: A Critical Review." *Child Abuse & Neglect* 2:37-49.

Belson, W. (1978). *Television Violence and the Adolescent Boy*. Westmead, England: Saxon House.

Bennett, G., P. Kingston and B. Penhale (1997). *The Dimensions of Elder Abuse: Perspectives for Practitioners*. London: Macmillan.

Bennett, T. (1995). "Identifying, Explaining and Targeting Burglary Hot Spots." *European Journal of Criminal Policy and Research* 3:113-123.

Bennett, T. (1986). "Situational Crime Prevention from the Offender's Perspective." In Heal, K., and G. Laycock (eds.), *Situational Crime Prevention: From Theory into Practice*. London: Her Majesty's Stationery Office.

Bennett, T., and R. Wright (1984). *Burglars on Burglary*. Brookfield, VT: Gower.

Benson, B.J., C.L. Gohm, and A.M. Gross (2007). "College Women and Sexual Assault: The Role of Sex-related Alcohol Expectancies." *Journal of Family Violence* 22:341-351.

Berger, R.J., W.L. Neuman, and P. Searles (1991). "The Social and Political Context of Rape Law Reform: An Aggregate Analysis." *Social Science Quarterly* 72:221-218.

Berger, R.J., P. Searles, and W.L. Neuman (1988). "The Dimensions of Rape Reform Legislation." *Law & Society Review* 22:329-349.

Berk, R.A., G.K. Smyth, and L.W. Sherman (1988). "When Random Assignment Fails: Some Lessons from the Minneapolis Spouse Abuse Experiment." *Journal of Quantitative Criminology* 4:209-223.

Berliner, L. (2003). "Making Domestic Violence Victims Testify." *Journal of Interpersonal Violence* 18:666-668.

Berliner, L. (1993). "When Should Children Be Allowed to Kill Abusers?" *Journal of Interpersonal Violence* 8:396-297.

Berliner, L. (1988). "Anatomical Dolls." *Journal of Interpersonal Violence* 3:468-470.

Bernard, M.L., and J.L. Bernard (1983). "Violent intimacy: The Family as a Model for Love Relationships." *Family Relations* 32:283-286.

Berryman, J. (2000). "Russia and the Illicit Arms Trade." *Crime, Law and Social Change* 33:85-104.

Besharov, D.J. (1991). "Reducing Unfounded Reports." *Journal of Interpersonal Violence* 16:112-115.

Besharov, D.J. (1990a). "Gaining Control over Child Abuse Reports." *Public Welfare* 48:34-40.

Besharov, D.J. (1990b). *Recognizing Child Abuse: A Guide for the Concerned.* New York: The Free Press.

Best, C.L., B.S. Dansky, and D.G. Kilpatrick (1992). "Medical Students' Attitudes about Female Rape Victims." *Journal of Interpersonal Violence* 7:175-188.

Biderman, A., and A. Reiss (1967). "On Exploring the 'Dark Figure' of Crime." *Annals of the American Academy of Political and Social Sciences* 374:1-15.

Bilchick, S. (1999). *Promising Strategies to Reduce Gun Violence.* Washington, DC: U.S. Department of Justice, Office of Juvenile Justice and Delinquency Prevention.

Binder, A., and J.W. Meeker (1988). "Experiments as Reforms." *Journal of Criminal Justice* 16:347-358.

Bjerregaard, B. (1996). "Stalking and the First Amendment: A Constitutional Analysis of State Stalking Laws." *Criminal Law Bulletin* 32:307-341.

Bjerregaard, B. (1989). "Televised Testimony as an Alternative in Child Sexual Abuse Cases." *Criminal Law Bulletin* 25:164-175.

Blackwell, B.S., and M.S. Vaughn (2003). "Police Civil Liability for Inappropriate Response to Domestic Assault Victims." *Journal of Criminal Justice* 31:129-146.

Blakely, B.E., and R. Dolon (1991). "Elder Mistreatment." In J.E. Hendricks (eds.), *Crisis Intervention in Criminal Justice/Social Service.* Springfield, IL: Charles C. Thomas Publisher.

Block, M.R., and J.D. Sinnott (1979). *The Battered Elder Syndrome: An Exploratory Study.* College Park, MD: University of Maryland.

Block, R.L., and C.R. Block (1995). "Space, Place and Crime: Hot Spot Areas and Hot Places of Liquor-Related Crime." In J.E. Eck and D. Weisburd (eds.), *Crime and Place.* Monsey, NY: Criminal Justice Press.

Blomberg, T.G., G.F. Waldo, and C.A. Bullock (1989). "An Assessment of Victim Service Needs." *Evaluation Review* 13:598-627.

Blomberg, T.G., G.F. Waldo, and D. Chester (2002). "Assessment of the Program Implementation of Comprehensive Victim Services in a One-Stop Location." *International Review of Victimology,* 9, 149-174.

Blumberg, M. (1989). "Transmission of the AIDS Virus through Criminal Activity." *Criminal Law Bulletin* 25:454-465.

Blumberg, M., and D. Langston (1991). "Mandatory HIV Testing in Criminal Justice Settings." *Crime & Delinquency* 37:5-18.

Boat, B.W., and M.D. Everson (1988). "Use of Anatomical Dolls among Professionals in Sexual Abuse Evaluations." *Child Abuse and Neglect* 12:171-179.

Boeringer, S.B. (1999). "Associations of Rape-Supportive Attitudes with Fraternal and Athletic Participation." *Violence Against Women* 5:81-90.

Bogard, M. (1990). "Why We Need Gender to Understand Human Violence." *Journal of Interpersonal Violence* 5:132-135.

Booth v. Maryland, 107 S. Ct. 2529 (1987), 482 U.S. 496 (1987).

Boscarino, J.A., C.R. Figley, and R.E. Adams (2004). "Evidence of Compassion Fatigue following the September 11 Terrorist Attacks: A Study of Secondary Trauma among Social Workers in New York." *International Journal of Emergency Mental Health*, 6, 98-108.

Bourke, L.B. (1989). *Defining Rape*. Durham, NC: Duke University Press.

Bowers, K.J., A. Hirschfield and S.D. Johnson (1998). "Victimization Revisited: A Case Study of On-residential Repeat Burglary on Merseyside." *British Journal of Criminology* 38:429-452.

Bowleg, L., and K.A. Stoll (1991). *More Harm Than Help: The Ramifications for Rape Survivors of Mandatory HIV Testing of Rapists*. Washington, DC: Center for Women Policy Studies.

Braithwaite, J. (2003). "Restorative Justice and a Better Future." In E. McLaughlin, R. Fergusson, G. Hughes and L. Westmarland (eds.), *Restorative Justice: Critical Issues*. Thousand Oaks, CA: Sage.

Braithwaite, J. (2002). *Restorative Justice and Responsive Regulation*. New York: Oxford University Press.

Braithwaite, J. (1999). "Restorative Justice: Assessing Optimistic and Pessimistic Accounts." In M. Tonry (ed.), *Crime and Justice: A Review of Research*, vol. 25. Chicago: University of Chicago Press.

Braithwaite, J. (1989). *Crime, Shame and Reintegration*. Cambridge: Cambridge University Press.

Braverman, M. (1999). *Preventing Workplace Violence: A Guide for Employers and Practitioners*. Thousand Oaks, CA: Sage.

Brecklin, L.E., and S.R. Ullman (2001). "The Role of Offender Alcohol Use in Rape Attacks: An Analysis of National Crime Victimization Survey Data." *Journal of Interpersonal Violence* 16:3-21.

Bridenback, M.L., P.L. Imhoff and J.P. Blanchard (1980). *The Use of Mediation/Arbitration in the Juvenile Justice Process: A Study of Three Programs*. Tallahassee, FL: Office of the State Court Administrator.

Bromley, M.L. (1999). "Community College Crime: An Exploratory Review." *Journal of Security Administration* 22:11-21.

Bromley, M.L. (1995). "Comparing Campus and City Crime Rates: A Descriptive Study." *American Journal of Police* 14(1): 131-148.

Brookman, F., and M. Maguire (2005). "Reducing Homicide: A Review of the Possibilities." *Crime, Law & Social Change* 42:325-403.

Brookoff, D. (1997). *Drugs, Alcohol, and Domestic Violence in Memphis.* Washington, DC: U.S. Department of Justice.

Brooks, A.D. (1996). "Megan's Law: Constitutionality and Policy." *Criminal Justice Ethics* 15:56-66.

Browne, A. (1987). *When Battered Women Kill.* New York: Free Press.

Browning, J., and D. Dutton (1986). "Assessment of Wife Assault with the Conflict Tactics Scale: Using Couple Data to Quantify the Differential Reporting Effect." *Journal of Marriage and the Family* 48:375-379.

Brownmiller, S. (1975). *Against Our Will: Men, Women and Rape.* New York: Simon and Schuster.

Bruinsma, G., and W. Bernasco (2004). "Criminal Groups and Transnational Criminal Networks." *Crime, Law & Social Change* 41:79-94.

Bruinsma, G.J.N., and J.P.S. Fiselier (1982). "The Poverty of Victimology." In H.J. Schneider (ed.), *The Victim in International Perspective.* New York: Walter de Gruyter & Company.

Bureau of Justice Assistance (1996). *Regional Seminar Series on Developing and Implementing Antistalking Codes.* Washington, DC: Bureau of Justice Assistance.

Bureau of Justice Statistics (1997). *Criminal Victimization in the United States, 1994.* Washington, DC: U.S. Government Printing Office.

Bureau of Justice Statistics (2003). *Criminal Victimization in the United States, 2002: Statistical Tables.* Washington, DC: United States Government Printing Office.

Bureau of Justice Statistics (2004). *National Crime Victimization Survey 1992-2002.* [Computer file] Ann Arbor, MI: ICPSR.

Burgess, A.W. (1995). "Rape Trauma Syndrome." In P. Searles and R.J. Berger (eds.), *Rape and Society: Readings on the Problem of Sexual Assault.* Boulder, CO: Westview Press.

Burgess, A.W., and P. Draper (1989). "The Explanation of Family Violence: The Role of Biological, Behavioral, and Cultural Selection." In L. Ohlin and N. Tonry (eds.), *Family Violence.* Chicago: University of Chicago Press.

Burgess, A.W., and L.L. Holmstrom (1974). "Rape Trauma Syndrome." *American Journal of Psychiatry* 131:981-986.

Burgess, A.W., and A.T. Laszlo (1976). "When the Prosecutrix Is a Child: The Victim Consultant in Cases of Sexual Assault." In E.C. Viano (ed.), *Victims & Society.* Washington, DC: Visage Press.

Burt, M.R., and R.E. Estep (1981). "Who Is a Victim?: Definitional Problems in Sexual Victimization." *Victimology* 6:15-28.

Burt, M.R., and B.L. Katz (1985). "Rape, Robbery, and Burglary: Responses to Actual and Feared Criminal Victimization, with Special Focus on Women and Elderly." *Victimology* 10:325-358.

Buzawa, E.S., and C.G. Buzawa (1990). *Domestic Violence: The Criminal Justice Response*. Newbury Park, CA: Sage.

Byers, B. (1991). "Death Notification." In J.E. Hendricks (ed.), *Crisis Intervention in Criminal Justice/Social Service*. Springfield, IL: Charles C. Thomas.

Caffey, J. (1946). "Multiple Fractures in the Long Bones of Infants Suffering from Chronic Subdural Hemotoma." *American Journal of Roentology* 56:163-173.

Calcutt, P.B. (1988). "The Victims' Rights Act of 1988, the Florida Constitution, and the New Struggle for Victims' Rights." *Florida State University Law Review* 16:811-834.

California Occupational Safety and Health Administration (1995). *Guidelines for Workplace Security*. Sacramento, CA: State of California Division of Occupational Safety and Health.

Call, J.E., D. Nice, and S.M. Talarico (1991). "An Analysis of State Rape Shield Laws." *Social Science Quarterly* 72:774-788.

Campbell, D.T., and J.C. Stanley (1963). *Experimental and Quasi-Experimental Designs for Research*. Chicago: Rand McNally & Company.

Campbell, R. (1995). "The Role of Work Experience and Individual Beliefs in Police Officers' Perceptions of Date Rape: An Integration of Quantitative and Qualitative Methods." *American Journal of Community Psychology* 23:249-277.

Campbell, R., and C.R. Johnson (1997). "Police Officers' Perception of Rape: Is There Consistency Between State Law and Individual Beliefs?" *Journal of Interpersonal Violence* 12:255-274.

Campbell, R., D. Patterson, and L.F. Lichty (2005). "The Effectiveness of Sexual Assault Nurse Examiner (SANE) Programs: A Review of Psychological, Medical, Legal, and Community Outcomes." *Trauma, Violence, & Abuse* 6:313-329.

Cancer Prevention Research Center (2007). *Detailed Overview of the Transtheoretical Model*. Kingston: University of Rhode Island. Retrieved on September 20, 2007, from http://www.uri.edu/research/cprc/transtheoretical.htm

Cannavale, F.J., Jr., and W.D. Falcon (1976). *Improving Witness Cooperation: Summary Report of the District of Columbia Witness Survey and a Handbook for Witness Management*. Washington, DC: U.S. Department of Justice.

Caringella-MacDonald, S. (1984). "Sexual Assault Prosecution: An Examination of Model Rape Legislation in Michigan." *Women and Politics* 4:65-82.

Carmody, D.C., and L.M . Washington (2001). "Rape Myth Acceptance among College Women: The Impact of Race and Prior Victimization." *Journal of Interpersonal Violence* 16:424-436.

Carrow, D.M. (1980). *Rape: Guidelines for a Community Response*. Washington, DC: U.S. Department of Justice.

Cassell, P.G. (1997). Statement before the Committee on the Judiciary, United States Senate, Concerning a Constitutional Amendment Protecting the Rights of Crime Victims on April 16, 1997.

Catalano, S. (2006a). *Intimate Partner Violence in the United States*. Washington, DC: Bureau of Justice Statistics. Retrieved on September 14, 2007 from http://www.ojp.usdoj.gov/bjs/intimate/ipv.htm

Catalano, S.M. (2006b). *Criminal Victimization, 2005*. Washington, DC: Bureau of Justice Statistics.

Cate, R.M., J.M. Henton, J. Kaval, F.S. Christopher, and S. Lloyd (1982). "Premarital Abuse: A Social Psychological Perspective." *Journal of Family Issues* 3:79-90.

Cazenave, N.A., and M.A. Straus (1979). "Race, Class, Network Embeddedness and Family Violence: A Search for Potent Support Systems." *Journal of Comparative Family Studies* 10:281-300.

Centers for Disease Control and Prevention (2007). "Homicides and Suicides, National Violent Death Reporting System, United States, 2003–2004." *Morbidity and Mortality Weekly Report* 55(July 7):721-724.

Chaffin, M. (2005). "Response to Letters." *Child Abuse & Neglect* 29:241-249.

Chaffin, M. (2004). "Is It Time to Rethink Healthy Start/Healthy Families?" *Child Abuse & Neglect* 28:589-595.

Chaffin, M., and D. Bard (2006). "Impact of Intervention Surveillance Bias on Analyses of Child Welfare Report Outcomes." *Child Maltreatment* 11:301-312.

Champlin, L. (1986). "The Battered Elderly." *Geriatrics* 37:115-116, 121.

Chan, R.N., D. Ainscow, and J.M. Sikorski (1980). "Diagnostic Failures in the Multiple Injured." *Journal of Trauma* 20:684-687.

Chan, W. (2005). "Crime, Deportation and the Regulation of Immigrants in Canada." *Crime, Law & Social Change* 44:153-180.

Chappel, D., and V. DiMartino (1998). *Violence at Work*. Geneva: International Labor Office.

Chelimsky, E. (1981). "Serving Victims: Agency Incentives and Individual Needs." In S.R. Salasin (ed.), *Evaluating Victim Services*. Beverly Hills: Sage.

Child Welfare Information Gateway (2006). *Child Abuse and Neglect Fatalities: Statistics and Interventions*. Washington, DC: U.S. Department of Health and Human Services.

Christoffel, K.K. (2007). "Firearm Injuries: Epidemic Then, Endemic Now." *American Journal of Public Health* 97:626-629.

Cohen, L.E., and M. Felson (1979). "Social Changes and Crime Rate Trends: A Routine Activities Approach." *American Sociological Review* 44:588-608.

Cicirelli, V.G. (1986). "The Helping Relationship and Family Neglect in Later Life." In K.A. Pillemer and R.S. Wolf (eds.), *Elder Abuse: Conflict in the Family*. Dover, MA: Auburn House.

Clay-Warner, J., and C.H. Burt (2005). "Rape Reporting after Reforms: Have Times Really Changed?" *Violence Against Women* 11:150-176.

Clemente, F., and M.B. Kleiman (1977). "Fear of Crime in the United States: A Multivariate Analysis." *Social Forces* 56:519-531.

Clery Act Summary. Retrieved on October 3, 2004 from http://www.securityoncampus.org/schools/cleryact/index.html

Coates, R.B., and J. Gehm (1989). "An Empirical Assessment." In M. Wright and B. Galaway (eds.), *Mediation and Criminal Justice: Victims, Offenders and Community*. Newbury Park, CA: Sage.

Cohen, F. (1995). "Sex Offender Registration Laws: Constitutional and Policy Issues." *Criminal Law Bulletin* 31:151-160.

Cohen, L.E., and M. Felson (1979). "Social Changes and Crime Rate Trends: A Routine Activities Approach." *American Sociological Review* 44:588-608.

Coleman, F.L. (1997). "Stalking Behavior and the Cycle of Domestic Violence." *Journal of Interpersonal Violence* 12:420-432.

Collins, J.J. (1989). "Alcohol and Interpersonal Violence: Less than Meets the Eye." In N.A. Weiner and M.E. Wolfgang (eds.), *Pathways to Criminal Violence*. Newbury Park, CA: Sage.

Colomb, W., and K. Damphousse (2004). Examination of Newspaper Coverage of Hate Crimes: A Moral Panic Perspective. *American Journal of Criminal Justice* 28:147-163.

Conrad, C. (2006). "Measuring Costs of Child Abuse and Neglect." *Journal of Health and Human Services Administration* 29:103-123.

Conte, J.R. (1991). "Child Sexual Abuse: Looking Backward and Forward." In M.Q. Patton (ed.), *Family Sexual Abuse: Frontline Research and Evaluation*. Newbury Park, CA: Sage.

Cook, R.F., J.A. Roehl and D.I. Sheppard (1980). *Neighborhood Justice Centers Field Test, Executive Summary*. Washington, DC: National Institute of Justice.

Cook, R.F., W.G. Skogan, T.D. Cook, and G.E. Antunes (1978). "Criminal Victimization of the Elderly: The Physical and Economic Consequences." *The Gerontologist* 18:338-349.

Cook, T.D., J. Flemming, and T.R. Tyler (1981). "Criminal Victimization of the Elderly: Validating the Policy Assumptions." In G.M. Stephenson and J.M. Davis (eds.), *Progress in Applied Social Psychology*. New York: Wiley.

Corbin, W.R., J.A. Bernat, K.S. Calhoun, L.D. McNair, and K.L. Seals (2001). "The Role of Alcohol Expectancies and Alcohol Consumption Among Sexually Victimized and Nonvictimized College Women." *Journal of Interpersonal Violence* 16:297-311.

Corrado, R.R., I.M. Cohen and C. Odgers (2003). "Multi-problem Violent Youths: A Challenge for the Restorative Justice Paradigm." In E.G.M. Weitekamp and H. Kerner (eds.), *Restorative Justice in Context: International Practice and Directions*. Portland, OR: Willan.

Corso, P.S., J.A. Mercy, T.R. Simon, E.A. Finkelstein, and T.R. Miller (2007). "Medical Costs and Productivity Losses Due to Interpersonal and Self-Directed Violence in the United States." *American Journal of Preventive Medicine* 32:474-484.

Costa, J.J. (1984). *Abuse of Women: Legislation, Reporting, and Prevention*. Lexington, MA: Lexington Books.

Costin, F., and N. Schwarz (1987). "Beliefs about Rape and Women's Social Roles: A Four-Nation Study." *Journal of Interpersonal Violence* 2:46-56.

Cotton, J.L. (1983). "Violence and High Temperature." *USA Today* August 12:13.

Crawford, A., and T. Newburn (2003). *Youth Offending and Restorative Justice: Implementing Reform in Youth Justice*. Portland, OR: Willan.

Crenshaw, W.B., L.M. Crenshaw, and J.W. Lichtenberg (1995). "When Educators Confront Child Abuse: An Analysis of the Decision to Report." *Child Abuse & Neglect* 19:1095-1113.

Cromwell, P.F., J.N. Olson and D.W. Avery (1991). *Breaking and Entering: An Ethnographic Analysis of Burglary*. Newbury Park, CA: Sage.

Cross, T.P., D. Finkelhor, and R. Ormrod (2005). "Police Involvement in Child Protective Services Investigations: Literature Review and Secondary Data Analysis." *Child Maltreatment* 10:224-244.

Crume, T.L., C. DiGuiseppi, T. Byers, A.P. Sirotnak, and C.J. Garrett (2002). "Under-ascertainment of Child Maltreatment Fatalities by Death Certificates, 1990–1998." *Pediatrics* 110:18. Retrieved on August 31, 2007 from http://www.pediatrics. org/cgi/content/full/110/2/e18

Crystal, S. (1986). "Social Policy and Elder Abuse." In K.A. Pillemer and R.S. Wolf (eds.), *Elder Abuse: Conflict in the Family*. Dover, MA: Auburn House.

Curtis, L.A. (1974). *Criminal Violence: National Patterns and Behavior*. Lexington, MA: D.C. Heath and Company.

Daly, K. (2003). "Making Variation a Virtue: Evaluating the Potential and Limits of Restorative Justice." In E.G.M. Weitekamp and H. Kerner (eds.), *Restorative Justice in Context: International Practices and Directions*. Portland, OR: Willan.

Daly, K. (2002). "Restorative Justice: The Real Story." *Punishment and Society* 4:5-79.

Dane, D.M. (1991). "Rape Intervention." In J.E. Hendricks (ed.), *Crisis Intervention in Criminal Justice/Social Service*. Springfield, IL: Charles C. Thomas.

Daro, D. (2005). "Response to Chaffin (2005)." *Child Abuse & Neglect* 29:237-240.

Davis, J.W., D.B. Hoyt, M.S. McArdle, R.C. Mackersie, S.R. Shackford, and A.B. Eastman (1991). "The Significance of Critical Care Errors in Causing Preventable Death in Trauma Patients in a Trauma System." *Journal of Trauma* 31:813-819.

Davis, K.C., J. Norris, W.H. George, J. Martell, and J.R. Heiman (2006). "Rape-Myth Congruent Beliefs in Women Resulting from Exposure to Pornography: Effects of Alcohol and Sexual Arousal." *Journal of Interpersonal Violence* 21:1208-1223.

Davis, P.W., J.L. Chandler, and R. LaRossa (2004). "'I've Tried the Switch but He Laughs through the Tears: The Use and Conceptualization of Corporal Punishment During the Machine Age, 1924–1939." *Child Abuse & Neglect* 28:1291-1310.

Davis, R.C. (1983). "Victim/Witness Noncooperation: A Second Look at a Persistent Phenomenon." *Journal of Criminal Justice* 11:287-299.

Davis, R.C. (1982). "Mediation: The Brooklyn experiment." In R. Tomasic and M.M. Feeley (eds.), *Neighborhood Justice: Assessment of an Emerging Idea*. New York: Longman.

Davis, R.C., M. Henley, and B. Smith (1990). *Victim Impact Statements: Their Effects on Court Outcomes and Victim Satisfaction*. Washington, DC: National Institute of Justice.

Davis, R.C., and B. Smith (1995). "Domestic Violence Reforms: Empty Promises or Fulfilled Expectations?" *Crime & Delinquency* 41:541-552.

Davis, R.C., and B.E. Smith (1994). "Victim Impact Statements and Victim Satisfaction: An Unfulfilled Promise?" *Journal of Criminal Justice* 22:1-12.

Davis, R.C., B.E. Smith, and B. Taylor (2003). "Increasing the Proportion of Domestic Violence Arrests That Are Prosecuted: A Natural Experiment in Milwaukee." *Criminology & Public Policy* 2:263-282.

Davis, R.C., and B.G. Taylor (1997). "A Proactive Response to Family Violence: The Results of a Randomized Experiment." *Criminology* 35:307-334.

Dawson, M., and R. Dinovitzer. (2001). "Victim Cooperation and the Prosecution of Domestic Violence in a Specialized Court." Justice Quarterly 18:593-622.

Day, L.E., and M. Vandiver (2000). "Criminology and Genocide Studies: Notes on What Might Have Been and What Still Could Be." *Crime, Law and Social Change* 34:43-59.

DeFrances, C.J., S.K. Smith, and L.V.D. Does (1996). *Prosecutors in State Courts, 1994.* Washington, DC: U.S. Department of Justice.

DeFrancis, V., and C.L. Lucht (1974). *Child Abuse in the 1970's.* Denver: The American Humane Association.

Deisz, R., J.H. Doueck, and N. George (1996). "Reasonable Cause: A Qualitative Study of Mandated Reporting." *Child Abuse & Neglect* 20:275-287.

DeJong, W. (1993). *Building the Peace: The Resolving Conflict Creatively Program* (RCCP). NIJ Program Focus. Washington, DC: U.S. Department of Justice.

DeKeseredy, W.S., and K. Kelly (1995). "Sexual Abuse in Canadian University and College Dating Relationships: The Contribution of Male Peer Support." *Journal of Family Violence* 10:41-53.

deMause, L. (1974). *The History of Childhood.* New York: Psycho-History Press.

Derene, S. (2005). *Crime Victims Fund Report: Past, Present, and Future.* Washington, DC: National Association of VOCA Assistance Administrators.

Detmer, C.M., and J.W. Lamberti (1991). "Family Grief." *Death Studies* 15:363-374.

DeVoe, J.F., K. Peter, P. Kaufman, S.A. Ruddy, A.K. Miller, M. Planty, T.D. Snyder and M.R. Rand (2003). *Indicators of School Crime and Safety: 2003.* Washington, DC: National Center for Educational Statistics and Bureau of Justice Statistics.

Dexter, E.G. (1904). *Weather Influences.* New York: Macmillan.

Dey, E.L., J.S. Korn, and L.J. Sax (1996). "Betrayed by the Academy: The Sexual Harassment of Women College Faculty." *Journal of Higher Education* 67:149-173.

Dible, D.A., and R.H.C. Teske, Jr. (1993). "An Analysis of the Prosecutory Effects of a Child Sexual Abuse Victim-Witness Program." *Journal of Criminal Justice* 21:79-85.

Dietz, T.L. (2000). "Disciplining Children: Characteristics Associated with the Use of Corporal Punishment." *Child Abuse & Neglect* 24:1529-1542.

Dinkes, R., E.F. Cataldi, G. Kena, and K. Baum (2006). *Indicators of School Crime and Safety, 2006.* Washington, DC: U.S. Department of Justice and U.S. Department of Education.

Dobash, R.E. (2003). "Domestic Violence: Arrest, Prosecution, and Reducing Violence." *Criminology & Public Policy* 2:313-318.

Dobash, R.E., and R.P. Dobash (1979). *Violence Against Wives: A Case Against the Patriarchy*. New York: Free Press.

Dobash, R.E., and R.P. Dobash (1977-78). "Wives: The 'Appropriate' Victims of Marital Violence." *Victimology* 2:426-242.

Dobash, R.E., R.P. Dobash, M. Wilson, and M. Daly (1992). "The Myth of Sexual Symmetry in Marital Violence." *Social Problems* 39:71-91.

Dodge, R.W. (1985). *Bureau of Justice Statistics Technical Report: Response to Screening Questions in the National Crime Survey*. Washington, DC: U.S. Government Printing Office.

Doerner, W.G. (2007). *Introduction to Law Enforcement: An Insider's View*, 3rd ed. Dubuque, IA: Kendall/Hunt.

Doerner, W.G. (2004). *Introduction to Law Enforcement: An Insider's View*, 2nd ed. Dubuque, IA: Kendall/Hunt.

Doerner, W.G. (1988). "The Impact of Medical Resources on Criminally Induced Lethality: A Further Examination." *Criminology* 26:171-179.

Doerner, W.G. (1987). "Child Maltreatment Seriousness and Juvenile Delinquency." *Youth & Society* 19:197-244.

Doerner, W.G. (1983). "Why Does Johnny Reb Die When Shot? The Impact of Medical Resources upon Lethality." *Sociological Inquiry* 53:1-15.

Doerner, W.G. (1980). "Trends in Southern Homicide: Is the South a 'Regional Culture of Violence?'" *Journal of Crime and Justice* 3:83-94.

Doerner, W.G. (1979). "The Violent World of Johnny Reb: An Attitudinal Analysis of the 'Regional Culture of Violence' Thesis." *Sociological Forum* 2:61-71.

Doerner, W.G. (1978a). "The Index of Southernness Revisited: The Influence of Wherefrom upon Whodunnit." *Criminology* 16:47-56.

Doerner, W.G. (1978b). "The Deadly World of Johnny Reb: Fact, Foible, or Fantasy?" in J.A. Inciardi and A.E. Pottieger (eds.), *Violent Crime: Historical and Contemporary Issues*. Beverly Hills: Sage.

Doerner, W.G. (1975). "A Regional Analysis of Homicide Rates in the United States." *Criminology* 13:90-101.

Doerner, W.G., M.S. Knudten, R.D. Knudten, and A.C. Meade (1976a). "Correspondence between Crime Victim Needs and Available Public Services." *Social Service Review* 50:482-490.

Doerner, W.G., and J.C. Speir (1986). "Stitch and Sew: The Impact of Medical Resources upon Criminally Induced Lethality." *Criminology* 24:319-330.

Doerner, W.G., and T. Tsai (1990). "Child Maltreatment and Juvenile Delinquency in Taiwan." *International Journal of Comparative and Applied Criminal Justice* 14:225-238.

Dollard, J. (1949). *Caste and Class in a Southern Town*. New Haven, CT: Yale University Press.

Dolliver, J.M. (1987). "Victims' Rights Constitutional Amendment: A Bad Idea Whose Time Should Not Come." *The Wayne Law Review* 34:87-93.

Dolon, R., and B. Blakely (1989). "Elder Abuse and Neglect: A Study of Adult Protective Service Workers in the United States." *Journal of Elder Abuse and Neglect* 1:31-49.

Dolon, R., and J.E. Hendricks (1989). "An Exploratory Study Comparing Attitudes and Practices of Police Officers and Social Service Providers in Elder Abuse and Neglect Cases." *Journal of Elder Abuse and Neglect* 1:75-90.

Dominick, J.R. (1978). "Crime and Law Enforcement in the Mass Media." In C. Winick (ed.), *Deviance and Mass Media*. Beverly Hills: Sage.

Donnerstein E. (1980). "Aggressive Erotica and Violence against Women." *Journal of Personality and Social Psychology* 39:269-277.

Donnerstein E., and J. Hallam (1978). "Effects of Erotic Stimuli on Male Aggression Toward Females." *Journal of Personality and Social Psychology* 32:237-244.

Dorne, C.K. (1989). *Crimes Against Children*. New York: Harrow and Heston, Publishers.

Doty, P., and E.W. Sullivan (1983). "Community Involvement in Combating Abuse, Neglect and Mistreatment in Nursing Homes." *Milbank Memorial Fund Quarterly/Health and Society* 37:115-121.

Dove, D.B., W.M. Stahl, and L.R.M. Delbuercio (1980). "A Five-Year Review of Deaths Following Urban Trauma." *Journal of Trauma* 20:760-765.

Dugan, L. (2003). "Domestic Violence Legislation: Exploring Its Impact on the Likelihood of Domestic Violence, Police Involvement, and Arrest." *Criminology & Public Policy* 2:283-312.

Duggan, A., L. Fuddy, L. Burrell, S.M. Higman, E. McFarlane, A. Windham, and C. Sia (2004). "Randomized Trial of a Statewide Home Visiting Program: Impact in Reducing Parental Risk Factors." *Child Abuse & Neglect* 28:623-643.

Duggan, A., E. McFarlane, L. Fuddy, L. Burrell, S.M. Higman, A. Windham, and C. Sia (2004). "Randomized Trial of a Statewide Home Visiting Program: Impact in Preventing Child Abuse and Neglect." *Child Abuse & Neglect* 28:597-622.

Duhart, D.T. (2001). *Violence in the Workplace, 1993-99*. Bureau of Justice Statistics Special Report. Washington, DC: Bureau of Justice Statistics.

Dunford, F.D. (1990). "System Initiated Warrants for Suspects of Misdemeanor Domestic Assault: A Pilot Study." *Justice Quarterly* 7:631-653.

Dunford, F.D., D. Huizinga, and D.S. Elliott (1989). *The Omaha Domestic Violence Police Experiments: Final Report*. Washington, DC: National Institute of Justice.

Durfee, M., D.T. Durfee, and M.P. West (2002). "Child Fatality Review: An International Movement." *Child Abuse & Neglect* 26:619-636.

Durkheim, E. (1951). *Suicide*. Glencoe, IL: Free Press.

Dutton, D.G., and A.J. Starzomski (1994). "Psychological Differences Between Court-Referred and Self-Referred Wife Assaulters." *Criminal Justice and Behavior* 21:203-221.

Earle, R.B. (1995). *Helping To Prevent Child Abuse—and Future Criminal Consequences: Hawai'i Healthy Start*. Washington, DC: U.S. Department of Justice.

Eber, L.P. (1981). "The Battered Wife's Dilemma: To Kill or to Be Killed." *Hastings Law Journal* 32:895-931.

Eckenrode, J., B. Ganzel, C.R. Henderson, Jr., E. Smith, D.L. Olds, J. Powers, R. Cole, H. Kitzman, and K. Sidora (2000). "Preventing Child Abuse and Neglect with a Program of Nurse Home Visitation: The Limiting Effects of Domestic Violence." *Journal of the American Medical Association* 284:1385-1391.

Edwards, S.S.M. (1989). *Policing 'Domestic' Violence: Women, the Law and the State*. Newbury Park, CA: Sage.

Ehrhardt, C.W., P.A. Hubbart, L.H. Levinson, W.M. Smiley, and T.A. Wills (1973). "The Aftermath of *Furman*: The Florida Experience." *Journal of Criminal Law and Criminology* 64:2-21.

Ehrhart, J.K., and B.R. Sandler (1985). *Myths and Realities about Rape*. Washington, DC: Project on the Status and Education of Women.

Eigenberg, H.M. (1990). "The National Crime Survey and Rape: The Case of the Missing Question." *Justice Quarterly* 7:655-671.

Eigenberg, H.M., K. McGuffee, P. Berry, and W.H. Hall (2003). "Protective Order Legislation: Trends in State Statutes." *Journal of Criminal Justice* 31:411-422.

Eigenberg, H.M., K.E. Scarborough, and V.E. Kappeler (1996). "Contributory Factors Affecting Arrest in Domestic and Non-Domestic Assaults." *American Journal of Police* 15:27-54. Eikenberry, K. (1987). "Victims of Crime/Victims of Justice." *The Wayne Law Review* 34:29-49.

Eikenberry, K. (1987). "Victims of Crime/Victims of Justice." *The Wayne Law Review* 34:29-49.

Eisikovits, Z. (1996). "The Aftermath of Wife Beating: Strategies of Bounding Violent Events." *Journal of Interpersonal Violence* 11:459-474.

Eisikovits, Z., and E. Buchbinder (1996). "Pathways to Disenchantment: Battered Women's Views of Their Social Workers." *Journal of Interpersonal Violence* 11:425-440.

Elias, R. (1990). "Which Victim Movement?: The Politics of Victim Policy." In A.J. Lurigio, W.G. Skogan and R.C. Davis (eds.), *Victims of Crime: Problems, Policies and Programs*. Newbury Park, CA: Sage.

Ellingworth, D., G. Farrell, and K. Pease (1995). "Victim is a Victim is a Victim?: Chronic Victimization in Four Sweeps of the British Crime Survey." *British Journal of Criminology* 35:360-365.

Elliott, D.S. (1989). "Criminal Justice Procedures in Family Violence Crimes." In L. Ohlin and M. Tonry (eds.), *Family Violence*. Chicago: University of Chicago.

Ellis, D. (1992). "Toward a Consistent Recognition of the Forbidden Inference: The Illinois Rape Shield Statute." *Journal of Criminal Law & Criminology* 83:395-436.

Ellis, L. (1989). *Theories of Rape*. New York: Hemisphere.

Enderson, B.L., D.B. Reath, J. Meadors, W. Dallas, J.M. DeBoo, and K.I. Maull (1990). "The Tertiary Trauma Survey: A Prospective Study of Missed Injury." *Journal of Trauma* 30:666-670.

Ennis, P. (1967). *Criminal Victimization in the United States: A Report of a National Survey*. Chicago: National Opinion Research Center.

Equal Employment Opportunity Commission (1999). *Enforcement Guidance: Vicarious Employer Liability for Unlawful Harassment by Supervisors*. http://www.eeoc.gov/docs/harassment.html.

Erez, E. (1990). "Victim Participation in Sentencing: Rhetoric and Reality." *Journal of Criminal Justice* 18:19-31.

Erez, E. (1989). "The Impact of Victimology on Criminal Justice Policy." *Criminal Justice Policy Review* 3:236-256.

Erez, E., and V. Guhlke (1988). "Victims in Court." Paper presented at the World Society of Victimology Sixth Annual Symposium.

Erez, E., and L. Roeger (1995). "The Effect of Victim Impact Statements on Sentencing Patterns and Outcomes: The Australian Experience." *Journal of Criminal Justice* 23:363-375.

Erez, E., and P. Tontodonato (1992). "Victim Participation in Sentencing and Satisfaction with Justice." *Justice Quarterly* 9:393-417.

Erez, E., and P. Tontodonato (1990). "The Effect of Victim Participation in Sentencing on Sentence Outcome." *Criminology* 28:451-474.

Erlanger, H.S. (1975). "Is There a 'Subculture of Violence' in the South?" *Journal of Criminal Law and Criminology* 66:483-490.

Erlanger, H.S. (1974). "The Empirical Status of the Subculture of Violence Thesis." *Social Problems* 20:280-292.

Erskine, H. (1974). "The Polls: Fear of Violence and Crime." *Public Opinion Quarterly* 38:131-145.

Everson, M.D., and B.W. Boat (1994). "Putting the Anatomical Doll Controversy in Perspective: An Examination of the Major Uses and Criticisms of the Dolls in Child Sexual Abuse Evaluations." *Child Abuse & Neglect* 18:113-129.

Everson, M.D., B.W. Boat, S. Bourg, and K.R. Robertson (1996). "Beliefs Among Professionals About Rates of False Allegations of Child Sexual Abuse." *Journal of Interpersonal Violence* 11:541-553.

Eyles, J., and K.J. Woods (1983). *The Social Geography of Medicine and Health*. New York: St. Martin's Press.

Fagan, A.A. (2005). "The Relationship Between Adolescent Physical Abuse and Criminal Offending: Support for an Enduring and Generalized Cycle of Violence." *Journal of Family Violence* 20:279-290.

Farley, R.H. (1987). "'Drawing Interviews': An Alternative Technique." *Police Chief* 54:37-38.

Farrell, A.D., and A.L. Meyer (1997). "The Effectiveness of a School-based Curriculum for Reducing Violence Among Urban Sixth-grade Students." *American Journal of Public Health* 87-979-988.

Farrell, G., and A.C. Bouloukos (2001). "International Overview: A Cross-national Comparison of Rates of Repeat Victimization." In G. Farrell and K. Pease (eds.), *Repeat Victimization*. Monsey, NY: Criminal Justice Press.

Farrell, G., and K. Pease (2003). "Measuring Repeat Victimization Using Police Data: An Analysis of Burglary Data and Policy for Charlotte, North Carolina." In M.J. Smith and D.B. Cornish (eds.), *Theory for Practice in Situational Crime Prevention*. Monsey, NY: Criminal Justice Press.

Farrell, G., C. Phillips, and K. Pease (1995). "Like Taking Candy: Why Does Repeat Victimization Occur?" *British Journal of Criminology* 35:384-399.

Farrell, G., W.H. Sousa, and D.L. Weisel (2002) "The Time-Window Effect in the Measurement of Repeat Victimization: A Methodology for Its Examination, and an Empirical Study." In N. Tilley (ed.) *Analysis for Crime Prevention*. Monsey, NY: Criminal Justice Press.

Fattah, E.A., and V.F. Sacco (1989). *Crime and Victimization of the Elderly*. New York: Springer-Verlag.

Feder, L., and L. Dugan (2002). "A Test of the Efficacy of Court-Mandated Counseling for Domestic Violence Offenders: The Broward Experiment." *Justice Quarterly* 19:343-375.

Federal Bureau of Investigation (2006). *Crime in the United States, 2005*. Washington, DC: U.S. Government Printing Office. Retrieved on August 21, 2007, from http://www.fbi.gov/ucr/05cius/offenses/violent_crime/forcible_rape.html

Federal Bureau of Investigation (2003). *Crime in the United States 2002: Uniform Crime Reports*. Washington, DC: U.S. Government Printing Office.

Federal Bureau of Investigation (2000). *Crime in the United States 1999*. Washington, DC: U.S. Government Printing Office.

Federal Bureau of Investigation (1999). *Crime in the United States 1998*. Washington, DC: U.S. Government Printing Office.

Feld. B.C. (1999). "Rehabilitation, retribution and restorative justice: Alternative conceptions of juvenile justice." In G. Bazemore and L. Walgrave (eds.), *Restorative Juvenile Justice: Repairing the Harm of Youth Crime*. Monsey, NY: Criminal Justice Press.

Feld, L.S., and M.A. Straus (1989). "Escalation and Desistance of Wife Assault in Marriage." *Criminology* 27:141-161.

Feinstein, D. (April 22, 2004). "Scott Campbell, Stephanie Roper, Wendy Preston, Louarna Gillis, and Nila Lynn Crime Victims' Rights Act." *Congressional Record* 150:S4260-S4265.

Felson, R.B., and H.J. Steadman (1983). "Situational Factors in Disputes Leading to Criminal Violence." *Criminology* 21:59-74.

Felstiner, W.L.F., and L.A. Williams (1982). "Community Mediation in Dorchester, Massachusetts." In R. Tomasic and M.M. Feeley (eds.), *Neighborhood Justice: Assessment of an Emerging Idea*. New York: Longman.

Felstiner, W.L.F., and L.A. Williams (1979). *Community Mediation in Dorchester, Massachusetts: Final Report*. Los Angeles, CA: University of Southern California.

Ferguson, C.J. (2007a). "Video Games: The Latest Scapegoat for Violence." *The Chronicle of Higher Education* (June 22):B20.

Ferguson, C.J. (2007b). "Evidence for Publication Bias in video Game Violence Effects Literature: A Meta-Analytic Review." *Aggression and Violent Behavior* 12:470-482.

Ferraro, K.F. (1995). *Fear of Crime: Interpreting Victimization Risk.* Albany, NY: SUNY Press.

Ferraro, K.F., and R.L. LaGrange (1988). "Are Older People Afraid of Crime?" *Journal of Aging Studies* 2:277-287.

Ferri, E. (1882). "Das Verbrechen in Seiner Abhangigkeit van Jahrlichen Temperaturewechse." *Zeitschrift fur die Gesammte Strufrechtswissenschaft* 2:38.

Fiegener, J.J., M. Fiegener, and J. Meszaros (1989). "Policy Implications of a Statewide Survey on Elder Abuse." *Journal of Elder Abuse and Neglect* 1:39-58.

Fields, M.D., and R.M. Kirchner (1978). "Battered Women Are Still in Need: A Reply to Steinmetz." *Victimology* 3:216-226.

Figley, C.R. (1995). *Compassion Fatigue: Coping with Secondary Traumatic Stress Disorder in Those Who Treat the Traumatized.* New York: Brunner/Mazel.

Fine, S.A. (1993). "Do Not Blur Self-Defense and Revenge." *Journal of Interpersonal Violence* 8:299-301.

Finkelhor, D. (1990). "Is Child Abuse Being Over-Reported? A Reply to Besharov." *Public Welfare* 48:22-29.

Finkelhor, D., and K. Yllo (1983). "Common Features of Family Abuse." In D. Finkelhor, R.J. Gelles, G.T. Hotaling, and M.A. Straus (eds.), *The Dark Side of Families: Family Violence Research.* Beverly Hills: Sage.

Finn, M.A., and L.J. Stalans (1995). "Police Referrals to Shelter and Mental Health Treatment: Examining Their Decisions in Domestic Assault Cases." *Crime & Delinquency* 41:467-480.

Finn, P., and S. Colson (1990). *Civil Protection Orders: Legislation, Current Court Practice, and Enforcement.* Washington, DC: U.S. Department of Justice.

Finn, P., and B.N.W. Lee (1987). *Serving Crime Victims and Witnesses.* Washington, DC: U.S. Department of Justice.

Finn-DeLuca, V. (1994). "Victim Participation at Sentencing." *Criminal Law Bulletin* 30:403-428.

Fisher, B.S. (2003b). "Acknowledging Sexual Victimization as Rape: Results from a National-Level Study." *Justice Quarterly* 20:535-574.

Fisher, B.S., F.T. Cullen, and M.G. Turner (2000). *The Sexual Victimization of College Women.* Washington, DC: U.S. Department of Justice.

Fisher, B.S., L.E. Daigle, F.T. Cullen, and M.G. Turner (2003a). "Reporting Sexual Victimization to the Police and Others: Results from a National-Level Study of College Women." *Criminal Justice and Behavior* 30:6-38.

Fisher, B.S., L.E. Daigle, F.T. Cullen, and M.G. Turner (2003b). "Acknowledging Sexual Victimization as Rape: Results from a National-Level Study." *Justice Quarterly* 20: 535-574.

Fisher, B.S., and J.J. Sloan (2003). "Unraveling the Fear of Victimization among College Women: Is the 'Shadow of Sexual Assault Hypothesis' Supported?" *Justice Quarterly* 20:633-659.

Fisher, B.S., J.J. Sloan, F.T. Cullen, and C. Lu (1998). "Crime in the Ivory Tower: The Level and Sources of Student Victimization." *Criminology* 36:671-710.

Fischer, K., and M. Rose (1995). "When 'Enough Is Enough:' Battered Women's Decision Making Around Court Orders of Protection." *Crime & Delinquency* 41:414-429.

Flaherty, E.G., R. Jones, and R. Sege (2004). "Telling Their Stories: Primary Care Practitioners' Experience Evaluating and Reporting Injuries Caused by Child Abuse." *Child Abuse & Neglect* 28:939-945.

Flaherty, E.G., R. Sege, L.L. Price, K.K. Christoffel, D.P. Norton, and K.G. O'Connor (2006). "Pediatrician Characteristics Associated with Child Abuse Identification and Reporting: Results from a National Survey of Pediatricians." *Child Maltreatment* 11:361-369.

Flavin, J. (2000). "(Mis)Representing Risk: Headline Accounts of HIV-Related Assaults." *American Journal of Criminal Justice* 25:119-136.

Flemming, B. (2003). "Equal Protection for Victims of Domestic Violence." *Journal of Interpersonal Violence* 18:685-692.

Florida Domestic Violence Fatality Review Team (2007). *2006 Annual Report Executive Summary*. Tallahassee: Florida Department of Law Enforcement. Retrieved on September 20, 2007, from http://www.fdle.state.fl.us/publications/Domestic_ Violence_Fatality_Report_2006.pdf

Florida Network of Victim Witness Services, Inc. (2004). *Code of Professional Ethics for Florida Victim Witness Service Providers*. Retrieved August 20, 2004 from http://www.fnvws.org/Code_of_Ethics/CodeofEthicsIndex.html

Florida Statutes (2007).

Florida Statutes (2004).

Fontana, V.J. (1973). *Somewhere A Child Is Crying*. New York: Macmillan.

Ford, D.A. (2003). "Coercing Victim Participation in Domestic Violence Prosecutions." *Journal of Interpersonal Violence* 18:669-684.

Forst, B.E., and J.C. Hernon (1985). *The Criminal Justice Response to Victim Harm*. Washington, DC: National Institute of Justice.

Fowler, T.K. (2003). *Report of the Panel to Review Sexual Misconduct Allegations at the Untied States Air Force Academy*. Arlington, VA: Department of Air Force.

Fox, J.A., and D.A. Hellman (1985). "Correlates of Campus Crime." *Journal of Criminal Justice* 13:429-444.

Fox, J.A., and M.W. Zawitz (2002). *Homicide Trends in the United States*. Washington, DC: Bureau of Justice Statistics.

Franklin II, C.W., and A.P. Franklin (1976). "Victimology Revisited: A Critique and Suggestions for Future Direction." *Criminology* 14:177-214.

Frazier, P.A., and E. Borgida (1992). "Rape Trauma Syndrome: A Review of Case Law and Psychological Research." *Law and Human Behavior* 16:293-311.

Freeman-Longo, R.E. (1996). "Feel Good Legislation: Prevention or Calamity." *Child Abuse & Neglect* 20:95-101.

Freilich, J.D., and C.J. Rivera (1999). "Mercy, Death, and Politics." *American Journal of Criminal Justice* 24:15-29.

Frenzen, P.D. (1991). "The Increasing Supply of Physicians in U.S. Urban and Rural areas, 1975 to 1988." *American Journal of Public Health* 81:1141-1147.

Frese, B., M. Moya, and J.L. Megias (2004). "Social Perception of Rape: How Rape Myth Acceptance Modulates the Influence of Situational Factors." *Journal of Interpersonal Violence* 19:143-161.

Friedman, J.J. (1973). "Structural Constraints on Community Action: The Case of Infant Mortality Rates." *Social Problems* 21:230-245.

Friedrichs, D.O. (2000). "The Crime of the Century? The Case for the Holocaust." *Crime, Law and Social Change* 23:21-41.

Frieze, I.H., and A. Browne (1989). "Violence in Marriage." In L. Ohlin and M. Tonry (eds.), *Family Violence*. Chicago: University of Chicago Press.

Fromm, S. (2001). *Total Estimated Cost of Child Abuse and Neglect in the United States: Statistical Evidence*. Chicago: Prevent Child Abuse America. Retrieved on September 29, 2004, from http://www.preventchildabuse.org/learn_more/research_docs/cost_analysis.pdf

Furman v. Georgia, 408 U.S. 238 (1972).

Gaboury, M.T., and R. Myers (1997). "Legal Developments in the Legislatures and the Courts." *The Crime Victims Report* 1:40-43.

Gagné, P. (1996). "Identity, Strategy, and Feminist Politics: Clemency for Battered Women Who Kill." *Social Problems* 43:77-93.

Galbraith, M.W. (1989). "A Critical Examination of the Definitional, Methodological and Theoretical Problems of Elder Abuse." In R. Filinson and S.R. Ingman (eds.), *Elder Abuse: Practice and Policy*. New York: Human Sciences Press.

Gallup, G., Jr. (1992). *The Gallup Poll Monthly, No. 318*. Princeton, NJ: The Gallup Poll.

Galvin J., and K. Polk (1983). "Attrition in Case Processing: Is Rape Unique?" *Journal of Research in Crime & Delinquency* 20:126-154.

Garbarino, J. (1976). "A Preliminary Study of Some Ecological Correlates of Child Abuse: The Impact of Socioeconomic Stress on Mothers." *Child Development* 47:178-185.

Garbarino, J., and G. Gilliam (1980). *Understanding Abusive Families*. Lexington, MA: Lexington Books.

Garcia, C.A. (2003). "Digital Photographic Evidence and the Adjudication of Domestic Violence Cases." *Journal of Criminal Justice* 31:579-587.

Garner, B.A. (1999). *Black's Law Dictionary*, 7th ed. St. Paul, MN: West.

Garner, J., and E. Clemmer (1986). *Danger to Police in Domestic Disturbances–New Look*. Washington, DC: U.S. Department of Justice.

Garner, J., J. Fagan, and C. Maxwell (1995). "Published Findings from the Spouse Assault Replication Program: A Critical Review." *Journal of Quantitative Criminology* 11:3-28.

Garofalo, J., and K.J. Connelly (1980a). "Dispute Resolution Centers, Part I: Major Features and Processes." *Criminal Justice Abstracts* 12:416-436.

Garofalol, J., and K.J. Connelly (1980b). "Dispute Resolution Centers, Part II: Outcomes, Issues, and Future Directions." *Criminal Justice Abstracts* 12:576-611.

Gartin, P.R. (1995a). "Examining Differential Officer Effects in the Minneapolis Domestic Violence Experiment." *American Journal of Police* 14:93-110.

Gartin, P.R. (1995b). "Dealing with Design Failures in Randomized Field Experiments: Analytic Issues Regarding the Evaluation of Treatment Effects." *Journal of Research in Crime & Delinquency* 32:425-445.

Gastil, R.D. (1978). "Comments." *Criminology* 16:60-64.

Gastil, R.D. (1971). "Homicide and a Regional Culture of Violence." *American Sociological Review* 36:412-427.

Geberth, V.J. (1992). "Stalkers." *Law and Order* 40:138-143.

Geis, G. (1977). "The Terrible Indignity: Crimes against the Elderly." In M.A.Y. Rifai (ed.), *Justice and Older Americans*. Lexington, MA: DC Heath.

Geiselman, R.E., G. Bornstein, and K.J. Saywitz (1992). *New Approach to Interviewing Children: A Test of Its Effectiveness*. Washington, DC: U.S. Department of Justice.

Gelles, R.J. (2000). "Estimating the Incidence and Prevalence of Violence against Women: National Data Systems and Sources." *Violence Against Women* 6:784-804.

Gelles, R.J. (1980). "Violence in the Family: A Review of Research in the 70's." *Journal of Marriage and the Family* 42:873-885.

Gelles, R.J. (1973). "Child Abuse as Psychopathology: A Sociological Critique and Reformulation." *American Journal of Orthopsychiatry* 43:611-621.

Gelles, R.J. (1975). "The Social Construction of Child Abuse." *American Journal of Orthopsychiatry* 45:363-371.

Gelles, R.J., and C.P. Cornell (1990). *Intimate Violence in Families*, 2nd ed. Beverly Hills: Sage.

Gelles, R.J., and C.P. Cornell (1985). *Intimate Violence in Families*. Beverly Hills: Sage.

Gelles, R.J., and M.A. Straus (1988). *Intimate Violence*. New York: Simon and Schuster.

Gelles, R.J., and M.A. Straus (1979). "Determinants of Violence in the Family: A Theoretical Integration." In W. Burr (ed.), *Contemporary Theories about the Family*. New York: Free Press.

George, L.K. (1986). "Caregiver Burden: Conflict between Norms of Reciprocity and Solidarity." In K.A. Pillemer and R.S. Wolf (eds.), *Elder Abuse: Conflict in the Family*. Dover, MA: Auburn House.

Gill, M., and K. Pease (1998). "Repeat Robbers: Are They Different?" In Gill, M. (ed.), *Crime at Work: Increasing the Risk for Offenders*. Leicester: Perpetuity Press.

Gerbner, G., L. Gross, M. Jackson-Beeck, S. Jeffries-Fox, and N. Signorielle (1978). "Cultural Indicators: Violence Profile No. 9." *Journal of Communication* 29:177-196.

Gerbner, G., L. Gross, N. Signorielle, and M. Morgan (1980). "Television Violence, Victimization, and Power." *American Behavioral Scientist* 23:705-716.

Giacopassi, D.J., and J.R. Sparger (1992). "The Effects of Emergency Medical Care on the Homicide Rate: Some Additional Evidence." *Journal of Criminal Justice* 20:249-259.

Giannelli, P. (1997). "Rape Trauma Syndrome." *Criminal Law Bulletin* 33:270-279.

Gil, D. (1971). *Violence Against Children: Physical Child Abuse in the United States.* Cambridge, MA: Harvard University Press.

Gilbert, N. (1993). "Examining the Facts: Advocacy Research Overstates the Incidence of Date and Acquaintance Rape." In R.J. Gelles and D.R. Loseke (eds.), *Current Controversies on Family Violence.* Newbury Park, CA: Sage.

Gioglio, G.R., and P. Blakemore (1983). *Elder Abuse in New Jersey: The Knowledge and Experience of Abuse Among Older New Jerseyans.* Trenton, NJ: New Jersey Department of Human Services.

Giordano, N., and J. Giordano (1984). "Elder Abuse: A Review of the Literature." *Social Work* 29:232-236.

Giovannoni, J.M., and R.M. Becerra (1979). *Defining Child Abuse.* New York: Free Press.

Glaser, D. (1956). "Criminality Theories and Behavioral Images." *American Journal of Sociology* 61:433-444.

Gold, M. (1958). "Suicide, Homicide, and the Socialization of Aggression." *American Journal of Sociology* 63:651-661.

Gomme, I.M. (1986). "Fear of Crime among Canadians: A Multi-Variate Analysis." *Journal of Criminal Justice* 14:249-258.

Gondolf, E.W. (2000). "Mandatory Court Review and Batterer Program Compliance." *Journal of Interpersonal Violence* 15:428-437.

Gondolf, E.W., J. McWilliams, B. Hart, and J. Stuehling (1994). "Court Response to Petitions for Civil Protection Orders." *Journal of Interpersonal Violence* 9:503-517.

Goodman, L.A., M.A. Dutton, and L. Bennett (2000). "Predicting Repeat Abuse Among Arrested Batterers: Use of the Danger Assessment Scale in the Criminal Justice System." *Journal of Interpersonal Violence* 15:63-74.

Gordon, J.A., and L.J. Moriarty (2003). "The Effects of Domestic Violence Batterer Treatment on Domestic Violence Recidivism: The Chesterfield County Experience." *Criminal Justice and Behavior* 30:118-134.

Gordon, M. (2000). "Definitional Issues in Violence against Women: Surveillance and Research from a Violence Research Perspective." *Violence Against Women* 6:747-783.

Gotsch, K.E., J.L. Annest, J.A. Mercy, and G.W. Ryan (2001). "Surveillance for Fatal and Nonfatal Firearm-Related Injuries—United States, 1993–1998." *Morbidity and Mortality Weekly Report* 50(April 13):1-32.

Graber, D. (1980). *Crime News and the Public.* New York: Praeger.

Graber, D. (1977). "Ideological Components in the Perceptions of Crime and Crime News." Paper presented to the meeting of the Society for the Study of Social Problems.

Greenberg, J., and B.J. Alge (1998). "Aggressive Reactions to Workplace Injustice." In Griffin, R.W., A. O'Leary-Kelly and J.M. Collins (eds.), *Dysfunctional Behavior in Organizations: Violence and Deviant Behavior.* Stamford, CT: JAI Press.

Greenberg, S.W., W.M. Rohe, and J.R. Williams (1985). *Informal Citizen Action and Crime Prevention at the Neighborhood Level: Synthesis and Assessment of the Research.* Washington, DC: National Institute of Justice.

Gregg v. Georgia, 428 U.S. 153 (1976).

Griffin, S. (1971). "Rape: The All-American Crime." *Ramparts* 10:26-36.

Gross, J.J. (1991). "Marital Rape—A Crime? A Comparative Law Study of the Laws of the United States and the State of Israel." *International Journal of Comparative and Applied Criminal Justice* 15:207-216.

Gross, M., E.P. Cramer, J. Forte, J.A. Gordon, T. Kunkel, and L.J. Moriarty (2000). "The Impact of Sentencing Options on Recidivism among Domestic Violence Offenders: A Case Study." *American Journal of Criminal Justice* 24:301-312.

Groth, A.N., and H.J. Birnbaum (1980). "The Rapist: Motivations for Sexual Violence. In S.L. McCombie (ed.), *The Rape Crisis Intervention Handbook: A Guide for Victim Care.* New York: Plenum Press.

Gutek, B. (1985). *Sex and the Workplace.* San Francisco: Jossey-Bass.

Hackney, S. (1969). "Southern Violence." In H.D. Graham and T.R. Gurr (eds.), *Violence in America.* New York: Signet.

Hahn, R.A., J. Mercy, O. Bilukha, and P. Briss (2005). "Assessing Home Visiting Programs to Prevent Child Abuse: Taking Silver and Bronze along with Gold." *Child Abuse & Neglect* 29:215-218.

Hamberger, L.K. (1993). "Comments on Pagelow's Myth of Psychopathology in Woman Battering." *Journal of Interpersonal Violence* 8:132-136.

Handelman, D. (1979). "The Interpretation of Child Abuse: Bureaucratic Relevance in Urban Newfoundland." *Journal of Sociology and Social Welfare* 6:70-88.

Hanke, P.J., and J.H. Gundlach (1995). "Damned on Arrival: A Preliminary Study of the Relationship between Homicide, Emergency Medical Care, and Race." *Journal of Criminal Justice* 23:313-323.

Harrington, N.T., and H. Leitenberg (1994). "Relationship Between Alcohol Consumption and Victim Behaviors Immediately Preceding Sexual Aggression by an Acquaintance." *Violence and Victims* 9:315-324.

Harris, A.R., S.H. Thomas, G.A. Fisher, and D.J. Hirsch (2002). "Murder and Medicine: The Lethality of Criminal Assault 1960-1999. *Homicide Studies,* 6:128-166.

Harris, D.K. (1999). "Elder Abuse in Nursing Homes: The Theft of Patients' Possessions." *Journal of Elder Abuse and Neglect* 10:141-151.

Harris, D.K., and M.L. Benson (1996). "Theft in Nursing Homes: An Overlooked Form of Elder Abuse." *Advances in Bioethics* 1:171-188.

Harris, N. (2003). "Evaluating the Practice of Restorative Justice: The Case of Family Group Conferencing." In L. Walgrave (ed.), *Repositioning Restorative Justice.* Portland, OR: Willan.

Hart, T.C. (2003). *Violent Victimization of College Students.* Washington, DC: U.S. Government Printing Office.

Hassell, I. (2005). "Response to Chaffin (2004)." *Child Abuse & Neglect* 29:235.

Hassler, R., B. Johnson, M. Town, and N. Websdale (1999). *Lethality Assessments as Integral Parts of Providing Full Faith and Credit Guarantees.* [Online]. Found at: http://www.vaw.umn.edu.

Hawes, C. (2003). "Elder Abuse in Residential Long-term Care Settings: What is Known and What Information is Needed?" In National Research Council,. *Elder Mistreatment: Abuse, Neglect, and Exploitation in an Aging America.* Washington, DC: National Academies Press.

Hawley, F.F., and S. Messner (1989). "The Southern Violence Construct: A Review of Arguments, Evidence, and the Normative Context." *Justice Quarterly* 6:481-511.

Hayes, H., and K. Daly (2004). "Conferencing and Re-offending in Queensland." *Australian and New Zealand Journal of Criminology* 37:167-191.

Hayward, R.A., and T.P. Hofer (2001). "Estimating Hospital Deaths Due to Medical Errors." *Journal of the American Medical Association* 286:415-420.

Healey, K.M. (1995). "Victim and Witness Intimidation: New Developments and Emerging Responses." *National Institute of Justice: Research in Action.* Washington, DC: U.S. Department of Justice.

Healey, K.M., and C. Smith (1998). *Batterer Programs: What Criminal Justice Agencies Need to Know.* Washington, DC: U.S. Department of Justice, National Institute of Justice.

Healey, K.M., C. Smith, and C. O'Sullivan (1998). *Batterer Intervention: Program Approaches and Criminal Justice Strategies.* Washington, DC: U.S. Department of Justice, National Institute of Justice.

Hearst, N., and S.B. Hulley (1988). "Preventing the Heterosexual Spread of AIDS: Are We Giving Our Patients the Best Advice?" *Journal of the American Medical Association* 259:2428-2432.

Heck, C., and A. Walsh (2000). "The Effects of Maltreatment and Family Structure on Minor and Serious Delinquency." *International Journal of Offender Therapy and Comparative Criminology* 44:178-193.

Heide, K.M. (1993). "Parents Who Get Killed and the Children Who Kill Them." *Journal of Interpersonal Violence* 8:531-544.

Heide, K.M. (1989). "Parricide: Incidence and Issues." *The Justice Professional* 4:19-41.

Hendricks, J.E. (1984). "Death Notification: The Theory and Practice of Informing Survivors." *Journal of Police Science and Administration* 12:109-116.

Henning, K., B. Renauer, and R. Holdford (2006). "Victim or Offender?: Heterogeneity Among Women Arrested for Intimate Partner Violence." Journal of Family Violence 21:351-368.

Henry, A.F., and J.F. Short, Jr. (1954). *Homicide and Suicide*. Glencoe, IL: The Free Press.

Henson, V.A., and W.E. Stone (1999). "Campus Crime: A Victimization Study." *Journal of Criminal Justice* 27:295-307.

Hepburn, J.R. (1973). "Violent Behavior in Interpersonal Relationships." *Sociological Quarterly* 14:419-429.

Herman-Giddens, M.E., G. Brown, S. Verbiest, P.J. Carlson, E.G. Hooten, E. Howell, and J.D. Butts (1999). "Underascertainment of Child Abuse mortality in the United States." *Journal of the American Medical Association* 282:463-467.

Hershkowitz, I. (2001). "A Case Study of Child Sexual False Allegation." *Child Abuse & Neglect* 25:1397-1411.

Hickey, E.W. (1997). *Serial Murderers and Their Victims*, 2nd ed. Belmont, CA: Wadsworth Publishing Company.

Hilberman, E. (1976). *The Rape Victim*. New York: Basic Books, Inc.

Hindelang, M.J. (1976). *Criminal Victimization in Eight American Cities: A Descriptive Analysis of Common Theft and Assault*. Cambridge, MA: Ballinger.

Hindelang, M.J. (1975). *Public Opinion Regarding Crime, Criminal Justice, and Related Topics*. Washington, DC: U.S. Department of Justice.

Hindelang, M.J., M.R. Gottfredson, and J. Garofalo (1978). *Victims of Personal Crime: An Empirical Foundation for a Theory of Personal Victimization*. Cambridge, MA: Ballinger.

Hirschel, J.D., C.W. Dean, and R.C. Lumb (1994). "The Relative Contribution of Domestic Violence to Assault and Injury of Police Officers." *Justice Quarterly* 11:99-117.

Hirschel, J.D., I.W. Hutchison III, and C.W. Dean (1992). "The Failure of Arrest to Deter Spouse Abuse." *Journal of Research in Crime & Delinquency* 29:7-33.

Hirschel, J.D., I.W. Hutchinson, C.W. Dean, J.J. Kelley, and C.E. Pesackis (1991). *Charlotte Spouse Assault Replication Project: Final Report*. Washington, DC: National Institute of Justice.

Ho, T. (2000). "Domestic Violence in a Southern City: The Effects of a Mandatory Arrest Policy on Male-versus-Female Aggravated Assault Incidents." *American Journal of Criminal Justice* 25:107-118.

Hochstedler, E. (1981). *Crimes against the Elderly in 26 Cities*. Washington, DC: Department of Justice.

Hoffman, M.H. (2000). "Emerging Combatants, War Crimes and the Future of International Humanitarian Law." *Crime, Law and Social Change* 34:99-110.

Hofstetter, E. (1981). *Bias in the News*. Columbus, OH: Ohio State University Press.

Hogben, M., D. Byrne, and M.E. Hamburger (1996). "Coercive Heterosexual Sexuality in Dating Relationships of College Students: Implications of Differential Male-Female Experiences." In E.S. Byers and L.F. O'Sullivan (eds.), *Sexual Coercion in Dating Relationships*. New York: The Hayworth Press.

Holmes, R.M. (1993). "Stalking in America: Types and Methods of Criminal Stalkers." *Journal of Contemporary Criminal Justice* 9:317-327.

Holmstrom, L.L., and A.W. Burgess (1978). *The Victim of Rape: Institutional Reactions*. New York: Wiley Interscience.

Holtfreter, K. (2004). "Fraud in American Organizations: An Examination of Control Mechanisms." *Journal of Financial Crime* 12:88-95.

Holtfreter, K., S. Van Slyke, and T.G. Blomberg (2005). "Sociolegal Change in Consumer Fraud: From Victim-Offender Interactions to Global Networks." *Crime, Law & Social Change* 44:251-275.

Hoover, E. (2004, May 28). "Alcohol Arrests on Campuses Increased Again in 2002." *The Chronicle of Higher Education* A33.

Horne, C. (2003). "Families of Homicide Victims: Service Utilization Patterns of Extra- and Intrafamilial Homicide Survivors." *Journal of Family Violence* 18:75-82.

Horney, J., and C. Spohn (1991). "Rape Law Reform and Instrumental Change in Six Urban Jurisdictions." *Law & Society Review* 25:117-153.

Horton, J.W. (1986). "Ethanol Impairs Cardiocirculatory Function in Treated Canine Hemorrhagic Shock." *Surgery* 100:520-530.

Hotaling, G.T., and D.B. Sugarman (1986). "An Analysis of Risk Markers in Husband to Wife Violence: The Current State of the Evidence." *Violence and Victims* 1:101-124.

Howeing, G.L., and Rumburg, D. (2005). *The Defense Task Force on Sexual Harassment & Violence at the Military Service Academies*. Washington, DC: Department of Defense.

Howlett, D. (1997). "Oklahoma Families Expand Victims' Rights." *USA Today* March 21:11A.

Hudson, J.E. (1988). "Elder Abuse: An Overview." In B. Schlesinger and R. Schlesinger (eds.), *Abuse of the Elderly: Issues and Annotated Bibliography*. Toronto: University of Toronto Press.

Hudson, M., and J. Carlson (1999). "Elder Abuse: Its Meaning to Caucasians, African Americans, and Native Americans". In Tatara, T. (ed.), *Understanding Elder Abuse in Minority Populations*. Philadelphia : Brunner/Mazel.

Hudson, M.F., C.M. Beasley, R.H. Benedict, J.R. Carlson, B.F. Craig, and S.C. Mason (1999). "Elder Abuse: Some African American Views." *Journal of Interpersonal Violence* 14:915-939.

Huesmann, L.E., and N.M. Malamuth (1986). "Media Violence and Antisocial Behavior: An Overview." *Journal of Social Issues* 42:1-6.

Humphrey, S.R., and A.S. Kahn (2000). "Fraternities, Athletic Teams, and Rape: Importance of Identification with a Risky Group." *Journal of Interpersonal Violence* 15:1313-1322.

Humphries, D. (2002). "No Easy Answers: Public Policy, Criminal Justice, and Domestic Violence." *Criminology & Public Policy* 2:91-96.

Hyman, I.A. (1982). "Corporal Punishment in the Schools: America's Officially Sanctioned Brand of Child Abuse." In G.J. Williams and J. Money (eds.), *Traumatic Abuse and Neglect of Children at Home*. Baltimore: John Hopkins University Press.

Illinois Compiled Statutes (2007). Chapter 720, 5/12-17. Retrieved on August 29, 2007, from http://www.ilga.gov/legislation/ilcs/documents/072000050K12-17.htm

International Association of Chiefs of Police (2000). *Guide for Preventing and Responding to School Violence*. Washington, DC: International Association of Chiefs of Police.

Ivatury, R.R., J. Kazigo, M. Rohman, J. Gaudio, R. Simon, and W.M. Stahl (1991). "'Directed' Emergency Room Thoracotomy: A Prognostic Prerequisite for Survival." *Journal of Trauma* 31:1076-1082.

Illinois Compiled Statutes (2007). Chapter 720, 5/12-17. Retrieved on August 29, 2007, from http://www.ilga.gov/legislation/ilcs/documents/072000050K12-17.htm

Jefferson, J. (2007). "Towns Invest in Medical Students." *Tallahassee Democrat* (May 26):3A.

Jensen, G.F., and M.A. Karpos (1993). "Managing Rape: Exploratory Research on the Behavior of Rape Statistics." *Criminology* 31:363-385.

Jensen, R.H. (1977-78). "Battered Women and the Law." *Victimology* 2:585-590.

Jerin, R.A., L.J. Moriarty, and M.A. Gibson (1995). "Victim Service or Self Service? An Analysis of Prosecution Based Victim-Witness Assistance Programs and Providers." *Criminal Justice Policy Review* 7:142-154.

Johnson, K.W. (1996). "Professional Help and Crime Victims." *Social Service Review* 71:89-109.

Johnson, N.C., and S.D. Young (1992). "Survivors' Response to Gang Violence." In R.C. Cervantes (ed.), *Substance Abuse and Gang Violence*. Newbury Park, CA: Sage.

Johnson, S.D., K. Bowers, and A. Hirschfield (1997). "New Insights into the Spatial and Temporal Distribution of Repeat Victimization." *British Journal of Criminology* 37:224-241.

Jones, A.S. (2000). "The Cost of Batterer Programs: How Much and Who Pays?" *Journal of Interpersonal Violence* 15:566-586.

Jurkovich, G.J., F.P. Rivara, H.G. Gurney, C. Fligner, R. Ries, B.A. Mueller, and M. Copass (1993). "The Effect of Acute Alcohol Intoxication and Chronic Alcohol Abuse on Outcome from Trauma." *Journal of the American Medical Association* 270:51-56.

Kalichman, S.C., M.E. Craig, and D.R. Follingstad (1990). "Professionals' Adherence to Mandatory Child Abuse Reporting Laws: Effects of Responsibility Attribution, Confidence Ratings, and Situational Factors." *Child Abuse & Neglect* 14:69-77.

Kama v. State, 507 So.2d 154 (Fla. 1st DCA 1987).

Kanin, E.J. (1957). "Male Aggression in Dating-Courtship Relations." *American Journal of Sociology* 63:197-204.

Kansas v. Hendricks, 117 S. Ct. 2072 (1997).

Kantor, G.K., and M.A. Straus (1987). "The 'Drunken Bum' Theory of Wife Beating." *Social Problems* 34:213-230.

Kapp, M.B. (1995). "Elder Mistreatment: Legal Interventions and Policy Uncertainties." *Behavioral Sciences and the Law* 13:365-380.

Kellerman, A.L. (1994). "Editorial: Firearm-Related Violence—What We Don't Know Is Killing Us." *American Journal of Public Health* 84:541-542.

Kelley, B.T., T.P. Thornberry, and C.A. Smith (1997). *In the Wake of Childhood Maltreatment*. Washington, DC: Office of Juvenile Justice and Delinquency Prevention.

Kelly, D.P. (1991). "Have Victim Reforms Gone Too Far—or Not Far Enough?" *Criminal Justice* 6:22-28, 38.

Kelly, D.P. (1987). "How Can We Help the Victim without Hurting the Defendant?" *Criminal Justice* 2:14-18, 38-39.

Kelly, D.P. (1984). "Delivering Legal Services to Victims: An Evaluation and Prescription." *The Justice System Journal* 9:62-86.

Kempe, C.H., F.N. Silverman, B.F. Steele, W. Droegemuller, and H.K. Silver (1962). "The Battered-Child Syndrome." *Journal of the American Medical Association* 181:105-112.

Kenna, W. Patrick v. U.S. District Court for the Central District of California, 435 F.3d 1011, 1016 (9th Cir. 2006).

Kennedy, E.M. (2007). "S.J. Res. 10: A Joint Resolution Proposing An Amendment to the Constitution of the United States Relative to Equal Rights for Men and Women; to the Committee on the Judiciary." *The Congressional Record* March 27:S3845.

Key, L.J. (1992). "A Working Typology of Grief among Homicide Survivors." In R.C. Cervantes (ed.), *Substance Abuse and Gang Violence*. Newbury Park, CA: Sage.

Killias, M. (1990). "Vulnerability: Towards a Better Understanding of a Key Variable in the Genesis of Fear of Crime." *Violence and Victims* 5:97-108.

Kilpatrick, D.G., C.L. Best, C.J. Veronen, A.E. Amick, L.A. Villenponteaux, and G.A. Ruff (1985). "Mental Health Correlates of Criminal Victimization: A Random Community Survey." *Journal of Consulting and Clinical Psychology* 53:873-886.

Kindermann, C., J. Lynch, and D. Cantor (1997). *Bureau of Justice Statistics: National Crime Victimization Survey: Effects of the Redesign on Victimization Estimates*. Washington, DC: U.S. Government Printing Office.

Kitson, G.C., R.D. Clark, D.S. DeGarmo, H. Dyches, and N. Rao (1991). "Bereavement in Natural and Violent Death." Paper presented at the Theory Construction and Research Methodology Workshop, National Council on Family Relations Annual Meeting.

Klappers, D. (1985). "Ident-A-Kid." *Police Chief* 52:30-31.

Kleemans, E.R. (2001). "Repeat Burglary Victimization: Results of Empirical Research in the Netherlands." In G. Farrell and K. Pease (eds.), *Repeat Victimization*. Monsey, NY: Criminal Justice Press.

Knudten, R.D., A.C. Meade, M.S. Knudten, and W.G. Doerner (1977). *Victims and Witnesses: Their Experiences with Crime and the Criminal Justice System: Executive Summary*. Washington, DC: National Institute of Law Enforcement and Criminal Justice.

Knudten, R.D., A.C. Meade, M.S. Knudten, and W.G. Doerner (1976). "The Victim in the Administration of Criminal Justice: Problems and Perceptions." In W.F. McDonald (ed.), *Criminal Justice and the Victim*. Beverly Hills: Sage.

Kolbos, J.R., E.H. Blakely, and D. Engleman (1996). "Children Who Witness Domestic Violence: A Review of Empirical Literature." *Journal of Interpersonal Violence* 11:281-293.

Konradi, A. (1996). "Preparing to Testify: Rape Survivors Negotiating the Criminal Justice Process." *Gender & Society* 10:404-432.

Kosberg, J.I. (1988). "Preventing Elder Abuse: Identification of High Risk Factors Prior to Placement Decisions." *The Gerontologist* 28:43-50.

Koss, M.P. (1995). "Hidden Rape: Sexual Aggression and Victimization in a National Sample of Students in Higher Education." In P. Pearles and R.J. Berger (eds.), *Rape and Society: Readings on the Problem of Sexual Assault*. Boulder, CO: Westview Press.

Koss, M.P., and H.H. Cleveland (1997). "Stepping on Toes: Social Roots of Date Rape Lead to Intractability and Politicization." in M.D. Schwartz (ed.), *Researching Sexual Violence Against Women: Methodological and Personal Perspectives*. Thousand Oaks, CA: Sage.

Koss, M.P., and J.A. Gaines (1993). "The Prediction of Sexual Aggression by Alcohol Use, Athletic Participation, and Fraternity Affiliation." *Journal of Interpersonal Violence* 8:94-108.

Koss, M.P., C.A. Gidycz, and N. Wisniewski (1987). "The Scope of Rape: Incidence and Prevalence of Sexual Aggression and Victimization in a National Sample of Students in Higher Education." *Journal of Consulting and Clinical Psychology* 55:162-170.

Koss, M.P., and K.E. Leonard (1984). "Sexually Aggressive Men: Empirical Findings and Theoretical Implications." In N. Malamuth and E. Donnerstein (eds.), *Pornography and Sexual Aggression*. New York: Academic Press.

Kreis, D.J., Jr., G. Plascencia, D. Augenstein, J.H. Davis, M. Echenique, J. Vopal, P. Byers, and G. Gomez (1986). "Preventable Trauma Deaths: Dade County, Florida." *Journal of Trauma* 26:649-654.

Kruzick, J.M., J.F. Clinton, and S.T. Kelber (1992). "Personal and Environmental Influences of Nursing Home Satisfaction." *The Gerontologist* 32:342-350.

Kübler-Ross, E. (1969). *On Death and Dying*. New York: Macmillan.

Kuehnle, K., and A. Sullivan (2003). "Gay and Lesbian Victimization: Reporting Factors in Domestic Violence and Bias Incidents." *Criminal Justice and Behavior* 30:85-96.

Kurki, L. (2000). "Restorative and Community Justice in the United States." In M. Tonry (ed.), *Crime and Justice: A Review of Research*, vol. 27. Chicago: Univ. of Chicago Press.

Lab, S.P. (1990). "Citizen Crime Prevention: Domains and Participation." *Justice Quarterly* 7:467-492.

Lab, S.P., and R.D. Clark (1996). *Discipline, Control and School Crime: Identifying Effective Intervention Strategies*. Final Report. Washington, DC: National Institute of Justice.

Lab, S.P., and J.D. Hirschel (1988). "Climatological Conditions and Crime: The Forecast is . . .?" *Justice Quarterly* 5:281-300.

Lab, S.P., and J.T. Whitehead (1994). "Avoidance Behavior as a Response to In-school Victimization." *Journal of Security Administration* 17(2):32-45.

Lamborn, L.L. (1987). "Victim Participation in the Criminal Justice Process: The Proposals for a Constitutional Amendment." *The Wayne Law Review* 34:125-220.

Lamond, D.A.P. (1989). "The Impact of Mandatory Reporting Legislation on Reporting Behavior." *Child Abuse & Neglect* 13:471-480.

Langen, P., and C. Innes (1986). *Preventing Domestic Violence against Women.* Washington, DC: U.S. Department of Justice.

Lansford, J.E., S. Miller-Johnson, L.J. Berlin, K.A. Dodge, J.E. Bates, and G.S. Pettit (2007). "Early Physical Abuse and Later Violent Delinquency: A Prospective Longitudinal Study." *Child Maltreatment* 12:233-245.

Largen, M.A. (1988). "Rape-Law Reform: An Analysis." In A.W. Burgess (ed.), *Rape and Sexual Assault, II.* New York: Garland Pub.

Lauritsen, J.L., and K.F. D. Quinet (1995). "Repeat Victimization Among Adolescents and Young Adults." *Journal of Quantitative Criminology* 11:143-166.

Leather, P., D. Beale, C. Lawrence, C. Brady and T. Cox (1999). "Violence and Work: Introduction and Overview." In Leather, P., C. Brady, C. Lawrence, D. Beale and T. Cox (eds.), *Work-related Violence: Assessment and Intervention.* London: Routledge.

LeBeau, J.L., and R.H. Langworthy (1986). "The Linkages between Routine Activities, Weather, and Calls for Police Service." *Journal of Police Science and Administration* 14:137-145.

LeCroy, C.W., and K. Whitaker (2005). "Improving the Quality of Home Visitation: An Exploratory Study of Difficult Situations." *Child Abuse & Neglect* 29:1003-1013.

LeDoux, J.C., and R.R. Hazelwood (1985). "Police Attitudes and Beliefs toward Rape." *Journal of Police Science and Administration* 13:211-220.

Ledray, L.E. (1999). *SANE: Sexual Assault Nurse Examiner: Development and Operation Guide.* Washington, DC: Office for Victims of Crime. Accessed on September 16, 2004, from http://www.ojp.usdoj.gov/ovc/publications/infores/sane/saneguide.pdf

Lempert, R.O. (1989). "Humility Is a Virtue: On the Publicization of Policy-Relevant Research." *Law & Society Review* 23:145-161.

Lerner, M.J. (1980). "The Desire for Justice and Reactions to Victims." In M. Walker and S. Brodsky (eds.), *Altruism and Helping Behavior.* New York: Academic Press.

Levenson, J.S., and L.P. Cotter (2005). "The Effect of Megan's Law on Sex Offender Reintegration." *Journal of Contemporary Criminal Justice* 21:49-66.

Leventhal, J.M. (2001). "The Prevention of Child Abuse and Neglect: Successfully Out of the Blocks." *Child Abuse & Neglect* 25:431-439.

Leventhal, J.M. (1999). "The Challenges of Recognizing Child Abuse." *Journal of the American Medical Association* 281:657-659.

Levi, B.H., G. Brown, and C. Erb (2006). "Reasonable Suspicion: A Pilot Study of Pediatric Residents." *Child Abuse & Neglect* 30:345-356.

Levin, J. (1993). "Swindled Seniors Testify on the Hill." *USA Today* (May 26):4B.

Levine, B.J. (1997). "Campaign Finance Reform Legislation in the United States Congress: A Critique." *Crime, Law and Social Change* 28:1-25.

Levine, K. (1978). "Empiricism in Victimological Research: A Critique." *Victimology* 3:77-90.

Levine, M., and L. Battistoni (1991). "The Corroboration Requirement in Child Sex Abuse Cases." *Behavioral Sciences and the Law* 9:3-20.

Levitt, C.J., G. Owen, and J. Truchsess (1991). "Families after Sexual Abuse: What Helps?" In M.Q. Patton (ed.), *Family Sexual Abuse: Frontline Research and Evaluation*. Newbury Park, CA: Sage.

Levrant, S., F.T. Cullen, B. Fulton, and J.F. Wozniak (1999) "Reconsidering Restorative Justice: The Corruption of Benevolence Revisited?" *Crime & Delinquency* 45:3-27.

Levy, H.B., J. Markovic, M.N. Kalinowski, S. Ahart, and H. Torres (1995). "Child Sexual Abuse Interviews: The Use of Anatomic Dolls and the Reliability of Information." *Journal of Interpersonal Violence* 10:334-353.

Lewis, A. (1996). "Mr. Clinton's Victims." *New York Times* June 28:A15.

Liang, J., and M.C. Sengstock (1983). "Personal Crimes against the Elderly." In J.I. Kosberg (ed.), *Abuse and Mistreatment of the Elderly: Causes and Interventions*. Littleton, MA: John Wright.

Liddick, D.R., Jr. (2000). "Campaign Fund-Raising Abuses and Money Laundering in Recent U.S. Elections: Criminal Networks in Action." *Crime, Law and Social Change* 34:111-157.

Lieb, R. (1996). "Community Notification Laws: 'A Step Toward More Effective Solutions.'" *Journal of Interpersonal Violence* 11:298-300.

Light, R.J. (1973). "Abused and Neglected in America: A Study of Alternative Policies." *Harvard Educational Review* 43:556-598.

Lindemann, E. (1944). "Symptomatology and Management of Acute Grief." *American Journal of Psychiatry* 101:141-148.

Lipovsky, J.A. (1994). "The Impact of Court on Children: Research Findings and Practical Recommendations." *Journal of Interpersonal Violence* 9:238-257.

Littel, K. (2001). *Sexual Assault Nurse Examiner (SANE) Programs: Improving the community Response to Sexual Assault Victims*. Washington, DC: Office for Victims of Crime.

Littlechild, B. (1995). "Violence Against Social Workers." *Journal of Interpersonal Violence* 10:123-130.

Lloyd, S., G. Farrell, and K. Pease (1994). *Preventing Repeated Domestic Violence: A Demonstration Project on Merseyside*. London: Home Office Police Research Group.

Lockhart, L.L., B.W. White, V. Causby, and A. Isaac (1994). "Letting Out the Secret: Violence in Lesbian Relationships." *Journal of Interpersonal Violence* 9:469-492.

Loftin, C., (1978). "Comments." *Criminology* 16:56-59.

Loftin, C., and R.H. Hill (1974). "Regional Subculture and Homicide: An Examination of the Gastil-Hackney Thesis." *American Sociological Review* 39:714-724.

Logan, T.K., L. Shannon, and R. Walker (2005). "Protective Orders in Rural and Urban Areas: A Multiple Perspective Study." *Violence Against Women* 11:876-911.

Logan, T.K., R. Walker, and C.G. Leukefeld. (2001). "Rural, Urban Influenced, and Urban Differences Among Domestic Violence Arrestees." *Journal of Interpersonal Violence*, 16:266-283.

Lombroso, C. (1968). *Crime, Its Causes and Remedies*. Montclair, NJ: Patterson.

Long-Onnen, J., and D. Cheatwood (1992). "Hospitals and Homicide: An Expansion of Current Theoretical Paradigms." *American Journal of Criminal Justice* 16:57-74.

Lottes, I.L. (1988). "Sexual Socialization and Attitudes toward Rape." In A.W. Burgess (ed.), *Rape and Sexual Assault, II*. New York: Garland.

Lowenstein, S.R., M.P. Weissberg, and D. Terry (1990). "Alcohol Intoxication, Injuries, and Dangerous Behaviors—and the Revolving Emergency Department Door." *Journal of Trauma* 30:1252-1258.

Lucal, B. (1995). "The Problem with 'Battered Husbands.'" *Deviant Behavior* 16:95-112.

Luckenbill, D.F. (1977). "Criminal Homicide as a Situated Transaction." *Social Problems* 25:176-186.

Luginbuhl, J., and M. Burkhead (1995). "Victim Impact Evidence in a Capital Trial: Encouraging Votes for Death." *American Journal of Criminal Justice* 20:1-16.

Lundberg-Love, P., and R. Geffner (1989). "Date Rape: Prevalence, Risk Factors, and a Proposed Model." In M.A. Pirog-Good and J.E. Stets (eds.), *Violence in Dating Relationships: Emerging Social Issues*. New York: Praeger.

Maan, C. (1991). "Assessment of Sexually Abused Children with Anatomically Detailed Dolls: A Critical Review." *Behavioral Sciences and the Law* 9:43-51.

MacDonald, P. (2000). *Make a Difference: Abuse/neglect Pilot Project*. Danvers, MA: North Shore Elder Services.

MacLeod, J., and G. Nelson (2000). "Programs for the Promotion of Family Wellness and the Prevention of Child Maltreatment: A Meta-Analytic Review." *Child Abuse & Neglect* 24:1127-1149.

Macolini, R.M. (1995). "Elder Abuse Policy: Considerations in Research and Legislation." *Behavioral Sciences and the Law* 13:349-363.

Maddock, J.W., P.R. Larson, and C.F. Lally (1991). "An Evaluation Protocol for Incest Family Functioning." In M.Q. Patton (ed.), *Family Sexual Abuse: Frontline Research and Evaluation*. Newbury Park, CA: Sage.

Maddox, G.L., and J. Wiley (1976). "Scope, Concepts and Methods in the Study of Aging." In R.G. Binstock and E. Shanas (eds.), *Handbook of Aging and the Social Sciences*. New York: Van Nostrand Reinhold.

Maden, M.F., and D.F. Wrench (1977). "Significant Findings in Child Abuse Research." *Victimology* 2:196-224.

Maguire, K., and A.L. Pastore (2005). *Sourcebook of Criminal Justice Statistics 2004*. Washington, DC: U.S. Department of Justice.

Maguire, K., and A.L. Pastore (2003). *Sourcebook of Criminal Justice Statistics 2002*. Washington, DC: U.S. Department of Justice.

Maguire, K., and A.L. Pastore (1996). *Sourcebook of Criminal Justice Statistics 1995*. Washington, DC: U.S. Department of Justice.

Makepeace, J.M. (1983). "Life Events Stress and Courtship Violence." *Family Relations* 32:101-109.

Makepeace, J.M. (1981). "Courtship Violence among College Students." *Family Relations* 30:97-102.

Mameli, P.A. (2002). "Stopping the Illegal Trafficking of Human Beings." *Crime, Law and Social Change* 38:67-80.

Maloney, C.B. (2007). "HJ. Res. 40. A Joint Resolution Proposing An Amendment to the Constitution of the United States Relative to Equal Rights for Men and Women; to the Committee on the Judiciary." *The Congressional Record* March 27:H3184.

Mann, C.R. (1990). "Black Female Homicide in the United States." *Journal of Interpersonal Violence* 5:176-201.

Mann, C.R. (1988). "Getting Even? Women Who Kill in Domestic Encounters." *Justice Quarterly* 5:33-51.

Marden, P.G. (1966). "A Demographic and Ecological Analysis of the Distribution of Physicians in Metropolitan America." *American Journal of Sociology* 72:290-300.

Marhoefer-Dvorak, A., P.A. Resick, C.K. Hutter, and S.A. Girelli (1988). "Single- Versus Multiple-Incident Rape Victims: A Comparison of Psychological Reactions to Rape." *Journal of Interpersonal Violence* 3:145-160.

Marquart, J.W. (2005). "Editorial Introduction: Bringing Victims In, But How Far?" *Criminology & Public Policy* 4:329-332.

Marsh, J.C., A. Geist, and N. Caplan (1982). *Rape and the Limits of Law Reform*. Boston, MA: Auburn House.

Martin, P.Y., and R. Hummer (1989). "Fraternities and Rape on Campus." *Gender & Society* 3:357-373.

Martin, P.Y., and R.M. Powell (1994). "Accounting for the 'Second Assault:' Legal Organizations' Framing of Rape Victims." *Law & Social Inquiry* 19:853-890.

Marwick, C. (1992). "Guns, Drugs Threaten to Raise Public Health Problem of Violence to Epidemic." *Journal of the American Medical Association* 267:2993.

Mawby, R.I., and S. Walklate (1994). *Critical Victimology*. Thousand Oaks, CA: Sage.

Maxwell, C.D., J.H. Garner, and J.A. Fagan (2002). "The Preventive Effects of Arrest on Intimate Partner Violence: Research, Policy and Theory." *Criminology & Public Policy* 2:51-80.

Maxwell, C.D., J.H. Garner, and J.A. Fagan (2001). *Research in Brief: The Effects of Arrest on Intimate Partner Violence: New Violence from the Spouse Assault Reduction Program*. Washington, DC: U.S. Department of Justice, National Institute of Justice.

McCarroll, J.E., R.J. Ursano, K.M. Wright, and C.S. Fullerton (1993). "Handling Bodies after Violent Death: Strategies for Coping." *American Journal of Orthopsychiatry* 63:209-214.

McCleary, R., B.C. Nienstedt, and J.M. Erven (1982). "Uniform Crime Reports as Organizational Outcomes: Three Time-Series Experiments." *Social Problems* 29:361-372.

McClennen, J.C. (2005). "Domestic Violence Between Same-Sex Partners: Recent Findings and Future Research." *Journal of Interpersonal Violence* 20:149-154.

McCold, P. (2003). "A Survey of Assessment Research on Mediation and Conferencing." In L. Walgrave (ed.), *Repositioning Restorative Justice*. Portland, OR: Willan.

McCold, P., and T. Wachtel (2002). "Restorative Justice Theory Validation." In E.G.M. Weitekamp and H. Kernere (eds.), *Restorative Justice: Theoretical Foundations*. Portland, OR: Willan.

McCold, P., and T. Wachtel (1998). *Restorative Policing Experiment: The Bethlehem, Pennsylvania, Police Family Group Conferencing Project*. Pipersville, PA: Community Service Foundation.

McCoy, H.V., J.D. Wooldredge, F.T. Cullen, P.J. Dubeck, and S.L. Browning (1996). "Lifestyles of the Old and Not So Fearful: Life Situation and Older Persons' Fear of Crime." *Journal of Criminal Justice* 24:191-205.

McCurdy, K., and D. Daro (1994). "Child Maltreatment: A National Study of Reports and Fatalities." *Journal of Interpersonal Violence* 9:75-94.

McFarlane, J., P. Wilson, A. Malecha, and D. Lemmy (2000). "Intimate Partner Violence: A Gender Comparison." *Journal of Interpersonal Violence* 15:158-169.

McGarrell, E.F., K. Olivares, K. Crawford, and N. Kroovand (2000). *Returning Justice to the Community: The Indianapolis Juvenile Restorative Justice Experiment*. Indianapolis: Hudson Institute.

McGhee, J.R. (1983). "The Vulnerability of Elderly Consumers." *International Journal of Aging and Human Development* 17:223-246.

McGillis, D., and J. Mullen (1977). *Neighborhood Justice Centers: An Analysis of Potential Models*. Washington, DC: Law Enforcement Assistance Administration.

McGuire, K.A. (1991). "AIDS and the Sexual Offender: The Epidemic Now Poses New Threats to the Victim and the Criminal Justice System." *Dickinson Law Review* 96:95-123.

McKinney, J.C. (1969). "Typification, Typologies, and Sociological Theory." *Social Forces* 48:1-12.

McKinney, J.C. (1950). "The Role of Constructive Typology in Scientific Sociological Analysis." *Social Forces* 28:235-240.

McKinney, K. (1990). "Sexual Harassment of University Faculty by Colleagues and Students." *Sex Roles* 23:421-438.

McLaughlin, E., R. Fergusson, G. Hughes, and L. Westmarland (2003). "Introduction: Justice in the Round– Contextualizing Restorative Justice." In E. McLaughlin, R. Fergusson, G. Hughes, and L. Westmarland (eds.), *Restorative Justice: Critical Issues*. Thousand Oaks, CA: Sage.

McLeod, M. (1987). "An Examination of the Victim's Role at Sentencing: Results of a Survey of Probation Administrators." *Judicature* 71:162-168.

McMahon, M., and E. Pence (1996). "Replaying to Dan O'Leary." *Journal of Interpersonal Violence* 11:452-455.

McNeely, R.L., and C.R. Mann (1990). "Domestic Violence Is a Human Issue." *Journal of Interpersonal Violence* 5:129-132.

McPheters, L.R. (1978). "Econometric Analysis of Factor Influencing Crime on the Campus." *Journal of Criminal Justice* 6:47-51.

McShane, M.D., and F.P. Williams III (1992). "Radical Victimology: A Critique of the Concept of Victim in Traditional Victimology." *Crime & Delinquency* 38:258-271.

Meeker, J.W., and A. Binder (1990). "Experiments as Reforms: The Impact of the 'Minneapolis Experiment' on Police Policy." *Journal of Police Science and Administration* 17:147-153.

Melton, G.B. (2005). "Mandated Reporting: A Policy without Reason." *Child Abuse & Neglect* 29-9-18.

Melton, G.B. (1980). "Psycholegal Issues in Child Victims' Interaction with the Legal System." *Victimology* 5:274-284.

Melton, G.B., and M.F. Flood (1994). "Research Policy and Child Maltreatment: Developing the Scientific Foundation for Effective Protection of Children." *Child Abuse & Neglect* 18:1-28.

Melton, H.C. (2007). "Predicting the Occurrence of Stalking in Relationships Characterized by Domestic Violence." *Journal of Interpersonal Violence* 22:3-25.

Melton, H.C., and J. Belknap (2003). "He Hits, She Hits: Assessing Gender Differences and Similarities in Officially Reported Intimate Partner Violence." *Criminal Justice and Behavior* 30:328-348.

Mendelsohn, B. (1982). "Socio-Analytic Introduction to Research in a General Victimological and Criminological Perspective." In H.J. Schneider (ed.), *The Victim in International Perspective*. New York: Walter de Gruyter & Company.

Mendelsohn, B. (1976). "Victimology and Contemporary Society's Trends." *Victimology* 1:8-28.

Mendelsohn, B. (1956). "The Victimology." *Etudes Internationale de Psycho-sociologie Criminelle* July:23-26.

Metropolitan Life (1993). *Violence in America's Public Schools*. New York: Louis Harris and Associates.

Meyer, T.P. (1972). "The Effects of Sexually Arousing and Violent Films on Aggressive Behavior." *Journal of Sex Research* 8:324-331.

Mignon, S.I., and W.M. Holmes (1995). "Police Response to Mandatory Arrest Laws." *Crime & Delinquency* 41:430-442.

Miller, J. (2006). "A Specification of the Types of Intimate Partner Violence Experienced by Women in the General Population." *Violence Against Women* 12:1105-1131.

Miller, T.R., M.A. Cohen, and B. Wiersema (1996). *Victim Costs and Consequences: A New Look*. Washington, DC: National Institute of Justice.

Mones, P. (1993). "When the Innocent Strike Back: Abused Children Who Kill Their Parents." *Journal of Interpersonal Violence* 8:297-299.

Monson, C.M., G.R. Byrd, and J. Langhinrichsen-Rohling (1996). "To Have and to Hold: Perceptions of Marital Rape." *Journal of Interpersonal Violence* 11:410-424.

Moore, D., and T. O'Connell (1994). "Family conferencing in Wagga Wagga: A communitarian model of justice." In C. Adler and J. Wundersitz (eds.), *Family Conferencing and Juvenile Justice: The Way Forward or Misplaced Optimism?* Canberra: Australian Institute of Criminology.

Morgan, F. (2001). "Repeat Burglary in a Perth Suburb: Indicator of Short-term or Long-term Risk?" In G. Farrell and K. Pease (eds.), *Repeat Victimization.* Monsey, NY: Criminal Justice Press.

Morgan, K., and B.L. Smith (2005). "Victims, Punishment, and Parole: The Effect of Victim Participation on Parole Hearings." *Criminology & Public Policy* 4:333-360.

Morse, B. (1995). "Beyond the Conflict Tactics Scale: Assessing Gender Differences in Partner Violence." *Violence & Victims,* 10:251-272.

Mouton, C.P., S. Rovi, K. Furniss, and N.L. Lasser (1999). "The Associations Between Health and Domestic Violence in Older Women: Results of a Pilot Study." *Journal of Women's Health and Gender-based Medicine* 8:1173-1179.

Murphy. C.M., and V.A. Baxter (1997). "Motivating Batterers to Change in the Treatment Context." *Journal of Interpersonal Violence* 12:607-619.

Murphy, S.M., A.E. Amick-McMullan, D.G. Kilpatrick, M.E. Haskett, L.J. Veronen, C.L. Best, and B.E. Saunders (1988). "Rape Victims' Self-Esteem: A Longitudinal Analysis." *Journal of Interpersonal Violence* 3:355-370.

Mustaine, E.E., R. Tewksbury, and K.M. Stengel (2006). "Residential Location and Mobility of Registered Sex Offenders." *American Journal of Criminal Justice* 30:177-192.

Myers, J.E.B. (1996). "Societal Self-Defense: New Laws to Protect Children from Sexual Abuse." *Child Abuse & Neglect* 20:255-258.

Myers, R.K. (1997a). "Victim Rights Clarification Act of 1997 Affects Victim Bill of Rights Act, Violent Crime Control Act, and Rule of Evidence." *The Crime Victims Report* 1:17, 29.

Myers, R.K. (1997b). "Supreme Court Finds Sexually Violent Predator Law Constitutional." *The Crime Victims Report* 1:56, 58-59.

Nathan, A.J. (2000). "At the Intersection of Domestic Violence and Guns: The Public Interest Exception and the Lautenberg Amendment." *Cornell Law Review* 85:822-858.

The National Archives Experience, *Constitution of the United States,* Retrieved September 14, 2007, from http://www.archives.gov/national-archives-experience/charters/constitution_amendments_11-27.htm

National Center on Elder Abuse (n.d.). *Frequently Asked Questions.* http://www.elderabusecenter.org

National Center for Health Statistics (2006). "Age-Adjusted Death Rates for Leading Causes of Injury Death by Year, United States, 1979–2004." *Morbidity and Mortality Weekly Report* 55(December 22):1363.

National Center for Injury Prevention and Control (2006). *CDC Injury Fact Book.* Atlanta, GA: Centers for Disease Control and Prevention, p. 55. Retrieved September 22, 2007, from http://www.cdc.gov/ncipc/fact_book/InjuryBook2006.pdf

National Center for Injury Prevention and Control (2004). *Youth Violence: Fact Sheet.* Atlanta, GA: Centers for Disease Control and Prevention. Retrieved August 22, 2004, from http://www.cdc.gov/ncipc/factsheets/yvfacts.htm

National Center for Injury Prevention and Control (2001). *Injury Mortality Maps of the United States, 1989-1998.* Atlanta, GA: Centers for Disease Control and Prevention. Retrieved August 22, 2004, from http://webappa.cdc.gov/cdc_mxt3

National Center for Victims of Crime (2007). *2007 National Crime Victims' Rights Week Resource Guide.* Washington, DC: U.S. Department of Justice.

National Center for Victims of Crime (1999). *HIV/AIDS Legislation.* Arlington, VA: National Victim Center. Retrieved on August 24, 2007, from http://www.ncvc.org/ncvc/main.aspx?dbName=DocumentViewer&DocumentID=32468

National Center for Victims of Crime (1996). *The 1996 Victims' Rights Sourcebook: A Compilation and Comparison of Victims' Rights Laws.* Arlington, VA: National Victim Center. Found at: http://www.ncvc.org/law/sbook/toc.htm.

National Child Abuse and Neglect Data System (2006). *Child Maltreatment 2005.* Washington, DC: U.S. Department of Health and Human Services.

National Children's Advocacy Center (2007). *Physical and Behaviorally Indicators of Abuse.* Huntsville, AL: The National Children's Advocacy Center. Retrieved on August 31, 2007, from http://www.nationalcac.org/families/for_workers/abuse_indicators.html

National Clearinghouse on Child Abuse and Neglect Information (2006). *Recognizing Child Abuse and Neglect: Signs and Symptoms.* Washington, DC: Child Welfare Information Gateway. Retrieved on September 4, 2007, from www.childwelfare.gov/pubs/factsheets/signs.cfm

National Clearinghouse on Child Abuse and Neglect Information (1999). *Child Abuse and Neglect State Statutes Series: Current Trends in Child Maltreatment Reporting Laws.* Washington, DC: U.S. Department of Health and Human Services. Government Printing Office.

National Clearinghouse on Child Abuse and Neglect Information (2003a). *Child Maltreatment 2002.* Washington, DC: U.S. Department of Health and Human Services .

National Clearinghouse on Child Abuse and Neglect Information (2003b). *Child Maltreatment 2002: Summary of Key Findings.* Washington, DC: U.S. Department of Health and Human Services.

National Clearinghouse on Child Abuse and Neglect Information (2003c). *Recognizing Child Abuse and Neglect: Signs and Symptoms.* Washington, DC: U.S. Department of Health and Human Services. Retrieved on September 29, 2004, from http://nccanch.acf.hhs.gov/pubs/factsheets/signs.cfm

National Coalition to Abolish Corporal Punishment in Schools (2007). "States Banning Corporal Punishment." Columbus, OH: The Center for Effective Discipline. Retrieved on August 30, 2007, from http://www.stophitting.com/disatschool/statesBanning.php

National Committee to Prevent Child Abuse (1996). *An Approach to Preventing Child Abuse*. Chicago: National Committee to Prevent Child Abuse, URL http://www.childabuse.org/fs15.html.

National Institute of Neurological Disorders and Stroke (2007). *Shaken Baby Syndrome*. Washington, DC: National Institutes of Health. Retrieved on August 31, 2007, from http://www.ninds.nih.gov/disorders/shakenbaby/shakenbaby.htm

National Institute of Neurological Disorders and Stroke (2001). "Shaken Baby Syndrome Information Page." Bethesda, MD: National Institutes of Health. Retrieved September 29, 2004, from http://www.doctorswhoswho.com/medical_library/diseases_conditions/children/shaken_baby_syndrome.htm

National Institute for Occupational Safety and Health (1997). *Violence in the Workplace*. NIOSH Facts. Found at: http://www.cdc.gov/niosh

National Institute for Occupational Safety and Health (1996). *Violence in the Workplace: Risk Factors and Prevention Strategies*. Found at: http://www.cdc.gov/niosh

National Institute for Occupational Safety and Health (1995). *Preventing Homicide in the Workplace*. NIOSH Alert. Found at: http://www.cdc.gov/niosh

National Research Council (2003). *Elder Mistreatment: Abuse, Neglect, and Exploitation in an Aging America*. Washington, DC: National Academies Press.

National Victim Center (1991). *America Speaks Out: Citizens' Attitudes About Victims' Rights and Violence*. Fort Worth, TX: National Victim Center.

National Victims' Constitutional Amendment Network (2004). *Crime Victims' Rights "Miranda Card."* Denver, CO: National Victims' Constitutional Amendment Passage. Retrieved September 8, 2007, from http://www.nvcan.org

National Violent Injury Statistics System (2005a). *Linking Data to Save Lives: How the National Violent Death Reporting System Will Help Break the Cycle of Violence in Our Communities*. Boston, MA: Harvard Injury Control Research Center, Harvard School of Public Health. Retrieved on August 19, 2007, from http://www.hsph.harvard.edu/hicrc/nviss/about_parent_nvdr.htm

National Violent Injury Statistics System (2005b). *Getting a Handle on Suicide*. Boston, MA: Harvard Injury Control Research Center, Harvard School of Public Health. Retrieved on August 19, 2007, from http://www.hsph.harvard.edu/hicrc/nviss/about_parent_nvdr.htm

National Violent Injury Statistics System (2004). *NVDRS in Thirteen States; More to Come*. Boston, MA: Harvard Injury Control Research Center, Harvard School of Public Health. Retrieved on August 19, 2007, from http://www.hsph.harvard.edu/hicrc/nviss/about_parent_nvdr.htm

Naylor, R.T. (2007). "The Alchemy of Fraud: Investment Scams in the Precious-Metals Mining Business." *Crime, Law & Social Change* 47:89-120.

Naylor, R.T. (2004). "The Underworld of Ivory." *Crime, Law & Social Change* 42:261-295.

Nelson, B.J. (1984). *Making An Issue of Child Abuse: Political Agenda Setting for Social Problems.* Chicago: University of Chicago Press.

Nelson, J.L. (1999). "The Lautenberg Amendment: An Essential Tool for Combating Domestic Violence." *North Dakota Law Review*, 75:365-390.

Newcomb, M.D., and T.F. Locke (2001). "Intergenerational Cycle of Maltreatment: A Popular Concept Obscured by Methodological Limitations." *Child Abuse & Neglect* 25:1219-1240.

Newman, D.W. (1995). "Jury Decision Making and the Effect of Victim Impact Statements in the Penalty Phase." *Criminal Justice Policy Review* 7:291-300.

Nicholl, C.G. (1999). *Community Policing, Community Justice, and Restorative Justice: Exploring the Links for the Delivery of a Balanced Approach to Public Safety.* Washington, DC: Office of Community Oriented Policing Services.

No Author (2004). *Overcoming Compassion Fatigue.* Retrieved August 20, 2004, from http://www.neurosy.org/caregiving/thecaregiver/compassion.shtml

No Author (2002). *National Victim Assistance Academy Brochure, 2002.* Washington, DC: Office for Victims of Crime.

No Author (1964). "Editorial." *Journal of the American Medical Association.* 188 (April 27):386.

Norris, J., and S. Feldman-Summers (1981). "Factors Related to the Psychological Impacts of Rape on the Victim." *Journal of Abnormal Psychology* 90:562-567.

Norton, J. (1987). "Robots Unlock Secrets of Child Sexual Abuse." *Police Chief* 54:31-36.

Norton, L. (1983). "Witness Involvement in the Criminal Justice System and Intention to Cooperate in Future Prosecutions." *Journal of Criminal Justice* 11:143-152.

Nugent, W.R., M.S. Umbreit, L. Wiinamaki, and J. Paddock (1999). "Participation in victim-offender mediation and severity of subsequent delinquent behavior: Successful replications?" *Journal of Research in Social Work Practice* 11:5-23.

O'Brien, R.M. (1985). *Crime and Victimization.* Beverly Hills: Sage.

Occupational Safety and Health Administration (2002). *Workplace Violence.* OSHA Fact Sheet. Washington, DC: Occupational Safety and Health Administration.

Office of the Florida Attorney General (1991). *Sexual Assault: Evidence Collection Protocol.* Tallahassee, FL: State of Florida.

Office of the Florida Attorney General, Florida Crime Prevention Training Institute, Victim Services Professional Development Program (2004). *Victim Services Practitioner Designation Requirements.* Retrieved August 20, 2004, from http://myfloridalegal.com/renewal.pdf

Office of Juvenile Justice and Delinquency Prevention (1999). *Violence After School, 1999.* Washington, DC: Office of Juvenile Justice and Delinquency Prevention.

Office of the Press Secretary (April 20, 1997). *National Crime Victims' Rights Week, 2007: A Proclamation by the President of the United States.* Washington, DC: The White House. Retrieved on September 9, 2007, from http://www.whitehouse.gov/news/releases/2007/04/20070420-12.html

Office of the State Attorney (No Date). *Policy Manual.* Second Judicial Circuit: Tallahassee, Florida.

Office of the U.S. Attorney General (2000). *Attorney General Guidelines for Victim and Witness Assistance.* Washington, DC: U.S. Department of Justice.

Office of the U.S. Attorney General (1992). *Attorney General Guidelines for Victim and Witness Assistance.* Washington, DC: U.S. Department of Justice.

Office for Victims of Crime (2002a). *Victim Input into Plea Agreements.* Washington, DC: U.S. Department of Justice.

Office for Victims of Crime (2002b). *Strengthening Antistalking Statutes.* Washington, DC: U.S. Department of Justice.

Office for Victims of Crime (2002c). *Privacy of Victims' Counseling Communications.* Washington, DC: U.S. Department of Justice.

Office for Victims of Crime (2002d). *Ordering Restitution to the Crime Victim.* Washington, DC: Office for Victims of Crime.

Office for Victims of Crime (2002e). *Restitution: Making It Work.* Washington, DC: Office for Victims of Crime.

Office for Victims of Crime (2001). *The Crime Victim's Right to Be Present.* Washington, DC: U.S. Department of Justice.

Office for Victims of Crime (1999). *Victims of Crime Act Crime Victims Fund. OVC Fact Sheet.* http://www.ojp.usdoj.gov/ovc/publications/factshts/cvfcva.htm.

Office for Victims of Crime (1998a). *New Directions from the Field: Victims' Rights and Services for the 21st Century.* Washington, DC: U.S. Department of Justice.

Office for Victims of Crime (1998b). *Victims' Rights Compliance Efforts: Experiences in Three States.* Washington, DC: U.S. Department of Justice.

Office for Victims of Crime (1997). *Civil Legal Remedies for Crime Victims,* 2nd ed. Washington, DC: U.S. Department of Justice. Found at: http://www.ncjrs.org.txtfiles/clr.txt

Office on Violence Against Women (2007). *About Domestic Violence.* Washington, DC: U.S. Department of Justice. Retrieved on September 20, 2007, from http://www.usdoj.gov/ovw/domviolence.htm

O'Grady, K., J. Waldon, W. Carlson, S. Street, and C. Cannizzaro (1992). "The Importance of Victim Satisfaction: A Commentary." *The Justice System Journal* 15:759-764.

Ohio Civil Rights Commission (1996). *Sexual Harassment in the Workplace.* Pamphlet. Columbus, OH: Ohio Civil Rights Commission.

Ohio State Medical Association (1994). *Ohio Physicians' Elder Abuse Prevention Project: Trust Talk.* Columbus, OH: Ohio State Medical Association.

Olds, D., J. Eckenrode, and H. Kitzman (2005). "Clarifying the Impact of the Nurse-Family Partnership on Child Maltreatment: Response to Chaffin (2004)." *Child Abuse & Neglect* 29:229-233.

Olds, D., P. Hill, and E. Rumsey (1998). *Prenatal and Early Childhood Nurse Home Visitation.* Washington, DC: U.S. Department of Justice, Office of Juvenile Justice and Delinquency Prevention.

O'Leary, K.A. (1996). "Physical Aggression in Intimate Relationships Can Be Treated Within a Marital Context Under Certain Circumstances." *Journal of Interpersonal Violence* 11:450-452.

Ohio Revised Code (2004).

Olweus, D. (1995). "Bullying or Peer Abuse at School: Facts and Intervention." *Current Directions in Psychological Science* 4:196-200.

Olweus, D. (1994). "Bullying at School: Basic Facts and Effects of a School-based Intervention Program." *Journal of Child Psychology and Psychiatry and Allied Disciplines* 35:1171-1190.

O'Malley, T.A., D.F. Everitt, H. O'Malley, and E. Campion (1983). "Identifying and Preventing Family-Mediated Abuse and Neglect of Elderly Persons." *Annals of Internal Medicine* 98:998-1004.

Orcutt, J.D., and R. Faison (1988). "Sex-Role Attitude Change and Reporting of Rape Victimization, 1973-1985." *Sociological Quarterly* 29:589-604.

Orr, D.A. (2000). "*Weiand v. State* and Battered Spouse Syndrome: The Toothless Tigress Can Now Roar." *Florida Bar Journal* 74:14-20.

Oshana, D., K. Harding, L. Friedman, and J.K. Holton (2005). "Rethinking Healthy Families: A Continuous Responsibility." Child Abuse & Neglect 29:219-228.

Owen, G., and N.M. Steele (1991). "Incest Offenders after Treatment." In M.Q. Patton (ed.), *Family Sexual Abuse: Frontline Research and Evaluation.* Newbury Park, CA: Sage.

Pagelow, M.D. (1993). "Response to Hamberger's Comments." *Journal of Interpersonal Violence* 8:137-139.

Pagelow, M.D. (1992). "Adult Victims of Domestic Violence: Battered Women." *Journal of Interpersonal Violence* 7:87-120.

Pagelow, M.D. (1984). *Family Violence.* New York: Greenwood Press.

Pallone, N.J. (2003). "Without Plea Bargaining, Megan Kanka Would Be Alive Today." *Criminology & Public Policy* 3:83-96.

Pallone, N.J. (1995). "A View from the Front Line." *Crime Justice Ethics* 14:9-16.

Parker, R.N. (1989). "Poverty, Subculture of Violence, and Type of Homicide." *Social Forces* 67:983-1007.

Parker, R.N., and M.D. Smith (1979). "Deterrence, Poverty, and Type of Homicide." *American Journal of Sociology* 85:614-624.

Parnas, R.I. (1967). "The Police Response to the Domestic Disturbance." *Wisconsin Law Review* 31:914-960.

Parry, J.K., and J. Thornwall (1992). "Death of a Father." *Death Studies* 16:173-181.

Parsonage, W.H., F.P. Bernat, and J. Helfgott (1994). "Victim Impact Testimony and Pennsylvania's Parole Decision Making Process: A Pilot Study." *Criminal Justice Policy Review* 6:187-206.

Pastore, A.L., and K. Maguire. *Sourcebook of Criminal Justice Statistics, 2007.* Washington, DC: U.S Department of Justice. Found at: http://www.albany.edu/sourcebook

Pastore, A.L., and K. Maguire (2006). *Sourcebook of Criminal Justice Statistics, 2005*. Washington, DC: U.S Department of Justice.

Paulsen, D.J. (2003). "Murder in Black and White: The Newspaper Coverage of Homicide in Houston." *Homicide Studies* 7:289-317.

Payne v. Tennessee, 111 S. Ct. 2597 (1991).

Pearlman, L.A., and K.W. Saakvitne (1995). *Trauma and the Therapist: Counter-transference and Vicarious Traumatization in Psychotherapy with Incest Survivors*. New York: W. W. Norton.

Pease, K. (1998). *Repeat Victimization: Taking Stock*. Crime Detection and Prevention Series, Paper 90. London: Home Office.

Penick, B.K., and M.B. Owens III (1976). *Surveying Crime: Panel for the Evaluation of Crime Surveys*. Washington, DC: National Academy of Sciences.

Pepper, C.D. (1983). "Frauds Against the Elderly." In J.I. Kosberg (ed.), *Abuse and Maltreatment of the Elderly: Causes and Interventions*. Littleton, MA: John Wright.

Peterson, R.R., and J. Dixon (2005). "Court Oversight and Conviction Under Mandatory and Nonmandatory Domestic Violence Case Filing Policies." *Criminology & Public Policy* 4:535-558.

Pfohl, S.J. (1977). "The 'Discovery' of Child Abuse." *Social Problems* 24:310-323.

Phillips, L.E. (1986). "Theoretical Explanations of Elder Abuse: Competing Hypotheses and Unresolved Issues." In K.A. Pillemer and R.S. Wolf (eds.), *Elder Abuse: Conflict in the Family*. Dover, MA: Auburn House.

Phillips, D.P. (1983). "The Impact of Mass Media Violence on U.S. Homicides." *American Sociological Review* 48:560-568.

Phillips, D.P. (1982). "The Impact of Fictional Television Stories on U.S. Adult Fatalities: New Evidence on the Effect of Mass Media on Violence." *American Journal of Sociology* 87:1340-1359.

Phythian, M. (2000). "The Illicit Arms Trade: Cold War and Post-Cold War." *Crime, Law and Social Change* 33:1-52.

Pillemer, K.A. (1988). "Maltreatment of Patients in Nursing Homes: Overview and Research Agenda." *Journal of Health and Social Behavior* 29:227-238.

Pillemer, K.A. (1986). "Risk Factors in Elder Abuse: Results from a Case-Control Study." In K.A. Pillemer and R.S. Wolf (eds.), *Elder Abuse: Conflict in the Family*. Dover, MA: Auburn House.

Pillemer, K.A., and D. Finkelhor (1988). "The Prevalence of Elder Abuse: A Random Sample Survey." *The Gerontologist* 28:51-57.

Pillemer, K.A., and D.W. Moore (1989). "Abuse of Patients in Nursing Homes: Findings from a Survey of Staff." *The Gerontologist* 29:314-320.

Pirog-Good, M.A., and J.E. Stets (eds.), *Violence in Dating Relationships: Emerging Social Issues*. New York: Praeger.

Pittman, D.J., and W., Handy (1964). "Patterns in Criminal Aggravated Assault." *Journal of Criminal Law, Criminology, and Police Science* 55:462-470.

Pleck, E. (1989). "Criminal Approaches to Family Violence, 1640-1980." In L. Ohlin and M. Tonry (eds.), *Family Violence*. Chicago: University of Chicago Press.

Pleck, E. (1979). "Wife Beating in Nineteenth-Century America." *Victimology* 4:60-74.

Police Executive Research Forum (2007). *Chief Concerns: Violent Crime in America: 24 Months of Alarming Trends*. Washington, DC: Police Executive Research Forum.

Pollak, J., and S. Levy (1988). "Countertransference and Failure to Report Child Abuse and Neglect." *Child Abuse & Neglect* 13:515-522.

Pollock, D.A., J.M. O'Neill, R.G. Parrish, D.L. Combs, and J.L. Annest (1993). "Temporal and Geographic Trends in the Autopsy Frequency of Blunt and Penetrating Trauma Deaths in the United States." *Journal of the American Medical Association* 269:1525-1531.

Polvi, N., T. Looman, C. Humphries, and K. Pease (1990). "Repeat Break and Enter Victimization: Time Curse and Crime Prevention Opportunity." *Journal of Police Science and Administration* 17:8-11.

Pontell, H.N. (2005). "White-Collar Crime or Just Risky Business? The Role of Fraud in Major Financial Debacles." *Crime, Law & Social Change* 42:309-324.

Poppen, J., and N.J. Segal (1988). "The Influence of Sex and Sex-Role Orientation on Sexual Coercion." *Sex Roles* 19:689-701.

Prentky, R.A. (1996). "Community Notification and Constructive Risk Reduction." *Journal of Interpersonal Violence* 11:295-298.

The President's Commission on Law Enforcement and Administration of Justice (1967). *Task Force Report: Crime and Its Impact—An Assessment*. Washington, DC: U.S. Government Printing Office.

The President's Task Force on Victims of Crime (1982). *Final Report*. Washington, DC: U.S. Government Printing Office.

Presley, M.M. (1999). "Jimmy Ryce Involuntary Civil Commitment for Sexually Violent Predators' Treatment and Care Act: Replacing Criminal Justice with Civil Commitment." *Florida State University Law Review* 26:487-516.

Prevent Child Abuse America (2002). *Resolution 11.14.02: Resolution on Corporal Punishment in Schools and Institutions*. Retrieved on September 29, 2004, from http://www.preventchildabuse.org/get_active/downloads/pcaa_res_corp_punish.pdf

Pridemore, W.A. (2000). "An Empirical Examination of Commutations and Executions in Post- *Furman* Capital Cases." *Justice Quarterly* 17:159-183.

Prochaska, J.O., and C.C. DiClemente (1984). *The Transtheoretical Approach: Crossing the Traditional Boundaries of Therapy*. Homewood IL: Dow Jones Irwin.

Pumphrey-Gordon, J.E., and A.M. Gross (2007). "Alcohol Consumption and Females' Recognition in Response to Date Rape Risk: The Role of Sex-Related Alcohol Expectancies." *Journal of Family Violence* 22:475-485.

Quetelet, A. (1835). *A Treatise on Man*. New York: Burt Franklin. Reprinted 1978.

Quinn, M.J. (1990). "Elder Abuse and Neglect: Treatment Issues." In S.M. Stith, M.B. Williams, and K. Rosen (eds.), *Violence Hits Home*. New York: Springer.

Quinn, M.J., and S.K. Tomita (1986). *Elder Abuse and Neglect: Causes, Diagnosis and Intervention Strategies.* New York: Springer.

Rafael, T., and L. Pion-Berlin (1999). *Parents Anonymous: Strengthening Families.* Washington, DC: U.S. Department of Justice.

Raford v. State, 27 Fla. L. Weekly S781, (Fla. 2002), No. SC01-379.

Rand, M.R., J.P. Lynch, and D. Cantor (1997). *Criminal Victimization, 1973-95.* Washington, DC: U.S. Bureau of Justice Statistics.

Range, L.M., and N.M. Niss (1990). "Long-Term Bereavement from Suicide, Homicide, Accidents, and Natural Deaths." *Death Studies* 14:423-433.

Ranish, D.R., and D. Shichor (1985). "The Victim's Role in the Penal Process: Recent Developments in California." *Federal Probation* 49:50-57.

Rantala, R.R. (2000). *Effects of NIBRS on Crime Statistics.* Bureau of Justice Statistics Special Report. Washington, DC: Bureau of Justice Statistics.

Rapoport, L. (1962). "The State of Crisis: Some Theoretical Considerations." *Social Service Review* 36:211-217.

Ray, L., P. Kestner, and L. Freedman (1986). "Dispute Resolution: From Examination to Experimentation." *Michigan Bar Journal* 65:898-903.

Reed, S.F. (2001). "Total Estimated Cost of Child Abuse and Neglect in the United States: Statistical Evidence." In B. Jacobs (ed.), Saving Lives, Saving Dollars: Mitigating the Impact of Child Maltreatment. Las Cruces: New Mexico State University. Retrieved on September 1, 2007, from http://spectre.nmsu.edu/dept/docs/fis/2006BriefingReport.pdf

Regehr, C., J. Hill, G. Goldberg, and J. Hughes (2003). "Postmortem Inquiries and Trauma Responses in Paramedics and Firefighters." *Journal of Interpersonal Violence,* 18:607-622.

Reichel, P., and C. Seyfrit (1984). "A Peer Jury in Juvenile Court." *Crime & Delinquency* 30:423-438.

Reifen, D. (1975). "Court Procedures in Israel to Protect Child-Victims of Sexual Assaults." In I. Drapkin and E. Viano (eds.), *Victimology: A New Focus. Volume 3: Crimes, Victims, and Justice.* Lexington, MA: Lexington Books.

Rennison, C.M. (2003). *Intimate Partner Violence, 1993–2001.* Washington, DC: U.S. Bureau of Justice Statistics.

Rennison, C.M. (2002a). *Criminal Victimization 2001: Changes 2000-2001 with Trends 1993-2001.* Washington, DC: U.S. Bureau of Justice Statistics.

Rennison, C.M. (2002b). *Rape and Sexual Assault: Reporting to Police and Medical Attention, 1992–2000.* Washington, DC: U.S. Bureau of Justice Statistics.

Rennison, C.M. (2001). *Criminal Victimization 20000: Changes 1999-2000 with Trends 1993-2000.* Washington, DC: U.S. Bureau of Justice Statistics.

Rennison, C.M., and S. Welchans (2000). *Intimate Partner Violence.* Bureau of Justice Statistics Special Report. Washington, DC: U.S. Department of Justice.

Resick, P.A. (1993). "The Psychological Impact of Rape." *Journal of Interpersonal Violence* 8:223-255.

Resick, P.A. (1990). "Victims of Sexual Assault." In A.J. Lurigio, W.G. Skogan, and R.C. Davis (eds.), *Victims of Crime: Problems, Policies, and Programs.* Newbury Park, CA: Sage.

Resick, P.A. (1987). *Reactions of Female and Male Victims of Rape or Robbery.* Washington, DC: National Institute of Mental Health.

Resick, P.A., K.S. Calhoun, B.M. Atkeson, and E.M. Ellis (1981). "Social Adjustment in Victims of Sexual Assault." *Journal of Consulting and Clinical Psychology* 49:705-712.

Reskin, B., and F. Campbell (1976). "Physician Distribution Across Metropolitan Areas." *American Journal of Sociology* 79:981-988.

Rich, J.A., and C.M. Grey (2005). "Pathways to Recurrent Trauma among Young Black Men: Traumatic Stress, Substance Use, and the "Code of the Street.'" *American Journal of Public Health* 95:816-824.

Riedel, M., M.A. Zahn, and L.F. Mock (1985). *The Nature and Patterns of American Homicide.* Washington, DC: U.S. Department of Justice.

Riger, S., M.T. Gordon, and R. LeBailly (1978). "Women's Fear of Crime: From Blaming to Restricting the Victim." *Victimology* 3:274-284.

Rights of Crime Victims, 18 U.S.C. §3771.

Ringwalt, C.L., P. Messerschmidt, L. Graham, and J. Collins (1992). *Youth's Victimization Experiences, Fear of Attack or Harm, and School Avoidance Behaviors.* Final Report. Washington, DC: National Institute of Justice.

Rinkle, V. (1989). "Federal Initiatives." In R. Filinson and S.R. Ingman (eds.), *Elder Abuse: Practice and Policy.* New York: Human Sciences Press.

Rivara, F.P., B.A. Mueller, G. Somes, C.T. Mendoza, H.B. Rushforth, and A.L. Kellerman (1997). "Alcohol and Illicit Drug Abuse and the Risk of Violent Death in the Home." *Journal of the American Medical Association* 278:569-575.

Rivo, M.L., T.M. Henderson, and D.M. Jackson (1995). "State Legislative Strategies to Improve the Supply and Distribution of Generalist Physicians, 1985 to 1992." *American Journal of Public Health* 85:405-407.

Roberts, A.R. (1992). "Victim/Witness programs: Questions and Answers." *FBI Law Enforcement Bulletin* 61:12-16.

Roberts, A.R. (1991). "Delivery of Services to Crime Victims: A National Survey." *American Journal of Orthopsychiatry* 6:128-137.

Roberts, K.A. (2005). "Women's Experience of Violence During Stalking by Former Romantic Partners: Factors Predictive of Stalking Violence." *Violence Against Women* 11:89-114.

Roberts, S., A.J. Weaver, K.J. Flannelly, and C.R. Figley (2003). "Compassion Fatigue Among Chaplains and Other Clergy after September 11th." *Journal of Nervous and Mental Disease,* 191:756-758.

Robinson, J. (1981). "Defense Strategies for Battered Women Who Assault Their Mates: *State v. Curry.*" *Harvard Women's Law Journal* 4:161-175.

Robinson, M.B. (1998). "Burglary Revictimization." *British Journal of Criminology* 33(1):78-87.

Robinson-Avila, K. (2006). "Child Abuse and Neglect Cost Billions." Found at: http://spectre.nmsu.edu/media/news2.lasso?i=892

Rodríguez, M.A., S.P. Wallace, N.H. Woolf, and C.M. Mangione (2006). "Mandatory Reporting of Elder Abuse: Between a Rock and a Hard Place." *The Annals of Family Medicine* 4:403-409.

Roehl, J.A., and R.F. Cook (1982). "The Neighborhood Justice Centers Field Test." In R. Tomasic and M.M. Feeley (eds.), *Neighborhood Justice: Assessment of an Emerging Idea*. New York: Longman.

Rosen, M.S. (2006). *Chief Concerns: A Gathering Storm—Violent Crime in America*. Washington, DC: Police Executive Research Forum.

Rounsaville, B.J. (1978). "Theories in Marital Violence: Evidence from a Study of Battered Women." *Victimology* 3:11-31.

Ruback, R.B., and M. Bergstrom (2006). "Economic Sanctions in Criminal Justice: Purposes, Effects, and Implications." *Criminal Justice and Behavior* 33:242-273.

Ruback, R.B., and J.N. Shaffer (2005). "The Role of Victim-related Factors in Victim Restitution: A Multi-method Analysis of Restitution in Pennsylvania." *Law and Human Behavior* 29(6): 657-681.

Ruback, R.B., G.R. Ruth, and J.N. Shaffer (2005). "Assessing the Impact of Statutory Change: A Statewide Multi-level Analysis of Restitution Orders." *Crime & Delinquency* 51(3): 318-342.

Ruback, R.B., J.N. Shaffer, and M. Logue (2004). "The Imposition and Effects of Restitution Orders in Four Pennsylvania Counties." *Crime & Delinquency* 50(2):168-188.

Rubin, P.N. (1995). "Civil Rights and Criminal Justice: Primer on Sexual Harassment." *National Institute of Justice: Research in Action*. Washington, DC: National Institute of Justice.

Rushing, W.A. (1975). *Community, Physicians and Inequality*. Lexington, MA: Lexington Books.

Rushing, W.A., and G.I. Wade (1973). "Community-Structure Constraints on the Distribution of Physicians." *Health Services Research* 8:283-297.

Russell, D.E.H. (1982). *Rape in Marriage*. New York: MacMillan.

Ryan, R.M. (1995). "The Sex Right: A Legal History of the Marital Rape Exemption." *Law & Social Inquiry* 20:941-1001.

Safarik, M.E., and J.P. Jarvis (2005). "Examining Attributes of Homicides: Toward Quantifying Qualitative Values of Injury Severity." *Homicide Studies* 9:183-203.

Saltzman, L.E., J.A. Mercy, P.W. O'Caroll, M.L. Rosenberg, and P.H. Rhodes (1992). "Weapon Involvement and Injury Outcomes in Family and Intimate Assaults." *Journal of the American Medical Association* 267:3043-3047.

Sample, L.L., and T.M. Bray (2003). "Are Sex Offenders Dangerous?" *Criminology & Public Policy* 3:59-82.

Sanders, W.B. (1980). *Rape and Woman's Identity*. Beverly Hills: Sage.

Sarri, R., and P.W. Bradley (1980). "Juvenile Aid Panels: An Alternative to Juvenile Court Processing in South Australia." *Crime & Delinquency* 26:42-62.

Saunders, E.J. (1988). "A Comparative Study of Attitudes Toward Child Sexual Abuse among Social Work and Judicial System Professionals." *Child Abuse & Neglect* 17:83-90.

Savitz, L.D., K.S. Kumar, and M.A. Zahn (1991). "Quantifying Luckenbill." *Deviant Behavior* 12:19-29.

Schafer, J. (1996). "Measuring Spousal Violence with the Conflict Tactics Scale: Notes on Reliability and Validity Issues." *Journal of Interpersonal Violence* 11:572-585.

Schafer, S. (1970). *Compensation and Restitution to Victims of Crime.* Montclair, NJ: Patterson Smith.

Schafer, S. (1968). *The Victim and His Criminal: A Study in Functional Responsibility.* New York: Random House.

Schaie, K.W. (1988). "Methodological Issues in Aging Research: An Introduction." In K.W. Schaie, R.T. Campbell, W. Meredith, and S.C. Rawlings (eds.), *Methodological Issues in Aging Research.* New York: Springer.

Schiff, A. (1999). "The Impact of Restorative Interventions on Juvenile Offenders." In G. Bazemore and L. Walgrave (eds.), *Restorative Juvenile Justice: Repairing the Harm of Youth Crime.* Monsey, NY: Criminal Justice Press.

Schissel, B. (1996). "Law Reform and Social Change: A Time-Series Analysis of Sexual Assault in Canada." *Journal of Criminal Justice* 24:123-138.

Schlesinger, B., and R. Schlesinger (1988). "Abuse of the Elderly: Knowns and Unknowns." In B. Schlesinger and R. Schlesinger (eds.), *Abuse of the Elderly: Issues and Annotated Bibliography.* Toronto: University of Toronto Press.

Schlesinger, R.A. (1988). "Grannybashing." In B. Schlesinger and R. Schlesinger (eds.), *Abuse of the Elderly: Issues and Annotated Bibliography.* Toronto: University of Toronto Press.

Schloenhardt, A. (1999). "Organized Crime and the Business of Migrant Trafficking." *Crime, Law and Social Change* 32:203-233.

Schmidt, J., and E.H. Steury (1989). "Prosecutorial Discretion in Filing Charges in Domestic Violence Cases." *Criminology* 27:487-510.

Schneid, T.D. (1999). *Occupational Health Guide to Violence in the Workplace.* Boca Raton, FL: Lewis.

Schneider, A.L., J.M. Burcart, and L.A. Wilson II (1976). "The Role of Attitudes in the Decision to Report Crimes to the Police." In W.F. McDonald (ed.), *Criminal Justice and the Victim.* Beverly Hills: Sage.

Schneider, A.L., W.R. Griffith, D.H. Sumi, and J.M. Burcart (1978). *Portland Forward Records Check of Crime Victims.* Washington, DC: National Institute of Law Enforcement and Criminal Justice.

Schneider, H.J. (1987). "Rape in Criminological and Victimological Perspective." *Eurocriminology* 1:15-29.

Schramberg, L.B., and D. Gaus (1999). "An Ecological Framework for Contextual Risk Factors in Elder Abuse by Adult Children." *Journal of Elder Abuse and Neglect* 11:79-103.

Schubot, D.R. (2001). "Date Rape Prevalence Among Female High School Students in a Rural Midwestern State During 1993, 1995, and 1997." *Journal of Interpersonal Violence* 16:291-296.

Schwartz, M.D. (2000). "Methodological Issues in the Use of Survey Data for Measuring and Characterizing Violence against Women." *Violence against Women* 6:815-838.

Schwartz, M.D. (1989). "Family Violence as a Cause of Crime: Rethinking Our Priorities." *Criminal Justice Policy Review* 3:115-132.

Schwartz, M.D., and V.L. Pitts (1995). "Exploring a Feminist Routine Activities Approach to Explaining Sexual Assault." *Justice Quarterly* 12:9-32.

Schwendinger, J.R., and H. Schwendinger (1983). *Rape and Inequality*. Beverly Hills: Sage.

Scully, D. (1990). *Understanding Sexual Violence*. Boston: Unwin Hyman.

Shapiro, B.L., and J.C. Schwartz (1997). "Date Rape: Its Relationship to Trauma Symptoms and Sexual Self-Esteem." *Journal of Interpersonal Violence* 12:407-419.

Shapiro, C. (1990). "Is Restitution Legislation the Chameleon of the Victims' Movement?" In B. Galaway and J. Hudson (eds.), *Criminal Justice, Restitution and Reconciliation*. Monsey, NY: Criminal Justice Press.

Shapland, J. (1983). "Victim-Witness Services and the Needs of the Victim." *Victimology* 8:233-237.

Shecter, J. (1996). "Fighting for Rape Victims." *The Chronicle of Higher Education*, April 19, p. A8.

Sheley, J.F., Z.T. McGee, and J.D. Wright (1995). *Weapon-related Victimization in Selected Inner-city High School Samples*. Washington, DC: National Institute of Justice.

Shell, D.J. (1982). *Protection of the Elderly: A Study of Elderly Abuse*. Winnipeg, MAN: Manitoba Council on Aging.

Shelley, L. (2003). "The Trade in People in and from the Former Soviet Union." *Crime, Law and Social Change* 40:231-250.

Sheridan, L., G.M. Davies, and J.C.W. Boon (2001). "Stalking: Perceptions and Prevalence." *Journal of Interpersonal Violence* 16:151-167.

Sherman, L.W. (1995). "Hot Spots of Crime and Criminal Careers of Places." In J.E. Eck and D. Weisburd (eds.), *Crime and Place*. Monsey, NY: Criminal Justice Press.

Sherman, L.W. (1992). *Policing Domestic Violence: Experiments and Dilemmas*. New York: The Free Press.

Sherman, L.W., and R.A. Berk (1984). "The Specific Deterrent Effects of Arrest for Domestic Assault." *American Sociological Review* 49:261-272.

Sherman, L.W., P.R. Garten, and M.E. Buerger (1989). "Hot Spots of Predatory Crime: Routine Activities and the Criminology of Place." *Criminology* 27:27-56.

Sherman, L.W., and H. Strang (2000). *Recidivism Patterns in the Canberra Reintegrative Shaming Experiments (RISE)*. Canberra: Center for Restorative Justice, Australian National University.

Sherman, L.W., and H. Strang (2003). "Captains of Restorative Justice: Experience, Legitimacy and Recidivism by Type of Offence." In E.G.M. Weitekamp and H. Kerner (eds.), *Restorative Justice in Context: International Practice and Directions*. Portland, OR: Willan.

Shope, J.H. (2004). "When Words Are Not Enough: The Search for the Effect of Pornography on Abused Women." *Violence Against Women* 10:56-72.

Shulman, L.P., D. Muran, and P.M. Speck (1992). "Counseling Sexual Assault Victims Who Become Pregnant after the Assault: Benefits and Limitations for First-Trimester Paternity Determination." *Journal of Interpersonal Violence* 7:205-210.

Siegel, J.M., J.M. Golding, J.A. Stein, M.A. Burnam, and S.B. Sorenson (1990). "Reactions to Sexual Assault: A Community Study." *Journal of Interpersonal Violence* 5:229-246.

Sigler, R.T., R.T., J.M. Crowley, and I. Johnson (1990). "Judicial and Prosecutorial Endorsement of Innovative Techniques in the Trial of Domestic Abuse Cases." *Journal of Crime and Justice* 18:443-454.

Sigler, R.T., and C.L. Shook (1997). "Judicial Acceptance of The Battered Woman Syndrome." *Criminal Justice Policy Review* 8:365-382.

Simons, R.L., C. Wu, C. Johnson, and R.D. Conger (1995). "A Test of Various Perspectives on the Intergenerational Transmission of Domestic Violence." *Criminology* 33:141-171.

Simpson, S.S., L.A. Bouffard, J. Garner, and L. Hickman (2006). "The Influence of Legal Reform on the Probability of Arrest in Domestic Violence Cases." *Justice Quarterly* 23:297-316.

Skinner, L. J., and K.K. Berry (1993). "Anatomically Detailed Dolls and the Evaluation of Child Sexual Abuse Allegations: Psychometric Considerations." *Law and Human Behavior* 17:399-421.

Skogan, W.G. (1981). *Issues in the Measurement of Victimization*. Washington, DC: U.S. Department of Justice.

Skogan, W.G. (1990). "The National Crime Survey Redesign." *Public Opinion Quarterly* 54:256-272.

Skogan, W.G., and M.G. Maxfield (1981). *Coping with Crime: Individual and Neighborhood Reactions*. Beverly Hills: Sage.

Skolnick, A.A. (1992). "Congress Acts to Resuscitate Nation's Financially Ailing Trauma Care Systems." *Journal of the American Medical Association* 267:2994.

Sloan, J.J. (1994). "The Correlates of Campus Crime: An Analysis of Reported Crimes on College and University Campuses." *Journal of Criminal Justice* 22:51-61.

Sloan, J.J. (1992). "Campus Crime and Campus Communities: An Analysis of Crimes Known to Campus Police and Security." *Journal of Security Administration* 15:31-47.

Smith, A. (2000). "It's My Decision, Isn't It? A Research Note on Battered Women's Perceptions of Mandatory Intervention Laws." *Violence Against Women* 6:1384-1402.

Smith, C., and T.P. Thornberry (1995). "The Relationship Between Childhood Maltreatment and Adolescent Involvement in Delinquency." *Criminology* 33:451-477.

Smith, D.L., and K. Weis (1976). "Toward an Open-System Approach to Studies in the Field of Victimology." In E.C. Viano (ed.), *Victims & Society*. Washington, DC: Visage Press Inc.

Smith, G.B., and S.P. Lab (1991). "Urban and Rural Attitudes Toward Participating in an Auxiliary Policing Crime Prevention Program." *Criminal Justice and Behavior* 18:202-216.

Smith, M.D. (2000). "A New Era of Homicide Studies?" *Homicide Studies* 4:3-17.

Smith, M.D., and R.N. Parker (1980). "Types of Homicide and Variation in Regional Rates." *Social Forces* 59:136-147.

Smith, R., and T. Smith (1979). "An Evaluation of the Akron 4-A Project." Paper presented to the Subcommittee on Courts, Civil Liberties, and the Administration of Justice, U.S. House of Representatives.

Smith et al. v. Doe et al., 538 U.S. 84 (2003).

Smithey, M. (1997). "Infant Homicide at the Hands of Mothers: Toward a Sociological Perspective." *Deviant Behavior* 18:255-272.

Smotas, L. (1991). "In Search of a Balance: AIDS, Rape, and the Special Needs Doctrine." *New York University Law Review* 66:1881-1928.

Snelling, H.A. (1975). "What Is Rape?" In L.G. Schultz (ed.), *Rape Victimology*. Springfield, IL: Charles C Thomas.

Snyder, H.N., and M. Sickmund (2006). *Juvenile Offenders and Victims: 2006 National Report*. Washington, DC: U.S. Department of Justice, Office of Justice Programs, Office of Juvenile Justice and Delinquency Prevention.

Snyder, H.N., and M. Sickmund (1999). *Juvenile Offenders and Victims: 1999 National Report*. Pittsburgh: National Center for Juvenile Justice.

Socolar, R.R.S., D.K. Runyan, and L. Amaya-Hackson (1995). "Methodological and Ethical Issues Related to Studying Child Maltreatment." *Journal of Family Issues* 16:565-586.

Soderstrom, C.A., and G.S. Smith (1993). "Alcohol's Effect on Trauma Outcomes: A Reappraisal of Conventional Wisdom." *Journal of the American Medical Association* 270:93-94.

Sohn, E.F. (1994). "Antistalking Laws: Do They Actually Protect Victims?" *Criminal Law Bulletin* 30:203-241.

Sorenson, S.B., B.A. Richardson, and J.G. Peterson (1993). "Race/Ethnicity Patterns in the Homicide of Children in Los Angeles, 1980 through 1989." *American Journal of Public Health* 83:725-727.

Sorenson, S.B., and H. Shen (2005). "Restraining Orders in California: A Look at Statewide Data." *Violence Against Women* 11:912-933.

South Carolina v. Gathers, 490 U.S. 805 (1989).

Spears, J.W., and C.C. Spohn (1996). "The Genuine Victim and Prosecutor's Charging Decisions in Sexual Assault Cases." *American Journal of Criminal Justice* 20:183-205.

Spelman, W. (1995). "Criminal Careers of Public Places." In J.E. Eck and D. Weisburd (eds.), *Crime and Place*. Monsey, NY: Criminal Justice Press.

Spence-Diehl, E., and Potocky-Tripodi (2001). "Victims of Stalking: A Study of Service Needs as Perceived by Victim Services Practitioners." *Journal of Interpersonal Violence* 16:86-94.

Spencer, B.J. (1987). "A Crime Victim's Views on a Constitutional Amendment for Victims." *The Wayne Law Review* 34:1-6.

Spinetta, J.J., and D. Rigler (1972). "The Child-Abusing Parent: A Psychological Review." *Psychological Bulletin* 77:296-304.

Spohn, C., and J. Horney (1990). "A Case of Unrealistic Expectations: The Impact of Rape Reform Legislation in Illinois." *Criminal Justice Policy Review* 4:1-18.

Spohn, C., and J. Spears (1996). "The Effect of Offender and Victim Characteristics on Sexual Assault Case Processing Decisions." *Justice Quarterly* 13:649-680.

Sprey, J., and S.H. Matthews (1989). "The Perils of Drawing Policy Implications from Research: The Case of Elder Mistreatment." In R. Filinson and S.R. Ingman (eds.), *Elder Abuse: Practice and Policy*. New York: Human Sciences Press.

Sproles, E.T., III (1985). *The Evaluation and Management of Rape and Sexual Abuse: A Physician's Guide*. Rockville, MD: U.S. National Center for Prevention and Control of Rape.

Stafford, M., and O.R. Galle (1984). "Victimization Rates, Exposure to Risk, and Fear of Crime." *Criminology* 22:173-185.

Stalans, L.J., and A.J. Lurigio (1995). "Responding to Domestic Violence Against Women." *Crime & Delinquency* 41:387-398.

Stanford, R.M., and B.L. Mowry (1990). "Domestic Disturbance Danger Rate." *Journal of Police Science and Administration* 17:244-249.

Stanley, J.L., K. Bartholomew, T. Taylor, D. Oram, and M. Landolt (2006). "Intimate Violence in Male Same-Sex Relationships." *Journal of Family Violence* 21:31-41.

Stearns, P.J. (1986). "Old Age Family Conflict: The Perspective of the Past." In K.A. Pillemer and R.S. Wolf (eds.), *Elder Abuse: Conflict in the Family*. Dover, MA: Auburn House.

Steele, B.F., and C. B. Pollock (1974). "A Psychiatric Study of Parents Who Abuse Infants and Small Children." In R.E. Helfer and C.H. Kempe (eds.), *The Battered Child*, 2nd ed. Chicago: University of Chicago Press.

Steinbock, B. (1995). "A Policy Perspective." *Criminal Justice Ethics* 14:4-9.

Steinman, L.I. (1993). "Despite Anti-stalking Laws, Stalkers Continue to Stalk: Are These Laws Constitutional and Effective?" *St. Thomas Law Review* 6:213-245.

Steinman, M. (1988). "Anticipating Rank and File Police Reactions to Arrest Policies Regarding Spouse Abuse." *Criminal Justice Research Bulletin* 4:1-5.

Steinmetz, S.K. (1988). *Duty Bound: Elder Abuse and Family Care*. Newbury Park, CA: Sage.

Steinmetz, S.K. (1983). "Dependency, Stress and Violence between Middle-Aged Caregivers and their Elderly Parents." In J.I. Kosberg (ed.), *Abuse and Maltreatment of the Elderly*. Boston: John Wright.

Steinmetz, S.K. (1978b). "Battered Parents." *Society* (July/August):54-55.

Steinmetz, S.K. (1978a). "Services to Battered Women: Our Greatest Need. A Reply to Field and Kirchner." *Victimology* 3:222-226.

Steinmetz, S.K. (1977-78). "The Battered Husband Syndrome." *Victimology* 2:499-509.

Stine, G.J. (1996). *Aids Update*. Englewood Cliffs, NJ: Prentice Hall.

Stitt, B.G., and S.A. Lentz (1996). "Consent and Its Meaning to the Sexual Victimization of Women." *American Journal of Criminal Justice* 20:237-257.

Stohert, J.C., G.B.M. Gbaanador, and D.N. Herndon (1990). "The Role of Autopsy in Death Resulting from Trauma." *Journal of Trauma* 30:1021-1026.

Stombler, M. (1994). "'Buddies' or 'Slutties:' The Collective Sexual Reputation of Fraternity Little Sisters." *Gender & Society* 8:297-323.

Stone, J.L., R.J. Lowe, O. Jonasson, R.J. Baker, J. Barrett, J.B. Oldershaw, R.M. Crowell, and R.J. Stein (1986). "Acute Subdural Hematoma: Direct Admission to a Trauma Center Yields Improved Results." *Journal of Trauma* 26:445-450.

Stout, K.A. (1991). "Intimate Femicide: A National Demographic Overview." *Journal of Interpersonal Violence* 6:476-485.

Stovall, C.J. (1997). Statement before the Committee on the Judiciary, United States Senate, Concerning a Constitutional Amendment Protecting the Rights of Crime Victims on April 16, 1997.

Straus, M.A. (1983). "Ordinary Violence Child Abuse, and Wife-Beating: What Do They Have in Common?" In D. Finkelhor, R.J. Gelles, G.T. Hotaling, and M.A. Straus, *The Dark Side of Families: Current Family Violence Research*. Beverly Hills: Sage.

Straus, M.A. (1978). "Wife-Beating: How Common and Why." *Victimology* 2:443-458.

Straus, M.A., R. Gelles, and S. Steinmetz (1980). *Behind Closed Doors: Violence in the American Family*. Garden City, NY: Anchor Press.

Straus, M.A., S.L. Hamby, S. Boney-McCoy, and D.B. Sugarman(1996). "The Revised Conflict Tactics Scales (CTS2): Development and Preliminary Psychometric Data." *Journal of Family Issues* 17:283-316.

Straus, M.A. (2000). "Corporal Punishment and Primary Prevention of Physical Abuse." *Child Abuse & Neglect* 24:1109-1114.

Struckman-Johnson, C. (1988). "Forced Sex on Dates: It Happens to Men, Too." *Journal of Sex Research* 24:234-240.

Stuart, B. (1996)."Circle sentencing: Turning swords into ploughshares." In B. Galaway and J. Hudson (eds.), *Restorative Justice: International Perspectives*. Monsey, NY: Criminal Justice Press.

Surette, R. (1998). *Media Crime and Criminal Justice: Images and Realities,* 2nd ed. Belmont, CA: Wadsworth.

Stuart, G.L., T.M. Moore, K.C. Gordon, S.E. Ramsey, and C.W. Kahler (2006). "Psychopathology in Women Arrested for Domestic Violence." *Journal of Interpersonal Violence* 21:376-389.

Sutherland, E.M. (1939). *Principles of Criminology*, 3rd ed. Philadelphia: Lippincott.

Sutocky, J.W., J.M. Shultz, and K.W. Kizer (1993). "Alcohol-Related Mortality in California, 1980 to 19889." *American Journal of Public Health* 83:817-823.

Swatt, M.L., and N.P. He (2006). "Exploring the Difference between Male and Female Intimate Partner Homicides: Revisiting the Concept of Situated Transactions." *Homicide Studies* 10:279-292.

Swisher, K. (1995). "Businesses Should Clearly Define Sexual Harassment." In K.L. Swisher (ed.), *What is Sexual Harassment?* San Diego: Greenhaven Press.

Tallahassee Police Department (2007). *Policy Manual: Death Notification*. Tallahassee: City of Tallahassee.

Tallahassee Police Department (no date). *Policy Manual*. Tallahassee: City of Tallahassee.

Tatara, T. (1993). "Understanding the Nature and Scope of Domestic Elder Abuse with the Use of State Aggregate Data: Summaries of the Key Findings of a National Survey of State APS and Aging Services." *Journal of Elder Abuse and Neglect* 5(4):35-57.

Tatara, T. (1990). *Summaries of National Elder Abuse Data: An Exploratory Study of Statistics Based on a Survey of State Adult Protective Service and Aging Agencies*. Washington, DC: National Aging Resource Center on Elder Abuse.

Tatara, T., L.M. Kuzmeskus, and E. Duckhom (1997). *Trends in Elder Abuse in Domestic Settings*. Elder Abuse Information Series No. 2. Washington, DC: National Center on Elder Abuse.

Taylor, B.G., R.C. Davis, and C.D. Maxwell. (2001). "The Effects of a Group Batterer Treatment Program: A Randomized Experiment in Brooklyn." *Justice Quarterly* 18:171-201.

Taylor, I., and R. Jamieson (1999). "Sex Trafficking and the Mainstream of Market Culture." *Crime, Law and Social Change* 32:257-278.

Taylor, L. (2000). "Patterns of Electoral Corruption in Peru: The April 2000 General Election." *Crime, Law and Social Change* 34:391-415.

Temkin, J. (1996). "Doctors, Rape and Criminal Justice." *The Howard Journal* 35:1-20.

Teret, S.P., G.J. Wintemute, and P.L. Beilsenson (1992). "The Firearm Fatality Reporting System: A Proposal." *Journal of the American Medical Association* 267:3073-3074.

Tewksbury, R. (2005). "Collateral Consequences of Sex Offender Registration." *Journal of Contemporary Criminal Justice* 21:67-81.

Tewksbury, R., and M.B. Lees (2007). "Perceptions of Punishment: How Registered Sex Offenders View Registries." *Crime & Delinquency* 53:380-407.

Tewksbury, R., and E.E. Mustaine (2003). "College Students' Lifestyles and Self-Protective Behaviors: Further Considerations of the Guardianship Concept in Routine Activity Theory." *Criminal Justice and Behavior* 30:302-327.

Texas Statutes (2004).

Thayer, T.A. (1997). "Triage: History and Horizons." *Topics in Emergency Medicine* 19:1-11.

Thobaben, M. (1989). "State Elder/Adult Abuse and Protection Laws." In R. Filinson and S.R. Ingman (eds.), *Elder Abuse: Practice and Policy*. New York: Human Sciences Press.

Thomas, K.R. (1997). "How to Stop the Stalker: State Antistalking Laws." *Criminal Law Bulletin* 29:124-136.

Thomas, M.P., Jr. (1972). "Child Abuse and Neglect, Part I: Historical Overview, Legal Matrix, and Social Perspectives." *North Carolina Law Review* 50:293-349.

Thompson, K.M., S.A. Wonderlich, R.D. Crosby, F.F. Ammerman, J.E. Mitchell, and D. Brownfield (2001). "An Assessment of the Recidivism Rates of Substantiated and Unsubstantiated Maltreatment Cases." *Child Abuse & Neglect* 251207-1218.

Tjaden, P., and N. Thoennes (2000). *Full Report of the Prevalence, Incidence, and Consequences of Violence Against Women: Findings from the National Violence Against Women Survey*. Washington, DC: U.S. Department of Justice.

Toennies, F. (1957). *Community and Society*. Trans. C.P. Loomis. East Lansing: Michigan State University.

Tolman, R.M., and A. Weisz (1995). "Coordinated Community Intervention for Domestic Violence: The Effects of Arrest and Prosecution on Recidivism of Woman Abuse Perpetrators." *Crime & Delinquency* 41:481-495.

Tomz, J.E., and D. McGillis (1997). *Serving Crime Victims and Witnesses*, 2nd ed. Washington, DC: U.S. Department of Justice.

Toseland, R.W. (1982). "Fear of Crime: Who Is Most Vulnerable?" *Journal of Criminal Justice* 10:199-210.

Ullman, S.R., G. Karabatsos, and M.P. Koss (1999). "Alcohol and Sexual Assault in a National Sample of College Women." *Journal of Interpersonal Violence* 14:603-625.

Ullman, S.R., and J.M. Siegel (1993). "Victim-Offender Relationship and Sexual Assault." *Violence and Victims* 8:121-133.

Umbreit, M.S., R.B. Coates, and B. Vos (2001). *Juvenile Offender Mediation in Six Oregon Counties*. Salem, OR: Oregon Dispute Resolution Commission.

Umbreit, M.S., B. Vos, R.B. Coates, and K.A. Brown (2003). *Facing Violence: The Path of Restorative Justice and Dialogue*. Monsey, NY: Criminal Justice Press.

United States v. Wood, CR. No. 05-00072DAE (D.Haw. July 17, 2006).

United States Code (2007).

U.S. Advisory Board on Child Abuse and Neglect (1995). *A Nation's Shame: Fatal Child Abuse and Neglect in the United States*. Washington, DC: U.S. Department of Health and Human Services, p. 13. Retrieved on September 1, 2007, from http://www.ican-ncfr.org/documents/Nations-Shame.pdf

U.S. Attorney General (2005). *Attorney General Guidelines for Victim and Witness Assistance*, pp. 51-55. Washington, DC: U.S. Department of Justice, Office for Victims of Crime. Retrieved on September 7, 2007, from http://www.usdoj.gov/olp/final.pdf

U.S. Attorney General's Commission on Pornography (1986). *Final Report*. Washington, DC: U.S. Government Printing Office.

U.S. Attorney General's Task Force (1984). *Family Violence*. Washington, DC: U.S. Government Printing Office.

U.S. Code (2004).

U.S. Department of Education, *Summary Campus Crime and Security Statistics — Criminal Offenses*. Retrieved on October 3, 2004, from http://www.ed.gov/admins/lead/safety/crime/criminaloffenses/index.html

U.S. Department of Justice (2006). *National Crime Victims' Rights Week Resource Guide, Crime Victims' Rights in America: A Historical Overview*. Washington, DC: National Center for Victims of Crime.

U.S. Department of Justice (2002). *Enforcement of Protective Orders*. Washington, DC: Office for Victims of Crime.

U.S. Department of Justice (1992). *Criminal Victimization in the United States, 1991*. Washington, DC: U.S. Government Printing Office.

U.S. Department of Justice (1989). *Redesign of the National Crime Survey*. Washington, DC: U.S. Government Printing Office.

U.S. Department of Justice (1986). *Four Years Later: A Report on the President's Task Force on Victims of Crime*. Washington, DC: U.S. Government Printing Office.

U.S. Equal Employment Opportunity Commission (n.d.). *Sexual Harassment Charges, EEOC & FEPAs Combined: FY1992-FY2003*. Found at: http://www.eeoc.gov/stats

U.S. General Accounting Office (2002). *Nursing Homes: More Can Be Done to Protect Residents from Abuse*. Washington, DC: U.S. General Accounting Office.

U.S. House of Representatives Select Committee on Aging (1981). *Elder Abuse: An Examination of a Hidden Problem*. Washington, DC: U.S. Government Printing Office.

U.S. National Archives and Records Administration. *The Ronald Reagan Presidential Library, Proclamation 4831 — Victims Rights Week, 1981*. Found at: http://www.reagan.utexas.edu/archives/speeches/1981/40881a.htm

U.S. Senate, Special Committee on Aging (1991). *Aging America: Trends and Projections*. Washington, DC: Department of Health and Human Services.

Ullman, S.R., G. Karabatsos, and M.P. Koss (1999). "Alcohol and Sexual Assault in a National Sample of College Women." *Journal of Interpersonal Violence* 14:603-625.

Ullman, S.R., and J.M. Siegel (1993). "Victim-Offender Relationship and Sexual Assault." *Violence and Victims* 8:121-133.

Umbreit, M.S. (1997). "Victim-Offender Dialogue: From the Margins to the Mainstream Throughout the World." *The Crime Victims Report* 1:35-36, 48.

Umbreit, M.S., and R.B. Coates (1993). "Cross-Site Analysis of Victim-Offender Mediation in four States." *Crime & Delinquency* 39:565-585.

United Nations (1985). *Declaration of Basic Principles of Justice for Victims of Crime and Abuse of Power*. Adopted November 29, 1985.

van Duyne, P.C. (2003). "Organizing Cigarette Smuggling and Policy Making, Ending Up in Smoke." *Crime, Law and Social Change* 39:285-317.

Van Ness, D.W. (1990). "Restorative Justice." In B. Galaway and J. Hudson (eds.), *Criminal Justice, Restitution, and Reconciliation*. Monsey, NY: Criminal Justice Press.

Van Ness, D.W., and K.H. Strong (2006). *Restoring Justice*, 3rd ed. Newark, NJ: LexisNexis Matthew Bender.

Van Voohrees, B.W. (2007). "Munchausen Syndrome by Proxy." Bethesda, MD: U.S. National Library of Medicine. Retrieved on August 31, 2007, from http://www.nlm.nih.gov/medlineplus/ency/article/001555.htm

Vandervort, F.E. (2006). "Videotaping Investigative Interviews of Children in Cases of Child Sexual Abuse: One Community's Approach." *Journal of Criminal Law & Criminology* 96:1353-1416.

Veevers, J. (1989). "Pre-court Diversion for Juvenile Offenders." In M. Wright and B. Galaway (eds.), *Mediation and Criminal Justice: Victims, Offenders and Community*. Newbury Park, CA: Sage.

Viano, E.C. (1987). "Victims' Rights and the Constitution: Reflections on a Bicentennial." *Crime & Delinquency* 33:438-451.

Viano, E.C. (1979). *Victim/Witness Services: A Review of the Model*. Washington, DC: U.S. Department of Justice.

Viano, E.C. (1976a). "Conclusions and Recommendations: International Study Institute on Victimology, Bellagio, Italy, July 1-12, 1975." In E.C. Viano (ed.), *Victims & Society*. Washington, DC: Visage Press Inc.

Viano, E.C. (1976b). "From the Editor: Victimology: The Study of the Victim." *Victimology* 1:1-7.

Villmoare, E., and V.V. Neto (1987). *Victim Appearances at Sentencing Under California's Victims' Bill of Rights*. Washington, DC: National Institute of Justice.

Violence Against Women Office (2004, August 29). *National Domestic Violence Hotline*. Found at: http://www.ndvh.org

Visher, C.A., A.V. Harrell, and L.C. Newmark (2007). *Pretrial Innovations for Domestic Violence Offenders and Victims: Lessons from the Judicial Oversight Demonstration Initiative*. Washington, DC: National Institute of Justice. Retrieved on September 21, 2007, from http://www.ncjrs.gov/pdffiles1/nij/216041.pdf

Volkwein, J., B. Szelest, and A.J. Lizotte (1995). "The Relationship of Campus Crime to Campus and Student Characteristics." *Research in Higher Education* 36:647-670.

von Hentig, H. (1948). *The Criminal and His Victim: Studies in the Sociobiology of Crime*. New Haven: Yale University Press.

von Hentig, H. (1941). "Remarks on the Interaction of Perpetrator and Victim." *Journal of Criminal Law, Criminology and Police Science* 31:303-309.

Vorenberg, E.W. (1981). *A State of the Art Survey of Dispute Resolution Programs Involving Juveniles*. Chicago: National Center for the Assessment of Alternatives to Juvenile Justice Processing, University of Chicago.

Wachtel, T. (1995). "Family Group Conferencing: Restorative Justice in Practice." *Juvenile Justice Update* 1(4):1-2,13-14.

Waldner-Haugrud, L.K., and B. Magruder (1995). "Male and Female Sexual Victimization in Dating Relationships: Gender Differences in Coercion Techniques and Outcomes." *Violence and Victims* 10:203-215.

Walker, G. (1990). "Crisis-Care in Critical Incident Debriefing." *Death Studies* 14:121-133.

Walker, L.E. (1988). "New Techniques for Assessment and Evaluation of Child Abuse Victims: Using Anatomically Correct Dolls and Videotape Procedures." In L.E.A. Walker (ed.), *Handbook on Sexual Abuse of Children*. New York: Springer-Verlag.

Walker, L.E. (1979). *The Battered Woman*. New York: Harper & Row.

Wallace, H., and K. Kelty (1995). "Stalking and Restraining Orders: A Legal and Psychological Perspective." *Journal of Crime and Justice* 18:99-111.

Walsh, A. (1986). "Placebo Justice: Victim Recommendations and Offender Sentences in Sexual Assault Cases." *Journal of Criminal Law & Criminology* 77:1126-1141.

Wan, A.M. (2000). "Battered Women in the Restraining Order Process: Observations on a Court Advocacy Program." *Violence Against Women* 6:606-632.

Ward, R.A., M. LaGory, and S.R. Sherman (1986). "Fear of Crime among the Elderly as Person/Environment Interaction." *Sociological Quarterly* 27:327-341.

Wardell, L., D.L. Gillespie, and A. Leffler (1983). "Science and Violence against Wives." In D. Finkelhor, R.J. Gelles, G.T. Hotaling, and M.A. Straus (eds.), *The Dark Side of Families: Current Family Violence Research*. Beverly Hills: Sage.

Warner, J.E., and D.J. Hansen (1994). "The Identification and Reporting of Physical Abuse by Physicians: A Review and Implications for Research." *Child Abuse & Neglect* 18:11-25.

Warr, M. (1984). "Fear of Victimization: Why Are Some Women and the Elderly More Afraid?" *Social Science Quarterly* 65:681-702.

Wasik, B.H., and R.N. Roberts (1994). "Survey of Home Visiting Programs for Abused and Neglected Children and Their Families." *Child Abuse & Neglect* 18:271-283.

Way, I., K.M. Van Deusen, G. Martin, B. Applegate, and D. Jandle (2004), "Vicarious Trauma: A Comparison of Clinicians Who Treat Survivors of Sexual Abuse and Sexual Offenders." *Journal of Interpersonal Violence*, 19:49-71.

Weaver, G.S., J.E.C. Wittekind, L. Huff-Corzine, J. Corzine, T.A. Petee, and J.P. Jarvis (2004). "Violent Encounters: A Criminal Event Analysis of Lethal and Nonlethal Outcomes." *Journal of Contemporary Criminal Justice* 20:348-368.

Websdale, N. (1998). *Rural Woman Battering and the Justice System: An Ethnography*. Thousand Oaks, CA: Sage.

Websdale, N., Sheeran, M., and B. Johnson. (1999). *Reviewing Domestic Violence Fatalities: Summarizing National Developments*. [Online]. Found at: http://www.vaw.umn.edu

Webster, B. (1988). "Victim Assistance Programs Report Increased Workloads." *National Institute of Justice: Research in Action*. Washington, DC: U.S. Department of Justice.

Webster, S.W., R. O'Toole, A.W. O'Toole, and B. Lucal (2005). "Overreporting and Underreporting of Child Abuse: Teachers' Use of Professional Discretion." *Child Abuse & Neglect* 29(11):1281-1296.

Weiand v. State, 732 So. 2d 1044 (Fla. 1999).

Weigend, T., (1983). "Problems of Victim/Witness Assistance Programs." *Victimology* 8:91-101.

Weis, K., and S.S. Borges (1976). "Rape as a Crime Without Victims and Offenders? A Methodological Critique." In E.C. Viano (ed.), *Victims & Society*. Washington, DC: Visage.

Weis, K., and S.S. Borges (1973). "Victimology and Rape: The Case of the Legitimate Victim." *Issues in Criminology* 8:71-115.

Weiss, A., and R.F. Boruch (1996). "On the Use of Police Officers in Randomized Field Experiments: Some Lessons from the Milwaukee Domestic Violence Experiment." *Police Studies* 19:45-52.

Weisz, A N., R.M. Tolman, and D.G. Saunders (2000). "Assessing the Risk of Severe Domestic Violence: The Importance of Survivors' Predictions." *Journal of Interpersonal Violence* 15:75-90.

Weitekamp, E.G.M. (1999). "The History of Restorative Justice." In G. Bazemore and L. Walgrave (eds.), *Restorative Juvenile Justice: Repairing the Harm of Youth Crime*. Monsey, NY: Criminal Justice Press.

West, J.G., R.H. Cales, and A.B. Gazzaniga (1983). "Impact of Regionalization: The Orange County Experience." *Archives of Surgery* 118:740-744.

Whitaker, C.J. (1989). *Bureau of Justice Statistics Special Report: The Redesigned National Crime Survey: Selected New Data*. Washington, DC: U.S. Government Printing Office.

Whitaker, D.J., J.R. Lutzker, and G.A. Shelley (2005). "Child Maltreatment Prevention Priorities at the Centers for Disease Control and Prevention." *Child Maltreatment* 10:245-259.

Whitby, D. (2001). "Conspiracy and Cover-Up." *Crime, Law and Social Change* 35:21-41.

White House News Release (July 27, 2006). "President Signs H.R. 447, the Adam Walsh Child Protection and Safety Act of 2006." Washington, DC: Office of the Press Secretary.

Whitehead, J.T., and S.P. Lab (2006). *Juvenile Justice: An Introduction*, 5th ed. Newark, NJ: LexisNexis Matthew Bender.

Whitehead, J.T., and S.P. Lab (2003). *Juvenile Justice: An Introduction*, 4th ed. Cincinnati: Anderson.

Widom, C.S. (1989). "Child Abuse, Neglect, and Violent Criminal Behavior." *Criminology* 27:251-271.

Widom, C.S., and M.G. Maxfield (2001). *An Update on the "Cycle of Violence."* Washington, DC: U.S. Department of Justice, National Institute of Justice.

Wilbanks, W. (1984). *Murder in Miami: An Analysis of Homicide Patterns and Trends in Dade County (Miami), Florida, 1917-1983*. Lanham, MD: University Press of America.

Williams, C.R., and B.A. Arrigo (1999). "Discerning the Margins of Constitutional Encroachment: The Drug Courier Profile in the Airport Milieu." *American Journal of Criminal Justice* 24:31-46.

Williams, S.D., J. Weiner, and H. MacMillan (2005). "Build-a-Person Technique: An Examination of the Validity of Human-Figure Features as Evidence of Childhood Sexual Abuse." *Child Abuse & Neglect* 29:701-713.

Willis, C.L., and R.H. Wells (1988). "The Police and Child Abuse: An Analysis of Police Decisions to Report Illegal Behavior." *Criminology* 26:695-715.

Wilson v. State, 744 So.2d 1237 (Fla. 1st DCA 1999).

Wintemute, G.J. (1999). "The Future of Firearm Violence Prevention: Building on Success." *Journal of the American Medical Association* 282:475-478.

Wisconsin Statutes (2003).

Wolf, R.S., and K.A. Pillemer (1989). *Helping Elderly Victims: The Reality of Elder Abuse*. New York: Columbia University Press.

Wolfgang, M.E. (1958). *Patterns in Criminal Homicide*. Montclair, NJ: Patterson Smith, Reprinted 1975.

Wolfgang, M.E., and F. Ferracuti (1967). *The Subculture of Violence: Towards an Integrated Theory of Criminology*. London: Tavistock.

Wolfner, G., D. Faust, and R.M. Dawes (1993). "The use of anatomically detailed dolls in sexual abuse evaluations: The state of the science." *Applied & Preventive Psychology* 2:1-11.

Women Against Violence Against Women (2005). *Rape Myths*. Vancouver, British Columbia, Canada: WAVAW. Retrieved August 23, 2007, from http://www.wavaw.ca/informed_myths.php

Woodworth, D.L. (1991). "Evaluation of a Multiple-Family Incest Treatment Program." In M.Q. Patton (ed.), *Family Sexual Abuse: Frontline Research and Evaluation*. Newbury Park, CA: Sage.

Woolf, P.D., C. Cox, J.V. McDonald, M. Kelly, D. Nichols, T. Hamill, and D.V. Feliciano (1991). "Effects of Intoxication on the Catecholamine Response to Multisystem Injury." *Journal of Trauma* 31:1271-1276.

Worth, D.M., P.A. Matthews, and W.R. Coleman (1990). "Sex, Role, Group Affiliation, Family Background, and Courtship Violence in College Students." *Journal of College Student Development* 31:250-254.

Wright, J.A., A.G. Burgess, A.W. Burgess, A.T. Laszlo, G.O. McCrary, and J.E. Douglas (1997). "A Typology of Interpersonal Stalking." *Journal of Interpersonal Violence* 11:487-502.

Wright, L. (1976). "The 'Sick but Slick' Syndrome as a Personality Component of Parents of Battered Children." *Journal of Clinical Psychology* 32:41-45.

Wright, M. (1991). *Justice for Victims and Offenders: A Restorative Response to Crime*. Philadelphia: Open University Press.

Wright, R.G. (2003). "Sex Offender Registration and Notification: Public Attention, Political Emphasis, and Fear." *Criminology & Public Policy* 3:97-104.

Wyatt, G.E., and M. Riederle (1995). "The Prevalence and Contact of Sexual Harassment among African American and White American Women." *Journal of Interpersonal Violence* 10:309-321.

Yacoubian, G.S., Jr. (2000). "The (In)significance of Genocidal Behavior to the Discipline of Criminology." *Crime, Law and Social Change* 34:7-19.

Yllo, K. (1999). "Wife Rape: A Social Problem for the 21st Century." *Violence Against Women* 5:1059-1063.

Young, M.A. (1987). "A Constitutional Amendment for Victims of Crime: The Victim's Perspective." *The Wayne Law Review* 34:51-68.

Younglove, J.A., M.G. Kerr, and C.J. Vitello (2002). "Law Enforcement Officers' Perceptions of Same Sex Domestic Violence: Reason for Cautious Optimism." *Criminal Justice and Behavior* 17:760-772.

Zehr, H. (1990). *Changing Lenses.* Scottsdale, PA: Herald Press.

Zehr, H., and H. Mika (2003). "Fundamental Concepts of Restorative Justice." In E. McLaughlin, R. Fergusson, G. Hughes, and L. Westmarland (eds.), *Restorative Justice: Critical Issues.* Thousand Oaks, CA: Sage.

Zellman, G.L. (1991). "Reducing Underresponding: Improving System Response to Mandated Reporters." *Journal of Interpersonal Violence* 16:115-118.

Zellman, G.L. (1990a). "Child Abuse Reporting and Failure to Report among Mandated Reporters: Prevalence, Incidence, and Reasons." *Journal of Interpersonal Violence* 5:3-22.

Zellman, G.L. (1990b). "Report Decision-Making Patterns among Mandated Child Abuse Reporters." *Child Abuse & Neglect* 14:325-336.

Zillman, G.L., J. Bryant, and R.A. Carveth (1981). "The Effects of Erotica Featuring Sadomasochism and Bestiality on Motivated Intermale Aggression." *Personality and Social Psychology Bulletin* 7:153-159.

Zingraff, M.T., J. Leiter, K.A. Myers, and M.C. Johnson (1993). "Child Maltreatment and Youthful Problem Behavior." *Criminology* 31:173-202.

Zirkel, P.A. (1990). "You Bruise, You Lose." *Phi Delta Kappan* 71:410-411.

Zoellner, L.A., N.C. Feeny, J. Alvarez, C. Watlington, M.L. O'Neill, R. Zager, and E.B. Foa (2000). "Factors Associated with Completion of the Restraining Order Process in Female Victims of Partner Violence." *Journal of Interpersonal Violence* 15:1081-1099.

Zona, M.A., K.K. Sharma, and J.L. Lane (1993). "A Comparative Study of Erotomania and Obsessional Subjects in a Forensic Sample." *Journal of Forensic Sciences* 65:894-903.

SUBJECT INDEX

AUTHOR INDEX